ROMANS

Also by James Montgomery Boice

Witness and Revelation in the Gospel of John
Philippians: An Expositional Commentary
The Minor Prophets: An Expositional Commentary (2 volumes)
How to Live the Christian Life (originally, *How to Really Live It Up*)
Ordinary Men Called by God (originally, *How God Can Use Nobodies*)
The Last and Future World
The Gospel of John: An Expositional Commentary (5 volumes)
The Epistles of John: An Expositional Commentary
"Galatians," in the *Expositor's Bible Commentary*
Can You Run Away from God?
Our Sovereign God, editor
Our Savior God: Studies on Man, Christ and the Atonement, editor
Does Inerrancy Matter?
The Foundation of Biblical Authority, editor
Making God's Word Plain, editor
The Sermon on the Mount
Genesis: An Expositional Commentary (3 volumes)
The Parables of Jesus
The Christ of Christmas
The Gospel of Matthew: An Expositional Commentary (2 volumes)
Standing on the Rock
The Christ of the Empty Tomb
Foundations of the Christian Faith (4 volumes in one)
Christ's Call to Discipleship
Transforming Our World: A Call to Action, editor
Ephesians: An Expositional Commentary
Daniel: An Expositional Commentary
Joshua: An Expositional Commentary
Nehemiah: An Expositional Commentary
The King Has Come
Romans: An Expositional Commentary (4 volumes)
Mind Renewal in a Mindless Age
The Glory of God's Grace (originally, *Amazing Grace*)
Psalms: An Expositional Commentary (3 volumes)
Sure I Believe, So What?
Hearing God When You Hurt
Foundations of God's City (originally, *Two Cities, Two Loves: Christian Responsibility in a Crumbling Culture*)
Here We Stand!: A Call from Confessing Evangelicals, editor
  with Benjamin E. Sasse
Living by the Book: The Joy of Loving and Trusting God's Word
Acts: An Expositional Commentary
The Heart of the Cross, with Philip G. Ryken
What Makes a Church Evangelical?
The Doctrines of Grace, with Philip G. Ryken

Romans

Volume 4
The New Humanity
Romans 12–16

JAMES
MONTGOMERY
BOICE

BakerBooks
Grand Rapids, Michigan

© 1995 by Baker Books

Published by Baker Books
a division of Baker Publishing Group
P.O. Box 6287, Grand Rapids, MI 49516-6287
www.bakerbooks.com

Paperback edition published 2005
ISBN 978-0-8010-6584-2

Printed in the United States of America

The Library of Congress has cataloged the hardcover edition as follows:
 Boice, James Montgomery, 1938-
  Romans.
   Includes bibliographical references and indexes.
   Contents: v. 1. Justification by faith, Romans 1–4—v. 2. The reign of grace,
   Romans 5:1–8:39—v. 3. God and history, Romans 9–11—v. 4. The new
  humanity, Romans 12–16.

   ISBN 10: 0-8010-1002-0 (v. 1)
   ISBN 978-0-8010-1002-6 (v. 1)
   ISBN 10: 0-8010-1003-9 (v. 2)
   ISBN 978-0-8010-1003-3 (v. 2)
   ISBN 10: 0-8010-1058-6 (v. 3)
   ISBN 978-0-8010-1058-3 (v. 3)
   ISBN 10: 0-8010-1039-X (v. 4)
   ISBN 978-0-8010-1039-2 (v. 4)
   1. Bible. N.T. Romans—Commentaries. I. Title.
 BS2665.3.B58 1991
 227´.1007   91-7204

Unless otherwise indicated, Scripture is taken from the Holy Bible, New International Version®. NIV®. Copyright © 1973, 1978, 1984 by Biblica, Inc.™ Used by permission of Zondervan. All rights reserved worldwide. www.zondervan.com

To **HIM**
who is able to establish you
by this gospel and the proclamation of Jesus Christ . . .
to the only wise God.

Contents

Preface

Ⅰt is always deeply satisfying to come
to the end of an important task, especially one that has taken a long time,
as these expositions of Paul's letter to the Romans have for me. I began teaching through the Book of Romans in the fall of 1986 and worked on these
studies as the major part of my weekly preaching ministry at Tenth Presbyterian Church in Philadelphia for the next eight years. Two years of preaching have gone into each of the four volumes of the series.

But it is not only a sense of satisfaction I feel as I come to the close of this
work. I have a deep gratitude to God for allowing me to finish such an
important and lengthy exposition, and also anticipation of what God may
be pleased to accomplish through it in the lives of those who will be helped
into the great doctrines of the Epistle by this gateway.

We live in mindless times, a point I make extensively in the studies dealing
with Romans 12:1–2. This is because of the fast pace of modern life, which
does not give people sufficient time to think; our materialism, which binds
us to things rather than freeing our minds for ideas; skepticism in philosophy,
which tells us that there is nothing to be gained by thinking anyway; and above
all the pervasiveness of television, which is destructive to rational thought
processes. But we need to think! And we need to think biblically! This is why
the last section of Paul's letter (chapters 12–16), dealing with the application
of the gospel treated in earlier chapters to various aspects of our lives, begins
with the need for mind renewal. Paul knew that if we are to act as Christians
we must first learn to think as Christians, since how we think will determine
what we do.

In our day people do not think deeply and seldom think about the truths
of Christianity. Unbelievers move through life in a spiritual daze unaware that

they have precious but impoverished and dying souls. Believers are often in a daze too. There is very little measurable difference in thought and action between believers and their unbelieving counterparts. One observer of the contemporary scene says that God lies weightlessly upon them and that Christian doctrines seem to have no consequences.

If a study of this nature helps people begin thinking about the great doctrines of Christianity and what they should mean for the living of our daily lives, then the benefit to them, their families, and their churches could be enormous. It is certainly what Paul intended when he wrote these chapters.

Think of what Paul covers in this application section. He writes about the need for mind renewal in 12:1–2; the Christian's relationship to other people, especially the need for love, in 12:3–21; issues involving the role of the state and a believer's relationship to it in 13:1–7; the law of love in 13:8–14; and Christian liberty, particularly how those who think they are theologically and spiritually strong are to treat their "weaker" brothers, in 14:1–15:33. Then there are closing sections dealing with Paul's plans for future ministry in 15:14–33, and final greetings from Christians in the church at Corinth to Christians in the church at Rome in 16:1–27.

It would make a tremendous difference to the lives of our churches and the impact of Christians on our world if we would just master and live by these teachings.

In each of my books I thank the elders and congregation of Tenth Presbyterian Church who encourage me to spend so much of my time in sermon preparation. Not all ministers have an inclination to study, nor are they encouraged by their congregations to spend substantial time doing it. I have had the benefit of this encouragement and have tried to take advantage of the time given. I believe this has been beneficial to the church, and I know has been beneficial to me.

Twice in the last two sections of Romans Paul writes that the goal of all things must be the glory of God. At the end of chapter eleven he says, "For from him and through him and to him are all things. To him be the glory forever! Amen" (Rom. 11:36). At the end of chapter 16 he likewise declares, "To the only wise God be glory forever through Jesus Christ! Amen" (Rom. 16:27). That is the purpose of all things, and it was Paul's deepest desire that everything he did and every thought he had might be to the glory of the great, sovereign, wise, holy, and compassionate God who had saved him through the gospel of his Son, Jesus Christ.

That is my desire too. And it is my special desire for this specific attempt to teach Romans. May God bless it to many people now and for many years to come. May it help them to come to know him better and obey him. To God alone be the glory.

Philadelphia, Pennsylvania

PART SIXTEEN

Applied Christianity

180

How Should We Then Live?

Romans 12:1–2

Therefore, I urge you, brothers, in view of God's mercy, to offer your bodies as living sacrifices, holy and pleasing to God—this is your spiritual act of worship. Do not conform any longer to the pattern of this world, but be transformed by the renewing of your mind. Then you will be able to test and approve what God's will is—his good, pleasing and perfect will.

Ｗith the start of chapter 12 we come in our study of Paul's letter to the practical section of the book. I am sure it is a point for which many readers have been eagerly waiting, since ours is a practical age and most people want practical teaching. But I begin by saying that I do not like this way of talking about the material in chapters 12–16. This is because to call these chapters practical suggests that the doctrinal sections are not practical, and whenever we find ourselves thinking along those lines we are making a mistake and contributing to great misunderstanding.

Doctrine is practical, and practical material must be doctrinal if it is to be of any help at all. A far better way to talk about Romans 12–16 is to say that these chapters contain applications of the very practical teaching Paul presented earlier.

John Murray, one of the best modern interpreters of Romans, uses the word *application* in his introduction to this section of the book. He says, "At this point the apostle comes to deal with concrete practical application."[1]

Perhaps an even better word is *consequences*. It occurs to me because of the compelling slogan of the Hillsdale College newsletter, *Imprimis:* "Because Ideas Have Consequences." We have had lots of ideas in the first great sections of Romans—truthful ideas, stirring ideas, ideas that have come to us by means of an inerrant and authoritative revelation. Now we are to explore their many important consequences.

Whose Values? And Why?

Let me make this point still another way by saying that this is the significance of the word *then* in the title of Francis Schaeffer's well-known study of the rise and fall of western culture, *How Should We Then Live?* Schaeffer had a gift for using words well, and this is nowhere seen more clearly than in this book's title. *Then* is a very simple word. We hardly think twice about our use of it. But when you reflect on the word in *How Should We Then Live?* it is clear at once that it is the most important word. Suppose the book were called *How Should We Live?* There would be nothing remarkable about that. How should we live? is a common question. It's not much different from asking, What shall we do today? or Where shall we have dinner tonight? But put *then* into the title, and the question becomes, How shall we live in light of the fact that God has redeemed us from sin's penalty by the death of Jesus Christ and freed us from sin's tyranny by the power of the Holy Spirit?

Schaeffer is very clear about where he thinks Western culture is headed. He looks at such current trends as increasing economic breakdown, violence in all areas of life and all countries, extreme poverty for many of the Third World's peoples, a love of affluence, and the underlying relativism of Western thought. He concludes that the choice before us is either totalitarianism—an imposed but arbitrary social order—or "once again affirming that base which gave freedom without chaos in the first place—God's revelation in the Bible and his revelation through Christ."[2]

Schaeffer's point is that those who have received this revelation must also act upon it, because that is the very nature of the revelation. It demands application. Writes Schaeffer, "As Christians we are not only to *know* the right world view, the world view that tells us the truth of what *is*, but consciously to *act* upon that world view so as to influence society in all its parts and facets across the whole spectrum of life, as much as we can to the extent of our individual and collective ability."[3]

1. John Murray, *The Epistle to the Romans*, 2 vols. in 1 (Grand Rapids: Wm. B. Eerdmans Publishing Company, 1968), vol. 2, p. 109.

2. Francis A. Schaeffer, *How Should We Then Live? The Rise and Decline of Western Thought and Culture* (Old Tappan, N.J.: Fleming H. Revell Company, 1976), p. 252.

3. Ibid., p. 256.

We are hearing a great deal about "family values" today, particularly in popular political campaigns. It was a Republican theme in the 1992 campaign, because the Republicans were using it to question Bill Clinton's morality. I believe in family values. I also supported Dan Quayle in what he said about them in that campaign. I think he wanted the right thing. But I must add that in the current political climate an appeal to "family values" without a corresponding acknowledgment of God's existence, God's law, and biblical revelation as a basis for all values will always have a hollow ring and sound purely political and manipulative.

Unless we acknowledge God and God's saving acts as the source and basis for our values, anyone who thinks clearly may refute our concern with such questions as these: What kind of family values are we talking about? A nuclear family? A single-parent family? A homosexual family? Why should any one be preferred above another? Or why should we want families at all? In other words, the call for values always invites these rejoinders: Whose values are we taking about? and Why those?

During a meeting of college educators at Harvard University in 1987, President Frank Rhodes of Cornell University suggested in an address on educational reforms that it was time for the universities to pay attention to values and the students' "moral well-being."

At once there were gasps from the audience, and one student jumped to his feet, demanding indignantly, "Whose values are to be taught? And who is to teach us?" The audience applauded loudly, which meant that in its judgment the student had rendered the president's suggestion foolish by these unanswerable questions.

President Rhodes sat down without even trying to answer them.[4]

A generation or so ago, it would have been natural for an educator to at least point to the accumulated wisdom of more than two millennia of Western history—to the writings of philosophers like Plato, Socrates, and Aristotle and to historians and modern thinkers, even if not to the Bible, though many would have included it as well. It is for a return to precisely this type of education that Allan Bloom called so eloquently in his book *The Closing of the American Mind*.[5] But all this has been forfeited today, as President Rhodes's capitulation showed. And it is not just that times have changed or that people today are skeptical. The problem is that without the absolutes provided by God's revelation of himself and his ways, all views are relative and there is no real reason for doing one thing rather than another—except for selfish, personal reasons, which obviously destroy morality rather than establish it. In other words, our days have become like the times of the Jewish judges when there was no king, the law was forgotten and, as a result, "everyone did as he [or she] saw fit" (Judg. 21:25).

4. Carl F. H. Henry, *Twilight of a Great Civilization* (Westchester, Ill.: Crossway Books, 1988), p. 170.
5. Allan Bloom, *The Closing of the American Mind* (New York: Simon and Schuster, 1987).

If revelation is the basis for social morality and ethics, then it is impossible to have valid, effective or lasting morals without it. We must have Romans 1–11 in order to have Romans 12–16.

John Calvin spoke about this at the start of his lectures on Romans 12, only he was comparing Christianity and philosophy. He said, "This is the main difference between the Gospel and philosophy. Although the philosophers speak on the subject of morals splendidly and with praiseworthy ability, yet all the embellishment which shines forth in their precepts is nothing more than a beautiful superstructure without a foundation, for by omitting principles, they propound a mutilated doctrine, like a body without a head. . . . Paul [in Romans 12:1–2] lays down the principle from which all the parts of holiness flow."[6]

"Therefore"

Above I commented on Francis Schaeffer's *How Should We Then Live?*, saying that *then* is the all-important word. When we come to the first verse of Romans 12 we discover exactly the same thing, only in this case the important word is *therefore*. "*Therefore*, I urge you, brothers, in view of God's mercy, to offer your bodies as living sacrifices." Paul means, "In view of what I have just been writing, you must not live for yourselves but rather give yourselves wholly to God."

I am sure you have heard some teacher say at one time or another that when you come to the word "therefore" in the Bible you should always pay close attention to it, because it is "there for" a purpose. *Therefore* always points back to something else, and this means that we can never understand the importance of what is coming or the connection between what is coming and what has been said until we know exactly what the "therefore" is referring to. We have already had to think this through several times in our study of Romans, because a couple of important *therefores* have already occurred: in 2:1, basing the condemnation of the allegedly moral person on the failure of the entire race as described in Romans 1; and in 5:1, linking the permanence of God's saving work as expounded in Romans 5–8 to the nature of that work as described in Romans 3 and 4.

These earlier *therefores* were important, but the *therefore* of 12:1 is more significant still.

What does the *therefore* of Romans 12:1 refer to? The immediately preceding verses, the doxology that ends Romans 11? The whole of the eleventh chapter, in which Paul explains the wisdom of God's saving acts in history and argues for the eventual restoration of Israel? Chapter 8, with its stirring assertion that nothing in heaven or earth will be able to separate us from

---

6. John Calvin, *The Epistles of Paul the Apostle to the Romans and to the Thessalonians*, trans. Ross MacKenzie (Grand Rapids: Wm. B. Eerdmans Publishing Company, 1973), p. 262.

the love of God in Christ Jesus? Or, to go back even further, the doctrine of justification by faith expounded in chapters 1–4?

There have been able defenders of each of these views, and with reason. Each can be defended by good arguments.

One summer, after I had been teaching the Book of Romans to a group of teaching leaders from Bible Study Fellowship, I received a letter in which a woman thanked me for the series and explained how she had come to understand the importance of God's grace in election for the first time. She wrote that for years she had considered election strange and dangerous but that her eyes had been opened. She wrote, "Not only was my mind opened, my heart was touched. The tears were impossible to restrict several times as I realized what a privileged and totally undeserving recipient of his grace I am. I can hardly believe what a gift I have received from him. It truly brings me to say, 'Yes, yes, yes' to Romans 12:1–2. It's the very least and only rational thing we can do in light of God's unimaginable gift."

This woman was moved by the doctrine of election, which is taught in Romans 9–11. But the answer to what the *therefore* of Romans 12:1 refers is probably *everything* in Romans that precedes it.

Charles Hodge summarizes this way: "All the doctrines of justification, grace, election, and final salvation, taught in the preceding part of the epistle, are made the foundation for the practical duties enjoined in this."[7]

This is Paul's normal pattern in his letters, of course. In the Book of Ephesians the first three doctrinal chapters are followed by three chapters dealing with spiritual gifts, morality, personal relationships, and spiritual warfare. In Galatians the doctrinal section in chapters 3 and 4 is followed in chapters 5 and 6 by material on Christian liberty, spiritual fruit, love, and the obligation to do good. In Colossians the doctrinal material is in 1:1–2:5. The application is in 2:5–4:18. The same pattern occurs in 1 and 2 Thessalonians. It is also in 1 and 2 Corinthians and Philippians, though it is not so apparent in those books. (Strikingly, this does not seem to be the case with the other New Testament writers, such as Peter and John. It seems to have been unique to Paul.)

Leon Morris says, "It is fundamental to [Paul] that the justified man does not live in the same way as the unrepentant sinner."[8]

Outline of Chapters 12–16

Therefore is a linking word, as I have said. We have looked back to what it refers to. Now we should look forward to see what the doctrinal material of

7. Charles Hodge, *A Commentary on Romans* (Edinburgh and Carlisle, Pa.: The Banner of Truth Trust, 1972), p. 393. Original edition 1835.

8. Leon Morris, *The Epistle to the Romans* (Grand Rapids: Wm. B. Eerdmans Publishing Company, and Leicester, England: Inter-Varsity Press, 1988), p. 431.

chapters 1–11 connects with. In this fourth volume of studies I am handling it in seven sections.

1. *Applied Christianity (12:1–2)*. Just as God is the basis of reality so that everything flows from him and takes its form from him ("For from him and through him and to him are all things," Rom. 11:36), so also our relationship to God is the basis of all other relationships and our duty to him the basis of all other duties. Because this is so, Paul sets out the principles that should govern our relationship to God in verses 1 and 2. He reminds us that we are not our own and that we should therefore present ourselves to God as willing and living sacrifices.

2. *The Christian and other people (12:3–21)*. There are three basic areas of application for the gospel, and they each involve relationships. The first two verses have outlined the right relationship of a Christian to God. The remainder of the chapter shows us: (1) the right relationship of a Christian to himself (he is not to think of himself more highly than he ought to think, but rather to be humble) and (2) the right relationship of a Christian to other people. The first is treated briefly, in verse 3. The second is dealt with at greater length, in verses 4–21.

3. *Church and state (13:1–7)*. The Christian does not have a relationship only to other individuals, however. He also has a relationship to institutions, particularly the state. What is the believer's relationship to the state to be? Is he to oppose it as an incorrigibly secular and godless entity? Is he to try to escape from it? Should the Christian submit to it? If we are to submit, is that submission to be without any qualification, regardless of what the state may do or ask us to do? Or are there limits? If there are limits, what are they? We know from history that these became very important matters for the early Christians, especially in the years when the emperors persecuted them, trying to abolish Christianity.

Paul answers many of these questions in the first half of chapter 13, providing a strong case for the validity and worth of secular governments.

4. *The law of love (13:8–14)*. Jesus said that the sum of morality is this: (1) that we love God with all our hearts, minds, souls, and strength and (2) that we love our neighbor as ourselves (cf. Matt. 22:34–40). Paul, who seems to reflect the explicit teaching of Jesus many times in these chapters, unfolds what that means in this section.

5. *Christian liberty (14:1–15:13)*. The longest part of these final chapters concerns Christian liberty. At first glance this seems surprising, given the many great personal, social, and cultural problems that existed in Paul's day as well as our own. Why did Paul not condemn slavery, develop a Christian view of economics, or comment on war? We cannot know with certainty why Paul chose to ignore these matters and address others, but his decision to deal with personal liberty at least indicates how important this matter was for him. He does not allow Christians to disobey God's moral law, and he offers no low standard of ethics. The standard is the highest: the yielding of our entire

selves to God as living sacrifices. But Paul was nevertheless firmly opposed to one group of Christians imposing extrabiblical (or nonbiblical) standards on other Christians.

The fact that Paul wrote the entire letter to the Galatians to defend the believer's liberty shows how strongly he felt about this. His advice to the Galatians was to "stand firm" in the liberty Christ has given us and not to be "burdened again by a yoke of slavery" (Gal. 5:1).

6. *Paul's personal ministry and plans (15:14–33)*. Having discussed the believer's personal liberty, Paul drops his ethical counsel and writes of his future plans. In these verses he picks up on matters he introduced at the start of the letter, explaining that he wants to come to Rome, why he has been hindered in coming earlier, and what he hopes to receive from the Romans when he does get to them.

7. *Final greetings (16:1–27)*. The last chapter of the book is often overlooked as little more than a list of names, but it is more important than that. The names in this chapter reveal much about the churches in Rome and Corinth and show how involved Paul was with the individuals who made up these early Christian communities. They show that Paul himself practiced the concern for others that he has been urging all along.

The New Humanity

As we plunge into the great forest of these remaining chapters we shall be looking very closely at the trees. But in this study we have been doing something equally valuable. We have been looking at the forest, and the bottom line of our study is that truth is a whole. Since we are talking about God's saving work for us, this means that everything God has done for us in salvation has bearing on everything we should do, on all of life. We must be different people because God has saved us from our sins.

And Christians are different. A number of years ago the Gallup Poll organization devised a scale to sort out those for whom religion seemed to be important and find out if it made any difference in their lives. America claims to be a very religious country, but the nation is increasingly immoral. Gallup wanted to know if serious religion made a difference for those who considered themselves to be "highly spiritually motivated" or committed.

He found that 12.5 percent of Americans are in this category, one person in eight. And he found that they really are different, so much so that he called them "a breed apart." He found that these people differed from the rest of the population in at least four key areas:

1. They are more satisfied with their lot in life. They are happier. Sixty-eight percent say they are "very happy" as compared with only 30 percent of those who are uncommitted.

2. Their families are stronger. The divorce rate among this group is far lower than among the less committed.

3. They tend to be more tolerant of persons of different races and religions. This is exactly opposite from what the media suggest when dealing with religion or religious leaders.

4. They are more involved in charitable activities than are their counterparts. A total of 46 percent of the highly spiritually committed say they are presently working among the poor, the infirm, and the elderly, compared to only 36 percent among the moderately committed, 28 percent among the moderately uncommitted, and 22 percent among the highly uncommitted.[9]

True conversion makes a difference in a person's life. If there are no differences, there is no genuine conversion. These differences are explained in the remaining chapters of this letter. Laws in themselves change little. Changed people change everything. And the only thing that ever really changes people is God himself through the gospel of our Lord Jesus Christ. If you have been called to faith in Jesus Christ, you are part of a radically changed community, the new humanity. It is your privilege to begin to make changes in our world.

9. George Gallup, Jr., "Is America's Faith for Real?" Princeton Theological Seminary *Alumni News*, vol. 22, no. 4, Summer 1982, pp. 15–17. For an earlier discussion of this poll see James Montgomery Boice, *Romans*, vol. 2, *The Reign of Grace: Romans 5:1–8:39* (Grand Rapids: Baker Book House, 1992), pp. 802–803.

181

Dying, We Live

Romans 12:1

Therefore, I urge you, brothers, in view of God's mercy, to offer your bodies as living sacrifices, holy and pleasing to God—this is your spiritual act of worship.

I do not like the word *paradox* used in reference to Christian teachings, because to most people the word refers to something that is self-contradictory or false. Christianity is not false. But the dictionary also defines *paradox* as a statement that *seems* to be contradictory yet may be true in fact, and in that sense there are paradoxes in Christianity. The most obvious is the doctrine of the Trinity. We speak of one God, but we also say that God exists in three persons: God the Father, God the Son, and God the Holy Spirit. We know the doctrine of the Trinity is true because God has revealed it to be true, but we are foolish if we think we can understand or explain it fully.

One of the great paradoxes of Christianity concerns the Christian life: We must die in order to live. We find this teaching many places in the Bible, particularly in the New Testament,[1] but the basic, foundational statement is by Jesus, who said, "If anyone would come after me, he must deny himself and

1. See Romans 6:1–14; Galatians 2:20, 5:24; Philippians 3:10; Colossians 3:3–5; 2 Timothy 2:11.

1491

take up his cross daily and follow me. For whoever wants to save his life will lose it, but whoever loses his life for me will save it" (Luke 9:23–24).

It was these words that inspired this well-known prayer of Saint Francis of Assisi:

> O Divine Master, grant that I may not so much
> Seek to be consoled as to console,
> To be understood as to understand,
> To be loved as to love.
> For it is by giving that we receive.
> It is in pardoning that we are pardoned,
> And it is by dying that we are born to eternal life.

I would not vouch for the theology implied in each of those impassioned sentences, but as a statement of principles governing the Christian life they are helpful.

More important, they are an expression of what Paul sets down at the start of Romans 12 as a first principle for learning to live the Christian life—self-sacrifice. "Therefore, I urge you, brothers, in view of God's mercy, to offer your bodies as living sacrifices, holy and pleasing to God—this is your spiritual act of worship." In Paul's culture a sacrifice was always an animal that was presented to a priest to be killed. So Paul is saying by this striking metaphor that the Christian life begins by offering ourselves to God for death. The paradox is that by offering ourselves to God we are enabled to live for him.

Therefore, it is by dying that we are enabled to live, period. For as Jesus said, trying to live, if it is living for ourselves, is actually death, while dying to self is actually the way to full living. What should we call this paradox? I call it "life-by-dying" or, as I have titled this study, "Dying, We Live."

Bought at a Price

This principle is so foundational to the doctrine of the Christian life that we must be very careful to lay it out correctly. After that we will go on to look at (1) the specific nature of this sacrifice, that it is an offering of our bodies presented to God as something holy and pleasing to him and (2) the specific motive for this sacrifice—why we should make it.

The first truth of this foundational teaching is that we are not our own but rather belong to Jesus, if we are truly Christians. Here is the way Paul puts it in 1 Corinthians: "Do you not know that your body is a temple of the Holy Spirit, who is in you, whom you have received from God? You are not your own; you were bought at a price" (1 Cor. 6:19–20). Again, just a chapter later, he says: "You were bought at a price; do not become slaves of men" (1 Cor. 7:23). Then, if we ask what that price is, well, the apostle Peter tells us in his first letter: "You know that it was not with perishable things such as silver and gold that you were redeemed from the empty way of life handed down to you from your forefathers, but with the precious blood of Christ, a lamb without blemish or defect" (1 Peter 1:18–19).

In that passage Peter uses the important word *redemption,* which means to buy back or to be bought again. It is one of the key words for describing what the Lord Jesus Christ accomplished for us by his death on the cross.

Since *redemption* refers to buying something or someone, the image is of a slave market in which we who are sinners are being offered to whomever will bid the highest price for us. The world is ready to bid, of course, particularly if we are attractive or in some other way seen as valuable. The world bids the world's currency.

It bids *fame.* Some people sell their souls to be famous; they will do almost anything to become well-known.

It bids *wealth.* Millions think that making money is the most important thing any person can do; they think that money will buy anything.

It bids *power.* Masses of people are on a power trip. They will wheel and deal and cheat and even trample on others to get to the top of the pyramid. It bids *sex.* Many have lost nearly everything of value in life for just a moment's indulgence.

But into the midst of this vast marketplace Jesus comes, and the price he bids to rescue enslaved sinners is his blood. He offers to die for them. God, who controls this auction, says, "Sold to the Lord Jesus Christ for the price of his blood." As a result we become Jesus' purchased possession and must live for him rather than ourselves, as Paul and Peter indicate.

The great preacher and biblical theologian John Calvin said rightly and precisely, "We are redeemed by the Lord for the purpose of consecrating ourselves and all our members to him."[2]

We need to remember that we are in the application section of Romans. Redemption was introduced earlier in the book, in chapter 3 (v. 24). So what we are finding here is an example of the truth that doctrine is practical and that practical material must be doctrinal if it is to be of any help at all. We are dealing with the practical question of "How should we then live?" But the very first thing to be said to explain how we should live is the meaning and implication of redemption. In other words, we cannot have true Christian living without the gospel.

Death to Our Past

Redemption from sin by Christ is not the only doctrine the Christian life of self-sacrifice is built on, however. A second truth is that we have died to the past by becoming new creatures in Christ, if we are truly converted. We studied this teaching in Romans 6, where Paul argued that because we have

2. John Calvin, *The Epistles of Paul the Apostle to the Romans and to the Thessalonians,* trans. Ross MacKenzie (Grand Rapids: Wm. B. Eerdmans Publishing Company, 1973), p. 262.

"died to sin" we are unable to "live in it any longer" (v. 2). Therefore, instead of offering the parts of our bodies "to sin, as instruments of wickedness," as we used to do, we must instead offer ourselves "to God, as those who have been brought from death to life; and . . . the parts of [our] bodies to him as instruments of righteousness" (Rom. 6:13).

When we studied this passage earlier I pointed out that it does not mean that we have become unresponsive to sin or that we should die to it or that we are dying to it day by day or that we have died to sin's guilt. The verb *die* is an aorist, which refers to something that has been done once for all. Here it refers to the change that has come about as a result of our being saved. "We died to sin" means that as a result of our union with Jesus Christ by the work of the Holy Spirit we have become new creatures in Christ so that we can never go back to being what we were. We are to start the Christian life with that knowledge. If we cannot go back, then we must go forward.

Let me review this teaching by summarizing what I wrote in my study of Romans 6:11 in volume 2. Dying to sin does not mean:

1. That it is my duty to die to sin.
2. That I am commanded to die to sin.
3. That I am to consider sin as a dead force within me.
4. That I am dead to sin so long as I am gaining mastery over it.
5. That sin in me has been eradicated.
6. That counting myself dead to sin makes me insensitive to it.[3]

What Paul is saying is that we have already died to sin in the sense that we cannot successfully return to our old lives. Therefore, since that is true, we might as well get on with the task of living for the Lord Jesus Christ. We need to forget about sinning and instead present our bodies as "living sacrifices" to God.

Dying to Live

The third foundational teaching for what it means to live by dying is the paradox itself, namely that it is by dying to our own desires in order to serve Christ that we actually learn to live.

It is not difficult to understand what this means. We understand only too well that dying to self means putting personal desires behind us in order to put the desires of God for us and the needs of other people first. We understand the promise too! If we do this, we will experience a full and rewarding life. We will be happy Christians. The problem is not with our understanding.

---

3. See James Montgomery Boice, *Romans*, vol. 2, *The Reign of Grace, Romans 5:1–8:39* (Grand Rapids: Baker Book House, 1992), p. 677.

The problem is that we do not believe it, or at least not in regard to ourselves. We think that if we deny ourselves, we will be miserable. Yet this is nothing less than disbelieving God. It is a failure of faith.

So I ask, Who are you willing to believe? Yourself, as reinforced by the world and its way of thinking? Or Jesus Christ?

I say Jesus specifically because I want to remind you of his teaching from the Sermon on the Mount. He speaks there about how to be happy. Indeed, the word is even stronger than that. It is the powerful word *blessed*, meaning to be favored by God:

> Blessed are the poor in spirit,
>   for theirs is the kingdom of heaven.
> Blessed are those who mourn,
>   for they will be comforted.
> Blessed are the meek,
>   for they will inherit the earth.
> Blessed are those who hunger and thirst for righteousness,
>   for they will be filled.
> Blessed are the merciful,
>   for they will be shown mercy.
> Blessed are the pure in heart,
>   for they will see God.
> Blessed are the peacemakers,
>   for they will be called sons of God.
> Blessed are those who are persecuted because of righteousness,
>   for theirs is the kingdom of heaven.
>
> Matthew 5:3–10

We call these statements the Beatitudes, which means the way to happiness or blessing. But this is not the way the world thinks one finds happiness. If a director of one of today's popular television sitcoms or the editor of a widely circulating fashion magazine were to rewrite the Beatitudes from a contemporary point of view, I suppose they would go like this: "Blessed are the rich, for they can have all they want; blessed are the powerful, for they can control others; blessed are the sexually liberated, for they can fully satisfy themselves; blessed are the famous, because they are envied." Isn't that the world's way, the way even Christians sometimes try to go, rather than the way of sacrifice?

But think it through carefully. The world promises blessings for those who follow these standards. But is this what they find? Do they actually find happiness?

Take for example a person who thinks that the way to happiness is wealth. He sets his heart on earning one hundred thousand dollars. He gets it, but he is not happy. He raises his goal to two hundred thousand dollars. When he gets that he tries to accumulate a million dollars, but still he is not happy. John D. Rockefeller, one of the richest men in the world in his day, was asked on one occasion, "How much money is enough?"

He was honest enough to answer wryly, "Just a little bit more."

A Texas millionaire once said, "I thought money could buy happiness. I have been miserably disillusioned."

Another person thinks that he will find happiness through power, so he goes into politics, where he thinks power lies. He runs in a local election and wins. After that he sets his sight on a congressional seat, then on a place in the Senate. If he is talented enough and the circumstances are favorable, he wants to be president. But power never satisfies. One of the world's great statesmen once told Billy Graham, "I am an old man. Life has lost all meaning. I am ready to take a fateful leap into the unknown."

Still another person tries the path of sexual liberation. She launches into the swinging singles scene, where the average week consists of "happy hours," Friday night parties, weekend overnight escapes into the country, and a rapid exchange of partners. But it does not work. Several years ago CBS did a television documentary on the swinging singles lifestyle in southern California, interviewing about half a dozen women who all said essentially the same thing: "We were told that this was the fun way to live, but all the men want to do is get in bed with you. We have had enough of that to last a lifetime."

Does the world's "me first" philosophy lead to happiness? Is personal indulgence the answer? You do not have to be a genius to see through that facade. It is an empty promise. Paul calls it "a lie" (Rom. 1:25).

So wake up, Christian. And listen to Paul when he pleads, "Therefore, I urge you, brothers, in view of God's mercy, to offer your bodies as living sacrifices, holy and pleasing to God—this is your spiritual act of worship. Do not conform any longer to the pattern of this world, but be transformed by the renewing of your mind. Then you will be able to test and approve what God's will is—his good, pleasing and perfect will" (Rom. 12:1–2).

God does not lie. His word is utterly reliable. You will find his way to be "good, pleasing, and perfect" if you will bend to it.

The Victim and the Priest

That brings us to the fourth and final foundational truth. The first two concerned what God has done for us in redeeming us and joining us to Jesus Christ by the Holy Spirit so that we become new creatures. The third point was the apparent paradox: life by dying. This last point is an urgent appeal for us to offer ourselves as living sacrifices to God. This is not done for us. It is something we must do.

This is the "obedience that comes from faith" that Paul wrote about early in the letter, saying, "Through him and for his name's sake, we received grace and apostleship to call people from among all the Gentiles to the obedience that comes from faith" (Rom. 1:5). So again we are back to one of the great doctrinal teachings.

What an interesting mental picture Paul creates for us in Romans 12:1. A sacrifice is something offered to God by a priest. A priest would take a sacrifice offered by a worshiper, carry it to the altar, kill it, pour out the blood, and then burn the victim's body. In that procedure the priest and the offering were two separate entities. But in this arresting image of what it is to live a genuinely Christian life, Paul shows that the priest and the offering are the same. Furthermore, we are the priests who present the offering, and the offerings we present are our own bodies.

Is there a model for this in Scripture? Of course. It is the model of Jesus himself, for he was both the sacrifice and the priest who made the sacrifice. We have a statement of this in one of our great communion hymns, translated from a sixth-century Latin text by the Scotsman Robert Campbell in 1849:

> At the Lamb's high feast we sing
> Praise to our victorious King,
> Who hath washed us in the tide
> Flowing from his pierced side;
> Praise we him whose love divine
> Gives his sacred blood for wine,
> Gives his body for the feast,
> Christ the Victim, Christ the Priest.

Yes, there is an enormous difference between the sacrifice Jesus made for us and our own sacrifices of ourselves. Jesus' sacrifice was an atoning sacrifice. He died in our place, bearing the punishment of God for our sin so that we might not have to bear it. His death was substitutionary. Our sacrifices are not at all like that. They are not an atonement for sin in any sense. Still, they are like Christ's sacrifice in that we are the ones who make them and that the sacrifices we offer are ourselves.

Another distinction is that in the Old Testament the priests made different kinds of sacrifices. There were sacrifices for sin, of course; they looked forward to the death of Jesus Christ and explained it as a substitutionary atonement. These were fulfilled by Jesus' death and are not repeatable. In this sense "we have been made holy through the sacrifice of the body of Jesus Christ once for all," as the author of Hebrews says (Heb. 10:10). But in addition to the sacrifices for sin there were also sacrifices of thanksgiving, offerings by worshipers who simply wanted to thank God for some great blessing or deliverance. It is this kind of a sacrifice that we offer when we offer God ourselves.

Sacrifice is an utterly unpleasant word in our day! No one wants to be a sacrifice. In fact, people do not want to sacrifice even a single little thing. We want to acquire things instead. Nevertheless, this is where the Christian life starts. It is God's instruction and desire for us, and it is "good, pleasing and perfect" even if it does not seem to be.

Will you trust God that he knows what he is doing? Will you believe him in this as in other matters? If you will believe him, you will do exactly what Paul urges you to do in Romans 12. You will offer your body as a "living sacrifice" to God and thereby prove that his will for you is indeed perfect.

182

Living Sacrifice: Its Nature

Romans 12:1

Therefore, I urge you, brothers, in view of God's mercy, to offer your bodies as living sacrifices, holy and pleasing to God—this is your spiritual act of worship.

Not long ago I reread parts of Charles Dickens's wonderful historical novel, *A Tale of Two Cities.* The cities are Paris and London, of course, and the story is set in the years of the French Revolution when thousands of innocent people were being executed on the guillotine by followers of the revolution. As usual with Dickens's stories, the plot is complex, but it reaches a never-to-be-forgotten climax when Sydney Carton, the disreputable character in the story, substitutes himself for his friend Charles Darney, who is being held for execution in the Bastille prison. Darney, who has been condemned to die, goes free, and Carton goes to the scaffold for him, saying, "It is a far, far better thing I do, than I have ever done; it is a far, far better rest I go to, than I have ever known." The tale is so well written that it still moves me to tears every time I read it.

Few things move us to hushed awe so much as a person's sacrifice of his or her life for someone else. It is the ultimate proof of true love.

1499

We are to sacrifice ourselves for Jesus if we love him. Jesus said, "Greater love has no one than this, that he lay down his life for his friends" (John 15:13), and he did it for us. The sacrifice of Sydney Carton for his friend Darney is only a story, albeit a moving one, but Jesus actually died on the cross for our salvation. Now, because he loved us and gave himself for us, we who love him are likewise to give ourselves to him as "living sacrifices."

But there is a tremendous difference. As I said in the last study, Jesus died in our place, bearing the punishment of God for our sin so that we would not have to bear it. Our sacrifices are not at all like that. They are not an atonement for sin in any sense. But they are like Christ's in this at least, that we are the ones who make them and that the sacrifices we make are ourselves. It is what Paul is talking about in Romans 12 when he writes, "Therefore, I urge you, brothers, in view of God's mercy, to offer your bodies as living sacrifices, holy and pleasing to God—this is your spiritual act of worship" (Rom. 12:1).

I introduced the matter of sacrifice in the last chapter. In this study I want to explore what exactly is meant by sacrifice, and how we are to do it.

Living Sacrifices

The first point is the obvious one: The sacrifice is to be a living sacrifice rather than a dead one. This was quite a novel idea in Paul's day, when sacrifices were always killed. The animal was brought to the priest. The sins of the person bringing the sacrifice were confessed over the animal, thereby transferring them to it symbolically. Then the animal was put to death. It was a vivid way of reminding everyone that "the wages of sin is death" (Rom. 6:23) and that the salvation of sinners is by substitution. In these sacrifices the animal died in place of the worshiper. It died so that he or she might not have to die. But now, with a burst of divinely inspired creativity, Paul reveals that the sacrifices we are to offer are not to be dead but rather living. We are to offer our lives to God so that, as a result, we might "no longer live for [ourselves] but for him who died for [us] and was raised again" (2 Cor. 5:15).

We are to be living sacrifices, yes. But with what life? Certainly not our old sinful lives in which, when we lived in them, we were dead already. Rather, we are to offer our new spiritual lives that have been given to us by Christ.

Robert Smith Candlish was a Scottish pastor who lived over a hundred years ago (1806–73) and who left us some marvelous studies of the Bible. In his study of Romans 12, he reflects on the nature of the life we are to offer God. "What life?" he asks. "Not merely animal life, the life that is common to all sentient and moving creatures; not merely, in addition to that, intelligent life, the life that characterizes all beings capable of thought and voluntary choice; but spiritual life: life in the highest sense; the very life which those on whose behalf the sacrifice of atonement is presented lost, when they fell into that state which makes a sacrifice of atonement necessary."[1]

1. Robert S. Candlish, *Studies in Romans 12: The Christian's Sacrifice and Service of Praise* (Grand Rapids: Kregel Publications, 1989), pp. 33–34. Original edition 1867.

What this means, among other things, is that we must be Christians if we are to give ourselves to God as he requires. Other people may give God their money or time or even take up a religious vocation, but only a Christian can give back to God that new spiritual life in Christ that he has first been given. Indeed, it is only because we have been made alive in Christ that we are able to do this or even want to.

Offering Our Bodies

The second thing we need to see about the nature of the sacrifice God requires is that it involves the giving to God of our bodies. Some of the earlier commentators stress that offering our bodies really means offering ourselves, all we are. Calvin wrote, "By *bodies* he means not only our skin and bones, but the totality of which we are composed."[2] But although it is true that we are to offer God all we are, most commentators today rightly refuse to pass over the word *bodies* quite this easily because they recognize how much the Bible stresses the importance of our bodies.

For example, Leon Morris says, "Paul surely expected Christians to offer to God not only their bodies but their whole selves. . . . But we should bear in mind that the body is very important in the Christian understanding of things. Our bodies may be 'implements of righteousness' (6:13) and 'members of Christ' (1 Cor. 6:15). The body is a temple of the Holy Spirit (1 Cor. 6:19); Paul can speak of being 'holy both in body and in spirit' (1 Cor. 7:34). He knows that there are possibilities of evil in the body but that in the believer 'the body of sin' has been brought to nothing (6:6)."[3]

In a similar manner, Robert Haldane says, "It is of the body that the apostle here speaks, and it is not proper to extract out of his language more than it contains. . . . This shows the importance of serving God with the body as well as with the soul."[4]

Paul does not elaborate upon what he means by presenting our bodies to God as living sacrifices in Romans 12, but has already presented this idea in chapter 6. There he said, "Therefore do not let sin reign in your mortal body so that you obey its evil desires. Do not offer the parts of your body to sin, as instruments of wickedness, but rather offer yourselves to God, as those who have been brought from death to life; and offer the parts of your body to him as instruments of righteousness. For sin shall not be your master,

2. John Calvin, *The Epistles of Paul the Apostle to the Romans and to the Thessalonians*, trans. Ross MacKenzie (Grand Rapids: Wm. B. Eerdmans Publishing Company, 1973), p. 264.

3. Leon Morris, *The Epistle to the Romans* (Grand Rapids: Wm. B. Eerdmans Publishing Company, and Leicester, England: Inter-Varsity Press, 1988), pp. 433–434.

4. Robert Haldane, *An Exposition of the Epistle to the Romans* (MacDill AFB: MacDonald Publishing Company, 1958), p. 554. See also John Murray, *The Epistle to the Romans*, 2 vols. in 1 (Grand Rapids: Wm. B. Eerdmans Publishing Company, 1968), vol. 2, p. 111. Murray notes the depreciation of the body in favor of the spirit in Greek thought and argues that against that background an emphasis upon the body by Paul was a Christian necessity.

because you are not under law, but under grace" (vv. 12–14). Paul is making the same point there, where he first begins to talk about sanctification, that he makes in 12:1—we are to serve God by offering him our bodies.

Sin can control us through our bodies, but it does not need to. So rather than offering our bodies as instruments of sin, we are to offer God our bodies as instruments for doing his will. This concerns specific body parts.

1. *Our minds.* Although we often think of our minds as separate from our bodies, our minds actually are parts of our bodies and the victory we need to achieve begins here. I will not dwell on this here because I will be treating it more fully later when I talk about mind renewal.[5] But I remind you that this is the point at which Paul himself begins in verse 2: "Do not conform any longer to the pattern of this world, but be transformed by *the renewing of your mind.*"

Have you ever considered that what you do with your mind will determine a great deal of what you will become as a Christian? If you fill your mind only with the products of our secular culture, you will remain secular and sinful. If you fill your head with trashy novels, you will begin to live like the characters you read about. If you do nothing but watch television, you will begin to act like the scoundrels on television. On the other hand, if you feed your mind on the Bible and Christian books, train it by godly conversation, and discipline it to critique what you see and hear by applying biblical truths to the world's ideas, you will grow in godliness and become increasingly useful to God.

When I wrote on this subject in my earlier study of Romans 6:12–14, I set out a simple goal in this area: "For every secular book you read, make it your goal also to read one good Christian book, a book that can stretch your mind spiritually."[6]

2. *Our eyes and ears.* The mind is not the only part of our body by which we receive impressions and that must therefore be offered to God as an instrument of righteousness. We also receive impressions through our eyes and ears, and these must be surrendered to God too.

Sociologists tell us that by the age of twenty-one the average young person has been bombarded by three hundred thousand commercial messages, all arguing from the assumption that personal gratification is the dominant goal in life.[7] Television and other modern means of communication put the acquisition of things before godliness; in fact, they never mention godliness at all. How are you going to grow in godliness if you are constantly watching television or reading printed ads or listening to secular radio?

I am not advocating an evangelical monasticism in which we retreat from the culture, though it is far better to retreat from it than perish in it. But

5. See chapters 187 and 188.

6. See James Montgomery Boice, *Romans,* vol. 2, *The Reign of Grace: Romans 5:1–8:39* (Grand Rapids: Baker Book House, 1992), p. 685.

7. Mike Bellah, *Baby Boom Believers: Why We Think We Need It All and How to Survive When We Don't Get It* (Wheaton: Tyndale House Publishers, 1988), p. 27.

somehow the secular input must be counterbalanced by the spiritual. As I wrote earlier, "Another simple goal might be for you to spend as many hours studying your Bible, praying, and going to church as watching television."

3. *Our tongues.* The tongue is also part of our body, and what we do with it is important either for good or evil. James, the Lord's brother, wrote, "The tongue is . . . a world of evil among the parts of the body. It corrupts the whole person, sets the whole course of his life on fire, and is itself set on fire by hell" (James 3:5–6). If your tongue is not given to God as an instrument of righteousness in his hands, this will be true of you. You do not need to be a Hitler and plunge the world into armed conflict to do evil with your tongue. A little bit of gossip or slander will suffice.

What you need to do is use your tongue to praise and serve God. For one thing, you should learn how to recite Scripture with it. You probably know the popular songs. Can you not also use your tongue to speak God's words? And how about worship? You should use your tongue to praise God by means of hymns and other Christian songs. Above all, you should use your tongue to witness to others about the person and work of Christ.

Here is another goal for you if you want to grow in godliness: Use your tongue as much to tell others about Jesus as for idle conversation.

4. *Our hands and feet.* There are several important passages about our hands and feet. In 1 Thessalonians 4:11–12, Paul tells us to work with our hands so that we will be self-supporting and not dependent on anybody: "Make it your ambition to lead a quiet life, to mind your own business and to work with your hands, just as we told you, so that your daily life may win the respect of outsiders and so that you will not be dependent on anybody." In Ephesians 4:28 he tells us to work so that we will have something to give to others who are in need: "He who has been stealing must steal no longer, but must work, doing something useful with his own hands, that he may have something to share with those in need."

As far as our feet are concerned, in Romans 10 Paul writes of the need others have for the gospel, saying, "How can they hear without someone preaching to them? And how can they preach unless they are sent? As it is written, 'How beautiful are the feet of those who bring good news!'" (Rom. 10:14–15).

What do you do with your hands? And where do your feet take you? Do you allow them to take you to where Christ is denied or blasphemed? To where sin is openly practiced? Are you spending most of your free time loitering in the hot singles clubs? You will not grow in godliness there. On the contrary, you will fall from righteous conduct. Let your feet carry you into the company of those who love and serve God. Or, if you go into the world, let it be to serve the world and witness to it in Christ's name. Use your feet and hands for him.

Here is another goal taken from the earlier study: "For every special secular function you attend, determine to attend a Christian function also. And when you attend a secular function, do so as a witness by word and action for the Lord Jesus Christ."[8]

Holiness

The third word Paul uses to indicate the nature of the sacrifices we are to offer God is *holy*. Any sacrifice must be holy, without spot or blemish and consecrated entirely to God. Anything less is an insult to the great and holy God we serve. How much more must we be holy who have been purchased "not with perishable things such as silver or gold . . . but with the precious blood of Christ" (1 Peter 1:18–19). Peter wrote, "But just as he who called you is holy, so be holy in all you do; for it is written: 'Be holy, because I am holy'" (1 Peter 1:15–16). The author of Hebrews said, "Without holiness no one will see the Lord" (Heb. 12:14).

This is the very heart of what we are talking about when we speak of living sacrifices: Holiness is the end of the matter, the point to which the entire Epistle of Romans has been heading. Romans is about salvation. But as someone wise has noted, salvation does not mean that Jesus died to save us *in* our sins but to save us *from* them.

Handley C. G. Moule expressed this well: "As we actually approach the rules of holiness now before us, let us once more recollect what we have seen all along in the Epistle, that holiness is the aim and issue of the entire Gospel. It is indeed an 'evidence of life,' infinitely weighty in the enquiry whether a man knows God indeed and is on the way to his heaven. But it is much more; it is the expression of life; it is the form and action in which life is intended to come out. . . . We who believe are 'chosen' and 'ordained' to 'bring forth fruit' (John 15:16), fruit much and lasting."[9]

I don't think any subject is more generally neglected among evangelicals in America in our day than holiness. Yet there was a time when holiness was a serious pursuit of anyone who called himself or herself a Christian, and how one lived and who one was inside was important.

England's J. I. Packer has written a book called *Rediscovering Holiness* in which he calls attention to this fact: "The Puritans insisted that all life and relationships must become 'holiness to the Lord.' John Wesley told the world that God had raised up methodism 'to spread scriptural holiness throughout the land.' Phoebe Palmer, Handley Moule, Andrew Murray, Jessie Penn-Lewis, F. B. Meyer, Oswald Chambers, Horatius Bonar, Amy Carmichael, and L. B. Maxwell are only a few of the leading figures in the 'holiness revival' that

---

8. Boice, *Romans*, vol. 2, p. 687. This entire discussion of what it means to offer our minds, ears, eyes, tongues, hands, and feet is borrowed with changes from the earlier study entitled, "God's Instruments" (Rom. 6:12–14).

9. Handley C. G. Moule, *The Epistle of St. Paul to the Romans* (London: Hodder and Stoughton, 1896), pp. 324–325.

touched all evangelical Christendom between the mid-nineteenth and mid-twentieth centuries."[10]

But today? Today holiness is largely forgotten as being important for Christians. We do not try to be holy, and we hardly know what holiness means. And we do not look for holiness in others. The great parish minister and revival preacher Robert Murray McCheyne once said, "My people's greatest need is my personal holiness." But pulpit committees hardly look for holiness in a new pastor today. They look for a winsome personality, communication skills, administrative ability, and other such things.

As for ourselves, we do not seek out books or tapes on holiness or attend seminars designed to draw us closer to God. We want seminars entitled "How to Be Happy," "How to Raise Children," "How to Have a Good Sex Life," "How to Succeed in Business," and so on.

Fortunately, this lack has begun to be noticed by some evangelical leaders who are disturbed by it and have begun to address the subject. I commend Packer's book, as well as a book written several years ago by Jerry Bridges called *The Pursuit of Holiness*. There is also the older classic by the English Bishop John Charles Ryle by the same title.[11]

Pleasing to God

The final word Paul uses to describe how we should present our bodies to God as living sacrifices is *pleasing*. If we do what Paul has urged us to do—offer our "bodies as living sacrifices, holy . . . to God"—then we will also find that what we have done is pleasing and acceptable to him.

That is an amazing thing to me, that God could find anything we might do to be pleasing. But it is so! I notice that the word *pleasing* occurs twice in this short paragraph. The first time, which is what we are looking at here, it indicates that our offering of ourselves to God pleases God. The second time, at the end of verse 2, it indicates that when we do this we will find God's will for our lives to be pleasing as well as good and perfect. That God's will for me should be pleasing, pleasing to me—that I understand. How could it be otherwise if God is all-wise and all-good? He must will what is good for me. But that my offering of myself to him should somehow also please him when I know myself to be sinful and ignorant and half-hearted even in my best efforts—that is astonishing.

10. J. I. Packer, *Rediscovering Holiness* (Ann Arbor, Mich.: Servant Publications, 1992), pp. 12–13.

11. J. C. Ryle, *Holiness: Its Nature, Hindrances, Difficulties and Roots* (Cambridge: James Clark, 1959) and Jerry Bridges, *The Pursuit of Holiness* (Colorado Springs: NavPress, 1978). Lately a number of important books have approached holiness from the side of the spiritual disciplines: R. Kent Hughes, *Disciplines of a Godly Man* (Wheaton: Crossway Books, 1991); Dallas Willard, *The Spirit of the Disciplines: Understanding How God Changes Lives* (San Francisco: Harper & Row, 1988); and Donald S. Whitney, *Spiritual Disciplines for the Christian Life* (Colorado Springs: NavPress, 1991).

But so it is! The Bible tells me that at my best I am to think of myself as an "unworthy" servant (Luke 17:10). But it also says that if I live for Jesus, offering back to him what he has first given to me, then one day I will hear him say, "Well done, good and faithful servant! . . . Come and share your master's happiness!" (Matt. 25:21).

Living for Christ may be hard. It always will be in this sinful, God-defying world. I may not understand what good it does either for me or for other people. But that commendation, the praise of the Lord Jesus Christ, will be enough for me. It will make it worthwhile.

183

Living Sacrifice: Its Motive

Romans 12:1

Therefore, I urge you, brothers, in view of God's mercy, to offer your bodies as living sacrifices, holy and pleasing to God—this is your spiritual act of worship.

What is it that motivates people to be "the best they can be," as the Army recruitment ads say? There are a number of answers.

One way to motivate people is to challenge them. Dale Carnegie, the author of *How to Win Friends and Influence People*, tells of a mill manager whose workers were not producing. The owner was named Charles Schwab, and he asked the manager what was wrong. "I have no idea," the manager said. "I've coaxed the men; I've pushed them; I've sworn and cussed; I've threatened them with damnation and being fired. Nothing works. They just won't produce."

"How many heats did your shift make today?" Schwab asked.

"Six."

Without saying anything else, Schwab picked up a piece of chalk and wrote a big number "6" on the floor. Then he walked away.

When the night shift came in they saw the "6" and asked what it meant. "The big boss was here today," someone said. "He asked how many heats the day shift made, and we told him six. He chalked it on the floor."

The next morning Schwab walked through the mill again. The night shift had rubbed out the "6" and replaced it with an even bigger "7." When the day shift reported the next day they saw the "7." So the night shift thought they were better than the day shift, did they? They'd show them. They pitched in furiously, and before they had left that evening they had rubbed out the "7" and replaced it with a "10." Schwab had increased production 66 percent in just twenty-four hours simply by throwing down a challenge.[1]

Napoleon said that men are moved by trinkets. He was referring to medals, and he meant that soldiers would risk even death for recognition.

Winston Churchill, the great British statesman and prime minister during the hard days of the Second World War, motivated the British people by his vision of victory and by brilliant speeches. We can remember some of his words today: "blood, toil, tears and sweat," "victory—victory at all costs, victory in spite of all terror; victory however long and hard the road may be," "their finest hour."

Moved by Mercy

What is it that motivates Christians to live a Christian life? Or to use Paul's language in Romans 12:1, what is it that motivates them "to offer [their] bodies as living sacrifices . . . to God"?

If you and I were as rational as we think we are and sometimes claim to be, we would not need any encouragement to offer our bodies to God as living sacrifices because it would be the most reasonable thing in the world for us to do it. God is our Creator. He has redeemed us from sin by the death of Jesus Christ. He has made us alive in Christ. He loves us and cares for us. It is reasonable to love God and serve him in return. But we are not as rational as that and do need urging, which is why Paul writes as he does in Romans 12. In verse 1 Paul urges us to offer our bodies to God as living sacrifices, and the motivation he provides is God's mercy: "Therefore, I urge you, brothers, *in view of God's mercy*, to offer your bodies as living sacrifices, holy and pleasing to God—this is your spiritual act of worship."

Romans 12:1 is an amazing verse. It is one of those portions of the Bible that is literally packed with meaning, which is why I have been trying to unpack it carefully in these opening studies.

I began by studying the word *therefore*, which links the urging of verses 1 and 2 to everything that Paul has already written about in the letter. Next we looked at the idea of sacrifice, finding that in genuine Christianity we live by dying to self, as strange as that may seem. Third, we explored the nature

---

1. Dale Carnegie, *How to Win Friends and Influence People* (New York: Simon & Schuster, 1963), pp. 173–76.

of these sacrifices, seeing that: (1) they are to be living, (2) they involve giving the specific individual parts of our bodies to God for his service, (3) they must be holy, and (4) if they are these things, they will be acceptable to God.

But why should we present our bodies as living sacrifices? The answer is simple: "In view of [or because of] God's mercy." In the Greek text the word *mercy* is plural rather than singular, so the reason for giving ourselves to God is literally because of God's manifold mercies—that is, because he has been good to us in many ways.

This is entirely different from the way the world looks at things. Assuming that people in today's world should even get concerned about living righteously—and it is doubtful that very many could—they would probably say, "The reason to live a moral life is because you are going to get in trouble if you don't." Or to give secular thinking the greatest possible credit, perhaps they might say, "Because it is good for you."

That is not what we have here.

In *Rediscovering Holiness,* J. I. Packer says,

> The secular world never understands Christian motivation. Faced with the question of what makes Christians tick, unbelievers maintain that Christianity is practiced only out of self-serving purposes. They see Christians as fearing the consequences of not being Christians (religion as fire insurance), or feeling the need of help and support to achieve their goals (religion as a crutch), or wishing to sustain a social identity (religion as a badge of respectability). No doubt all these motivations can be found among the membership of churches: it would be futile to dispute that. But just as a horse brought into a house is not thereby made human, so a self-seeking motivation brought into the church is not thereby made Christian, nor will holiness ever be the right name for religious routines thus motivated. From the plan of salvation I learn that the true driving force in authentic Christian living is, and ever must be, not the hope of gain, but the heart of gratitude.[2]

That is exactly what Paul is teaching. As John Calvin wrote, "Paul's entreaty teaches us that men will never worship God with a sincere heart, or be roused to fear and obey him with sufficient zeal, until they properly understand how much they are indebted to his mercy."[3]

What Is Mercy?

This is not the first time we have had to think about mercy in studying Romans. Mercy is one of three words often found together: goodness, grace and mercy. *Goodness* is the most general term, involving all that emanates from God: his decrees, his creation, his laws, his providences. It extends to

---

2. J. I. Packer, *Rediscovering Holiness* (Ann Arbor, Mich.: Servant Publications, 1992), p. 75.
3. John Calvin, *The Epistles of Paul the Apostle to the Romans and to the Thessalonians,* trans. Ross MacKenzie (Grand Rapids: Wm. B. Eerdmans Publishing Company, 1973), p. 263.

the elect and to the nonelect, though not in the same way. God is good, and everything he does is good. *Grace* denotes favor, particularly toward the undeserving. There is common grace, the kind of favor God shows to all persons in that he sends rain on the just and unjust alike. There is also special, or saving, grace, which is what he shows to those he is saving from their sins. *Mercy* is an aspect of grace, but the unique quality of mercy is that it is given to the pitiful.

Arthur W. Pink says, "Mercy . . . denotes the ready inclination of God to relieve the misery of fallen creatures. Thus 'mercy' presupposes sin."[4]

Let me show how this works by three examples.

In the Beginning

The first is Adam. Try to put yourself in Adam's position at the very beginning of human history and imagine how he must have felt when God came to him in the garden after he and Eve had sinned by eating from the forbidden tree. God had warned Adam about eating, saying, "You are free to eat from any tree in the garden; but you must not eat from the tree of the knowledge of good and evil, for when you eat of it you will surely die" (Gen. 2:16–17). The Hebrew text actually says, "*On the day* you eat of it you will die." But Adam and Eve had eaten of it, and now God had come to them to demand an accounting and pronounce judgment.

"Where are you?" God called.

Adam and his wife had hidden among the trees when they heard God coming; they were terrified. God had said that they would die on the day they ate of the forbidden tree. Eve must have expected to die. Adam must have expected to die. "I heard you in the garden, and I was afraid because I was naked; so I hid," Adam said.

"Who told you that you were naked?" God asked. "Have you eaten from the tree that I commanded you not to eat from?"

Adam confessed that he had eaten, though he blamed the woman for getting him to do it.

God addressed the woman. "What is this you have done?"

Eve blamed the serpent (Gen. 3:9–13).

At last God began his judgments, beginning with the serpent:

> Cursed are you above all the livestock
>   and all the wild animals!
> You will crawl on your belly
>   and you will eat dust
>   all the days of your life.
> And I will put enmity
>   between you and the woman,

4. Arthur W. Pink, *The Attributes of God* (Grand Rapids: Baker Book House, 1975), pp. 83–84.

> and between your offspring and hers;
>> he will crush your head,
>> and you will strike his heel.

Genesis 3:14–15

God spoke to Eve next, foretelling pain in childbirth and harsh struggle within the marriage. We call it the battle of the sexes.

Finally, God addressed Adam:

> Cursed is the ground because of you;
>> through painful toil you will eat of it
>> all the days of your life.
> It will produce thorns and thistles for you,
>> and you will eat the plants of the field.
> By the sweat of your brow
>> you will eat your food
> until you return to the ground,
>> since from it you were taken;
> for dust you are
>> and to dust you will return.

Genesis 3:17–19

Imagine yourself in Adam's place, living through what I have described. God had told Adam and Eve that they would die, but they had not died. There had been judgments, of course, consequences. Sin always has consequences. But they had not been struck down; and, in fact, God had even announced the coming of a Redeemer who one day would crush Satan's head and undo his work. Even more, God had illustrated the nature of Christ's atonement by killing animals, the innocent dying for the guilty, and then by clothing Adam and Eve with the animals' skins. It was a picture of imputed righteousness.

Adam must have been overwhelmed by an awareness of God's mercy. Adam deserved to die, but instead of killing him, God spared him and promised a Savior instead.

No wonder Adam then named his wife "Eve," meaning life-giver or mother. It was his way of expressing faith in God's promise, for God had said that it was from the seed of the woman that the Redeemer would come. The memory of God's mercy must have kept Adam looking to God in faith and living for God by faith through his long life from that time forward, for Adam lived to be eight hundred years old and was the father of the line of godly patriarchs that extended from him through his third son Seth to Noah.

The Worst of Sinners

My second example is Paul. In his earlier days Paul was called Saul, and he was a fierce opponent of Christianity. He was a Pharisee, the strictest sect of the Jews, and he was zealous for the traditions of his fathers. This led him to participate in the martyrdom of Stephen, and he followed that by arresting and otherwise persecuting many of the early Christians. Having done what he could in Jerusalem, Paul obtained letters to the leaders of the synagogues in Damascus and went there to arrest any Christians he could find and carry them off to Jerusalem for trial and possible execution.

On the way Jesus stopped him. There was a bright light from heaven, and when Saul fell to the ground, blinded by the light, he heard a voice speaking to him. "Saul, Saul, why do you persecute me?"

"Who are you, Lord?" Saul asked.

"I am Jesus, whom you are persecuting," the voice replied.

At this point Paul must have had feelings similar to those of Adam when God had appeared to him in the garden of Eden. True, God had not told Paul that he would die if he persecuted Christians. He was persecuting them in ignorance, supposing that he was serving God. But he had been terribly mistaken. He had done great harm, and he had even participated in the killing of Stephen. In that first moment of Paul's dawning apprehension, when he recognized that it was Jesus of Nazareth who was speaking to him, he must have thought that Jesus had appeared to him to judge him. He certainly deserved it. He must have expected to have been struck down and to die.

Instead Jesus sent him to Damascus, where he was to be told what he should do. When the message came to him by a disciple named Ananias, it was that he was to be God's "chosen instrument to carry [God's] name before the Gentiles and their kings and before the people of Israel" (Acts 9:1–15).

Mercy? I should say it was. Paul never forgot it.

That is why, years later, he could write to his young friend and co-worker Timothy, saying, "Here is a trustworthy saying that deserves full acceptance: Christ Jesus came into the world to save sinners—of whom I am the worst. But for that very reason I was shown mercy so that in me, the worst of sinners, Christ Jesus might display his unlimited patience as an example for those who would believe on him and receive eternal life" (1 Tim. 1:15–16). It was because he knew himself to be a sinner saved only by the mercy and grace of God that Paul joyfully gave himself to God as a living sacrifice and worked tirelessly to please him.

A Slave of Slaves

My third example is John Newton. Newton ran away to sea as a young boy and eventually went to Africa to participate in the slave trade. His reason for going, as he later wrote in his autobiography, was that he might "sin his fill."

Sin he did! But the path of sin is downhill, and Newton's path descended so low that he was eventually reduced to the position of a slave in his master's African compound. This man dealt in slaves, and when he went off on slaving expeditions Newton fell into the hands of the slave trader's African wife, who hated white men and vented her venom on Newton. Newton was forced to eat his food off the dusty floor like a dog, and at one point he was actually placed in chains. Sick and emaciated, he nearly died.

Newton escaped from this form of his slavery eventually. But he was still chained to sin and again went to sea transporting slaves from the west coast of Africa to the New World. It was on his return from one of these slave voyages that Newton was wondrously converted.

The ship was overtaken by a fierce storm in the north Atlantic and was nearly sinking. The rigging was destroyed; water was pouring in. The hands tried to seal the many leaks and brace the siding. Newton was sent down into the hold to pump water. He pumped for days, certain that the ship would sink and that he would be taken under with it and be drowned. As he pumped water in the hold of that ship, God brought to Newton's mind verses he had learned from his mother as a child, and they led to his conversion. When the ship survived the storm and the sailors were again in England, Newton left the slave trade, studied for the Christian ministry, and finally became a great preacher. He even preached before the queen.

What was Newton's motivation? It was a profound awareness of the grace and mercy of God toward him, a wretched sinner. Newton wrote these words:

> Amazing grace—how sweet the sound—
> That saved a wretch like me!
> I once was lost, but now am found—
> Was blind, but now I see.

Newton never forgot God's mercy to him. Once a friend was complaining about someone who was resistant to the gospel and living a life of great sin. "Sometimes I almost despair of that man," the friend remarked.

"I never did despair of any man since God saved me," said Newton.

In his most advanced years Newton's mind began to fail and he had to stop preaching. But when friends came to visit him he frequently remarked, "I am an old man. My mind is almost gone. But I can remember two things: I am a great sinner, and Jesus is a great Savior." Certainly the mercy of God moved Newton to offer his body as a living sacrifice to God and to seek to please him.

Love So Amazing

Now I come to you. Up to this point I have been asking you to put yourself in the place of Adam, Paul, and John Newton, trying to feel what they must have felt as an awareness of the greatness of the mercy of God swept over them. But if you are a Christian, you should be feeling the same things yourself even without reference to Adam or Paul or other characters.

Ephesians 2 describes your experience. It says that before God revealed his mercy to you, you were "dead in your transgressions and sins" (v. 1). You "followed the ways of this world and of the ruler of the kingdom of the air" (v. 2) and were "by nature [an object of God's] wrath" (v. 3). "You were separate from Christ, excluded from citizenship in Israel and [a foreigner] to the covenants of the promise, without hope and without God in the world" (v. 12). That was your condition.

But now listen to what God did.

"Because of his great love for us, God, who is rich in mercy, made us alive with Christ even when we were dead in transgressions—it is by grace you have been saved. And God raised us up with Christ and seated us with him in the heavenly realms in Christ Jesus, in order that in the coming ages he might show the incomparable riches of his grace, expressed in his kindness to us in Christ Jesus" (vv. 4–7).

That is the nature of the goodness, love, grace, and mercy of our great God. If you are a Christian, shouldn't it motivate you to the most complete offer of your body to him as a living sacrifice and to the highest possible level of obedience and service? How can it do otherwise? In my opinion, you can never understand and accurately appreciate what God has done in showing you mercy in Christ without replying wholeheartedly, as did Isaac Watts in his great hymn "When I Survey the Wondrous Cross" (1709):

> Love so amazing, so divine,
> Demands my soul, my life, my all.

184

Service That Makes Sense

Romans 12:1

Therefore, I urge you, brothers, in view of God's mercy, to offer your bodies as living sacrifices, holy and pleasing to God—this is your spiritual act of worship.

The Greek words of the last phrase of Romans 12:1 are ambiguous and have been translated different ways. For example, there are two different ways the words *spiritual act of worship* in Romans 12:1 may be understood. The noun translated *worship* is *latreia*, which can mean either service or worship. The plural of *latreia* can even mean rites or duties. The adjective in this important combination of words is *logikos*, however, which can mean either spiritual or rational, and when it is coupled to the noun two rather different meanings are possible.

One meaning is preserved in the King James Version: "your reasonable service." The newer translation is "your spiritual worship," which appears in the New International Version.

What is it? Is it "reasonable service" or "spiritual act of worship"? One answer is that the Greek words may actually embrace both ideas at the same time, spiritual worship being thought of also as rational service. But if I am forced to make a choice, I find myself siding with John Murray, who notes

1515

that "reasonable or rational is a more literal rendering."[1] *Logikos* has given us the English word *logical,* which means reasonable or according to reason, and this should also be the preferred meaning, if for no other reason than because in the next verse Paul talks about Christians being transformed by "the renewing of [their] mind[s]."

So Paul really is talking about something reasonable, saying that the living sacrifice that he is urging upon us here is logical.

Even more, the service itself is to be performed reasonably, or with the mind. "The service here in view is worshipful service and the apostle characterizes it as 'rational' because it is worship that derives its character as acceptable to God from the fact that it enlists our mind, our reason, our intellect. It is rational in contrast with what is mechanical or automatic. . . . The lesson to be derived from the term 'rational' is that we are not 'spiritual' in the biblical sense except as the use of our bodies is characterized by conscious, intelligent, consecrated devotion to the service of God."[2]

To understand these words well we must comprehend two things. First, we must understand the kind of service that is required. Second, we need to see why such demanding service is so reasonable.

Giving God Ourselves

As far as the first of these two matters is concerned, we have already spent a good bit of time exploring what this kind of service is about. It concerns what Paul calls "sacrifice." When we were looking at it in detail earlier we saw that it involves three things. First, it must be a *living* sacrifice. That is, our lives are to be given to God in active, continuing service. Second, it involves the offering of our *bodies.* In other words, we must give God the use of our minds, eyes, ears, tongues, hands, feet, and other body parts. Third, we must be *holy.* Moreover, we saw that if we do this, then the sacrifices we make to God will be *pleasing* to him.

Our problem, of course, is that we do not want to give God ourselves. We will give him things. It is relatively easy to give God money, though even here we are frequently far less than generous. We will even give God a certain amount of our time. We will volunteer for charitable work. But we will not give ourselves. Yet without ourselves these other "gifts" mean nothing to the Almighty.

1. John Murray, *The Epistle to the Romans,* 2 vols. in 1 (Grand Rapids: Wm. B. Eerdmans Publishing Company, 1968), vol. 2, p. 112.

2. Ibid. Leon Morris says, "Today most interpreters understand the adjective as *spiritual,* which makes good sense and is certainly in mind. But it is hard to think that the connection with 'reason' has been completely lost, and there is something to be said for 'intelligent worship' (Phillips) or JB's 'that is worthy of thinking beings.'" (Leon Morris, *The Epistle to the Romans* [Grand Rapids: Wm. B. Eerdmans Publishing Company, and Leicester, England: Inter-Varsity Press, 1988], p. 434). The New American Standard Bible translates the words as "spiritual service," but the New English Bible by a longer phrasing probably comes closest to the meaning by saying "worship offered by the mind and the heart."

You will begin to understand the Christian life only when you understand that God does not want your money or your time without yourself. You are the one for whom Jesus died. You are the one he loves. So when the Bible speaks of reasonable service, as it does here, it means that you are the one God wants. It is sad if you try to substitute things for that, the greatest gift.

A wonderful illustration of how we do sometimes substitute things for ourselves is the story of Jacob's return to his own country as related in Genesis 32. He had cheated his brother Esau out of his father Isaac's blessing about twenty years before, and he had been forced to run away because his brother was threatening to kill him. Twenty years is a long time. Over those two decades Jacob had gradually forgotten his brother's threats. But when it came time to go home, which is what this chapter describes, Jacob began to remember the past and grew increasingly fearful of what might happen.

Moving along toward Canaan with Laban behind him and his own country in front of him, Jacob had time to think. He remembered his own disreputable conduct. He recollected Esau's murderous threats. Every step became more difficult. Finally he came to the brook Jabbok that marked the border of his brother's territory, looked across to where Esau lived, and was terrified. If he could have gone back, he would have. But there was no way to go except forward.

What was he to do?

The first thing he did was send some servants ahead to see if they could find Esau and perhaps get a feeling for what he was planning to do. They had not gone very far when they ran into Esau, who was actually coming to meet Jacob. Unfortunately, he had four hundred men with him. This was a huge army from Jacob's point of view, and he could only assume the worst—that Esau was coming to kill him. He thought quickly, then divided his family, servants, and flocks into two groups, reasoning that if Esau attacked one group, the other might escape.

Ah, but what if Jacob was in the group Esau attacked?

On second thought, that didn't seem to be a very good plan, so he decided to appease his brother with gifts. First he sent him a present of two hundred female goats. He sent a servant along to drive the herd, and he gave the servant these instructions: "When my brother Esau meets you and asks, 'To whom do you belong, and where are you going, and who owns all these animals in front of you?' then you are to say, 'They belong to your servant Jacob. They are a gift to my lord Esau, and he is coming behind us'" (Gen. 32:17–18).

After this he sent another group of twenty male goats, and he gave the servant in charge of this flock the same instructions, to say that they belonged to Jacob and were being sent as a gift to Esau, with Jacob to come after them.

Just in case Esau was not satisfied with the goats, Jacob decided to send two hundred ewes, then twenty rams. After this he sent over the rest of his livestock: "thirty female camels with their young, forty cows and ten bulls, and twenty female donkeys and ten male donkeys" (v. 15). Each group had its servants in charge, and to each servant he gave the same message. It must have been an amusing picture—all Jacob's possessions stretched out across the desert going toward Esau.

But there was more. After he had sent the animals Jacob sent his least favored wife Leah with her children ahead of him across the Jabbok, followed by his favored wife Rachel with her children. Then there was the Jabbok. And then there at last, all alone and trembling, was Jacob.

I suppose that if he had known the chorus, he might have been singing "I surrender all." All the goats, that is. All the sheep. All the camels. All the cows. All the bulls. All the donkeys. He had given up everything, but he had still not given himself. That is what some of us do. We tell God that we will give him some time. We volunteer to help with something around the church. We give him our money. We do not give ourselves.

That night the angel came and wrestled with Jacob to bring him to the point of personal submission, after which this scheming, stiff-necked man was never the same again. When is the angel going to come and wrestle with you? Does he need to?

Why Is It Reasonable?

Let's not wait for the angel. Let's deal with this matter of sacrificial service to God now. Let's examine why it is reasonable to serve God sacrificially.

1. *It is reasonable because of what God has already done for us.* We touched on this point in the first of our studies of Romans 12, because it is implied in the word with which Paul begins this final major section of the letter: *therefore.* *Therefore* refers back to everything Paul said earlier. He discussed our need as sinners. We are under the wrath of God, on a destructive downhill path and unable to help ourselves. Paul has shown that we are not even inclined to help ourselves. Instead of drawing close to God, who is our only hope, we run away from him, suppressing even the truths about God known from the revelation of himself in nature.

Yet God has not let it go at that. God intervened to save us by the work of Jesus Christ, who died for us, and by the work of the Holy Spirit, who enables us to understand what Jesus has accomplished, repent of our sin, and trust him for our salvation. Then he has also joined us to Jesus Christ to make us different people from what we were before. Paul expounded on that in the letter's first eleven chapters. So now, when he gets to chapter 12, he says, "Look what God has done. Is it not reasonable to give yourself utterly and sacrificially to a God who has given himself utterly and sacrificially for you?"

Let me make that personal. Are you a believer in Jesus Christ? Are you trusting him for your salvation? Has the Holy Spirit made you alive in Jesus Christ? If he has, what can be more reasonable than to give yourself to him? What is more logical than to serve God wholeheartedly in this way?

2. *It is reasonable because of what God is continuing to do.* The salvation of a Christian is not just a past thing. It is also a present experience, because God

is continuing to work in those whom he has brought to faith in Jesus Christ. It is difficult to make changes in our lives, break destructive habits, form new ways of thinking, and please God. But this is exactly what God is doing in us. It is what this text is about. God does not start a thing and abandon it. When God starts something he always brings it to completion. He is doing this with you. Therefore, it is absurd to oppose his purposes. It is futile. The only reasonable thing is to join God and get on with what he is enabling you to do.

3. *It is reasonable because such service is God's will for us, and his is a good, pleasing and perfect will.* This point anticipates Romans 12:2, which says, "Do not conform any longer to the pattern of this world, but be transformed by the renewing of your mind. Then you will be able to test and approve what God's will is—his good, pleasing and perfect will."

Christians often get greatly hung up on the idea of discovering what God's specific will is for their lives. There has been great debate on this, some of which I reviewed earlier in my study of Romans 8.[3] In my judgment, there clearly are specific plans for our lives that God had determined in advance, because he has predetermined all things. The difficulty is that he has not revealed these to us. They are part of the hidden counsels of God, and they are not known by us simply because they are hidden. But although these specific details are not made known, general but very important things are, and the most important of these is that God wants us to be like Jesus Christ.

This is what Romans 8:28–29 says. "We know that in all things God works for the good of those who love him, who have been called according to his purpose. For those God foreknew he also predestined to be conformed to the likeness of his Son, that he might be the firstborn among many brothers." This is what Romans 12:2 is getting at as well.

Sometimes we also get hung up on the idea that God's will must be something hard, difficult, or irrational. Paul corrects that error by giving us three adjectives to describe the nature of God's will.

It is *good*, he says. God is the master of the understatement. So if God says his will is good, he means good with a capital *G*. He means that his will for us is the best thing that could possibly be.

God's will is also *acceptable*, says Paul. This means acceptable to us, since the fact that God's will is acceptable to God goes without saying. Do not say that the will of God is hard. Or difficult. Or irrational. If you are thinking along those lines, it is because you have not yet learned to surrender to it. Those who do surrender to God's will, offering their whole selves as sacrifices to him, find that the will of God is the most acceptable thing there can be.

Finally, Paul argues that the will of God is *perfect*. No one can say more than that. Our ways are not perfect. They can always be improved upon and

3. See chapter 108, "Knowing the Will of God" (Romans 8:27) in James Montgomery Boice, *Romans*, vol. 2, *The Reign of Grace, Romans 5:1–8:39* (Grand Rapids: Baker Book House, 1992), pp. 893–900.

often must be corrected. God's ways are perfect. They can never be made better. So isn't it the most reasonable thing in the world to serve God and to do so without reservation, with all your heart?

4. *It is reasonable because God is worthy of our very best efforts.* We read in Revelation 4:11:

> You are worthy, our Lord and God,
>   to receive glory and honor and power,
> for you created all things,
>   and by your will they were created
>   and have their being.

And again, of Jesus in Revelation 5:9–10:

> You are worthy to take the scroll
>   and to open its seals,
> because you were slain,
>   and with your blood you purchased men for God
>   from every tribe and language and people and nation.
> You have made them to be a kingdom and priests to serve our God,
>   and they will reign on the earth.

And yet again in Revelation 5:12:

> Worthy is the Lamb, who was slain,
> to receive power and wealth and wisdom and strength
> and honor and glory and praise!

That is the testimony of the elders, the four living creatures, the angels, and the entire company of the redeemed. It means that God is worthy of all honor, including the very best we have to offer.

Do you believe that?

I think that is the problem. If we did believe it, we would judge it reasonable to live for Jesus now and we would do it. Instead, in many cases we only say, "Jesus is worthy of all honor," and then go out and fail to live for him. Our actions refute our profession. On the other hand, if you do live for him, giving God all you can ever hope to be, then you are testifying that God truly is a great God and that he is worthy of the best you or anyone else can offer.

5. *It is reasonable because only spiritual things will last.* My last point is that it is reasonable to give everything you have for God because in the final analysis only that which is spiritual will last. Everything else—everything we see and touch and handle—will pass away. Jesus said, "Heaven and earth will pass away" (Matt. 24:35). If that is true of the heavens and the earth, it is certainly true of the small perishable things you and I give so much of our lives for.

Although "the world and its desires pass away," we are also told that the one who "does the will of God lives forever" (1 John 2:17). And so do his works! The Bible says, "Blessed are the dead who die in the Lord. . . . They will rest from their labor, for their deeds will follow them" (Rev. 14:13). Learning to think this way is part of what it means to think spiritually. It is a start in developing a truly Christian mind.

I close with two illustrations. Jim Elliot wrote as a young missionary, "He is no fool who gives what he cannot keep to gain what he cannot lose." He gave his life to God in what he judged to be the most reasonable service, and he gained a spiritual inheritance forever.

Another missionary, William Borden, came from a wealthy privileged family, was a graduate of Yale University, and had the promise of a wonderful and lucrative career before him. But he felt a call to serve God as a missionary in China and left for the field even though his family and friends thought him a fool for going. After a short time away and even before he reached China, Borden contracted a fatal disease and died. He had given up everything to follow Jesus. He died possessing nothing in this world. But Borden of Yale did not regret it. We know this because he left a note as he lay dying that said, "No reserve, no retreat, and no regrets." Like so many others, he found the service of Christ to be eminently reasonable, and he gained a lasting reward.

185

The Pattern of This Age

Romans 12:2

Do not conform any longer to the pattern of this world, but be transformed by the renewing of your mind. Then you will be able to test and approve what God's will is—his good, pleasing and perfect will.

Some verses in the Bible are enriched when we read them in several translations, and Romans 12:2 is one of them. In the New International Version the first part of Romans 12:2 says, "Do not conform any longer to the pattern of this world."

This verse has two key words: *world*, which in Greek is literally *age* (*aiôn*, meaning this present age, in contrast to "the age to come"), and *do not conform*, which is a compound having at its root the word *scheme*. So the verse means "Do not let the age in which you live force you into its scheme of thinking and behaving." This is what some of the translations try to bring out. The New American Catholic Bible says, "Do not conform yourselves to this age." The Jerusalem Bible says, "Do not model yourselves on the behaviour of the world around you." The Living Bible reads, "Don't copy the behavior and customs of this world." Best known of all is the paraphrase of J. B. Phillips, which states, "Don't let the world around you squeeze you into its own mold."

The idea in each of these renderings is that the world has its ways of thinking and doing things and is exerting pressure on Christians to conform to them. But instead of being conformed, Christians are to be changed from within to be increasingly like Jesus Christ.

What Is Worldliness?

The first phrase of verse 2 is a warning against worldliness. But as soon as we say *worldly* we have to stop and make clear what real worldliness is. When I was growing up in a rather fundamentalist church I was taught that worldliness was following such "worldly" pursuits as smoking, drinking, dancing, and playing cards. A Christian girl would say:

> I don't smoke, and I don't chew,
> And I don't go with boys who do.

That is not what Romans 12:2 is about, however. To think of worldliness only in those terms is to trivialize what is a far more serious and far more subtle problem.

The clue to what is in view here is that in the next phrase Paul urges, as an alternative to being "conformed" to this world, being "transformed *by the renewing of your mind.*" This means that he is concerned about a way of thinking rather than merely behaving, though right behavior will follow naturally if our thinking is set straight. In other words, the worldliness we are to break away from and repudiate is the world's "worldview," what the Germans call *Weltanschauung,* a systematic way of looking at all things. We are to break out of the world's way of thinking and instead let our minds be molded by the Word of God.

In our day Christians have not done this very well, and that is the reason why they are so often "worldly" in the other senses too. In fact, it is a sad commentary on our time, verified by surveys, that American Christians in general have mostly the same values and behavior patterns as the world around them.

Secularism: "The Cosmos Is All That Is"

If worldliness is not smoking, drinking, dancing, and playing cards, what is it? If it is a way of thinking, what is a worldly worldview? There is no single word that perfectly describes how the world thinks, but *secularism* is good for general purposes. It is an umbrella term that covers a number of other "isms," like humanism, relativism, pragmatism, pluralism, hedonism, and materialism. *Secularism,* more than any other single word, aptly describes the mental framework and value structure of the people of our time.

The word *secular* also comes closest to what Paul says when he refers to "the pattern of this world." *Secular* is derived from the Latin word *saeculum,* which means age. And the word found in Paul's phrase in verse 2 is the exact

Greek equivalent. The NIV uses the word *world,* but the Greek actually says, "Do not be conformed to this *age.*" In other words, "Do not be 'secularist' in your worldview."

There is a right way to be secular, of course. Christians live in the world and are therefore rightly concerned about the world's affairs. We have legitimate secular concerns. But secularism (note the "ism") is more than this. It is a philosophy that does not look beyond this world but instead operates as if this age is all there is.

The best single statement of secularism I know is something Carl Sagan said in the television series *Cosmos.* He was pictured standing before a spectacular view of the heavens with its many swirling galaxies, saying in a hushed, almost reverential tone of voice, "The cosmos is all that is or ever was or ever will be." That is bold-faced secularism. It is bound up entirely by the limits of the material universe, by what we can see and touch and weigh and measure. If we think in terms of our existence here, it means operating within the limits of life on earth. If we are thinking of time, it means disregarding the eternal and thinking only of the now.

We have it expressed in popular advertising slogans like "You only go around once" and Pepsi's "Now Generation." These slogans dominate our culture and express an outlook that has become increasingly harmful. If now is the only thing that matters, why should we worry about the national debt, for example? That's not our problem. Let our children worry about it. Or why should we study hard preparing to do meaningful work later on in life, as long as we can have a good time now? Most important, why should I worry about God or righteousness or sin or judgment or salvation, if now is all that really matters?

R. C. Sproul writes, "For secularism, all life, every human value, every human activity must be understood in light of this present time. . . . What matters is *now* and only *now.* All access to the above and the beyond is *blocked.* There is no exit from the confines of this present world. The secular is all that we have. We must make our decisions, live our lives, make our plans, all within the closed arena of this time—the here and now."[1]

Each of us should understand that description instantly, because it is the viewpoint we are surrounded with every single day of our lives and in every conceivable place and circumstance.

Yet that is the outlook to which we must refuse to be conformed. Instead of being conformed to this world, as if that is all there is, we are to see all things as relating to God and to eternity. Here is the contrast, as expressed by Harry Blamires: "To think secularly is to think within a frame of reference bounded by the limits of our life on earth; it is to keep one's calculations rooted in this-worldly criteria. To think Christianly is to accept all things with

---

1. R. C. Sproul, *Lifeviews: Understanding the Ideas that Shape Society Today* (Old Tappan, N.J.: Fleming H. Revell, 1986), p. 35.

the mind as related, directly or indirectly, to man's eternal destiny as the redeemed and chosen child of God."[2]

Humanism: "You Will Be Like God"

There is a proper kind of humanism, meaning a proper concern for human beings. Humanitarianism is a better word for it. People who care for other people are humanitarians. But there is also a philosophical humanism, which is a way of looking at people, particularly ourselves, apart from God, and this is wrong and harmful. This is a secular way of looking at them, which is why we so often speak not just of humanism but of "secular humanism."

The best example of secular humanism I know is in the Book of Daniel. One day Nebuchadnezzar, the great king of Babylon, was on the roof of his palace looking out over his splendid hanging gardens to the prosperous city beyond. He was impressed with his handiwork and said, "Is this not the great Babylon I have built as the royal residence, by my mighty power and for the glory of my majesty?" (Dan. 4:30). It was a statement that everything he saw was "of" him, "by" him, and "for" the glory of his majesty, which is humanism. Humanism says that everything revolves around man and exists for man's glory.

God would not tolerate this arrogance. So he judged Nebuchadnezzar with insanity, indicating that this is a crazy philosophy. Nebuchadnezzar was then driven out to live with the beasts and acted like a beast until at last he acknowledged that God alone is the true ruler of the universe and that everything exists for his glory rather than ours.

I, Nebuchadnezzar, raised my eyes toward heaven, and my sanity was restored.
Then I praised the Most High; I honored and glorified him who lives forever.

His dominion is an eternal dominion. . . .
He does as he pleases
    with the powers of heaven
    and the peoples of the earth.

Daniel 4:34–35

Humanism is opposed to God and hostile to Christianity. This has always been so, but it is especially evident in the public statements of modern humanism: *A Humanist Manifesto* (1933), *Humanist Manifesto II* (1973), and *The Secularist Humanist Declaration* (1980). The first of these, the 1933 document, said, "Traditional theism, especially faith in the prayer-hearing God, assumed to love and care for persons, to hear and understand their prayers, and to be able to do something about them, is an unproved and outmoded faith. Salvationism, based on mere affirmation, still appears as harmful, diverting

2. Harry Blamires, *The Christian Mind: How Should a Christian Think?* (Ann Arbor, Mich.: Servant Books, 1978), p. 44.

people with false hopes of heaven hereafter. Reasonable minds look to other means for survival."[3]

The 1973 *Humanist Manifesto II* said, "We find insufficient evidence for belief in the existence of a supernatural"[4] and "There is no credible evidence that life survives the death of the body."[5]

Humanism leads to a deification of self and, contrary to what it professes, to an utter disregard for other people.

In deifying self, humanism actually deifies nearly everything but God. Several years ago Herbert Schlossberg, one of the project directors for the Fieldstead Institute, wrote a book titled *Idols for Destruction,* in which he showed how humanism has made a god of history, mammon, nature, power, religion, and, of course, humanity itself.[6] It is brilliantly done.

As far as disregarding other people, well, look at the best-sellers of the 1970s. You will find titles like *Winning through Intimidation* and *Looking Out for Number One.* These books say, in a manner utterly consistent with secular humanism, "Forget about other people; look out for yourself; you are what matters." What emerged in those years is what Thomas Wolfe, the social critic, called the "Me Decade." And the 1970s gave way to the 1980s, which others have aptly called the "Golden Age of Greed."

Remember, too, that this is the philosophy (some would say religion) underlying public school education. This is ironic, of course, since humanism is an irrational philosophy. How so? Because it is impossible to establish humanistic or any other values or goals without a transcendent point of reference, and it is precisely that transcendent point that is being repudiated by the humanists. Frighteningly, the irrationalism of humanism is appearing in the chaos of the schools, where students are using guns to kill other students and threaten teachers.

In the fall of 1992 an ABC *Prime Time Live* television special, featuring Diane Sawyer, reported that in this country one in five students come to school with a handgun somewhat regularly and that there are ten times as many knives in schools as there are guns. This is as true of the suburbs as it is of the inner city. In Wichita, Kansas, which calls itself mid-America, students must pass through metal detectors in order to enter school, and there are still guns and other weapons in the buildings.

For humanism as well as for secularism, the word for Christians is "do not conform any longer." We remember that the first expression of humanism was not the *Humanist Manifesto* of 1933 or even the arrogant words of Nebuchadnezzar spoken about six hundred years before Christ, but rather

3. *Humanist Manifestos I and II* (New York: Prometheus Books, 1973), p. 13.
4. Ibid., p. 16.
5. Ibid., p. 17.
6. Herbert Schlossberg, *Idols for Destruction: Christian Faith and Its Confrontation with American Society* (Washington, D.C.: Regnery Gateway, 1990).

the words of Satan in the Garden of Eden, who told Eve, "You will be like God, knowing good and evil" (Gen. 3:5).

Relativism: "A Moral Morass"

While we are talking about humanism we also have to talk briefly about *relativism*, because if man is the focal point of everything, then there are no absolutes in any area of life and everything is up for grabs. Some years ago Professor Allan Bloom of the University of Chicago wrote a book called *The Closing of the American Mind*, in which he said on the very first page, "There is one thing a professor can be absolutely certain of: almost every student entering the university believes, or says he believes, that truth is relative."[7]

What that book set out to prove is that education is impossible in such a climate. People can learn skills, of course. You can learn to drive a truck, work a computer, handle financial transactions, and do scores of other things. But real education, which means learning to sift through error to discover what is true, good, and beautiful, is impossible, because the goals of real education—truth, goodness, and beauty—do not exist. And even if they did exist in some far-off metaphysical never-never-land, it would be impossible to find them, because it requires absolutes even to discover absolutes. It requires such absolutes as the laws of logic, for example.

Is it any wonder that with such an underlying destructive philosophy as relativism, not to mention secularism and humanism, America is experiencing what *Time* magazine called "a moral morass" and "a values vacuum"?[8]

Materialism: "The Material Girl"

The final "ism" to which Christians are not to be conformed is *materialism*. This takes us back to secularism, since it is a part of it. If "the cosmos is all there is or ever was or ever will be," as Carl Sagan says, then nothing exists but what is material or measurable, and if there is any value to be found in life, it must be in material terms. Be as healthy as you can. Live as long as you can. Get as rich as you can.

When today's young people are asked to name their heroes or heroines, what comes out rather quickly is that they have no people they actually look up to except possibly the rich and the famous—people like Michael Jordan and Madonna. And speaking of Madonna, isn't it interesting that she is referred to most often not as a singer or entertainer or even a sex symbol but as "the material girl." That is, she represents the material things of this world, clothes (or the lack of them), money, fame, and above all, pleasure. And this is what today's young people want to be like! They want to be rich and famous and have things and enjoy them. They want to be like Madonna.

7. Allan Bloom, *The Closing of the American Mind* (New York: Simon & Schuster, 1987), p. 25.
8. *Time*, May 25, 1987, p. 14.

The poet T. S. Eliot wrote an epitaph for our materialistic generation:

> Here were decent godless people:
> Their only monument the asphalt road
> And a thousand lost golf balls.[9]

How different the Lord Jesus Christ! He was born into a poor family, was laid in a borrowed manger at his birth, never had a home or a bank account or a family of his own.

He said of himself, "Foxes have holes and birds of the air have nests, but the Son of Man has no place to lay his head" (Matt. 8:20).

At his trial before Pilate he said, "My kingdom is not of this world. If it were, my servants would fight . . . My kingdom is from another place" (John 18:36).

When he died he was laid in a borrowed tomb.

If there was ever an individual who operated on the basis of values above and beyond the world in which we live, it was Jesus Christ. He was the polar opposite of "the material girl." But at the same time no one has ever affected this world for good as much as Jesus. It is into his image that we are to be transformed rather than being forced into the mold of this world's sinful and destructive "isms."

No One But Jesus

In the next few studies we are going to explore another aspect of the problem presented by today's world and begin to look at the solution proposed in Romans 12:2. But I want to close this study by looking ahead one phrase to what Paul says we are to be: not *conformed* but *transformed* by the renewing of our minds. There is a deliberate distinction between those two words. Conformity is something that happens to you outwardly. Transformation happens inwardly. The Greek word translated *transformed* is *metamorphoô*, from which we get *metamorphosis*. It is what happens to the lowly caterpillar when it turns into a beautiful butterfly.

This Greek word is found four times in the New Testament: once here, once in 2 Corinthians 3:18 to describe our being transformed into the glorious likeness of Jesus Christ, and twice in the gospels of the transfiguration of Jesus on the mountain where he had gone with Peter, James, and John. Those verses say, "There he was transfigured before them" (Matt. 17:2; Mark 9:2). The same word used by Paul to describe our transformation by the renewing of our minds so that we will not be conformed to this world is used by the gospel writers to describe the transfiguration of Jesus from the form of his earthly humiliation to the radiance that Peter, James, and John were privileged to witness for a time.

And that is why Paul writes as he does in 2 Corinthians, saying, "We, who with unveiled faces all reflect the Lord's glory, are being transformed into

---

9. T. S. Eliot, "Choruses from 'The Rock,'" *The Complete Poems and Plays: 1909–1950* (New York: Harcourt Brace and Company, 1952), p. 103.

his likeness with ever-increasing glory, which comes from the Lord, who is the Spirit" (2 Cor. 3:18).

In 2 Corinthians Paul says, "It is happening." In Romans 12 he says, "Let it happen," thus putting the responsibility, though not the power to accomplish this necessary transformation, upon us. How does it happen? Through the renewing of our minds; and the way our minds become renewed is by study of the life-giving and renewing Word of God. Without that study we will remain in the world's mold, unable to think and therefore also unable to act as Christians. With that study, blessed and empowered as it will be by the Holy Spirit, we will begin to take on something of the glorious luster of the Lord Jesus Christ and become increasingly like him.

186

This Mindless Age

Romans 12:2

Do not conform any longer to the pattern of this world, but be transformed by the renewing of your mind. Then you will be able to test and approve what God's will is—his good, pleasing and perfect will.

In the last chapter I referred to Harry Blamires, an Englishman who wrote an important Christian book in 1963 titled *The Christian Mind: How Should a Christian Think?*[1] Blamires was a student of C. S. Lewis. His book's main thesis, repeated over and over in chapter 1, is that "There is no longer a Christian mind," meaning that in our time there is no longer a distinctly Christian way of thinking. There is to some extent a Christian ethic and even a somewhat Christian way of life and piety. But there is no distinctly Christian frame of reference, no uniquely Christian worldview, to guide our thinking in distinction from the thought of the secular world around us.

Unfortunately, the situation has not improved over the past thirty years. In fact, it has grown worse. Today, not only is there little or no genuine Christian thinking, there is very little thinking of any kind. The Western world (and perhaps even the world as a whole) is well on its way to becoming what I have frequently called a "mindless society."

---

1. Harry Blamires, *The Christian Mind: How Should a Christian Think?* (Ann Arbor, Mich.: Servant Books, 1978). Original edition 1963.

Since Christians are called to mind renewal—our text says, "Do not conform any longer to the pattern of this world, but be transformed *by the renewing of your mind*"—this cultural mindlessness is a major aspect of the "pattern of this world" that we are to recognize, understand, repudiate, and overcome. We are to be many things as Christians, but we are especially to be thinking people. We are to possess a "Christian mind."

America Has Been "Vannatized"

There are a number of causes for our present mindlessness—Western materialism, the fast pace of modern life, and philosophical skepticism, to name a few—but I believe that the chief cause is television.

I began to study television as a cultural problem several years ago, and the thing that got me started was a 1987 graduation address at Duke University by Ted Koppel of ABC's *Nightline*. Following this address Koppel was frequently quoted by Christian communicators because of something he said about the Ten Commandments. He was deploring the declining moral tone of our country and reminded his predominantly secular audience of the abiding validity of this religious standard. He said that they are Ten Commandments, not "ten suggestions," and that they "are," not "were" the standard. But to me the most interesting thing about Koppel's address was his opening sentence, in which he said that America has been "Vannatized."

Koppel was referring to Vanna White, the beautiful and extraordinarily popular hostess of the television game show *Wheel of Fortune*. Vanna White is something of a phenomenon on television. Her actual work is simple. She stands on one side of a large game board that holds blocks representing the letters of words the contestants are supposed to guess. As they guess correctly, Vanna walks across the platform and turns the blocks around to reveal the letters. When she gets to the other side she claps her hands. It is simple work, but Vanna seems to like it. No, "like" is too mild a term, as Koppel notes. Vanna "thrills, rejoices, adores everything she sees." People respond to her so well that books about her have appeared in bookstores, and she is well up on that magical but elusive list of the most admired people in America.

But here is the interesting thing. Until recently Vanna never said a word on *Wheel of Fortune*, and Koppel asked how a person who says nothing and who is therefore basically unknown to us can be so popular. That is just the point, he answered. Since we do not know what Vanna White is actually like, she is whatever you want her to be. "Is she a feminist or every male chauvinist's dream? She is whatever you want her to be. Sister, lover, daughter, friend, never cross, non-threatening, and non-judgmental to a fault."[2] She is popular because we project our own deep feelings, needs, or fantasies onto the television image.

2. Ted Koppel, "Viewpoints," Commencement Address, Duke University, May 10, 1987.

Koppel does not care very much about *Wheel of Fortune*'s success, of course. He was analyzing our culture. And his point is that Vanna White's appeal is the very essence of television and that television forms our way of thinking or, to be more accurate, of not thinking. It has been hailed as the great teaching tool, but that is precisely what it does not do, because it seldom presents anything in enough depth for a person actually to think about it. Instead, it presents thirty-second flashes of events and offers images upon which we are invited to project our own vague feelings.

If all we are talking about is game shows and other forms of television entertainment, none of this would matter very much, except for the amount of time our children spend watching these banal, mind-numbing diversions rather than disciplining their minds by serious study. But if television is really conditioning us not to think, as Koppel and I maintain, then television is a serious intellectual, social, and spiritual problem.

Amusing Ourselves to Death

A more academic study of the negative impact of television on culture has been provided by Neil Postman, a professor of communication arts and sciences at New York University, in a book called *Amusing Ourselves to Death: Public Discourse in the Age of Show Business.*[3]

Amusing Ourselves to Death was published in 1985, one year after 1984, the year popularized as the title of George Orwell's futuristic novel, with its dark vision of a society controlled by fear. In Orwell's novel Big Brother rules everything with a ruthless iron fist. But Postman reminds us that there was another novel written slightly earlier with an equally chilling but quite different vision of the future: *Brave New World* by Aldous Huxley. In Huxley's novel there is no need for Big Brother, because in this ominous vision of the future people have come to love their oppression as well as the technologies that strip away their capacities to think:

> What Orwell feared were those who would ban books. What Huxley feared was that there would be no reason to ban a book, for there would be no one who wanted to read one. Orwell feared those who would deprive us of information. Huxley feared those who would give us so much that we would be reduced to passivity and egoism. Orwell feared that the truth would be concealed from us. Huxley feared the truth would be drowned in a sea of irrelevance. Orwell feared we would become a captive culture. Huxley feared we would become a trivial culture. . . . As Huxley remarked in *Brave New World Revisited,* the civil libertarians and rationalists who are ever on the alert to oppose tyranny "failed to take into account man's almost infinite appetite for diversions."[4]

3. Neil Postman, *Amusing Ourselves to Death: Public Discourse in the Age of Show Business* (New York: Penguin Books, 1986). Original edition 1985.
4. Ibid., pp. vii–viii.

Obviously, as Postman suggests, the Western cultures have succumbed to the second of these two oppressions, just as the communist countries fell victim to the first.

The first half of Postman's book is a study of the difference between what he calls "the age of typography" and our present television age, which he calls "the age of show business." Typography refers to words in print, and it concerns the communication of ideas by newspapers, pamphlets, and books. It is rational and analytic, because that is the way written words work. He writes:

> To engage the written word means to follow a line of thought, which requires considerable powers of classifying, inference-making and reasoning. It means to uncover lies, confusions, and over-generalizations, to detect abuses of logic and common sense. It also means to weigh ideas, to compare and contrast assertions, to connect one generalization to another. To accomplish this, one must achieve a certain distance from the words themselves, which is, in fact, encouraged by the isolated and impersonal text. That is why a good reader does not cheer an apt sentence or pause to applaud even an inspired paragraph. Analytic thought is too busy for that, and too detached.[5]

He illustrates the strength of the age of typography by public attention to the famous Lincoln-Douglas debates of the mid-eighteen hundreds, which people were capable of hearing, understanding, and forming opinions about, even though they lasted three to seven hours. In the eighteenth and nineteenth centuries "America was as dominated by the printed word and an oratory based on the printed word as any society we know of,"[6] Postman says. The country could think.

Unfortunately, television does not operate by rational means of communication but by images, as Ted Koppel pointed out, and as a result we are becoming a mindless culture.

News on Television: "Now . . . This"

A great deal of what Postman develops in his book is reinforcement for what I have been describing as mindlessness. So let me review three specific areas of bad influence, as he sees it.

A chapter in the book that deals with news on television is entitled "Now . . . This." That is because these are the words most used on television to link one brief televised news segment—the average news segment on network news programs is only forty-five seconds long—to the next news segment or commercial. What the phrase means is that what one has just seen has no relevance to what one is about to see or, for that matter, to anything. Rational thought requires such connections. It depends on similarities, contradictions,

5. Postman, Amusing Ourselves, p. 51.
6. Ibid., p. 41.

deductions, and the development of probable consequences. It requires time. It is what books and other serious print media give us. But this is precisely what television does not give. It does not give time for thought, and if it does not give time for thought or promote thought, what it essentially amounts to is "diversion."

Postman says that television gives us "news without consequences, without value, and therefore without essential seriousness; that is to say, news as pure entertainment."[7] In other words, it is not only mindless, it is teaching us to be mindless, to the point at which we even suppose that our ignorance is great knowledge.

Reach Out and Elect Someone

A second area of bad influence is politics. Postman calls this chapter "Reach Out and Elect Someone." Ronald Reagan once said, "Politics is just like show business."[8] But if this is so, then the object of politics on television is not to pursue excellence, clarity, or honesty, or any other generally recognized virtue, but to *appear* as if you are pursuing these things.

After the 1968 presidential campaign, in which Richard Nixon finally won the White House, a political writer named Joe McGinniss wrote a book titled *The Selling of the President 1968*. In it he described the strategy of the Nixon advisors who felt that their candidate had lost the 1960 election to John Kennedy because of Kennedy's better television image. He reports William Gavin, one of Nixon's chief aids, as advising, "Break away from linear logic: present a barrage of impressions, of attitudes. Break off in mid-sentence and skip to something half a world away. . . . Reason pushes the viewer back, it assaults him, it demands that he agree or disagree; impression can envelop him, invite him in, without making an intellectual demand. . . . Get the voters to like the guy, and the battle's two-thirds won."[9]

How do campaign managers get their candidates elected today? Not by discussing issues, because that is a sure way to get defeated—any position on any issue, unless it is utterly meaningless, is certain to offend somebody. The way to win elections is to present a pleasant television image and to keep the candidate out of trouble for as long as possible.

That is why Ronald Reagan won in 1980 and even more decisively in 1984. It was not his positions, though they were substantially different from those of his predecessors and were, in my opinion, generally right. There really was "a Reagan revolution." But this was not why he won. He won because he had a long career in movies and was a master of the television medium. He projected an image of a strong decent man we could trust.

7. Ibid., p. 100.
8. Ibid., p. 125.
9. From memorandums prepared by William Gavin. Quoted by Joe McGinniss, *The Selling of the President* (New York: Penguin Books, 1988), pp. 208, 188, 189. Original edition 1969.

The 1988 presidential election, in which George Bush defeated Michael Dukakis, involved issues about which every intelligent voter should have been carefully informed. Television is supposed to be the medium through which this is done. But a discussion of the issues is precisely what the voters did not get. Where did George Bush and Michael Dukakis differ in their politics? In regard to domestic programs such as Social Security, child care, education, taxes, abortion? In international affairs? The military? Relations with Russia, Eastern Europe, China, Japan? It was only specialists in government who knew the true answers to those questions, not the voters, because those were not the issues of the campaign.

What were the issues then? Actually, there was only one issue, and it was this: Is George Bush a "wimp"? That question was raised because he looked like a wimp on television; he is thin, seems to be frail, and held his head slightly to one side in a way that looked deferential. If the Dukakis camp could encourage voters to think of Bush that way, they would vote for Dukakis, because no one wants a wimp for president. On the other hand, Bush's task was to convince the voters that he would actually be a strong president, and the strategy of his camp was therefore to wage a strong, aggressive—many said unfair and nasty—campaign against Dukakis.

The media complained! Dan Rather, Tom Brokaw, and Peter Jennings were predictably self-righteous and offended. They called it the least substantial, meanest campaign in memory. But how hypocritical! It was mindless, but it was mindless precisely because that is what television demands. It demands images and not thought.

The campaign of 1992 is another example. I said from the beginning that Bill Clinton would win the election, not because he might have a better program for getting this country out of debt or even because the electorate was unhappy with America's slow rate of economic growth in the previous two years, but because Clinton looks better on television. Clinton is the perfect television candidate, and so he won.

Marshall McLuhan, the television "guru," was right when he said, "The medium *is* the message." The campaign managers have learned that, which is why they organize the kinds of campaigns they do.

I know someone will say, "But Reagan *was* a decent, strong man." Or, "George Bush really *is* a wimp (or 'is *not* a wimp')." Or, "Bill Clinton is the stronger candidate." But my point is that we do not actually know those things and cannot know them, at least from television, until events perhaps support or fail to support our perceptions. The most serious thing of all perhaps is not that we do not know, but that we think we do know because of television.

Religion as Entertainment

The third area of bad influence is religion. Postman's chapter on religion is called "Shuffle Off to Bethlehem." Religion is on television chiefly in an entertainment format. With the possible exception of Billy Graham, who has an international following quite apart from the television medium, and some other teaching pastors such as Charles Stanley and D. James Kennedy, the religious television stars are mostly entertainers. Pat Robertson is a master of ceremonies along the lines of Merv Griffin. Jimmy Swaggart is a piano player and singer as well as having been a vivacious and entertaining speaker. Even televised church services, like those of Jerry Falwell and Robert Schuller, contain their requisite musical numbers and pop testimonies, just like variety shows on secular television. The proper name for them is vaudeville.

Nearly everything that makes religion real is lost in the translation of church to television. The chief loss is a sense of the transcendent. God is missing. Postman says:

> Everything that makes religion an historic, profound and sacred human activity is stripped away; there is no ritual, no dogma, no tradition, no theology, and above all, no sense of spiritual transcendence. On these shows, the preacher is tops. God comes out as second banana. . . .
>
> CBS knows that Walter Cronkite plays better on television than the Milky Way. And Jimmy Swaggart plays better than God. For God exists only in our minds, whereas Swaggart is *there*, to be seen, admired, adored. Which is why he is the star of the show. . . . If I am not mistaken, the word for this is blasphemy.[10]

An observer who likes such religious entertainment might object, "Well, what harm is done as long as genuine religion is still to be found in church on Sundays?" I would argue that so pervasive and normalizing is the impact of television that pressures have inevitably come to make church services as irrelevant and entertaining as the tube.

In the vast majority of church services today there are virtually no pastoral prayers, while there is much brainless music, chummy chatter, and abbreviated sermons. Preachers are told to be personable, to relate funny stories, to smile, and above all to stay away from topics that might cause people to become unhappy with the church and leave it. They are to preach to felt needs, not necessarily real needs. This generally means telling people only what they want to hear.

Your Mind Matters

This is the point at which we need to talk about genuine mind renewal for Christians, which is what I will continue with in the next study. But I close here by mentioning a helpful little book by John Stott, the Rector Emeritus of All Souls Church in London, titled *Your Mind Matters*. It deals with six spheres of Christian living, and it argues that each one is impossible without a proper and energetic use of our minds: Christian worship, Christian faith,

10. McGinniss, *The Selling*, pp. 116–17, 123.

Christian holiness, Christian guidance, Christian evangelism, and Christian ministry. We need to think.

Stott argues that "anti-intellectualism . . . is . . . part of the fashion of the world and therefore a form of worldliness. To denigrate the mind is to undermine foundational Christian doctrines." He asks pointedly, "Has God created us rational beings, and shall we deny our humanity which he has given us? Has God spoken to us, and shall we not listen to his words? Has God renewed our mind through Christ, and shall we not think with it? Is God going to judge us by his Word, and shall we not be wise and build our house upon this rock?"[11]

They are important and helpful questions, if you *think* about them.

---

11. John R. W. Stott, *Your Mind Matters: The Place of the Mind in the Christian Life* (Downers Grove, Ill: InterVarsity Press, 1972), p. 26.

187

Mind Renewal in a Mindless Age: Part 1

Romans 12:2

Do not conform any longer to the pattern of this world, but be transformed by the renewing of your mind. Then you will be able to test and approve what God's will is—his good, pleasing and perfect will.

In each of the last two studies dealing with what it means to think as a Christian rather than in a worldly or secular way, I have mentioned Harry Blamires, an Englishman who has written two good books on this subject: *The Christian Mind: How Should a Christian Think?* (1963) and *Recovering the Christian Mind: Meeting the Challenge of Secularism* (1988). In each of these books Blamires encourages us to reject the world's thinking and begin to think as Christians. This is what Paul is writing about in our text from Romans 12: "Do not conform any longer to the pattern of this world, but be transformed by the renewing of your mind" (v. 2). This means that our thinking is not to be determined by the culture of the world around us but rather that we are to have a distinctly different and growing Christian worldview.

But what does it actually mean to have an outlook like that? How are we to experience mind renewal in our exceedingly mindless age?

Thinking Christianly and Thinking Secularly

The one thing this does not mean is what most people probably assume it does, and that is to start thinking mainly about Christian things. We do need to think about Christian subjects, of course. In fact, it is from that base of revealed doctrine and its applications to life that we can begin to think Christianly about other matters. I am going to pursue exactly that line of thought in this study. But to think Christianity itself is not a matter of thinking about Christian subjects as opposed to thinking about secular subjects, as we suppose, but rather to think in a Christian way about everything. It means to have a Christian mind.

This is because, by contrast, it is possible to think in a secular way even about religious things. Take the Lord's Supper, for instance. For most Christians the Lord's Supper is probably the most spiritual of all spiritual matters, and yet it is possible to think about even it in a worldly manner. For example, a trustee of the church might be thinking that he forgot to include the cost of the communion elements in the next year's budget. Another person might be looking at the minister and criticizing his way of handling the elements. "He's so awkward," this person might be thinking. Still another person might be reflecting on how good it is for people to have spiritual thoughts or to observe religious ceremonies. "This is good for people," he might be reflecting. Each of these persons is thinking secularly about the most sacred of Christian practices.

On the other hand, it is possible to think Christianly about even the most mundane matters. Blamires suggests how we might do this at a gasoline station while we are waiting for our tank to be filled with gas. We might be reflecting on how a mechanized world with cars and other machines tends to make God seem unnecessary for people, or how a speeded-up world in which we use our cars to race from one appointment to another makes it difficult to think deeply about or even care for other people. Even further, we might be wondering, do material things like cars serve us, or are we enslaved to them? Do they cause us to covet and therefore break the tenth commandment? How do they impact the environment over which God has made us stewards?

Blamires says, "There is nothing in our experience, however trivial, worldly, or even evil, which cannot be thought about Christianly. There is likewise nothing in our experience, however sacred, which cannot be thought about secularly—considered, that is to say, simply in its relationship to the passing existence of bodies and psyches in a time-locked universe."[1]

---

1. Harry Blamires, *The Christian Mind: How Should a Christian Think?* (Ann Arbor, Mich.: Servant Books, 1978), p. 45. Original edition 1963.

The God Who Is There

So I ask again, Where do we start? How do we begin to think and act as Christians? There is a sense in which we could begin at any point, since truth is a whole and truth in any area will inevitably lead to truth in every other area. But if the dominant philosophy of our day is secularism, which means viewing all of life only in terms of the visible world and in terms of the here and now, then the best of all possible starting places is the doctrine of God, for God alone is above and beyond the world and is eternal. Even more, the doctrine of God is a necessary and inevitable starting place if we are to produce a genuinely Christian response to secularism.

What does that mean for our thinking?

Well, if there is a God, that very fact means that there is literally such a thing as the supernatural. *Supernatural* means over, above, or in addition to nature. In other words, to go back to Carl Sagan's popular credo, the cosmos is *not* all there is or was or ever will be. God is. God exists. He is there, whether we acknowledge it or not, and he stands behind the cosmos. In fact, it is only because there is a God that there is a cosmos, since without God nothing else could possibly have come to be.

If anything exists, there must be an inevitable, self-existent, uncaused first cause that stands behind it.

Several years ago at the Philadelphia Conference on Reformed Theology Professor John H. Gerstner was talking about creation and referred to something his high school physics teacher once said: "The most profound question that has ever been asked by anybody is: Why is there something rather than nothing?"

Gerstner said that he was quite impressed with that at the time. But later, as he sharpened his ability to think, he recognized that it was not a profound question at all. In fact, it was not even a true question. It posed an alternative, something rather than nothing. "But what is nothing?" Gerstner asked. "Nothing" eludes definition. It even defies conception. For as soon as you say, "Nothing is . . ." nothing ceases to be nothing and becomes something. Gerstner referred to Jonathan Edwards, who is not noted for being funny but who was at least a slight bit humorous on one occasion when he said, "Nothing is what the sleeping rocks dream of."

So, said Gerstner, "Anyone who thinks he knows what nothing is must have those rocks in his head."[2]

As soon as you ask, "Why is there something rather than nothing?" the alternative vanishes, you are left with something, and the only possible explanation for that something is "In the beginning God created the heavens and the earth" (Gen. 1:1), which is what Christianity teaches.

2. John H. Gerstner, "Man as God Made Him" in James M. Boice, editor, *Our Savior God: Man, Christ, and the Atonement* (Grand Rapids: Baker Book House, 1980), p. 20.

"He Is There and He Is Not Silent"

The God who exists has revealed himself. This is the doctrine of revelation. Francis Schaeffer titled one of his books *He Is There and He Is Not Silent* [3] to make this point. God is there, and he has not kept himself hidden from us. He has revealed himself—in nature, in history, and especially in the Scriptures.

In chapter 185 I mentioned four "ism"s that are part of the pattern of this age: secularism, humanism, relativism, and materialism. The doctrine of God is the specific Christian answer to secularism. Revelation is the specific answer to relativism. If God has spoken, then what he has said is truthful and can be trusted absolutely, since God is truthful. This gives us absolutes in an otherwise relative and therefore ultimately chaotic universe.

That God has spoken and that God's Word to us can be trusted has always been the conviction of the church, at least until relatively modern times. Today the truthfulness of the Bible has been challenged, but with disastrous results. For without a sure word from God all words are equally valid, and Christianity is neither more certain nor more compelling than any other merely human word or philosophy.

But notice this: If God has spoken, there will always be a certain hardness about the Christian faith and Christians. I do not mean that we will be hard on others or insensitive to them. Rather, there will be a certain unyielding quality to our convictions.

For one thing, we will insist upon truth and will not bow to the notion, however strongly it is pressed upon us, that "that's just your opinion."

Several years ago when I was flying to Chicago from the West Coast I got into a conversation with the woman seated next to me. We talked about religion, and whenever I made a statement about the gospel she replied, "But that's just your opinion." She was out of the relativistic mold.

I hit upon a way of answering her that preserved the hardness of what I was trying to say and yet did it nicely. I said, "You're right; that is my opinion, but that's not really what matters. What matters is: Is it true?"

She did not know quite what to say to that. So the conversation went on, and after a while she replied to something else I was saying in the same way: "But that's just your opinion."

I said, "You're right; that is my opinion, but that's not really what matters. What matters is: Is it true?" This happened about a dozen times, and after a while she began to smile and then laugh as she anticipated my comment coming. When I got home I sent her a copy of *Mere Christianity*.

Another thing the doctrine of revelation will mean for us is that we will not back down or compromise on moral issues. You know how it is whenever you speak out against some particularly bad act. If people do not say, "But

---

3. Francis A. Schaeffer, *He Is There and He Is Not Silent* (Wheaton, Ill.: Tyndale House, 1972).

that's just your opinion," they are likely to attack you personally, saying things like, "You'd do the same thing if you were in her situation" or "Do you think you're better than he is?" We must not be put off by such attacks. Our response should be something like this: "Please, I wasn't talking about what I would do if I were in her shoes. I'm a sinner too. I might have acted much worse. I would probably have failed sooner. I wasn't talking about that. I was talking about what is right, and I think that is what we need to talk about. None of us is ever going to do better than we are doing unless we talk about it and decide what's right to do."

"What the secular mind is ill-equipped to grasp is that the Christian faith leaves Christians with no choice at all on many matters of this kind," writes Blamires.[4] We are people under God's authority, and that authority is expressed for us in the Bible.

The West's Spiritual Exhaustion

Now let's return to some implications of the doctrine of God. First, if there is a God and if he has made us to have eternal fellowship with him, then we are going to look at failure, suffering, pain, and even death differently than non-Christians do. For the Christian these can never be the greatest of all tragedies. They are bad. Death is an enemy (1 Cor. 15:26). But they are over-balanced by eternal matters.

Second, success and pleasure will not be the greatest of all goods for us. They are good, but they will never compare with salvation from sin or knowing God. Jesus said it clearly: "What good will it be for a man if he gains the whole world, yet forfeits his soul?" (Matt. 16:26). Or, from the other side, "Do not be afraid of those who kill the body but who cannot kill the soul. Rather, be afraid of the One who can destroy both soul and body in hell" (Matt. 10:28).

That leads to a Christian response to materialism. There are two kinds of materialism, a philosophical materialism like that of doctrinaire communism and a practical materialism that is most characteristic of the West. We have been raised with a false kind of syllogism that says that because we are not communists and communists are materialists, therefore we are not materialists. But that is not necessarily true. Most of us embrace a practical materialism that warps our souls, stunts our spiritual growth, and hinders the advance of the gospel in our time.

The best critique of Western materialism that I know was presented by Aleksandr Solzhenitsyn, the well-known Soviet dissident and writer, in an address given to the graduating class of Harvard University in 1978. Up to that point Solzhenitsyn had been somewhat of an American hero. He had suffered in the Soviet Union's infamous gulag prison system and had later defected. That's why he was invited to speak at Harvard. But in this address

4. Blamires, *The Christian Mind*, p. 141.

he was so blunt in his criticism of the West that his popularity vanished almost overnight, and he was almost never heard from, though he continued to write voluminously from a retreat in New England.

Solzhenitsyn's address was no defense of socialism. Quite the contrary. He celebrated its ideological defeat in Eastern Europe, saying, "It is zero and less than zero." But he declared, "Should someone ask me whether I would indicate the West such as it is today as a model to my country, frankly I would have to answer negatively. . . . Through intense suffering our own country has now achieved a spiritual development of such intensity that the Western system in its present state of spiritual exhaustion does not look attractive." He maintained that "after the suffering of decades of violence and oppression, the human soul longs for things higher, warmer, and purer than those offered by today's mass living habits, introduced by the revolting invasion of publicity, by TV stupor and by intolerable music."[5]

According to Solzhenitsyn, the West has pursued physical well-being and the acquiring of material goods to the exclusion of almost everything spiritual.

"We Do Not Mind That We Die"

In 1989 Westerners were astounded by the political changes in Eastern Europe. Country after country repudiated its seventy-two-year communist heritage and replaced its leaders with democratically elected officials. We rejoiced in these changes, and rightly so. But we need to remember two things.

First, while the former communist lands have moved in a more democratic direction, we have moved in the direction of their materialism, living as if the only thing that matters is how many earthly goods we can acquire now. We marveled at the moving scenes of East Germans passing through the openings in the infamous Berlin Wall. We saw them gazing in amazement at the abundance of goods on West Berlin shelves. But what is the good of their being able to come to the West if all they discover here is a spiritual climate vastly inferior to their own?

And that is the second thing we need to remember. Though the American media with its blindness to things spiritual did not acknowledge it, the changes in the Eastern Bloc came about not by anyone's will, that of Mikhail Gorbachev or any other, but by the spiritual vitality of the people.

The strength of the Polish Solidarity movement, where the breakthrough first came, is that of the Roman Catholic Church. Pope John Paul II was a strong supporter of the people's faith and dreams.

Faith and spiritual strength also lay behind the changes in East Germany. Conventional wisdom in Germany has it that the turning point was on October 9, 1989, when seventy thousand demonstrators marched in Leipzig.

---

5. Aleksandr Solzhenitsyn, "A World Split Apart," The 1978 Commencement Address at Harvard University, *Harvard Gazette*, June 8, 1978, pp. 17–19.

The army was placed on full alert, and under normal circumstances it would have attacked the demonstrators violently. But the protesters' rallying cry was, "Let them shoot, we will still march." The army did not attack, and after that the protests grew until the government was overthrown.

In Romania, where President Nicolae Ceauşescu just weeks before had declared that apple trees would bear pears before socialism should be endangered in Romania, the end began in the house of a Protestant pastor whose parishioners surrounded him, declaring that they were willing to die rather than let him be arrested by the state police.[6]

Josef Tson, founder and president of the Romanian Missionary Society, was in Romania just after the death of Ceauşescu and reported the details of the story. The pastor was from the city of Timisoara, and his name was Laszlo Tokes. On Saturday, December 16, 1989, just a few days before Christmas, hundreds and then thousands of people joined the courageous parishioners who had surrounded his house trying to defend him. One was a twenty-four-year-old Baptist church worker who decided to distribute candles to the ever-growing multitude. He lit his candle, and then the others lit theirs. This transformed the protective strategy into a contagious demonstration, and it was the beginning of the revolution. The next day, when the secret police opened fire on the people, the young man was shot in the leg, and the doctors had to amputate it. But on his hospital bed this young man told his pastor, "I lost a leg, but I am happy. I lit the first light."

The people in Romania do not call the events of December 1989 a national revolution. They say rather, "Call it God's miracle." The rallying cry of the masses was "God lives!" That from a former fiercely atheistic country! The people shouted, "Freedom! Freedom! We do not mind that we die!"[7]

Willing to die? Ah, that is the only ultimately valid test of whether one is a practical materialist at heart or whether one believes in something greater and more important than things. Do we? No doubt there are Westerners who are willing to die for things intangible. The people who were willing to die for civil rights during the Civil Rights Movement in the 1960s are examples. But today the masses of individuals in America no longer share this high standard of commitment and sacrifice. In 1978, during President Jimmy Carter's abortive attempt to reinstate draft registration for the young, newspapers carried a photograph of a Princeton University student defiantly waving a poster marked with the words: "Nothing is worth dying for."

"But if nothing is worth dying for, is anything worth living for?" asks Charles Colson, who comments on this photograph in *Against the Night: Living in the*

---

6. The generally neglected story of the role of the church in the changes that have come to Eastern Europe is told in part in the January 22, 1990, issue of *National Review*, "How the East Was Won: Reports on the Rebirth of Christianity under Communism," pp. 22–28.

7. *Voice of Truth* magazine, Romanian Missionary Society, January-February 1990, p. 2.

New Dark Ages.[8] If there is nothing worth living for or dying for, then the chief end of man might as well be cruising the malls, which is the number one activity of today's teenagers, according to the pollsters.

Solzhenitsyn summarizes our weak thinking at this point when he says of today's Americans: "Every citizen has been granted the desired freedom and material goods in such quantity and of such quality as to guarantee in theory the achievement of happiness, in the morally inferior sense which has come into being during [these last] decades. . . . So who should now renounce all this? Why and for what should one risk one's precious life in defense of common values?"[9]

Christianity has the answer to that, and Christians in past ages have known it. It is to "gain a better resurrection" (Heb. 11:35), which means to do what is right because what is right pleases God and that is what ultimately matters. But those who do it must be thinking Christians.

---

8. Charles Colson, *Against the Night: Living in the New Dark Ages* (Ann Arbor, Mich.: Servant Publications, 1989), p. 33.

9. Solzhenitsyn, "A World Split Apart," p. 17.

188

Mind Renewal in a Mindless Age: Part 2

Romans 12:2

Do not conform any longer to the pattern of this world, but be transformed by the renewing of your mind. Then you will be able to test and approve what God's will is—his good, pleasing and perfect will.

In the last study I introduced the Christian doctrines of God and revelation as the biblical answer to secularism, humanism, relativism, and materialism, but I did not write about humanism in detail. The answer to humanism is the Christian doctrine of man.

Humanism is the philosophy to which human beings inevitably come if they are secularists. Secularism means eliminating God or anything else that may be transcendent from the universe and focusing instead on only what we can see and measure now. When God is eliminated in this process, man himself is left as the pinnacle of creation and becomes the inadequate and unworthy core for everything. In philosophy we usually trace the beginnings of this outlook to the pre-Socratic Greek philosopher Protagoras. Protagoras expressed his viewpoint in Greek words that have given us the better known

Latin concept *homo mensura*, which means "Man, the measure" or, as it is often expressed, "Man is the measure of all things." The idea is that man is the norm by which everything is to be evaluated. He is the ultimate creature and thus the ultimate authority.

This seems to elevate man, but in practice it does exactly the opposite. It deifies man, but this deification always debases man in the end, turning him into an animal or even less than an animal. Moreover, it causes him to manipulate, ignore, disparage, wound, hate, abuse, and even murder other people.

What's Wrong with *Me?*

In the last twenty years something terrible has happened to Americans in the way we relate to other people, and it is due to the twisted humanism about which I have been writing. Prior to that time there was still something of a Christian ethos in this country and people used to care about and help other people. It was the natural thing to do. Today we focus on ourselves and deal with others only for what we can get out of them. This approach is materialistic and utilitarian.

In 1981 a sociologist-pollster, Daniel Yankelovich, published a study of the 1970s titled *New Rules: Searching for Self-Fulfillment in a World Turned Upside Down.* This book documented a tidal shift in values by which many and eventually most Americans began to seek personal self-fulfillment as the ultimate goal in life rather than operating on the principle that we are here to serve and even sacrifice for others, as Americans for the most part really had done previously.[1] He found that by the late 1970s, 72 percent of Americans spent much time thinking about themselves and their inner lives.[2] So pervasive was this change that as early as 1976 Tom Wolfe called the seventies the "Me Decade" and compared it to a third religious awakening.[3]

But isn't this a good thing? Shouldn't thinking about ourselves make us happy? If we redirect our energy to fulfilling ourselves and earn as much as we can to indulge even our tiniest desires, shouldn't we be satisfied with life? No! It doesn't work that way. It fails on the personal level, and it fails in the area of our relationships with other people also.

In 1978 Margaret Halsey wrote an article for *Newsweek* magazine titled "What's Wrong with Me, Me, Me?" Halsey referred to Wolfe's description of the seventies as the "me" generation, highlighting the belief that "inside every human being, however unprepossessing, there is a glorious, talented and overwhelmingly attractive personality [which] will be revealed in all its splendor

1. Daniel Yankelovich, *New Rules: Searching for Self-Fulfillment in a World Turned Upside Down* (New York: Random House, 1981), pp. 10–11.

2. Ibid., p. 5.

3. Tom Wolfe, "The 'Me-Decade' and the Third Great Awakening," *New York* magazine, August 23, 1976, pp. 26–40.

if the individual just forgets about courtesy, cooperativeness and consideration for others and proceeds to do exactly what he or she feels like doing."

The problem, as Halsey pointed out, is not that there are not attractive characteristics in everyone (or at least in most people) but that human nature consists even more basically of "a mess of unruly primitive elements" which spoil the "self-discovery." These unruly elements need to be overcome, not indulged. And this means that the attractive personalities we seek really are not there to be discovered but rather are natures that need to be developed through choices, hard work, and lasting commitments to others. When we ask "What's wrong with me?" it is the "me, me, me" that is the problem.[4]

This affects our relationships with other people too, because it makes our world impersonal. Charles Reich in his best-selling book *The Greening of America* wrote:

> Modern living has obliterated place, locality and neighborhood, and given us the anonymous separateness of our existence. The family, the most basic social system, has been ruthlessly stripped to its functional essentials. Friendship has been coated over with a layer of impenetrable artificiality as men strive to live roles designed for them. Protocol, competition, hostility, and fear have replaced the warmth of the circle of affection which might sustain man against a hostile environment. . . . America [has become] one vast, terrifying anti-community.[5]

The Christian Doctrine of Man

The Christian answer to this is the biblical doctrine of man, which means that if we are to have renewed minds in this area, we need to stop thinking about ourselves and other people as the world does and instead begin operating within a biblical framework.

When we turn to the Bible to see what it has to say about human beings, we find two surprising things. First, we find that man is a uniquely valuable being, far more important than the humanists imagine him to be. But, second, in his fallen condition we also find that he is much worse than the humanists suppose.

Let's take the fact that human beings are more valuable than humanists imagine first. The Bible teaches this at the very beginning of Genesis when it reports God as saying, "Let us make man in our image, in our likeness" (Gen. 1:26). We are then told, "So God created man in his own image, in the image of God he created him; male and female he created them" (v. 27).

In ancient times books were copied by hand with rough letters. There was no typesetting, so it was not possible to emphasize one idea over another by such devices as italics, capital letters, boldface, and centered headings. Instead

4. Margaret Halsey, "What's Wrong with Me, Me, Me?" *Newsweek*, April 17, 1978, p. 25.
5. Charles Reich, *The Greening of America: The Coming of a New Consciousness and the Rebirth of a Future* (New York: Bantam Books, 1971), p. 7.

emphasis was made by repetition. For example, when Jesus wanted to stress something as unusually important, he began with the words "verily, verily" or "truly, truly." We have the same thing in the first chapter of Genesis with the phrases "in our image," "in his own image," and "in the image of God." That idea is repeated three times, which is a way of saying that man being created in God's image is important. It is what makes man distinct from the animals. He is to value this distinction greatly.

Just a few chapters later in Genesis, the fact that man is made in God's image is given as the reason why we are not to murder other people and why murderers should be punished by death, since they devalue another individual's life, taking it lightly: "Whoever sheds the blood of man, by man shall his blood be shed; for in the image of God has God made man" (Gen. 9:6).

Bible students have debated the full meaning of what it means to be made in the image of God for centuries. This is not surprising since being made in God's image means to be like God and God is above and far beyond us, beyond even our full understanding. Nevertheless, we can know a few things:

1. *Personality.* To be made in God's image means to possess the attributes of personality, as God himself does, but animals, plants, and matter do not. This involves knowledge, memory, feelings, and a will. Of course, there is a sense in which animals have what we call personalities, meaning that individuals in a species sometimes behave differently than others in the species. But animals do not create. They do not love or worship. Personality, in the sense I am writing about here, is something that links human beings to God but does not link either God or man to the rest of creation.

2. *Morality.* The second characteristic of being made in the image of God is morality, for God is a moral God and those made in his image are made with the capacity to discern between what is right and wrong, between good and evil. This involves the further elements of freedom and responsibility. To be sure, the freedom of human beings is not absolute, as God's freedom is. We are not free to do all things. We are limited. Nevertheless, our freedom is a true freedom, even when we use it wrongly as Adam and Eve did when they sinned. They lost their original righteousness as a result. But they were still free to sin, and they were free in their sinful state afterward in the sense that they were still able to make right and wrong choices. Moreover, they continued to be responsible for them.

3. *Spirituality.* The third feature of being made in the image of God is spirituality, which means that human beings are able to have fellowship with God. Another way of saying this is to say that "God is spirit" (John 4:24) and that we are also spirits meant for eternal fellowship with him. Nothing can be greater than that for human beings, and the Westminster Shorter Catechism states it well when it says in the answer to the first question: "Man's chief end is to glorify God and to enjoy him forever."

Perhaps at this point we are beginning to see why secular humanism is so bad and not just a less attractive option than Christianity. Humanism sounds like it is focusing on man and elevating man, but it actually strips away the most valuable parts of human nature. As far as personality goes, it reduces us to mere animal urges, as Sigmund Freud tried to do. Regarding morality, instead of remaining responsible moral agents, which is our glory, we are turned into mere products of our environment or our genetic makeup, as B. F. Skinner asserts. As far as spirituality is concerned, how can we maintain a relationship to God if there is no God and we are made the measure of all things?

To refer again to Aleksandr Solzhenitsyn, in humanism "things higher, warmer, and purer" are drowned out by "today's mass living habits and TV stupor." We can make engrossing five-minute TV videos or commercials, but we no longer build cathedrals.

The Doctrine of the Fall

What is the problem, then? If human beings are more important and more valuable than the humanists imagine, why is it that things are so bad? The answer is the Christian doctrine of sin, which tells us that although people are more valuable than secularists imagine, they are in worse trouble than the humanists can admit. We have been made in God's image, but we have lost that image, which means that we are no longer fully human or as human as God intends us to be. We are fallen creatures.

Here I think of something I wrote about in the first volume of these studies, when I was looking closely at Romans 1. Romans 1 is about human beings falling down a steep slippery slope when they abandon God, and I pointed out that the conceptual framework for this downbound slide is found in Psalm 8. Psalm 8 both begins and ends with the words: "O Lord, our Lord, how majestic is your name in all the earth" (vv. 1, 9). In the middle it talks about the created order. So the beginning and ending teach that everything begins and ends with God, rather than with man, and that if we think clearly we will agree with this.

Then it describes men and women particularly:

> When I consider your heavens,
>   the work of your fingers,
> the moon and the stars,
>   which you have set in place,
> what is man that you are mindful of him,
>   the son of man that you care for him?
> You made him a little lower than the heavenly beings
>   and crowned him with glory and honor.
> You made him ruler over the works of your hands;
>   you put everything under his feet:
> all flocks and herds,
>   and the beasts of the field.

Psalm 8:3–7

These verses fix man at a very interesting place in the created order: lower than the angels ("the heavenly beings") but higher than the animals—somewhere in between. This is what Thomas Aquinas saw when he described man as a mediating being. He is like the angels in that he has a soul. He is like the beasts in that he has a body. The angels have souls but not bodies, while the animals have bodies but not souls.

But here is the point. Although man is a mediating being, created to be somewhere between the angels and the animals, in Psalm 8 he is nevertheless described as being somewhat lower than the angels rather than as being somewhat higher than the beasts, which means that he is destined to look not downward to the beasts, but upward to the angels and beyond them to God and so to become increasingly like him. But if we will not look up, if we reject God, as secularism does, then we will inevitably look downward and so become increasingly like the lower creatures and behave like them. We will become beastlike, which is exactly what is happening in our society. People are acting like animals, and even worse.

Over the last few decades I have noticed that our culture is tending to justify bad human behavior on the ground that we are, after all, just animals. I saw an article in a scientific journal about a certain kind of duck. Two scientists had been observing a family of these ducks, and they reported something in this duck family that they called "gang rape." I am sure they did not want to excuse this crime among humans by the comparison they were making, but they were suggesting that gang rape among humans is at least understandable given our animal ancestry. The inference comes from the evolutionary, naturalistic worldview they espoused.

A story of a similar nature appeared in the September 6, 1982, issue of *Newsweek* magazine. It was accompanied by a picture of an adult baboon holding a dead infant baboon, and over this there was a headline that read: "Biologists Say Infanticide Is as Normal as the Sex Drive—And That Most Animals, Including Man, Practice It." The title is as revealing in its way as Carl Sagan's "The cosmos is all that is or ever was or ever will be." It identifies man as an animal, and it justifies his behavior on the basis of that identification. The sequence of thought goes like this: (1) Man is an animal, (2) Animals kill their offspring, (3) Therefore, it is all right (or at least understandable) that human beings kill their offspring.

The argument is fallacious, of course. Most animals do not kill their offspring. They protect their young and care for them. But even if in a few instances some animals do kill their offspring, this is still not comparable to the crimes of which human beings are capable. In the United States alone we kill over one and a half million babies each year by abortion—usually just for the convenience of the mother.[6] And the number of outright murders is soaring.

6. See chapter 22, "How Low Can You Go?" in James Montgomery Boice, *Romans,* vol. 1, *Justification by Faith: Romans 1–4* (Grand Rapids: Baker Book House, 1991), pp. 196–98.

The Doctrine of Redemption

My point in these last two studies has been that renewing our minds begins with understanding and applying the great Christian doctrines, and thus far we have at least touched on four of them: the doctrines of God, revelation, man, and the fall. This is a proper starting place for our thinking if we are serious about what Paul is urging upon us in our text from Romans, "be transformed by the renewing of your mind."

In the next study I will move on to the final phrase of verse 2 to ponder what it means to "test and approve what God's will is." But before I do that I want to mention the doctrine of redemption, without which nothing in either of these last two studies would be complete.

The doctrine of redemption—the fact that "God so loved the world that he gave his one and only Son, that whoever believes in him shall not perish but have eternal life" (John 3:16)—infinitely intensifies everything I have been saying about man being both more valuable than the humanists can imagine as well as also being worse than they can possibly suppose.

The doctrine of redemption intensifies man's value because it teaches that even in his fallen state, a condition in which he hates God and kills his fellow creatures, man is still so valuable to God that God planned for and carried out the death of his own precious Son to save him. At the same time, this doctrine teaches that man's state is indescribably dreadful, because it took nothing less than the death of the very Son of God to accomplish it.

I want to close this study by referring again to what I regard as the greatest single piece of writing produced by the great Christian scholar and apologist C. S. Lewis. It was preached as a sermon in the summer of 1941, but it is known to us as an essay called "The Weight of Glory."[7] Lewis begins by probing for the meaning of glory, recognizing that it is something of the very essence of God that we desire. It is something "no natural happiness will satisfy."[8] At the same time it is also something from which we, in our sinful state, have been shut out. We want it. We sense that we are destined for it. But glory is beyond us—apart from what God has done to save us and make us like himself.

At the end of the essay, Lewis applies this to how we should learn to think about other people. We should understand that they are either going to be brought into glory, which is a supreme and indescribable blessing, or else they are going to be shut out from it—forever. Here he says, "It is a serious thing to live in a society of possible gods and goddesses, to remember that the dullest and most uninteresting person you can talk to may one day be a creature which, if you saw it now, you would be strongly tempted to worship, or else a horror and a corruption such as you now meet, if at all, only in a

7. C. S. Lewis, "The Weight of Glory" in *The Weight of Glory and Other Addresses* (New York: Macmillan Publishing Company/Collier Books, 1980). I refer to this essay in two places in *Romans*, vol. 2—pp. 703–4 and 862–63.

8. Lewis, "The Weight of Glory," p. 8.

nightmare. . . . There are no *ordinary* people. You have never talked to a mere mortal. Nations, cultures, arts, civilizations—these are mortal, and their life is to ours as the life of a gnat. But it is immortals whom we joke with, work with, marry, snub, and exploit—immortal horrors or everlasting splendors."[9]

What Lewis is doing in that essay is helping us to develop a Christian mind about other people, and his bottom line is that we will treat others better only if we learn to think of them in these terms.

9. Lewis, "The Weight of Glory," 18–19.

189

God's Good, Pleasing, and Perfect Will

Romans 12:2

Do not conform any longer to the pattern of this world, but be transformed by the renewing of your mind. Then you will be able to test and approve what God's will is—his good, pleasing and perfect will.

Some time ago the staff of the Bible Study Hour prepared a brochure that compared the world's thinking and the Bible's teaching in six important areas: God, man, the Bible, money, sex, and success. The differences were striking, but what impressed me most as I read over the brochure was how right many of the world's ideas seemed if not considered critically and biblically. We hear the world's approach given out so often, so attractively, and so persuasively, especially on television, that it's imperative that we think critically about it.

Here are some of the world's statements we printed:

"I matter most, and the world exists to serve me. Whatever satisfies me is what's important."

"If I earn enough money, I'll be happy. I need money to provide security for me and my family. Financial security will protect me from hardship."

"Anything is acceptable as long as it doesn't hurt another person."

"Success is the path to fame, wealth, pleasure, and power. Look out for number one."

How about the Christian way? From the world's perspective the Christian way does not look attractive or even right. It says such things as:

"God is in control of all things and has a purpose for everything that happens."

"Man exists to glorify God."

"Money cannot shield us against heartbreak, failure, sin, disease, or disaster."

"Success in God's kingdom means humility and service to others."

Because we are so much part of the world and so little like Jesus Christ, even Christians find God's way unappealing. Nevertheless, we are to press on in that way and prove by our lives that the will of God really is good, pleasing, and perfect in all things.

I find it significant that this is where Paul's statements about being transformed by the renewing of our minds—rather than being conformed to the patterns of this world—end. They end with proving the way of God to be the best way and the will of God to be perfect. This means that action is needed: God is not producing hothouse or ivory-tower Christians. He is forming people who will prove the value of God's way by conscious choices and deliberate obedience.

This point was expressed well by Robert Candlish, one of the best Scottish exegetes of the last century. He wrote, "The believer's transformation by the renewing of his mind is not the ultimate end which the Holy Spirit seeks in his regenerating and renovating work. It is the immediate and primary design of that work, in one sense. We are created anew in Christ Jesus. That new creation is what the Holy Spirit first aims at and effects. But 'we are created in Christ Jesus unto good works, which God hath before ordained that we should walk in them' (Eph. 2:10). The essence of a good work is the doing of the will of God. The proving of the will of God, therefore, is a fitting sequel of our 'being transformed by the renewing of our mind.'"[1]

---

1. Robert S. Candlish, *Studies in Romans 12: The Christian's Sacrifice and Service of Praise* (Grand Rapids: Kregel Publications, 1989), pp. 80–81. Original edition 1867.

God Has a Will for Each of Us

This last part of Romans 12:1–2 is not difficult to handle because the points are obvious. The first is this: God has a good, pleasing, and perfect will for each of us. Otherwise, how would it be possible for us to test and approve what that will is?

But this requires some explanation. Today when Christians talk about discovering the will of God what they usually have in mind is praying until God somehow discloses a specific direction for their lives—who they should marry, what job they should take, whether they should be missionaries, what house they should buy, and so forth. This is not exactly what proving the will of God means, nor is it what Romans 12:2 is teaching. The will of God is far more important than that.

You may recall that I discussed the matter of knowing the will of God earlier in this series, when I was writing on Romans 8:27, the verse that speaks about the Holy Spirit interceding "for the saints in accordance with God's will."[2] I pointed out that Garry Friesen, a professor at Multnomah School of the Bible, and J. Robin Maxson, a pastor from Klamath, Oregon, had written a very good book on that subject entitled *Decision Making and the Will of God*.[3] They distinguished between three meanings of the word *will:* first, God's *sovereign will,* which is hidden and is not revealed to us except as it unfolds in history; second, God's *moral will,* which is revealed in Scripture; and third, God's *specific will for individuals,* which is what people are usually thinking about when they speak of searching for or finding God's will. These authors rightly accepted the first two of these *wills,* but they disagreed with the idea that God has a specific will for each life and that it is the duty of the individual believer to find that will or "live in the center of it."

My evaluation of this book was that it is helpful in cutting away many of the hang-ups that have nearly incapacitated some Christians. Its exposure of the weakness of subjective methods of determining guidance is astute. Its stress on the sufficiency of Scripture in all moral matters is essential. My only reservation was that it does not acknowledge that God does indeed have a specific (though usually hidden) will for us or adequately recognize that God does sometimes reveal that will in special situations.

We may not know what that specific will is, and we do not need to be under pressure to "discover" it, fearing that if we miss it, somehow we will be doomed to a life outside the center of God's will. We are free to make decisions with what light and wisdom we possess.

Nevertheless, we can know that God does have a perfect will for us, that the Holy Spirit is praying for us in accordance with that will, and that this

2. See James Montgomery Boice, "Knowing the Will of God" (Romans 8:27) in *Romans,* vol. 2, *The Reign of Grace: Romans 5:1–8:39* (Grand Rapids: Baker Book House, 1992), pp. 893–900.
3. Garry Friesen with J. Robin Maxson, *Decision Making and the Will of God: An Alternative to the Traditional View* (Portland, Oreg.: Multnomah Press, 1980).

will of God for us will be done—because God has decreed it and because the Holy Spirit is praying for us in this area.

Still, having said all this, I need to add that this is not primarily what Romans 12:2 is talking about when it speaks of God's will. In this verse *will* is to be interpreted in its context, and the context indicates that the will of God that we are encouraged to follow is the general will of offering our bodies to God as living sacrifices, refusing to be conformed to the world's ways, and instead being transformed from within by the renewing of our minds. It is this that we are to pursue and thus find to be good, pleasing, and perfect, though, of course, if we do it, we will also find ourselves working out the details of God's specific will for our lives.

Good, Pleasing, and Perfect

The second obvious point about the ending of Romans 12:2 is that the will of God is good, pleasing, and perfect. It teaches about the nature of God's will for us.

1. *The will of God is good.* In a general way the will of God for every Christian is revealed in the Bible. Romans 8 contains a broad expression of this plan: that we might be delivered from God's judgment upon us for our sin and instead be made increasingly like Jesus Christ. The five specifically highlighted steps of this plan, as presented in verses 29–30, include (1) foreknowledge, (2) predestination, (3) effectual calling, (4) justification, and (5) glorification.

But there are also many specifics. The Ten Commandments contain some of these. It is God's will that we have no other gods before him, that we do not worship even him by the use of images, that we do not misuse his name, that we remember the Sabbath day by keeping it holy, that we honor our parents, that we do not murder or commit adultery or steal or give false testimony or covet (Exod. 20). The Lord Jesus Christ amplified upon many of these commandments and added others. It is God's will that we be holy (1 Thess. 4:3). It is God's will that we should pray (1 Thess. 5:17). Above all Jesus taught that we are to "love each other" (John 15:12).

These things often do not seem good to us, because we are far from God and are still thinking in the world's way. Nevertheless, they are good, which we will discover if we will obey God in these areas and put his will into practice. As one of the great Romans commentators, Robert Haldane, says, "The will of God is here distinguished as good, because, however much the mind may be opposed to it and how much soever we may think that it curtails our pleasures and mars our enjoyments, obedience to God conduces to our happiness."[4]

2. *The will of God is pleasing.* Pleasing to whom? Not to God, of course. That is obvious. Besides, we do not have to prove that God is pleased by his own will, nor could we. When Paul encourages us to prove that God's will is a pleas-

---

4. Robert Haldane, *An Exposition of the Epistle to the Romans* (MacDill AFB: MacDonald Publishing Company, 1958), p. 557.

ing will, he obviously means pleasing to us. That is, if we determine to walk in God's way, refusing to be conformed to the world and being transformed instead by the renewing of our minds, we will not have to fear that at the end of our lives we will look back and be dissatisfied or bitter, judging our lives to have been an utter waste. On the contrary, we will look back and conclude that our lives were well lived and be satisfied with them.

I was talking with a Christian man whose mother was dying. The mother was not a Christian, and she had become very bitter, although she had not been a bitter person before. She felt that everyone was turning against her, even her children, who actually were trying to help her. This man said to me, "I am convinced that Christians and non-Christians come to the end of their lives very differently. Those who are not Christians feel that they do not deserve to end their lives with failing health and pain, and they think their lives have been wasted. Christians are satisfied with what God has led them through and has done for them. It is better to die as a Christian."

I think that is exactly right. It is what Paul is saying.

3. *The will of God is perfect.* There are a number of words in the Greek language that are translated by our word *perfect.* One is *akribôs,* from which we get our word *accurate,* meaning correct. Another is *katartizô,* which means well fitted to a specific end, like a perfect solution to a puzzle. The word in Romans 12:2 is different. It is *teleios,* which has the thought of something that has attained its full destiny, is complete. It can be used of one who is mature, a mature adult. It is used of Jesus, who became a complete, or perfect, man. It is used of the end of history. In our text it means that those who do the will of God discover that it is not lacking in any respect. There is a satisfying wholeness about it.

To put this in negative form, it means that if we reach the end of our lives and are dissatisfied with them, this will only mean that we have been living in the world's way and have been conformed to it rather than having been transformed by the renewing of our minds. We will have been living for ourselves rather than for God and others.

We Need to Check It Out

The third obvious point of this verse is that we need to prove by our experience that the will of God is indeed what Paul tells us it is—good, pleasing, and perfect. We need to check it out. It is by checking it out that we will begin to find out what it actually is.

This is the exact opposite of our normal way of thinking. Usually we want God to tell us what his will for us is, and after that we want to be able to decide whether it is good, pleasing, or perfect, and thus whether or not we want to do it. Romans 12:2 tells us that we have to start living in God's way and that it is only as we do that we will begin to know it in its fullness and learn how good it really is. Robert Candlish says, "The will of God . . . can be known only by trial. . . . No one who is partaker of a finite nature and who occupies the position of a subject or servant under the authority of God, under his law, can understand what . . . the will of God is otherwise than through actual experience. You cannot explain to him beforehand what the will of God is and what are its attributes or characteristics. He must learn this for himself. And he must learn it experimentally. He must prove in his own person and in his own personal history what is . . . 'that good and acceptable and perfect will of God.'"[5]

God's Creatures and Probation

One of the most valuable parts of Candlish's study is the way he follows up on this idea, noting that the idea of proving the will of God experimentally goes a long way toward explaining the Bible's teaching about probation. This word is derived from the word *prove* and refers to a trial or test. According to Candlish, every order of free and intelligent being has been called upon to stand trial in the sense that ultimately it was created to prove that the will of God is good, pleasing, and perfect—or, if the creature should reject that will and fail the test, to prove that the contrary will of the world is disappointing and defective. Candlish reminds us of the following biblical examples.

1. *The angels.* We are not told much in the Bible about the trial of the angels, but it is certain that they did stand trial and that some of them failed that trial and so entered into the rebellion led by Satan and passed under the severe judgment of Almighty God.

Candlish speculates that the specific issue of that trial may have been the command to worship the Son of God: "When God brings his firstborn into the world, he says, 'Let all God's angels worship him'" (Heb. 1:6). But whether or not this was the specific matter the angels of God were to prove good, pleasing, and perfect, it is clear that many did not regard God's will as such. It is why they rebelled against it. And even those who did adhere to God's will must have done so not knowing then the full goodness, satisfaction, or perfection of what they were being called upon to do. They have been learning it since by their doing of it; that is, they have been learning it experimentally (cf. Eph. 3:8–11).

2. *Man in his pristine state.* The second case of probation is man in his pristine state. We know a great deal more about this than we do about the trial of the angels, since it concerns us most directly and is revealed to us for that reason. Adam and Eve were required to prove the good, pleasing, and perfect will of God in the matter of the tree of the knowledge of good and evil, refusing to eat of it because God had forbidden it to them. We know how this turned out. When weighed against what they considered to be more desirable ("you will be like God, knowing good and evil," Gen. 3:5), our first parents chose the way of sin, ate of the tree, and paid the price of their transgression.

5. Candlish, *Studies in Romans 12*, p. 81.

Candlish argues that if Adam and Eve had kept the will of God, though it did not seem desirable at that stage of their lives, "They would have found by experience that what God announced to them as his will was really in itself, as the seal of his previous covenant of life and as the preparation for the unfolding of his higher providence, fair, reasonable [and] good. . . . They would have learned experimentally that it was suited to their case and circumstances, deserving of their acceptance, sure to become more and more pleasing as they entered more and more into its spirit and became more and more thoroughly reconciled to the quiet simplicity of submission which it fostered."[6]

But they did not prove it to be such and therefore brought sin, judgment, and death upon the race.

3. *The Lord Jesus Christ.* The third example is Jesus Christ, who in his incarnate state took it upon himself to prove that God's will was indeed good, pleasing, and perfect, even though it involved the pain of the cross, which in itself hardly seemed good, pleasing, or even acceptable.

In the garden Jesus prayed that the cross might be taken from him, adding, "Yet not as I will, but as you will" (Matt. 26:39). The author of Hebrews says, "During the days of Jesus' life on earth, he offered up prayers and petitions with loud cries and tears to the one who could save him from death, and he was heard because of his reverent submission. Although he was a son, he learned obedience from what he suffered" (Heb. 5:7–8). In the Book of Philippians Paul speaks of Jesus humbling himself and becoming "obedient to death—even death on a cross!" (Phil. 2:8).

Writes Candlish, "It must have been, it often was, with him a struggle—an effort—to do the will of God. It was not easy, it was not pleasant. It was self-denial, self-sacrifice, self-crucifixion throughout. It was repulsive to the highest and holiest instincts of his pure humanity. It laid upon him most oppressive burdens; it brought him into most distressing scenes; it involved him in ceaseless, often thankless toil; it exposed him to all sorts of uncongenial encounters with evil men and evil angels. But he proved it. And in the proving of it, and as he was proving it, he found it to be good and acceptable and perfect."[7]

4. *Christians.* And what of ourselves, we who confess Jesus Christ to be our Lord and Savior? We are on trial now, and the matter of our probation is whether or not we will embrace the will of God for our lives, turning from the world and its ways, and so prove by the very embracing of that will that it is exactly what God declares it to be when he calls it perfect.

Who is to do that? You are, and you are to do it in the precise earthly circumstances into which God has placed you.

How are you to do it? You are to do it experimentally—that is, by actually putting the revealed will of God to the test.

6. Ibid., p. 85.
7. Ibid., p. 89.

When are you to do it? Right now and tomorrow and the day after that. You are to do it repeatedly and consistently and faithfully all through your life until the day of your death or until Jesus comes again.

Why are you to do it? Because it is the right thing to do, and because the will of God really is good, pleasing, and perfect.

Candlish says this:

> Of the fashion of the world, it may be truly said that the more you try it, the less you find it to be satisfying. It looks well; it looks fair, at first. But who that has lived long has not found it to be vanity at last?
>
> It is altogether otherwise with the will of God. That often looks worst at the beginning. It seems hard and dark. But on! On with you in the proving of it! Prove it patiently, perseveringly, with prayer and pains. And you will get growing clearness, light, enlargement, joy. You will more and more find that "the path of the just is as the shining light, that shineth more and more unto the perfect day." For "wisdom's ways are ways of pleasantness, and all her paths are peace." "The judgments of the Lord are true and righteous altogether. More to be desired are they than gold, yea, than much fine gold; sweeter also than honey, and the honeycomb. Moreover by them is thy servant warned; and in keeping of them there is great reward."[8]

8. Candlish, *Studies,* pp. 96–97.

PART SEVENTEEN

The Christian and Other People

190

First Things First

Romans 12:3

For by the grace given me I say to every one of you: Do not think of yourself more highly than you ought, but rather think of yourself with sober judgment, in accordance with the measure of faith God has given you.

Some time ago I came across the story of a man who imagined himself to be quite spiritual. He was talking with a more mature friend, and he asked his friend to pray for him that he might be humble. "Pray for me that I might be nothing," he said.

His friend replied with some wisdom, probably thinking of 1 Corinthians 1:28, "You *are* nothing, brother. Take it by faith."

This is what Paul wants us to do in Romans 12:3, as he moves from his profound development of the first principles of the Christian life in Romans 12:1–2 to a discussion of a Christian's right relationship to other people that fills the remainder of the chapter. His words specifically combine a right estimation of ourselves with faith, though in a slightly different sense from my story. "For by the grace given me I say to every one of you: Do not think of yourself more highly than you ought, but rather think of yourself with sober judgment, in accordance with the measure of faith God has given you," Paul says.

1565

Robert S. Candlish outlines Romans 12 in three parts: (1) the Christian's relationship to God (vv. 1–2), (2) the Christian's relationship to the church (vv. 3–13), and (3) the Christian's relationship to a hostile world (vv. 14–21).[1] If we follow his outline, we are at the start of section two, the Christian's relationship to the church. Much of what follows is indeed about the church, but it is important to see that in starting this discussion Paul focuses first on the Christian's estimate of himself alone, since he knows that none of us will ever properly evaluate and esteem other Christians within the fellowship of the church if our pride is in the way.

It is a matter of dealing with first things first—first, a right relationship with God; second, a proper evaluation of myself; third, a right relationship with other people.

Two Ways of Thinking

All of these relationships involve the mind, of course. Paul has been telling us not to be conformed to the pattern of this world but rather "to be transformed by the renewing of your mind." Now he spells out what this means, beginning, "Do not *think* of yourself more highly than you ought, but rather *think* of yourself with sober judgment."

Even in this English translation we cannot miss the fact that verse 3 repeats twice the idea of thinking. There is a wrong kind of thinking that we are to reject (thinking too highly of ourselves) and a right kind of thinking that we are to embrace (thinking soberly).

In the Greek text, however, the emphasis on right as opposed to wrong thinking is even stronger than this, since the word for thinking (*phronein*), occurs four times, twice with prefixes. *Phronein* means to make a right estimate of things. A fairly literal translation of verse 3 would go like this: "I say through the grace that is given to me, to every one of you, that you should not estimate yourself beyond what you should estimate, but that you should estimate yourself in such a way as to have a sensible estimate of yourself."

Two Common Errors

There are two possible errors in this kind of self-evaluation:

1. *To think of ourselves more highly than we ought to think.* This is the greater of the two dangers, because it is the one that comes to us most naturally. The reason it does is that it is linked to pride, the first and most deadly of the seven deadly sins. Almost everyone thinks more highly of himself than he ought, and we also want other people to have similarly exalted opinions of us.

How do we think more highly of ourselves than we ought? Some people have high opinions of themselves because of their having been born into a

---

1. Robert S. Candlish, *Studies in Romans 12: The Christian's Sacrifice and Service of Praise* (Grand Rapids: Kregel Publications, 1989). Original edition 1867.

family distinguished because of its wealth or the achievement of some illustrious ancestor. People like this have a recognizable name—Astor, Rockefeller, or Dupont, for example. Perhaps they are related to someone who has achieved recognition in the media or because of public office. Name-droppers fit into this category. They are always telling you about the celebrity they had lunch with last week or the congressmen they will be speaking to tomorrow. Perhaps the person has achieved a recognizable name himself. She is mentioned in the press, or he has appeared on the major television talk shows.

In the last century in England there was a snob by the name of Oscar Browning. He wanted to meet Alfred Lord Tennyson, so he sought him out on the Isle of Wight, where Tennyson was staying, marched up to him, shook him by the hand and announced, "I am Browning."

Tennyson knew only one Browning, the poet Robert Browning. He looked at Oscar Browning carefully. "No, no you're not," he said and walked away.

It would be nice if this type of pride did not exist among Christians, but unfortunately, it does. Some take pride simply in knowing a Christian leader, or in working with him or her. Some take pride in their denomination or their particular church. They act as if it is more important to be a Presbyterian or an Episcopalian or a Baptist (or whatever else they might be) than to be a Christian.

Other people think more highly of themselves than they should because of their exceptional education. That is, they think they know more than other people or are simply smarter than others.

Still other individuals have high opinions of themselves because they have been given unusual power, or seek it. Not long ago Michael Scott Horton edited a book titled *Power Religion: The Selling Out of the Evangelical Church?* in which he documented the pursuit of worldly power by evangelicals. He covered such important subjects as power politics, power evangelism, power growth, the power within, and power preachers. His conclusion:

> Even in the Christian world there is a tremendous spirit of self-confidence and pride: our church growth projects will at last usher in the kingdom; or we will do it by performing signs and wonders, what some proponents even refer to as "magic," or perhaps we will rule by taking over the public institutions and exerting political, social and economic pressure on the enemies of Christ; others may wish to achieve power through tapping the inner resources of the individual through the latest offerings of pop-psychology; some will demonstrate this self-confidence by reinforcing personality cults, legalistic restrictions and peer pressure; finally, some will appeal to the power of fear and paranoia to gather followings, as if they had an inside tract on such divine secrets as the date of our Lord's return. Evangelical gatherings are often marked by a certain smugness about the uniqueness of our generation in God's plan.[2]

2. Michael Scott Horton, ed., *Power Religion: The Selling Out of the Evangelical Church?* (Chicago: Moody Press, 1992), pp. 13–14.

None of this is unique to our time, of course. We see it in all ages of the Christian church. We remember, for instance, that Paul was writing Romans from Corinth on his third missionary journey—that is, while he was living in the midst of a church that had been marked by the pursuit of such worldly goals as family prestige, education, and political power. He reminded these people of their humble origin, thus encouraging them not to think of themselves more highly than they ought to think—the very thing he is doing in Romans: "Brothers, think of what you were when you were called. Not many of you were wise by human standards; not many were influential; not many were of noble birth. But God chose the foolish things of the world to shame the wise; God chose the weak things of the world to shame the strong. He chose the lowly things of this world and the despised things—and the things that are not—to nullify the things that are, so that no one may boast before him" (1 Cor. 1:26–29).

2. *To think too lowly of ourselves, a false humility.* The second error in our evaluation of ourselves is to think too lowly of ourselves and so exude a false kind of humility. Sometimes this is really pride, because when we tell people bad things about ourselves what we really want them to say is, "No, I don't think you're like that at all. I think you're really intelligent (or wise or attractive or kind or whatever)."

"That helps," we say. "Keep it up. Tell me more. I'd like you to talk me out of this."

When we act like that we are really being proud rather than humble, and we show it at once if the other person agrees with our earlier negative self-evaluation. We are offended when a friend says, "Yes, I guess you really are stupid" (or ugly or ineffective or a hopeless case).

On the other hand, some people really do have too low an opinion of themselves and need to find a proper self-esteem. These people need to do this not by propping themselves up artificially—that is, by telling themselves that they are brilliant when they are not, or beautiful when they are plain, or effective when they are actually ineffective and bungling—but rather by finding a proper self-evaluation in spiritual terms. If they are Christians, they need to recognize that they have been made by God and that, however ineffective they may feel—and actually be—in themselves, they are important to God, who has made them to do "good works" (Eph. 2:10).

The Right Way to Think about Ourselves

One of the problems we have is that we usually think about ourselves too much. Yet the solution Paul offers is not to stop thinking about ourselves entirely but instead to start thinking about ourselves in a right way. This has two parts: (1) We are to think of ourselves "with sober judgment" and (2) We are to think of ourselves "in accordance with the measure of faith God has given."

1. *With sober judgment.* Not long ago I was reading a study of Romans by the late Ray Stedman, former pastor of the Peninsula Bible Church of Palo Alto, California. He said that every morning when he got up he tried to remind himself of three things:

> First, I am made in the image of God. I am not an animal and I don't have to behave like an animal. I have an ability within me, given to me by God himself, to respond and relate to God. Therefore I can behave as a man and not as a beast.
>
> Second, I am filled with the Spirit of God. The most amazing thing has happened! Though I don't deserve it in the least degree, I have the power of God at work within me. I have become, in some sense, the bearer of God, and God himself is willing to be at work in me through the problems and pressures I go through this day.
>
> Third, I am part of the plan of God. God is working out all things to a great and final purpose in the earth, and I am part of it. What I do today has purpose and significance and meaning. This is not a meaningless day I am going through. Even the smallest incident, the most apparently insignificant word or relationship, is involved in his great plan. Therefore all of it has meaning and purpose.[3]

Stedman says rightly that there is nothing better than this to set us up on our feet and give us "confidence without conceit." When we think of ourselves in this way we are indeed thinking soberly and evaluating ourselves as God's creatures without either vanity or a lack of proper self-esteem.

2. *In accordance with the measure of faith God has given.* The second phrase Paul uses for thinking rightly about ourselves is "in accordance with the measure of faith God has given you." This is a little bit more than simply seeing ourselves as made in the image of God, given the Holy Spirit of God, and having part in the overall plan of God. It involves what each one of us is uniquely—that is, as different from other people—and it leads to the discussion of spiritual gifts that follows in this chapter.

Faith here can be taken in three ways: (1) our confidence or trust in God—hence, "Think of yourself... in accordance with the measure of your actual trust in God" (that is, "not as trusting God more than you actually do"); (2) our knowledge of God or of "the faith" God has revealed—hence, "Think of yourself... according to the degree of knowledge about yourself and all people that you have attained" (that is, don't exaggerate the human condition); or (3) our individual spiritual gifts received by faith—hence, "Think of yourself... in accordance with the specific gifts or talents God has given you."

3. Ray C. Stedman, *From Guilt to Glory*, vol. 2, *Reveling in God's Salvation* (Portland, Oreg.: Multnomah, 1978), pp. 109–110.

This last meaning is the most unusual, but it is the one to be preferred here because of the context. The first part of verse 3 looks back to what Paul has said in verses 1 and 2. We are to think "soberly" as one aspect of what it means to have a renewed mind. The second part of verse 3 looks ahead to what is going to be said about gifts. We are to understand that the church contains many members and that these have been given and exercise diverse endowments. We do not have all of these gifts ourselves, and we are to evaluate our contribution to the church on the basis of the gifts we have, not on the basis of another's talents.

John Murray says, "It is called the measure of faith in the restricted sense of the faith that is suited to the exercise of this gift, and this nomenclature is used to emphasize the cardinal place which faith occupies not only in our becoming members of this community but also in the specific functions performed as members of it."[4]

So part of a genuine humility has to do with understanding the spiritual endowments God has given us, taking this seriously, and beginning to use those gifts for God. This is exactly where the remainder of this paragraph is going, of course. For after teaching us in the next two sentences that the church is made up of many diverse members and that these members possess different spiritual gifts, Paul continues: "If a man's gift is prophesying, let him use it in proportion to his faith. If it is serving, let him serve; if it is teaching, let him teach; if it is encouraging, let him encourage; if it is contributing to the needs of others, let him give generously; if it is leadership, let him govern diligently; if it is showing mercy, let him do it cheerfully" (vv. 6–8).

Each of us is responsible for discovering what our particular gifts are and using them. It is a false humility that says, "I don't have anything to offer to anyone. God can't use me."

For the Glory of God

In Romans 12 Paul is speaking specifically of spiritual gifts—those that are to be exercised for spiritual ends within the fellowship and outreach of the church: prophesying, serving, teaching, encouraging, contributing to the needs of others, leadership, and showing mercy. But I think we are also to have a sober assessment of our natural abilities and acquired skills and that we are to use these to God's glory also. This is particularly true in our secular employment.

I think of a story told by Harry Ironside, a great Bible teacher of an earlier generation. Ironside's father died when he was quite young, so during his school days, on vacations, and on Saturdays, Ironside used to work for a

4. John Murray, *The Epistle to the Romans*, 2 vols. in 1 (Grand Rapids: Wm. B. Eerdmans Publishing Company, 1968), vol. 2, p. 119 (cp. p. 118). See also Charles Hodge, *A Commentary on Romans* (Edinburgh and Carlisle, Pa.: The Banner of Truth Trust, 1972), pp. 386–87. Original edition 1835.

Scottish shoemaker named Dan Mackay. The man was a Christian from the Orkney Islands who did his work well, and as he had opportunity he would speak to his customers about the importance of being born again.

Ironside's responsibility was to pound leather for the soles of the shoes. The cut cowhide was soaked in water and then placed on a piece of iron and pounded until it was hard and dry. This toughened the leather and made the soles last longer, but the pounding took a long time.

One day Ironside was walking by another cobbler's shop, and he saw that the owner was not pounding the leather soles at all. He simply took the soles out of the water and nailed them to the upper portion of the shoes with the water splashing out as he drove the nails in. Ironside went inside and asked him why he was doing his work that way. "Are they just as good as if they were pounded?" he asked.

The cobbler gave him a naughty wink and answered, "They come back all the quicker this way, my boy!"

Ironside thought he had learned something important. So he went back to the Christian cobbler, his boss, and suggested that maybe he was wasting his time pounding the leather to toughen it and get it dry. Mr. Mackay stopped his work and opened his Bible to Colossians 3:23–24, where he read, "Whatever you do, work at it with all your heart, as working for the Lord, not for men, since you know that you will receive an inheritance from the Lord as a reward."

He said, "Harry, I don't cobble shoes just for the money I get from my customers. I am doing this for the glory of God. I expect to see every shoe I have ever repaired in a big pile at the judgment seat of Christ, and I do not want the Lord to say to me in that day, 'Dan, this was a poor job. You did not do your best here.' I want him to be able to say, 'Well done, good and faithful servant.'"[5]

Let me give a more recent example. Several years ago Charles Colson, the head of Prison Fellowship, and Jack Eckerd, founder of the well-known Eckerd Drug Store chain, teamed up on a book called *Why America Doesn't Work*, which examines America's loss of a sound work ethic. Their conclusion is that the problem is spiritual and that it requires spiritual solutions. Their suggestions concern a sober evaluation of ourselves as God's work and of why God has given us the work we have to do in life. "Why, then, should we work?" they ask. Here are their answers:

Because work gives expression to our creative gifts and thus fulfills our need for meaning and purpose.

Because work is intrinsically good when done with the proper attitude and motive.

Because we are commanded to exercise stewardship over the earth, participating in the work of creation in a way that glorifies God.

5. H. A. Ironside, *Illustrations of Bible Truth* (Chicago: Moody Press, 1945), pp. 37–39.

Because we are citizens of this earth and have certain responsibilities to our fellow citizens.

It is this moral character of work that historically has been the very heart of the work ethic.[6]

So you see how practical this all is. A proper humility in which we learn to think soberly about ourselves does not lead to self-abnegation or inactivity, which honors no one. Instead it leads to the energetic use of every gift and talent God has given, knowing that they have come from him—that no glory is ever due to us—but because they do come from him, they must be used faithfully and wholeheartedly for his glory.

6. Chuck Colson and Jack Eckerd, *Why America Doesn't Work* (Dallas, London, Vancouver, Melbourne: Word Publishing, 1991), p. 178.

191

One Body in Christ

Romans 12:4-5

Just as each of us has one body with many members, and these members do not all have the same function, so in Christ we who are many form one body, and each member belongs to all the others.

Anyone who is interested in the doctrine of the church and senses its importance must be a bit surprised to notice how little the word *church* actually occurs in the Bible. It is not found in the Old Testament at all. The first time it occurs is in Matthew 16:18, then again in Matthew 18:17. It is not in the other gospels. It is scattered throughout Acts, of course (about eighteen times), but it is found only five times in Romans, all in chapter 16 (vv. 1, 3, 5, 16, 23). There are quite a few instances in 1 Corinthians and Ephesians (eighteen and nine times respectively), but then the references become infrequent again. In the New International Version of the Bible the singular word *church* occurs only seventy-nine times.

The explanation, of course, is that although the word *church* is itself relatively infrequent, the doctrine of the church is discussed many more times by other words and images.

That is the case in our text. Paul is beginning to talk about the church in Romans 12:4–5. His discussion is going to deal with church unity, the distribution of diverse gifts among the members of the church, and the way Christians in the church are to behave toward one another. But Paul does not use the word *church*. Instead he speaks of Christ's body: "Just as each of us has one body with many members, and these members do not all have the same function, so in Christ we who are many form *one body*, and each member belongs to all the others." This is an important text, because "the body of Christ" is a powerful image for the church. As we might expect, it is also found numerous other places in Paul's writings.[1]

What Is the Church?

Most of us know that the church is not a building, though we say, "I'm going to church," meaning a building, or we speak about "building a church," again meaning a building. We know that the church is people. But how do these people fit into a particular congregation or a denomination in our thinking? We talk about the Episcopal Church or the Presbyterian Church or the Baptist Church. Are they "churches," even "the one true church" as some claim? Are they even churches at all? And what about the people in these denominations? Are all of them members of the church? If so, in what sense? Does membership in a particular organization make you a church member? What about those who watch services on television? Or what about those who were baptized and attended church at one time but who no longer attend?

Paul's image is very helpful at this point. For when he speaks of the body of Christ, obviously he is speaking of those who belong to Christ, who are joined to him in exactly the sense in which he speaks about our being joined to Christ in Romans 5 and elsewhere. This is a spiritual reality, invisible but supremely real. It is something that is accomplished by the Holy Spirit, and it has to do with faith in Christ, by which we become new creatures, having passed out of our death-union with Adam to a new life-union with the Savior.

Charles Colson has written a book on the church called *The Body*, in which he complains of a lack of definition and identity by supposedly Christian people. "The church—the body of God's people—has little to do with slick marketing or fancy facilities. It has everything to do with the people and the Spirit of God in their midst," he says.[2]

John Stott has written, "The church is a people, a community of people, who owe their existence, their solidarity and their corporate distinctness from other communities to one thing only—the call of God."[3]

1. The idea of the church being one body with a multiplicity of members occurs in 1 Corinthians 10:17, 12:12–30; Ephesians 1:23, 4:4–16, 5:23–30; and Colossians 1:18, 1:24, 2:19, 3:15.
2. Charles Colson with Ellen Santilli Vaughn, *The Body* (Dallas, London, Vancouver, and Melbourne: Word Publishing, 1992), p. 49.
3. John R. W. Stott, *One People* (London: Falcon Books, 1969), p. 15.

Strictly speaking, the church of Jesus Christ, created by Jesus from among all peoples, is a New Testament reality. That is why the word *church* is found only in the New Testament. It is why Jesus used the future tense when he replied to Peter's great confession in Matthew 16 by saying, "On this rock *I will build my church*" (v. 18). This church began at Pentecost when people from all nations were brought to faith in Jesus by the Holy Spirit. Acts lists them as having been "Parthians, Medes and Elamites; residents of Mesopotamia, Judea and Cappadocia, Pontus and Asia, Phrygia and Pamphylia, Egypt and the parts of Libya near Cyrene; visitors from Rome (both Jews and converts to Judaism); Cretans and Arabs" (2:9–11).

But this is not quite the whole story. If the church is the community of those who have been called by God, as Stott suggests in his definition of the church, then the Old Testament believers belonged to the church of Jesus Christ too. This is because they looked forward to Christ's coming and were joined to him by faith, just as we look back.

The key concept here is the covenant. This covenant is expressed in God's call of particular individuals (and not others) and by his entering into a formal agreement to save, protect, and bless them. For their part, the individuals are required to believe, worship, and obey God. Adam and Eve were part of this initial covenant, and so were their godly descendants listed in Genesis 5. We see the idea of a covenant formally and most clearly set out in God's calling of Abraham, with whom a special stage in the history of the Old Testament "church" begins. God said, "Leave your country, your people and your father's household and go to the land I will show you. I will make you into a great nation and I will bless you" (Gen. 12:1–2). Later that covenant was ratified by a ceremony in which God foretold the future history of Abraham's descendants and promised them a land of their own, "from the river of Egypt to the great river, the Euphrates" (Gen. 15:18; see vv. 12–21). Abraham's response was to believe God and worship him.

We find the same pattern in God's dealings with Isaac, Abraham's son, and with Jacob, his grandson. In each case the call of God is joined to a covenant promise, and this is followed by faith, worship, and obedience on the people's part. The church consists of all these people, those whom God has called from all times and from all places and has joined to Jesus Christ.

There Is One Body, One Church

Paul's image of the church as Christ's body not only defines the church as the community of those who have been joined to Christ, but it also teaches that there is only one church. There is but one church because Jesus has but one body.

Ephesians 4:4–6 parallels the ideas we find in Romans 12, only with greater elaboration since Ephesians is essentially a book about the church. Significantly, this passage occurs at the same point in Ephesians as our passage in Romans does, where Paul begins to apply the earlier doctrine of salvation to

Christian living. He talks about believers being "humble and gentle," for example. Then he talks about the unity of the church, saying, "There is one body and one Spirit—just as you were called to one hope when you were called—one Lord, one faith, one baptism; one God and Father of all, who is over all and through all and in all" (Eph. 4:4–6).

There are seven important unities in this passage:

1. *One body.* This is an important image for the church, because it pictures it as an organic whole rather than as a machine that is made up of independent parts. The church is not an airplane, a train, or an automobile. It is an organism in which the parts are alive and both support and depend on one another. In 1 Corinthians Paul writes, "God has combined the members of the body and has given greater honor to the parts that lacked it, so that there should be no division in the body, but that its parts should have equal concern for each other. If one part suffers, every part suffers with it; if one part is honored, every part rejoices with it" (1 Cor. 12:24–26).

2. *One Spirit.* The word *Spirit* is capitalized in this phrase because Paul is not thinking here that Christians share the same spirit in the sense that they are one in their enthusiasms and goals. He is referring to the work of the Holy Spirit in drawing us to Christ. We are all different. We have come to Christ along different roads. Nevertheless, the reason we have come along those roads at all is that the same Holy Spirit has been drawing us, so that at the theological level our conversion experiences are the same. We have all been awakened to our need. We have all been made alive in Christ. We have all believed on him. Moreover, the Holy Spirit is performing a work of sanctification in each of us, so that we are all working for Christ and are beginning to produce the fruit of the Holy Spirit, which is "love, joy, peace, patience, kindness, goodness, faithfulness, gentleness and self-control" (Gal. 5:22–23).

3. *One hope.* Today the word *hope* usually means something that is uncertain. But in the New Testament it refers to what is sure and certain but for which we wait. Paul calls this "*one* hope" because it embraces a unifying set of beliefs among Christians—namely, the return of Jesus Christ, the Resurrection, and the Final Judgment. Another way of thinking about the Christian's hope is to say that when Jesus returns we are going to be with him, all of us. People from all races and nations and economic backgrounds will be together with Jesus, and the many things that divide us now will be forgotten. If that is so, shouldn't there be ways in which we reach across denominational, racial, and other barriers and work together now? Shouldn't we be able to demonstrate our unity better than we do?

4. *One Lord.* To hear some Christians talk, you would think that there are many Lords. "I know a Jesus who causes me to do this, which excludes you," some say. Or, "Your Jesus isn't the Jesus I know." Well, there is such a thing as believing in or proclaiming a false Christ, who is not the Lord. We are not to have fellowship with unbelief. But usually that is not our problem. Our real problem is that we distrust Christians who are not made precisely in our

mold. We need to realize that if others really believe in Christ, then the fact that we have this same Lord should draw us together.

5. *One faith.* This is not the subjective *faith* that we must have to be Christians. Here the word is being used objectively to refer to the content of faith, or the gospel, and it is teaching that there is only one body of genuine Christian doctrine, whatever our own limited understanding of it may be. Indeed, if we are really Christians, our differences must be in minor areas since by definition we all believe the major doctrines. As a rule, it would be helpful for us to explore the areas in which we agree with other Christians before we explore the points at which we differ.

6. *One baptism.* It is interesting that Paul should include baptism in a list of things that unite us since a diverse understanding of baptism is one of the things that has divided denominations most severely. The explanation, of course, is that Paul is not thinking of modes of baptism or even whether infants should be baptized. He is thinking of baptism as the sacrament in which we are publicly identified with Christ. If you have been identified with Jesus Christ by baptism, then you are also identified with all others who have likewise been baptized in his name.

7. *One God.* The final point of unity is "one God." We notice here that the first three of these points are grouped around the Holy Spirit: one body, one Spirit, one hope. The next three are grouped around the Lord Jesus Christ: one Lord, one faith, one baptism. This last item concerns the first person of the Godhead only.

Why is this the order? Probably because Paul is thinking from the effect to the cause. He begins with our being part of the church, and he asks, in effect, "How did we get to be part of the church?" The answer is: By the Holy Spirit joining us to Christ. The Holy Spirit made us part of one body and gave us one hope. Next question: "What, then, is the church?" Answer: Those who have Jesus Christ as Lord, who have believed on him and his work, and who have been identified with him publicly by baptism. The final questions are: But why did Jesus do this? And where did the idea of the church come from anyway? The answer is: Because it was God the Father's plan. The idea of the church comes from God the "Father of all, who is over all and through all and in all" (Eph. 4:6).

John Stott talks about the Trinity as the essential basis for church unity and sums it up like this: "There can be only one Christian family, only one Christian faith, hope and baptism, and only one Christian body, because there is only One God, Father, Son and Holy Spirit. You can no more multiply churches than you can multiply Gods. Is there only one God? Then he has only one church. Is the unity of God inviolable? Then so is the unity of the church. . . . It is no more possible to split the church than it is possible to split the Godhead."[4]

4. John R. W. Stott, *God's New Society: The Message of Ephesians* (Downers Grove, Ill.: InterVarsity Press, 1979), p. 151.

The Problem with the Church Today

And yet we have split the church, or at least the visible church that people see. John Stott's concern in the book *One People* is that we have done it by dividing the clergy from the laity. His book is designed to recapture a proper lay ministry. Charles Colson is concerned about our institutions and our individualism. He wants to revive the spiritual vitality of Christ's body. Donald Grey Barnhouse, in his studies of Romans, was troubled by the way we have turned minor points of doctrine into major causes for division. He wanted to overcome that arrogance.

We see this problem on several levels today:

1. *The institutional problem.* The division or disunity of the church is a problem at the institutional level, of course. In the hymn "Onward, Christian Soldiers," we sing:

> We are not divided, all one body we;
> one in hope and doctrine, one in charity.

But even as we sing it, we know it is not true. Or we recite the Apostles' Creed, containing the words, "I believe in . . . the holy catholic church." *Catholic* means universal, broad, diverse, united. But though we may believe in a universal church, we seem to restrict our thoughts of the church to our own particular fellowship or denomination. It is this institutional problem that has captured the attention of some Christian leaders and through them has been a driving force behind the well-intentioned but misdirected and mostly unsuccessful ecumenical movement.

2. *Individualism.* It strikes me, however, that today the problem is not so much our institutions, since they do not mean a whole lot to most people anyway, but rather our individualism, which I would define as hyperpersonalized religion. It is the religion of "Jesus and me only." It is what sociologists and pollsters uncover whenever they explore America's religious attitudes and practices.

Many people know the name of Robert Bellah, author of the sociological study of American life called *The Habits of the Heart*.[5] Bellah says that America has been infected with a virulent virus that he calls "radical individualism." It affects every area of life. People make up their own rules for everything, entirely apart from other people, and as a result they sometimes do terrible things to others. This "radical individualism" is particularly noticeable in religion. According to a *USA Today* survey, of the 56 percent of Americans who attend church, 46 percent do so because "it is good for you" (that is, "good for *me*"), and 26 percent go because it is where they hope to find "peace of

5. Robert N. Bellah et al., *The Habits of the Heart: Individualism and Commitment in American Life* (New York: Harper and Row, 1986).

mind and spiritual well-being." Truth—that is, specific doctrine—does not seem important to these people.[6]

In Bellah's study there is a report of a woman named Sheila who considers herself to be very religious. "What is your religion?" she was asked.

"I call it 'Sheilaism,'" she answered. "It's just my own little voice."

The word for this is *narcissism,* derived from the ancient story of Narcissus, a young Greek athlete who was in love with himself and spent his time by a quiet pool staring at his own reflection. It is a part of being conformed to this world rather than being transformed by the renewing of our minds, and it is a radical departure from what religion in America used to be, and should be. "Today religion in America is as private and diverse as New England colonial religion was public and unified," says Robert Bellah.[7] Clearly you cannot have "one body in Christ" if everyone is creating a private little a la carte religion for himself.

Maintain the Bond

So what is the challenge to informed biblical Christians in an age like ours? Well, the answer is not the ecumenical movement. Our task is not to create the unity of the body, above all not from the top down. The unity of the body is a given for those who are "in Christ." Nevertheless, we should work for any valid visible expression of our oneness in Christ that is attainable, and we should avoid unnecessary divisions and even try to learn from one another in a humble, teachable spirit, which is the point at which Paul started in verse 3.

In his study of this passage in his volumes on Romans, Donald Grey Barnhouse tells how he once made slighting remarks about a denomination he considered to be on the fringe of genuine Christianity. A minister from this denomination was present and afterwards told Barnhouse how grieved he was at what he considered an unjust judgment. Barnhouse apologized, and it was agreed that he would meet for lunch with four or five ministers from this particular church.

When they got together, Barnhouse, who had suggested the luncheon, made the additional suggestion that during lunch they should discuss only the points on which they agreed. Afterwards, when they had finished, they could talk about their differences. They began to talk about Jesus Christ and what he meant to each of them. The tension abated, and there was a measure of joy as each confessed that Jesus was born of a virgin, that he came to die for our sins and then rose again bodily. Each acknowledged Jesus Christ as Lord. Each agreed that Jesus was now in heaven at the right hand of God the Father praying for his church. They confessed that he had sent his Holy Spirit at Pentecost and that the Lord was living in each of his children by means of the Holy Spirit. They acknowledged the reality of the new birth

6. Cited in "Events and People," *The Christian Century,* September 30, 1987.
7. Bellah, *The Habits of the Heart,* p. 220.

and that they were looking forward to the return of Jesus Christ, after which they would be spending eternity together.

By this time the meal was drawing to a close. And when they turned to the matters that divided them, they found that they were indeed secondary—not unimportant, but secondary—and they recognized that they were areas in which they could agree to disagree without denying that each was nevertheless a member of Christ's body. Barnhouse confessed, "Though separated by a continent, I have often prayed for these men and am confident that they have prayed for me. We know that we are one in Christ. They made a distinct contribution to my spiritual life, and I contributed to theirs. I am the richer since I became acquainted with them."[8] Something like that would be a very good experience for most of us.

---

8. Donald Grey Barnhouse, *One Body in Christ*, booklet 68 in the series of expositions on Romans (Philadelphia: The Bible Study Hour, 1956), p. 11.

192

God's Gifts to Christ's Body

Romans 12:6–8

We have different gifts, according to the grace given us. If a man's gift is prophesying, let him use it in proportion to his faith. If it is serving, let him serve; if it is teaching, let him teach; if it is encouraging, let him encourage; if it is contributing to the needs of others, let him give generously; if it is leadership, let him govern diligently; if it is showing mercy, let him do it cheerfully.

In the last study we began to look at the doctrine of the church as it is presented to us under the image of Christ's body. This is a very rich image, and we saw two things it teaches. First, it teaches what it is to be a member of the church. To be a church member means to be a part of Christ's body, and this means that a person who is a member of the church must be joined to him. It is not a question of merely belonging to an organization, though that is also important in its place. It means to be united to Jesus Christ by the Holy Spirit so that we are no longer in Adam but "in Jesus." It is a spiritual reality.

The second thing we have seen about the church presented under the image of Christ's body is that it is a unity. That is, there is only one church

1581

just as there is only one body. You can no more have multiple churches than you can have multiple Christs or a multiple Godhead.

But the image of the church as Christ's body also signifies something else, and that is diversity in unity. It is what Paul is chiefly talking about in Romans 12, for he has just written, "Just as each of us has one body with many members, and these members do not all have the same function, so in Christ we who are many form one body, and each member belongs to all the others" (vv. 4–5). Paul calls the parts of the body "members." We are those members. So the image teaches that Christians have different gifts and are to function differently from others in the use of these gifts, while nevertheless being a part of the body and contributing to the body's unity.

Diversity of Gifts

Different gifts! It is hard for many of us to recognize this and accept it, because we are always wanting other Christians to be like us and function like us, or be cogs in our machine rather than contributing to another Christian's work. Paul knew Christians who had this trouble too, but he tells everyone that we must accept this diversity if the church is to function as it should.

This was important to Paul. *Charismata,* the word translated *gifts,* occurs seventeen times in the New Testament; sixteen of those occurrences are in Paul's writings.

Charismata is based on the word *grace (charis)* and actually means "a grace gift." It is something given to the people of God by God or, as can also be said, by Jesus Christ. Since grace is God's unmerited favor, the word indicates that spiritual gifts are dispensed by God according to his pleasure and that the gifts will differ. Every Christian has at least one gift, like the people who received talents in Christ's parables. Moreover, since these are given by God, they are to be used for his glory and according to his plans rather than to enhance our own glory or further our plans. This is where the thrust toward unity comes in. Each member of the body is to work toward the well-being of the whole so that when one member does well all the others do well and when one member suffers the entire body suffers.

Another way of saying this is to say that we not only belong to Christ, we also belong to one another. John Murray says of Christians, "They have property in one another and therefore in one another's gifts and graces."[1] It would be correct to add that you, as a Christian, have a right to the gifts the other members of the body have been given, and they have a right to your gift. You cheat them if you do not use it, and you are poorer if you do not depend on them.

---

1. John Murray, *The Epistle to the Romans,* 2 vols. in 1 (Grand Rapids: Wm. B. Eerdmans Publishing Company, 1968), vol. 2, p. 120.

Exercising the Gifts

What these spiritual gifts are is not easy to say, because every time there is a listing of the gifts in the New Testament—five times in all (Rom. 12:6–8, 1 Cor. 12:8–10 and 28–30, Eph. 4:11, 1 Peter 4:11)—the specific items differ. Ephesians 4:11 seems to give the most basic list: apostles, prophets, evangelists, pastor/teachers. This is the way 1 Corinthians 12:28–30 starts too, but then it moves from what seems to be offices in the church to specific functions like working miracles, healing, helping, administering, speaking in tongues, and interpreting tongues. Romans 12:6–8 has a bit of both. First Peter 4:11 has only service and speaking, but these two items are categories into which other gifts fit.

Nineteen gifts are mentioned in these five lists, but the number is not absolute. Different words may describe the same gift, as with serving and helping, and there are probably gifts that could be mentioned but are not. Seven gifts are mentioned in Romans 12:

1. *Prophesying.* The first is prophesying. In 1 Corinthians 12:28 and Ephesians 4:11 this gift comes immediately after and is closely linked to the gift of "apostles." There were no apostles in the church at Rome at this time, so Paul does not mention apostles in the Romans list.

In our day the word *prophesy* retains only a shade of its former meaning, "foretelling the future." In the Old and New Testaments a prophet is one who speaks the words of God. The Greek word for prophet literally means "one who stood in front of another person and spoke for him." An example is the relationship between Moses and his brother Aaron. Moses was unwilling to accept God's call to go to Egypt, stand before Pharaoh, and demand that he let Israel go, because, as he said, "I have never been eloquent" (Exod. 4:10). God answered that he would send Aaron to speak for him. "You shall speak to him and put words in his mouth. . . . He will speak to the people for you, and it will be as if he were your mouth and as if you were God to him" (vv. 15–16). Later this is explained by these words: "See, I have made you like God to Pharaoh, and your brother Aaron will be your prophet" (Exod. 7:1).

This is the sense in which Abraham is called a prophet in Genesis 20:7, because God spoke to him and he spoke God's words to other people. It is the same in the New Testament (Luke 7:26–28, John 4:19; cf. Matt. 10:41; 13:57; Luke 4:24). There seem to have been quite a few such prophets in the early church, so much so that Paul devotes nearly the whole of 1 Corinthians 14 to discussing the gift of prophecy and the gift of tongues, which is closely linked to it. From this and other passages it would seem that the prophets were men who spoke under the immediate influence of the Holy Spirit to communicate a doctrine, remind people of a duty, or give a warning (cf. Acts 21:10–14).

Charles Hodge expresses it this way in his commentary on Romans: "The point of distinction between them [prophets] and the apostles, considered as religious teachers, appears to have been that the inspiration of the apostles was abiding, they were the infallible and authoritative messengers of Christ; whereas the inspiration of the prophets was occasional and transient. The latter differed from the teachers *(didaskaloi),* inasmuch as these were not necessarily inspired, but taught to others what they themselves had learned from the Scriptures or from inspired men."[2]

The gift of prophecy in this sense, like the gift of apostleship, is something that is no longer with the church since, having the completed Old and New Testaments, we no longer need it. The Bible is for us the recorded testimony of these inspired men.

The really fascinating item in this mention of prophecy is the attached phrase "let him use it in proportion to his faith." The word translated *proportion* is the word *analogia* (analogue or analogy), which has given expositors the important hermeneutical principle known as the analogy of faith. This is the only place where these words occur in the Bible, but they have been seen to teach what is usually described as the need to compare one Scripture with another so that a passage that is clearly understood throws light on one less clear. From this principle derive the additional guidelines of a necessary unity and noncontradiction in the Bible.

There is some doubt as to whether this is exactly what is meant here. But whatever Paul means, he is implying some control of or limitation on the prophet. The last words of the phrase are literally "the faith" (not "his faith," as in the NIV). So if "the analogy of *the* faith" is meant, it would mean that even the prophet is bound by prior revelation. He is not to propound anything contrary to "the faith" that has already been delivered to the saints. We remember that in Galatians 1:8, Paul applied this test to both the apostles and angels, insisting that even they have to conform to the standard of right doctrine: "Even if we or an angel from heaven should preach a gospel other than the one we preached to you, let him be eternally condemned!"

If this does not refer to the analogy of faith and means only that the prophet is to speak in accordance with the measure of his own personal faith, it still implies a limitation, because the prophet is not to go beyond what God has given him to speak.[3] So here is a contemporary application. If that was true of the ancient prophets, how much more true ought it to be of Bible teachers today. Anyone who is called to teach must be rigidly disciplined so as not to go beyond what God has actually revealed in Scripture. Our task is to expound the whole counsels, but *only* the whole counsels of God.

2. *Serving.* The next spiritual gift is serving. This Greek word is sometimes also translated *ministry* and applied to the "ministry [that is, teaching] of the word [of God]" (cf. Acts 6:4). But since teaching is mentioned next we should

---

2. Charles Hodge, *A Commentary on Romans* (Edinburgh and Carlisle, Pa.: The Banner of Truth Trust, 1972), p. 389. Original edition 1835.

3. For a balanced treatment of the ways this phrase can be understood, see Murray, *The Epistle to the Romans,* vol. 2, pp. 122–23.

probably think of ministry more broadly here, that is, as embracing all kinds of ministry for the sake of Christ.

What is important to note is that the Greek word *diakonian* is the root of our word *deacon*. So what is being spoken of here is a diaconal, or service, ministry. Does this refer to the specific office of a deacon or deaconess in the church, as in Acts 6:1–6? Yes, but not only that. In the church all are called to serve others, though some are given this gift in special measure in order to lead others in the work. We need to remember that even Jesus was a deacon in that, as he said, "The Son of Man did not come to be served, but to serve, and to give his life as a ransom for many" (Matt. 20:28).

So let's do it! That is what the text says. In the case of prophecy, we are told that the prophet is to prophesy according to the "analogy" of faith or "in proportion to his faith." That is a qualification or directive. That is not the case here. Here the text just says, "If it is serving, let him serve." In other words, just do it!

In Charles Colson's book *The Body*, there are three quotations that stress service. William Booth, the founder of the Salvation Army, said to his missionaries to India: "Go to the Indian as a brother, which indeed you are, and show the love which none can doubt you feel . . . eat, drink and dress and live by his side. Speak his language, share his sorrow."

Count Zinzendorf, the founder of the Moravians, told his missionaries: "Do not lord it over the unbelievers but simply live among them; preach not theology but the crucified Christ."

Dietrich Bonhoeffer said, "The church is herself only when she exists for humanity. . . . She must take her part in the social life of the world, not lording it over men, but helping and serving them. She must tell men, whatever their calling, what it means to live in Christ, to live for others."[4] In *Life Together*, a study of the meaning of Christian fellowship, Bonhoeffer has a whole chapter stressing the ministry of Christians to other Christians. It is, he says, a ministry of holding one's tongue, meekness, listening, helping, bearing burdens, yes, and also speaking the truth when it is needed.[5] Each of us has a service ministry to perform, because each of us is called to be like Jesus Christ. Where can you serve? Where can you serve that you are not serving now?

3. *Teaching.* In one way or another, by one word or another, this gift occurs in each of the five New Testament lists. It is a critical gift, of course, the more so today since the gifts of apostleship and prophecy have ceased. I am sure that many have this gift. Ray Stedman says that in his opinion probably a third

---

4. Charles Colson, with Ellen Santilli Vaughn, *The Body* (Dallas, London, Vancouver, and Melbourne: Word Publishing, 1992), pp. 312–13. The quotations are from F. Booth Tucker, *Muktifanj, or Forty Years with the Salvation Army in India and Ceylon* (London: Marshall Brothers, n.d.); William P. Showalter, "Zinzendorf, That Remarkable Man of God," *Crosspoint*, Summer 1991, p. 25; and Dietrich Bonhoeffer, *Letters and Papers from Prison*, ed. Eberhard Bethge (New York: Macmillan, 1967), pp. 11–12.

5. Dietrich Bonhoeffer, *Life Together*, trans. by John W. Doberstein (New York, Hagerstown, San Francisco, and London: Harper & Row, 1954), pp. 90–109.

of all Christians have it and should be using it. If you know anything about Jesus and the gospel, you should teach what you know, formally if you have the opportunity but also informally by a casual word or testimony. You will be surprised what you are able to teach others.

I am a pastor. This is the preeminent gift of pastors, and this leads me to say to pastors that, having been called to teach, they must teach. No one has the opportunity a pastor has for carefully studying and faithfully expounding the Bible. What is more, if he does not do it, then in most churches it will not be done at all. Teaching is hard work, because we must learn ourselves before we teach. But what better calling can one have? So get on with it, and be faithful in it, if that is your gift. I notice that Paul handles his admonition here exactly as he handled it when he spoke of serving earlier, and as he will speak of encouraging later. No fuss. No fanfare. Just do it.

4. *Encouraging.* Encouragement has become a rather weak word for us, usually meaning little more than giving someone a slap on the back and saying "Good job" or "Well done." When we study the use of this word in the Bible, however, we find it is much more than this. The Greek word appears 107 times in the New Testament, and it is translated by such additional, powerful verbs as *beseech, comfort, desire, pray, entreat,* and *console.* It is the same word used of the Holy Spirit and his ministry in John 14–16. The New International Version translates it as *Counselor* (in John 14:15, 26; 15:26; 16:7), but the Greek is *paraklētos,* which literally means "one who is called in alongside another to help out." Counselor is a synonym for *lawyer,* and it is worth noting that the precise Latin translation of *paraklētos* is *advocatus,* which also means "one who is called alongside of," and that *advocate* is also a synonym for *lawyer.* If we put this thought into our passage, we get something like "Let the person who has the gift of getting alongside another person to help him or her, really do it. Let him stand by his friend and really help him."

What a tremendous need we have for those who are like that. Many people are hurting, but there are not many helping, because we are all so absorbed in ourselves and our own private affairs. We are living in a narcissistic age, another "Me Decade."

Exhortation was the gift of Barnabas, who traveled with Paul. In Acts 4:36 we are told that his real name was Joseph but that he was named Barnabas because Barnabas means "Son of Encouragement," and that is what he was. We may remember how he stood by John Mark to help him when Paul refused to take Mark along on one of his missionary journeys because he had deserted them earlier. Barnabas got alongside Mark, lifted him up, and reestablished him as a useful servant of Christ, which Paul acknowledged later (2 Tim. 4:11).

5. *Contributing to the needs of others.* John Calvin and some of the earlier commentators thought that this gift referred to an official church office—that is, to the diaconate that is particularly entrusted with this task. But there is no need to limit this to some official position, and most modern scholars do

not. The deciding element seems to be Paul's teaching that those who have this gift are to give "generously." That is an appropriate thing to say if the person involved is giving out of his or her own funds. But the deacons administer the church's funds, and if this refers to deacons, it would be more appropriate to tell them to give carefully, judiciously, or prayerfully, realizing that it is other people's money they are handling.

Are you generous with what you have been given? Some people are so poor it is hard to imagine how they could give anything. But statistics tell us that it is the poor who are most generous in terms of proportionate giving. The very rich are the least generous. Do you have enough to eat, clothes to wear, a place to live, even money in the bank? Then think how you can best be generous with those who are needy or have nothing.

6. *Leadership.* It is interesting that Paul includes leadership in his list of Christian gifts. The word actually means government or good administration, and it includes the task of management. This is an important quality to look for in elders, since they need to "manage," or "take care of God's church" (1 Tim. 3:5).

The excellent Swiss commentator F. Godet points out how important this must have been in the early church, when so many of the institutions we take for granted were lacking:

> Think of the numerous works of private charity which believers then had to found and maintain! Pagan society had neither hospitals nor orphanages, free schools or refuges [rescue missions], like those of our day. The church impelled by the instinct of Christian charity, had to introduce all these institutions into the world; hence no doubt, in every community, spontaneous gatherings of devout men and women who, like our present Christian committees, took up one or other of these needful objects, and had of course at their head directors charged with the responsibility of the work. Such are the persons certainly whom the apostle has in view in our passage.[6]

I am not sure that this is exactly what Paul had in mind when he wrote this. But it is certainly one way this gift functions in the church, and it points to a similar and continuing need today. All the organizations we have require management. Those who manage well deserve honor.

7. *Showing mercy.* The final gift is showing mercy, and Paul's point is that this should be done cheerfully, not begrudgingly. The Greek word is *hilarotēti*, which gives us our word *hilarious*. How much we need a cheerful, hilarious spirit in the church! Too often our faces are grim and there is no spirit of joy to be found anywhere.

6. F. Godet, *Commentary on St. Paul's Epistle to the Romans*, trans. by A. Cusin (Edinburgh: T. & T. Clark, 1892), vol. 2, p. 293.

You and the Gift God Has Given

I close with a paragraph from Ray Stedman, who has written on spiritual gifts in a more helpful way than anyone I know. He asks in his study of Romans 12, "Who are you anyway?" It is a good question for us to ask. Stedman answers:

> I am a son of God among the sons of men. I am equipped with the power of God to labor today. In the very work given me today God will be with me, doing it through me. I am gifted with special abilities to help people in various areas, and I don't have to wait until Sunday to use these gifts. I can use them anywhere. I can exercise the gift God has given me as soon as I find out what it is, by taking note of my desires and by asking others what they see in me and by trying out various things. I am going to set myself to the lifelong task of keeping that gift busy.[7]

Paul told Timothy, "Fan into flame the gift of God, which is in you" (2 Tim. 1:6). That is exactly what you should do. You have a gift. The rest of the body needs it. You will be accountable for what you do with it. Use it so that one day you will hear Jesus say, "Well done, good and faithful servant! You have been faithful with a few things; I will put you in charge of many things. Come and share your master's happiness" (Matt. 25:21, 23).

---

7. Ray C. Stedman, *From Guilt to Glory*, vol. 2, *Reveling in God's Salvation* (Portland, Oreg.: Multnomah Press, 1978), p. 118.

*

193

The Greatest Thing in the World

Romans 12:9

Love must be sincere. Hate what is evil; cling to what is good.

fter the first two verses of Romans 12, which establish the principles by which sound doctrine is to be applied to godly living, Paul has begun to write about the church. His words are not abstract theologizing: He is thinking of the people who make up the church, and his words have to do first with the humility that allows each to assess himself with sober judgment, and second with the knowledge that God has given spiritual gifts to all members of the church and that these must be exercised faithfully for the benefit of all. This line of thought continues in what follows, although in verse 9 the apostle moves from his discussion of spiritual gifts, which are of various sorts and appear in various individuals, to virtues that must be seen in all who call themselves Christians.

"Characteristically," says Australian professor Leon Morris, "he begins with love."[1]

This same sequence, from a discussion of spiritual gifts to discussion of love, is found in 1 Corinthians, though on a larger scale. In that letter Paul

1. Leon Morris, *The Epistle to the Romans* (Grand Rapids: Wm. B. Eerdmans Publishing Company, and Leicester, England: Inter-Varsity Press, 1988), p. 443.

talks about the gifts in chapter 12. This corresponds to Romans 12:4–8. Then he passes to the well-known hymn about love that is chapter 13. Romans 12:9–13 corresponds to 1 Corinthians 13.

In this study we begin with verse 9, which introduces the subject. What follows, in verses 10–13, is a further elaboration of how love functions. We will look at those verses in the next study.

Henry Drummond's Sermon

In 1883 the Scottish scientist and evangelist Henry Drummond gave a famous inspirational lecture at a mission station in central Africa called "The Greatest Thing in the World." It was about love, and it was based on 1 Corinthians 13, the great chapter on love—particularly on the last words: "But the greatest of these is love" (v. 13). Drummond was not what we would call an evangelical. I would judge from this and others of his writings I have read that he was basically a Christian humanist in that he believed that the Christian virtues could themselves, if sincerely practiced, save the world. There is not much about the cross or the atonement or the work of the Holy Spirit in his work. Still, "The Greatest Thing in the World" is a classic, and no less an evangelical than D. L. Moody, who heard Drummond give this talk in America the following year, said he had never listened to "anything so beautiful."

Drummond was right in at least one thing. In terms of the Christian virtues, love is preeminent; and if it is truly felt and practiced, the other requirements will follow. After all, even Jesus said that love of God and neighbor sums up the Law and the Prophets (Matt. 22:34–40).

Drummond wrote:

Take any of the commandments. "Thou shalt have no other gods before me." If a man love God, you will not have to tell him that. Love is the fulfilling of that law. "Take not his name in vain." Would he ever dream of taking his name in vain if he loved him? "Remember the Sabbath day to keep it holy." Would he not be too glad to have one day in seven to dedicate more exclusively to the object of his affection? Love would fulfill all these laws regarding God. And so, if he loved man, you would never think of telling him to honor his father and mother. He could not do anything else. It would be preposterous to tell him not to kill. You could only insult him if you suggested that he should not steal—how could he steal from those he loved? It would be superfluous to beg him not to bear false witness against his neighbor. If he loved him, it would be the last thing he would do. And you would never dream of urging him not to covet what his neighbors had. He would rather they possessed it than himself. In this way, "Love is the fulfilling of the law." It is the rule for fulfilling all rules, the new commandment for keeping all the old commandments, Christ's one secret of the Christian life.[2]

2. Henry Drummond, *The Greatest Thing in the World* with other selected essays, ed. William R. Webb (Kansas City, Mo.: Halmark Editions, 1967), pp. 10–11.

At the end of this essay Drummond said that, as he looked back over his life and all the beautiful things he had seen and enjoyed, he was convinced that it was only the small, seemingly insignificant acts of the love of one individual for another that will last forever.

The Nature of Love

But we must not get overly sentimental at this point, since love is not some mushy emotion that embraces all, forgives all, forgets all, and requires nothing. The danger of an essay like Henry Drummond's is that it encourages just those sentiments. The Bible never does. In fact, you will notice at once that in our text Paul does not even define love. He passes immediately to how love functions. It is the same in 1 Corinthians 13. Chapter 13 seems to be defining love, but it does so only in the sense that it tells us what love does and does not do.

Romans 12:9 states two specific things about love. First, true love is genuine. "Love must be sincere," says the author. Second, love must be discriminating. "Hate what is evil; cling to what is good," is how Paul puts it. In the Greek text *hate* and *cling* are participles, meaning hating and clinging. So it is clear that they are linked to the former statement and describe how love is to operate, rather than being independent statements or commands.

1. *Love is genuine.* The New International Version translates the first half of verse 9 as "Love must be sincere." *Sincere* is an English word based on the Latin words *sine cera*, meaning without wax, and it refers to the ancient practice of using wax to hide cracks in inferior pottery so the vessel could be sold for a higher price than it could be otherwise. Quality ware was stamped *sine cera* ("without wax") to show that it had not been doctored. In regard to people, this says that a sincere person is one who is not hiding his true nature by hypocritical words or actions.

In the Greek text the word translated *sincere* is *anupokritos*, the latter part of which has given us the word *hypocritical*, which I have used to describe speech that is insincere. *Anupokritos* means without a mask, and it refers to the way in which, in the Greek theater, actors would carry tragic, comic, or melodramatic masks to signal the role they were playing. When Paul tells us that love is to be *an* ("not") hypocritical, he is saying that those who love are not to play a role but rather are to be genuine. In other words, we are to get off the stage and drop our masks.

But that is not easy. John Calvin remarks in his treatment of Romans 12:9 that "it is difficult to express how ingenious almost all men are in counterfeiting a love which they do not really possess. They deceive not only others, but also themselves, while they persuade themselves that they have a true love for those whom they not only treat with neglect, but also in fact reject."[3]

3. John Calvin, *The Epistles of Paul the Apostle to the Romans and to the Thessalonians*, trans. Ross MacKenzie (Grand Rapids: Wm. B. Eerdmans Publishing Company, 1973), p. 271.

It may help us to realize that the love that is commended here is the love of God that is shown to fallen creatures through the death of God's Son, the Lord Jesus Christ, and which is developed in Christians by the Holy Spirit. In all, there are four Greek words that may be translated *love: storgê*, which refers to family affection; *philia*, which denotes love between friends; *eros*, which is sexual love; and *agapê*, which is God-love and is therefore pure, holy, unvarying, and unfeigned. It is the latter word that is used in verse 9. This love is sincere by definition, since God is utterly unvarying and unfeigned. It is this true, Godlike love that we are to have for other people.

If we are new creatures in Christ, then we must love without hypocrisy, since this is the very nature of the love that has been placed within us by the Father. We must be *sine cera*.

2. *Love is discriminating*. For some people it may come as a shock to discover the word *hate* immediately after the words *love must be sincere*. First, love; then hate! The two seem incompatible to most of us. But they are not, and their juxtaposition in this verse teaches an important truth; love must be discriminating. Real love does not love everything. On the contrary, it hates what is evil and clings to what is good.

"God is love" (1 John 4:8). That is one of the most sublime statements in the Bible, but God is not only love. He is also hate in the sense that he hates what is evil with a proper, righteous hatred. Proverbs 6:16–19 tells us seven things that God hates: "haughty eyes, a lying tongue, hands that shed innocent blood, a heart that devises wicked schemes, feet that are quick to rush into evil, a false witness who pours out lies and a man who stirs up dissension among brothers." Isaiah 1:12–15 tells us that God hates religion that is merely formal:

> When you come to appear before me,
>> who has asked this of you,
>> this trampling of my courts?
> Stop bringing meaningless offerings!
>> Your incense is detestable to me.
> New Moons, Sabbaths and convocations—
>> I cannot bear your evil assemblies.
> Your New Moon festivals and your appointed feasts
>> my soul hates.
> They have become a burden to me;
>> I am weary of bearing them.
> When you spread out your hands in prayer,
>> I will hide my eyes from you;
>> even if you offer many prayers,
>> I will not listen.

In Amos 5:21 God says, "I hate, I despise your religious feasts; I cannot stand your assemblies." The reason, of course, is that these merely formal observances are hypocritical, and love is not hypocritical.

Therefore, if we love as God loves—and we must if we are Christians—then there will be things for us to hate, just as there will also be things we must love. We will hate the violence done to people by whatever name—nationalism, ethnic cleansing, racial or religious pride, war, keeping the peace, even "necessity." But we will love the humble and those who work for peace, yes, and even those who are guilty of the violence, because we will want to turn them from their ways. We will hate lying, especially by those who are in important positions—CEOs and other heads of corporations, political figures, presidents, and even ministers. We will hate what their lies do to others. Yet we will love the truth and will at the same time also love those who are lying, for we will see them as people who need the Savior.

That is what love does. Love *hates* evil—an intentionally strong word. But love also clings to what is good. The Greek word rendered *cling* in some of its forms means to glue. So the idea is that true love will bond us to the good. We will stick to it like epoxy.

The Greatest of These

We can hardly discuss what love is like, even on the basis of these two powerful terms—hating evil and loving good—without also turning to what Paul says about love in 1 Corinthians 13:

> If I speak in the tongues of men and of angels, but have not love, I am only a resounding gong or a clanging cymbal. If I have the gift of prophecy and can fathom all mysteries and all knowledge, and if I have a faith that can move mountains, but have not love, I am nothing. If I give all I possess to the poor and surrender my body to the flames, but have not love, I gain nothing.
>
> Love is patient, love is kind. It does not envy, it does not boast, it is not proud. It is not rude, it is not self-seeking, it is not easily angered, it keeps no record of wrongs. Love does not delight in evil but rejoices with the truth. It always protects, always trusts, always hopes, always perseveres.
>
> Love never fails. But where there are prophecies, they will cease; where there are tongues, they will be stilled; where there is knowledge, it will pass away. For we know in part and we prophesy in part, but when perfection comes, the imperfect disappears. When I was a child, I talked like a child, I thought like a child, I reasoned like a child. When I became a man, I put childish ways behind me. Now we see but a poor reflection as in a mirror; then we shall see face to face. Now I know in part; then I shall know fully, even as I am fully known.
>
> And now these three remain: faith, hope and love. But the greatest of these is love.

It should be evident to anyone that the most important paragraph of this chapter is the second. The first tells us how important love is. The third says that love will endure even when things like prophecies, tongues, and the quest for knowledge have ceased. The final paragraph says that love is more important even than such enduring things as faith and hope. But it is the second paragraph that lists love's wonderful qualities and functions. There are fifteen statements in all.

1. *Love is patient.* Drummond says that this is "the normal attitude of love."[4] This is because people are difficult, exasperating, and slow. Love understands this and so waits patiently. It knows that God is patient and that he has been wonderfully patient with us.

2. *Love is kind.* The world is filled with hurting, suffering people. Love knows this and does what it can to help, uplift, serve, encourage, and otherwise embrace them in their misery. It is quick to speak an encouraging word, quick to offer everyone a willing, outstretched hand.

3. *Love does not envy.* The first two descriptions of love have been positive. Here is the first of eight negative statements, saying what love is *not* and does *not* do. Love is not jealous. It is glad when other people win honors, achieve fame, strike it rich, and are praised. This is because love knows God and is content with the life God has given. Only a believer can be truly happy when others are preferred before himself.

4. *Love does not boast.* The world is filled with boasters, people who in one way or another are calling attention to who they are, how important they are, and how much they have achieved. Love does not do this, because love does not think highly of itself and because it is glad when others are exalted. A wise man once said, "There is no limit to what a man can achieve if he is not worried about who gets the credit." This is love.

5. *Love is not proud.* The opposite of pride is humility, and love is humble. Love does not have inflated ideas of itself. Love is gracious.

6. *Love is not rude.* The opposite of rudeness is courtesy, and love has good manners. It thinks of others. It holds its tongue and waits for others to speak. Love listens. Love does not dominate a social setting and will not blurt out things that wound another person.

7. *Love is not self-seeking.* The world looks at something and asks, "What's in it for me?" Love does not seek for self, because it is not thinking of self. Love thinks of the one it loves. Jesus did not seek his own advantage when he came to earth to save us. Rather, he "made himself nothing, taking the very nature of a servant, . . . he humbled himself and became obedient to death—even death on a cross" (Phil. 2:7–8).

8. *Love is not easily angered.* "For embittering life, for breaking up communities, for destroying the most sacred relationships, for devastating homes, for withering up men and women, for taking the bloom off childhood; in short, for sheer gratuitous misery-producing power, [anger] stands alone," says Henry Drummond.[5] But love is not easily angered. It does not have a

4. Drummond, *The Greatest Thing in the World,* p. 13.
5. Ibid., p. 17.

short fuse. It is not irritable, not easily provoked. It is not touchy. Love is patient and kind.

9. *Love keeps no record of wrongs.* Some people have a knack for bringing up mistakes we have made and wounds we have inflicted even decades afterwards. Love forgets these wrongs. It does not compile statistics. It is not resentful. It is not vindictive.

10. *Love does not delight in evil.* Love is not amused by wrongdoing. It is not attracted by vice. It does not find trash intriguing, even when it is dressed up for prime time television or published in glossy magazines. Dishonest schemes do not please it. Love hates wickedness.

11. *Love rejoices with the truth.* This is the other half of the only two-part description in this paragraph. It shows that the evil Paul is thinking of when he says "does not delight in evil" is chiefly the evil that tells lies. Love loves truth, above all the truth that is God's. Love loves the Bible. It delights to speak about it.

12. *Love always protects.* The last four descriptions say what love *always* does. First, it always protects the other person. It sides with the weak. It rallies around the one who has been oppressed, attacked, abused, hurt, slandered, or otherwise made a victim. Love protects children, because it knows that "the kingdom of heaven belongs to such as these" (Matt. 19:14).

13. *Love always trusts.* Love is never suspicious. Love is not trying to see under the surface or pry out the hidden motives of another. Love is not stupid or gullible, but it always thinks the best. It is the quality that brings out the best in other people. A mother shows love when she tells her struggling son that she believes in him, or her discouraged daughter that she knows she will do well.

14. *Love always hopes.* Love does not stop loving because it is not loved in return or because it is deceived. Love hopes for the best, and it forgives not once or even seven times, but seventy times seven. Love is not even counting.

15. *Love always perseveres.* Love never gives up. It is unconquerable, indomitable. Love can outlast hate and evil and indifference. Love can outlast anything. Donald Grey Barnhouse wrote, "It is . . . the one thing that stands after all else has fallen."[6]

Because He First Loved Us

We live in a skeptical world, and it would be safe to say that there are not many worldly people who believe in a love like this. They may wish for it, wanting to be loved in this way. But most would say with some bitterness that to hope for true love in this world is a delusion.

What a pity this is! Because exactly this love has come into our world in the person of Jesus Christ, and love is to be shown by those who are his dis-

6. Donald Grey Barnhouse, "Love—the Great Indispensable" in *Lest You Be Hypocrites,* booklet 70 in the series of expositions on Romans (Philadelphia: The Bible Study Hour, 1957), p. 11.

ciples. In 1 John 4, the disciple who leaned on Christ's bosom at the Last Supper tells us that "God is love" (v. 8). He follows it up by saying that the exhibition of God's love is in the death of Jesus for our sins. "No one has ever seen God," he says. But then, "If we love each other, God lives in us and his love is made complete in us" (v. 12). In other words, the world cannot see God, but they can see him in the way Christians love each other.

In ancient times the pagans marvelled at such love. "Behold how these Christians love one another!" they cried. Do you love like that? Remember that this is where the apostle Paul *begins* the list of Christian virtues.

194

Love in Action

Romans 12:10-13

Be devoted to one another in brotherly love. Honor one another above yourselves. Never be lacking in zeal, but keep your spiritual fervor, serving the Lord. Be joyful in hope, patient in affliction, faithful in prayer. Share with God's people who are in need. Practice hospitality.

I pointed out in the last study that although the various exhortations of Romans 12:9–13 seem in most translations merely to be strung together in no specific order and with no apparent relationship to one another, in the Greek they are arranged quite carefully. To begin with, they fall into two separate portions: verse 9, which introduces the subject of love in a general way, and verses 10–13, which show how genuine love is to function. We saw that the Greek words for *hate* and *cling* in verse 9 are actually participles linked to the words "love must be sincere." So the sentence actually reads, "Love must be sincere, hating what is evil and clinging to what is good." This tells us that the love Paul is talking about is no mere sentimental mush but rather is concerned for what is good. It is both genuine and discriminating. In the next verses, after describing this love generally, Paul shows how it is to operate in nine areas.

That is the second important fact about this arrangement. In the Greek text these are nine nouns in the dative case, each of which comes first in its clause for emphasis. We usually translate a dative with the word *to*, as in "to the store" or "to church." But in this case the meaning is something like "as regards" or "with respect to." John Murray does not stick to the nine items specifically, but he provides a translation of verses 10–13 that gives a good idea how this goes: "*In brotherly love* being kindly affectioned to one another, *in honor* preferring one another, *in zeal* not flagging, *in spirit* fervent, serving the Lord, *in hope* rejoicing, *in affliction* being patient, *in prayer* continuing instant, *in the needs of the saints* partaking, hospitality pursuing."[1]

This is how the love introduced in verse 9 is to function.

Kindness to One Another

The first thing Paul writes about is being kind to one another. Our translation says, "Be devoted to one another in brotherly love." I pointed out in the last study that in the Greek language there are four words for love: *agapê, philia, storgê,* and *eros*. The last word refers to sexual love and does not occur in the New Testament, no doubt because this kind of love had become so debased among the heathen. The first word, *agapê,* is the great New Testament word for God's love and for the love of Christians for God and one another. It is the word used in verse 9. The remaining two words, *philia* and *storgê,* are in this verse, which means that all three of the New Testament's words for love are in verses 9 and 10.

But they occur in combinations. In the Greek text the first words of Paul's command are "in brotherly love." That is *philadelphia* in Greek, the word for *love* being combined with the word for *brother.* The second combination is the Greek word *philostorgoi,* rendered *devoted* in the New International Version. These words mean that "in respect to the love of our Christian brothers and sisters, we are to be marked by a devotion that is characteristic of a loving, close-knit, and mutually supportive family."

The King James Version reads, "Be *kindly affectionate* to one another with brotherly love." *Kindly* is based on the word *kin,* meaning *family.* So again, we are being told that we are to love and treat Christians as we would members of our family.

Christians are our family, of course, regardless of their background, race, nationality, occupation, wealth, or education—or even whether we are attracted to or like another believer. That is irrelevant. The first verse of "Blessed Be the Tie That Binds" goes like this:

> Blessed be the tie that binds
> Our hearts in Christian love;

1. John Murray, *The Epistle to the Romans,* 2 vols. in 1 (Grand Rapids: Wm. B. Eerdmans Publishing Company, 1968), vol. 2, p. 129.

> The fellowship of kindred minds
> Is like to that above.

"Kindred minds" means the minds of those who are spiritual kin—members of God's new family on earth. So our devotion to one another is not to be a matter of liking but of life. The contemporary church will never have the power of the early church until today's Christians love one another as a close-knit family.

Preferring One Another

The second of Paul's datives is about honor and is closely related to what has just been said. A literal translation might be, "And in respect to honor, lead the way for each another." In other words, "Don't wait around for people to recognize your contributions and praise you. Instead, be alert to what they are contributing and honor them."[2]

Unfortunately, if we look at today's church, we must conclude that the exact opposite is more often the case. Instead of thinking about and appreciating other Christians and what they are doing, our minds are usually on ourselves, and we are resentful that we are not sufficiently recognized or appreciated. Therefore we are jealous of other Christians. Great harm has been done by such jealousy. Ministries have been seriously weakened. Churches have been split. Valuable causes have been set back for generations and sometimes for good. Paul must have seen this as a potential danger for the church at Philippi, for he wrote to those believers: "Do nothing out of selfish ambition or vain conceit, but in humility consider others better than yourselves. Each of you should look not only to your own interests, but also to the interests of others" (Phil. 2:3–4).

This is how true love functions. It gets to the front of the line not to receive its own honors, but to show honor and respect for other people.

Never Flagging in Zeal

Verse 11 contains three statements about true love, beginning with a negative: "Never be lacking in zeal." A more literal rendering, highlighting the dative construction, would be: "In regard to what you ought to be doing, don't be lazy." This is directed against weariness in well-doing (Gal. 6:9), and it is

2. The verb *proêgoumenoi* in this sentence is hard to translate. It may mean "Be eager to show respect for one another," which is what the NIV seems to indicate, but this is not the way it is used in other places. As Hodge points out, it normally means to go before, or to lead, hence to set an example. Most modern commentators think of it in this way. So the idea would be "Set an example for others by honoring and respecting one another." See Charles Hodge, *A Commentary on Romans* (Edinburgh and Carlisle, Pa.: The Banner of Truth Trust, 1972), p. 396. Original edition 1835.

a real problem when trying to live the Christian life for any length of time. It is easy to get discouraged. It is hard to keep on steadily.

At this point the King James Version says, "Not slothful in business." To most people *business* suggests commercial dealings only, which is why newer versions drop that word. But it is helpful to think of it in this way.

1. *The business of being a Christian.* It is a puzzle to me how anyone can take on the most important business of all, the business of being a follower of Jesus Christ, and do it in a passive, apathetic, part-time, or slovenly manner. Yet many do. What we should do is follow after Jesus Christ with all our hearts and minds and with all the energy at our disposal. We should work at being Christians. Robert Candlish writes about this wisely: "Your sanctification must be made a matter of business. It must be cared for and prosecuted in a business-like way; not indolently and slothfully, as if it were a process that might be left to itself, but industriously, sedulously, diligently, with regularity and punctuality, as you would manage a worldly concern, on the common principles of worldly energy and worldly care and worldly zeal."[3]

2. *The business of being a Christian father or mother.* Raising a family takes work, and Christian love demands that this too be done steadily and without being lazy. Children will not raise themselves in godliness. Left to themselves they will grow up like an untended garden, full of weeds and other wild things. It takes work to raise children well.

3. *Church business.* I am always surprised how church leaders will so often conduct the work of the church in a slipshod manner, doing whatever needs to be done to just get by, when they would never think of conducting their own business in that way or running their own home on such principles. The work of the church, including how we manage the building, should be done in the best possible way we know how. After all, if it is done well, the church will remain as a place for worship and work long after we are gone and our businesses and homes have passed to other hands.

We should be diligent in our spiritual battles too. Candlish says, "If you would fight for Christ, you must fight deliberately, with [a] cool head as well as [a] warm heart; with fixed and resolute determination, upon principle rather than upon impulse. If you would work for Christ, you must work systematically, and you must work on with patient and persevering energy, with firm purpose not to give up or to give in."[4]

4. *The business of earning a living.* I said earlier that the word *business* in verse 11 (KJV) does not refer to commercial enterprises, but to everything we should be doing. On the other hand, it does not exclude the ways in which we make our livings but rather embraces them. Christians should excel in how they work. Paul told the Colossians, "Whatever you do, work at it with all your heart,

3. Robert S. Candlish, *Studies in Romans 12: The Christian's Sacrifice and Service of Praise* (Grand Rapids: Kregel Publications, 1989), p. 168. Original edition 1867.
4. Ibid., p. 170.

as working for the Lord, not for men, since you know that you will receive an inheritance from the Lord as a reward. It is the Lord Christ you are serving" (Col. 3:23–24). The last sentence means that love for Christ should prod us to work both well and hard in everything.

Fervent in Spirit

The word *fervor* (NIV) or *fervent* (KJV) is from a verb meaning to boil. So a literal translation of this phrase would be: "In respect to the spirit (or Spirit), boiling." Unfortunately, since boiling suggests heat and we think of heat as having to do with anger, it would be better to think of this as a Christian "bubbling over" or even, as the Revised Standard Version has it, "being aglow with the Spirit."

This probably refers not to the Holy Spirit, but to a personality that radiates the presence of Jesus Christ. On the other hand, this does not happen apart from the Holy Spirit, and in this sense the translation *Spirit* is not wrong. Donald Grey Barnhouse wrote, "The glow of the Spirit is the warmth of the soul touched by the love of Christ. It cannot exist apart from the knowledge that we have been loved, that Christ gave himself for our sins, that we have been redeemed, and that the Holy Spirit has come to dwell in our hearts. Such knowledge causes us to yield in full surrender to him as Lord of all. The Holy Spirit, who dwells in all believers, will glow through those who allow him to fill and direct their lives."[5]

Serving the Lord

"Serving the Lord" has probably been added to "keep your spiritual fervor" to show that the "glow" of the Spirit is not without direction but is instead focused on the work and cause of Christ. Still, this is another dative construction that sets it apart as a separate item. Literally it reads, "As regards the Lord, serving."[6] We remember how Jesus once asked, "Why do you call me, 'Lord, Lord,' and do not do what I say?" (Luke 6:46), meaning that if he is our Lord, we must obey and serve him. We will do no less if we truly love him. Moreover, the way we will show we love other people is by serving them. Even Jesus "did not come to be served, but to serve, and to give his life as a ransom for many" (Matt. 20:28).

5. Donald Grey Barnhouse, *God's Discipline: Exposition of Bible Doctrines, Taking the Epistle to the Romans as a Point of Departure,* vol. 9, *Romans 12:1–14:12* (Grand Rapids: Wm. B. Eerdmans Publishing Company 1964), p. 74.
6. Some Greek manuscripts read *kairô,* which together with the verb would mean serving the time, or even making the most of time. It has been argued that this must be the original meaning since it would be a natural mistake to change *time* to *Lord* but not the reverse. Notwithstanding such views, an error in reverse could happen, and the great weight of manuscript evidence is in favor of "serving the Lord."

Rejoicing in Hope

Verse 12 introduces three more items, which also go together. It might be paraphrased, "In so far as we have cause to hope, let us be joyful; in so far as we have cause of pain, let us hold out; in so far as the door of prayer is open to us, let us continue to use it."[7]

In the Bible hope always has to do with what God has promised but that we have not seen or received yet. In particular it refers to that "blessed hope," which is "the glorious appearing of our great God and Savior, Jesus Christ" (Titus 2:13) and to the fact that when he appears "we shall be like him, for we shall see him as he is" (1 John 3:2). The fact that we do not see this yet is important, for it means that as Christians we will have our eyes fixed on invisible, spiritual things, like Abraham, who did not set his affection on the things of this life but who "was looking forward to the city with foundations, whose architect and builder is God" (Heb. 11:10).

More than anything else, this is what sets Christians apart from those about us who are merely secular. Others have their horizons bounded by what is seen. Like Carl Sagan, for them "the cosmos is all that is or ever was or ever will be." The horizons of Christians are not cut off like this. They are wider even than the universe, for Christians look to God, hope in God, and look forward expectantly to an eternity with him.

And what a difference this makes in daily life. Robert Haldane says, "The hope of the glory of God, in which the apostle here affirms that Christians ought to rejoice, is provided as an important part of the believer's armor—a helmet to cover his head to defend him against the attacks of spiritual enemies (1 Thess. 5:8). It supports him when [he is] ready to be cast down. . . . It soothes the bitterness of affliction when the believer is resting on the promises of God. In prosperity it elevates his affections, and fixing his expectation of the glory that shall be revealed, disengages him from the love of this world. . . . It comforts him in the prospect of death."[8]

Patient in Affliction

While waiting for the glory that is still to be revealed the Christian sometimes suffers persecution or affliction. Therefore, Paul adds that "in respect to affliction" the one who trusts God should be "patient"—not just resigned in a fatalistic, stoic sense, accepting what cannot be changed, but waiting confidently for God's own resolution of the problem, knowing that he will reward the good and punish evil in his own time.

---

7. Godet attributes this paraphrase to Hofmann (F. Godet, *Commentary on St. Paul's Epistle to the Romans*, trans. by A. Cusin (Edinburgh: T. & T. Clark, 1892), vol. 2, p. 297.

8. Robert Haldane, *An Exposition of the Epistle to the Romans* (MacDill AFB: MacDonald Publishing Company, 1958), pp. 566–567.

Meanwhile, we should not to be overly confident that we are among the good or that our actions, especially those that are criticized, are without any evil motives or are beyond reproach. Rather, we must be careful to "make [our] calling and election sure" (2 Peter 1:10) and examine ourselves to see whether we truly love Jesus Christ and are serving him or are merely pursuing our own interests.

In Prayer Continuing Faithful

A literal translation of this verse might be "and in regard to prayer, continuing." *Continuing* is an interesting word to use. We might have expected any one of a number of other words. But Paul says *continuing* because he was aware that this is just the problem. It is not that we never pray. We almost have to, if we are Christians. But we get tired of praying, our minds wander, and we neglect prayer precisely when we most need it.

Our Lord was aware of this too, which is why he said so much about prayer. If you go through the gospels and study what he said, you will find that in nearly all instances the bottom line of his teaching was simply that we should pray—not that we should be paragons of prayer, or eloquent in prayer, or even that we pray on until we get what we desire, though that is sometimes implied—simply that we should pray. He said this because we don't, at least not when we most need to.

Do you remember Jesus' teaching about prayer in Luke 11? After he had given the Lord's Prayer, Jesus told about a man who knocked on a neighbor's door late at night because a friend had come and he had nothing to give him, and although the neighbor did not want to get out of bed to help, eventually he did because of the man's persistence. Jesus also told about human fathers who willingly give their children food when they ask for it, not substituting a snake for a fish or a scorpion for an egg. Those stories were meant to illustrate our need on the one hand, and God's willingness to meet that need on the other.

Then Jesus said, "So . . . *ask* and it will be given to you; *seek* and you will find; *knock* and the door will be opened to you" (Luke 11:9). In other words, "Pray." Just pray! The only reasons we might fail to pray are that: (1) we do not think we need God's help, thinking that we are adequate of ourselves, or (2) we do not believe God really is a loving heavenly father. Why else would we not pray or even be in prayer continually?

Participating in the Need of the Saints

The last of Paul's nine datives is a compound phrase that fills all of verse 13. In our translation it appears as two distinct ideas: (1) "Share with God's people who are in need" and (2) "Practice hospitality." But the Greek text actually combines the ideas, saying, "In regard to the need of the saints, participating, practicing hospitality."

This means that Paul is not just talking about giving money to poor Christians. In fact, he is not thinking about money specifically at all. He is thinking about the needs of Christians and about identifying with them in those needs. If a person is mourning, we should identify with him in his sorrow and give what comfort we can. If another is lonely or abandoned, we should be company for her to the degree we are able. We should give to the financial needs of impoverished people, too. Jesus made such things a test of whether a person is truly a Christian, saying in Matthew 25, "Come, you who are blessed by my Father; take your inheritance, the kingdom prepared for you since the creation of the world. For I was hungry and you gave me something to eat, I was thirsty and you gave me something to drink, I was a stranger and you invited me in, I needed clothes and you clothed me, I was sick and you looked after me, I was in prison and you came to visit me" (Matt. 25:34–36). Those who had not done that were sent away "to eternal punishment" (v. 46).

I do not know how anything can be more practical than this. To love one another, to honor one another, to serve one another, to pray for one another, and to meet one another's needs is the very heart of applied Christianity.

195

The Christian and His Enemies

Romans 12:14–16

Bless those who persecute you; bless and do not curse. Rejoice with those who rejoice; mourn with those who mourn. Live in harmony with one another. Do not be proud, but be willing to associate with people of low position. Do not be conceited.

My good friend Michael Scott Horton has written a book called *Made in America,* in which he examines the impact of American culture on Christianity, especially evangelical Christianity. The impact comes from a variety of cultural sources, he says, but one of these is our consumerism. In America everything is sold—from toothpaste to politicians—and the way it is sold is by appealing to the dreams and desires of the people. Nothing bad is ever faced. Disappointments are ruled out. This has its effect on Christianity. In order to sell Christianity—and selling it is big business today—anything unpleasant or demanding is suppressed, and the gospel is commended rather as a cure for failure and low self-esteem, as well as the path to power.

"In consumer religion, Christianity becomes trivialized. Its great mysteries become cheap slogans. Its majestic hymns are traded in for shallow jingles. . . . And its parishioners, now unashamedly called audiences, have come to expect dazzling testimonies, happy anecdotes, and fail-proof schemes for successful living that will satiate spiritual consumption," he says.[1]

1. Michael Scott Horton, *Made in America: The Shaping of Modern American Evangelicalism* (Grand Rapids: Baker Book House, 1991), p. 70.

How different is biblical Christianity! In the Gospels Jesus spoke often of the cost of following after him in faithful discipleship, without which there is no salvation and no Christianity. What is more—and here the situation becomes even more impossible for today's marketers of religion—he warned that those who identify with him would be hated. Instead of being popular and successful, Christians would be hated and rejected, as he was.

What a way to "sell" Christianity!

A Radical Ethic

But we must be truthful as God is truthful. Therefore, we must not pretend that the followers of Jesus will always have a smooth path in which to walk or be carried to the skies on "flowery beds of ease."

In Romans 12, Paul has been discussing the application of theology to daily life. He has said that the underlying principle is that Christians are to cease thinking as the world thinks and begin to think as Christians—a radical proposal. First, we are to think of ourselves with sober judgment. Next, we are to see others in the church as members of Christ's body.

But now we come upon an even more radical proposal—we are to love our enemies. Paul says that instead of hating those who hate us, we are to love them and pray for them, even as Christ loved us and prayed for us. "Bless those who persecute you; bless and do not curse," is his instruction.

Christians Will Be Persecuted

Paul's words come directly from Jesus' teaching, of course: first, the certainty of persecution; then, the way we should respond to it.

All through his ministry Jesus alluded to the fact that the world would hate and persecute his followers. But in the last discourses, recorded in John's gospel, Jesus became explicit in these predictions:

> If the world hates you, keep in mind that it hated me first. If you belonged to the world, it would love you as its own. As it is, you do not belong to the world, but I have chosen you out of the world. That is why the world hates you. Remember the words I spoke to you: "No servant is greater than his master." If they persecuted me, they will persecute you also. If they obeyed my teaching, they will obey yours also. They will treat you this way because of my name, for they do not know the one who sent me. . . .
>
> All this I have told you so that you will not go astray. They will put you out of the synagogue; in fact, a time is coming when anyone who kills you will think he is offering a service to God. They will do such things because they have not known the Father or me.
>
> John 15:18–21; 16:1–3

These words predict the world's hatred of Christ's followers and explain why the world will hate Christians. There are three reasons:

1. *Christians "do not belong to the world."* There is a natural but sinful tendency among people to dislike those who are different from them. This explains much racial hatred as well as the dislike people of one ethnic background frequently feel for people of another or why people feel uneasy when visiting the sick or dying. This can be quite trivial, or it can have stronger motivations. In his *Daily Study Bible* on John, William Barclay tells how Jonas Hanway, the man who invented the umbrella, was persecuted. When he tried to introduce his idea into England, where the umbrella should have been welcomed as a wonderful gift from a rainy heaven, Hanway was pelted with dirt and stones. Barclay also mentions the great Aristides of Athens, an outstanding leader who was called "Aristides the Just." He was banished by the citizens of Athens. Afterward, when one of the people was asked why he had voted to banish so outstanding a leader, the man replied only, "It was because I am tired of hearing him always called 'the Just.'"[2]

The world's people like those who are like themselves. Anyone who does not conform to the pattern, who is different, will meet trouble. But if that is so of people who are basically the world's type anyway, how much more true must it be of those who have been lifted out of the world and its way of thinking by Jesus Christ. The Bible calls them "a new creation" in Christ (2 Cor. 5:17). They are truly different. So the world hates them and tries to persecute them, sometimes in the open, sometimes in subtle ways.

2. *Christians have been "chosen . . . out of the world."* There is probably no doctrine of the Christian faith that is more hated by the world than the doctrine of election. People hated it when Jesus first taught it, so much so that on one occasion they responded by trying to kill him (Luke 4:24–29). People hate it just as much today. They hate it even if they just suspect we believe it, even when we do not teach it openly.

3. *Christians are identified with Christ.* The third reason why the world hates and persecutes Christians is the chief reason and the one Jesus stresses most in John's gospel—because believers are identified with Christ. Moreover, since Jesus is God and since unbelievers hate God—they would murder him if they could get their hands on him—their hatred for God, whom they cannot reach, is vented against Christians. To put it in other words, the world does not hate Christians because of what they are in themselves. In ourselves we are nothing. The world hates Christians because it hates Christ and because we are followers of Christ and stand for his cause against the standards of the world.

"Bless and Do Not Curse"

The fact of persecution is well established. If we are Christ's and if we stand for Christ against the world, we will experience it. But now the question is

[2]William Barclay, *The Gospel of John* (Philadelphia: The Westminster Press, 1956), vol. 2, p. 217.

this: How are we to respond to persecution? In Romans 12:14 Paul tells us that we are to bless our persecutors. We are to "bless" and "not curse." Again, this is a conscious reflection of Jesus' common teaching.

Jesus' best-known teaching on this subject is from the Sermon on the Mount. In that sermon, uttered near the beginning of his ministry, the Lord spoke of those who will persecute Christians, saying:

> You have heard that it was said, "Love your neighbor and hate your enemy." But I tell you: Love your enemies and pray for those who persecute you, that you may be sons of your Father in heaven. He causes his sun to rise on the evil and the good, and sends rain on the righteous and the unrighteous. If you love those who love you, what reward will you get? Are not even the tax collectors doing that? And if you greet only your brothers, what are you doing more than others? Do not even pagans do that? Be perfect, therefore, as your heavenly Father is perfect.
>
> Matthew 5:43–48

We will never be able to do what Christ is saying (and Paul is repeating in Romans) unless we understand two things. First, it is natural to strike back at people who are hurting us. It is natural to wish them harm, to "curse" them, to use Paul's word. Moreover, there will be more persecution, and thus a greater danger of cursing, the more pronounced is our Christianity. The more we stand out for Christ, the more we will be persecuted and the greater the danger of our wanting to strike back at our tormentors.

Robert S. Candlish, devotes several pages in his study of Romans 12 to this problem, pointing out that if our Christianity is lukewarm, if we seldom openly identify with Christ's cause, the danger of persecution and the resulting temptation to retaliate will be slight. But if we stand for Christ, for righteousness, and are persecuted, what then? "Can flesh and blood stand it?" he asks. "Can you abstain in your hearts from venting what is but too near akin to a malediction or a curse? Can you help yourselves from partly giving way to what may seem fully justifiable emotions of personal resentment and a personal sense of unprovoked and undeserved wrong?"

"No!" he answers. "Not unless you make conscience of blessing those whom you are thus tempted to curse."[3]

And that is the second thing we need to understand, that the only way to overcome our natural tendency to fight back is to work for our persecutors' good. That is, we have to bless and not curse.

The word *bless* has different meanings. When we bless God we ascribe to him the praise that is his due. When God blesses us he bestows blessing upon us. When we bless others we ask God to bless them.[4] It is in this sense that

---

3. Robert S. Candlish, *Studies in Romans 12: The Christian's Sacrifice and Service of Praise* (Grand Rapids: Kregel Publications, 1989), p. 237. Original edition 1867.

4. See John Murray, *The Epistle to the Romans*, 2 vols. in 1 (Grand Rapids: Wm. B. Eerdmans Publishing Company, 1968), vol. 2, p. 134.

we are told to bless and not curse. We are to pray for our enemies, asking God to bless them. But, then, if we are asking God to do good to them, it is patently clear that we must also seek every honest means of doing good to them too.

This brings us back to Jesus' teaching. Toward the beginning of his ministry, in the Sermon on the Mount, he uttered what we know as the Golden Rule: "In everything, do to others what you would have them do to you" (Matt. 7:12). Many of the world's cultures have it in negative form: "Do not do anything to another that you would not want them to do to you." This is not surprising. It simply amounts to: "Don't hit someone else unless you want to get hit yourself." Anyone with even the smallest amount of wisdom can see the sense of that.

But that is not what Jesus said. He expressed his "rule" in a positive form, saying that we are to seek out and, as far as possible, effect the good of other people, even our enemies.

We have in Stephen, the first martyr, an example of this principle in action. As Stephen was being stoned to death he prayed for those who were killing him, saying, "Lord, do not hold this sin against them" (Acts 7:60). His prayer was heard too. We do not know what happened to everyone who was present at the stoning of Stephen that day, but we do know what happened to one of them. His name was Saul, later known as Paul, the author of this very letter. He was profoundly moved by the way Stephen prayed for his antagonists, and Stephen's death won (or at least pricked the heart of) his tormentor (Acts 26:14).

Saint Augustine once said wisely, "The Church owes Paul to the prayer of Stephen."[5]

So let's learn to pray for and bless others. Robert Candlish says:

> When you suffer wrong, call to mind the considerations which should bring the wrong-doer before you in a very different light. Look at his case rather than your own. . . . If you put yourself in his place, you will see much, very much, that should charm all your resentment away and turn it into tenderest pity and concern. . . . Ask yourself what, if his history had been yours, you would have been, how you—if his lot were yours, his training, his habits, his companions—would be inclined to think and feel and act. You cease to wonder at his obtuseness and his opposition. You are drawn and not repelled by that too easily accounted for infatuation of his, which really hurts not you, but, alas! is ruining his own benighted soul. No thought of self can find harbor within you. All your thought is of him. Your bowels yearn over him and more for the very blindness and madness which make him a persecutor. And so you bless, and do not curse.[6]

5. Quoted by William Barclay, *The Letter to the Romans* (Edinburgh: The Saint Andrew Press, 1969), p. 182.
6. Candlish, *Studies in Romans 12*, p. 244.

Four Important Characteristics

In verses 15 and 16 Paul lists four characteristics of those who are true Christians. These verses bear the same relationship to verse 14 as verses 10–13 bore to verse 9 in the preceding paragraph. In verse 9 Paul set forth a love that is sincere and discriminating. Then in verses 10–13 he listed nine areas in which that love is to function. In this paragraph he has explained that in regard to our enemies we are to bless and not curse. That is the general statement. Next he lists four areas in which that should be done.

The way they are written, verses 15 and 16 could apply to Christians as well as to enemies. But since they are bracketed by references to those who persecute us, in verse 14 which comes before and verse 17 which comes after, Paul must be thinking of how Christians should relate to unbelievers.

1. *Empathy.* Empathy describes what Paul is talking about when he says, "Rejoice with those who rejoice; mourn with those who mourn." Empathy is the ability to identify closely with someone else, to make his case your own and allow what has happened to him to affect you also.

But this is not easy to do. We often do it superficially. We would not think of joking at a funeral, for example, and we express our condolences to those who suffer loss. Again, when a friend is promoted we send congratulations and may even attend a party in his honor. But when someone does very well we find it hard to be anything but jealous, even when we are congratulating him or her. There is only one way to break out of this. We have to stop thinking of ourselves and our own interests all the time, and the only way we can do that is by a transformation accomplished in us by Jesus Christ. Jesus set the example, of course, since he did not exalt himself but rather took "the very nature of a servant . . . and became obedient to death—even death on a cross!" (Phil. 2:7–8).

2. *Amicability.* Christians should be easy to get along with. This is what Paul is thinking of when he says that we should "live in harmony with one another." He is not talking about making peace, which is a positive thing. He will deal with that later (in v. 18). He is talking about not making sparks or causing turmoil. If this is still dealing with enemies, as it must be since the verses both before and after speak of them, then he is saying that we should not be like those Christian crusaders who are always looking for a fight or hunting down "Christ's enemies." We are to love and win people, not root them out to beat them senseless.

3. *The common touch.* Christians should "be willing to associate with people of low position" even more than others, because that is what most of us are. God did not choose "many who were wise by human standards," many who were "influential" or "of noble birth." Rather "God chose the foolish things of the world to shame the wise; God chose the weak things of the world to shame the strong. He chose the lowly things of this world and the despised things—and the things that are not—to nullify the things that are, so that no one may boast before him" (1 Cor. 1:26–29).

We are to associate with those who seem unimportant even if we have a high position. Jesus did it and was criticized for it (Matt. 11:19). We need to stop thinking of other people as being beneath us and instead come to regard them as people made for everlasting fellowship with God.

4. *Humility.* The last sentence in this paragraph takes us back to where Paul began. He said in verse 3, "Do not think of yourself more highly than you ought, but rather think of yourself with sober judgment." Right thinking, about both ourselves and others, dominates verse 16, as it did the earlier statement.[7] Can we do it? Leon Morris has a helpful suggestion when he reminds us that "the person who is wise in his own eyes is rarely so in the eyes of other people."[8]

Our Great Example

The trouble with exhortations of this nature, practical as they may be, is that they seem far beyond us and therefore discourage us if we start to take them seriously. They are not discouraging if we do not think deeply, for then we just assume that we are like this. But if we examine ourselves, we will have to admit that we do not pray for God's blessing on our enemies very often, empathize with others, act agreeably, or associate with those the world scorns and be humble. And that is discouraging.

Perhaps what we need to do here is simply get our minds off ourselves entirely and begin to think of Christ. Because if we think of him, we will become increasingly like him, even if we are not especially conscious of it.

Donald Grey Barnhouse writes:

When the nations were raging and the peoples imagining a vain thing, he did not move to destroy them. He did not destroy Adam when he sinned, but promised a Savior and began the long course of history so that man could have opportunity upon opportunity to repent and return to God. . . . He did not destroy us when we were ungodly sinners. He came from heaven to save us. He came into the camp of his enemies and allowed them to do their will against him in order to establish the foundation for our redemption. When we were without strength, when we were enemies, Christ died for us. Note that he did not save us by demonstrating his mighty power in some miracle. He saved us—He saved us by letting us kill him. How astonishing this is!

And when he rose from the dead he did not judge those who behaved so wickedly against him. The Jerusalem to which he held out his arms before he

---

7. This is obscured by the New International Version's characteristically idiomatic translation. In the Greek text the word for *thinking (phroneō)*, which occurs four times in verse 3, occurs three more times here. The King James Version captures the idea a little better by using the word *mind* twice and *wise* once. It says, "Be of the same *mind* one toward another. *Mind* not high things, but condescend to men of low estate. Be not *wise* in your own conceits."

8. Leon Morris, *The Epistle to the Romans* (Grand Rapids: Wm B. Eerdmans, and Leicester, England: Inter-Varsity Press, 1988), p. 451.

died was still the center of his loving thought. He commanded his disciples to go into all the world and preach the gospel to every creature, but he commanded them to begin at Jerusalem. Was this not heaping coals of fire upon the heads of his enemies? And did it not melt the hearts of many?[9]

It did, of course. It still does. It can through you.

---

9. Donald Grey Barnhouse, *How to Get Along with People*, booklet 72 of the exposition on Romans (Philadelphia: The Bible Study Hour, 1957), p. 33.

196

Right Living at All Times

Romans 12:17

Do not repay anyone evil for evil. Be careful to do what is right in the eyes of everybody.

Not long ago I came across an elaborate poll on the values and conduct of Americans. It appeared as a book called *The Day America Told the Truth*, and it was described as "the most massive in-depth survey of what Americans really believe that has ever been conducted."[1] The survey was based on a sampling of more than two thousand people in one week, each person answering over eighteen hundred questions, and there were follow-up interviews with thousands more.

A survey of this scope reveals a lot of things, of course. But one of the dominant findings—perhaps the most important of all—is that America no longer has a sense of right and wrong. "A letdown in moral values is now considered the number one problem facing our country," the pollsters wrote.[2] Our political and business leaders have betrayed us. We lie all the time. "Only 13 per-

---

1. James Patterson and Peter Kim, *The Day America Told the Truth: What People Really Believe about Everything that Really Matters* (New York: Prentice Hall Press, 1991), p. 4.
2. Ibid., p. 8.

cent of us believe in all of the Ten Commandments," the book reports. "Forty percent of us believe in five of the Ten Commandments. . . . There is absolutely no moral consensus in this country as there was in the 1950s, when all our institutions commanded more respect. Today there is very little respect for the law—for any kind of law."[3]

The number one rationalization for lawless and immoral behavior is that everyone else is doing it. "If everybody else is doing it, why shouldn't I?" is our argument.[4]

Making the distinction between right and wrong is what civilization—not to mention right religious behavior—is all about. But that is what we have lost in America. We do not believe in right and wrong. Therefore, it is against that serious national problem that we come to Paul's challenge to Christians in Romans 12:17, where we read, "Be careful to do what is *right* in the eyes of everybody."

All Things Right and Beautiful

The verse has two parts: (1) "Do not repay anyone evil for evil" and (2) "Be careful to do what is right in the eyes of everybody." The first part is the negative version of the Golden Rule ("Bless those who persecute you; bless and do not curse"). The second part is where Paul gets into the need for right conduct.

The King James Version of this verse seems to say something very different. It says, "Provide things honest in the sight of all men," which sounds like a command to support your family, to see that they have food to eat and a place to live, to pay the children's college tuition. That is not what the KJV translators meant, but the problem arises from the fact that the key word in this verse has several meanings. The word is *kalos*, which one Greek dictionary defines as good, right, proper, fitting, better, honorable, honest, fine, beautiful, or precious. The earlier translation selected the word *honest*. The New International Version uses the word *right*.

This does not mean that either translation is mistaken, however. It is just a case of the Greek word being more inclusive than any one of our many English terms.

The way to understand *kalos* is to know that it was the word used by the Greek philosophers, especially Plato, to describe the goal of sound thinking. Usually we think of this goal as "the good," which Plato proposed as the right pursuit of all rational beings. But if we are working in the area of aesthetics, the "good" that we are pursuing becomes "the beautiful." In philosophy it is "the truth." If we are thinking of morals, it is what is "right." If we are thinking of character, it is what is "honorable."

3. Patterson and Kim, *The Day America Told the Truth*, p. 6.
4. Ibid., p. 31.

The point is that this is what all people should aim at. So when Paul told the Romans that they were to "be careful to do what is *right* in the eyes of everybody," he was saying that Christians are to lead the way in good or right things, and they are to do this always. We are to be known as those who always pursue the very best in all areas.

Leon Morris puts it in other terms. He says that Paul "is calling on them to live out the implications of the gospel. Their lives are to be lived on such a high plane that even the heathen will recognize the fact. They will always be living in the sight of non-Christians, and the way they live should be such as to commend the essential Christian message."[5]

The Need for Ethics

It is evident that if we are to pursue what is good, true, right, honest, or beautiful in life, there must be something good, true, right, honest, or beautiful to pursue. And this means that there must be absolutes. Otherwise, we would be looking for something that is not there, and looking for something that does not exist is insanity. This is exactly the problem, of course, and it is why America is experiencing its present "values vacuum" or "morals morass," as *Time* magazine reported several years ago.[6] In other words, our problem is relativism.

This is what Allan Bloom expressed so powerfully in *The Closing of the American Mind*, an exposé of the failure of American higher education during the seventies and eighties.[7] Bloom is a Platonist, or at least he shares the educational goals of the Greek philosophers. He wants to pursue the "good." He thinks that is what higher education is all about. But today, he says, people no longer believe that there is a higher, absolute truth or good to be discovered, especially in education, and as a result the whole educational enterprise is in chaos.

In order to pursue a goal, there must be a goal. To have a strong moral society, we must have moral absolutes. Otherwise, all we can have is what is pragmatic or expedient, which is what education, politics, and American life as a whole have come to. It is why we do not have any heroes today and why we do not have any moral leadership in this country.

A generation or two ago there were heroes, people like Charles Lindbergh, Babe Ruth, Henry Ford, Douglas MacArthur, George Washington Carver, and many others. Today's heroes are celebrities—people like Michael Jordan and Madonna. Why are there no heroes? *The Day America Told the Truth* says, "There are no heroes because we have ceased to believe in anything strongly enough to be impressed by its attainment."[8]

5. Leon Morris, *The Epistle to the Romans* (Grand Rapids: Wm. B. Eerdmans Publishing Company, and Leicester, England: Inter-Varsity Press, 1988), p. 452.

6. *Time*, May 25, 1987, p. 14.

7. Allan Bloom, *The Closing of the American Mind* (New York: Simon & Schuster, 1987).

8. Patterson and Kim, *The Day America Told the Truth*, p. 208.

We are not getting leadership from our elected officials, either. We do not even trust them to be honest. In *The Day America Told the Truth* there is this sad anecdote. In 1987 a university president was teaching an adult Sunday school class in his local church. It included bankers, business executives, and college professors. He asked this question, based on a recent news event: "We hear on the news that an Iranian ship has been sunk in the Persian Gulf. The Iranian government says that it was sunk by American torpedoes. The U.S. government says that the ship hit Iranian mines. Whom do you believe?" The class was silent. No one answered. Everyone wanted more information before deciding what they thought had happened. Not one person in the class trusted his own government enough to believe it would be telling the truth.[9]

We need to have our national morality renewed. But, of course, this cannot happen if the only thing we can say about values is that they are relative. This is what Charles Colson told the Harvard Business School when he was invited to address it as part of Harvard's Distinguished Lecturer series. He told them they could not teach ethics because ethics requires absolutes but the philosophical basis of American higher education, including education at Harvard, is relativism. He distinguished between "ethics" and "morals." Here is what he told them: "The word 'ethics' derives from the Greek word *ethos*, which literally means 'stall'—a hiding place. It was the one place you could go and find security. There could be rest and something that you could depend on; it was unmovable. 'Morals' derives from the word *mores*, which means 'always changing.' Ethics or *ethos* is the normative, what *ought* to be. Morals is what *is*. Unfortunately, in American life today we are totally guided by moral determinations. So, we're not even looking at ethical standards."[10] He argued that in order to have ethics a nation must have access to a set of absolute values, or at least believe they can be found.

But the only place those values can be found is in the biblical revelation, which is why the Judeo-Christian value system has served so well and for so long as the soul of Western civilization. It is also why we need it again today, and so desperately.

Do the "Right" Thing

Several years ago a movie came out called *Do the Right Thing*. This is good advice, even if our culture is unable to tell us what the right thing is. The Bible tells us we need to do what is right in several areas.

1. *Handling money.* In 2 Corinthians 8 Paul writes about the way he was handling a large sum of money given by the Gentile churches for the poor Christians of Jerusalem. There had been a famine in Judea. Many were starving, and the Gentiles had given money for these poor people. In these chap-

---

9. Patterson and Kim, *The Day America Told the Truth*, pp. 208–9.
10. Charles W. Colson, *The Problem of Ethics*, number 2 in the Sources series (Washington: The Wilberforce Forum, 1992), p. 9.

ters Paul explains that he was committing the money to a group of men appointed by the various churches so there would be accountability and no questions about any mishandling of the funds. He explains his reasoning in verses 20–21, using the word *kalos*, the word found in Romans 12:17: "We want to avoid any criticism of the way we administer this liberal gift. For we are taking pains to do what is right *[kalos]*, not only in the eyes of the Lord but also in the eyes of men" (2 Cor. 8:20–21).

The church has suffered scandals over money. Jim Bakker went to jail because of money, and he is only the most visible and recent of many prominent religious figures who have mishandled their supporters' funds. If we are to be "careful to do what is right in the eyes of everybody," we must begin here. We should be utterly honest and entirely above board in how we handle money.

That is why at Tenth Presbyterian Church we have our books audited and why the Bible Study Hour does the same thing as well as holding membership in the Evangelical Council for Financial Accountability.

2. *Fair treatment of those who work for you.* In Colossians Paul writes to those who own slaves, saying, "Masters, provide your slaves with what is *right* and fair, because you know that you also have a Master in heaven" (Col. 4:1). The word that is translated *right* in this verse is not the same word as in Romans 12:17. In this verse the word is *dikaios*, from which we get the Greek word for *righteousness (dikaiosunê)*. It means conforming to a standard, right, proper, fair, honest, innocent. It is a different word, but it means the same or nearly the same thing, and it would be fair to say that *dikaios* is a near biblical equivalent of the secular philosophical Greek term *kalos*.

This means that we should treat those who work for us fairly, not using them only for what we can get out of them or always trying to get the highest profit at the lowest cost, at their expense. It means that Christians should lead the way in fair labor relations and work always for the good of their employees.

Wayne Alderson is one person who has shown how this can be done. He was a coal miner's son who pioneered constructive rather than antagonistic labor-management relations in a steel foundry in western Pennsylvania known as Pitron. When he entered the plant, Pitron was in the throes of a ruinous and potentially explosive strike. But Alderson identified with the workers, respected them, and treated them fairly, and as a result he soon turned the plant into one of the nation's most productive and profitable operations. He now heads an organization known as Value of the Person, which is trying to apply biblical principles to labor-management relations nationwide.[11]

3. *Respect of one's parents.* One sad part of the loss of values in America surveyed in *The Day America Told the Truth* is a breakdown in filial piety, more

---

11. See R. C. Sproul, *Stronger Than Steel: The Wayne Alderson Story* (New York: Harper & Row, 1980).

than half of all Americans admitting that they do not plan to take care of their parents in their old age. Nor do the parents expect to be taken care of.[12] The Bible's standard is quite different. The fifth of the Ten Commandments says, "Honor your father and your mother" (Exod. 20:12), and Paul wrote thoughtfully, "Children, obey your parents in the Lord, for this is right [dikaios]" (Eph. 6:1).

4. *The pursuit of all good things.* A list of this kind might go on indefinitely since right conduct needs to be a part of everything we think, say, and do. But I have been restricting myself to verses in which the word *right* actually occurs in the NIV. Here is a final one that I have put last only because it comes close to embracing nearly everything else: "Finally, brothers, whatever is true, whatever is noble, whatever is right [dikaios], whatever is pure, whatever is lovely, whatever is admirable—if anything is excellent or praiseworthy—think about such things" (Phil. 4:8).

We live in a sinful, evil, perverted culture. It is hard not to be sullied by it. Yet it was no different in Paul's day. The Greek and Roman world of the first century was a slime pit. But in spite of it, Paul says that Christians are to set their minds on good things, things that are true, noble, right, pure, lovely, admirable, excellent, and praiseworthy. We are to seek the best rather than the worst of the world around us.

Just One More Problem

The first problem I discussed is knowing what the "right" thing is so we might do it. I pointed out that it is impossible to know what the right thing is in a relativistic culture like ours. We need absolutes. Above all we need the absolutes that can only come from God. We need the biblical revelation.

But here is the second problem: having the will to do what is right even when we know what it is. I say this because in spite of everything I have said about America's moral decline and the loss of a fixed moral standard for most people, many nevertheless believe they should do what is right, and in some cases they even believe they know what is right. It is just that they do not do it. Even if they want to! Even if they are sure they can!

Above I wrote about Charles Colson and his address on ethics given to the Harvard Business School in 1991. In that address he recognized both of these problems—first, knowing what is right and, second, having the will to do it—and he illustrated the problems by his own experience. Here is part of his testimony.

> I grew up in America during the great Depression and thought that the great goal of life was success, material gain, power and influence. That's why I went into politics. I believed I could gain power and influence how people lived. If I earned a law degree—and I did at night—and accumulated academic honors

12. Patterson and Kim, *The Day America Told the Truth*, p. 8.

and awards, it would enable me to find success, power, fulfillment, and meaning in life.

I had a great respect for the law. When I went through law school, I had a love for the law. I learned the history of jurisprudence and the philosophy underlying it.

I studied Locke, the Enlightenment, and social contract theories as an undergraduate at Brown, and had great respect for the political process. I also had a well-above-average I.Q. and some academic honors. I became very self-righteous.

When I went to the White House, I gave up a law practice that was making almost $200,000 a year (and that was back in 1969, which wasn't bad in those days). It's kind of ordinary now for graduates of Harvard Business School, but then it was a lot of money. . . . I took a job in the White House at $40,000 a year. . . .

There was one thing about which I was absolutely certain—that no one could corrupt me. *Positive!* And if anybody ever gave me a present at Christmas time, it went right to the driver of my limousine. They used to send in bottles of whiskey, boxes of candy, and all sorts of things. Right to the driver of my automobile. I wouldn't accept a thing.

Patty and I were taken out on someone's boat one day. I discovered it was a chartered boat, and ended up paying for half of if because I didn't want to give the appearance of impropriety. Imagine me worried about things like that.

I ended up going to prison. . . .

I never once in my life thought I was breaking the law. I would have been *terrified* to do it because I would jeopardize the law degree I had worked four years at night to earn. I had worked my way onto the Law Review, Order of Coif, and Moot Court—all the things that lawyers do—and I graduated in the top of my class. I wouldn't put that in jeopardy for anything in the world!

I was so sure. But, you see, there are two problems. Every human being has an infinite capacity for self-rationalization and self-delusion. You get caught up in a situation where you are absolutely convinced that the fate of the republic rests on the reelection of, in my case, Richard Nixon. . . . There's an enormous amount of peer pressure, and you don't take time to stop and think, "Wait a minute. Is this right by some absolute standard or does this seem right in the circumstances? Is it okay?" . . .

Second, and even more important—and this goes to the heart of the ethical dilemma in America today—even if I had known I was doing wrong, would I have had the *will* to do what is right? It isn't hindsight. I have to tell you the answer is no. . . .

I discovered that there was no restraint on the evil in me. In my self-righteousness I was never more dangerous.

I discovered what Solzhenitsyn wrote so brilliantly from a prison—that the line between good and evil passes not between principalities and powers, but it oscillates within the human heart. Even the most rational approach to ethics is defenseless if there isn't the will to do what is right. On my own—and I can only speak for myself—I do not have that will. That which I want to do, I do not do; that which I do, I do not want to do.

It is only when I can turn to the One whom we celebrate at Easter—the One who was raised from the dead—that I can find the will to do what is right. It's only when that value and that sense of righteousness pervade a society that there can be a moral consensus. I would hope I might leave you, as future business leaders, the thought that society of which we are a part—and for which you should have a great sense of responsibility and stewardship—desperately needs those kind of values. And, if I might say so, each one of us does as well.[13]

Colson was referring to the Apostle Paul when he said, "That which I want to do, I do not do; that which I do, I do not want to do" (see Rom. 7:15). But Colson, like Paul, found that what is impossible for us as mere human beings becomes possible through the power of Jesus Christ working within. "Who will rescue me from this body of death?" Paul queried. But he had the answer: "Thanks be to God—through Jesus Christ our Lord!" (v. 25).

13. Colson, *The Problem of Ethics,* pp. 11–13, 22–23.

197

Keeping the Peace

Romans 12:18–20

If it is possible, as far as it depends on you, live at peace with everyone. Do not take revenge, my friends, but leave room for God's wrath, for it is written: "It is mine to avenge; I will repay," says the Lord. On the contrary:

> *"If your enemy is hungry, feed him;*
> *if he is thirsty, give him something to drink.*
> *In doing this, you will heap burning coals on his head."*

Whenever the subject of peace comes up Christians tend to get a bad rap, because the people discussing it think immediately of the Crusades of the Middle Ages or Protestants fighting Catholics in Northern Ireland today. We are supposed to be people of peace. Jesus is the "Prince of Peace" (Isa. 9:6). Yet Christianity seems to go hand in hand with political disruptions, internecine strife, and war.

These associations are not entirely fair. The Crusades were not really Christian. And in any case, they are only examples of the many thousands of wars that have scarred the face of human history. One writer has estimated that in the last four thousand years of human history there have been only three hundred years of peace. Human nature is vindictive, and the fights in which Christians have been involved are merely examples of the innumerable battles that have divided and continue to divide nations, races, families, and people of all backgrounds, beliefs, and dispositions. One of the songs I remember from my college days had this verse:

> The whole world is festering with unhappy souls.
> The French hate the Germans. The Germans hate the Poles.
> Italians hate Yugoslavs. South Africans hate the Dutch.
> And I don't like anybody very much.

Neither United nor Reformed

There is some truth to the complaint that Christians have not always been a peace-loving people. Wars among nations are seldom in our control. But what about the battles that have divided Christians from Christians? In 1054 the Eastern Orthodox church divided from the Catholic church over one word in the Nicene Creed, *filioque*. It means "and the Son," and it had to do with whether it is right to say that the Holy Spirit proceeds "from the Father *and the Son*" or whether the Holy Spirit proceeds only "from the Father."

The leaders of the Reformation divided over how Jesus was present in the communion service, Martin Luther insisting on a literal physical presence ("This is my body," Matt. 26:26) and Zwingli on a mere remembrance ("Do this in remembrance of me," Luke 22:19).

And what of today? One writer tells of a crossroads in a small town where there were churches on three of the four corners. When a stranger asked what churches they were he was told, "Well, that one is United Presbyterian. This one is Reformed Presbyterian. And this one," pointing to the third, "is for Presbyterians who are neither united nor reformed."

Some divisions are based on important matters of theology and practice, of course. But many are not, and the self-righteous, antagonistic, fighting spirits that lie behind these unnecessary divisions and perpetuate them are a scandal among those who profess to follow Jesus Christ. Jesus said, "Blessed are the peacemakers" (Matt. 5:9). He asserted, "By this all men will know that you are my disciples, if you love one another" (John 13:35).

Paul gets to this important matter in Romans 12:18–20, when he says:

If it is possible, as far as it depends on you, live at peace with everyone. Do not take revenge, my friends, but leave room for God's wrath, for it is written: "It is mine to avenge; I will repay," says the Lord. On the contrary:

> "If your enemy is hungry, feed him;
>   if he is thirsty, give him something to drink.
> In doing this, you will heap burning coals on his head."

These are important statements about what it means to be a peacekeeper, especially because this is the first time in the letter that Paul has discussed the subject of peace between human beings. He discussed what it means to have peace with God in the first chapters of the letter (see Rom. 5:1). But this is the first consideration of what it means to be a peacemaker. There are three verses in this section, and they make three important points.

Realism

The first thing we notice about Paul's challenge to Christians to live a life of peace is his sobering realism. He begins, "If it is possible" and "as far as it depends on you. . . " (v. 18).

This way of speaking recognizes two potential sources of difficulty: (1) the behavior of other people may negate peace and (2) there may be issues at stake that will make peace impossible even from the side of the Christian. For example, truth cannot be bartered away or sacrificed just to maintain peace. Purity cannot be violated. Injustice cannot be condoned. James 3:17 says, "The wisdom that comes from heaven is *first* of all pure, *then* peace-loving. . . ." So a prior, necessary Christian commitment to purity, truth, honesty, justice, and other indispensable matters may make peace unattainable.

Realism recognizes that this is a very wicked world. It knows that evil exists and affirms that it must be resisted by all right-thinking people, sometimes even to the point of armed conflict.

In September 1938 Prime Minister Neville Chamberlain returned from Munich following his much-watched meeting with Adolf Hitler and greeted enthusiastic London crowds with the promise of "peace in our time." He had just signed the infamous four-party agreement giving Germany the right to invade and occupy portions of Czechoslovakia. To maintain peace he had gone against his better judgment and had betrayed an ally. But it was not Chamberlain's motive that was at fault. He was a man of peace who wanted to avoid a threatened bloodbath. What was lacking was his judgment. He was not sufficiently realistic about evil, and World War II was the result.

We also need realism of a positive nature: We should realize that some things contribute to peace just as other things cause conflict and that, if we are Christians, we need to be on the side of the one rather than the other.

Here is some practical realism from the Book of Proverbs:

1. "Hatred stirs up dissension, but love covers all wrongs" (Prov. 10:12).

2. "A fool shows his annoyance at once, but a prudent man overlooks an insult" (Prov. 12:16).

3. "Fools mock at making amends for sin, but goodwill is found among the upright" (Prov. 14:9).

4. "A gentle answer turns away wrath, but a harsh word stirs up anger" (Prov. 15:1).

5. "He who covers over an offense promotes love, but whoever repeats the matter separates close friends" (Prov. 17:9).

6. "Starting a quarrel is like breaching a dam; so drop the matter before a dispute breaks out" (Prov. 17:14).

7. "An angry man stirs up dissension" (Prov. 29:22).

These verses tell us many things we can do to promote or encourage peace even if the other person does not want it.

Forbearance

The second important point Paul has to make about keeping peace is forbearance. He says, "Do not take revenge, my friends, but leave room for God's wrath, for it is written: 'It is mine to avenge; I will repay,' says the Lord" (v. 19). This is categorical teaching. It does not say, "Do not avenge yourselves except under the following three or four conditions" or "except under extreme circumstances." It says, "Do not avenge yourselves." That means never. Fighting back is not Christian.

"But surely I have to stand up for my rights," you say. Do you? If you want to stand up for someone's rights, I'll tell you what to do: Stand up for someone else's rights, fight for them. Do not fight for yourself, at least not if you are serious about obeying God and following Jesus Christ.

This verse tell us something else we should do as well, but it is no more acceptable to our natural way of thinking than what I have just said: Leave room for God's wrath.

In the Greek text of Romans these words are literally, "Give place to wrath," which is how the King James translators rendered the verse. In other words, there is no specific reference to God, which means that there is some question as to what the verse actually teaches. It could mean four things:

1. Give place to *your enemy's wrath*. That is, step aside and let it pass by you. If there is to be wrath, let it be his rather than yours.

2. Give place to *your own wrath*. That is, give it time to expend itself. Don't do anything hasty. Let the pressure in you dissipate.

3. Give place to *the wrath of the civil magistrate*. That is, let the case come before the courts. That is what they are for.

4. Give place to *God's wrath*. This is the view of the translators of the New International Version, who have added the word "God's" to clarify what they believe the text is teaching.

Of these four interpretations, the middle two can probably be eliminated quickly. The second, giving place to your own wrath, is just a modern idea. We speak of "letting it all hang out" or "getting it off your chest," but that is hardly biblical. In fact, the point of this passage is the precise opposite. We are not to let our wrath out. We are to forego it. The third interpretation, giving place to the proper function of the civil courts, is not in view either. It is true that the next chapter begins to talk about the role of the civil magistrate, but it does not develop the government's role in providing justice for us when we are wronged but rather the state's role in either punishing or commending us for our behavior.

That leaves either the first or fourth interpretation: (1) that we are to give place to our enemy's wrath, allowing it to work or (4) that we are to leave vengeance to God. The choice here is difficult, because both are true and both have something to commend them. Those who argue for the first view note that stepping back to allow something to pass by is the natural meaning of the Greek verb. Donald Grey Barnhouse says, "Here we are being told simply to endure patiently the wrath of the man who does us wrong. If evil rushes toward us, we are to love the evildoer and stand aside while he strikes out in blind selfishness; for we know that he cannot hurt us in the citadel of the heart where Jesus Christ holds sway."[1] Jesus' command, "Do not resist an evil person. If someone strikes you on the right cheek, turn to him the other also" (Matt. 5:39), is along this exact line.

On the other hand, since the verse goes on to speak of God's wrath, saying, "For it is written: 'It is mine to avenge; I will repay,' says the Lord," most commentators feel that the idea of giving place to God's wrath is almost inescapable. John Murray says, "Here we have what belongs to the essence of piety. The essence of ungodliness is that we presume to take the place of God, to take everything into our own hands. It is faith to commit ourselves to God, to cast all our care on him and to vest all our interests in him. In reference to the matter in hand, the wrongdoing of which we are the victims, the way of faith is to recognize that God is judge and to leave the execution of vengeance and retribution to him. Never may we in our private personal relations execute the vengeance which wrongdoing merits."[2]

The statement "It is mine to avenge; I will repay" is from Deuteronomy 32:35, but it is also quoted in Hebrews 10:30. It is an essential truth to keep in mind, but it is difficult, especially when we are under attack. Times of attack are a profound test of faith and of whether or not we really do have an otherworldly perspective.

When we were studying the "pattern of this age" in our exposition of Romans 12:1–2, I contrasted the Christian worldview with that of secularism. Secularism rejects a beyond or a hereafter and sees life only as the now. So, for the secularist, to suggest leaving vengeance to God is utter foolishness.

---

1. Donald Grey Barnhouse, *God's Discipline: Exposition of Bible Doctrines, Taking the Epistle to the Romans as a Point of Departure,* vol. 9, *Romans 12:1–14:12* (Grand Rapids: Wm. B. Eerdmans Publishing Company, 1964), p. 95.

2. John Murray, *The Epistle to the Romans,* 2 vols. in 1 (Grand Rapids: Wm. B. Eerdmans Publishing Company, 1968), vol. 2, pp. 141–42. Murray has the best discussion of the four options.

If the secularist is going to get what he wants, it will have to be now. And if justice is going to be done, it will have to be done in this life. Hence retaliation is the answer. It is only a person who sees beyond the now and is willing to trust God to establish justice and meet out punishments and awards hereafter who can be forebearing and hence be a peacemaker.

Remember these words: "'It is mine to avenge; I will repay,' says the Lord." They are important.

Active Goodness

The third verse dealing with what it means to "live at peace with everyone" is verse 20, which develops a contrast with the thought of taking vengeance into our own hands. "On the contrary," it says,

> "If your enemy is hungry, feed him;
>   if he is thirsty, give him something to drink.
> In doing this, you will heap burning coals on his head."

The thrust of this verse is clear enough. We are to do good even to those who do evil to us. This is the positive way in which we are to work toward peace or be peacemakers. Moreover, it is a third step in an obvious progression. First, we are to forebear doing evil, not retaliating for wrongs done. Second, we are to do good instead of doing evil. Third, we are to do good even to our enemies. The quotation is from Proverbs 25:21–22.

The difficult part of this is the last line, which as Leon Morris notes in a classic understatement, is "a metaphorical expression whose meaning is not obvious."[3] What does it mean to "heap burning coals" on our enemy's head? And why should we want to?

Charles Hodge suggests three possible interpretations.

1. *Increasing the enemy's guilt and thus his eventual punishment.* This is the oldest and probably the most widely received interpretation of the metaphor. But this is hardly the thrust of this passage, not to mention that it is also a revolting idea. It amounts to using good as a weapon. That is, "Be good to your enemy, because in the end your good will harm him more than if you were mean." It is hard to imagine Jesus or even a nice worldly person seriously saying that.

2. *Kindness will cause your enemy to become guilty and feel shame.* This is not much better. To be sure, shame might lead to repentance and thus eventually to salvation. But initially it is pain itself that we would be trying to inflict, and this hardly sits well with the idea of doing good to one's enemies or blessing those who curse us, which Paul has expounded just a few verses earlier.

3. Leon Morris, *The Epistle to the Romans* (Grand Rapids: Wm. B. Eerdmans Publishing Company, and Leicester, England: Inter-Varsity Press, 1988), p. 454.

3. *Doing good to one's enemy is the best means of subduing him or winning him over.* Hodge calls this the simplest and natural meaning, saying, "To heap coals of fire on anyone is a punishment which no one can bear; he must yield to it. Kindness is no less effectual; the most malignant enemy cannot always withstand it. The true and Christian method, therefore, to subdue an enemy is to 'overcome evil with good.'"[4] This is where the next verse takes us, of course. For the end of the matter is that evil is to be overcome by good, not good by evil or even evil by evil. Hodge says, "Nothing is so powerful as goodness. . . . Men whose minds can withstand argument, and whose hearts rebel against threats, are not proof against the persuasive influence of unfeigned love."[5]

And isn't that exactly how the Lord Jesus Christ subdued us to himself? No one was ever reviled so much or as unjustly as Jesus. Yet, as Peter wrote, "When they hurled their insults at him, he did not retaliate; when he suffered, he made no threats. Instead, he entrusted himself to him who judges justly. He himself bore our sins in his body on the tree, so that we might die to sins and live for righteousness; by his wounds you have been healed. For you were like sheep going astray, but now you have returned to the Shepherd and Overseer of your souls" (1 Peter 2:23–25).

It was by his conduct in suffering and before his enemies that Jesus won us, and it is by his death and the power of his resurrection that he enables us to live like him.

His Mind in Us

This leads me to the last point, a very important one. I have been working through what Paul is teaching about peacekeeping or peacemaking, and I have stressed that it requires realism, forbearance, and active goodness to those who do wrong. But perhaps you have been thinking—I know the thought comes to me—"But I can't do it. I don't care if this is the Christian way or is the example of Christ, I can't do it. Nothing is ever going to get me to the point of wanting to do good to those who hate me."

Fair enough. You have to start where you are, and if that is where you are, you have to recognize it. But also recognize that those who belong to Jesus Christ do not have a choice about whether they are going to follow and obey him or not. We must, if we are Christians. Therefore, we must be peacekeepers and peacemakers. We must be like him.

So the question is not Will you? The question is merely How? Let me make two suggestions.

First, you will never make any progress in making peace between yourself and other people until you have first found peace with God. You must be a Christian. Our relationship with God is the most important of all relation-

---

4. Charles Hodge, *A Commentary on Romans* (Edinburgh and Carlisle, Pa.: The Banner of Truth Trust, 1972), p. 402. Original edition 1835.

5. Ibid., p. 404.

ships, and if we are not at peace with him, we will never be at peace with others. We will be fighting constantly. That is why Peter went right on to discuss Jesus' death. On the cross Jesus made peace between rebellious sinners like us and the sovereign, holy God against whom we have rebelled. It is by believing that and trusting in Jesus' finished work that peace with God may be found.

Paul told the Colossians, "God was pleased to have all his fullness dwell in him [Christ], and through him to reconcile to himself all things, whether things on earth or things in heaven, by making peace through his blood, shed on the cross" (Col. 1:19–20).

Second, if you are to be a peacemaker, you must be at peace yourself, and this means you must have experienced what Paul in Philippians calls the peace of God. "Let your gentleness be evident to all. The Lord is near. Do not be anxious about anything, but in everything, by prayer and petition, with thanksgiving, present your requests to God. And the peace of God, which transcends all understanding, will guard your hearts and your minds in Christ Jesus" (Phil. 4:5–7).

First, peace with God. Second, the peace of God. Then, at the last, you will be able to start being a peacekeeper and a peacemaker. For when you are at peace with God and when the life of the Prince of Peace is in you, Jesus will be doing through you what he himself was doing when he was in the world. And while you are at it, do not forget the seventh of the eight Beatitudes, which promises a blessing to peacemakers, adding, "For they will be called sons of God" (Matt. 5:9).

198

The Triumph of Good over Evil

Romans 12:21

Do not be overcome by evil, but overcome evil with good.

W̲e have come to the last sentence of Romans 12, and it is worth noting, as we look back over the preceding verses, that Paul has said three times that we are not to return evil for evil. Verse 14 commands, "Bless those who persecute you; bless and do not curse." Verse 17 urges, "Do not repay anyone evil for evil." Now, verse 21, the last verse in the chapter, demands, "Do not be overcome by evil, but overcome evil with good." This is Paul's overriding theme in this section. It is why he repeats the idea. But these verses also establish a progression leading from what we must admit is already a very difficult standard to a standard that is even higher—in fact, some would say it's nearly impossible.

Here is how it develops. Verse 14 tells us that we are not to *speak* badly of another person but rather to speak good instead. Verse 17 tells us that we are not to *retaliate* for evil done to us. That concerns *actions*. At the end, in verse 21, Paul takes us beyond anything we might anticipate and tells us that not only are we not to retaliate for evil done to us, but that we are actually

1629

to do good to others and, amazingly, actually to *overcome* the evil of those other persons by our good conduct.

Love Stronger Than Hate

The standard Paul lays down in this chapter is so unnatural to us and seemingly impossible that I want to begin with the story of a man who has actually lived up to it. His name is John Perkins, a black man who dropped out of school in the third grade but who became a pastor and founder of the Voice of Calvary Ministries in Mendenhall, Mississippi. He has received national recognition for his leadership in race relations, has an honorary doctorate from Wheaton College, and even served on a presidential commission for inner-city problems under President Ronald Reagan.

John Perkins was born in Mississippi. He left the south for California when he was still a teenager, became a Christian in California, and later returned to Mississippi because he believed God was calling him to preach the gospel to the poor black people he had been raised with and help them by developing and supporting black leadership.

On February 7, 1970, a Saturday night, a van of black college students who had been taking part in a civil rights march was pulled over by highway patrolmen from Brandon, Mississippi, and the students were arrested. Perkins and two of his associates went to the jail to post bail, but when they arrived they were surrounded by five deputy sheriffs and several highway patrolmen who arrested them and began to beat them.

Perkins had not been speeding, taking drugs, or resisting arrest. He didn't even have a police record. All he had done was go to the jail to post bail for the students. But he was a black leader, and he was hated.

Perkins was beaten most of that night, along with some of the others. They stomped on him and kicked him in the head, ribs, and groin. One officer brought a fork over to him and said, "Do you see this?" Then he jammed it up his nose. After that he shoved it down his throat. For part of that terrible evening Perkins was unconscious and so mutilated that the students who were watching over him in his cell thought that he was either dead or about to die. It was a case of evil in a particularly vicious, violent, racist form.

Yet it did something good for Perkins. Up to this point he had been in Mississippi to preach to black people only. It was all he was allowed to do, of course. The doors of virtually all white churches were closed to him. But the beating changed him and gave him a new vision. He wrote:

> I remembered their faces—so twisted with hate. It was like looking at white-faced demons. For the first time I saw what hate had done to those people. These policemen were poor. They saw themselves as failures. The only way they knew how to find a sense of worth was by beating us. Their racism made them feel like "somebody."

When I saw that, I just couldn't hate back. I could only pity them. I said to God that night, "God, if you will get me out of this jail alive"—and I really didn't think I would, maybe I was trying to bargain with him—"I really want to preach a gospel that will heal these people, too."[1]

Perkins's recovery took some time, since he needed to heal both physically and emotionally. The physical recovery was assisted by a pair of compassionate doctors, one white and one black. The emotional healing was accomplished by God, who taught him that the same gospel that frees blacks also frees whites and that real justice, if it was to come, would come "only as people's hearts were made right with God and God's love motivated them to be reconciled to each other."[2]

"Now that God had enabled me to forgive the many whites who had wronged me, I found myself able to truly love them," said Perkins. "I wanted to return good for evil."[3] And Perkins did! His ministry is the proof of that desire, and it is continuing. It is a striking case of a believer refusing to be overcome by evil but instead overcoming evil with good.

Do Not Be Overcome, but Overcome

Our text has two parts. The first says, "Do not be overcome by evil." That is the negative. The second part says, "But overcome evil with good." That is the positive. Of the two it is the hardest to accomplish.

1. *Do not be overcome by evil.* The negative part is hard enough, of course. This is because to be overcome by evil means to respond to evil with evil, that is, to fight back, and that is the most natural thing for a sinful human being to do. It was summed up in a recent comic strip in which Hagar the Horrible tells his son, "Son, don't let the sun go down upon your wrath. . . . Attack your enemy at once and waste him while what he did to you is still fresh in your mind."

Unfortunately, there are many examples of just that kind of retaliation and of the evil that comes from it. There is the example of Mattathias, one of the Maccabees, who commanded his followers, "Avenge the wrong done to your people. Pay back the Gentiles in full" (1 Macc. 2:67–68 NRSV). They tried, but much damage to Israel and an untold loss of lives was the result. We have seen the attitude in Israel in a tit-for-tat policy against the Arabs of the Gaza Strip and the West Bank. We have seen it in South Africa, which seemed on the very edge of a genocidal civil war in spite of the heroic efforts of some leaders, both black and white, to avoid it and move toward reconciliation and justice. We have seen the identical attitude in the former Yugoslavia, where centuries old racial and religious hatred have fueled one

---

1. John Perkins, *With Justice for All* (Ventura, Calif.: Regal Books/GL Publications, 1982), pp. 98–99.
2. Ibid., p.102.
3. Ibid., p.102–3.

of the most destructive wars of recent history. Indeed, this is the case in every place where the normal human instinct for retaliation and the cherishing of hatreds holds sway.

This must not be the case with Christians. Christians are not to avenge themselves. Instead, as Jesus said, "Do not resist an evil person. If someone strikes you on the right cheek, turn to him the other also. And if someone wants to sue you and take your tunic, let him have your cloak as well" (Matt. 5:39–40).

2. *Overcome evil with good.* Yet not only are we not to strike back, thus being overcome by evil, with evil ruling the day, we are to respond positively in love, thus overcoming the evil in the situation and in the other person with our good.

Every time I get on the positive side of this matter I feel that the standard is so far above most of us as to seem almost unreal. I have already given a great living example of this principle in the life of John Perkins. David and his treatment of King Saul is a good illustration of this from the Old Testament.

David had served Saul faithfully, killed Goliath, fought his battles, and become a hero of the nation. But that had incited Saul to jealousy, and at this point Saul was pursuing David ruthlessly to put him to death. Taking three thousand men with him, Saul pursued David into the wilderness of En Gedi. David was hiding in a cave, and Saul entered, not even suspecting he was there. While the king was in the cave David crept forward and cut off a corner of Saul's robe, which he used to prove his love for the king. Yet so far was David from wanting to do any evil to Saul that he was conscience-stricken just for having cut off the corner of the robe.

When Saul went out again David followed and called to him, "My lord the king!" (1 Sam. 24:8). Saul looked back. David continued. "Why do you listen when men say, 'David is bent on harming you'? This day you have seen with your own eyes how the Lord delivered you into my hands in the cave. Some urged me to kill you, but I spared you; I said, 'I will not lift my hand against my master, because he is the Lord's anointed.' See, my father, look at this piece of your robe in my hand! I cut off the corner of your robe but did not kill you. Now understand and recognize that I am not guilty of wrongdoing or rebellion. I have not wronged you, but you are hunting me down to take my life. May the LORD judge between you and me. And may the LORD avenge the wrongs you have done to me, but my hand will not touch you. As the old saying goes, 'From evildoers come evil deeds,' so my hand will not touch you" (1 Sam. 24:9–13).

When Saul heard this he was stricken with guilt and wept aloud. "You are more righteous than I," he said. "You have treated me well, but I have treated you badly. . . . May the LORD reward you well for the way you treated me today. I know that you will surely be king and that the kingdom of Israel will be established in your hands. Now swear to me by the LORD that you will not cut off my descendants or wipe out my name from my father's family" (1 Sam. 24:16–21). David promised this and they parted on good terms, at least temporarily.

A short time later a similar incident occurred. Saul and his guard of soldiers were sleeping in their camp, and David and his friend Abishai went to it secretly and removed Saul's spear and water bottle. Then they called to the king from a hilltop some distance away, showing the spear and water bottle as proof that once again the Lord had placed Saul in David's power and that he had spared him graciously, since David could have killed Saul if he had wanted to. "Why is my lord pursuing his servant?" David cried. "What have I done, and what wrong am I guilty of?" (1 Sam. 26:18).

Saul answered, "I have sinned. Come back, David my son. Because you considered my life precious today, I will not try to harm you again. Surely I have acted like a fool and have erred greatly" (1 Sam. 26:21).

We know, of course, that Saul was unable to change his character, and therefore these were only temporary embarrassments and confessions. He never stopped trying to kill David, and he was stopped only when God allowed Saul and his son Jonathan to be slain in battle with the Philistines. But on these two occasions, for a short time at least, good triumphed gloriously, and good attended David's long reign in no small measure because of the way he was known to have conducted himself then. "Do not be overcome by evil, but overcome evil with good." David triumphed in both of these areas and prospered because of it.

Who Is Sufficient for This?

How are we to live like this? How can we, being what we are? In his study of Romans 12, Robert Candlish observes, "This surely is a very holy calling. It is a very awful calling. We may well ask, 'Who is sufficient for these things?' And we can be sustained only when we are enabled to add, 'Our sufficiency is of God'—of that God who has so dealt with us as he would have us to deal with our fellow-men and fellow-sinners."[4]

How are we to overcome evil with good, when our natures are so contrary to this standard? Candlish has suggested a first means. I want to develop it and add two more suggestions.

1. *We must know with deep gratitude that this is how God has treated us.* We deserved to be condemned, but God was good to us and overcame our evil by his good. If we appreciate this rightly, it will empower us to do the same. In fact, if we do not have this spirit, it will be sound evidence that we do not know God and have not experienced his grace in salvation.

I think of the story Jesus told about the unmerciful servant. This man owed the king ten thousand talents, the equivalent of several million dollars. Since

4. Robert S. Candlish, *Studies in Romans 12: The Christian's Sacrifice and Service of Praise* (Grand Rapids: Kregel Publications, 1989), p. 339. Original edition 1867.

he was unable to pay, the king was going to sell him, his wife, and his children into slavery. But the servant fell on his knees and begged for mercy, promising to pay back everything. This was an impossible thing to do, of course. But the king took pity on him, canceled the debt, and let him go.

This servant then found another servant who owed him a mere pittance. He demanded repayment. The servant who owed only a little pleaded for a chance to pay his debt, but the first man refused and had the other cast into prison. When the king heard this, he recalled the first servant, rebuked him, and had him jailed too. "This is how my heavenly Father will treat each of you unless you forgive your brother from your heart," Jesus concluded (see Matt. 18:21–35).

The parable does not teach that we are saved from sin by good works, of course. We are saved by grace alone. It does teach, however, that if we have been saved by grace we will be gracious and that, if we are not, we have never actually known the grace of God and will be judged for our sins at the final judgment. If it does nothing else, the parable shows why overcoming evil with good is not optional for Christians. We must forgive because we have been forgiven. We must overcome evil with good because God has overcome our even greater evil in saving us.

2. *We must study the example of Jesus Christ.* The second thing we need if we are to learn what it is to overcome evil with good and actually overcome it is the example of Jesus Christ. For this is what Jesus did, and if he is our Savior, we will love him and want to be like him.

Charles Hodge has written:

> One of the most beautiful exhibitions of the character of our Savior was afforded by his conduct under persecution. "He was led as a lamb to the slaughter"; "when he was reviled, he reviled not again; when he suffered, he threatened not." Even martyrs dying for the truth have not always been able to avoid the prediction of evil to their persecutors, so much easier is it to abstain from recompensing evil for evil than really to love and pray for the good of our enemies. This, however, is Christian duty; such is the spirit of the gospel.[5]

This is what moved John Perkins. He saw the enslaving nature of white racial hatred as he was being beaten. But it was later, as he was recovering in the hospital that God directed him to Jesus and by this means began to work powerfully on his heart. He wrote:

> The Spirit of God worked on me as I lay in that bed. An image formed in my mind—the image of a cross, of Christ on the cross. This Jesus knew what I had suffered. He understood. He cared. Because he had gone through it all himself.

5. Charles Hodge, *A Commentary on Romans* (Edinburgh and Carlisle, Pa.: The Banner of Truth Trust, 1972), p. 404. Original edition 1835.

He too was arrested and falsely accused. He too had an unjust trial. He too was beaten. Then he was nailed to a cross and killed like a common criminal. But when he looked at the mob who had crucified him, he didn't hate them; he loved them. And he prayed, "Father, forgive them, for they do not know what they are doing" (Luke 23:34).

His enemies hated, but he forgave. God wouldn't let me escape that. He showed me that however unjustly I had been treated, in my bitterness and hatred I was just as sinful as those who had beaten me. And I needed forgiveness for my bitterness.

I read Matthew 6:14, 15 again and again in that bed: "For if you forgive men for their transgressions, your heavenly Father will also forgive you. But if you do not forgive men, then your heavenly Father will not forgive your transgressions." To receive God's forgiveness, I was going to have to forgive those who had hurt me. As I prayed, the faces of those policemen passed before me one by one, and I forgave each one. Faces of other white people from the past came before me, and I forgave them. I could sense that God was working a deep inner healing in me that went far back beyond February 7, 1970. It went clear back to my earliest memories of childhood. God was healing all those wounds that had kept me from loving whites. How sweet God's forgiveness and healing was.[6]

Nothing in all history has done so much to heal deep human hurts and redirect otherwise resentful and retaliating lives than the example of Jesus Christ, who "suffered for [us] . . . that [we] should follow in his steps. . . . He himself bore our sins in his body on the tree, so that we might die to sins and live for righteousness; by his wounds you have been healed. For you were like sheep going astray, but now you have returned to the Shepherd and Overseer of your souls" (1 Peter 2:21, 24–25).

3. *We must be close to Christ and strive to draw closer to him always.* Important as the example of Jesus Christ is, that example alone is not enough. Nor is merely being saved enough, otherwise Paul would not be urging the Romans to this high standard of conduct, as he is doing. It would be automatic. In order to live as Christ we must first belong to Christ and second draw close to Christ, indeed striving to draw closer to him always. Charles Hodge says, "We must remember that without Christ we can do nothing. . . . If, therefore, we attempt to discharge the duties here enjoined apart from him, we shall be as a branch severed from the vine; and unless we are 'instant in prayer,' this union with Christ cannot be kept up."[7]

Paul himself was weak. He called himself "the worst" of sinners (1 Tim. 1:15). Yet he also said, "I can do everything through him who gives me strength" (Phil. 4:13). So can you, if you stay close to Jesus.

6. Perkins, *With Justice for All*, pp. 100–101.
7. Hodge, *A Commentary on Romans*, p. 404.

A Remarkable Chapter

As we look back over this remarkable chapter, starting with the offering of our bodies to God as living sacrifices and ending with the offering of ourselves and own best efforts to others in order that, by the grace of God, we might overcome their evil with good, we marvel at the wisdom, scope, and power of a gospel that can do that. It is a gospel that can take sinners who have lived only for themselves and turn them into men and women who actually overcome the evil of this world. Who could ever think up a gospel like that? Not us, for sure. Only God could devise such a powerful gospel.

Here is how Robert Haldane describes it:

> In the above remarkable portion of Scripture, we learn the true tendency of the doctrine of salvation wholly by grace, established in a manner so powerful in the preceding part of this epistle, by which men are created in Christ Jesus unto good works. How beautiful is it, and how sublime when displayed in all its practical effects in the duties which flow from it. . . . We may search all the works of the most admired writers and, so far as they have not borrowed from the fountain of inspired truth, we shall find in them nothing comparable to the elevated maxims contained in this chapter. Especially we shall not discover the faintest shadow of resemblance to the motives by which these duties are here inculcated. If the heavens declare the glory of God, and the firmament showeth forth his handiworks—if the invisible things of him from the creation of the world are clearly seen by the things that are made, even his eternal power and Godhead, so that the heathen are without excuse—how much more clearly do the Scriptures proclaim their Divine origin, and the majesty of their Author! God hath magnified his word above all his name.[8]

Indeed, he has! God has exalted his truth above anything else that we can possibly hope to understand or know. It is for us now to exalt God's name and Word by living out his truth in the way we go about our daily lives.

8. Robert Haldane, *An Exposition of the Epistle to the Romans* (MacDill AFB: MacDonald Publishng Company, 1958), p. 575.

PART EIGHTEEN

Church and State

199

Authority

Romans 13:1

Everyone must submit himself to the governing authorities, for there is no authority except that which God has established. The authorities that exist have been established by God.

In the fall of 1561 an important conversation took place in Scotland between Queen Mary and the Calvinistic Protestant preacher John Knox.

Mary was a Catholic. She had been educated in Catholic France, and she believed that sovereigns—she herself was one—had absolute power over the consciences of their subjects. Knox was a reformer. For his uncompromising preaching he had been sentenced to serve as a galley slave for nineteen months. After his release, he had studied in Geneva under John Calvin from 1553 to 1559. Then, in the summer of 1560, he had participated in the drafting of the Scottish Confession of Faith that stated that Jesus Christ "is the only Head of His Kirk" (sections 11 and 18). Knox had returned just two years before his celebrated conversation with Queen Mary.

In the interview Mary accused Knox of having wrongly taught the people to receive another religion than their princes allow. "And how can that doc-

trine be of God, seeing that God commands subjects to obey their princes?"
she asked. She was referring to Romans 13:1 and other texts.

Knox answered, "Madam, as right religion took neither [its] origin nor
authority from worldly princes, but from the Eternal God alone, so are not
subjects bound to frame their religion according to the appetites of their
princes."

He admonished Mary, "God commands queens to be nurses unto his
people."

"Yes, but you are not the church that I will nourish," she retorted.

Knox replied, "Your will, Madam, is no reason."[1] In this way the issues of
church and state and the proper role and function of the state were framed
in Scotland in the sixteenth century. There was no relief in Scotland until
Mary's forced abdication in 1567.

Christians and the State

What is the role of the state in human affairs? How is the state to relate
to the church of Jesus Christ? How are Christian people to relate to the government's authority? It is these questions that Paul raises and answers in the
first seven verses of Romans 13.

What a source of controversy they have been! J. C. O'Neill in *Paul's Letter to
The Romans* wrote, "These seven verses have caused more unhappiness and misery
in the Christian East and West than any other seven verses in the New Testament."[2]
That is probably not true. But they have certainly puzzled many and caused
unhappiness among some scholars. Some of them, like the one I just quoted,
have attempted to eliminate the verses from the letter, reasoning that they are
un-Pauline and come rather from a Stoic source. Such persons think the verses
have been interpolated, arguing that verse 8 would follow nicely after 12:21, and
that there is nothing quite like this section anywhere else in Paul's writing.

This is true, but that does not mean that Paul did not write it. Furthermore,
it can be argued equally well that his discussion of the legitimate authority
and proper function of the state is a natural follow-up to the immediately
preceding section in which he presented the duty of the Christian to return
good for evil, since to do that does not mean that a Christian always has to
be victimized by evil persons. It is the state's duty to restrain and punish evil.

Again, a discussion of the role of the state is natural in a letter to Christians
living at the center of the Roman world. Jews were notoriously resistant to all outside authority. They had fomented numerous rebellions, and the greatest one of
all, the rebellion that was to be crushed by the Roman general Titus in 70 A.D.,

1. J. Marcellus Kik, *Church and State: The Story of Two Kingdoms* (London, New York, and
Toronto: Thomas Nelson & Sons, 1963), pp. 92–93. Kik draws the quotations from Knox's own
work, *The History of the Reformation of Religion in Scotland* (London, 1905).

2. Cited by Leon Morris, *The Epistle to the Romans* (Grand Rapids: Wm. B. Eerdmans Publishing
Company, and Leicester, England: Inter-Varsity Press, 1988), p. 457.

was only a decade away from the time Paul wrote this letter. In the sixties Christians were shielded under a law originally promulgated by Julius Caesar, but turmoil was coming. Were the followers of Christ to align themselves with the coming revolution, or were they to be loyal citizens of the all-encompassing Roman empire? If so, what about the lordship of Jesus Christ? Was he King, or was he not? If they were not to be loyal citizens, what was their position regarding Rome to be?

The Starting Point: God Is Sovereign

The starting point of Paul's argument is found in the reason he gives for his categorical opening statement that "everyone," not only Christians, "must submit himself to the governing authorities" (Rom. 13:1). Why? The answer is not that you will get into trouble if you don't, or even that obedience is necessary for maintaining social order. Those are excellent pragmatic reasons that Paul understands and will bring into the discussion in due time, but they are not the reasons he gives at the beginning. What he says in verse 1 is that we must obey the authorities because "there is no authority except that which God has established" and "the authorities that exist have been established by God."

In other words, the starting point for Paul's argument is the doctrine of the sovereignty of God, in this case in regard to human rulers. God is sovereign. Therefore, those who exercise authority do so because God has established them in their positions.

We have to take this sovereignty seriously, because it is easy for us to accept God's being sovereign when we are given Christian rulers or when people of high moral character are elevated to positions of responsibility. But what about evil rulers? What about Nero, the corrupt emperor who was reigning in Rome at the very time Paul was writing this letter? What about rulers who persecuted the church? Or, for that matter, what about such evil leaders as Adolf Hitler, Joseph Stalin, and Idi Amin, or even elected officials like Richard Nixon, who betrayed our trust and disappointed us?

Romans 13:1 tells us that even these authorities have been established by God, and that we have a legitimate (though not unlimited) responsibility to obey even them.

We have already come across one example of an evil but nevertheless God-established ruler in Romans, though Paul was not specifically thinking about the role of the state when he brought him into his discussion. This example is Pharaoh, the oppressor of the Jews. He worked them as slaves and arrogantly resisted Moses' demand that he let God's people go. God judged this arrogance. Egypt was ruined by a series of ten plagues, culminating in the death of all the firstborn children of the country. In the end Pharaoh and his armies were destroyed by drowning in the Red Sea. But evil as this man was, he had nevertheless been put into his position by God, which Paul clearly says.

That is the teaching of Romans 9:17, where Paul quotes God as telling Pharaoh, "*I raised you up* for this very purpose, that I might display my power in you and that my name might be proclaimed in all the earth" (quoting Exod. 9:16). God raised Pharaoh up so that he might display his wrath in judging him. It was not a desirable appointment, but still it was God who had raised him up simply because God is sovereign in all things.

A second example is Nebuchadnezzar, another arrogant ruler. He thought he was superior to Jehovah because he had been able to conquer Jerusalem, raze the temple, and carry off to Babylon the gold and silver objects that had been used by the Jewish priests in their worship. The first four chapters of Daniel are a record of the struggle that took place as Nebuchadnezzar contended for sovereignty and God worked to humble him and show him that God alone, not Nebuchadnezzar, is the Most High God and ruler of all.

Three times in Daniel 4 the text says that "the Most High is sovereign over the kingdoms of men and gives them to anyone he wishes" (vv. 17, 25, 32): (1) Nebuchadnezzar heard these words in his dream; (2) Daniel recited them to him as the words of God; (3) Nebuchadnezzar heard them from heaven when God uttered his important, symbolic judgment of insanity upon the stiff-necked ruler. This is an important truth, and in the end Nebuchadnezzar seems to have gotten the message, for he confessed:

I, Nebuchadnezzar, raised my eyes toward heaven, and my sanity was restored. Then I praised the Most High; I honored and glorified him who lives forever.

His dominion is an eternal dominion;
    his kingdom endures from generation to generation.
All the peoples of the earth
    are regarded as nothing.
He does as he pleases
    with the powers of heaven
    and the peoples of the earth.
No one can hold back his hand
    or say to him: "What have you done?" . . .

Everything he does is right and all his ways are just. And those who walk in pride he is able to humble.

                                                            Daniel 4:34–35, 37

Another example is Cyrus the Persian, who is also mentioned in Daniel (1:21, 6:28, 10:1). He was an unusually humane ruler, whom God used to bring the Jews back to Jerusalem from Babylon. In Isaiah 45:1 this pagan king is even called the Lord's "anointed," which means messiah, the very title given to Jesus as the Messiah of God.

These rulers—Nero, Pharaoh, Nebuchadnezzar, Cyrus—and all others have been set in their places by God, simply because God is sovereign and, as the Westminster Confession of Faith says, "God from all eternity did, by the most wise and holy counsel of his own will, freely and unchangeably ordain whatsoever comes to pass" (III, 1). There is no ruler anywhere or from any time in history who was not set in his exalted position by God.

Obeying the Sovereign

Of course, the problem for us is not so much that God has established whatever rulers there may be. We can believe that abstractly and either like and approve of our rulers, or not like them and disapprove of them, or perhaps even reject them. The problem is that we are told that it is the duty of Christians to obey those who exercise such authority, and that includes *all* authorities, not just kings and presidents but also policemen, judges, schoolteachers, bosses, and other such "governing authorities." We do not want to do that.

Paul is writing about the civil government in Romans 13, but these other authorities come into the picture tangentially because they have governing roles and have been set in place by God.

There are many obvious problems at this point. First, Paul does not answer a lot of our questions. For example, when is a government a legitimate government, and when isn't it? When is it right to rebel against an unjust or tyrannical government, or isn't it permitted at all? What about our own American War of Independence? If we had been living then, what side should we have been on, with England or with the colonists? What are we to do when there are rival claimants to the throne? Which one should we obey? Again, at what point does an unjust ruler become legitimate?

Or what about limits? Paul says we are to obey the governing authorities. But does this mean that we are to obey everything they command? What about unjust acts commanded by an evil government? Killing civilians? Lying? Clandestine operations even for such an important branch of government as the CIA? Are there no limits to what must be obeyed?

We are going to explore the limits to the obedience Christians can give a civil government in the next study. But the point I am making here is that the matter of obedience to those in authority cannot be taken lightly, as we are so often inclined to do.

As far as Romans 13:1 is concerned, it would be difficult, probably impossible, for anyone to write a more all-encompassing, absolute, or utterly unqualified statement than the one Paul has given: "Everyone [literally, 'every soul'] must submit himself to the governing authorities."

This is written so strongly that Robert Haldane thinks that it requires an obedience to secular rulers that is almost absolute: "Everyone, without exception, is, by the command of God, to be subject to the existing powers, whatever were the means by which they became possessed of the situation in which they stand. . . . If God has appointed every government that exists in the world, his people are bound to submit to every government under which their lot has been cast."[3]

3. Robert Haldane, *An Exposition of the Epistle to the Romans* (MacDill AFB: MacDonald Publishing Company, 1958), pp. 577, 579.

Power or Authority?

There *are* limits, of course, but the place to begin is not with the limits, but by trying to understand the nature of the authority that has been given to civil rulers. The key word is *authority*, which occurs six times in these verses.

Two Greek words are used of political power that are closely connected but need to be distinguished. The first is *kratos,* which refers to what we might call "the naked power of rule." It can be legitimate or illegitimate, as in the case of the devil, who, we are told, has "the power of death" (Heb. 2:14) but who will lose it when Jesus returns. His power will be taken away, and he will be cast into the lake of fire. This word has proved useful in describing the various types of government. For example, we speak of democracy. *Dêmos* means people, crowd, or public assembly. *Kratos* means rule. So democracy means rule by the people (or by many people). A plutocracy is a system in which the rich (or aristocrats) rule, because *ploutos* means wealth.

So when we speak of *power (kratos)* we recognize that there can be both legitimate and illegitimate power. And, of course, Christians are under no obligation to obey a power that is illegitimate. Just because a man with a gun orders us to do something does not mean that we should do it necessarily. The man has power, but it is illegitimate. What we need is a legitimate power—a policeman—to subdue him.

The other word that is used of political as well as other kinds of power is *exousia,* which is the word Paul uses in Romans 13. *Exousia* is a delegated power, power that is given to a person or group of persons by another. Paul uses it in Romans 13 because he wants to make explicit that the authority of the governing powers is from God.

Nevertheless, they are responsible for how they exercise it. That is the important thing. They are responsible to God, precisely because God has given them the power. So here in one word is both the legitimacy and the necessary accountability of human government.

Jesus before Pilate

An important example is Jesus Christ's trial before Pontius Pilate. Jesus was tried for treason because, as his accusers put it, he "claim[ed] to be a king" (John 19:12). It did not take Pilate long to discover that the kind of kingdom Jesus was talking about was no direct threat to Rome, because it was a kingdom of truth. Jesus told him, "I am a king. In fact, for this reason I was born, and for this I came into the world, to testify to the truth. Everyone on the side of truth listens to me" (John 18:37). After he had heard that, Pilate knew that this was a religious matter and was of no concern to him.

Yet the leaders of the people were still clamoring for Jesus' death, and it became clear that Pilate was soon going to bow to their wishes. He wanted to help Jesus, but Jesus was not speaking to him. "Do you refuse to speak to me?" Pilate said. "Don't you realize I have power either to free you or to crucify you?" (John 19:10).

At this point Jesus replied with one of two classic texts for helping us understand the God-given role of civil government and the right relationship of the church to the state.[4] He answered, "You would have no power over me if it were not given to you from above. Therefore the one who handed me over to you is guilty of a greater sin" (John 19:11).

The word that is translated *power* in this verse is the same word that Paul uses in Romans 13, and it is used in exactly the same way. The authority that was given to Pilate was a delegated authority, because it had been given to him by God. It was a true authority. Pilate had the right to try Jesus and render judgment as he thought right. But he was responsible to God for what he did and for how he did it. That is why Jesus was able to remind him, "Therefore the one who handed me over to you is guilty of *a greater sin.*" The sin of the Jewish leaders was greater than the sin of Pilate, because they were sinning against the Scriptures, which pointed to Jesus and were fulfilled by Jesus, and against their consciences, as even Pilate recognized ("It was out of envy that they had handed Jesus over to him," Matt. 27:18). Nevertheless, Pilate was also sinning by condemning an innocent man, and he would have to answer to God for it.

Pilate had authority in Christ's trial. He could decide as he wished. He decided wrongly, but he had authority to make that decision even if it was wrong. This is because his authority was from God, and Jesus did not suggest that it be wrested from him even because he had made so great an error as condemning the Son of God. If nothing else, the example of Jesus before Pilate shows us that for Christians revolution for the sake of revolution alone ("I would rather be king than you") is wrong.

Indeed, instead of being revolutionaries, Christians are obligated to be the very best citizens possible. We should obey speed limits, pay our taxes honestly, vote in elections, and in all other respects respond with respect and compliance to those who are over us.

To Tell the Truth

Yet this does not mean that Christians are merely to be pliant, lying down in the face of evil and doing nothing to oppose it. Again, we have the example of Jesus. Jesus did not show disrespect to Pilate. He did not warn him that if he failed to rule justly, Jesus' followers would rise up and do their best to unseat him and the Roman government. Jesus knew what the governor would do, and he accepted it as from God, which it surely was. But Jesus was not silent. He spoke of the truth, which he had been sent to make known, and

---

4. The other classic text is Matthew 22:21 ("Give to Caesar what is Caesar's, and to God what is God's"). We will consider it in the next study.

he reminded Pilate that Pilate was sinning and would therefore one day himself have to answer for it.

That is our role. We speak often today of the separation of church and state, and we should be thankful for that separation. It is a dearly won liberty to have a church free from government interference or control and to have a state free from clerical domination.[5] *But the separation of church and state does not mean the separation of God and state.* And though we do not rule the state, nor should we, it is nevertheless our duty as Christians to speak out against the civil ruler's sins and remind the governing authorities that they are ultimately accountable to him from whom their authority comes.

So we are accountable too! We are accountable to speak up. We do not have the power of the sword. That is reserved for the civil authorities, as Paul will show in Romans 13:4. Our weapon is truth, for we are a kingdom of the truth. The truth is stronger than the sword. But woe to us if we do not wield the sword of truth powerfully.

---

5. For a stirring account of the struggle going back to the earliest days of the church see Kik, *Church and State: The Story of Two Kingdoms.*

200

Must Caesar Always Be Obeyed?

Romans 13:2

Consequently, he who rebels against the authority is rebelling against what God has instituted, and those who do so will bring judgment on themselves.

Left to ourselves we are like those described in the last verse of the Book of Judges when "Israel had no king; [and] everyone did as he saw fit" (Judg. 21:25). That is why Paul insists in Romans 13:1 that we are to obey secular authorities: The state is God's wise provision for avoiding anarchy.

Having been told that we must obey the authorities, the next two verses of Romans 13 give us reasons why we should. First, if we disobey the state we will be disobeying God, and God will punish us (v. 2). Second, the government will also punish us (v. 3). Verse 2, which we are to study carefully now says, "Consequently, he who rebels against the authority is rebelling against what God has instituted, and those who do so will bring judgment on themselves."

Must Obedience Be Absolute?

This raises some important questions. For example, are there no conditions under which rebellion against the existing authority is justified? Or demanded? Suppose the state is tyrannical. Suppose it is violating human rights. And what about obedience itself? Must obedience be absolute, or are there limits? Can we obey in some areas and not others? Must Caesar *always* be obeyed?

That question alludes to Jesus' celebrated response to the question his enemies raised about taxes, and is one of two classic texts for helping us understand the God-given role of government and our rightful relationship to it.

We examined the first of these two classic texts in the last study: Jesus' reply to Pilate at his trial. Pilate had asked him if he were not aware that Pilate had power either to free Jesus or to crucify him. Jesus replied, "You would have no power over me if it were not given you from above. Therefore the one who handed me over to you is guilty of the greater sin" (John 19:11). We saw that the word translated as *power* is actually the word *authority* and that it refers to an authority that is delegated. In other words, Jesus said that although Pilate had a true authority, that authority had been given to him by God and he was therefore responsible to God for how he used it. This verse lays the groundwork for the limitations of the state's authority.

The setting for the second classic text is this. Jesus' enemies had come to him with a trick question: "Is it right to pay taxes to Caesar or not?" (Matt. 22:17). They thought that if he said it was right to pay taxes, they could discredit him with the people who hated Rome and for whom taxes were a greatly resented burden. He would be dismissed as a collaborator. On the other hand, if Jesus said that they should resist Rome by refusing to pay their taxes, then his enemies could denounce him to the Roman authorities as an insurrectionist.

Jesus asked for a coin. When they produced it, he asked whose portrait was on it and whose inscription, probably holding it out to them so they could see it. "Caesar's," they replied.

"Give to Caesar what is Caesar's," Jesus said, thus laying the basis for the exact teaching Paul gives in Romans 13:7, when he says, "Give everyone what you owe him: If you owe taxes, pay taxes." However, at this point I think Jesus must have flipped the coin over, exposing the back on which there would have been a portrait of one of the Roman gods or goddesses. And he continued, making the contrast, "*and to God what is God's*" (Matt. 22:21).

The first part of Jesus' answer reinforced Caesar's authority, even in such an unpopular matter as taxes. His second part drew limits. Although the state has a God-given and therefore legitimate authority, the authority of God is greater. Therefore, those who know God must worship and obey him, even if it means disobeying Caesar.

Four Logical Options

Jesus' words in response to the question about taxes suggest four options that I have found useful in dealing with this matter of the state's authority and the rightful limits of a Christian's compliance with it: (1) God alone as an authority with the authority of Caesar denied, (2) Caesar alone as an authority with the authority of God denied, (3) the authority of both God and Caesar but with Caesar in the dominant position, and (4) the authority of God and Caesar but with God in the dominant position.

1. *God alone as an authority.* The first option is one some Christians have embraced at some periods of history, especially when the state has become excessively oppressive or corrupt. In the early church, some people called anchorites went off into the desert, thus separating themselves from all social contacts and living, as they believed, solely for the service of God. From that early movement monasticism was born.

It would be an error to think that this has been practiced only in the early church or by members of monastic orders. Monasticism is also the practical approach of evangelical Christians who so separate themselves from the secular world that they withdraw from the surrounding culture, refuse to participate in elections, have only Christian friends, or will work only for Christian companies.

2. *Caesar alone as an authority.* The second option is that of most secularists and sometimes even of so-called Christians: the choice of Caesar alone. It was the way chosen by the Jewish leaders at the time of Christ's trial, when they told Caesar (incredibly, in view of their past and their knowledge of the Old Testament), "We have no king but Caesar" (John 19:15).

This is the most dangerous of the four options, because if God is left out, Caesar is left with no ultimate accountability. He has nothing to restrain his whims or cruelty.

In America we recognize the need for checks upon governmental power, so each of our three main branches of government has a check on the others. The president (of the executive branch) appoints Supreme Court justices (of the judicial branch); but if the president gets out of line, the Senate (part of the legislative branch) can impeach him. The president initiates programs, but Congress must fund them. As for Congress, it can make laws, but the president can refuse to sign them (the power of the veto), or the judicial branch can declare them unconstitutional. The Supreme Court is carefully protected out of respect for our laws. We claim to be a nation governed by laws, not by men. But the court cannot initiate legislation; it can only pass on it, and the president has the power to appoint the justices.

We have created this system of checks and balances because we recognize that people in positions of power are untrustworthy. But if that is true on the merely human level, how much truer is it on the cosmic level. Human rulers regularly conspire against God (Ps. 2). So if we forsake God, we are at the mercy of our governors.

3. *The authority of God and Caesar but with Caesar in the dominant position.*
The third option is one many persons would claim, but it is the position of
cowards. This is because if God's authority is recognized at all, it must be
supreme simply because God is supreme by definition. That is what it means
to be God. So if anyone claims to obey the state before God or rather than
God, while nevertheless still believing in God, it can only be because he is
afraid of what Caesar can do to him.

This was the case with Pilate. He knew Jesus was innocent of the charges
brought against him. He declared him innocent and even tried to release
him. But in the end he gave in and had Jesus crucified. Why? Because he
was afraid of Caesar. Toward the end of the trial, when Pilate was holding
out against their wishes, the Jewish authorities played their trump card, crying
out, "If you let this man go, you are no friend of Caesar" (John 19:12). Pilate,
who feared Caesar and wanted to be a friend of Caesar more than anything
else in the entire world, gave in and thus condemned the sinless Son of God.

The irony is that Pilate failed to secure Caesar's friendship even so, because
a few years later he was removed from office by the proconsul of Syria and
banished to France, where he died.

4. *The authority of God and Caesar but with God in the dominant position.* The
last option is the only valid one: God and Caesar, but with God in the dominant position. It was the position Jesus articulated when he said, "Give to
Caesar what is Caesar's, and to God what is God's."

Because Christians recognize the authority of the state, they are (or should
be) the very best of citizens, in two ways. First, they should obey the state in
all areas of its legitimate authority. As I said in the last study, we should obey
the speed limits, pay our taxes honestly, vote in elections, support worthy
civic endeavors, speak well of our rulers, and support and pray for them.
Calvin expressed this well when he wrote, "We are not only subject to the
authority of princes who perform their office toward us uprightly and faithfully as they ought, but also to the authority of all who, by whatever means,
have got control of affairs, even though they perform not a whit of the
princes' office."[1]

However, the other way Christians should be the very best of citizens is by
opposing the state verbally and by acts of noncompliance whenever the government strays from its legitimate God-given function or transgresses the
moral law of God. In the last study we saw that we are to do this chiefly by
words—that is, by rational argument, not by coercive power. The power of
the sword is the state's, not ours. Nevertheless, we are also to resist and even
disobey the state when necessary.

---

1. John Calvin, *Institutes of the Christian Religion,* 2 vols., ed. John T. McNeill, trans. by Ford
Lewis Battles (Philadelphia: Westminster Press, 1960), p. 1512.

Limitation Number One: Evangelism

The first area in which Christians cannot recognize the authority of the government and must therefore disobey it is whenever the state forbids the preaching of the gospel or evangelism. This is because Christians have a God-given duty to evangelize. We call it the Great Commission. Jesus said, "Go into all the world and preach the good news to all creation" (Mark 16:15). He told the eleven, "Go and make disciples of all nations" (Matt. 28:19). He said, "You will be my witnesses in Jerusalem, and in all Judea and Samaria, and to the ends of the earth" (Acts 1:8).

What must happen when the authorities demand differently is illustrated in Acts 4 and 5. The disciples had been preaching in Jerusalem, but they had created such a stir that the leaders of the people called them in and, meeting in solemn assembly, commanded that the apostles keep silent. Peter and John replied, "Judge for yourselves whether it is right in God's sight to obey you rather than God. For we cannot help speaking about what we have seen and heard" (Acts 4:19–20).

The apostles were threatened and released, but they went right back to their preaching. They were arrested again. "We gave you strict orders not to teach in this name [the high priest said]. Yet you have filled Jerusalem with your teaching and are determined to make us guilty of this man's blood" (Acts 5:28).

The apostles replied, "We must obey God rather than men" (v. 29).

This incident makes clear that Christians are to give preference to the preaching of the gospel and are not to cease from it even though commanded to do so by the civil authorities. They may suffer for it. Many of the early preachers were arrested and beaten. Some were killed. But they evangelized anyway. We need to remember this in our age, which is becoming increasingly intolerant of any public articulation of Christian faith and truth.

Limitation Number Two: Morality

A second biblical limit on obedience to human authorities is in moral areas affecting Christian conduct. No government has the right to command Christians to perform immoral or non-Christian acts. During the Nazi era Christians in Germany were faced with a devilish state and its openly anti-Christian and even antihuman practices. German citizens were commanded to have no dealings with the Jews. They were not to trade with them, have friendships with them, or even acknowledge them. This was an unjustified demand on Christians to behave immorally, and those who disobeyed these laws were right to do so.

Corrie ten Boom and her family were right to hide Jews and thus try to save their lives.

Dietrich Bonhoeffer was right to speak out against Hitler, organize an underground church, and strengthen its opposition and witness.

Martin Niemoeller was right to go on preaching the truth even to the point of being imprisoned for it. We are told that another minister visited him in jail and argued that he would be set free if only he would agree to keep silent about certain subjects. "So why are you in jail?" he concluded.

"Why aren't you in jail?" Niemoeller countered.

In our country Christians must also speak out against racism, government and corporate corruption, sex and age discrimination, and other evils. At the present moment in America it is unlikely that you will be imprisoned for speaking the truth, though that may come in time. But you might lose your job for refusing to be dishonest or for calling those who are not honest to account. You might lose your chance for promotion. You might be cut out of the leadership circle. No matter. You must still speak up, and you must act justly even if you are pressured to comply.

Limitation Number Three: Civil Disobedience

There is a third area in which Christians must disobey the state, but it is a difficult one in which to remain truly biblical—when the state flagrantly ignores either righteousness or justice and those who are sensitive to these wrongs feel the need to do more than merely speak out. This differs from the previous area in that the former limitation concerned times in which Christians are pressured to act immorally themselves and must refuse, while this refers to government immorality and the need for Christians to do something to change it.

We generally speak of this as civil disobedience, and there are many excellent examples of it having been done rightly and with success. The Civil Rights movement of the sixties is a good example.

The problem is that as soon as we move away from words only (that is, speaking the truth and calling the rulers to account) and into the area of direct action, it is easy to cross over the line into a wrong method of responding and thus become guilty not merely of breaking an unjust law but of breaking just and even moral laws. Let me give two examples.

1. *Dietrich Bonhoeffer.* I have already commended Dietrich Bonhoeffer for his stand against the evils of the Nazi state. He is also to be commended for courageously returning to Germany from America, where he was living at the time, to help the struggling church and give it leadership. But Bonhoeffer was not executed for speaking out against Nazism. He was executed for being involved in a plot to assassinate Adolf Hitler. We can understand how he might have felt that assassination was the only course left to him to stop the growing evil, but desperation does not make murder right, and at this point he clearly went beyond any possible biblical sanction.

We can contrast his conduct with that of David in his struggle against King Saul. God had already removed his blessing from Saul, and Saul was seeking David's life. David did not have to wait in Jerusalem to be killed. He had every right to flee. This was a form of disobedience. But David did not cross over the line and try to kill Saul. On the contrary, he spared his life on at least two occasions while he waited for God to remove him, which God did in the end.

Jesus told Peter, "All who draw the sword will die by the sword" (Matt. 26:52).

2. *Operation Rescue.* The second example is often on our minds because it is current: the attempt of Christians to stem the terrible destruction of human life through abortions, which are legal by today's laws. This effort is best exemplified by a group called Operation Rescue, although other organizations are also involved.

When I am talking about the abortion problem, as I often do, I usually challenge the blockading of abortion clinics on the basis of the methodology being used. I say that we live in a television age and that television turns our tactics against us to the point of our losing the battle against this great evil. I say that television will never record a serious discussion about the true nature of abortion or the value of a life made in the image of God conducted between an anti-abortionist and a woman who is considering an abortion. It is not good television. But as soon as a restraining order is issued and the police arrive to begin arresting the demonstrators and placing them in paddy wagons, then the cameras roll. For this makes good television, and we who oppose abortion appear on television as people who are violent and who want to take away other people's rights. That is a problem the pro-life people need to consider carefully.

But that is not the issue here. There is nothing wrong with being arrested in itself. The problem in this area is the carryover from mere protest and the attempt to persuade people by speaking the truth to breaking otherwise perfectly valid laws, like rights of private property, freedom of movement, and so forth.

We can applaud the courage of those who demonstrate. We should endorse the issue they represent. We must love them as Christian brothers and sisters. But we must still say that it is not right to trespass on others' property. It is not right to make it difficult for people to enter abortion clinics, if they choose to do so. Above all, it is not right to invade the clinics, destroy records and equipment, or do things that are even worse.

The problem in this area can be seen in the Florida case in which one demonstrator shot and killed a doctor who had been performing abortions. The act was not courageous or godly. It was murder.

I want to make every allowance for the right exercise of the consciences of other people in these areas. I understand that many feel they must do something to attract attention to the evil that exists rather than do nothing. But as Charles Colson observes in *Kingdoms in Conflict*, "In our day, breaking laws to make a dramatic point is the ultimate logic of terrorism, not civil disobedience."[2] And what is also true, "Civil disobedience, like law itself, is habit-

2. Charles Colson, with Ellen Santilli Vaughn, *Kingdoms in Conflict* (Grand Rapids: a co-publication of William Morrow and Zondervan Publishing House, 1987), p. 250.

forming, and the habit it forms is destructive of law."[3] Rightly practiced civil disobedience has its place. But we have to be very careful how we use it and what we may be unleashing if we do.

What Is Needed

There is no moment in all of life in which we must be more diligent to hear and obey the Word of God in Scripture as when we are calling on another person or group to do the same. We tend to be self-righteous at the best of times. But we are especially self-righteous when we embark on a crusade. At times we must indeed disobey. Caesar is not God, and though we must render to Caesar what is Caesar's, we must be careful to give God what is God's. May God give us grace to know the difference.

---

3. A statement made by Harvard law professor Alexander Bickel, quoted in Colson, *Kingdoms in Conflict*, p. 251.

201

The Power of the Sword

Romans 13:3–4

For rulers hold no terror for those who do right, but for those who do wrong. Do you want to be free from fear of the one in authority? Then do what is right and he will commend you. For he is God's servant to do you good. But if you do wrong, be afraid, for he does not bear the sword for nothing. He is God's servant, an agent of wrath to bring punishment on the wrongdoer.

We are studying the Christian doctrine of the state—that is, of God-ordained government—and we come in this study to a word that in our day is often on people's tongues: *power.* Everyone is interested in power. We want to have power over our own lives. We speak about empowering people. We refer to power trips. Men buy power ties. Even the church is into power, so much so that recently a book called *Power Religion* appeared to oppose this sad trend.[1]

The reason we come to power now is that it emerges in Romans 13 as a second reason why Christians should submit to the secular authorities. We

1. Michael Scott Horton, editor, *Power Religion: The Selling Out of the Evangelical Church?* (Chicago: Moody Press, 1992).

examined the first reason in our study of verse 2: God has established them, so if we resist those who have been raised up to govern us, we are resisting God and God will judge us accordingly. The second reason we should obey is that the state will judge us too. That is, we will get in trouble because the state has *power* to enforce its decrees and laws.

Paul expressed this idea by writing, "For rulers hold no terror for those who do right, but for those who do wrong. Do you want to be free from fear of the one in authority? Then do what is right and he will commend you. For he is God's servant to do you good. But if you do wrong, be afraid, for he does not bear the sword for nothing. He is God's servant, an agent of wrath to bring punishment on the wrongdoer" (Rom. 13:3–4). In these verses the power of government is expressed by the symbol of a sword.

Government by Force

Power of the sword means force. This is what the state has been given by God, and it is the very basis for how the state conducts its affairs.

We do not like to think about this very much, because forcing someone to do something is not supposed to be good in our "free" society. Think of raising children, for example. Most people today think it is bad to force children to do anything. So instead of saying, "Make your bed" or "Eat your dinner or else," we give them options, presenting the good as "being in their best interest," or offering them rewards instead of punishments. We say, "Would you rather eat your dinner now or for breakfast?" or even "Would you rather eat your potatoes or your spinach first?" Even as adults we often bristle as soon as someone says that we have to do something.

Because of this cultural mind-set, whenever we think of government, especially if it is one we favor, we refuse to think of it as existing or operating by force. Instead we think of it as giving moral guidance and appealing to the best in its people while providing an environment for self-fulfillment or expression. We will admit that totalitarian systems like the former communist states of Eastern Europe operated by force. That is what was wrong with them, we think. But we suppose that our government must be different—or at least we hope it is.

But it is not! "Kinder and gentler" perhaps, its cast-iron fist hidden by a velvet glove. But it too is based on force, for the simple reason that every government is based on force. That is the nature of governments. There is no other way in which they can operate.

For example, we have a system of so-called voluntary self-assessment of income tax in this country. When you fill out your form each April you can read on the front of the tax booklet that we are a country unique in the world in that each year millions of Americans "voluntarily" assess their own tax and "voluntarily" pay those billions of dollars that keep the government running. How wonderful—"voluntary self-assessment." But it is not truly voluntary, of course. If you refuse to pay your income tax, you will be billed for the deficient amount, plus interest. And if you refuse to pay even then, you will be arrested and your assets seized to pay the delinquent taxes.

Paying taxes is not voluntary at all. It is mandatory, and the proof that it is mandatory is the government's final use of force to accomplish its objectives.

Let me give you another example. Suppose you are a businessman who is becoming bogged down by the increasing number of government laws regulating your business. You have so many areas in which you need to comply and so many forms to fill out that you decide that you just will not fill them out this year. What will happen? The government will close your business and possibly even arrest you.

In this study I want to explore the areas in which this power, given to the state by God, is to operate. But before I do that, let me note that the right to enforce laws by force is a right given to the state and not the church. When Jesus was tried by Pilate he acknowledged Pilate's authority over him, which included the right even to put him to death. But Jesus did not claim that power for himself or his followers. When questioned about his kingdom, he replied that his kingdom was a kingdom of truth: "For this I came into the world, to testify to the truth. Everyone on the side of truth listens to me" (John 18:37).

The church has always gotten into trouble when it has tried to take the state's power—that is, force—into its own hands. The church tried to do this in the Middle Ages, after Christianity had been embraced by Constantine as the religion of the empire. But the result was disastrous for the church. The leaders of the church became power hungry, true religion diminished, and corruption increased.

Religious leaders make bad rulers, because secular power seems to corrupt them even more than it corrupts secular rulers. Therefore, the power of the sword has been given to Caesar, not the church, and it must not be used to advance the cause of Christ. Caesar alone has the right to cut off heads.

Civil and Social Order

Nevertheless, when we say that the power of the sword has been given to the state, we do not mean that this power can be exercised in any way whatsoever, or that the state can do by the exercise of power what the church alone is able to do by its proclamation of the gospel and the truth. Let's look at each of these.

1. *The state's power, however legitimate it may be when used in the areas for which God has given it, cannot be exercised in any way whatsoever.* The state has no God-given right to massacre its citizens, for instance. It has no right to use its power to advance evil. Paul makes this clear in Romans 13:3–4, when he speaks repeatedly of those who do good and those who do evil, and of the state's exercise of its power to reward those who do the one and punish those who do the other.

How, then, is the power of the sword to be used? First, the state is given power to defend its citizens from both enemies outside the state and evildoers within. It has power to wage war, including all necessary powers that go with it: power to conscript its people into the armed forces, power to tax for the war effort, power to redirect the nation's economy to a wartime footing. These are legitimate powers, but they are justified only by the need for the common defense. The power to regulate the economy in order to wage war does not necessarily carry over into peacetime, for example.

The state also has power to defend its citizens from evildoers within. That is, it has been given responsibility to provide and maintain social order. The biblical writers seem to have been particularly concerned about this, probably because they were more aware than most of us of how terrible anarchy can be. Nobody is safe in such times, so even a bad government is to be preferred to chaos. That is one reason why we are told to pray even for evil rulers. Paul told Timothy, "I urge, then, first of all, that requests, prayers, intercession and thanksgiving be made *for everyone*—for kings and all those in authority, that we may live peaceful and quiet lives in all godliness and holiness" (1 Tim. 2:1–2). Social order is good by itself, but it is particularly good for Christians because it gives us an opportunity to advance the gospel.

The church can remind the authorities of this good role and urge them to it. John Calvin said, "Magistrates may learn from this the nature of their calling. They are not to rule on their own account, but for the public good. Nor do they have unbridled power, but power that is restricted to the welfare of their subjects."[2]

The second area in which government has been given power by God is in establishing, exercising, and maintaining justice—that is, in rewarding good behavior and punishing bad behavior. This is what Paul chiefly has in mind in these verses when he says, "For rulers hold no terror for those who do right, but for those who do wrong. Do you want to be free from fear of the one in authority? Then do what is right and he will commend you. For he is God's servant to do you good. But if you do wrong, be afraid, for he does not bear the sword for nothing. He is God's servant, an agent of wrath to bring punishment on the wrongdoer."

There are two matters here, each enormously important now. First, a conviction that there are such things as good and evil is critical. For when Paul says that the state has been given power to punish evil, he is assuming a moral standard to which not only the individual citizen but also the state must conform. In other words, the state should reward what is good and punish what is evil, but in order to do that the state must know what the good is, and for that there must be an objective moral standard outside itself, either discovered by it or given to it.

2. John Calvin, *The Epistles of Paul the Apostle to the Romans and to the Thessalonians*, trans. Ross MacKenzie (Grand Rapids: Wm. B. Eerdmans Publishing Company, 1973), p. 282.

This is extremely relevant today because American law has gone through a revolution in this area. John W. Whitehead has written a book about this called *The Second American Revolution*.[3] This revolution Whitehead is writing about is the current rejection of rule by law that is objective and unchanging for a malleable sociological law that can be determined by the jurists.

Let me explain. In 1907 Supreme Court Justice Charles Evans Hughes expressed the sociological understanding of law for the first time officially when he said, "The Constitution is what the judges say it is." He meant that the justices are not bound by an absolute law. Instead, they are free to find whatever they want in the law and even to change it. So there is no appeal beyond what the Supreme Court decides, even if it is contrary to what the Constitution or any other laws meant years ago.

When the Constitution was written, however, its authors intended something very different. They meant that law was supreme. Therefore, ours was to be a country governed by laws and not by men, even Supreme Court justices. This idea came into American jurisprudence from the Scottish Presbyterian Samuel Rutherford and his monumental work *Lex Rex*, meaning "law is king," and through such figures as the English jurist William Blackstone, who worked it into English common law, and John Witherspoon, the only minister to sign the Declaration of Independence, who worked it into our Constitution.

Incidentally, it is only because the colonists believed in an absolute law to which even magistrates were responsible that they judged themselves right to rebel against England. It was because King George had violated the rights of "life and liberty," which had been given to them by "the Laws of Nature and of Nature's God," that they rebelled.

The points here are that the state's ability to act justly depends upon absolute law and that this approach to the state's authority is the only genuinely Christian one. Apart from this everything becomes relative, the possibility of achieving equal justice for all is eventually destroyed, and the citizens become subject to the changing whims of their judges.

2. *The state cannot reform evildoers by power.* The power of the sword has been given to the state to defend its citizens and to punish wrongdoing only. Or, to put it in other words, the state has a God-given responsibility to punish bad or evil behavior, but it has no authority—and even less power—to actually change or reform the evildoer.

No one has seen this with greater clarity or expressed it with greater insight than C. S. Lewis in an essay called "The Humanitarian Theory of Punishment."[4] In this essay Lewis distinguishes between the old idea of retributive justice, in which a person who has done something bad is punished in accor-

---

3. John W. Whitehead, *The Second American Revolution* (Elgin, Ill.: David C. Cook, 1982).

4. C. S. Lewis, "The Humanitarian Theory of Punishment" in *God in the Dock: Essays on Theology and Ethics* (Grand Rapids: Wm. B. Eerdmans Publishing Company, 1970), pp. 287–94.

dance with what he or she has done, and the humanitarian idea of justice, in which the person is disciplined in order to reform him.

The first is based on "desert," to use the old word for it. It means that the murderer is given a longer time in jail than the petty thief because the first is a greater crime and the murderer deserves a greater punishment. The second is based on what someone thinks might help or cure the criminal.

Our system is a mixture, of course. Jail sentences are proportionate to the degree of crimes involved. But we also mitigate these on the basis of whether a prisoner is well-behaved or, in the case of crime judged to flow from mental illness, whether the person is cured. We see a practical expression of the second idea in the fact that we call our prisons penitentiaries—places where people are to do penance—or reformatories—places where they can be reformed.

Lewis argues that, although the humanitarian view seems compassionate and thus enlightened (it claims to want only the well-being of the criminal), it is actually cruel, for several reasons.

First, it takes determination of the nature and length of the penalty out of the hands of judges, who affix it for all according to an objective legal standard, and places it in the hands of psychological experts who alone may determine when the criminal is well.

Second, it debases the person involved. Instead of being a responsible moral agent, capable of doing wrong but also capable of paying a proper punishment for it, the criminal becomes a thing to be worked upon by the experts until he is "well" by their definition. This is what was done in the Soviet Union to political prisoners, for example.

And that leads to the third reason. Lewis writes, "If crime and disease are to be regarded as the same thing, it follows that any state of mind which our masters choose to call 'disease' can be treated as crime; and compulsorily cured."[5] That should be of concern to Christians, if to no one else, because Christianity has never been popular, and in the name of curing our "antisocial" or "humanity-hating" beliefs or actions, any government that is powerful enough could lock us up until we are "cured" ideologically.

Of course, what Romans 13 is saying is that the state has no business trying to cure people, only that it is mandated by God to punish bad behavior and reward good actions. Therefore, the state must have a standard of right and wrong, and it must administer that standard impartially. That is all government really can do in the long run.

Where Are God's People?

Two final points are needed to round out this picture of government and its proper use of power:

5. Lewis, "The Humanitarian Theory," p. 293.

1. *Government cannot develop morality.* Government can only punish; it cannot develop morality in its citizens. The important word in that statement is *develop,* of course. For I am not saying that government is not to be concerned with morality. On the contrary, morality is precisely what it is to be concerned with, for morality is the only true basis for law.

For example, if the government passes a law against stealing and enforces it with the power of the sword, the only valid basis for the law and the penalty affixed for breaking it is that stealing is wrong. Or to put it another way, there is a God-given right to private property. If stealing is not wrong, then the act of government to oppose it and punish it is tyranny—an unjustifiable restriction of freedom. If stealing is wrong, then the government is acting properly. It is the same with all laws. The only valid basis for any law is a previously existing morality.

To give another example, in the case of capital punishment the only valid base for the right of the government to take a life of one who has taken the life of another is Genesis 9:6, which says that the murderer may be killed because he has killed one made "in the image of God." This means that his act was a violation of the law of God and an offense to God.

Nevertheless, this valid concern for morality does not mean that the government can develop morality in its citizens, for it cannot. It can proscribe penalties. It can enforce them and thus perhaps also restrain evil somewhat. But it cannot change the people involved.

A case in point was Prohibition. Government outlawed traffic in alcoholic beverages. But although the trade was restricted a bit, the sale of alcohol nevertheless flourished, and it erupted into a storm as soon as Prohibition was repealed.

2. *Morality comes from revealed religion.* If government cannot develop morality in its citizens, then morality must come in another way and from another source. What can that source be? Where can morality come from? There is only one answer. It comes from revealed religion, and it must work its way into national life through those citizens who know and sincerely desire to please God.

Religious people are, therefore, the best asset a country can have and the only thing that will advance it in the direction of justice and true righteousness. So today the need is not for more laws. If we do not have a moral citizenry, even the laws can be used immorally. They can be used to get out of paying one's debts, escape a prison sentence, cheat the innocent, oppress the poor, and many such things. What we need are people who know and are willing to live by the moral laws of God.

Remember 2 Chronicles 7:14. That great Old Testament text does not offer healing for a nation through the election of a better president or the ouster of an old one. It does not even recommend passing better laws. It proscribes renewal through the repentance of God's people: "If my people, who are called by my name, will humble themselves and pray and seek my face and turn from their wicked ways, then will I hear from heaven and will forgive their sin and will heal their land."

202

Because of Conscience

Romans 13:5

Therefore, it is necessary to submit to the authorities, not only because of possible punishment but also because of conscience.

One of the greatest delights of studying the Bible carefully, as all of us should do, is that we frequently come upon unexpected but very wonderful things.

For example, the account of God's creation of the heavenly bodies in Genesis 1 reads: "And God said, 'Let there be lights in the expanse of the sky to separate the day from the night, and let them serve as signs to mark seasons and days and years, and let them be lights in the expanse of the sky to give light on the earth.' And it was so. God made two great lights—the greater light to govern the day and the lesser light to govern the night. *He also made the stars*" (Gen. 1:14–16).

"He also made the stars!"

What an amazing, unexpected and utterly understated line—"Oh, yes, and also the billions of blazing stars, supernovas, black holes, galaxies and quasars. That, too." I remember that Malcolm Muggeridge called those five words one of the greatest "throw-away lines" in literary history.

1663

And Don't Forget Conscience

There is something like that in the verse we come to in this study, particularly in the word with which it ends: "conscience."

Paul is writing about the proper function of government and why Christians should be exemplary in their submission to its legitimate authority. There are two reasons, and they are both powerful. First, we should submit to the governing authorities because "the authorities that exist have been established by God. Consequently, he who rebels against the authority is rebelling against what God has instituted, and those who do so will bring judgment on themselves" (Rom. 13:1–2). That is, if we resist the state, we are resisting God and God will judge us. The second reason, which we examined in the last study, is that the state will judge us too. "If you do wrong, be afraid, for he does not bear the sword for nothing" (v. 4). The state will insist that we obey it and will punish us if we do not.

Here are two good reasons for submitting to the civil government. But then, just when we think Paul has made his point thoroughly and is about to wrap up, he adds almost as an afterthought, "Oh, yes, and also because of conscience." The full verse says, "Therefore, it is necessary to submit to the authorities, not only because of possible punishment but also because of conscience."

I call this an understatement, or a throw-away line compared to "he also made the stars," because conscience is not a small thing of little importance but rather a large thing of very great importance. Conscience involves our sense of what is right and wrong and, even more importantly, our awareness that we ought to do what is right. In other words, when Paul speaks of conscience, as he does here, he suddenly lifts the discussion of submission to the governing authorities from what we might call a merely pragmatic level to the highest possible plane. For now, instead of saying, "You should obey the state because you will get in trouble if you don't," he says, "You should obey the state because that is the right thing to do, and you know you should do what is right."

Let me say this another way. Instead of treating us as we might treat an animal, training it to respond mechanically by rewarding desired behavior and punishing undesirable behavior, Paul treats people as responsible moral agents—that is, as human beings made in God's image—by appealing to our consciences.

What Is the Conscience?

The conscience seems to have been more important to Paul than to any other biblical writer. In the New International Version of the Bible the word *conscience* occurs twenty-nine times, but only four of those occurrences are in the Old Testament.[1] Twenty-five are in the New Testament, and twenty of those are in Paul's speeches or writings, quite a few being in 1 and

---

1. Genesis 20:5–6; 1 Samuel 25:31; Job 27:6.

2 Corinthians.[2] Aside from Paul's use of the word, there are in addition only three occurrences in Hebrews and two in 1 Peter.[3]

The word *conscience* is composed of two Latin words: *con*, meaning with, and *scientia*, meaning knowledge. So conscience means "with knowledge." Specifically, it has to do with knowledge of one's heart or inner motivations as contrasted with one's actions.

This is the way the word normally appears in English literature. But because we are sinners and know ourselves to be sinners, "conscience" usually is employed in a negative way as something that condemns us. For example, in *Richard III*, Richard, who was a very evil king, says:

> My conscience hath a thousand several tongues,
> And every tongue brings in a several tale,
> And every tale condemns me for a villain.
>
> *Richard III*, Act 5, Scene 3

The word is used the same way in *Hamlet*. Referring to the play that Hamlet uses to expose the king's treacherous murder of his father, Hamlet says:

> The play's the thing
> Wherein I'll catch the conscience of the king.
>
> *Hamlet*, Act 2, Scene 2

In *Paradise Lost* John Milton says of Satan:

> Now conscience wakes despair
> That slumber'd, wakes the bitter memory
> Of what he was, what is, and what must be.
>
> *Paradise Lost*, Book 4, Line 23

These uses of the word, and others like them, are mostly negative, and with reason. We are guilty of many offenses and our consciences usually condemn us.

But now consider Paul's use of the word. Paul is aware that a person's conscience can be weak (1 Cor. 8:7, 10, 12), and he knows that our consciences can condemn us, since he speaks of striving "always to keep my conscience clear before God and man" (Acts 24:16). But generally Paul speaks of a "good conscience" (1 Tim. 1:5, 19) and a "clear conscience" (1 Tim. 3:9; 2 Tim. 1:3). He told the Sanhedrin, "My brothers, I have fulfilled my duty to God in all good conscience to this day" (Acts 23:1). To the Corinthians he wrote, "Our conscience testifies that we have conducted ourselves in the world, and especially in our relations with you, in the holiness and sincerity that are from

2. Acts 23:1, 24:16; Romans 9:1, 13:5; 1 Corinthians 4:4, 8:7, 8:10, 8:12, 10:25, 10:27 (twice); 2 Corinthians 1:12, 4:2, 5:11; 1 Timothy 1:5, 1:19, 3:9; 2 Timothy 1:3.
3. Hebrews 9:9, 10:22, 13:18; 1 Peter 3:16, 3:21.

God" (2 Cor. 1:12). Again, "By setting forth the truth plainly we commend ourselves to every man's conscience in the sight of God" (2 Cor. 4:2).

There is an enormous difference here between the use of *conscience* by secular writers and its characteristic biblical use. The reason is that God has quickened the Christian's moral nature so that he or she not only knows what is right as opposed to what is wrong but also has been given a true desire and ability to do what conscience demands.

What This Means for Government

But we are talking about the role of conscience as it applies to the Christian's relationship to civil government, not to moral matters in general. So we need to ask what is involved here when Paul says, "Therefore, it is necessary to submit to the authorities, not only because of possible punishment but also because of conscience."

1. *We have a higher motive for obeying than others have.* Paul's main point in this section is that Christians are to obey the secular authorities, and the first reason he has given is that God has established human governments. That is something that Christians can alone fully appreciate. But even this can appeal to a low motivation if all we mean by it is that God will punish those who disobey the civil governments he has set up. However, when Paul brings in the matter of the conscience, he is saying also that we must obey because obedience is right and because, being responsible moral agents, we ought to do the right thing.

In adding this standard Paul also raises our significance as responsible agents and tells us that what we do really matters. Paul is telling us that our obedience to the secular authorities matters, and that this is a very good reason why we should be careful to do it. It matters to God, of course. He cares whether or not you obey him. But it also matters to society. If you take obedience to the laws of the country lightly—if you say, "Well, everyone is doing it" or "They're crazy laws anyway" or "It's not my law; I didn't write it or vote for it"—if you do that, then you are contributing to a spirit of lawlessness that will issue in anarchy and eventually lead to the loss of civil liberties and to a dictatorial government. On the other hand, if you obey the laws of the land, you will be contributing to society by helping to sustain a stable and liberty-respecting government.

One of the great tragedies of our country today is that many people have little or no respect for authority and therefore feel free to break any laws that seem inconvenient to them. So civil disorder is rising. The police are unable to contain the disorder. The courts are overworked, and the nation's prisons are overflowing.

2. *We have a stronger reason for disobeying when disobedience becomes necessary.* I pointed out in an earlier study that there are limits to the authority that has been granted civil government. This is because authority by its very nature is "given," in this case God-given, and the one given governmental authority

is therefore responsible to God. The government has no right to forbid the free exercise or propagation of religion. No secular ruler has the right to violate the Ten Commandments or force others to do so. The government has no right to compel Christians to commit unjust acts or to act contrary to an informed Christian conscience.

But that is the important point here. Conscience! A Christian should have an enlightened moral conscience because he should know the Word of God, and because he possesses the Holy Spirit to help him understand it. Also, because he has a new nature the Christian should have a stronger desire to exercise that conscience rightly. A secular ruler might know a right course of action but decide not to pursue it simply because it might be inconvenient, not in his own selfish interests, opposed by his friends, or for any other number of reasons.

The Christian cannot think this way. Therefore, regardless of whether an action is convenient, personally advantageous, or popular, the Christian ought to pursue the right course of action.

This means that a Christian will stand against the state when it does wrong, regardless of the consequences. The world may say, "You'll never get ahead if you do that." But the Christian will ask not whether the position is advantageous or popular, but whether the position itself is right and will act accordingly. Governments have often been wrong. Our own government is frequently wrong. Christians will stand against those wrong actions and for the right "because of conscience."

The Exercise of Conscience

As soon as I write that "our own government is frequently wrong" I am sure I stir up defensive reactions in some people, and many will ask for examples.

1. *Abortion.* Most evangelical people think of abortion when we think of the government being wrong, and we are dismayed that the Clinton administration favors the right of abortion on demand. We believe abortion is wrong because the fetus is not "tissue," as the pro-choice forces like to think of it, but a tiny human being. We believe abortion is murder and that God will not hold us guiltless for the murder of more than a million and a half babies every year.

What are we to do about it? We are to protest it, of course, explaining our position and arguing our case. I have already pointed out that we will get nowhere if all we do is adopt the world's methodology—sit-ins and pressure tactics and more laws. The world will use that against us, and has. Instead, we need to explain that the only view of mankind that protects us from exploitation by tyrannical rulers or others is that we are made in the image of God and are therefore valuable to God, even in an embryonic state. We need to show that the disenfranchising of the unborn child is no different than the once-popular defense of slavery by calling blacks less than human or the murder of Jews by calling them a threat to society. We must show that human beings are *all* made in God's image and therefore must not be destroyed for anyone's convenience, even that of the mother.

2. *Pornography.* We have a strong and valuable tradition of the right of free speech and free expression in this country, and it is something we do not want to lose. We do not want to take away people's right to express their opinions in print or by graphic media. But no freedom is utterly without limits. Someone said, "Your freedom ends where my nose begins." So when we deal with pornography we need to say that freedom to print sexually obscene material stops at the point at which it harms others.

And it does harm others. Defenders of the pornography industry deny this, of course, just as makers of cigarettes deny that cigarettes cause lung cancer, emphysema, and other lung-related illnesses. But in this case, it is our job to show that pornography really is harmful. We need to document our case. We need to remind people that Ted Bundy, who in 1989 was executed for multiple serial murders of young women in Florida and elsewhere, said on death row that the chief contributing influence to his violent murderous course was pornography. We need to highlight the Federal Bureau of Investigation report that convincingly links pornography to sex-related murders and the study of the Michigan State Police that linked pornography to 40 percent of its assault cases.[4]

The Reverend Donald E. Wildmon has been making this case through the American Family Association (formerly the National Federation for Decency), which he has directed since its founding in 1977.

What can one person do, or even a group of persons? I can tell you what one man did. His name is Jack Eckerd, and when he became a Christian in 1983 he decided that selling *Playboy* and *Penthouse* magazines in his extensive drugstore chain was displeasing to God. He called his company's president and told him that he wanted the pornographic magazines removed from all seventeen hundred Eckerd drugstores. The president protested because the sales brought in millions of dollars for the firm, but Eckerd persisted and won. He owned the stores.

Moreover, his action caused something of a chain reaction. One by one Revco, Peoples, Rite-Aid, Dart Drug, Grey Drug, and High's Dairy Stores followed Eckerd's lead. The last hold-out was 7-Eleven, which in 1986 finally removed pornography from all forty-five hundred of its stores and recommended that its thirty-six hundred franchises do the same.[5]

All this happened without a single law being passed. Why? Because of conscience.

3. *Gun control.* It is incredible to me that there are so few serious actions being taken in our country to control the use of guns, particularly since scores of people are being shot in America every single hour. Our papers and television news shows are full of the stories. The reason why there is so little action is the powerful gun

4. See Charles Colson, with Ellen Santilli Vaughn, *The God of Stones and Spiders: Letters to a Church in Exile* (Wheaton: Crossway Books, 1990), p. 42.

5. Ibid., p. 40.

lobby. It argues that the right to bear arms is guaranteed by our Constitution, and that is right. But the Constitution does not mean that we cannot insist on licensing guns, just as we license cars, or that we cannot ban the use of some guns in the same way we do not allow people to drive tanks or armored personnel carriers on our highways. We should not allow felons to own guns.

People argue that criminals will get guns anyway; we cannot stop them. But that is irrelevant. Of course, they will. But when they are caught with an unlicensed gun, they need to be prosecuted for that. Yet this is not my chief concern. My concern is not with the specific laws to be passed. I am not in the business of writing laws. What I am calling for is an outpouring of conscience in the matter of gun availability and the mushrooming of gun-caused murders. The Christian's task is to cry out against the evil and not stop crying until something is done about it.

4. *Public schools.* And what about the public schools? I am not insisting here that prayers and Bible readings ought to be reinstated. Many Christians doubt that is a good idea. My concern is with the education itself. In many schools education is not even happening. And even where it does happen, it happens in an ethical environment that is destructive of character and even sound citizenship. People who have values should not be forced to submit to this system. They should be free to create other options and not be penalized even financially by having to pay for their own systems while at the same time being required to support the disasters that pass for schools in their communities.

Our task should be to expose the failures and encourage alternatives, even good secular ones. We need to defend everybody, not just our own interests. We need to call for voucher systems or something like them.

Conscience and the Word of God

This is far from a full social agenda for the Christian community but only an example of the function of Christian conscience in our world.

But let me caution that one of our great dangers as Christians is pride, and by that I mean that we easily assume that only our consciences have been enlightened and that we alone have the right answers. We do not. We need to listen to others, particularly well-informed non-Christians. And we need to remember that our consciences are valuable only when they are themselves enlightened by the written Word of God.

One writer has compared the human conscience to a sundial. It is not a perfect timepiece, but it is fairly accurate—as long as the sun is shining on it. Suppose you consult it by moonlight. In that case, it might tell any time at all. It might say that it is noon when it is actually three o'clock in the morning. The sundial is only valuable when the sun is shining on it. In the same manner, the conscience is only valuable when it is illuminated by the Word of God. We need people who will stand for the right and do the right "because of conscience." But if you start a crusade, be sure the position you take is biblical and that you are not merely serving yourself or enhancing your own crusading reputation.

203

To Each His Due

Romans 13:6-7

This is also why you pay taxes, for the authorities are God's servants, who give their full time to governing. Give everyone what you owe him: If you owe taxes, pay taxes; if revenue, then revenue; if respect, then respect; if honor, then honor.

No one likes to pay taxes or, for that matter, thinks very charitably about tax collectors. Yet that is the point at which Paul's treatment of the rights of civil government and a Christian's responsibility to it end. We are to pay our taxes and in every other way rightly honor those who are in authority over us, even tax collectors.

When we analyze what this means we find that these last two verses of Paul's teaching about the Christian and his or her relationship to civil government have two parts. The first part says we need to pay taxes. The second part is about showing respect and giving honor to those who deserve respect and who should be shown honor. The verses say, "This is also why you pay taxes, for the authorities are God's servants, who give their full time to governing. Give everyone what you owe him: If you owe taxes, pay taxes; if revenue, then revenue; if respect, then respect; if honor, then honor" (Rom. 13:6-7).

No One Likes to Pay Taxes

This is hard to do. The famous French philosopher and author François Voltaire was having a dinner party with two of his witty friends, and he suggested that they entertain themselves by each improvising a story about thieves. His two friends each told an amusing story and was praised for it. It was then Voltaire's turn. "Gentlemen," he said, "there was once a tax collector. . . . Good Lord, I've forgotten the rest of the story."

Victor Amadeus, the Duke of Savoy who became King of Sicily and later King of Sardinia, taxed his subjects severely. Once he stopped a working man and asked how he was getting along. "About as well as things can go in a holy land like ours," he answered.

"Holy land?" said Amadeus. "I don't understand."

"Well, we must be a holy land because here the Passion of our Savior repeats itself, only in reverse."

"Reverse?"

"Yes," said the peasant. "In those olden days One died for all. Here all of us die for one."[1]

Supporting Government through Taxes

There are probably a hundred stories like these because no one likes to pay taxes. Yet in Romans 13:6–7 Paul joins with Jesus in saying that this is one important responsibility of a Christian. A Christian is to support his government by paying taxes.

The reason, of course, is that government is expensive and we benefit by it in countless ways, even if we have a bad government. In his commentary on Romans, Ray Stedman, the former senior minister of the Peninsula Bible Church near San Francisco, tells how when he was first a minister he made so little money that for years he didn't have to pay any taxes at all and that it came as a shock to him when one year he finally had to do so. He resented it. So when he mailed in his tax return that year he addressed it to "The *Infernal* Revenue Service." That didn't seem to bother the tax collectors. They took his money anyway. The next year he addressed it to "The *Eternal* Revenue Service," but that didn't bother them either. After that he gave up and settled into the same resigned attitude that most of us have for at least the first two weeks in April every year.[2]

But resignation is not the right attitude. Rather, when we pay our federal taxes we should be thankful for the armed forces those taxes support and for the peace and national security we enjoy because of them. Taxes support the courts and numerous federal agencies from which we benefit. We have

---

1. The stories are from Clifton Fadiman, general editor, *The Little, Brown Book of Anecdotes* (Boston and Toronto: Little, Brown and Company, 1985), pp. 562, 566.

2. Ray C. Stedman, *From Guilt to Glory*, vol. 2, *Reveling in God's Salvation* (Portland, Oreg.: Multnomah, 1978), p. 145.

national parks, federal drug enforcement agencies, food inspectors, the center for infectious diseases, the Federal Bureau of Investigation, air traffic controllers, and other indispensable services. When we pay our state taxes we should be thankful for the state's funding of universities, some city services, maintenance of state highways, and the courts. City taxes fund schools, garbage collection, firefighters, and police.

We may complain about taxes, but without them government could not function, civilization would be impossible, and our lives and property would be in jeopardy every moment of every day.

Responsible Taxation

But although the state's authority and power are from God and are therefore to be respected, the state is nevertheless responsible to God for what it does with that power. This is true in the area of taxation also.

1. *A responsible use of taxed money.* One limitation on government in the area of taxation is that taxes are not to be used merely to increase the luxury and elevate the lifestyle of our governors. This is clear from the way Paul sets down these verses. For when he says that "the authorities are God's servants," he is saying that government officials are to use our taxes to serve the people and not to enrich themselves.

John Calvin expressed this well in his commentary:

Paul takes the opportunity of mentioning tributes, and he bases his reason for paying taxes on the office of the magistrates. If it is their responsibility to defend and preserve uninjured the peace of the upright and to resist the impious attempts of the wicked, they cannot do this unless they are assisted by force and strong protection. Tributes, therefore, are paid by law to support such necessities. . . . It is right, however, that they should remember that all that they receive from the people is public property, and not a means of satisfying private lust and luxury.[3]

We do not see abuses of this nature very much among the highest elected officials in our country because presidents, senators, and congressmen are under intense public scrutiny, and abuses in this area can be detected and used against them politically. Abuses that are too flagrant will result in their being put out of office at the next election.

However, we do have much abuse of public monies further down the scale. We see featherbedding of government agencies, far more people being employed than are necessary to do the job. We see bloated budgets and sometimes outright graft or the placing of family members on the payroll to do nonexistent jobs. Many abuses occur at the level of city government, and from

---

3. John Calvin, *The Epistles of Paul the Apostle to the Romans and to the Thessalonians*, trans. Ross MacKenzie (Grand Rapids: Wm. B. Eerdmans Publishing Company, 1973), pp. 283–84.

time to time these bring even the largest and most prosperous cities to the brink of bankruptcy.

2. *Confiscatory taxation.* The second abuse about which the government needs to be especially on guard is confiscatory taxation, which means making taxes so high that the government is, in effect, stealing from its people and thus eventually ruining both itself and the country.

This is a tremendous danger, and it is one the founders and early leaders of our country recognized. In fact, it is why they insisted on "no taxation without representation" in the struggles with England that led to the War of Independence. Our forefathers recognized that representative government is the only safeguard against having one's possessions at the mercy of a king or any other strong ruler, and they were willing to venture their lives and sacred honor for that safeguard. One of our earliest chief justices, John Marshall, said, "The power to tax is the power to destroy." Another justice, Oliver Wendell Holmes, expressed this same concern from the point of view of prohibiting destructive tax legislation. He said, "The power to tax [will not be] the power to destroy while this court sits."

This is a difficult area, of course. For it is like asking, "When is long too long?" or "When is short too short?" Those are relative terms, and everything depends on the objects involved and the circumstances.

When are taxes too much? That depends on the condition of the economy and of the world. In a robust economy taxation can be higher as the state uses its higher share of taxes to do more to develop the country and enrich people's lives. In times when people are struggling just to make ends meet, the government has to ease up. Greater taxation is required in times of war than when the country is at peace. In peacetime there really should be something like a "peace dividend," as there was after World War II. It should not be an open door for the state merely to spend more on government programs.

What about the graded income tax? Is that just? No, of course it is not just. We speak of the rich paying their "fair" share. But fairness is the one thing that cannot be said of taking more taxes from those who make more. Fairness would require that we tax everyone equally. Taxing the rich more may be expedient. It may be the only place money can be found in recessionary times or in a failing economy. But it is not just, and in the long run it hurts the national economy since accumulated capital is the only source of funding for new business projects. When the government taxes the rich excessively it mortgages the future for short-term economic gain.

Today spending by our national government is out of control. Most of our elected officials lack courage to stop the excess and reduce the federal budget, not to mention the escalating deficit. Some officials actually want to spend more.

Let me make a radical proposal. Under our system those who do well by making more money are penalized. They are taxed more than others. Shouldn't there be a system under which, if you make more money (or at least if you develop or control a business that makes more money), you should be rewarded? Wouldn't we see greater prosperity if, when people made more, taxes for those people actually went down? In one of Jesus' parables the servant who invested the ten talents he had in order to make ten more was rewarded by being given ten cities, and the man who increased his five talents by adding five more talents was given five cities. As for the man who had been given one talent but failed to use it, his talent was taken away from him and given to the man who had ten! (Luke 19:11–27).

Respect and Honor

How government should conduct itself in the area of taxation was not Paul's concern, of course. He was concerned about how Christians are to function. So at this point he broadens his words from taxes to talk about proper respect and honor. "Give everyone what you owe him," he says, adding after taxes, "if respect, then respect; if honor, then honor." This verse is a bridge to the next section of Romans, in which Paul writes about loving one another, because honor should be shown to many kinds of people and not only to government officials.

A quick look through a concordance brings out several categories of those we are to honor.

1. *The king.* We have been studying a Christian's responsibility to those exercising civic responsibilities, so a good place to start is with the Bible's commands to "honor the king" and all who, like him, are in high positions of authority.

In words that are very close to Paul's, Peter writes:

Submit yourselves for the Lord's sake to every authority instituted among men: whether to the king, as the supreme authority, or to governors, who are sent by him to punish those who do wrong and to commend those who do right. For it is God's will that by doing good you should silence the ignorant talk of foolish men. Live as free men, but do not use your freedom as a cover-up for evil; live as servants of God. Show proper respect to everyone: Love the brotherhood of believers, fear God, *honor the king.*

1 Peter 2:13–17

When Paul was arrested and brought before the Sanhedrin he spoke of having fulfilled his duty to God in all good conscience, and at that point the high priest ordered those standing near him to strike him on the mouth because they thought his words were arrogant. Paul knew this was illegal under Jewish law since he had not been convicted of anything. So he replied, "God will strike you, you whitewashed wall! You sit there to judge me according to the law, yet you yourself violate the law by commanding that I be struck" (Acts 23:3).

Those who were standing by rebuked Paul for talking so disrespectfully to the high priest. Paul then replied, "Brothers, I did not realize that he was the high priest; for it is written: 'Do not speak evil about the ruler of your people'" (v. 5). The quotation is from Exodus 22:28.

We honor the king and those who are over us by refusing to speak of them disrespectfully, and we exercise a genuinely Christian responsibility toward them by praying for them. This includes officials of our city government as well as federal officials, police, firefighters, and schoolteachers.

2. *Church officers.* There are a number of verses that tell us to honor those who have been given authority in the churches. Paul told Timothy, "The elders who direct the affairs of the church well are *worthy of double honor*, especially those whose work is preaching and teaching" (1 Tim. 5:17). The author of Hebrews wrote of church leaders, "*Obey your leaders and submit* to their authority" (Heb. 13:17).

Again, there are helpful biblical examples of this. When Aaron led the people into idolatry by making the golden calf and Moses came down the mountain to the camp to punish the offenders, Moses did not dishonor Aaron publicly. He demanded to know what he had done. Aaron gave a lame excuse, blaming Moses for taking so long on the mountain, the people for their stiff-necked ways, and even magical circumstances, claiming that all he had done was throw the people's gold into the furnace and the calf had come out. Moses understood these excuses and lies for what they were, but he did not rebuke Aaron since Aaron had been appointed by God and it was for God to rebuke or remove him, not Moses. Moses seems to have let the interrogation of Aaron drop at this point (Exod. 32:21–24).

On the other side we have the story of Miriam, Moses' sister, who opposed Moses because he had married a Cushite woman—that is, probably a black woman. Moses did not defend himself, but God heard and punished Miriam with leprosy. It is a serious thing to speak or work against those whom God has appointed to positions of church authority.

3. *Parents.* The Ten Commandments contain another verse about those we are to honor, our parents. "*Honor your father and your mother*, so that you may live long in the land the Lord your God is giving you" (Exod. 20:12). Paul quotes this verse in Ephesians 6:2, noting that it is "the first commandment with a promise."

This is an important command and rightly heads the list of those on the second table of the law, commands expressing our duty toward other people. It is first because the family is the smallest unit of society and respect for family members, particularly parents, is foundational to family order and discipline. Children should be taught to respect their parents and should be punished if they do not. Because if we teach children to obey their parents, when they grow up they will be able to respect and obey others—teachers, policemen, magistrates, and God. We need to speak kindly to our parents, listen to their opinions, remember their birthdays, and care for them in their old age. If we do not respect our parents, whom we can see, how will we be able to respect and obey God, whom we cannot see?

4. *Older persons.* Leviticus is a difficult book, but it is filled with many important verses, and one of them is this: "Rise in the presence of the aged, *show respect for the elderly* and revere your God" (Lev. 19:32). How little we do that today! Instead of respecting older people we often despise them, thinking instead that the only people of value are the young. "Never trust anyone over thirty," they said in the sixties—but the sixties was not a decade of great wisdom.

5. *God.* If we are called to honor people who are in authority over us because of their appointments to office, because they are our parents, or because of their age, we obviously also need to respect and honor God. First Timothy 6:16 says of God the Father, "*To him be honor* and might forever. Amen." Similarly, John 5:22–23 says, "The Father judges no one, but has entrusted all judgment to the Son, *that all may honor the Son just as they honor the Father.* He who does not honor the Son does not honor the Father, who sent him."

How do we honor God? We do it by studying his Word that we may come to know him. When we discover something in his Word that he requires of us, we honor him by doing what he has commanded. We honor him by thanking him for all he has given and by praising him for all he is in and of himself. We honor God by trusting him through all the many trials and disappointments of life. We honor him by praising him as the source of whatever good may be found in us or whatever good we may do in this life.

We remember that in that wonderful scene in Revelation, when the saints stand before God represented by the twenty-four elders.

They lay their crowns before the throne and say:

"You are worthy, our Lord and God,
　　to receive glory and honor and power,
for you created all things,
　　and by your will they were created
　　and have their being."

　　　　　　　　　　　　Revelation 4:10–11

It is the elders' way of showing that anything they have accomplished has been accomplished by the grace of God and by him only. So they give their crowns to God and praise him.

The Character of Citizens

It is only as Christian people capture the high ground of doing what they do for the honor and glory of God that they can be used of God to elevate society to where those who deserve honor are given honor and those who deserve respect are given respect. And it is only when that happens that a nation becomes morally strong and justice becomes a reality and not just a hollow word. In other words, a nation does not become strong by laws but by the character of its citizens.

The former British Prime Minister Margaret Thatcher was an unusual politician in that she understood the limits of government and called for its renewal by people able to live a life of true faith. Addressing the General Assembly of the Church of Scotland, she said, "The truths of the Judaic-Christian tradition are infinitely precious, not only, as I believe, because they are true, but also because they provide the moral impulse which alone can lead to that peace . . . for which we all long. . . . There is little hope for democracy if the hearts of men and women in democratic societies cannot be touched by a call to something greater than themselves. Political structures, state institutions, collective ideals are not enough. We parliamentarians can legislate for the rule of law. You, the church, can teach the life of faith."[4]

The wonderful thing about this is that if we begin by showing respect to those to whom respect is due and honor to those to whom honor is due, above all showing honor and respect to God, then others may learn something of God through us and eventually come to respect, honor, and love him too, which is salvation and the beginning of wisdom. "To each his due" is not only a word about taxes. It is about justice too, and about the foundation of a free and just society.

---

4. Quoted in Charles Colson, with Ellen Santilli Vaughn, *Against the Night: Living in the New Dark Ages* (Ann Arbor, Mich.: Servant Publications, 1989), p. 120.

PART NINETEEN

The Law of Love

204

Debt and How to Get Out of It

Romans 13:8

Let no debt remain outstanding, except the continuing debt to love one another, for he who loves his fellowman has fulfilled the law.

Romans 13:8 begins a new section of Paul's letter in which Paul turns from the way believers are to relate to the governing authorities to how they are to treat other people in general. Our text is an effective transition, because it picks up on verse 7 ("Give everyone what you owe him: If you owe taxes, pay taxes; if revenue, then revenue; if respect, then respect; if honor, then honor") and bridges to the ongoing Christian responsibility to love other people.

Verse 8 says, "Let no debt remain outstanding, except the continuing debt to love one another, for he who loves his fellowman has fulfilled the law."

Borrowing or Failing to Repay?

The King James Version began this verse a bit differently: "Owe no man any thing" ("Owe no one anything," RSV). This is a literal translation of the Greek. But the New International Version is closer to the actual meaning when it says, "Let no debt remain outstanding," because the Bible does not forbid borrowing. Jesus assumed the right to borrow in Matthew 5:42, when he said, "Give to the one who asks you, and do not turn away from the one who wants to borrow from you." Other texts assume this also (see Exod. 22:25;

1681

Ps. 37:26; Luke 6:35). The point of Romans 13:8 is not that Christians should never borrow, but that they should never leave their debts unpaid. As Leon Morris points out, being a present imperative, the verb even has a continuous force: "Don't continue owing. Pay your debts."[1]

John Murray says, "This cannot be taken to mean that we may never incur financial obligations. . . . But it does condemn the looseness with which we contract debts and particularly the indifference so often displayed in the discharging of them."[2]

The difference between borrowing under certain circumstances and failure to repay what is borrowed can be illustrated as follows. Suppose you are renting a house. You do not own the house. You are only benefiting from it through the willingness of the owner to rent it to you. All you owe is the rent. In this case, the words of our text, "Let no debt remain outstanding," mean that you are to pay the rent on time. Suppose now that you need to borrow capital for a business. The situation is exactly the same. You do not own the capital. All you are doing is renting it through the willingness of the owner to loan it to you. What you owe is the interest—plus the repayment of the capital on whatever schedule has been agreed upon between you and the lender. There is no sin in borrowing the money as long as you are able to pay the interest and premiums according to that schedule.

America: A Debtor Nation

But the problem for many Americans, including our government, is that debt financing has become a way of life, and those who borrow are frequently enticed, misled, or trapped into borrowing more than they are able to repay. Then they default on their payments and often escape the weight of their financial obligations by declaring personal bankruptcy. Bankruptcy means cheating the person or company that has lent the money, and it is an unjust and impermissible course of action for a Christian. It is at this point that Romans 13:8 speaks most forcefully to people today when it says, "Let no debt remain outstanding."

The United States began to go into serious debt only after World War II. Before that we were living within our means. Income paid for the debt on bonds, inflation was negligible, and the country had a positive balance of trade. Today our national debt has passed $4 trillion. None of us really knows how much $1 million is, let alone $1 billion or $1 trillion. Breaking it down may help: $4 trillion dollars is $16,000 for every man, woman, and child in the United States ($4 trillion divided by 250 million). If we wanted to pay this debt off, we would first have to stop going into debt, which our leaders

---

1. Leon Morris, *The Epistle to the Romans* (Grand Rapids: Wm. B. Eerdmans Publishing Company, and Leicester, England: Inter-Varsity Press, 1988), p. 467.

2. John Murray, *The Epistle to the Romans*, 2 vols. in 1 (Grand Rapids: Wm. B. Eerdmans Publishing Company, 1968), vol. 2, pp. 158–59.

are unwilling or unable to do. (They are actually increasing the debt at an accelerating rate, rather than decreasing it.) Then we would have to repay what we have borrowed. At what rate? And for how long? Well, at 6 percent the interest alone is $657 million per day ($240 billion divided by 365). If we started a repayment plan of, say, $1 billion per day ($343 million per day on top of the interest payments), it would take us more than eleven thousand years to pay off $4 trillion.

People think it does not really matter that our government owes money since, as they say, we owe it to ourselves. But that is unsound reasoning. Money borrowed by government always has to be repaid by someone. It can be repaid literally by future taxes or deceitfully by future inflation, in which the dollars are simply made to be worth less. Or it can be repudiated during a period of political upheaval. In other words, it can be stolen from the lenders, who are the people. There are no other possibilities. Debt simply does not go away.

We can't do anything about the government's debt, of course, except perhaps trying to elect representatives with enough courage to fight it. But we can do something about our own debt, which for many people today is a serious problem.

The difficulty is that our consumer-oriented culture has deceived many people into living beyond their means on the assumption that they will have more money in the future so they can buy on credit now, enjoy their possessions, and pay later. That is a dangerous assumption, of course. We cannot count on earning more in the future than the present. But even if we could count on this, to live by debt financing is still foolish.

The problem is that you not only have to repay the amount borrowed plus interest, you also have to repay interest on the interest still owed. This is known as compounding, and it is the exact opposite of the way money invested early and regularly grows into substantial amounts over a lifetime. This is why if you buy a $100,000 house with a thirty-year mortgage at 10 percent interest, you will have made total payments of over $315,000 by the end of the thirty years. If you live within your means and save, compounding works for you. A person who saves can actually become wealthy by the time of retirement, even if his or her salary is small. On the other hand, if you live beyond your means by borrowing, compounding works against you and can trap you before you are even aware of what is happening.

The biggest trap is credit cards. Almost all creditworthy adults have at least one credit card, and the average cardholder has seven. If you have credit cards and use them only for convenience, paying the full amount due each month so that you never have to pay interest, you are in fine shape. But if you use them to borrow on time, you are headed for trouble. Unfortunately, most people use them as a revolving line of credit.

In 1988 *Money* magazine reported that the average balance on these cards per person was $1,450 and that millions of Americans had outstanding debts of $2,500 or more. In their judgment, more than twenty million households were living beyond their means.[3] Today, of course, the problem is even worse, and the inability of these millions of people to repay their debts is contributing to our current sluggish economy.

Yet consumer credit companies continue to bombard us with appeals to add just one more credit card. This is not because our credit is so good they just cannot resist wanting us as clients, but that they get 18 to 21 percent interest on whatever we fail to pay monthly, and that is much more than they can get by lending their money at today's competitive bank rates. If you fall for their seductive appeals and end up buying *anything* on credit, you are foolish.

Ron Blue is a Christian financial planning expert who has written a good book on biblical principles for personal finance called *Master Your Money*. In it he tells an interesting story. When the Sears company introduced its Discover Card they used Atlanta as a test market, and the Atlanta papers reported that Sears officials expected credit card usage to go up by thirty-five billion dollars as a result of introducing the new card. Their studies showed that the new card would be used for incremental borrowing. That is, it would not be a case of people borrowing on the Discover card rather than on some other card, like American Express, Visa, or MasterCard, for instance. It would be additional borrowing, because the new card would be an additional credit line for those who had it.

Blue talked to a banking friend about the way banks view people who pay credit card bills on time, thus avoiding the high interest. The banker told him that in the banking industry a person who pays his bills right away is known as a "deadbeat," because the company is unable to make much money from him. A decade or so ago a deadbeat was someone who failed to pay his bills. Now he is someone who pays his bills promptly.[4]

Climbing Out of the Debt Pit

There are few ministers today who are not frequently called upon to counsel persons who have been trapped by debt. In fact, the problem has become so serious, even among otherwise solid evangelical people, that many churches have developed financial counseling classes to help parishioners with their debt problems.

Suppose you have been trapped by debt. You cannot pay your bills each month, and the problem is getting worse rather than better. What are you going to do about it? Our text says, "Let no debt remain outstanding." How are you going to obey this vital biblical command? Let me suggest the following practical steps.

1. *Recognize that you have a spiritual problem.* If you are a Christian, this is the place you need to start, because it will place the responsibility for your

---

3. *Money 1988*, compiled by the editors of *Money* (Birmingham: Oxmoor House, 1988), p. 98.
4. Ron Blue, *Master Your Money: A Step-by-Step Plan for Financial Freedom, Revised and Updated for the Financial Realities of the 90s* (Nashville: Thomas Nelson Publishers, 1991), pp. 119–20.

condition on you and not on God or adverse circumstances, and assuming responsibility for your own life is the healthiest and most important course for anyone.

Sometimes when Christians get trapped by debt they go to their ministers and ask why God hasn't fulfilled his promise. Hasn't he said that he will "meet all [our] needs" (cf. Phil. 4:19)? Does God break his promises? Does he fail to keep his word? You know the answer to that. God never breaks his word. Therefore, God has not failed you. Rather it is you who have failed him.

Instead of being spiritual, you have become secular in your thinking. You have listened to the siren song of the secular culture surrounding you, and you have adopted a consumptive lifestyle on the world's recommendation and urging. You have been adopting the world's hedonistic philosophy: "Do it now." "Live it up." "You only go around once." "You're worth it."

Earlier in this volume I addressed the harmful effects of television. Ron Blue makes this observation:

> The more television a person watches, the higher lifestyle the person is apt to desire. Television advertising is extremely sophisticated and effective. In a similar way, the more time you spend in shopping malls, the higher lifestyle you are apt to want because you are surrounding yourself with temptation. It is much like going to the grocery store just before mealtime to do your weekly shopping. Chances are that you will spend substantially more than if you went after a meal and with a specific list in mind.[5]

2. *Stop buying on time.* Simply stop taking on more debt, in any way or for any reason. There are reasons why debt is sometimes a right strategy—to buy a house, for example, assuming that you are able to afford it and still meet your other financial obligations. But if you are trapped by debt, as many are, it is essential that you absolutely stop adding to it. How? Well, one way would be to cut up your credit cards or lock them away.

Money magazine is not in the business of discouraging borrowing. But in the 1988 issue I cited earlier the editors wrote, "If willpower alone cannot stop your borrowing, try plastic surgery: cut up your cards, cancel your credit lines, and close your overdraft accounts."[6]

3. *Reduce your expenditures to below your current income.* Live within your means. Blue says it like this: "Spend less than you earn and do it for a long time, and you will be financially successful."[7]

Do you remember Charles Dickens's touching character Mr. Micawber from *David Copperfield?* Micawber was always living a bit beyond his means, which led to the loss of everything he owned, eventually even to his being put in prison. Micawber understood his problem, as many today do not, and

5. Ibid., p. 114.
6. *Money 1988*, p. 100.
7. Blue, *Master Your Money*, p. 35.

he gave Copperfield this warning: "Annual income twenty pounds, annual expenditure nineteen, nineteen six, result happiness. Annual income twenty pounds, annual expenditure twenty pounds ought and six, result misery. The blossom is blighted, the leaf is withered, the God of day goes down upon the dreary scene, and—in short you are for ever floored. As I am!"[8]

If you have trouble reducing your expenditures, you need to prepare a budget and stick to it. If you cannot do that, you need to seek help from a professional counselor about where cuts in your spending should be made.

And this might be helpful. Blue says that at one point in his career he read that using credit cards will cause a family to spend 34 percent more than they would if they were to pay for everything they purchased with cash. That was supposed to be true even if they always paid their credit card bills immediately. Blue found this hard to believe. But he decided to try it. He had always paid his credit card bills at once, because he resented having to pay interest on the money. Nevertheless, he and his wife talked it over, put their credit cards away, and for a year lived strictly on cash.

Were they inconvenienced? Yes. It meant carrying a lot of cash around, and it took a lot to pay for such high-priced items as household appliances, car repairs, and airplane tickets. But having to pay with cash changed Blue's thinking. Paying cash at the drugstore caused him to think carefully about what he was buying and in some cases to eliminate impulsive purchases. Paying cash for clothes caused him to ask whether he really needed them or whether something cheaper might be equally as good.

The bottom line is that at the end of his experimental year, when he added up what he had spent, Blue found that his living expenses had decreased 33 percent from what they had been the year before when he had been using his credit cards. And he had thought that he was living on a bare-bones budget even then![9] That might be a good strategy for you, if you are having trouble living within your current income.

4. *Sell assets to reduce your current debt.* There are only two ways to get out of debt after you have decided to do it: (1) sell off unnecessary assets in order to repay the debt and (2) begin a repayment schedule and stick to it. Neither of these is easy, which is one reason why getting into debt is so bad. But of the two, the easiest is to sell off assets. You will not be able to do this with everything. But there are probably some things you can sell—a high-priced or second car perhaps, a recreational vehicle, a boat, stereo equipment, or other such items.

5. *Pay something on each debt each month.* Not everyone has the luxury of being able to sell off assets to repay debt. In fact, 80 percent of Americans owe more than they own, which means that selling assets is not much of an option in

8. Charles Dickens, *David Copperfield* (New York and Toronto: The New American Library, 1962), p. 182.

9. Blue, *Master Your Money*, pp. 123–24.

their cases, though they may be able to reduce their debt by selling some items. Therefore, for most people the only remaining way to get out of the debt trap is by carefully preparing and rigidly following a debt repayment schedule.

Blue has two additional suggestions at this point. First, concentrate on eliminating the smallest debts first. This will make the repayment project simpler, and it will be good for you to have some reward for what may be a long and difficult effort. When you have eliminated the smallest debts, you can apply what you would have been spending on those debts to the other, greater liabilities. Thus, you will be building momentum that will itself be encouraging.

Second, precommit any unexpected income to your debt repayment. If you are a Christian, this will alert you to God's providential oversight of your financial life. If you are seriously trying to obey God in respect to the text we are studying— "Let no debt remain outstanding"—God will most likely provide funds you have not been expecting, and you will be able to thank him for it. When that happens, you will have come far from the attitude that asks, "Why did God let me get into this mess?" or "Why hasn't God kept his promises?" And you will be thinking instead, "What is God trying to teach me through this bad situation?"

He Never Earned More Than $8,000

I want to end with this story, again from the book by Ron Blue. On one occasion a retired pastor came to him for some financial advice. He had never earned more than $8,000 in any one year, and he wanted to know if he would have enough money to live out his life in retirement. At this point the man was eighty years old, and he had been retired for twenty years.

Blue began to ask about his finances. Did he have any debts? No. Why not? Because he knew he would have to repay them someday, and he wasn't earning enough money to pay off debt, feed his family, and give his tithe. Did he have any assets? Yes. He had $250,000 in cash and money market funds in his wife's name and an additional $350,000 in his own name, a total of $600,000. Oh and, yes, he had also invested $10,000 in a new company some years ago, and the value of the stock had by this time grown to $1,063,000. Total assets $1,663,000! And he had never earned more than $8,000 a year! Blue sent him away with no advice at all and told him not to listen to anybody else, either. What he was doing was just fine.

That is a remarkable story, of course. Not everyone will invest in a company that can grow assets from $10,000 to $1,000,000 in a lifetime. But it is a striking illustration of what can happen if a person handles his or her finances as a Christian should.[10]

10. Ibid., pp. 13–14.

205

The Debt of Love

Romans 13:8–10

Let no debt remain outstanding, except the continuing debt to love one another, for he who loves his fellowman has fulfilled the law. The commandments, "Do not commit adultery," "Do not murder," "Do not steal," "Do not covet," and whatever other commandment there may be, are summed up in this one rule: "Love your neighbor as yourself." Love does no harm to its neighbor. Therefore love is the fulfillment of the law.

After I had preached the sermon that was the basis for the previous chapter, a number of people told me about their experiences of getting out of debt. The most moving stories were those that told of the tremendous relief and sense of new freedom when the last of the person's burdensome debts was paid off. One person said that it was an experience second only to having been set free from the burden of sin through faith in Jesus Christ.

I have never been in debt financially, but I can understand how immense the relief of getting out of debt must be. Yet there is one debt we can never get out from under, and that is the debt to love.

Our text says, "Let no debt remain outstanding, except the continuing debt to love one another, for he who loves his fellowman has fulfilled the law. The commandments, 'Do not commit adultery,' 'Do not murder,' 'Do not steal,' 'Do not covet,' and whatever other commandments there may be, are summed up in this one rule: 'Love your neighbor as yourself.' Love does no harm to its neighbor. Therefore love is the fulfillment of the law" (Rom. 13:8–10).

A Permanent Obligation

What this means, in very simple terms, is that we can never say that we have satisfied our obligations in this area. Leon Morris puts it like this: "We can never say, 'I have done all the loving I need to.' [This is because] love is a permanent obligation, a debt impossible to discharge."[1] This is not the first time Paul has written about the Christian's obligation to love. He wrote about Christian love in chapter 12 (vv. 9–13), where he showed both what love is like and how it is to function.

1. *What love is like.* Love must be both sincere and discriminating: (1) "Love must be sincere" and (2) "Hate what is evil; cling to what is good" (Rom. 12:9).

The Greek word translated *sincere* is *anupokritos*, the latter part of which has given us *hypocrisy* and *hypocritical. Anupokritos* means without a mask, referring to the way in which, in the Greek theater, actors would carry masks to signal the role they were playing. When Paul tells us that love is to be *an* (that is, "not") hypocritical, he is saying that those who love are not to play a role but are rather to drop their masks and be genuine.

The second part of Romans 12:9 teaches that love is also to be wise or discriminating. Real love does not love everything. On the contrary, it hates what is evil and clings to what is good. If we truly love, we will hate violence done to other people by whatever means. But we will love those who work for peace and even those who are guilty of the violence, because we will want to turn them from their ways. We will hate lying, but we will love the truth and will at the same time even love those who are lying, for we will see them as people who need the Savior.

2. *How love is to function.* In the verses following verse 9, where he speaks of love's nature, Paul highlights nine specific functions of love. As we saw in chapter 194, in the Greek text of these verses there are nine nouns in the dative case, each of which comes first in its phrase for emphasis. A literal translation of Romans 12:10–13 would be something like this: "*As regards brotherly love,* be devoted to one another; *as regards honor,* honor others above yourselves; *as regards zeal,* never be lacking; *as regards service,* always keep your spiritual fervor, serving the Lord; *as regards hope,* joyful; *as regards affliction,* patient; *as regards prayer,* faithful; *as regards the needs of God's people,* sharing; *as regards hospitality,* pursuing."[2]

---

1. Leon Morris, *The Epistle to the Romans* (Grand Rapids: Wm. B. Eerdmans Publishing Company, and Leicester, England: Inter-Varsity Press, 1988), pp. 467–68.
2. See chapter 193, "The Greatest Thing in the World" (Romans 12:9), and chapter 194, "Love in Action" (Romans 12:10–13).

In his description of love's nature and function in chapter 12, Paul had the love of believers for one another specifically in mind (though he broadens his outlook toward the end of the chapter), and he was emphasizing love of the good as opposed to love of evil. The new elements in chapter 13 are: (1) he is talking about all people, not just Christians, and (2) as far as the nature of love is concerned, he is teaching that love is the fulfillment of the moral law.

Love for all Persons

In Paul's writings the words "one another," as in the phrase "except the continuing debt to love one another," usually refer to Christians.[3] But in this case they surely, though uncharacteristically, refer to all people. This is because immediately after this Paul begins to discuss the moral law, which is binding upon all and is for all, indicating that love for others is the fulfillment of this law, and also because he immediately broadens the statement about loving "one another" by adding, "He who loves *his fellowman* has fulfilled the law." The word *fellowman* gives the earlier phrase its full meaning.

This is in line with Jesus' teaching about love. On one occasion an expert in the law asked Jesus what was necessary to earn eternal life, and Jesus replied by referring to the moral law, as he often did. He taught that one is to "Love the Lord your God with all your heart and with all your soul and with all your strength and with all your mind" and, second, "Love your neighbor as yourself" (Luke 10:27).

"Who is my neighbor?" the expert demanded.

Jesus answered by telling the parable of the Good Samaritan:

A man was going down from Jerusalem to Jericho, when he fell into the hands of robbers. They stripped him of his clothes, beat him and went away, leaving him half dead. A priest happened to be going down the same road, and when he saw the man, he passed by on the other side. So too, a Levite, when he came to the place and saw him, passed by on the other side. But a Samaritan, as he traveled, came where the man was; and when he saw him, he took pity on him. He went to him and bandaged his wounds, pouring on oil and wine. Then he put the man on his own donkey, took him to an inn and took care of him. The next day he took out two silver coins and gave them to the innkeeper. "Look after him," he said, "and when I return, I will reimburse you for any extra expense you may have."

Luke 10:30–35

Jesus concluded that the neighbor was the Samaritan, though he was of a different racial stock than the man who had been robbed, and that he was a neighbor simply because he had acted to help the unfortunate victim. Jesus

---

3. See Romans 15:14; Galatians 5:13, 6:2; Ephesians 4:2, 4:32; Colossians 3:13; 1 Thessalonians 3:12, 4:9, 4:18. See also John 13:34–35, 15:12, 15:17; James 5:16; 1 John 3:11, 3:23, 4:7, 4:11–12.

taught that anyone who wanted to follow after him and be his disciple would
have to show that love to everyone.

Love's Fulfilling of the Law

Jesus quoted Leviticus in the introduction to that parable: "Love your
neighbor as yourself" (Lev. 19:18). It was what occasioned the expert's quib-
ble. Jesus elsewhere called loving our neighbors as ourselves the second greatest commandment (Matt. 22:39), after loving "the Lord your God with all
your heart and with all your soul and with all your mind" (v. 37), which was
the first. It is significant that Paul quotes that same verse in order to make
exactly the same point in Romans 13: "Love your neighbor as yourself" (v. 9).

It seems to me that Paul must have been thinking of Jesus' words specifically, since Jesus ended his teaching about the first and second great commandments by saying, "All the Law and the Prophets hang on these two commandments" (Matt. 22:40), and Paul concludes the same way here (v. 10).
True, Jesus spoke both of the first table of the law (love for God) as well as
the second table (love for man) and Paul speaks only of love for our fellowman, but that is what the context demands since he is writing about how
Christians are to act toward others in this world.

To illustrate his point he lists four of the Ten Commandments.

1. *"Do not commit adultery."* Love will not commit adultery, because this is
a sin against both God and others, and love will not harm others. We think
of Joseph and the way he was tempted to sin by the wife of Potiphar. He told
her, "With me in charge . . . my master does not concern himself with anything
in the house; everything he owns he has entrusted to my care. No one is
greater in this house than I am. My master has withheld nothing from me
except you, because you are his wife. How then could I do such a wicked thing
and sin against God?" (Gen. 39:8–9). In Joseph's case, love was the fulfillment
of the law against adultery.

2. *"Do not murder."* If love will not harm another person, it surely will not
murder another person, even in the sense of attacking him with words (see
Matt. 5:21–22). On the contrary, instead of tearing down, love will use words
to edify and build up others. Paul told the Corinthians, "Knowledge puffs
up, but love builds up" (1 Cor. 8:1). It does that especially for one who is a
"weaker" brother.

3. *"Do not steal."* There are many ways we can steal. We steal from an
employer when we do not give him or her the best work of which we are capable. We steal if we overextend our coffee breaks or leave work early. We steal
if we waste the products with which we are working. We steal if, as businessmen, we charge too much for our products or try to make a killing in a lucrative field. We steal if we sell an inferior product, pretending that it is better
than it is. We steal when we mismanage another person's money, or if we borrow but do not repay what we have borrowed.

If we love other people, we will do none of these things. Instead, we will work so we will not be dependent on others to support us (1 Thess. 4:11) and will have something to share with those in need (Eph. 4:28).

4. *"Do not covet."* The last of the Ten Commandments strikes at the heart of our materialistic, consumer-oriented culture, which teaches us to covet everything. This is the chief cause behind the debt trap so many have fallen into.

The biggest problem with covetousness is not the trouble it gets us into, however, bad as that is. It is rather that it makes us insensitive to the needs of other people. For instead of helping us to see who they are and what their needs are, covetousness makes us jealous of others with the result that we see only what they have—and want it. Covetousness destroyed Aachan, when he saw the wealth of Jericho and took it secretly, contrary to God's express command. Covetousness and grasping after material things has destroyed the usefulness of many contemporary Christians.

If we loved other people, we would want good things for them rather than letting their good things make us want more for ourselves. In this area, as in the others, love truly is the fulfillment of the law.

Love in Action

It can hardly fail to strike anyone who reads these verses carefully that the examples Paul offers in the form of samples from the moral law are all negative: "Do *not* commit adultery," "Do *not* murder," "Do *not* steal," "Do *not* covet." This is important, because we are hardly in position to do good to another person until we are ready at least to stop doing him or her harm. Still, we must know that real love is also positive. It "does" for the other. This is involved in the very first thing Paul says, for he writes of the "continuing debt to love one another" (v. 8).

Let's think about this "continuing debt" positively, and ask, What does it mean to discharge this debt honestly? Here are some extremely simple but important and often neglected ways.

1. *Listen to one another.* We live in an age in which few people really listen to one another. We talk to or at one another, of course. And the media are always talking at us. But we do not listen, and as a result ours is a lonely age in which community has largely disappeared and hundreds of thousands of people live daily within a soundproofed cocoon.

Quite a few years ago a movie called *Network* provided an excellent critique of our modern, impersonal, television-dominated age. The two main characters were an older man played by William Holden and a young product of the TV generation played by Faye Dunaway. The two were having an affair, but they were not connecting at the personal level. The man, who still remembered what relationships should and could be, was dissatisfied. The woman didn't know what he wanted.

"What do you want from me?" she asked at one point.

"I want you to love me," he answered.

This was a desire she did not understand. So she replied honestly, "I don't know how to do that." The two then stood staring at one another, not speaking, and the viewer became aware of how fragile their relationship was. They could not communicate. There was nothing to hold them together. At that moment the telephone rang. What would happen now? Could the woman ignore the telephone and actually listen to the man? For a moment she seemed to try. But then, as she still stood facing him, her eyes shot sideways to the phone and the opportunity was gone forever. To really love another person we must listen. If we do not know how to listen, we must learn how. And we must take time to do it.

2. *Share with one another.* The second thing we need to do is share ourselves with each other. The problem is that sharing ourselves makes us vulnerable, especially if we are trying to share with a person we care deeply about. We are afraid to be vulnerable.

No wonder the world's people do not share. They usually hate each other below the smooth surface of their relationships, and often their hatreds are not even buried that far. This should not be the case for Christians. We do not need to be afraid to be vulnerable, because we have already become vulnerable before God, meaning that we have already been exposed as sinners before him. There is nothing about us that God does not know. He knows all sins, all our faults, all our miserable failures as human beings. Yet here is the wonderful thing: God loves us anyway and is working in us to make us different people. God has accepted us just as we are, and he is making us to be like Jesus Christ. Therefore, since God has accepted us we do not need to fear rejection by anybody.

Sharing is the reverse side of listening. We listen to the other person as he or she shares. Then we share ourselves. This is the only way to show real love and build real relationships.

3. *Forgive one another.* None of us is without sin. Therefore, we are all guilty of sinning against others. For this reason, listening and sharing also involve forgiveness. Sharing means expressing our hurts, and listening means hearing how we have hurt the other person.

Francis Schaeffer developed this well in a study of love called "The Mark of the Christian."[4] When we have hurt another person we must say, "I am sorry," he said. But love is more than this. Love is also giving and receiving forgiveness. He referred to the Lord's Prayer, in which Jesus taught us to pray, "Forgive us our sins, for we also forgive everyone who sins against us" (Luke 11:4). This does not suggest that we are only to forgive when the other person is sorry, though we must forgive them. Schaeffer says:

4. Appendix II in Francis A. Schaeffer, *The Church at the End of the Twentieth Century* (Downers Grove, Ill.: InterVarsity Press, 1970), pp. 133–53. This material was also published separately by InterVarsity Press as *The Mark of the Christian* (1970).

Rather, we are called upon to have a forgiving spirit without the other man having made the first step. We may still say that he is wrong, but in the midst of saying that he is wrong, we must be forgiving. . . .

Such a forgiving spirit registers an attitude of love toward others. But, even though one can call this an attitude, true forgiveness is observable. Believe me, you can look on a man's face and know where he is as far as forgiveness is concerned. And the world is called on to look upon us and see whether we have love across the groups, across the party lines. Do they observe that we say, "I'm sorry," and do they observe a forgiving heart? . . . Our love will not be perfect, but it must be substantial enough for the world to be able to observe it.[5]

And let's remember how Jesus said, "If you forgive men when they sin against you, your heavenly Father will also forgive you. But if you do not forgive men their sins, your Father will not forgive your sins" (Matt. 6:14–15). That is the equivalent of saying that you must forgive others to be a true Christian.

4. *Serve one another.* The fourth practical expression of what it means to love one another is service. This does not come to us naturally, which is one reason the Bible mentions and illustrates it so often.

This was practically the last lesson Jesus left with the disciples. In the Upper Room at the time of the institution of the Lord's Supper, Jesus got up from the meal, took off his outer clothing, wrapped a towel around his waist, and began to wash the disciples' feet. Peter was appalled. "You shall never wash my feet," he said (John 13:8).

Jesus replied that it was necessary if Peter was to be his disciple, and Peter relented. Still none of them understood what Jesus meant or why he was doing what he was doing (John 13:2–11).

So Jesus explained, "You call me 'Teacher' and 'Lord,' and rightly so, for that is what I am. Now that I, your Lord and Teacher, have washed your feet, you also should wash one another's feet. I have set you an example that you should do as I have done for you. I tell you the truth, no servant is greater than his master, nor is a messenger greater than the one who sent him. Now that you know these things, you will be blessed if you do them" (John 13:13–17).

Jesus was giving an example of menial service, teaching that we are to serve others. On another occasion he said, "Whoever wants to become great among you must be your servant, and whoever wants to be first must be your slave—just as the Son of Man did not come to be served, but to serve, and to give his life as a ransom for many" (Matt. 20:26–28).

What the World Needs

Some time ago there was a popular song with the words, "What the world needs now is love, sweet love." Love *is* exactly what the world needs—the song was right about that. But it was also wrong, because the love it was singing

5. Ibid., p. 145.

about was only the sweet, sentimental love of our empty, commercial age, and that love is not good enough. What the world needs is the sincere, selfless, sacrificial, serving love of God displayed in those who know him and are determined to obey him faithfully.

If you know Jesus, you will not follow after the world's selfish ways but instead will love as God loves. You will keep the law: "Love is the fulfillment of the law." But you will also go out of your way to listen to, share with, forgive, and serve all other people.

206

Understanding the Times

Romans 13:11

And do this, understanding the present time.

This study is about "understanding the times," a challenge suggested by the first half of Romans 13:11. I begin by referring to two other sections of the Bible.

First, Matthew 16:1–3. The leaders of the people had come to Jesus to ask for a sign from heaven, and he replied by saying that they already been given signs and that their problem was that they would not understand the ones they had. Then he used a popular saying similar to our adage: "Red sky at night, sailors' delight. Red sky in the morning, sailors take warning."

Jesus said, "When evening comes, you say, 'It will be fair weather, for the sky is red,' and in the morning, 'Today it will be stormy, for the sky is red and overcast.' You know how to interpret the appearance of the sky, but you cannot interpret the signs of the times" (Matt. 16:2–3). His point was that they could not interpret the signs of his coming.

The second passage is from 1 Chronicles 12, which lists the warriors who came to David when he was king at Hebron. The men of Issachar were among

1697

them, and they are described as those "who understood the times and knew what Israel should do" (1 Chron. 12:32).

So we have, on the one hand, those who could not "interpret the signs of the times" and, on the other hand, those who "understood the times and knew what Israel should do." It is against this background that I set Romans 13:11, our text: "And do this, *understanding the present time.*"

The combination of verses causes us to ask: Do we understand the times in which we live? If not, why not? If we do, what are we doing about it? The bottom line is that if we understand the present time, we will know what to do with our time—and will do it, if we are wise.

This Present Time

I have been surprised by the way some commentators have used this text to discuss eschatology. Because the verse goes on to say, "The hour has come for you to wake up from your slumber, because our salvation is nearer now than when we first believed," they speculate about how close that final deliverance (or salvation) really is.

But that is not what this verse is about. The Greek words say merely, "And this, knowing the time." Yet the New International Version is surely correct when it adds the word "present" to indicate that the time Paul is concerned about is not some future time when the Lord Jesus Christ will return, but rather the present time. And he is concerned that we understand it and use it wisely, knowing that it will be gone forever and the opportunities it holds will be lost forever, when Jesus comes.

So what about this present time? What kind of time is it? Let's look at several passages that describe it clearly.[1]

This Present *Evil* Time

Galatians 1:4 lays the groundwork for our thinking in this area, saying that Jesus "gave himself for our sins to rescue us from *the present evil age*, according to the will of our God and Father." Obviously, in this verse Paul is thinking of this world's time as a whole, all time prior to the return of Jesus Christ in glory, and he is telling us that it is an evil time out of which we need to be rescued.

---

1. The Greek word translated *time* in this verse is *kairos.* This word occurs eighty-five times in the New Testament, and thirty of these are in Paul's writings. Usually *kairos* is defined as "meaningful time" or "a time holding or presenting unusual opportunity." Examples in Paul's writings would be Romans 3:26 and 1 Corinthians 4:5. *Kairos* is usually contrasted with *chronos*, also translated *time* but understood to describe time only chronologically, that is, as a sequence of mere moments. Most of the word books make this distinction, and Switzerland's Oscar Cullmann made much of it in his studies in biblical theology (for example, in *Christ and Time*, 1951). However, James Baar has criticized this and similar linguistic distinctions in *Biblical Words for Time* (Naperville, Ill.: Alec R. Allenson, 1962).

I wonder if we really believe that this is a "present evil age." I suspect that what we really believe is that this age is really rather nice, something to be sought after and enjoyed as much as possible.

You are never going to make any true progress in wisdom unless you begin by realizing that this world is hostile to God and opposed to any desires for godliness on the part of God's people. Jesus said it clearly. He told his disciples just before his arrest and crucifixion, "If the world hates you, keep in mind that it hated me first. If you belonged to the world, it would love you as its own. As it is, you do not belong to the world, but I have chosen you out of the world. That is why the world hates you" (John 15:18–19). Later he prayed, "My prayer is not that you take them out of the world but that you protect them from the evil one" (John 17:15).

What this means is that all cultures decline to the degree that they reject Christ. And the more radical the rejection, the more rapid the disintegration. Our own Western culture is declining rapidly.

A number of contemporary writers are saying this, and not all are Christians. Allan Bloom's book, *The Closing of the American Mind*, is one example.[2] It deplores the decline of Western standards of education due to the overthrow of moral and cultural values by philosophic relativism. Another book that deals with the impact of relativism and the abolishing of Christian absolutes in twentieth-century history is English historian Paul Johnson's masterful study, *Modern Times: The World from the Twenties to the Nineties*.[3] I think too of Malcolm Muggeridge's *The End of Christendom*,[4] Carl F. H. Henry's *Twilight of a Great Civilization*,[5] Herbert Schlossberg's *Idols for Destruction*,[6] and Charles Colson's *Against the Night: Living in the New Dark Ages*.[7] I encourage you to read them, if you want honest, penetrating studies of this age.

In *Against the Night*, Charles Colson quotes Whittaker Chambers, a former communist spy who became a Christian and a passionate defender of the West, but who died despairing of it:

> It is idle to talk about preventing the wreck of Western civilization. It is already a wreck from within. This is why we can hope to do little more now than snatch a fingernail of a saint from the rack or a handful of ashes from the fire, and bury them secretly in a flower pot against the day, ages hence, when a few men begin again to dare to believe that there was once something else, that something else is thinkable, and need some evidence of what it was and the fortifying

2. Allan Bloom, *The Closing of the American Mind* (New York: Simon and Schuster, 1987).

3. Paul Johnson, *Modern Times: The World from the Twenties to the Nineties*, revised edition (New York: Harper & Row, 1991).

4. Malcolm Muggeridge, *The End of Christendom* (Grand Rapids: Wm. B. Eerdmans Publishing Company, 1980).

5. Carl F. H. Henry, *Twilight of a Great Civilization* (Westchester, Ill.: Crossway Books, 1988).

6. Herbert Schlossberg, *Idols for Destruction* (Washington, D.C.: Regnery Gateway, 1990).

7. Charles Colson, with Ellen Santilli Vaughn, *Against the Night: Living in the New Dark Ages* (Ann Arbor, Mich.: Servant Publications, 1989).

knowledge that there were those who, at the great nightfall, took loving thought
to preserve the tokens of hope and truth.[8]

Those are grim words, but they are an honest reflection on this present
(or any other) age apart from the true God and the power of true Christianity.

The Sign of Jonah

In 2 Corinthians 6:2, Paul writes, "I tell you, now is *the time of God's favor,*
now is the day of salvation." In other words, although this is indeed an evil
age, it is nevertheless also the age in which God has accomplished our salvation.

We see this too in Matthew 16:4, the verse immediately following Jesus'
words about the Pharisees and Sadducees' failure to interpret the signs of
the times. Jesus told them, "A wicked and adulterous generation looks for a
miraculous sign, but none will be given it except the sign of Jonah." It is clear
from the way he had spoken of Jonah four chapters earlier that he was referring to his own upcoming death and resurrection.[9]

And that is exactly the way the rest of Matthew 16 unfolds. You will recall
that immediately after this and after warning his disciples of what he called
"the yeast of the Pharisees and Sadducees"—that is, their teaching—Jesus
asked the disciples who the people thought he was.

They replied, "Some say John the Baptist; others say Elijah; and still others,
Jeremiah or one of the prophets."

"But what about you?" Jesus asked. "Who do you say I am?"

Peter answered for the others: "You are the Christ, the Son of the living
God" (Matt. 16:13–15). Jesus then explained how Peter's answer was right
and that it was something that had been revealed to him by God. In other
words, he put his seal of approval on Peter's true answer, affirming that
Peter (and eventually the other disciples too) had interpreted the signs of
the times correctly. They had observed what was happening in Christ's ministry and had therefore come to understand that he was the Son of God
and to believe on him.

But the salvation Jesus was bringing was by way of the cross. At the time
this was something Peter did not understand at all. He believed that Jesus
was the Messiah. But when Jesus went on to teach that "he must go to
Jerusalem and suffer many things at the hands of the elders, chief priests
and teachers of the law, and that he must be killed and on the third day be

8. In Charles Colson, with Ellen Santilli Vaughn, *Against the Night,* p. 110. The quote is from
an article by Russell Kirk titled, "Wise Men Know What Wicked Things Are Written on the Sky,"
Modern Age (Spring 1985), p. 113.

9. "A wicked and adulterous generation asks for a miraculous sign! But none will be given
it except the sign of the prophet Jonah. For as Jonah was three days and three nights in the
belly of a huge fish, so the Son of Man will be three days and three nights in the heart of the
earth" (Matt. 12:39–40).

raised to life" (Matt. 16:21), Peter rebuked him, saying that he didn't want that to happen to Jesus. Peter needed to be rebuked by Jesus instead.

If we are to understand this present time, we must understand that this is also a time marked out by the cross of Jesus Christ, whom God sent to be our Savior. Paul wrote, "But when the time had fully come, God sent his Son, born of a woman, born under law, to redeem those under law, that we might receive the full rights of sons" (Gal. 4:4–5).

A Time to Repent and Believe

A third passage is from the day, a week before his death, when Jesus was approaching Jerusalem. When he saw it he began to weep, saying, "If you, even you, had known on this day what would bring you peace—but now it is hidden from your eyes. The days will come upon you when your enemies will build an embankment against you and encircle you and hem you in on every side. They will dash you to the ground, you and the children within your walls. They will not leave one stone on another, because you did not recognize *the time of God's coming to you*" (Luke 19:41–44).

What Jesus meant was that the people had been given time to repent of their sins and turn to him and be saved. But they had refused to do it, and as a result the time of their opportunity was drawing to an end.

That is exactly the condition of people in our world today, since the destruction of Jerusalem, which overtook the people of that city within a generation of Jesus' death and resurrection, was a foretaste and warning of the final judgment that is to come upon every member of our race. Judgment will fall on you, if you are not trusting Jesus Christ for your salvation. He himself will be judge. But here is the good news. Today is the day of God's grace. Judgment has not yet come. Therefore, turn from your sin and believe on Jesus. Perhaps this is the very moment of God's coming to you personally.

A Time of Gospel Proclamation

In the first chapter of Acts, at the very beginning of the account of the founding and growth of the Christian church, the disciples asked Jesus, "Lord, are you *at this time* going to restore the kingdom to Israel" (Acts 1:6). Their question showed that they were still thinking in unbiblical categories. The Jews expected the Messiah to drive out the Romans, who occupied their country, and reestablish David's dynasty and an independent state of Israel. They believed that Jesus was the Messiah, so they anticipated that he would fulfill this popular expectation.

Jesus replied that this is not what this age is about. This age is one of gospel proclamation. He said, "It is not for you to know the times or dates the Father has set by his own authority. But you will receive power when the Holy Spirit comes on you; and you will be my witnesses in Jerusalem, and in all Judea and Samaria, and to the ends of the earth" (Acts 1:7–8).

That is the fourth text needed to explain the nature of the times in which we live. It tells us that it is not for us to know the times God has set for the end of all things. That alone should rebuke the many extravagant attempts to discern the end of the age from Romans 13 or any other passage touching on eschatology. What we are to know is that these are gospel times, times given to us by God to take the good news about the death and resurrection of Jesus Christ, which is the way of salvation, to all people throughout the whole world.

Going back to Romans 13:11, this means that if you really do understand the present time, which is what the text is asking you to do, you will be in the vanguard of those who are seeking to lead others to faith in Jesus Christ as Savior.

What else is time for, if it is not for that? It is not time for you merely to make money or a name for yourself or to have a good time. How could you even suppose that merely making money or becoming famous or enjoying yourself is what life is about? Life is from God, and the time you have has been given to you by him. Time is for Jesus, and history is about God calling a people out of this present evil age to believe in and also live for him. Your role in this present time, if you are a believer, is to live for Jesus—and witness for him too.

Jesus told his disciples, "All authority in heaven and on earth has been given to me. Therefore go and make disciples of all nations, baptizing them in the name of the Father and of the Son and of the Holy Spirit, and teaching them to obey everything I have commanded you. And surely I will be with you always, to the very end of the age" (Matt. 28:18–20).

The Time Is Short

In 1 Corinthians 7:29 Paul adds something else about time that fits perfectly with what he is saying in Romans 13: "*The time is short.*" If we are going to serve Jesus Christ, we had better do it now, because we do not have forever. In Romans Paul develops this same idea by saying, "The hour has come for you to wake from your slumber, because our salvation is nearer now than when we first believed."

This is true in two senses, and each can be applied both to believers and to unbelievers.

1. *The return of Jesus Christ is imminent. Imminent* is not a calendar term, as if we might be saying that Jesus' return is going to take place tomorrow or, at the latest, the day after that or the day after that. Some Bible teachers have fallen into the error of saying this and even of setting dates.[10] But imminent does not mean immediate. It means it could be at any moment—nothing stands in its way. Of course, that is important all by itself. Since Jesus could return to wrap up this age and usher in the final judgment at any moment,

10. One of the most recent, sad attempts to do this is Harold Camping's *1994?* (New York: Vantage Press, 1992).

it is urgent that you be ready to meet him, whoever you are and whenever he may come.

If you are a Christian, you must be ready to render account for what you have done with the talents and opportunities he has given you. If you are not a Christian, you will be judged. Anyone who understands this about the times will flee from sin to Jesus and then live for him and serve him with all the strength he provides.

2. *The time when you must stand before Jesus Christ is close.* That is, regardless of the time when Jesus will return, your personal end is very close. At the best you will die in seventy or eighty years. You may die tomorrow, or today.

If you are trusting Christ, that time is "nearer . . . than when [you] first believed," to use Paul's words. Soon *you* will stand before Jesus to give your accounting. Will you acquit yourself well on that day of final reckoning? Will you hear Jesus say, "Well done, good and faithful servant! You have been faithful with a few things; I will put you in charge of many things. Come and share your master's happiness!" (Matt. 25:23)? Or will you be ashamed to stand before him?

If you are not a Christian, tremble! And know no peace until you do trust Jesus. In that same parable, the master says of the unbelieving person, "Throw that worthless servant outside, into the darkness, where there will be weeping and gnashing of teeth" (Matt. 25:30).

Redeeming the Time Because . . .

The sixth and final text having to do with the time in which we live and how we are to understand it is Ephesians 5:16, which brings us back to what Paul wrote in Romans 13 as well as to the evil of this present time: "Be very careful, then, how you live—not as unwise but as wise, making the most of every opportunity, because the days are evil." The King James Version says, "*Redeeming the time*, because the days are evil."

The great American Puritan Jonathan Edwards was aware of how important time is. In his youth, before the age of twenty, he wrote out as a personal resolution: "Never to lose one moment of time, but to improve it in the most profitable way I possibly can." He did this faithfully himself. So it is not at all surprising to find him urging the same on those he taught for so many years in Northampton.

One of his sermons, preached in December 1734, is called "The Preciousness of Time and the Importance of Redeeming It"[11] and is based on Ephesians 5:16. One section of that sermon was on improving the time we have. Among his points were these:

11. Jonathan Edwards, "The Preciousness of Time and the Importance of Redeeming It," *The Works of Jonathan Edwards*, vol. 2 (Edinburgh and Carlisle, Pa.: The Banner of Truth Trust, 1976), pp. 233–36.

1. *"Consider . . . that you are accountable to God for your time."* Time is as much a talent given you by God as your natural attributes or advantages. If you were really convinced that you will have to give God an accounting for what you do with your time, would you not use it otherwise than you do? Would you not resolve "never to lose one moment of time, but to improve it in the most profitable way [you] possibly can"? If you believe that, all that is left is to do it.

2. *"Consider how much time you have lost already."* If you are old or in middle age, you need to pay special attention to this. If you have not been active in Christ's service, you have wasted many precious moments. You can never make them up. But should you not then make every effort to use the remaining time well? Should you not "redeem the time" you do have, knowing the evil of the age and the value of the gospel?

3. *Consider how you may "improve the present time without delay."* There is nothing you can do about the past, but you should at least make sure that you do not repeat your former errors. Turn from your idleness, sin, or unbelief. Believe on the Lord Jesus Christ and determine to follow him. Witness for him. Remember that you are to understand the times and use time wisely. The time is coming when "time shall be no more."

207

Sleepers Awake!

Romans 13:11

And do this, understanding the present time. The hour has come for you to wake up from your slumber, because our salvation is nearer now than when we first believed.

My favorite radio station has a unique feature of its early-morning programming called the "Sousalarm." They play a lively Sousa march at 7:15 A.M. sharp to rouse listeners out of bed and get them started on the day. In this text we have a "gospel alarm," taken from Paul's call to Christians in Romans 13. It is an insistent wake-up call: "The hour has come for you to wake up from your slumber, because our salvation is nearer now than when we first believed" (Rom. 13:11).

Paul's Teaching and Jesus' Teaching

I have had several occasions in these studies of Romans 12 and 13 to show that Paul is reflecting the teaching of the Lord Jesus Christ in what he says. Since this is nowhere clearer than in the very last part of Romans 13, let me take just a moment to point up three references. As I see it, these references follow the same sequence as in the gospels. Conventional dating of the New Testament books places the Pauline epistles early and the gospels late, but this does not mean that Paul was necessarily unfamiliar with the material

1705

about Jesus' life that was later included in the gospels. Consider what we have in Romans 13:8–11.

1. *"Love your neighbor as yourself."* In verses 8–10 Paul discussed the law of love, probably with an awareness of Jesus' teaching about the greatest and second greatest of the commandments. That specific teaching is found in Matthew 22.

2. *"Understand . . . the present time."* In verse 11 Paul urged his readers to live godly lives because they understand the present time. This reminds us of Jesus' instructions to his disciples found in the sermon given on the Mount of Olives before his crucifixion (Matt. 24).

3. *"Wake up from your slumber."* In verse 11 we have Paul's call to Christians to wake up. This bears a striking resemblance to Jesus' parable of the five wise and five foolish women recorded in Matthew 25.

Since Paul is probably echoing Jesus' teaching in this verse, we can conclude that our Lord himself as well as the great apostle to the Gentiles, the leading theologian of the early Church, combine in these words to call each of us to wake up. So I ask, Are you awake? Are you awake to your calling, to your unique opportunities for service as a Christian? Are you using the time the Lord has given you to be a witness for him?

The Sleeping Christian

I begin by reminding you that these words are written to professed believers in Jesus Christ and not to non-Christians. Many who claim to be Christians are asleep. Christians are called to behave in a Christlike way to all people—above all, living out the law of love (v. 10)—but many are not actually doing it. As far as all outward appearances are concerned, they are like those unbelievers around them who are spiritually dead. They are not active for God. They are slumbering.

They are like Jonah when he was running away from God. Jonah was a prophet whom God had called to go to Nineveh, the capital city of the great Assyrian empire. He was to preach a message of judgment against it. But Jonah wouldn't go. As he later explained it, he was aware that God was "a gracious and compassionate God, slow to anger and abounding in love, a God who relents from sending calamity" (Jonah 4:2; cf. Exod. 34:5–7), and he reasoned that if God was like that, then the only possible reason for God's sending him to Nineveh with a message of judgment was so that the people might repent and be saved. Since the Assyrians were the hated enemies of his own people, the Jews, Jonah didn't want to preach anything to them.

So he ran away to Tarshish, a city on the far side of the Straits of Gibraltar in Spain. He did it by taking a ship from the Jewish port city of Joppa, paying his full fare.

Jonah could take the ship, but God was not obliged to take this disobedience from Jonah. So God sent a storm onto the Mediterranean Sea that threatened to sink the vessel, drowning not only Jonah but also the pagans who were sailing it. It was a furious storm, fierce beyond anything these experienced sailors had ever encountered before. So they were praying desperately, all of them—all, that is, but Jonah. Jonah had gone below deck where he had fallen into a deep sleep.

At this point the captain went to him and rebuked him: "How can you sleep? Get up and call on your god! Maybe he will take notice of us, and we will not perish" (Jonah 1:6).

What a sobering picture this is! The sailors were doing everything they knew to do to save the ship, even praying in their ignorance to whatever gods there might be! But Jonah, the one person who actually knew the great God who controls everything, even the winds and the waves, and who also knew why the storm had been sent, was asleep in the ship's dark hold.

The great French thinker and writer Jacques Ellul wrote a study of Jonah in which he viewed the sailors as standing for the unsaved, perishing world, and Jonah as standing for the insensitive, sleeping church. He notes that in this world (not the world to come, but this world) the destinies of both are linked:

> The safety of all depends on what each does. But each has his own thing to do. They are in the same storm, subject to the same peril, and they want the same outcome. They are in a unique enterprise, and this ship typifies our situation. What do these sailors do? First, they do all they humanly can; while Jonah sleeps, they try all human methods to save the vessel, to keep the enterprise going (v. 5). What experience, nautical science, reason, and common sense teach them to do, they do. In this sense they do their duty. The sailors are in charge of the world, and in normal conditions they discharge their task correctly. We can ask no more of them. The tragic thing here, however, is that if conditions cease to be normal, it is not the fault of the sailors, the pagans; it is the fault of the Christian who has sailed with them. It is because of him that the situation is such that the knowledge and tradition of the sailors can do no more.
>
> We have to realize once again that this is how it usually is with the world; the storm is unleashed because of the unfaithfulness of the church and Christians. This being so, if the tempest is God's will to constrain his church, a will by which the whole human enterprise is endangered, one can easily see why man's technical devices are of no avail.[1]

When Jonah finally did wake up—or rather was awakened by the captain—he had a valuable message to deliver to the sailors, even though he was running away and had been disobedient. He pointed to the Hebrew God as the true God ("the God of heaven, who made the sea and the land," Jonah 1:9), explained what was going on, which the sailors had no way of knowing ("It is my fault that this great storm has come upon you," Jonah 1:12), and proposed a solution ("Pick me up and throw me into the sea," Jonah 1:12).

1. Jacques Ellul, trans. by Geoffrey W. Bromiley, *The Judgment of Jonah* (Grand Rapids: Wm. B. Eerdmans Publishing Company, 1971), pp. 29–30.

In fact, as I read the story I sense that the sailors became believers in God as a result of Jonah's testimony. For we are told at the end of the first chapter, after they had thrown Jonah overboard and the sea had become calm, "At this the men greatly feared the Lord, and they offered a sacrifice to the Lord and made vows to him" (Jonah 1:16).

Do you know people who need to hear your testimony about the God who is able to save sinners? Of course, you do. They are perishing, and they have no idea what to do. You have the answer. The answer is that God sent his Son, the Lord Jesus Christ, to be their Savior by dying for them and in their place. They need to believe on him. Isn't it time for you to wake up and tell them about Jesus?

He Found Them Sleeping

There is another Bible story that we also need to think about at this point, and that is the story of the disciples sleeping in the garden on the night of Jesus' arrest by the temple authorities. Jesus was praying in great agony, saying to the Father, "My Father, if it is possible, may this cup be taken from me. Yet not as I will, but as you will" (Matt. 26:39). Jesus asked the disciples to keep him company, to watch and pray. But they failed to do it. Instead of praying, they were soon fast asleep even as the enemies of Christ made their way into the garden to carry him off to trial and crucifixion.

The disciples, who had not prayed and therefore had not been fortified by God for what was coming, quickly fled. And a short time later, Peter, who followed the arresting party into the courtyard of the Jewish high priest, denied that he ever knew Jesus (Matt. 26:69–75).

In Jonah's case, the sleeper missed the opportunity to testify about God to the unbelieving world—at least until he was awakened by the world and by circumstances. In the second case, the sleeping disciples failed to pray and were therefore useless when the hour of crisis came.

Is it any different today? Are believers not as much asleep in our day as ever they were? The need of the world is apparent, but we do not see it. We have the answer to the world's troubles, but we don't know it. Or if we do, we fail to make it known. Is that true of you? Awake, sleepers! That is the message. If you have been asleep, you need to wake up right now.

Sounding of the "Gospel Alarm"

Have you ever gone into someone's bedroom to wake him up and found him so deeply asleep that all he wanted to do was keep on sleeping? I am sure you have. So I am sure you can understand that the situation of the church in our day is very much like that. The world is perishing. Christians are sleeping. And Christians do not even want to wake up! It is easier and far more pleasant to go on sleeping. Why should we wake up? Why should we even want to wake up? Let me give you some reasons.

1. *Because our salvation is nearer now than when we first believed.* This is the reason Paul himself gives, and it is a powerful one. Whenever it was that you first believed on Jesus Christ as your Savior and promised to follow him as his disciple—whether five years ago, fifty years ago, or just recently—you have less time to serve him now than you did when you first believed. Your time is not unlimited. Besides, it is slipping away with every passing moment. When are you going to live for Jesus, if not now?

If you are a young person, it is easy to suppose that life is long and that you still have plenty of time to serve Jesus. You do not know that, of course. There is no guarantee that you will live through today, let alone for forty, fifty, or sixty more years. But even if you do have a very long life before you, why should you want to waste the time you have? Or if you waste it now, forming a pattern of living for yourself rather than for God, what is to make you think that you will change your self-centered ways and be of any use to others later? If you do not wake up and live for Jesus now, it is likely that you will continue sleeping into old age and die having done nothing at all of value for the Lord Jesus Christ or his kingdom.

If you are an old person, you may have wasted many years—just as I have been describing. You are willing to confess that what I have just said is very true. Past days are indeed lost opportunities. But you are still here, you are still listening, and what I am saying is, "Wake up!" Even on his deathbed, young David Brainard, a missionary to the American Indians and close friend of Jonathan Edwards, took time to teach a young Indian boy to read so he could read the Bible. He was glad that there was still something, even in his weakened state, that he could do for Jesus. Is there nothing you can do, even in your old age?

2. *Because you have no right to sleep when there is work to do.* The great Baptist preacher Charles Haddon Spurgeon gave a sermon on Romans 13:11 in which he explained why believers have no right to be asleep. He showed that Christians have been rescued from death to be Christ's witnesses and that they are called to be alert and working until Jesus comes.

He developed this from the case of the ten virgins in Christ's parable:

> When the five wise virgins went out to meet the bridegroom, and took their lamps with them, what right had they to be asleep? I can very well understand those sleeping who had no oil in the vessels with their lamps, because when their lamps went out they would be in the dark, and darkness suggests sleep. But those who had their lamps well trimmed, should they go asleep in the light? Those that had the oil, should they go to sleep while the oil was illuminating them? They needed to be awake to put the oil into the lamp. Besides, they had come out to meet the bridegroom. Could they meet him asleep? When he should come, would it be fit that he should find those who attended his wedding all asleep in a row, insulting his dignity and treating his glory with scorn?[2]

---

2. Charles Haddon Spurgeon, "Wake up! Wake up!" in *Metropolitan Tabernacle Pulpit*, vol. 24 (Pasadena, Tex.: Pilgrim Publications, 1972), p. 655.

We might argue that if they had been awake they might have been able to instruct and help those other women who were not ready for the Lord's return and who were eventually shut out of the wedding banquet.

3. *Because we have many enemies who are awake and working even if we are not.* This is a point Spurgeon also makes, pointing to the enemy who sowed the tares in the gospel field "while everyone was sleeping" (Matt. 13:25). He said:

> You may sleep, but you cannot induce the devil to close his eyes. . . . You may see evangelicals asleep, but you will not find ritualists slumbering. The prince of the power of the air keeps his servants well up to their work. Is it not a strange thing that the servants of the Lord often serve him at a poor, cold, dead-alive rate? Oh, may the Lord quicken us! If we could with a glance see the activities of the servants of Satan, we should be astonished at our own sluggishness.[3]

At the height of the cold war Robert McNamara, who was at the time United States secretary of state, said that he always had to remember that "when we are sleeping the other two-thirds of the world is awake and up to some mischief." As for ourselves, if we understood that the enemies of the gospel are always awake, wouldn't we be more alert in opposing them and speaking up for Jesus?

4. *Because there is something worth waking up for.* I am told that one of the saddest things about the prisons of this country is that so many prisoners fall into what the wardens call a prison shuffle, moving at the slowest possible speed, and that many who are imprisoned spend long hours in their beds trying to sleep the lengthy years of their sentences away. That is sad, but understandable. It is understandable that people who have nothing to live for should want to kill time.

But that is not our case. We have meaningful work to do. We have the task of telling men and women of that Savior who, if they believe on him, will lift them out of darkness into light and out of death into life. Moreover, that life is an eternal life, so the fruit of what we are given to do as Christians is eternal. Those who are saved through our witness will be in heaven with God forever. They will be part of that everlasting chorus that will be praising God. Likewise, the good works we do will be remembered before God forever. Not even a cup of water given to a thirsty person in Christ's name will be forgotten.

What else in all of life is like that? Everything else is going to pass away. It will perish. So why live for things that perish? Live for God. The Bible says, "The world and its desires pass away, but the man who does the will of God lives forever" (1 John 2:17). Our text says, "The hour has come for you to wake up from your slumber." Or as the King James version has it, "It is high time" to wake up! And so it is!

---

3. Spurgeon, "Wake up," p. 657.

The Sad Case of Unbelievers

Romans 13:11 is directed to Christians, but it is legitimate to address unbelievers also. Some Christians are asleep in respect to spiritual things, but unbelievers are more than asleep—they are spiritually dead, because unaided by God they are unable to respond to, understand, or even hear the gospel.

Here I turn back to Matthew 25:1–13, which contains the parable of the five wise and the five foolish women. In Spurgeon's handling of the story, the focus was on those who had no right to be asleep. Spurgeon applied it to people who know Jesus Christ but who are asleep and therefore fail properly to wait for or serve him. But what of the other five women? They were not true believers; they were lost. What of them?

The important thing about this part of the parable is that those who were lost actually thought they were saved and, in fact, for a time were indistinguishable from their believing sisters. This is a point made in each of the three parables in this chapter. The five women had received the bridegroom's invitation, had responded positively, and were even waiting for his coming. They were sure they would be admitted to the wedding banquet. Therefore, even though they were not ready when he came because they were off buying oil, trying to get ready, they expected him to open the door to them and were incredulous when he turned them away.

"Sir! Sir! Open the door for us!" they cried.

He replied, "I tell you the truth, I don't know you" (Matt. 25:11–12).

In the next story the servant who buried his master's talent and did not use it was amazed when the master disapproved of his actions. He thought he had done well, but his master called him wicked and lazy and had him cast "outside, into the darkness, where there will be weeping and gnashing of teeth" (Matt. 25:26–30).

In the third parable recounted in Matthew 25, the goats could not understand why they were rejected since, as they implied, they would have fed Jesus if they had seen him and understood that he was hungry, or given him something to drink if they had seen him and understood that he was thirsty, or invited him in, or clothed him, or looked after him, or gone to visit him. They did not understand that they would have been able to do that only by helping other people or understand that their opportunity to do it was now past. They too were asleep. They also perished.

In each of these cases, the people involved were members of what we would call the visible church. So the parables are to warn such people, people who think everything is well with their souls, that they need to wake up to their true spiritual condition.

This is what happened during the American revivals that took place in the colonies under the preaching of such godly men as Jonathan Edwards, Gilbert Tennent, and George Whitfield. The movement was called the Great Awakening because this was the first effect the preachers of the gospel noticed. They noticed that people who had been thinking of themselves as

Christians woke up to the fact that they were not actually born-again children of God and were distressed by that fact. Once awakened, they were able to hear the gospel and believe it. By believing they gave evidence that they were spiritually regenerated or revived.

What we need today is another Great Awakening. It is what you need if you only *think* you are a Christian.

208

Saint Augustine's Text

Romans 13:12–14

The night is nearly over; the day is almost here. So let us put aside the deeds of darkness and put on the armor of light. Let us behave decently, as in the daytime, not in orgies and drunkenness, not in sexual immorality and debauchery, not in dissension and jealousy. Rather, clothe yourselves with the Lord Jesus Christ, and do not think about how to gratify the desires of the sinful nature.

There are some verses in the Bible that immediately bring to mind some great Christian leader or hero of the faith, just because they are so closely associated with that person's life or testimony. Romans 1:17 is the best-known example, because it was used of God in the conversion of Martin Luther, the father of the Protestant Reformation: "The just shall live by faith" (KJV). But how about Matthew 28:20, "Lo, I am with you alway, even unto the end of the world" (KJV)? That was the life verse of David Livingstone, the great pioneer missionary to central Africa. Or John Newton's text: "Thou shalt remember that thou wast a bondsman in the land of Egypt, and the Lord thy God redeemed thee" (Deut. 15:15, KJV)? Newton, the former "slave of slaves," regarded those words as a description of his early dissolute life and of God's deliverance of him from it.

There are so many of these verses, all linked to the conversion or life work of some great Christian leader, that earlier in this century an Australian pastor named Frank W. Boreham produced a series of books on them that proved immensely popular.[1] Most bore as a subtitle the words: "Texts That Made History."

At the end of Romans 13, we arrive at three verses that make anyone who knows anything of church history think at once of Saint Augustine, the words God used in his conversion: "The night is nearly over; the day is almost here. So let us put aside the deeds of darkness and put on the armor of light. Let us behave decently, as in the daytime, not in orgies and drunkenness, not in sexual immorality and debauchery, not in dissension and jealousy. Rather, clothe yourselves with the Lord Jesus Christ, and do not think about how to gratify the desires of the sinful nature" (Rom. 13:12–14). How it came about is a fascinating story.

Augustine's Early Life

Saint Augustine's first name was Aurelius, though he himself never used it—we know it only from those who wrote about him. Augustine was born on November 13, 354 A.D., of mixed pagan and Christian parentage—his mother was a Christian, his father was not—at Tagaste, a small provincial town in North Africa.

His parents had great ambitions for him, though their desires differed greatly. His mother's name was Monnica, and the passion of her life was that her son might become a Christian. His father wanted him to have a superior liberal education and by this means eventually become a great and wealthy man. So Augustine was educated first in his hometown, then at the renowned but notoriously corrupt city of Carthage, also on the northern coast of Africa across from Sicily. Augustine was trained as a rhetorician, one who made his living by arguing cases of law or giving speeches. He was brilliant and was so successful that he later moved from Carthage to Rome, and eventually, in 384 A.D., from Rome to Milan, where he had been appointed government professor of rhetoric. This post gave him high social standing and brought him into contact with the most influential people in Italy, even members of the Roman court.

In 400 A.D., about fourteen years after his conversion, which took place in Milan in 386 A.D., Augustine published his *Confessions*. This was a book of thirteen relatively short chapters in which he tells of the grace of God in his early life and how God led him to faith in Jesus Christ.

On the very first page, Augustine wrote this sentence: "Thou hast formed us for thyself, and our hearts are restless till they find rest in thee."[2] He meant that of everyone, of course, but it was especially true of himself and is there-

---

1. The series began in 1920, continued until 1928, and contained such titles as *A Bunch of Everlastings, A Handful of Stars, A Casket of Cameos, A Faggot of Torches,* and *A Temple of Topaz.*

2. Saint Augustine, *The Confessions of St. Augustine,* in *A Select Library of the Nicene and Post-Nicene Fathers of the Christian Church,* ed. Philip Schaff, vol. 1 (Grand Rapids: Wm. B. Eerdmans Publishing Company, 1974), p. 45.

fore the major testimony of his life. Augustine tried everything the world had to offer, but he found it all empty. He was indeed restless until he came to rest in Christ.

1. *His youthful pleasures.* To many people one of the most fascinating parts of the *Confessions* is Augustine's description of his early life. Because of what he says, Augustine has been thought of as having lived a wild and wasteful life, being something of an abandoned libertine and a rake. But there are two things wrong with this way of thinking. First, he was not as depraved as we suppose. He was promiscuous, sleeping with many women at age sixteen, but by the age of seventeen he had formed a long-lasting relationship with a woman whom he did not marry—his parents did not want him to marry, supposing that marriage at an early age would be an obstacle to his career—and Augustine and this woman were faithful to each other until they were eventually forced apart to make way for a "proper" legal marriage some fourteen years later. Augustine wrote that while they were together he was faithful to her, and the *Confessions* contain a tragic passage describing his personal heartbreak when they were forced apart.[3]

The second thing wrong with thinking of Augustine as a great libertine is that it somehow makes him worse than we ourselves are. Augustine was no better but also not much worse than everyone else in his time, and the way he lived is all too common even today. We live in an age of similar sexual "liberation," and the pattern of Augustine's early years is duplicated today many millions of times over, even by Christian people. So we are no better. And while it is true that he confessed his sins openly, and we usually do not, his sins were only those of which many of us are also guilty.

But here is the point. With ruthless self-examination and logic this great saint—for such he became—explains that even in his indulgences his heart remained restless. For a time he indeed lived for fleshly pleasures. But he found that even surfeited with all the pleasures of the flesh "our hearts are restless till they find rest in thee."

2. *His quest for philosophical truth.* Augustine did not only have a strong sexual nature, however. He also had a strong and restless mind, and his *Confessions* tell how he journeyed from one popular philosophical system to another to try to discover truth. He was awakened to this pursuit by reading a book of Cicero's, since lost, called *Hortensius.* The great Latin writer had written it to encourage love for philosophy, and this was its immediate effect on Augustine. From this point on Augustine resolved to make truth his sole pursuit.

His strong mind led him into the philosophy of the Manichaeans, who were the rationalists of their age. They expressed a high reverence for Jesus Christ, but their religion was all naturalistic, or antisupernatural. They were

---

3. "My mistress being torn from my side as an impediment to my marriage, my heart, which clave to her, was racked, and wounded, and bleeding. And she went back to Africa, making a vow unto thee never to know another man, leaving with me my natural son by her" (Augustine, *Confessions,* p. 100).

critical of the Bible and had developed a way of looking at evil that relieved man of responsibility for personal sins or failures. This was appealing to a young man, as you can imagine. It bolstered Augustine's intellectual pride, allowed him to speak well of his mother's religion, excused his moral failings, and freed him to live in any manner he pleased.

Augustine drifted away from the Manichees at about the time he left North Africa for Rome. For a short while he was disillusioned and skeptical about everything, but he was then introduced to the Platonists, who sought for an immaterial reality, good, or truth behind the observable phenomena of life. This had a deep effect on Augustine since, up to this point, he had been unable to think of anything immaterial as real.

But even this was unsatisfactory. Augustine was on the way toward true faith and God, but he still had not found what he was seeking. In a wonderfully perceptive passage he compares the books of the Platonists with what he later found in Scripture:

> I read, not indeed in the same words, but to the selfsame effect, enforced by many and divers reasons, that, "In the beginning was the Word, and the Word was with God, and the Word was God. The same was in the beginning with God. All things were made by him; and without him was not anything made that was made." . . . But that "he came unto his own, and his own received him not. But as many as received him, to them he gave power to become the sons of God, even to them that believe on his name." That I did not read there.
>
> In like manner, I read there that God the Word was born not of flesh, nor of blood, nor of the will of man, nor of the will of the flesh, but of God. But that "the Word was made flesh, and dwelt among us," I read not there. . . .
>
> That before all times, and above all times, thy only-begotten Son remaineth unchangeably co-eternal with thee . . . is there. But that "in due time Christ died for the ungodly," and that "thou sparedst not thine only Son, but deliveredst him up for us all," is not there.[4]

In other words, Augustine learned about the immaterial, unchangeable mind, or *logos*, of God from the Platonists. The Platonists had surmised many true things about God. But Augustine did not find the incarnation of Jesus Christ or the atonement in their writings. He did not find the gospel. Therefore, he did not find forgiveness for his sins, and his heart remained restless because it had not yet come to rest in God.

3. *His fame.* When Augustine arrived in Milan as government professor of rhetoric at the university, he was immediately launched into the highest and most influential circles of Italian society. His mother was brought over from Africa. The circle of his old intimates gathered around him. Wealthy and influential friends sought him out. He had achieved the fame he sought. But, as often happens when people finally find the thing they have been fervently

---

4. Saint Augustine, *Confessions*, pp. 107–8.

seeking, Augustine discovered that the realization of his life goal was unsatisfying. In fact, this became the most miserable time of his life. He even became sick of a chest or lung infection, and it was doubtful whether he would be able to continue his career in oratory.

4. *His exposure to religion.* Augustine was always somewhat religious, and his religion was never very far from the true evangelical religion of his mother, which was Christianity. Augustine was skeptical, but he almost always believed in God, and in these early days he would probably have said that in one way or another he was always striving to know him.

When Augustine arrived in Milan he came under the influence of Ambrose, the bishop of that city. Ambrose was a man of towering intellect, massive learning, and great godliness. Moreover, he was an outstanding preacher. So Augustine, who loved the technical skills of good speaking, went to hear him. At first Augustine was interested only in his homiletical style. But Ambrose was really an expositor of the Bible and thus also an outstanding teacher of Christian doctrine. Almost in spite of himself, Augustine was led deeper into understanding what the gospel of salvation through Jesus Christ was all about, though he had not yet come to a point at which he could commit himself to Jesus and become his disciple. He began to read the Bible.

Augustine was also introduced to the lives of several very prominent Christians. One was Victorinus, a rhetorician like Augustine. He made public profession of his faith in Rome, though he was then well known and his identification with Christ was costly. Augustine was likewise influenced by the story of Antony and the legendary monks of Egypt. Antony renounced the world for Christ. This moved Augustine, who loved the world, but he did not believe the gospel. Augustine understood much about Christianity. But his heart was restless, because he had not yet come to rest in Christ.

"Save Me, But Not Yet!"

Augustine wrote of these days, "To thee, showing me on every side that what thou saidst was true, I, convicted by the truth, had nothing at all to reply, but the drawling and drowsy words: 'Presently, lo, presently'; 'Leave me a little while.' But 'presently, presently,' had no present; and my 'leave me a little while' went on for a long while."[5] He looked to his past and observed, "But I, miserable young man, supremely miserable even in the very outset of my youth, had entreated chastity of thee, and said, 'Grant me chastity and continency, but not yet.' For I was afraid lest thou shouldest hear me soon, and soon deliver me."[6]

On one occasion he cried out to his good friend Alypius, "What is wrong with us? . . . The unlearned start up and 'take' heaven, but we, with our learning, but wanting heart, see where we wallow in flesh and blood! Because others

5. Ibid., p. 121.
6. Ibid., p. 124.

have preceded us, are we ashamed to follow, and not rather ashamed at not following?"[7]

The Scene in the Garden

At last there came the well-known scene in the garden of a friend's estate near Milan, where Augustine was converted. He and Alypius had been reading the Bible together, but Augustine became so distressed at his own lack of spiritual resolution that he withdrew to a distant part of the garden so he could give vent to his emotion and Alypius would not see his tears.

These are Augustine's words:

I flung myself down, how, I know not, under a certain fig-tree, giving free course to my tears. . . . And, not indeed in these words, yet to this effect, spake I much unto thee—"But thou, O Lord, how long?" "How long, Lord? Wilt thou be angry forever? O, remember not against us former iniquities"; for I felt that I was enthralled by them. . . . "Why not now? Why is there not this hour an end to my uncleanness?"

I was saying these things and weeping in the most bitter contrition of my heart, when, lo, I heard the voice as of a boy or girl, I know not which, coming from a neighboring house, chanting, and oft repeating, "Take up and read; take up and read." Immediately my countenance was changed, and I began most earnestly to consider whether it was usual for children in any kind of game to sing such words; nor could I remember ever to have heard the like. So, restraining the torrent of my tears, I rose up, interpreting it no other way than as a command to me from heaven to open the book, and to read the first chapter I should light upon. For I had heard of Antony, that, accidentally coming in whilst the gospel was being read, he received the admonition as if what was read were addressed to him: "Go and sell that thou hast, and give to the poor, and thou shalt have treasure in heaven; and come and follow me." And by such oracle was he forthwith converted unto thee.

So quickly I returned to the place where Alypius was sitting; for there had I put down the volume of the apostles, when I rose thence. I grasped, opened, and in silence read that paragraph on which my eyes first fell,—"Not in rioting and drunkenness, not in chambering and wantonness, not in strife and envying; but put ye on the Lord Jesus Christ, and make not provision for the flesh, to fulfill the lusts thereof." No further would I read, nor did I need; for instantly, as the sentence ended—by a light, as it were, of security infused into my heart—all the gloom of doubt vanished away.[8]

Alypius was converted himself at this time, and both of them went to tell Augustine's mother, Monnica, who had been praying for her son for years and now rejoiced and praised God for his conversion. It was not long after this that Monnica died, as she and Augustine were on their way back to North

---

7. Saint Augustine, *Confessions,* p. 124.
8. Ibid., pp. 127–128.

Africa, where Augustine eventually became a presbyter and then Bishop of
Hippo Regius, serving the Lord there for more than forty years until his death
on August 28, 430 A.D., at the age of seventy-six.

Augustine's Later Life

It is hard to overestimate the importance of Augustine's contribution to
Christian theology and the church. Hippo was a second-rate diocese, having
no special prominence in itself. Besides, it was overrun by the Vandals at the
very time Augustine was dying, and the bishopric, the school, and the clergy
that Augustine had established and trained were all either widely scattered
or destroyed. Nevertheless, Augustine's influence lived on, perhaps more than
any other nonbiblical figure, through his writings. They gave form to the best
of the church's life during the Middle Ages and were in a sense the true foundation of the Holy Roman Empire.

Adolf Harnack was no conservative theologian, but he called Augustine
the greatest man whom, "between Paul the Apostle and Luther the Reformer,
the Christian Church has possessed."[9]

After his conversion Augustine produced many polemical works against
the Manichaeans, Donatists, and Pelagians, interspersed with Bible expositions and theological studies. He is best known for four works that aptly crown
the whole: (1) *The Confessions*, written about 400 A.D.; (2) *On Christian Doctrine*,
written from 397–426; (3) *On the Holy Trinity*, written from 395–420; and (4)
The City of God, written from 413–426. The fourth volume was the first attempt
by any Christian writer to produce a philosophy of history, and it has become
an acknowledged classic. In it Augustine describes two rival cities or societies
". . . formed by two loves: the earthly by the love of self, even to the contempt
of God; the heavenly by the love of God, even to the contempt of self."[10] It
is a masterful way of analyzing history.

Don't Put Off Putting On!

Romans 13:13–14 was not only God's means of leading Saint Augustine
to faith in Christ, it was also a summary of his life. Verse 13 describes what
he was. Verse 14 describes what he became. The passage from the first condition to the second is what the Bible urges upon everyone.

These two verses are best known for effecting the conversion of Saint
Augustine. But if we think about them for a moment, it is evident that they
are not in the first instance written to unbelievers to urge them to become

9. Adolf Harnack in "Monasticism and the Confessions of St. Augustine." Cited by Benjamin
Breckinridge Warfield, *Calvin and Augustine* (Philadelphia: Presbyterian and Reformed
Publishing Company, 1956), p. 306.

10. Saint Augustine, *The City of God*, in *A Select Library of the Nicene and Post–Nicene Fathers of
the Christian Church*, ed. Philip Schaff, vol. 2 (Grand Rapids: Wm. B. Eerdmans Publishing
Company, 1977), pp. 282–83.

Christians at all. This part of Romans, beginning with the first verse of chapter 12, is written to Christians to explain how they are to live. It really means that we who profess Christ are to live godly lives.

But God uses his Word in unexpected ways, and it is impossible to imagine any passage of the Bible that could not be used by God sometime for the conversion of someone. Is that how God has been using these verses in your life? Has he been using Romans 13:13–14 to move you from sinful self-indulgence, a pursuit of wealth and fame, or even religion, to faith in Jesus Christ? If God has been doing that with you, let me say clearly that now is the time to commit yourself to him. Do not say, "Presently, presently" or "In a little while." The present is now. This is the only perfect time to "clothe yourself with the Lord Jesus Christ" and become a Christian.

PART TWENTY

Christian Liberty

209

Where Is the Chasm?

Romans 14:1

Accept him whose faith is weak, without passing judgment on disputable matters.

If someone spends a lot of time talking about a particular subject, it is usually because the person is interested in it and thinks it's important. So apparently Paul is very interested in the way Christians treat other Christians, since he writes on this subject at length.

Romans 14 begins a new section (Rom. 14:1–15:13), and it is one of the book's longest parts—certainly the longest single part of the closing application portion of the letter (Rom. 12:1–16:27). Why does Paul give so much space to discussing why Christians need to accept those with whom they disagree on less than essential matters? What about matters that in our judgment are much more important, like Christian economics, politics, ecology, or the emancipation of oppressed peoples? Is something as "insignificant" as accepting and getting along with other Christians really that important?

Apparently Paul thought so.

His instruction about developing a Christian mind, which I personally think is very important, was completed in two verses. To discuss a right estimate of oneself and others and the need to encourage others took six verses.

1723

A call to love one another filled thirteen verses; material on the question of church and state, seven verses; right conduct in light of the imminent return of Jesus Christ, seven verses more. But now his discussion of how Christians are to accept and support other Christians when they do not think or behave as we think they should fills all of chapter 14 and the first half of chapter 15, a total of thirty-five verses. Moreover, this is the last major subject Paul discusses, since following this he begins to talk about his own future plans and sends his final greetings. Apparently, this is the matter he wants to leave before our minds in closing.

There are two main parts to this section: (1) how people with tender consciences are to be treated (14:1–12), and (2) how the "strong" are to use their liberty (14:13–15:13). This is written for the "strong." So if you think you are a strong Christian, both these parts are for you.

What Is the Issue?

The first verse of chapter 14 is a thematic statement. In the New International Version it reads: "Accept him whose faith is weak, without passing judgment on disputable matters." Some people will know it better in the King James Version: "Him that is weak in the faith, receive ye, but not to doubtful disputations." Phillips paraphrases, "Welcome a man whose faith is weak, but not with the idea of arguing over his scruples."

There has been a great deal of debate over what Paul is specifically concerned about in this verse and those following. He is talking about people who are "weak" versus those who are "strong." But who are these weak and strong people? Paul does not spell out exactly who they are, nor why the views of the one party are weak or weaker than the other.

Later on in this section Paul mentions two specific matters: (1) the idea that a Christian is free to eat anything versus the idea that he should eat only vegetables, and (2) the keeping of special "holy" days. This makes us think of other passages in Paul's writings in which these matters are mentioned, but there are differences that make it hard to use those passages to explain what Paul is concerned about here.

For instance, in 1 Corinthians 8:1–13 and 10:23–33 Paul also uses the word *weak* while speaking of those who had reservations about eating meat from animals that had been sacrificed to one of the pagan gods or goddesses. But nothing in Romans mentions idols, and a concern for a vegetarian diet is not an issue in 1 Corinthians. There are similarities, but there is no reason to assume that the two situations were the same.

Again, Paul is concerned with the observance of special "holy" days in Galatians and Colossians. Galatians 4:10–11 says, "You are observing special days and months and seasons and years! I fear for you, that somehow I have wasted my efforts on you." In Colossians 2:16–17 he warns his readers about those who would impose the observance of such days upon them: "Therefore do not let anyone judge you by what you eat or drink, or with regard to a religious festival, a New Moon celebration or a Sabbath day. These are a shadow of the things that were to come; the reality, however, is found in Christ." Obviously, these are similar texts. But what is most noticeable about them is that Paul takes an entirely different approach in Galatians and Colossians from what he does in Romans. In the shorter Epistles he tells his readers not to become entangled in such things. In Romans he says that none of this matters.

Is Paul being inconsistent, then? Has his mind changed? No! He is merely dealing with different things. John Murray explains it like this:

> In Galatians Paul is dealing with the Judaizers who were perverting the gospel at its center. They were the propagandists of a legalism which maintained that the observance of days and seasons was necessary to justification and acceptance with God. This . . . was "a different gospel which is not another." . . . In Romans 14 there is no evidence that those esteeming one day above another were involved in any respect in this fatal error. They were not propagandists for a ceremonialism that was aimed at the heart of the gospel. Hence Paul's tolerance and restraint.[1]

A bit further on in this section, in chapter 15, Paul also speaks of differences between Jews and Gentiles, but he is not specific there, either. That is, he does not link the eating of meat or the observance of special days, or their opposites, to either group. So it is not a Jewish asceticism in food versus a Gentile laxity or indulgence that he has in mind.

When we put this together we are probably right to conclude that Paul is not thinking of any one area of action or belief specifically, though he throws out suggestions, but rather that he is intentionally being quite general. To use our common expression, the problem is that Christians are always dumping on one another. Instead of getting on with living their own lives as best they can to the glory of God or, which is also necessary, living so as to win nonbelievers to Christ, they are wasting their time trying to find fault with one another. They do not trust what God is doing in the other Christian.

We have to stop that behavior, Paul says. We must accept and support one another if we are to hear and heed what Paul is saying in this last major section of the letter.

Today's Issues, Not Yesterday's

Another matter we need to think about as we begin to get into this section is that when we are thinking about accepting other Christians as they are we need to grapple with the issues that are dividing believers today and not those that troubled Christians yesterday.

1. John Murray, *The Epistle to the Romans*, 2 vols. in 1 (Grand Rapids: Wm. B. Eerdmans Publishing Company, 1968), vol. 2, pp. 172–73.

I can think of several behavioral issues that years ago caused Christians to look down on other Christians and judge them and their conduct unfavorably: drinking, smoking, dancing, and going to movies. I did not spend much time in excessively narrow or legalistic church circles while I was growing up, but if I had, the list might have been expanded to include such things as the length of a boy's hair or the length of a girl's skirt.

In my youth those were the issues that would have fallen into the category Paul is writing about in Romans 14 and 15. And one of the sad things about those years is that what Paul wrote about in these chapters was not heeded. That is, the older generation made such a watershed issue of these things that many young people were turned off to religion, or at least to evangelical or fundamentalist religion, rather than conform to what they understood quite rightly to be other than the essence of the gospel.

Many unbelievers must have been turned off or at least confused by this as well. Many of them undoubtedly got the impression that being a Christian essentially meant giving up these so-called worldly vices, rather than trusting Jesus Christ as one's personal Savior and Lord.

But here is the problem. If that is all Paul is writing about in Romans 14 and 15, then he really doesn't have much to say to our generation. This is because ours is an antinomian, liberal, all-accepting generation, and except for a few narrow circles that most of us have little or no contact with, most Christians are all too accepting of what used to be called worldly conduct. We don't care whether people smoke or drink or play cards or so forth. That may be good in some ways, though I would argue that it is also bad in others. But that is not the point here. The question here is this: Is this all that Paul is talking about in these chapters; and if it is, shouldn't we just skip ahead to Romans 15:14 and congratulate ourselves on having already mastered this teaching?

I hope we know that this isn't right. The specifics may have changed, but the problem is with us somewhere, and it is probably greater in us than with others, especially if we do not think we have a problem. Let me suggest a few areas where we can apply this today.

1. *When another Christian is going through hard times.* I suppose this is the area in which I see the failure of the self-styled "strong" toward the "weak" brother or sister most often. Christians go through hard times. Sometimes it is in the family. A husband is deserted by his wife, or a wife is abandoned by her husband. Sometimes a Christian loses his job and, if the individual is a husband, may come to a point where he is unable to support his family. Sometimes there is sickness or an accident that brings a person to the very edge of life.

When Christians go through such difficult periods, their fellow believers should rally around them, support and encourage them, and help them financially. But instead, what often happens is that those who ought to help sit in judgment. They say, or at least they think, "That person must be out of the will of God, or this wouldn't have happened to her." Or a man loses his job and another Christian accuses him of failing to support his family, noting cruelly—he has a verse for the occasion—"If anyone does not provide for his relatives, and especially for his immediate family, he has denied the faith and is worse than an unbeliever" (1 Tim. 5:8). When a person has a serious car accident or falls or is struck with a serious disease, someone will say smugly, "God must be trying to get your attention."

What a terrible situation! Such "friends" speak like Job's counselors, and they do not even sit down and empathize with the struggling believer first, as those shallow but at least empathetic men did. Unfortunately, many Christians today lack empathy.

2. *Variations in individual piety.* A second area where Christians continue to judge one another is personal piety. Do you have a "quiet time" every morning? How long per day do you pray? Are you reading good Christian books? How often do you witness?

Don't get me wrong. I think a daily (or at least a regular) quiet time is important. It is essential that we pray, and none of us prays as much as would be profitable. I am constantly saying, "Turn off the television and read a worthwhile Christian book." We are commanded to witness. The problem is that we judge other Christians by whether they measure up to what we ourselves do, forgetting that we are probably not very good models in these areas ourselves, at least if we are to measure our performance by the saints of a past era, and that the other Christian may be excelling in areas with which we are not even familiar.

One very common form of this is the way a "spiritual" wife will judge a husband who does not read the Bible or Christian books as much as she does. He is not thinking about spiritual things all the time; he has his work to think about, and when he comes home he may be tired and perhaps only wants to watch the ball game on television. The wife, if she does not work outside the home and does not have her time entirely taken up with raising young children, has time to read and think. When her husband gets home she wants to talk about what she has been thinking about that day. If he doesn't, she thinks it is because he is not very spiritual or is "not right with God."

It may well be that the husband is not spiritual, of course. But whether he is or not, the attitude that judges him for what he is not doing and fails to appreciate him for what he is doing is wrong. And it is also wrong when the husband dismisses his wife and her concerns. In this case, it does not matter who is "weak" or who is "strong." What matters is that we accept the other Christian as a believer and trust God for what he is doing in that person's life.

Donald Grey Barnhouse told of being at a luncheon with a group of ministers where someone spoke disparagingly about the clergy in another denomination. They didn't seem to accomplish anything, he said. Barnhouse entered the conversation by telling about one of those ministers whom he had known personally. The man had gone through seminary and had been ordained. But he seldom preached, never went to prayer meetings, and often failed to attend church for weeks at a time. Worse than that, he spent all his time in his library and indulged in habits that others felt were intemperate and un-Christian. He lived this way for more than twenty years. The ministers concluded that a man like that was no credit to the ministry and perhaps was not even a Christian.

Later in the luncheon Barnhouse turned the conversation to the subject of Bible study helps and asked what the others thought was the best Bible concordance. They said that the best was *Strong's Exhaustive Concordance,* which contains Hebrew and Greek word lists and comparative helps. Barnhouse then pointed out that the minister he had described earlier, of whom they had all disapproved, was James Strong, the author of this invaluable volume.[2]

The point was obvious. God has given his servants diverse talents, and he uses them in ways that please him. How we feel about them is irrelevant, since they answer to God rather than to us. Our part is to accept these others as fellow believers and support them and pray for their work.

3. *Denominational affiliation.* Church affiliations also often wrongly divide believers and produce judgmental attitudes. I am not saying that we have to consider other denominations to be right in their distinctives, any more than we have to consider other Christians as always right when they differ from us. But just as we are to accept other Christians as Christians, so must we accept other denominations as true elements of the one body of Christ—if they acknowledge him as Lord and confess the gospel as the one way of salvation.

4. *Personality differences.* What about personality differences? Does every Christian have to be grim like an undertaker, or always smiling like a stand-up comedian? Charles Spurgeon was the greatest preacher of his age, but he was frequently criticized for being funny. When one woman objected to the humor he inserted into his sermons Spurgeon told her, "Madam, you would think a great deal better of me if you knew the funny things I kept out."

Spurgeon was a character. A young man asked what he should do about a box of cigars he had been given. Spurgeon solved his problem. "Give them to me," he said, "and I will smoke them to the glory of God."

On another occasion Spurgeon was criticized for traveling to meetings in a first class railway carriage. His antagonist said, "Mr. Spurgeon, what are you doing up here? I am riding back there in the third class carriage taking care of the Lord's money." Spurgeon replied, "And I am up here in the first class carriage taking care of the Lord's servant."

Let's stop dumping on one another, and let's allow God to deal with each of his servants how, when, and as kindly as he will. And while we are at it, let's be thankful that he has dealt as kindly as he has with us. If he had not, we would all be in deep trouble.

2. Donald Grey Barnhouse, *God's Freedom: Exposition of Bible Doctrines, Taking the Epistle to the Romans as a Point of Departure,* vol. 5, *Romans 6:1–7:25* (Grand Rapids: Wm. B. Eerdmans Publishing Company, 1961), p. 217.

What Does Paul Advise?

We are only at the beginning of this important section of Romans, of course. There is much more to come. But we should notice clearly even here that Paul has two initial points of advice. In fact, what he says is stronger than advice—these are commands, and the whole sentence is made up of them: "Accept him whose faith is weak" and "Do not pass judgment in disputable matters."

1. *Accept him whose faith is weak*. This means that we are to accept other Christians as Christians and that, as John Murray says, "There is to be no discrimination in respect of confidence, esteem, and affection."[3]

Accept is a strong term, because it is used of God's acceptance of us in verse 3 and of Christ's acceptance of us in 15:7. Verse 3 says, "The man who does not eat everything must not condemn the man who does, for God has accepted him." The other verse says, "Accept one another, then, just as Christ accepted you." If God has accepted the other person, who are you not to accept him?

2. *Do not pass judgment in disputable matters.* Recognize that some standards of right conduct are unclear and that other matters really do not matter. In those areas, let the matter drop and get on with things that do matter. Above all, accept the other believer for what he or she has to offer to the whole body of Christ. And do your own part too! Tell someone about Jesus. Certainly you have better things to do than to hunt out the speck in the eye of your fellow Christian while overlooking the plank in your own.

Francis Schaeffer used to talk about "the chasm." He said that we put it in the wrong place, dividing ourselves from other Christians. It shouldn't be there. True, there is a chasm between those who know Jesus Christ and those who do not, between Christians and the world, and it is a deep one. But that is where it lies, between Christians and the world, not between Christians and Christians. All who know Jesus Christ are on this side of the chasm, and we must stand with them for Christ's kingdom.

---

3. Murray, *The Epistle to the Romans*, vol. 2, p. 175.

210

Kosher Cooking and All That

Romans 14:2–4

One man's faith allows him to eat everything, but another man, whose faith is weak, eats only vegetables. The man who eats everything must not look down on him who does not, and the man who does not eat must not condemn the man who does, for God has accepted him. Who are you to judge someone else's servant? To his own master he stands or falls. And he will stand, for the Lord is able to make him stand.

Out in Arizona there is a great rift in the surface of the earth known as the Grand Canyon. On the map it appears only as a slightly shaded area that is not at all imposing. But if you are staying at a hotel on the north rim of the Grand Canyon and want to go to the south rim, you will discover that the only way you can get there is by driving over several hundred miles of hot desert roads.

I do not know if this is what Francis Schaeffer was thinking about when he spoke and wrote about "the chasm," as he often did. He was an American, but he lived in Switzerland and may have been thinking about some deep chasm in the Alps. But the particular chasm he had in mind is irrelevant. What this great contemporary apologist was thinking about was the way

Christians place chasms between themselves and other people, and his concern was that we get our chasms in the right place.

At the end of the last study, I pointed out that Christians tend to place chasms between themselves and other Christians, either judging them not to be Christians at all because of some offensive detail of their conduct or else regarding them as Christians but as those with whom they should have no contact. That is wrong. It is what Paul is denouncing in Romans 14, where he begins by saying, "Accept him who is weak in the faith, without passing judgment on disputable matters" (v. 1).

There is a true chasm, of course, and it is a frightening one. It is between those who are Christians and those who are not, between those who have been made spiritually alive and those who remain spiritually dead. That chasm can only be bridged by God through the utterly supernatural and spiritual work of regeneration. The chasm is not to be placed between any who truly believe on Jesus Christ as their Savior.

Christians Are Not Clones

Christians have plenty of problems with the world. The world has a different master, pursues different goals, and lives according to a different set of rules. We are not part of it. But the worst problems we face are on this side of the chasm, between Christians who all confess Jesus Christ to be Lord and Savior but who look at some things differently.

Christians are not clones. God could have made us identical copies of one another, I suppose, though that would not have been very interesting. But he did not. He made us very different, and as a result we inevitably act differently and also think differently about the things we do. These variations put strains on us all, and the end result is that we have difficulty getting along. People in the world have problems too, of course. Don't think that it is nicer out there. It isn't. But the fact that unbelievers have trouble getting along with one another does not mean that Christians should be blind to the problems we ourselves have.

What do we do when we encounter Christians who behave differently from us? Paul highlights two wrong responses here.

First, those who consider themselves to be strong in faith frequently look down on or despise the weak—they sneer. On the other hand, the weak usually condemn the strong—they frown.

Using the example of different opinions about what a Christian should eat or not eat, Paul says, "The man who eats everything must not look down on him who does not, and the man who does not eat must not condemn the man who does" (v. 3).

The First of Paul's Examples: Diet

In the introductory study to this section, Romans 14:1–15:13, I pointed out that Paul is approaching this matter broadly because this is a broad, generic problem in the church. But the problem expresses itself in specifics, and for that reason he gives two examples of what he has in mind. The first is the matter of eating or not eating certain foods. The second is observing or not observing special days.

Let's examine the first example, about what we eat or do not eat. Paul introduces it by saying: "One man's faith allows him to eat everything, but another man, whose faith is weak, eats only vegetables" (v. 2). What is he thinking about here? There are several possibilities.

1. *Keeping kosher.* We have already seen that nothing we know about the Jewish community or practice in the first Christian century perfectly fits what Paul says, nor does anything we know about conditions or religious practices among the Gentiles. On the other hand, what we know about each is a legitimate example.

Let's take the Jewish community first. There is nothing in the Old Testament law that required Jews to be vegetarians, which is what Paul says the "weak" brothers were in his example, but the Jews did have dietary restrictions. In Leviticus 11, careful distinctions are made between "clean" and "unclean" animals. Jews were free to eat the first but not the second. In Leviticus 17, the people were told not to eat blood, which had to be properly drained even from edible meat before it could be eaten. For Jews who "keep kosher" today this means that specifically appointed rabbis must oversee the slaughtering of animals and place kosher labels on the meat. Again, Exodus 23:19 (also 34:26) is a verse that has become the basis for Jews keeping two sets of dishes, one to hold foods made with milk and the other for those without milk. The verse merely says, "Do not cook a young goat in its mother's milk."

Even though there is nothing in Romans 14 to indicate that this is specifically what Paul has in mind, it is significant, as the great *Theological Dictionary of the New Testament* edited by Gerhard Kittel points out, that the word Paul uses to describe the "weak" brother, *astheneô*, is often used for the word *kosher* in the Greek translation of the Old Testament.[1] So it is highly likely that Jewish scruples about diet were at least one thing the apostle had in mind.

2. *Gentile asceticism.* Since Paul mentions vegetarianism, which the Jews as a whole did not practice, it is probably also right to suppose that he is thinking of certain kinds of Gentile asceticism, too, which we find in the writings of some of the Greek and Roman philosophers. At certain periods of ancient history life became so excessively indulgent that many of the pagans adopted a rigidly ascetic lifestyle, dressing in plain clothes, eating simple vegetables, and drinking only water.

---

1. Gerhard Kittel, editor, *Theological Dictionary of the New Testament,* vol. 1, trans. Geoffrey W. Bromiley (Grand Rapids: Wm. B. Eerdmans Publishing Company, 1964), p. 490.

In those days some people who thought like this would have become Christians, and it is easy to see how they might have carried their views over into Christianity as something of great importance to them. "After all," they might have said, "if I lived a simple lifestyle before I became a Christian, I am certainly not going to live a less pure life now." They had not learned that what they ate or did not eat was unimportant, and they would easily have become judges of their Christian brothers and sisters who lived like those whose lifestyle they were protesting even before they became believers.

3. *The Corinthian problem.* Finally, we can't overlook the fact that Paul was writing to Rome from Corinth, and he had faced one particular form of the eating problem there (see 1 Cor. 8:1–13 and 10:23–33).

In the pagan world of Paul's day the practice of religion consisted to a large extent of the offering of sacrifices at pagan temples. The animals were not just burnt up, of course, nor thrown away. Rather, after the offerings were made, the priests would present the carcasses for sale in the marketplaces, and as a result those who went to the market to buy meat would end up with meat from animals that had been sacrificed to the pagan idols. What was a Christian to do if he or she went to a friend's home and meat like this was served? Wouldn't eating it somehow defile the Christian or at least give legitimacy to pagan practices?

Paul answered that "an idol is nothing at all" and that a Christian should feel perfectly free to eat the meat. For the sake of those whose consciences might be wounded by such eating, however, a Christian should be sensitive on this issue and not impose his freedom on his weaker brothers or sisters unnecessarily. In a manner exactly parallel to what he says a bit further on in Romans, Paul wrote, "Therefore, if what I eat causes my brother to fall into sin, I will never eat meat again, so that I will not cause him to fall" (1 Cor. 8:13).

What are we to do about matters of eating or drinking, or not eating or not drinking, or similar matters? The important thing about Romans is that Paul is not even dealing with this issue as one to be resolved, but rather with the attitude that either scorns or condemns the other Christian. *That* is the issue! Not the eating or not eating. In other words, what you eat or do not eat or drink or do not drink does not matter, so stop arguing about it, and stop letting it determine with whom you will associate or with whom you will work in Christ's service.

Jesus' Revolutionary Teaching

There is something else we need to think about before we turn to Paul's specific instructions or advice, and that is the teaching of Jesus Christ on this issue, which Paul certainly knew.

Jesus' ministry was conducted almost entirely within Israel within Jewish circles, and the matter of keeping kosher was of great importance to Judaism. Jesus was revolutionary in what he taught on this issue, however. He had been talking about the Pharisees, who had objected to the fact that Jesus' disciples often ate without washing their hands ceremonially according to their law, and he replied by attacking their legalism, which, he said, was exercised without their actually obeying God's commands. One example was the way they avoided taking care of their elderly parents, saying that the money they could have used for this purpose had been dedicated to God. "You nullify the word of God by your tradition that you have handed down. And you do many things like that" (Mark 7:13; cf. vv. 1–13).

"Many things?" they might have objected. "For instance . . ."

How about your laws regarding kosher? Jesus asked. "Nothing outside a man can make him 'unclean' by going into him. Rather, it is what comes out of a man that makes him 'unclean'" (Mark 7:15).

When the disciples looked puzzled and later asked him what he meant, Jesus elaborated. "Don't you see that nothing that enters a man from the outside can make him 'unclean'? For it doesn't go into his heart but into his stomach, and then out of his body." Mark adds significantly, "In saying this, Jesus declared all foods 'clean'" (Mark 7:18–19).

Jesus continued, "What comes out of a man is what makes him 'unclean.' For from within, out of men's hearts, come evil thoughts, sexual immorality, theft, murder, adultery, greed, malice, deceit, lewdness, envy, slander, arrogance and folly. All these evils come from inside and make a man 'unclean'" (Mark 7:20–23). In Matthew Jesus adds, "But eating with unwashed hands does not make him 'unclean'" (Matt. 15:20; cf. vv. 16–20).

Obviously, Jesus was not concerned with external matters but with issues of the heart. So if Jesus was not concerned with external matters, God also is not concerned about them and we should not be either. As I say, this was radical teaching in that day in view of the Jews' well-known and rigorously observed laws of purification.

God is not concerned with what you eat!

But there is something about which God *is* concerned, and that is what comes out of our hearts. That is what makes a man "unclean," said Jesus. If it is not what goes into a person's mouth that defiles the person but what comes out, then we should exercise even more care than the ancient Jews did to get, have, and keep a pure heart. Our hearts are not pure naturally. Jeremiah said, "The heart is deceitful above all things and beyond cure" (Jer. 17:9). But because "with God all things are possible" (Matt. 19:26), my heart and your heart can be changed. They can be changed by Jesus and by the power of the Holy Spirit. That is what we should be concerned about. If we had any idea how impure our own hearts were and were concerned about them, we would be far less inclined to scorn and judge other believers.

Points for the "Strong" Believer

How do we get over our natural but destructive tendency to scorn or judge believers who do not behave exactly like we do? In these verses Paul gives several truths from which to start.

1. *The other Christian does not answer to you but to God.* Paul teaches this when he asks the self-styled "strong" believer, "Who are you to judge someone else's servant" (v. 4).

Why is it so hard for us to realize this? We understand how this works in everyday life. If you run a business and have people reporting to you, you have a right to determine their work goals, hours, terms of compensation, and performance standards. Your employees are accountable to you. But people who work for your competitor, the business down the street, or your neighbor are not accountable to you. You may not like what they are doing. You may disapprove of their objectives or work. But what they do is none of your business.

It is exactly the same in Christianity. I do not mean by this that we should not have a mutual concern for one another. Jesus taught that we are our brother's keeper (read the story of the Good Samaritan), and if that is true of other people in general, it is certainly true of our brothers and sisters in Christ. We have to pray for them, help them, urge them on, and do everything possible to see that they do well and succeed as Christians. But this does not include scorning them or judging them if in Jesus' service they see things differently and act differently than you do. This is because they do not answer to you. They answer to Jesus. Therefore, leave it with him. And remember that Jesus cares about them and is more concerned that they live an upright, strong, and spiritually profitable life than you are.

2. *God has already accepted the other Christian as he or she is.* We know this by definition since a Christian is one who stands before God not on the basis of his or her own righteousness but because of the work of Jesus Christ. Since the other believer has been accepted and not rejected by Jesus, you should accept him or her too.

This does not mean that everything the other Christian does is right any more than everything you do is right. But it means that the Christian is accepted because of Christ's death on his or her behalf and the gift of Christ's righteousness to such a one by God. In other words, the basis of his or her acceptance is not works. If you are making the other person's acceptance (by you or, as your own conduct implies, by God) depend on what he or she is doing, you are operating on the basis of salvation by works and are denying the gospel.

You do not have to agree that everything the other person is doing is right, any more than he has to agree that everything you are doing is right. But it does mean that you have to accept the person as a believer with whom you must be in fellowship, because God has himself accepted him, just as he has accepted you. In the last study I pointed out that the same word that is used in verse 1, where we are told to "accept" him whose faith is weak, is used in verse 3 of God's acceptance of us and in 15:7 of Christ's acceptance of us. So it is because God has accepted us that we are to accept others. Moreover, since *we* are accepted by grace apart from our works, obviously we need to accept other believers on the same basis.

We have to remember that "it is by grace [we all] have been saved, through faith—and this not from yourselves, it is the gift of God—not by works, so that no one can boast" (Eph. 2:8–9).

3. *The other Christian stands by the grace of God, just as you do.* Let's remember that it is also by grace that we stand and function in the Christian life. Paul indicates this when he says, "To his own master he stands or falls. And he will stand, for the Lord is able to make him stand" (v. 4).

Some commentators take this matter of standing or falling as referring to the final judgment because the words are often used in that context, but this is not what is in view here. "Acceptance" *does* refer to the basis on which we stand before God or are justified. We are accepted because of Christ's death here, and we will be accepted exactly for that reason at the final judgment. But as far as standing or falling is concerned, this is in the context of the servant's relationship to his master and of the master's ability to bear him or her up. It is a promise that Jesus will be with his people, that he has useful and important work for them to do, and that he will see that they are kept upright to accomplish it.

If Jesus feels that the other believer needs to change something about how he is living in order to accomplish the work he has ordained for him to do, Jesus will see to the change. You can't bring it about by yourself anyway. But if in the meantime Jesus does not bother to change that conduct, then it does not matter to him and is not hurting what he has appointed the other one to do. As a matter of fact, it is possible that what you are so concerned about does not matter under any circumstances—simply because you and I tend to get hung up on things that do not matter while we overlook the things that do.

Remember that Jesus told the Pharisees, "Woe to you, teachers of the law and Pharisees, you hypocrites! You give a tenth of your spices—mint, dill and cummin. But you have neglected the more important matters of the law—justice, mercy and faithfulness. You should have practiced the latter, without neglecting the former" (Matt. 23:23). The Pharisees would have looked down on the common people, who perhaps failed to tithe rigorously. But they had no trouble breaking scores of their other laws in order to arrest, try, and dispose of Jesus Christ.

4. *You too are accountable to God.* Finally, we need to remember that it is not only the other Christian who is going to give an account to God, but you will have to do it too. In one place Jesus said that you will have to give an account even of every careless word you have spoken (Matt. 12:36).

If that is true, don't you think you have enough to be concerned about without trying to straighten out the other Christian? Of course, no one is always right in everything he or she does, but let Jesus worry about straightening the other Christian out, especially in those areas that probably don't really matter anyway. In the meantime, worry about your own accountability and determine that, regardless of the case of others, when you stand before the judgment seat of Jesus Christ you will hear him say of you, "Well done, good and faithful servant" (Matt. 25:21, 23).

211

Holy Days or Holy People?

Romans 14:5–6

One man considers one day more sacred than another; another man considers every day alike. Each one should be fully convinced in his own mind. He who regards one day as special, does so to the Lord. He who eats meat, eats to the Lord, for he gives thanks to God; and he who abstains, does so to the Lord and gives thanks to God.

I t is sad to think about the things that have divided Christians. In the Middle Ages the Catholic and Eastern Orthodox branches of the church divided over the *filioque* clause in the Nicene Creed. The words mean "and the Son," and the point in dispute was whether the Holy Spirit proceeds from the Father alone or from both the first and second persons of the Trinity. At the time of the Reformation the Lutherans, Zwinglians, and Calvinists divided over how Christ was thought to be present in the Lord's Supper. Luther's followers insisted on the Roman Catholic view, that the communion bread and wine are transformed literally into the body and blood of Christ. *"Hoc est corpus meum* ('This is my body')," insisted Luther. The Zwinglians understood the Lord's Supper to be a remembrance service only. They emphasized, "Do this in remembrance of me" (Luke 22:19). Calvin spoke of a "real presence" of Jesus, but insisted that it was a spiritual and not a physical presence.

1739

It is sad that these divisions took place, but at least these were over theological or biblical issues. The matters Paul mentions in Romans 14 are not even great theological issues: what kind of food should be eaten or whether Christians should set aside special days for their religious observances. Paul's point is that issues like these should never divide Christians, that differences of conviction here must be respected. Unfortunately, these matters do divide us, and those who disagree often look down on one another.

Divisions over Days

We have already looked at the issue of eating meat or not, and we have seen that Paul says that which a Christian chooses doesn't matter. His second example, in verses 5 and 6, is about observing special days as holy.

I pointed out in chapter 209 that this matter is also mentioned by Paul in Galatians 4:10–11 and in Colossians 2:16–17. In those verses he denounces special day observances: "You are observing special days and months and seasons and years! I fear for you, that somehow I have wasted my efforts on you" (Gal. 4:10–11), and "Therefore do not let anyone judge you by what you eat or drink, or with regard to a religious festival, a New Moon celebration or a Sabbath day. These are a shadow of the things that were to come; the reality, however, is found in Christ" (Col. 2:16–17).

It is different here in Romans. In Galatians and Colossians the people Paul is writing against wanted to mingle diet or celebrations of days with grace as a way of salvation, and that was "a different gospel—which is really no gospel at all" (Gal. 1:6–7). It had to be opposed. By contrast, the people Paul is thinking about in Romans 14 were not observing diet or days as a way to get to heaven but were doing it because they were convinced that it was necessary to obey or please God.

It is significant that Paul drops the terms "weak" and "strong" at this point. This suggests that the issue he is dealing with now is even less a part of a mature understanding of the gospel than eating meat or being a vegetarian. For now it is not even a question of weakness or strength, but only different ideas of what will please God.

Yet, it is still a contemporary and divisive issue. Even today it produces divisions and distrust. In our day the focus is mostly on what day of the week Christians should worship God and how they should keep that day. There are three main views.

1. *Saturday or Sabbath worship.* Some Christians hold that we should worship on Saturday since this is the biblical day, according to their view. This is the position of the Seventh-Day Adventists, for example, and of some others.

2. *Sunday worship but as the Sabbath.* The second position is that Christians are to worship on Sunday but that Sunday should be the equivalent of the Old Testament Sabbath, meaning that Christians are to observe it as the Jews observed Saturday. The Westminster Confession of Faith takes this view, calling the Lord's Day "the Christian Sabbath." It says that "this Sabbath is then

kept holy unto the Lord, when men, after a due preparing of their hearts, and ordering of their common affairs beforehand, do not only observe an holy rest all the day from their own works, words, and thoughts, about their worldly enjoyments and recreations; but also are taken up the whole time in the public and private exercises of his worship, and in the duties of necessity and mercy" (Chapter XXI, Sections 7, 8).

This was the view of the English and American Puritans. It is held by many in the Reformed churches today.

3. *Sunday worship as a new "Lord's Day."* This view holds that the Sabbath has been abolished by the death and resurrection of Jesus Christ and that a new day, the Lord's Day, which has its own characteristics, has replaced it. This was the view of John Calvin, who said that "the day sacred to the Jews was set aside" and that "another was appointed" for it.[1] This is my position also.

Differences on this matter are divisive in some cases. The most serious conflicts within my denomination, the conservative Presbyterian Church in America, are between those who insist on a strict adherence to the Westminster Standards, with its "Sabbatarian" view, and others who hold to the Standards more loosely, at least at this point, and agree instead with Calvin that Sunday has replaced the Sabbath. In our denomination there are people who would like to get pastors like me excluded, because we think this is a nonessential matter on which the Westminster Confession of Faith simply has gone beyond what ought to be required of anyone.

The Sabbatarian Position

What should we think of this disagreement? Let's take the Sabbatarian position, first of all. In the Presbyterian church, the strength of this position is not in the fact that it is found in the Westminster Confession of Faith, though some use that as a club to try to force other people to adopt their position, but rather that it is found in the Bible, in fact, in the Ten Commandments. If it is found in the Ten Commandments, it must be binding on us just as the other commandments are, these people argue.

The fourth commandment says, "Remember the Sabbath day by keeping it holy. Six days you shall labor and do all your work, but the seventh day is a Sabbath to the LORD your God. On it you shall not do any work, neither you, nor your son or daughter, not your manservant or maidservant, nor your animals, nor the alien within your gates. For in six days the LORD made the heavens and the earth, the sea, and all that is in them, but he rested on the seventh day. Therefore the LORD blessed the Sabbath day and made it holy" (Exod. 20:8–11). The reasoning is that if God has set the seventh day apart as something holy and has given instructions as to how it should be observed, then we must observe it.

---

1. John Calvin, *Institutes of the Christian Religion*, 2 vols., ed. John T. McNeill, trans. Ford Lewis Battles (Philadelphia: The Westminster Press, 1960), p. 399.

There are some good arguments against this view, of course, which I have developed elsewhere.[2] I have argued that the Sabbath was a uniquely Jewish institution, that there is no evidence that it was ever observed by any other ancient race or nation, and that it was observed for the first time by Israel only after the people had received the law at Sinai. It is true that Genesis 2:2–3 says that on the seventh day God "rested from all his work" and that he therefore "blessed the seventh day and made it holy," but it doesn't say he did it then. And there is no indication that Adam and Eve, Noah, Abraham, Isaac, Jacob, or any of the patriarchs observed or even knew about the Sabbath.

In fact, we read in Nehemiah, "You came down on Mount Sinai; you spoke to them from heaven. You gave them regulations and laws that are just and right, and decrees and commands that are good. *You made known to them your holy Sabbath*" (Neh. 9:13–14). This implies that the Sabbath was not known to Israel before Sinai but was part of the special arrangements God made with Israel then for the ordering of the life of that unique nation.

Similarly, Exodus 31:13 calls the Sabbath "a sign between me and you for the generations to come, so you may know that I am the LORD, who makes you holy." And later, "It will be *a sign between me and the Israelites forever*" (v. 17). This portrays the Sabbath as something established between God and Israel only.

It's important to remember that an emphasis on Sabbath-keeping leads easily to harmful legalism. It clearly did among the Jews. In fact, this was the first (and later proved to be the ultimately fatal) point of contention between the Jewish leaders and Jesus Christ. Neither he nor his disciples held to the leaders' strict ideas of how the Sabbath should be observed, and when Jesus was challenged at the point of his "unorthodox" behavior, he replied by telling these legalists, "The Sabbath was made for man, not man for the Sabbath. So the Son of Man is Lord even of the Sabbath" (Mark 2:27). In saying this, he pointed to the limited value of the seventh day, even as they observed it, and at the same time asserted his right to amend its observance or even abolish it or replace it if he wished.

The Pharisees didn't agree with him on this. In fact, they hated him for striking at something that was especially dear to them, and as a result they plotted to kill him. Mark tells us that it was on the basis of this issue and after he had healed a man on the Sabbath that the Pharisees first "began to plot with the Herodians how they might kill Jesus" (Mark 3:6). Even today, people who insist on a strict Sabbath tend to be legalistic in other matters also.

Sunday as a New "Lord's Day"

What about the alternate view, then, that Sunday is a new day of Christian worship and that it has characteristics different from the Sabbath? This is

2. See James Montgomery Boice, *The Gospel of John: An Expositional Commentary*, 5 vols. in 1 (Grand Rapids: Zondervan Publishing House, 1985), pp. 316–320, and *Foundations of the Christian Faith* (Downers Grove, Ill.: InterVarsity Press, 1986), pp. 233–35.

my view, and I have what I believe are good reasons for it. For example, although the word *sabbath* is found nine times in Acts, not once is it said to have been a day observed by Christians. Acts 1:12 uses the phrase "a Sabbath day's walk [journey]." In chapter 13 the word occurs four times in describing how Paul used the Sabbath for his evangelistic ends, going into the synagogues to preach to Jews who were assembled there (vv. 14, 27, 42, 44). Similar references occur in chapters 15 (v. 21), 17 (v. 2), and 18 (v. 4). Nowhere is it said that the church met on the Sabbath or that Christians even thought of their own day, Sunday, as being like or continuing the Sabbath.

Nor did they observe Sunday as the Jews observed Saturday. The Jews abstained from all work. But to judge from the early records, the Christians used Sunday as a day of vigorous spiritual activity and observed it not with long faces but with thanksgiving and joy.[3]

Although the danger of the Sabbatarian position is that it leads to legalism, observing the Lord's Day freely can lead to libertinism—that is, to a complete disregard of the day so that, although Christians are not bound to any special form of activity, many do nothing. They even fail to go to church or go only in a perfunctory way, to get the "duty" over with quickly so they can spend the rest of the day on worldly activities.

Let me say that I do not believe you are "breaking the Sabbath" by eating out on Sunday, playing ball with your children, going to a football game, or even going to a movie. But surely we are missing the boat if Sunday is not a day of spiritual refreshment, an evangelistic opportunity, hours of genuine worship, and a time of joy for us.

Three Guidelines from Romans

Having given both the pros and cons of these two main views—I have overlooked Saturday worship as a minority view that does not affect very many of today's Christians—let me say here that, just as in the case of whether Christians are free to eat meat or should be vegetarians, the important point of Romans 14 is that Paul does not take sides on the issue. He does not rule on the Sabbath question.

So I am not going to insist on my view either. I have friends who think differently. In fact, one of my best friends, a pastor, observes Sunday by eliminating all worldly activities, spending the time after services either in visiting his people and the sick, or in Bible study, prayer, or other reading. How could I possibly suggest that the way he keeps the "Sabbath" is wrong? It isn't. He is serving the Lord by what he does. At the same time, he does not look down on those who, like me, are engaged in so many "Sabbath" activities that we can hardly think of resting until sometime on Monday.

What Paul does give are three helpful guidelines in this area.

[3]Boice, *The Gospel of John*, pp. 321–25.

1. *Each must be convinced in his or her own mind.* Notice that verse 5 does not say, "Let everyone do what he or she feels is right, because, after all, the person is convinced in his or her own mind." He does not say the person involved is convinced and therefore should not be challenged, but rather that he should be convinced. This means that Paul is willing to treat each believer as a responsible, thinking person, not merely one to be led about docilely by a self-styled "stronger" believer. Therefore, we have a responsibility, each one of us, to search out these matters for ourselves.

The words "in his own mind" are important too. For we remember that this last section of Romans began with an emphasis on the mind, saying that a Christian is not to be conformed "any longer to the pattern of this world" but to be transformed by mind renewal (Rom. 12:2).

There is no escaping our individual responsibility. It is not enough to say, "Well, I grew up in a church where no one paid any special attention to Sunday," or "My pastor is a strict Sabbatarian, so I suppose I should be also," or "Since it doesn't really matter, I just won't think about it; I'll drift along." Paul is not condemning anyone, but the reason he is not saying that either position is wrong is that he considers Christians to be responsible, thinking individuals who should be working through each of these matters for themselves. If we are really doing this, perhaps we will even come to a new sense of agreement or at least cooperation on these matters.

2. *It is possible to serve the Lord either way.* This must be a major emphasis of Paul's, because he repeats the idea three times in verse 6 alone: "He who regards one day as special, does so *to the Lord.* He who eats meat, eats *to the Lord*, for he gives thanks to God; and he who abstains, does so *to the Lord* and gives thanks to God."

In this verse Paul brings the two examples of diet and the keeping of days together and says that it is possible to serve the Lord either way in either area. The person who is a vegetarian for religious reasons is (or should be) so because he believes that this is a testimony to God. He does not want to eat meat that has been offered to idols, for instance, or perhaps because he considers life, even the life of animals, to be sacred. On the other hand, the person who eats anything receives his more abundant meals as having come from God and he rejoices that religion does not really consist in eating or not eating. He knows, as Paul says just a few verses further on in chapter 14, "The kingdom of God is not a matter of eating and drinking, but of righteousness, peace and joy in the Holy Spirit" (v. 17).

And what about the observance of special days? The one who stops all worldly activity on Sunday does so in order to serve the Lord, in his case by worship, study, and acts of mercy. The one who is free to do anything should do what he or she does in order to serve God too.

The critical question is this: Are you really serving God by what you do? Does Sunday really count for you in your Christian life and walk? Are you using it well? Do you benefit from it? And for that matter, how about the other days of the week? Are you serving God in those days too, as you should? If you are in a job where you cannot serve God, should you get out of it? It is probably the case that you should simply learn to do whatever you are doing for God's glory. Are you doing that? It is important that you answer these questions. You are not called to be a robot. You are to be a significant, thinking Christian.

3. *The diagnostic question: Can you be thankful?* Paul mentions the matter of serving the Lord three times in verse 6, but he also speaks of giving "thanks to God" twice. He mentions it in connection with eating either meat or vegetables because we naturally and rightly give thanks at mealtimes. But it should also be true of anything we do or do not feel led to do, including how we conduct ourselves on Sunday.

This third guideline cuts two ways.

First, if the other Christian is giving thanks to God for his food or for the line of work or conduct into which he has been led, then his thanks to God should be proof to you that he is doing it "unto the Lord." This takes us back to verse 4: "Who are you to judge someone else's servant? To his own master he stands or falls. And he will stand, for the Lord is able to make him stand." If he is serving the Lord, then you should keep out of his way and allow God to work through the other believer as he sees fit.

Second, the principle of giving thanks is a great help for discerning what we ourselves should do in doubtful situations. What may I do in such and such a situation where the Bible is not explicit or at least where I do not understand how it is explicit? One very good answer is this: Can you enjoy it in the Lord and give thanks for it? The Swiss commentator F. Godet asks, "May I allow myself this or that pleasure? Yes, if I can enjoy it to the Lord, and while giving him thanks for it; no, if I cannot receive it as a gift from his hand, and bless him for it. This mode of solution respects at once the rights of the Lord and those of individual liberty."[4]

And while I am at it, let me say that even the Jewish Sabbath, for all its tendency toward legalism, was meant to be a time of thanksgiving and joy for Israel. Here is how Isaiah writes about it in chapter 58:

> If you keep your feet from breaking the Sabbath
>   and from doing as you please on my holy day,
> if you call the Sabbath a delight
>   and the LORD's holy day honorable,
> and if you honor it by not going your own way
>   and not doing as you please or speaking idle words,
> then you will find your joy in the LORD,
>   and I will cause you to ride on the heights of the land
>   and to feast on the inheritance of your father Jacob.
>
> Isaiah 58:13–14

I do not see how any child of God could desire more from God than that.

---

4. F. Godet, *Commentary on St. Paul's Epistle to the Romans*, trans. A. Cusin (Edinburgh: T. & T. Clark, 1892), vol. 2, p. 334.

212

God, Other People, and Ourselves

Romans 14:7–9

For none of us lives to himself alone and none of us dies to himself alone. If we live, we live to the Lord; and if we die, we die to the Lord. So, whether we live or die, we belong to the Lord.

For this very reason, Christ died and returned to life so that he might be the Lord of both the dead and the living.

There are not many people who have studied seventeenth-century English prose literature even if they were English majors in college. But I had a good college course on it and found the prose of that time to be a treasure.

That was the century of John Donne, best known for his "Songs and Sonnets." But Donne became a preacher and also wrote great sermons as well as other prose literature. Among his prose writings are some "Meditations" he composed while confined to bed recovering from a serious illness. At one point he heard a church bell ringing the death toll of some other person, and he reasoned that it is never merely for other people the bell rings. Since each of us is mortal, it rings for us. Donne wrote, "No man is an island, entire of itself; every man is a piece of the continent, a part of the maine; if a clod be washed away by the sea, Europe is the less, as well as if a promontory were, as well as if a manor of thy friends, or of thine own were; any man's death diminishes me, because I am involved in mankind. And therefore never send to know for whom the bell tolls; it tolls for thee."[1]

Those last words are well known. They are the source of the title of one of Ernest Hemingway's best known novels, for example. But they come to mind now not because of Hemingway, but because of Paul's teaching in Romans 14:7–8: "For none of us lives to himself alone and none of us dies to himself alone. If we live, we live to the Lord; and if we die, we die to the Lord. So, whether we live or die, we belong to the Lord."

The Believer and Other People

In this passage the apostle is reflecting not so much on a Christian's relationship to other people—being a part of the much greater community of mankind or of the body of believers—as John Donne did, but rather on each Christian's relationship to God. That is, he is saying not that we belong to one another but that we belong to Jesus. Most commentators point this out.

Yet it is also true that we belong to one another, Christians to other Christians, and this is also appropriate to the context of Romans 14. That those who belong to Christ also belong to one another is a natural extension of what Paul has been saying in verses 1–6, for he said there that Christians are to respect the convictions and spiritual experience of others, meaning that they are not to harm them. Moreover, the fact that we belong to one another is also connected to what follows, for beginning with verse 13 Paul says that for the sake of other believers we ought to abstain from some things we consider permissible.

What you do affects others. Therefore you are not acting in isolation when you either live for Christ or fail to live for him.

This is said many times in the Bible, including numerous occasions in Paul's writings. But one passage that says it exceptionally well is 1 Corinthians 12:12–26, where Paul compares the church to a human body:

> The body is a unit, though it is made up of many parts; and though all its parts are many, they form one body. So it is with Christ. For we were all baptized by one Spirit into one body—whether Jews or Greeks, slave or free—and we were all given the one Spirit to drink.
> . . . If the foot should say, "Because I am not a hand, I do not belong to the body," it would not for that reason cease to be a part of the body. And if the ear should say, "Because I am not an eye, I do not belong to the body," it would not for that reason cease to be part of the body. . . .

1. John Donne, *The Complete Poetry and Selected Prose*, ed. Charles M. Coffin (New York: The Modern Library/Random House, 1952), p. 441. I have modernized Donne's spelling and some of his punctuation.

The eye cannot say to the hand, "I don't need you!" And the head cannot say to the feet, "I don't need you!" On the contrary, those parts of the body that seem to be weaker are indispensable, and the parts that we think are less honorable we treat with special honor. . . . But God has combined the members of the body and has given greater honor to the parts that lacked it, so that there should be no division in the body, but that its parts should have equal concern for each other. *If one part suffers, every part suffers with it; if one part is honored, every part rejoices with it.*

Now you are the body of Christ, and each one of you is a part of it.

It might go far to establish us in godliness and cause us to live for Christ wholeheartedly if we really understood that in one way or another everything we do, whether for good or ill, always affects other Christians, usually beginning with those who are closest to us.

The Believer and God

Yet the world can say much of this quite apart from the biblical revelation. It is commonplace today to talk about living in a global village so that what we do in America in terms of our economics or morals or politics affects, for example, what happens to people in Japan or Brazil or Eastern Europe. If we raise tariffs on imports from South America so that the sales of certain products are reduced and American products are protected, we hurt the livelihood of poor people there. If we make morally degenerative movies and export them to the world, as we are doing, the harmful moral climate of America damages countless other people.

What is profound in Paul's teaching is that none of us is isolated from God with the result that what we do in terms of that vertical relationship deeply affects how we either help or harm other people.

Notice the threefold repetition of the words "to the Lord" in verse 8. "If we live, we live *to the Lord*; and if we die, we die *to the Lord*. So, whether we live or die, we belong *to the Lord.*" The point is that we are to be in a right relationship to the Lord and serve the Lord in everything—indeed, everything we do is related to God in one way or another, either good or bad and whether or not we realize it—so that we do not hurt other people.

Not long ago I heard an illustration of this principle that showed how those who are not Christians sometimes understand this better than some believers. The first king to unite the warring tribes of the great Arabian peninsula was King 'Abd al-'Aziz. He ruled in the earlier years of this century and died in 1951. In the late 1930s and early 1940s American oil companies were starting to develop the great Arabian oil fields, and this meant that many foreigners, particularly Americans, were beginning to move into this strongly Islamic country. Some of them were Christians, and early in this development a number of expatriates approached the Saudi king to ask if they could establish churches in Arabia. He said he would think about it, telling them to come back in several weeks for his answer.

About a week later, another group of oil company employees came to the king to ask if they could have alcohol in the company camps. Alcohol is forbidden to Moslems. The king replied by a question. He asked the Americans, "If you could have either churches or alcohol, which of the two would you choose?"

This became an important issue for the company, and the answer was debated carefully. At last the Americans returned and said they would prefer to have the alcohol. King 'Abd al-'Aziz replied, "If you had said churches, I would have given you permission to have both. But since you chose alcohol, you can have neither." In his own way, this wise Moslem ruler understood that if people are right with God, they can be expected to order life in a responsible way not only for themselves but also for other people. But if, on the contrary, they will not submit to God, they cannot be trusted to care for one another.

Living for God

Our text tells us that believers in Christ do not live to themselves but "to the Lord" and that they die "to the Lord" too. What does this mean? Let's start with the purpose of our being here on earth.

The best known Christian answer to our purpose here is the one found in the first response of the Westminster Shorter Catechism. The catechism asks, "What is the chief end of man?" It answers, "Man's chief end is to glorify God and to enjoy him forever." The catechism teaches that our chief purpose in life is not our own self-fulfillment or the achievement of a sense of self-worth or even helping others, important as that may be, but the glory of God. That is, God must always come first in everything, for he *is* first. He is the first and greatest of all realities. As Paul wrote in the great doxology that ends Romans 11, "For from him and through him and to him are all things. To him be the glory forever! Amen" (v. 36). Therefore, in the most literal sense, each of us is to live "to the Lord."

But strikingly and brilliantly, the catechism also adds the words "and to enjoy him forever," thereby indicating that this living to God or pursuit of God's glory is not a painful, self-denying, grim, or grievous thing, but rather a joy and delight for those who do it.

I have been greatly blessed in this respect by some reading I have been doing recently in the writings of John Piper, the pastor of Bethlehem Baptist Church in Minneapolis.[2] Piper is insistent that the glory of God is the end of life and indeed of all creation. But he also insists that we are to enjoy God and even that the way in which we best glorify God *is* by enjoying him. In a book titled *The Supremacy of God in Preaching* Piper writes:

2. Piper is the author of the careful exegetical study of Romans 9 that proved so helpful in my own study of that important chapter. See James Montgomery Boice, *Romans*, vol. 3, *God and History: Romans 9–11* (Grand Rapids: Baker Book House, 1993), chs. 129, 130.

God's deepest purpose for the world is to fill it with reverberations of his glory in the lives of a new humanity, ransomed from every people, tribe, tongue, and nation (Rev. 5:9). But the glory of God does not reflect brightly in the hearts of men and women when they cower unwillingly in submission to his authority or when they obey in servile fear or when there is no gladness in response to the glory of their king.

. . . When God sends his emissaries to declare, "Your God reigns!" his aim is not to constrain man's submission by an act of raw authority; his aim is to ravish our affections with irresistible displays of glory. The only submission that fully reflects the worth and glory of the King is glad submission. Begrudging submission berates the King. No gladness in the subject, no glory to the King.[3]

No one of the world's people has any idea what this means, of course. On the contrary, the world is determined instead to suppress all true knowledge of God and live for self (Rom. 1:18–32). This way of living leads downhill so that we begin to act like beasts. And we not only do what the animals do, being beastlike in our behavior, we do things the animals would not do. The only way we ever learn to live uprightly and actually experience the power to live uprightly is when we live our lives to the Lord.

R. C. Sproul, the founder and president of Ligonier Ministries, has adopted the Latin phrase *coram deo* as the title of a column in his monthly publication *Table Talk*. It means "before God" or "before the face of God" or "in the light of God's all-seeing presence." That is the idea we are dealing with here. Only the Christian can and does live *coram deo*. In fact, he or she must live for God, for this is one thing being a Christian truly means. The non-Christian does not live *coram deo*. On the contrary, it can be said of him that his chief end is to glorify himself and to enjoy himself forever.

There is one more matter here. This way of living, that is, living "to the Lord," will enable us to take whatever comes into our lives as from the Lord and enable us to live each moment for him. John Calvin saw the importance of this and wrote about it in his treatment of our text:

God claims such power over life and death that every individual is to bear his own condition in life as a yoke laid on him by God. It is just that God should assign to every man his station and course in life. In this way we are not only forbidden to attempt to do anything hastily without a command from God, but we are also commanded to be patient in all trouble and loss. If, therefore, the flesh at any time shrinks from adversity, let us remember that a man who is not free and master of himself perverts law and order if he does not depend on the will of his Lord.[4]

---

3. John Piper, *The Supremacy of God in Preaching* (Grand Rapids: Baker Book House, 1990), pp. 24–25.

4. John Calvin, *The Epistles of Paul the Apostle to the Romans and to the Thessalonians*, trans. Ross MacKenzie (Grand Rapids: Wm. B. Eerdmans Publishing Company, 1973), p. 294.

Calvin knew that if we live "to the Lord," we will be able to receive every-thing "from the Lord" joyfully and with thanksgiving.

Dying to God

Verse 8 also says that if we are believers in Christ, we also "die to the Lord." The phrase embraces two things.

1. *The manner of our deaths.* One thing "dying to the Lord" means is that the way in which we are called to die is from God and therefore we can trust the manner of our deaths to him. Not long ago I was with a man who was two weeks from retirement. He was thinking about what was going to happen to him in the future, and he talked about dying. "The desirable thing is to die all at once and not in pieces," he said. I suppose that is right. It *is* desirable. I have always said that I would prefer to die in a plane crash. But death does not always come all at one time. Sometimes it does come in pieces, and it usually does if we live long enough. Our eyesight fails, then our hearing. Our memories begin to fade. Parts of our body break down—our hearts, kidneys, lungs. Our muscles weaken. In our day, with our advances in medicine, it is possible to be kept alive for ten or twenty years even though we may be little more than a noncommunicating invalid, completely confined to a wheelchair, or even worse.

How are we to think about such things as Christians? The answer, if we believe God to be sovereign in our deaths as well as over our lives, is that we can receive all these circumstances as being from him and can serve and love him in whatever conditions we are. The world cannot even think of doing this, but Christians can. Believers can do all things to God's glory.

2. *The timing of our deaths.* The second way in which we can "die to the Lord" concerns the timing of our deaths. Sometimes Christians live out full and useful lives and die in mature old age. At other times Christians die in the midst of life, often leaving a wife, husband, or children behind. Sometimes they die young. Sometimes Christians even die as children. How are we to think about this? Are we to consider the death of the young believer a tragedy? Is it a cosmic mistake? We can never think this way if we believe in God's sovereignty! If God is truly sovereign, he must be as sovereign over the timing of our deaths as the manner of them and as over life itself.

Speaking of our text, Calvin said, "Thus too we are taught the rule by which to live and die, so that if he [God] lengthens out life in the midst of continual sorrow and weariness, we are not to seek to depart before our time. But if he should suddenly recall us in the prime of our life, we must always be ready for our departure."[5]

5. Calvin, *The Epistles of Paul,* p. 294.

Jesus, the Lord of All

The last phrase of verse 8 and the whole of verse 9 are written to strengthen our belief in God's sovereignty, for they tell us that if we are Christians, "we belong to the Lord" and that it was to make this possible that Jesus "died and returned to life," that is, rose again.

There is a sense in which Jesus is and has always been the Lord of all things. For Jesus is God, and lordship actually means God's sovereignty. There is nothing in all creation nor anything that has ever happened in all the history of the earth or universe over which Jesus has not been Lord. Yet Paul is writing here about Jesus' special lordship over his own saved people, and he is saying that he has become their Lord by dying for them and then rising again. By his death he achieved their deliverance from sin's dread penalty and power, and by his resurrection he has established an ongoing relationship with them by which he guides, protects, and saves them day by day until they come at last to be with him in heaven.

The Sadducees tried to trap Jesus with a question about the resurrection. They were the liberals of their day, and they thought belief in a physical resurrection was foolish. Jesus told them they had erred for two reasons. First, they did not know the Bible, which taught that there is a resurrection. And second, they did not know the power of God that makes resurrections and any other supposedly impossible thing possible. The Scripture he quoted was Exodus 3:6, where God declares, "I am the God of your father, the God of Abraham, the God of Isaac, and the God of Jacob." Because the verb "I am" is in the present tense, not the past, Jesus concluded that Abraham, Isaac, and Jacob must still be alive, since God "is not the God of the dead but of the living" (Matt. 22:29).

That is exactly what we have in Romans 14, except that now the chapter is talking about the second person of the Trinity rather than the first. It tells us that Jesus is "Lord of both the dead and the living" (v. 9). In other words, those who are his belong to him now and will still belong to him in the future, beyond death. They will belong to him forever.

Something very important happened to me between the preaching of the sermon that appears as the previous chapter and the preparation of this study. It was the death of my father. He had been failing for some time, particularly in his mind. But his death nevertheless came suddenly, and within a few days my mother, sisters, and I had arranged for a double funeral—one in Hamilton, Massachusetts, where my parents had been living, and a second one in Philadelphia, where my father was to be buried. Everyone came—my mother, my parents' children, their children, and their children's children, four generations in all. When we were all together there were four pews of descendants from this one marriage, every one of them professing to believe on Jesus Christ as his or her Savior.

One of my associates conducted the funeral; but I was also to speak, and I was mulling over of what I might say when my mind ran ahead to these verses: "For none of us lives to himself alone and none of us dies to himself alone. If we live, we live to the Lord; and if we die, we die to the Lord. So, whether we live or die, we belong to the Lord. For this very reason, Christ died and returned to life so that he might be the Lord of both the dead and the living."

When I thought of them it seemed to me that this was exactly what needed to be said. For this is the sole but nevertheless extraordinary comfort for all who know Jesus Christ in this life. If we live, we live to the Lord. If we die, we die to the Lord. So whether we live or die, whichever it is, we are the Lord's. Do you know any comfort equal to that? I don't. Our sole comfort is that we belong to Jesus Christ. But because of who he is, that is also a great and all-sufficient comfort. Because we know Jesus to be a wise and utterly sovereign God, we can trust him with whatever comes into our lives and with the manner and timing of our deaths, too. Do you trust him? You can. I commend him to you as a trustworthy Savior.

213

Answerable to God

Romans 14:10–12

You, then, why do you judge your brother? Or why do you look down on your brother?
For we shall all stand before God's judgment seat. It is written:

"'As surely as I live,' says the Lord,
'Every knee will bow before me;
  every tongue will confess to God.'"

So then, each of us will give an account of himself to God.

In the fourteenth chapter of Romans Paul has been explaining why Christians must not be judgmental where the conduct of other believers is concerned, and one of the reasons he has given is that none of us exists in isolation. We belong to each other and need each other. Moreover, being Christians, we belong to God. So we must not spend our time putting the other Christian down but rather we must accept as brothers and sisters those who are also trying to serve the Lord as best they know how and try earnestly to build up those other persons.

Paul argued that "none of us lives to himself alone and none of us dies to himself alone" (Rom. 14:7). In the last study I cited John Donne's "No Man Is an Island" to make that point.

But there is one situation in which a man or woman *is* isolated, and that is when he or she stands before the judgment seat of God, as we each must do. On that day there will be no pleading someone else's responsibility for what we have done or blaming another person for our faults or taking another's credit for our own. As Paul writes to the Corinthians, "We must all appear before the judgment seat of Christ, that *each one may receive what is due him* for the things done while in the body, whether good or bad" (2 Cor. 5:10). If nothing else is able to get us thinking about our conduct rather than someone else's, it should be this extremely serious, awesome, and inescapable moment of personal accountability.

Christians Must Give an Accounting

Our text is referring to Christians when it says, "For we will all stand before God's judgment seat" (v. 10). It is true that unbelievers will also be judged at the final judgment, but that is not what Paul is writing about here. In this chapter he is reminding his readers that Christians will also be judged, since *all* must appear before God and give an accounting.

I am sure this does not seem right to many Christians, because they understand rightly that because they have trusted Jesus Christ as their Savior they have passed from a state of being under judgment or condemnation to one of being justified before God. Even more, they remember how Jesus said, "Whoever hears my word and believes him who sent me has eternal life and will not be condemned [the King James Version said, 'shall not come into condemnation']; he has crossed over from death to life" (John 5:24). If that is true, how can a Christian possibly be judged? Or to think about Paul's words in Romans 14, how can the apostle say, speaking specifically of Christians, "We will all stand before God's judgment seat"?

The answer, of course, is that there are various judgments spoken of in the Bible and that the word *judge* is used in various ways.

Whenever we speak of the judgments mentioned in the Bible we are moving into the area of Bible prophecy, and this is an area in which Christians have very different views. (It is another area in which we need to be unusually understanding and accepting of one another.) However, as I read the Bible it seems to me that at least seven different judgments are mentioned: (1) a judgment of believers at the judgment seat of Christ (Rom. 14:10–12; 1 Cor. 3:11–15; 2 Cor. 5:10); (2) a series of judgments on the earth (Rev. 6–11, 15–16); (3) a judgment of the beast and the false prophet, at which time the devil will be imprisoned (Rev. 19:20; 20:1–3); (4) a judgment of the Gentile nations (Ps. 2); (5) a judgment of Israel (Ezek. 20:32–38); (6) the final judgment of Satan (Rev. 20:1–10); and (7) the final judgment of unbelievers at the Great White Throne (Rev. 20:11–15).

All these judgments except the first are judicial judgments: They involve God's punishments of individuals or nations for those peoples' specific sins. The punishments involve spiritual or eternal death and hell suffering. The first of these judgments stands apart from the rest, because it is a judgment of believers, which means that it is not for sin and does not involve spiritual death or suffering. Nevertheless, it is still a real judgment in which the followers of Christ are to give an accounting for what they have done in this life and are either rewarded or disapproved by God on that basis.

It helps to get a picture of what this involves by realizing that the phrases in Romans 14:10 rendered "God's judgment seat" and in 2 Corinthians 5:10 rendered "the judgment seat of Christ" each contain the Greek word *bêma,* which refers not to the judge's seat in a court of law but to the bench upon which the referees or judges sat at an athletic contest. It was the place from which those who did well in the contest and triumphed were rewarded with a laurel wreath and from which those who broke the rules were disqualified or disapproved.

This was a well-known concept for the ancient Greeks and Romans, and Paul drew on it more than once in his writings. Thus, although Romans 14:10 and 2 Corinthians 5:10 are the only two verses in which the word *bêma* actually is used, we find Paul alluding to this idea elsewhere as well:

1. *1 Corinthians 9:25–27.* "Everyone who competes in the games goes into strict training. They do it to get a crown that will not last; but we do it to get a crown that will last forever. Therefore I do not run like a man running aimlessly; I do not fight like a man beating the air. No, I beat my body and make it my slave so that after I have preached to others, I myself will not be disqualified for the prize."

2. *Philippians 3:12–14.* "I press on to take hold of that for which Christ Jesus took hold of me. Brothers, I do not consider myself yet to have taken hold of it. But one thing I do: Forgetting what is behind and straining toward what is ahead, I press on toward the goal to win the prize for which God has called me heavenward in Christ Jesus."

3. *2 Timothy 4:7–8.* "I have fought the good fight, I have finished the race, I have kept the faith. Now there is in store for me the crown of righteousness, which the Lord, the righteous Judge, will award to me on that day—and not only to me, but also to all who have longed for his appearing."

The man who wrote Romans 8:38–39 ("For I am convinced that neither death nor life, neither angels nor demons, neither the present nor the future, nor any powers, neither height nor depth, nor anything else in all creation, will be able to separate us from the love of God that is in Christ Jesus our Lord") is not worrying about his eternal salvation. He is not afraid that he may be sent to hell. But he is aware that he is going to have to give an account to God of every word he has spoken and everything he has done. And he is taking that moment of personal accountability very, very seriously.

You Must Give an Accounting

We can see how seriously he takes this by the way he writes about it in Romans 14:10–12. Notice three things. First, he emphasizes the word *you* by putting it in an emphatic position and repeating it twice. This is more obvious in the Greek text than in the English translations, but the New International Version tries to capture the idea by asking in verse 10, "*You*, then, why do *you* judge your brother?" Paul is referring both to the one whom he called weak earlier and to the one he called strong. That is, he is writing to *you*, whoever you may be.

Second, Paul brings in a quotation from the Old Testament, which he often does when he comes to the end of an argument:

It is written:

> "'As surely as I live,' says the Lord,
> 'Every knee will bow before me;
>   every tongue will confess to God.'"

This quotation is taken somewhat loosely from Isaiah 49:23 (see Isa. 49:18), and it is a solemn reminder of how God has said that every person who has ever lived will appear before him for judgment. So we must not think that just because we are Christians, somehow we are going to get off without an accounting.

Third, Paul repeats his point in different words but with emphasis in verse 12: "So then, each of us will give an account of himself to God." This includes you and me.

Accountable for All Things

But for what will we be held accountable? This is a serious and very practical matter, so let's look at some of the verses that tell exactly what we are accountable for.

1. *We are accountable for every word we have spoken.* There are many verses in the Bible that tell us this. For example, Jesus spoke about how words come from the heart, a good heart producing good words and a bad heart producing bad words. He said, "I tell you that men will have to give account on the day of judgment for every careless word they have spoken. For by your words you will be acquitted, and by your words you will be condemned" (Matt. 12:36–37). In the letter to the Ephesians Paul wrote, "Do not let any unwholesome talk come out of your mouths, but only what is helpful for building

others up according to their needs" (Eph. 4:29) and "Nor should there be obscenity, foolish talk or coarse joking, which are out of place, but rather thanksgiving" (Eph. 5:4).

This does not mean that a Christian can never laugh or tell jokes. We do not have to be serious all the time. But it does mean that there should be a certain gravity about us as befits those who are aware of the gospel of the grace of God and of the fact that many are perishing because they will not turn from their sins and believe on Jesus Christ. And even if we laugh and tell jokes, which we will at times, we will not be telling dirty jokes. On the contrary, we will try to edify others even by our humor.

We will pay attention to the words we hear and read too. Donald Grey Barnhouse had some useful thoughts on this in his study of Romans:

> I think it is fair and logical to conclude that if the believer must account for every careless word, this applies not only to what he says, but to what he allows himself to hear and read. If you spend several hours a week watching television, you can be almost certain that the thing has mastery over you; but if you watch it only occasionally and in order to relax after a long period of work or study, that is a different matter. I know people who are better acquainted with the comic strips than they are with the Bible. They say that they are too busy for Bible study, but they have at least fifteen minutes a day for the comics and another fifteen to listen to news broadcasts. I read some magazines from back to front, just to laugh at the cartoons, and throw them down without reading any of their articles or stories. However, I am not your judge, and you may not be mine. We are each answerable to the Lord.[1]

There is a positive side to this, however. Although our idle words will be condemned, our public confessions of Jesus Christ and words that are spoken in praise of God to bring him glory will also be remembered forever. For the text in Matthew also says, "By your words you will be acquitted" (Matt. 12:37).

I have always been encouraged by what is said concerning the people of God who lived in the time of Malachi: "Then those who feared the Lord talked with each other, and the Lord listened and heard. A scroll of remembrance was written in his presence concerning those who feared the Lord and honored his name" (Mal. 3:16). This means that God hears our good, faithful, and true words too, and that he remembers them forever. I believe that no word spoken for Jesus or in Jesus' name will ever be wasted or fail of its reward.

2. *We are accountable for the talents that have been given to us.* We should remember the parable Jesus told in various forms in which a king or owner of an estate left cities to be managed by his servants or gave varying numbers of talents to them, returning later to demand an accounting. In one of these,

---

1. Donald Grey Barnhouse, *God's Discipline: Exposition of Bible Doctrines, Taking the Epistle to the Romans as a Point of Departure,* vol. 9, *Romans 12:1–14:12* (Grand Rapids: Wm. B. Eerdmans Publishing Company, 1964), p. 218.

he dismissed the manager, saying, "What is this I hear about you? Give an account of your management, because you cannot be manager any longer" (Luke 16:2). In another he condemned the faithless steward for being "wicked" and "lazy" (Matt. 25:26) but praised the faithful servants, saying, "Well done, good and faithful servant! You have been faithful with a few things; I will put you in charge of many things. Come and share your master's happiness" (Matt. 25:21, 23).

Have you ever taken stock of the talents God has given you? I do not mean just your particularly strong points or strong skills, but everything you are. Have you ever done a complete inventory of who you are so that you may give it all to God for his service and glory?

I am a fifty-five-year-old white male whom God called to the ministry at an early age so I would be able to direct every stage of my education to that end. I was raised in a Christian home, taught the Bible from childhood onward, was influenced by strong men and women of God, and was placed in Philadelphia in a strong city church to teach the Bible to the people God sends to serve there. We are called to model city ministry at Tenth Presbyterian Church, and we have done it. Everything that is good in me has come from God, and my responsibility is to take those good gifts and offer them up to God in his service, making them count for him in every way I can.

That is my inventory. It is that for which I must give an accounting. Your case is different. You have an entirely different background and entirely different training. You may have been called to be a teacher or a doctor or a secretary or the CEO of some company. You may be black or white or some other color. You may have a high IQ or a low IQ. Whatever you have, it has been given to you by God, and you are responsible to God for how you use it. Are you using it for him? If you do not know the answer to that question, you need to sit down quietly, take personal inventory, and ask God to show you what you can do that will make a difference for him in this life and for eternity.

3. *We are accountable for how we use our money.* Nothing in life so mirrors our values and priorities as what we do with our money, which is why someone has said, "Let me look at your checkbook, and I will tell you what you are." What you do with your money tells volumes about you.

This is why the Bible has so much to say about money. It is why Jesus spoke about it. Jesus said:

> Do not store up for yourselves treasures on earth, where moth and rust destroy, and where thieves break in and steal. But store up for yourselves treasures in heaven, where moth and rust do not destroy, and where thieves do not break in and steal. For where your treasure is, there your heart will be also. . . . No one can serve two masters. Either he will hate the one and love the other, or he will be devoted to the one and despise the other. You cannot serve God and Money.

Matthew 6:19–21, 24

What would I discover if I were to examine your checkbook? You would have payments on the house, checks for the heating and electricity, money for food, hospital and doctors' bills, perhaps education bills—and taxes, of course, lots of taxes. But what beyond that? Would I find more money being spent on a second home, a luxury car, the country club, or entertainment than for Christian work? What percentage of your income would I find given to the support of your local church? Or to missions? Or to help people you know who are in serious financial need? If you give anything to your church or charitable causes, you probably consider yourself to be very generous, a great philanthropist. But would that judgment hold up to a really objective scrutiny? Would God be satisfied with your priorities?

Earlier I mentioned Donald Grey Barnhouse. In his study he refers to a cartoon in which a farmer is sitting at a table with nine giant potatoes in front of him and a tenth potato, his tithe to God, sitting off by itself. The isolated potato is marked "The Lord's portion," and the caption expresses the words of the farmer who is saying, "I don't see how any fellow could be mean enough to give less."

True enough. The caption is meant to commend the farmer as a man with a surrendered heart. But I find myself thinking, "Nine for me and one for God? Is even that a strong enough priority? When we have been given so much and have such abundance, is that all we can do, should do, or would do if we really loved the Lord with all our hearts and minds and souls and were aware that one day we will have to give an accounting of how we have spent our money?"

4. *We are accountable for how we have used our time.* Finally, you will have to give an accounting for your time. How are you using your time? Do you waste long hours watching television? Or if you work all the time, are you working for yourself only, or do you work for others and share your time with your family, or with others you could help? Do you invest some of your time in Bible study, witnessing, or some type of Christian work?

What You Do Now Counts

Let's close by returning to the points Paul is making.

1. *Stop judging your neighbor.* Most of us are guilty of this, and it is one of the most harmful things that takes place in Christian churches. We think that because there are standards to be maintained we must be snooping out the shortcomings of others. We are not called to do this. If you are worried about standards, make sure you live up to them yourself. Or let the people God has appointed to deal with them—the elders in a local church—do the shepherding work.

2. *Take inventory of your own actions and behavior.* Unless you are perfect or nearly perfect, which I doubt you are, that will be enough to keep you busy for a very long time, and we will all be better off. Besides, you will help others

better that way, because people are always helped more by a loving example of what should be done than by moral nitpicking or outright condemnation.

3. *Do what you can to build up the body.* Being judgmental tears down. Modeling builds up, and that is what we most need. And remember that it is spiritual work that will last. Most of what you have been spending your time on will pass with the passing of this world and be gone forever.

Accountability is always a sobering message. But it is also encouraging, because it means that what you do really counts.

214

Responsible Christianity

Romans 14:13-16

Therefore let us stop passing judgment on one another. Instead, make up your mind not to put any stumbling block or obstacle in your brother's way. As one who is in the Lord Jesus, I am fully convinced that no food is unclean in itself. But if anyone regards something as unclean, then for him it is unclean. If your brother is distressed because of what you eat, you are no longer acting in love. Do not by your eating destroy your brother for whom Christ died. Do not allow what you consider good to be spoken of as evil.

We live in a day when people are impatient with theology. If they are willing to listen to Christian teaching at all, they want it to be practical. Is it? Well, teaching about the Christian life is practical, and it is the Christian life with which Paul is dealing in this, the last major section of Romans (chaps. 12–16).

Yet the way he does it is surprising. When people ask for practical teaching about how Christians should live, they usually want a list of things Christians should do or not do: read your Bible, come to church, spend quality time with your children, and so on. If their concern is for values or Christian morality, they want a list of rules approaching legalism: Don't smoke. Don't drink. Don't go to bad movies. Don't cheat on your income tax. Have you noticed how little there is of anything like that in these last chapters of Romans? Paul gives commands. Indeed, this is the place in the letter where they are particularly found: "Hate what is evil; cling to what is good" (Rom. 12:9); "Live at peace with everyone" (v. 18); "Do not take revenge" (v. 19); "Let no debt remain outstanding" (Rom. 13:8). But these are general statements, not a list of practical dos and don'ts, and they are introduced by the important general teaching that the way we are to approach everything is from the perspective of a renewed Christian mind:

> Therefore, I urge you, brothers, in view of God's mercy, to offer your bodies as living sacrifices, holy and pleasing to God—this is your spiritual act of worship. Do not conform any longer to the pattern of this world, but be transformed by the renewing of your mind. Then you will be able to test and approve what God's will is—his good, pleasing and perfect will.

> Romans 12:1–2

Is Legalism the Answer?

But what about dos and don'ts? Isn't there a list of things we should do and not do? There is, of course. The Ten Commandments is one important list. Nothing in Paul's writings suggests that we are free to violate the moral law of God. But when he writes about specific details of the Christian life, as he does here, it is important to see that the approach he takes is not legalism. He does not provide a list of acceptable and nonacceptable things, above all not in gray areas. In fact, in these areas he teaches that Christians are free to do anything, and they must allow other Christians to do the same. In other words, the way to move forward in the Christian life is not for one group of believers to lay down a set of rules for other Christians.

One commentator writes, "We may advise, we may cite our own experiences, we may pray, we may point to the Word of God, we may seek to enlighten, but *we may never command the conscience of another believer.*"[1]

How those who know the nature of true Christian freedom are to use their liberty is precisely what Paul discusses in the section of Romans to which we come now. Romans 14:13–15:13 is the second part of a long section in which Paul addresses the way Christians are to relate to others with whom they disagree on some matters. The first part was about how people who disagree on such matters are to treat each other (Rom. 14:1–12). The second part is about how the "strong" are to use their liberty (Rom. 14:13–15:13). In other words, the first part deals with Christian liberty itself, the second part with how it should be exercised.

---

1. Donald Grey Barnhouse, *One Lord, One Master,* booklet 84 in the radio series on Romans (Philadelphia: The Bible Study Hour, 1959), p. 13.

The key concept is *responsibility*. We are free as Christians, but we must use our freedom in a way that supports, helps or builds up the other person, not in a way that harms him or tears him down.

The Basic Principle: Verse 13

Verse 13 is a restatement of the principle Paul has been explaining from the start—we must stop passing judgment on one another. It is something he has been saying to both the weak and the strong. The "weak" brother or sister is the one who is bothered by scruples over things that should not matter. The person he calls "strong" is the one who knows that in principle what one does in these areas really doesn't matter.

Paul has provided two examples of what he is talking about: first, care about what one eats—believing that a Christian should not eat meat but should be a vegetarian; second, a scrupulous observance of days. This involved the Jewish passion for the faithful observance of the Sabbath, new moons, and other feast days mentioned in the Old Testament. These matters do not mean much to most people today, so in our first study of this section I suggested some modern equivalents: (1) the judgmental way some Christians look at others who are going through hard times, reasoning that the other person must have done something wrong for which he or she is being punished; (2) variations in individual piety, some practices or lack of them being judged "unspiritual" by those who think otherwise; (3) denominational affiliations, some being judged apostate by narrower brethren; and (4) personality differences—because some people are shy and cannot speak easily about their faith to other people, they are often thought to be unspiritual or even disobedient believers.

Scripture does not give us merely negative commands, but also gives us positive injunctions, which is the case here. In the Greek text of verse 13 the word *judge* is used twice. In the first case, the verse tells us to stop judging other people. In the second, it tells us to start judging ourselves. This is a word play in the original language that does not work so well in English because our meanings of the word *judge* are more restricted. This is why the New International Version translates the verse as it does. The King James Version was more literal: "Let us not therefore *judge* one another any more; but *judge* this rather . . ." The NIV conveys the idea better when it departs from the literal rendering and says, "Therefore let us stop passing judgment on one another. Instead, make up your mind not to put any stumbling block or obstacle in your brother's way."

Here the best recourse may be a paraphrase. Ray Stedman does this: "Scripture does not merely say, 'Stop judging'; it says, 'Stop judging others; if you want to judge, start with yourself.'"[2] I referred to this in chapter 209

2. Ray C. Stedman, *From Guilt to Glory*, vol. 2, *Reveling in God's Salvation* (Portland, Oreg.: Multnomah Press, 1978), p. 174.

when I wrote, "You have better things to do than to hunt out the speck in the eye of your fellow Christian while overlooking the plank in your own."

When Paul says, "Therefore let us stop passing judgment on one another," he is speaking to both the weak and the strong believer. The weak are not to judge the strong by considering them unspiritual, and the strong are not to judge the weak by considering them immature. This picks up on what was said in the first section of the chapter and is a natural bridge to what follows.

At this point, however, Paul becomes more directive, speaking to those who considered themselves to be strong, saying, "Instead, make up your mind not to put any stumbling block or obstacle in your brother's way." In fact, from this point on nearly everything he writes is to them. The strong believer has more latitude in these matters and can accommodate the weaker brother, while the weaker brother cannot accommodate him. The weak brother can only abstain from what he believes to be wrong. The strong Christian can either abstain or not abstain. Therefore, he has it within his power to accommodate the other person, which is what Paul tells him to do.

The Underlying Truth: Verse 14

The second verse of this section is a parenthesis. For although Paul will say that the strong believer should forgo what his principles would otherwise permit for the sake of the weaker brother, the underlying truth nevertheless is that the strong believer is right: No food is unclean of itself.

We know that Paul felt this strongly, first because of the way he writes here and also because he has said the same thing explicitly in other letters. Here he appeals to his being "in the Lord Jesus" (v. 14). This does not mean that he has a specific saying of Jesus to appeal to, though he might have been thinking of Christ's words in Mark 7:1–13. It only means that he is close to the Lord and is speaking in accord with Jesus' spirit. In the mouth of an apostle, this is a very close claim to speaking by inspiration.

In 1 Corinthians 8 he answers the Corinthians' questions about eating meat that has been sacrificed to idols by writing, "We know that an idol is nothing at all in the world and there is no God but one" (v. 4) and "Food does not bring us near to God; we are no worse if we do not eat, and no better if we do" (v. 8). Similarly, in 1 Timothy 4:4 he says, "Everything God created is good, and nothing is to be rejected if it is received with thanksgiving." What this means is that, in principle, the strong are right. Nothing that goes into the body defiles the person, only what comes out.

Nevertheless, Paul adds that for the one who thinks something is unclean it truly is. Therefore, for his sake the strong believer should be willing to forgo many things that he would otherwise be able to enjoy because of his own sense of spiritual freedom.

The Strong's Responsibility: Verses 15–16

This brings us to the main point of this passage, but at the same time also to something that must be handled very carefully. To see why we only have to ask this question: Do the strong in faith have to forgo anything about which some weaker believer might object? In a world with so much variety there is hardly anything you or I might do that will not be objected to by some other believer. Moreover, there are believers on both sides of most issues. If we were to listen to what all these other Christians have to say and try to live by their standards, we would either fall into a new legalism or go crazy trying to balance thousands of conflicting claims on our behavior.

William Barclay expresses this well when he writes, "Paul is not saying that we must always allow our conduct to be dominated and dictated by the views, and even the prejudices, of others; there are matters which are essentially matters of principle, and in them a man must take his own way. But there are a great many things which are neutral and indifferent, . . . and it is Paul's conviction that in such things we have no right to give offence to the more scrupulous brother."[3]

Barclay says, "It is a Christian duty to think of everything, not as it affects ourselves only, but also as it affects others."[4] This is part of what it means for a believer in Christ to be guided by a Christian mind.

At this point let's think about the decree of the first church council described in Acts 15. The question that made the meeting necessary was whether Gentiles, who were becoming Christians in large numbers, needed to be circumcised to be saved. The Jewish legalists thought they did; after all, circumcision is the Old Testament sign of membership in the covenant people. Paul and his party believed they did not. According to Paul's account of the same council in his letter to the Galatians, Paul had brought along a young Gentile missionary worker named Titus as a test case. Titus, being a Gentile, had not been circumcised. Would he be compelled to be, or would the council come out on the side of pure grace?

We know how the council decided. After much debate Peter gave a strong decisive speech in which he argued, "Now then, why do you try to test God by putting on the necks of the disciples a yoke that neither we nor our fathers have been able to bear? No! We believe it is through the grace of our Lord Jesus Christ that we are saved, just as they are" (Acts 15:10–11).

This was heeded, and the council adopted the advice of James, the Lord's brother: "It is my judgment, therefore, that we should not make it difficult for the Gentiles who are turning to God. Instead we should write to them, telling them to abstain from food polluted by idols, from sexual immorality, from the meat of strangled animals and from blood. For Moses has been

3. William Barclay, *The Letter to the Romans* (Edinburgh: Saint Andrew Press, 1969), p. 207.
4. Ibid.

preached in every city from the earliest times and is read in the synagogues on every Sabbath" (vv. 19–21).

This was done. The council sent a letter to the Gentile believers in Antioch, Syria, and Cilicia, saying, "It seemed good to the Holy Spirit and to us not to burden you with anything beyond the following requirements: You are to abstain from food sacrificed to idols, from blood, from the meat of strangled animals and from sexual immorality" (vv. 28–29).

This has been judged an unfortunate compromise by some students of the Book of Acts, but it was nothing of the sort. It was a perfect example of the teaching Paul has included in Romans. First and most important, it upheld the cause of Gentile liberty, excluding legalism. It decreed that it was not necessary for Gentiles to become circumcised in order to be saved. Nothing is required but faith in Christ's atoning work. It was because of this that Paul was able to write to the Galatians, saying that the council had declared for Gentile liberty and that "not even Titus, who was with me, was compelled to be circumcised, even though he was a Greek" (Gal. 2:3).

At the same time, the council showed concern for the consciences of the weaker, Jewish brethren. For that is what three of the four forbidden actions were about. The demand for sexual morality was required by the moral law of God, of course. The Gentiles needed to hear it. But the other three items all had to do with Jewish scruples about food. In writing to the Corinthians Paul says that it does not matter whether an animal has been sacrificed to an idol or not. A Christian is free to eat it. "We are no worse if we do not eat, and no better if we do" (1 Cor. 8:8). But not all Jews saw it this way, and for their sakes the council ruled that Gentiles should avoid practices that were offensive to their Jewish brethren. James made this reasoning explicit when he said, "For Moses has been preached in every city from the earliest times and is read in the synagogues on every Sabbath" (Acts 15:21). That is, Jews are found everywhere; their law forbids such practices and we want to win them rather than repel them. Moreover, if they are Christians, we want to live with them within the one strong fellowship of the Christian church.

Strikingly therefore, in the same chapter of Corinthians in which Paul argues that "an idol is nothing" (1 Cor. 8:4) and that "we are no worse if we do not eat, and no better if we do" (v. 8), he immediately goes on to say this:

> Be careful, however, that the exercise of your freedom does not become a stumbling block to the weak. For if anyone with a weak conscience sees you who have this knowledge eating in an idol's temple, won't he be emboldened to eat what has been sacrificed to idols? So this weak brother, for whom Christ died, is destroyed by your knowledge. When you sin against your brothers in this way and wound their weak conscience, you sin against Christ. Therefore,

if what I eat causes my brother to fall into sin, I will never eat meat again, so
that I will not cause him to fall.

1 Corinthians 8:9–13

The last line is particularly powerful. For Paul, the great champion of
Gentile liberty, is not saying merely that he will forgo his privilege to eat meat
as long as the scrupulous believer is around, but that he will do it forever if
that is what is necessary for the spiritual health of the other believer.

Why the Strong Should Forgo Privileges

But it is hard to see things that way, especially in this day of passionate
emphasis upon our own "rights." That is why the last two verses supply such
forceful reasons why the advice not to do anything to harm the other believer
should be heeded. There are three of them. This is the way John Calvin
expresses them in his commentary.[5]

1. *Love is violated if our brother is made to grieve for so slight a reason, for it is
contrary to love to cause anyone distress.*

If the truth of the gospel was at stake, Paul would fight to the last ditch to
defend it. But if it is not a matter of God's grace in saving sinners, it is clear
that the demands of love should override one's personal freedom in periph-
eral matters. Paul has stressed the demands of Christian love earlier in this
section, in chapter 12:9–21 and chapter 13:8–14. "Love does no harm to its
neighbor," Paul said (Rom. 13:10). But if this is so and if we do love, then
we will not harm our Christian brothers or sisters for so slight a matter as
what we eat or drink. To insist on our own way at this point would be selfish
at best and most likely be wicked.

2. *The price of the blood of Christ is wasted when a weak conscience is wounded,
for the most contemptible brother has been redeemed by the blood of Christ.*

In verse 15, Paul uses a strong word when he says that we are not to
"destroy" the brother "for whom Christ died." He does not mean that we
might cause our brother to perish eternally by some sin. He means that sin
is destructive and that if your actions cause the other person to do what he
or she believes to be sinful, then you are harming that person because for
him that behavior is wrong. How can you do that if you understand, as you
should, that the other person is one for whom Christ died? Jesus gave his
life for that other believer. How can you refuse to give up a merely questionable practice? In this area comparison with our Lord would put most of us
to shame.

3. *If the liberty which Christ has attained for us is good, we ought to see that men
do not slander it and rightly disparage it when we abuse the gifts of God.*

5. John Calvin, *The Epistles of Paul the Apostle to the Romans and to the Thessalonians,* trans. Ross
MacKenzie (Grand Rapids: Wm. B. Eerdmans Publishing Company, 1973), p. 298.

The *good* of this verse is not the disputed matter that might be spoken of as *evil* by the weaker brother. It is the strong believer's liberty, and the point is that our freedom must not be thought by unbelievers to be merely an excuse for Christian license. We are responsible to God, first of all, but also to our weaker brethren and to the watching world. This is a short life. Its pleasures are passing and will be vastly overshadowed by the far greater pleasures and joys of heaven. Should we not willingly give up a little more here for the sake of that which is eternal, and that others might be saved?

215

God's Kingdom

Romans 14:17

For the kingdom of God is not a matter of eating and drinking, but of righteousness, peace and joy in the Holy Spirit.

One of the saddest things about church history is that early Christian leaders forgot that the kingdom of God is not the exercise of civil authority but "righteousness, peace and joy in the Holy Spirit" and began to contend for civil power over the bodies and consciences of men.

We think of the scene on Christmas day in 800 A.D. when Pope Leo III placed a golden crown upon the head of Charlemagne while he knelt before him and the people shouted, "To Charles Augustus, crowned by God, the great and pacific emperor of the Romans, life and victory." Or we recall an even more powerful scene nearly three centuries later, in 1077, when the German emperor Henry IV stood barefoot in the snow and in penitent's garb before the castle gate of Canossa, pleading for mercy from Pope Gregory VII, who two years earlier had deposed him, forbidden anyone to acknowledge his authority, and had even excommunicated him from the saving ordinances of the church. Henry was suing to save his kingdom. These were examples of power politics and power religion at their highest pitch, as both popes and emperors contended for who should have the highest earthly authority.

Gregory VII, better known as Hildebrand, had declared in the bull *Dictatus Papae*, "The Roman Church was founded by God alone; the Roman pope alone can with right be called universal; he alone may use the imperial insignia; his feet only shall be kissed by all princes; he may depose the emperors; he himself may be judged by no one; the Roman Church has never erred, nor will it err in all eternity."[1]

Is that what the Bible means when it talks about God's kingdom—the rule of popes or other church leaders over kings and their kingdoms? Or is God's kingdom something else? It obviously is something else, and church leaders have erred whenever they have tried to make the church a temporal kingdom. The periods of history in which they have done this have become the most oppressive, secular, corrupt, and violent the world has seen.

God's Kingdom and Human Kingdoms

Paul has been writing about the demands of Christian love and the obligation each believer has to protect and edify his Christian brother or sister. But now, suddenly in the midst of all this, there comes a definition of the kingdom of God that is almost a thunderbolt in view of some Christians' forceful and repeated attempts to impose their earthly wills on other people: "For the kingdom of God is not a matter of eating and drinking, but of righteousness, peace and joy in the Holy Spirit" (v. 17).

Romans 14:17 is a key verse for any biblical study of the true nature of the church, yet this is the only time in Romans that Paul employs the word *kingdom*, and he uses it only sixteen times in all his writings.[2] It is, however, a common and important term in the gospels. There are fifty-five occurrences of *kingdom* in Matthew, twenty in Mark, forty-six in Luke, and five in John.

God's kingdom is difficult to define because it is so important and so extensive. Sometimes the word is used of the universal reign of God over his creation. At other times it is used of the Messianic reign of Jesus Christ, as God promised David: "Your house and your kingdom will endure forever before me; your throne will be established forever" (2 Sam. 7:16). Later, when the house of David was in evident decline, the prophet Isaiah made clear that this promise was to be fulfilled in the divine Messiah who was to come: "He will be called Wonderful Counselor, Mighty God, Everlasting Father, Prince of Peace. Of the increase of his government and peace there will be no end. He will reign on David's throne and over his kingdom, establishing and upholding it with

---

1. Quoted by J. Marcellus Kik, *Church and State: The Story of Two Kingdoms* (New York, London, and Toronto: Thomas Nelson & Sons, 1963), p. 6.

2. 1 Corinthians 4:20, 6:9–10, 15:50; Galatians 5:21; Colossians 4:11; 1 Thessalonians 2:12; 2 Thessalonians 1:5; cf. 1 Corinthians 15:24; Ephesians 2:2, 5:5; Colossians 1:12, 13; 2 Timothy 4:1, 18.

justice and righteousness from that time on and forever" (Isa. 9:6–7). In still other passages, as in Romans 14, the word refers to the church.

Perhaps the most important thing to be said about the kingdom of God is that it is *God's* kingdom. It is *the realm in which God rules.* Moreover, because it is a case of *God* ruling, his kingdom must by definition be over and above any of the kingdoms of men and be infinitely superior to them. The kingdoms of men may endure for a time, but they eventually pass away. The kingdom of God is forever.

The normal course of the kingdoms of this world is described in a striking way in the Book of Daniel. After the early chapters in which the divine humbling of Nebuchadnezzar is recounted, his son Belshazzar comes to the throne. We are told that Belshazzar gave a party, during the course of which he defiled the vessels that had been used for God's worship in the temple in Jerusalem but had been brought to Babylon by Nebuchadnezzar after he had conquered the Jews' capital city. While Belshazzar was doing this, the fingers of a hand appeared and wrote on the plaster of the wall of the banqueting room: MENE, MENE, TEKEL, PARSIN.

The king and his nobles were frightened, and when none of the king's wise men could decipher the words, they sent for Daniel, who explained what the writing meant. "*Mene:* God has numbered the days of your reign and brought it to an end. *Tekel:* You have been weighed on the scales and found wanting. *Peres:* Your kingdom is divided and given to the Medes and Persians" (Dan. 5:26–28).

Daniel said this:

> O king, the Most High God gave your father Nebuchadnezzar sovereignty and greatness and glory and splendor. Because of the high position he gave him, all the peoples and nations and men of every language dreaded and feared him. Those the king wanted to put to death, he put to death; those he wanted to spare, he spared; those he wanted to promote, he promoted; and those he wanted to humble, he humbled. But when his heart became arrogant and hardened with pride, he was deposed from his royal throne and stripped of his glory. He was driven away from people and given the mind of an animal; he lived with the wild donkeys and ate grass like cattle; and his body was drenched with the dew of heaven, until he acknowledged that the Most High God is sovereign over the kingdoms of men and sets over them anyone he wishes.
>
> But you his son, O Belshazzar, have not humbled yourself, though you knew all this. . . . You did not honor the God who holds in his hand your life and all your ways.
>
> Daniel 5:18–23

That very night the Medes and Persians overran the palace, Belshazzar was killed, and Darius reigned in his stead.

That is the course of every human kingdom. God allows an individual or group to rise above their peers in power, their victories bring pride, and God removes them and allows others to reign in their place. Arnold Toynbee, the great British historian, wrote that the world has known thirty-four major civilizations, but all have endured only for a time. Egypt was once mighty, but it fell. Greece and Rome have fallen. The Soviet Union has collapsed. In time the United States of America will also succumb to this inevitable law of history: "Righteousness exalts a nation, but sin is a disgrace to any people" (Prov. 14:34). Pride and sin will also bring America down.

God's Kingdom and the Church

But what of the church? Is it to be an earthly kingdom? If it is, what should its relationship to the civil authorities be? If not, of what does it actually consist?

A great many errors about the church and its proper relationship to the secular powers could have been avoided if Bible students had begun with the definition I have just given and then carried it over to the church consistently. The kingdom of God is *the realm in which God rules*. That is why there is a sense in which the whole world is God's kingdom; he is sovereign over his entire creation. At the same time, the rule of God describes his relationship to those who acknowledge his rule—that is, to those into whom he has entered by his Holy Spirit. This means that the kingdom of God is present in this important spiritual sense whenever individuals come to acknowledge God's rule and reflect his character.

How is that expressed? That is the question Paul answers in the verse we are studying. For when he writes, "The kingdom of God is not a matter of eating and drinking, but of righteousness, peace and joy in the Holy Spirit," Paul is saying that the kingdom of God is present and is seen in whatever God does in the lives of Christians. And what God does is bestow righteousness, grant peace, and bring joy in the Holy Spirit. This has nothing to do with what we eat or drink (or what we do not eat or drink) or whether, to use Paul's first example, believers observe certain days. God is not concerned about these things, which is why we are not to be concerned about them, except to the extent that our conduct may hurt others. What we must be concerned about are the three items Paul mentions: "righteousness, peace and joy in the Holy Spirit."

God's Kingdom and the Christian

Unfortunately, commentators are divided about the way these three terms are to be understood, since they are used in various ways in the Bible. One approach is to see these words as expressions of God's progressive saving work in the Christian: first, God gives the righteousness of Christ to the believer; second, this imparted righteousness becomes the basis for a new peace between God and the sinner, spilling over into a peacemaking approach to other persons; third, a life of divine joy results. The other approach is to see these as moral qualities to be developed within the Christian: righteousness or just dealings toward others, peacemaking toward others, and a joyful disposition toward others.

A number of important commentators hold to the latter view, that these are moral qualities developed in the Christian.[3] John Murray makes three good arguments for it: "(1) 'Joy in the Holy Spirit' is subjective; it is joy in the believer's heart. Since this joy is coordinated with righteousness and peace we would expect the two latter to be in the same category. (2) Verse 18 points back to verse 17. 'Herein' ['in this way,' NIV] refers to the elements specified in verse 17. In these elements the believer is said to serve Christ, be well-pleasing to God, and approved of men. The service of Christ is, without question, an obligation devolving upon us and the discharge is said to make us well-pleasing to God. These ideas do not accord with forensic righteousness and peace. (3) Likewise in verse 19 we have hortatory terms directed to our responsibility. Of particular relevance are the words, 'follow after things which make for peace.' . . . For these reasons 'righteousness' and 'peace' should be taken as the rectitude and harmony that must govern the attitude and behavior of the believer within the fellowship of the church."[4]

In my opinion, however, this is not a place where arguing from the drift of Paul's argument is terribly persuasive. Normally it would be, but in verse 17 Paul is simply injecting another reason why Christians are not to be bound by man-made rules and regulations. He is emphasizing that the kingdom of God does not consist of such things but is actually righteousness, peace, and joy in the Holy Spirit.

Moreover, it is most natural to view righteousness in the same way Paul has been developing this term throughout the letter, as the righteousness of Christ imparted to us. With the whole letter behind him, why would he change his usage now?

Charles Hodge clearly thought as I do when he expressed the alternative view like this:

> Paul does not mean to say that Christianity consists in morality; that the man who is just, peaceful and cheerful is a true Christian. This would be to contradict the whole argument of this epistle. The righteousness, peace and joy intended are those of which the Holy Spirit is the author. Righteousness is that which enables us to stand before God, because it satisfies the demands of the law. It is the righteousness of faith, both objective and subjective; peace is the concord between God and the soul, between reason and conscience, between the heart and our fellowmen. And the joy is the joy of salvation; that joy which only those who are in the fellowship of the Holy Ghost ever can experience.[5]

---

[3]See Robert Haldane, *An Exposition of the Epistle to the Romans* (MacDill AFB: MacDonald Publishing Company, 1958), pp. 604–5; and John Murray, *The Epistle to the Romans*, 2 vols. in 1 (Grand Rapids: Wm. B. Eerdmans Publishing Company, 1968), vol. 2, pp. 193–94.

[4]Murray, *The Epistle to the Romans*, vol. 2, p. 194.

[5]Charles Hodge, *A Commentary on Romans* (Edinburgh and Carlisle, Pa.: The Banner of Truth Trust, 1972), p. 425. Original edition 1835 It may be noted on this point that John Calvin is a bit unclear (*The Epistles of Paul the Apostle to the Romans and to the Thessalonians*, trans. Ross MacKenzie [Grand Rapids: Wm. B. Eerdmans Publishing Company, 1973], pp. 298–99) and Leon Morris is nondiscriminating. Morris says, "It seems likely that Paul is not differentiating sharply between these two views and that he is using the expression in a way that suggests both" (*The Epistle to the Romans* [Grand Rapids: Wm. B. Eerdmans Publishing Company, and Leicester, England: Inter-Varsity Press, 1988], p. 489).

It might be added that if this is the case, if the righteousness in view is the righteousness of Christ imparted to us; peace, the peace we have with God the Father; and joy, the joy of the Holy Spirit, which is a fruit of his work within us, then Paul's definition of God's kingdom is trinitarian. The gift of righteousness pertains to God the Son, peace to God the Father, and joy to God the Holy Spirit—a very satisfactory form of definition.

1. *The righteousness of Jesus Christ.* Righteousness is one of the most important words in Romans. It is used thirty-five times in this one letter alone, and it more than any other single word is used by Paul to sum up the salvation that comes to us through the work of Jesus Christ. Since the kingdom of God means among other things the reign of God in us through the work of Christ, it is nearly impossible to think of the kingdom of God in us without reference to this imparted righteousness.

In volume one of these studies I made three important points about this New Testament concept:[6]

First, this righteousness from God is the righteousness of the Lord Jesus Christ. We have no righteousness of ourselves. "There is no one righteous, not even one" (Rom. 3:10). If we are to have any righteousness at all—which we must if we are to stand before the holy presence of Almighty God—we must receive it from Christ.

Second, God offers this righteousness of Jesus Christ freely, apart from any need to work for it on our part. This is critical, since the mere existence of righteousness would do us no good unless God were willing to give it to us freely; we could never deserve or earn it. It was a discovery of this great truth that transformed Martin Luther and launched the Reformation. Before he discovered that God offered the righteousness of Christ as a free gift, Luther hated God for demanding what he could never produce. But after he discovered God's grace in the gospel, Luther became a champion of grace and was willing to perish for that truth.

Third, faith is the channel by which sinners receive Christ's righteousness. Initially Luther thought of faith as a work, but he came to see it merely as a hand opening to receive what God offers. We can say then that the kingdom of God comes to those who by God's grace open their hearts to receive Christ's righteousness and God's rule.

Augustus M. Toplady expressed this movingly when he wrote this hymn:

> Nothing in my hand I bring.
> Simply to thy cross I cling;
> Naked, come to thee for dress;

---

6. James Montgomery Boice, *Romans,* vol. 1, *Justification by Faith: Romans 1–4* (Grand Rapids: Baker Book House, 1991), pp. 105–9.

> Helpless, look to thee for grace;
> Foul, I to the fountain fly;
> Wash me, Savior, or I die.
> Rock of Ages, cleft for me.
> Let me hide myself in thee.

2. *The peace of God the Father.* The second of Paul's three terms is *peace*, and this certainly means, at least in the first instance, the peace with God that we have as a result of Jesus Christ's work for us and God's justification of us because of that work.

The Bible speaks of two kinds of peace: "peace *with* God" because of Christ's work and the "peace *of* God," which he imparts as we lay our concerns before him. Paul mentions the first type in Romans 5:1: "Therefore, since we have been justified through faith, we have peace with God through our Lord Jesus Christ." He refers to the second peace in Philippians 4:6–7: "Do not be anxious about anything, but in everything, by prayer and petition, with thanksgiving, present your requests to God. And the peace of God, which transcends all understanding, will guard your hearts and your minds in Christ Jesus."

3. *The joy of the Holy Spirit.* And last of all is joy, though it is the first of the marks of the church as Jesus developed them in his great prayer for the church recorded in John 17 (see v. 13). Indeed, it is even first here in the sense that it is the first evidence of the work that has been done for us and in us by God. When we have been justified by God as a result of receiving Christ's righteousness and have been brought into a relationship with God that may be described as peace after warfare, the natural expression of that in us is the superabounding joy of the Holy Spirit.

Have you experienced that joy? One of the sad things about so many Christians is that they do not seem to be cheerful. One Sunday afternoon in Scotland a church janitor picked up a piece of paper on which one of the worshipers had been doodling, probably during a particularly long sermon. It contained this bit of wry doggerel:

> To dwell above with saints in love,
> Aye, that will be glory!
> To dwell below with saints I know,
> Now that's a different story.

It shouldn't be different, of course. It is true that nothing here will ever equal our joy in heaven—that joy will be full, matchless, and unalloyed. But something of that joy, something of the joy of our salvation, should be observable now in all who are truly believing members of God's kingdom.

First Righteousness and Peace

But we must get the order right! There are many people who would love to have the joy that trusting Christians have. In fact, they envy them that joy. But they are unwilling to have it on God's terms, which is the only way it can be had, and that is through faith in the perfect and completed work of Christ. First righteousness, followed by peace with God. Then joy!

Remember what the angel said to the shepherds when the heavenly legions appeared in the night sky over Bethlehem to announce Jesus' birth: "Do not be afraid. I bring you good news of great joy that will be for all the people. Today in the town of David a Savior has been born to you; he is Christ the Lord" (Luke 2:10). It is because we have a Savior, who is also our king, that we have peace with God and joy that is full of glory.

216

Approved by God and Man

Romans 14:17–18

For the kingdom of God is not a matter of eating and drinking, but of righteousness, peace and joy in the Holy Spirit, because anyone who serves Christ in this way is pleasing to God and approved by men.

At the end of Luke 2, the chapter that contains Luke's account of the birth of Jesus Christ, there is a fascinating verse that is particularly meaningful if we consider it together with our text in Romans. Luke is writing of Jesus, who, he says, "grew in wisdom and stature, and *in favor with God and men*" (v. 52). In Romans, Paul writes that the Christian "who serves Christ in this way is *pleasing to God and approved by men.*" The correspondence between these two verses suggests that Christians serve Christ by becoming like Jesus Christ and that if they do this they will receive both divine and human approval.

Serving Jesus "In This Way"

The key terms in Romans 14:18 are the Greek words *en touto* (possibly *en toutois*), which the New International Version translates as *in this way*, the Revised Standard Version as *thus*, and the J. B. Phillips paraphrase as *in these things.*

1779

The proper translation has been a matter of some controversy because of uncertainty about the Greek text. In most of the ancient manuscripts the Greek words are singular: "in this." But in some they are plural: "in these things." If the latter is right, Paul would be referring to the three items mentioned in the previous verse (righteousness, peace, and joy in the Holy Spirit), and this would dispose us to think of them as virtues rightly to be seen in every Christian: righteous dealings with other people, peacemaking among other people, and a cheerful disposition.

If the majority of the manuscripts are right—that is, if the words are singular ("in this")—then Paul would be referring to the nonjudgmental attitude he has been commending since the beginning of the chapter. That is, he would be promoting a right way of Christian thinking and behaving—knowing that the kingdom of God does not consist in eating and drinking or other nonessential matters but is rather something else entirely: the righteousness of Christ imputed to the sinner, which the believer will want to make known to other people; peace with God achieved by the work of Christ on his or her behalf; and joy, which is a mark of the Holy Spirit of God in the regenerated person's life. In other words, the person who serves Christ will do it by living out a truly vital faith and not by trying to sustain a false, judgmental, and barren legalism.

Paul is not introducing a new subject. He is pointing out that God is looking for a living, vital faith, not legalism. Legalism contributes to the pride of the flesh, because whenever we measure up to some moral code of our own or some other person's devising we think of ourselves as being better than people who do not measure up to it. Jesus is not served in that way or with that kind of thinking. He is served when we understand that we are accepted by God through the work of Jesus Christ alone and are therefore able joyfully to accept and love all others for whom Jesus died. These other believers may be wrong in many respects, in our opinion. But we will know that we are all nevertheless part of one spiritual body, the body of Christ, and that we belong together with all other Christians as together we seek to live for Christ and bear a strong witness for him in this world.

Paul's Personal Example

When we read this passage in light of what we know about Paul and his background in Pharisaic Judaism, it is impossible not to sense that he is writing out of his own experience and with a strong sense of gratitude for the liberty he had himself found in Jesus Christ.

We remember that Paul had been a Pharisee and that the Pharisees were the strictest religious sect of the Jews. There were never very many Pharisees, but they were highly regarded because they made it their life endeavor and passion to keep the law of God in its entirety. If the law said, "Remember the Sabbath day by keeping it holy" and "on it you shall not do any work," they asked, What is work? Then they devised a detailed list of what was and was not forbidden labor. A godly person could not cook on the Sabbath; that was work. So the food to be eaten had to be cooked the day before. Carrying something was work. Even something like a handkerchief could not be carried from one room to another; that would mean breaking the law. If the hand-kerchief were worn around the neck as a piece of clothing, however, it fell into a different category and was allowed.

There were thousands of regulating definitions like this, and not only for the Sabbath observance but for every other Old Testament precept as well. Food laws were strictly observed. Kosher cooking was demanded. Tithes were obligatory. The Pharisees tithed their possessions as well as their money, which Jesus acknowledged even when he was chiding them for their hypocrisy: "Woe to you, teachers of the law and Pharisees, you hypocrites! You give a tenth of your spices—mint, dill and cummin. But you have neglected the more important matters of the law—justice, mercy and faithfulness. You should have practiced the latter, without neglecting the former" (Matt. 23:23).

That was exactly the problem. In the days before his conversion Paul had been meticulous in keeping these man-made regulations, but he had neglected the more important matters. In fact, he had not even begun to appreciate their importance. For that is what legalism does. It bogs us down in trivia while making us dull, impervious, and then blind to things that are essential. Paul thought he was righteous, but he had not even begun to under-stand the scope of God's righteousness. He did not know that pleasing God by human righteousness was beyond his ability. He knew the word *grace*, but he did not understand the nature of God's great and abundant grace or that he needed that grace. Most important, he did not recognize that his attempts to attain to his own righteousness had actually been keeping him from sal-vation through Christ by the grace of God.

One day that changed. Paul was on his way to Damascus to arrest Chris-tians, whom he believed were enemies of the true faith given to his people. Instead he was arrested by Jesus. A bright light flashed from heaven, and when Paul saw it he fell to the ground blinded. He heard a voice saying, "Saul, Saul, why do you persecute me?" (Acts 9:4).

Paul knew this was a theophany, a revelation or appearance of God. So he asked, "Who are you, Lord?" (v. 5).

He was shocked when the divine voice replied, "I am Jesus, whom you are persecuting. Now get up and go into the city, and you will be told what you must do" (vv. 5–6).

Paul was forever changed by this revelation. He became an entirely dif-ferent man, and he thought differently too. In Philippians he tells us what this encounter meant to him, comparing what he found in Christ with what he had been trying to achieve for himself before that time:

> If anyone else thinks he has reasons to put confidence in the flesh, I have more:
> circumcised on the eighth day, of the people of Israel, of the tribe of Benjamin,

a Hebrew of the Hebrews; in regard to the law, a Pharisee; as for zeal, persecuting the church; as for legalistic righteousness, faultless. But whatever was
to my profit I now consider loss for the sake of Christ. What is more, I consider
everything a loss compared to the surpassing greatness of knowing Christ Jesus
my Lord, for whose sake I have lost all things. I consider them rubbish, that I
may gain Christ and be found in him, not having a righteousness of my own
that comes from the law, but that which is through faith in Christ—the righteousness that comes from God and is by faith. I want to know Christ and the
power of his resurrection and the fellowship of sharing in his sufferings, becoming like him in his death, and so, somehow, to attain to the resurrection from
the dead.

Philippians 3:4–11

Paul is saying that before he met Jesus in that vision he thought that he
had pleased God by his inherited religious advantages coupled to his own
numerous achievements:

Circumcised on the eighth day. That was a claim to having been born into a
true Jewish family rather than being a proselyte, who would be circumcised
as an adult, or an Ishmaelite, who would be circumcised when he was thirteen
years old.

An Israelite. Israel was the covenant name of God's elect people. So this word
brings in Paul's inherited claim to all the covenant privileges and blessings.

The tribe of Benjamin. When the civil war that came after the death of Solomon
divided the northern kingdom from the southern kingdom, Benjamin was the
one tribe that remained with Judah in the south, therefore remaining close
to the proscribed place of worship, which was Jerusalem. Both kingdoms fell
away from God. But the decline was about one hundred years slower in the
south, and Benjamin benefited from the geographical association.

A Hebrew of Hebrews. This is a way of saying that Paul was a pure-blooded
Jew, born of a Jewish father as well as a Jewish mother. Being a Jew brought
great spiritual advantages, which Paul has already listed in Romans 9:4–5:
"Theirs is the adoption as sons; theirs the divine glory, the covenants, the
receiving of the law, the temple worship and the promises. Theirs are the
patriarchs, and from them is traced the human ancestry of Christ, who is God
over all, forever praised!"

But Paul was not only counting on the spiritual advantages he had inherited, he was counting on the things he had achieved for himself, too. He was
also a *Pharisee,* as we have seen. He was a *zealous* Pharisee, which he proved
by his persecution of the infant church. Finally, he was at least in his own
eyes *faultless* in regard to *legalistic righteousness.* Like a good Pharisee he had
done what he believed he should do.

Yet once he saw Jesus and learned how empty all these human achievements were and how far short he had fallen of the inner righteousness that
the holy God requires, he counted all of that as "loss compared to the surpassing greatness of knowing Christ." That is, he reckoned his former assets

as liabilities. He moved them over to the liabilities column. Under assets he wrote "Jesus Christ alone."

When we read Paul's testimony we can understand in a moment why a man like Paul was never going to go back to legalism and why he was so eager to urge an entirely different approach on other Christians. He didn't want any more of that; it hadn't worked. We can understand why he says categorically and without any qualification, "The kingdom of God is not a matter of eating and drinking, but of righteousness, peace and joy in the Holy Spirit."

Pleasing to God

When Paul was in Judaism he must have believed that what he was doing pleased God, or at least he must have hoped that God was pleased. But after he was converted he knew that it was actually this new liberated life, lived by the grace of God in Christ, that pleased him.

The aim of every believer must be to please God, and our example in doing so must be the Lord Jesus Christ. On the occasion of Jesus' public baptism by John, recorded in three of the gospels, a voice came from heaven declaring, "This is my Son, whom I love; with him I am well pleased" (Matt. 3:17; cf. Mark 1:11; Luke 3:22). Toward the end of his ministry, on the occasion of his transfiguration, the voice from heaven came again, saying to Peter, James, and John, "This is my Son, whom I love; with him I am well pleased. Listen to him" (Matt. 17:5).

Jesus pleased his Father perfectly. So if you are striving to be like Jesus, you will please God too. Paul had this mind when he wrote of his own aspirations, saying, "We make it our goal to please him" (2 Cor. 5:9).

Is that your goal? If it is, you will stop judging other Christians and instead live in a way that manifests the grace of God in your own life. Above all, you will remember that you are only a sinner and that you have been saved solely by God's grace. People who understand that know they are not better than other people, even if they have come to understand the Bible better than others and obey it more completely. The truth is that such people are not comparing themselves with other people at all. Their minds are on Jesus. They know only that they belong to Jesus and love him, and that they want other people to know and love him too.

Approved by Men

The final phrase of our text is startling, for it tells us that the one who serves Jesus Christ in this way will not only be pleasing to God but will also be "approved by men." What is startling about that statement is that we often are not at all pleasing to non-Christians. We are scorned and even hated by them.

The Bible seems to be contradictory here. On the one hand, Jesus told his disciples, "If the world hates you, keep in mind that it hated me first. If you belonged to the world, it would love you as its own. As it is, you do not belong to the world, but I have chosen you out of the world. That is why the world hates you" (John 15:18–19). He also said this:

> Blessed are you when men hate you,
>   when they exclude you and insult you
>   and reject your name as evil,
>   because of the Son of Man. . . .
> Woe to you when all men speak well of you,
>   for that is how their fathers treated the false prophets.
>
> Luke 6:22, 26

On the other hand, Paul listed human approval as a qualification of one who wanted to be an officer in the church: "He must also have a good reputation with outsiders, so that he will not fall into disgrace and into the devil's trap" (1 Tim. 3:7). As far as the example of Jesus himself is concerned, although he "grew in wisdom and stature, and in favor with God and men" (Luke 2:52), he also was despised by many (Isa. 53:3).

Perhaps this illustration will help explain this paradox. Years ago one of my predecessors at Tenth Presbyterian Church, Donald Grey Barnhouse, was teaching about Christians being in the world but not a part of the world, and he concluded by saying, "You may be sure that if nobody thinks you are strange and out of step, you are not a good Christian." After the meeting a friend who had been present and had heard that remark added wisely, "However, you should also say that if *everybody* thinks you are strange and out of step, you are not a good Christian."[1]

Clearly we are not out to please the world, and we will not please it. If the world hated our Lord and Master enough to crucify him, we can be sure that it will hate us too. At the same time, there should be within the true follower of Jesus Christ enough of his character, truth, love, and integrity that some looking on will, reluctantly perhaps but nevertheless genuinely, acknowledge that the believer is indeed living an exemplary and truly pious life. They should be able to acknowledge that Christians are real. The world must not be able to wag its finger at us and call us hypocrites.

A brief study of the word *approved* (*dokimos* in Greek) will also help us understand what is required of one who is serious about serving Jesus Christ. In the ancient world there was no paper money as we know it today, and until a rudimentary banking system grew up for the sake of international trade during the Middle Ages, all financial transactions were in gold, silver, or base metal coin. There were no great coin presses, so in order to make coins the metal was heated until liquid, then poured into molds where it was allowed to cool. After cooling, the irregular edges of the rough coins were trimmed

---

1. See Donald Grey Barnhouse, *God's Glory: Exposition of Bible Doctrines, Taking the Epistle to the Romans as a Point of Departure,* vol. 10, *Romans 14:13–16:27* (Grand Rapids: Wm. B. Eerdmans Publishing Company, 1964), p. 17.

away. This was an inexact method, of course. Moreover, the metal was soft because it was not mixed with alloys, and people frequently shaved away at the edges and kept the metal, in time collecting enough to make up the equivalent of a new coin. We know this was a problem because many laws were passed against it. In one century alone, the city of Athens passed over eighty laws intended to stop this practice.

What happened, of course, was that in time some coins would become so whittled down that the merchants would reject them as obviously lacking their full weight or value. At this point the coins were said to be *adokimos*—"disapproved." On the other hand, merchants who were upright and would therefore neither give nor accept "light" money, were said to be *dokimos*—honest men. And their coins were *dokimos* too.

That is the sense in which the word *approved* is used of the followers of Jesus Christ. They are to be approved by the world in the sense that the world is to recognize that they have their full weight, that they are people of genuine spiritual substance. Moreover, when we remember that one meaning of the Hebrew word *kabod* (usually translated *glory* in the Bible) is weight or weightiness, we see that in this sense Christians are to be those who show forth something of the glory of Jesus Christ and are recognized by the world as doing so. We might say that the world is to recognize that believers in Christ are the genuine article and that they show forth something that is better than anything the world knows and that goes beyond its experience.

It is tragic that it should ever be any other way. Somewhere in his writings, John R. W. Stott, the wise Church of England rector, tells about two Englishmen who were riding in a railway carriage. In the next carriage was a man whom one of the first two thought looked like the presiding Archbishop of Canterbury. "No, he's not," said the friend.

"Yes, he is," said the first.

Eventually they decided to make a bet on whether the third gentleman was the archbishop or not. They agreed on their terms. Then the traveler who thought the man was the well-known leader of the Church of England crossed over to the other compartment and asked him if he were by any chance the Archbishop of Canterbury. The man replied with a curse, swearing that blankety-blank he was not the blankety-blank Archbishop of Canterbury. The questioner went back to his compartment and told his companion, "The bet's off. There's no way to tell whether he's the archbishop or not."

Getting Our Priorities Right

Our text tells us that if we are determined to serve Jesus Christ by living for him and not by legalism, then we will be "pleasing to God and approved by men." But notice that if we do please men (which is not always the case but should frequently be), we will not please them by setting out to please them, but rather by setting out to serve Christ. That is, we must put things in the right order and get our priorities straight. If you try to please men, you will never please them all the time, though you may please some occasionally. But what is really important, you will never please God. God cannot be put in second place. On the other hand, if you determine to please God, you will certainly please him and you may even get a begrudging approval by some fairly reasonable human beings too.

The Book of Revelation says, "To him who loves us and has freed us from our sins by his blood, and has made us to be a kingdom and priests *to serve his God and Father*—to him be glory and power for ever and ever! Amen" (Rev. 1:5–6). So let's be sure that we really do serve God.

217

Building Up or Tearing Down

Romans 14:19–15:2

Let us therefore make every effort to do what leads to peace and to mutual edification. Do not destroy the work of God for the sake of food. All food is clean, but it is wrong for a man to eat anything that causes someone else to stumble. It is better not to eat meat or drink wine or do anything else that will cause your brother to fall.

So whatever you believe about these things keep between yourself and God. Blessed is the man who does not condemn himself by what he approves. But the man who has doubts is condemned if he eats, because his eating is not from faith; and everything that does not come from faith is sin.

We who are strong ought to bear with the failings of the weak and not to please ourselves. Each of us should please his neighbor for his good, to build him up.

Most of us get impatient with repetition. In fact, if the repetition is also admonition, we get hostile: "Why are you telling me that again? I heard you the first time. I'll get to it when I am good and ready." Children get impatient when their parents remind them to eat their cereal, make their beds, clean up their rooms, or wash their faces. The attitude doesn't stop with childhood either. As adults we get impatient with repetitions from God and find them offensive.

1787

The fact that something is repeated shows that we need to hear it. I say this here because nearly everything in the verses that end Romans 14 and begin Romans 15 has been said before. Paul is still talking about our tendencies to judge other Christians, fighting over things that are not important, and he tells us not to do this, encouraging the strong to bear with the convictions of the weak. In fact, the very same words occur in these two sections: *peace* (verses 17 and 19), *destroy* (verses 15 and 20), *clean* and *unclean* (verses 14 and 20), *stumble* (verses 13 and 20), *fall* (verses 4 and 21), *condemned* (verses 3 and 23), and *weak* and *strong* (verses 1 and 15:1).

I often say that if God tells us something once, we should pay attention. It is God speaking. But when he says something twice or even three times, surely we should stop anything else we are doing, focus our minds, seize upon each individual word, memorize what is being said, ponder its meaning, and seek to apply it to every aspect of our lives.

The Building That Is Christ's Church

Nevertheless, the passage we come to now is not entirely repetitious. The main points are, but the section as a whole is bracketed with a concept that has not yet appeared in Romans—to *edify* or *build up*. This word pictures Christians as a building (or part of a building) that needs to be carefully constructed, and it contrasts this work with actions or attitudes that would tend to tear the building down. The word occurs in verse 19: "Let us therefore make every effort to do what leads to peace and to mutual *edification*." Then, although the New International Version translates it as *build up*, it occurs again in Romans 15:2, where we read: "Each of us should please his neighbor for his good, *to build him up*."[1]

Edification is mostly a Pauline concept, since fifteen out of eighteen occurrences of the word (*oikodomē*) in the New Testament are in Paul's writings. Yet the roots of the idea probably go back to Jesus' words to Peter at the time of Peter's great confession of faith in Jesus as the Son of God. Jesus had asked his disciples who other people thought he was. They gave the popular answers: John the Baptist, Elijah, Jeremiah, or one of the prophets. "But what about you?" he then asked. "Who do you say I am?" (Matt. 16:15).

Peter answered, "You are the Christ, the Son of the living God" (v. 16).

Then Jesus said, "Blessed are you, Simon son of Jonah, for this was not revealed to you by man, but by my Father in heaven. And I tell you that you are Peter, and on this rock I will *build* my church, and the gates of Hades will not overcome it" (vv. 17–18).

1. The fact that this section both begins and ends with "edification" shows that these verses belong together and that the chapter division in our Bibles is not as helpful or wise as it could be. Charles Hodge wrote that "the separation of this passage [Romans 15:1–13] from the preceding chapter is obviously unhappy" (Charles Hodge, *A Commentary on Romans* [Edinburgh and Carlisle, Pa.: The Banner of Truth Trust, 1972], p. 432. Original edition 1835).

Jesus was speaking of the corporate body of believers, of course. Paul usually employs the word to refer to building up individual Christians, helping individuals grow spiritually. But the words in the Greek text are exactly the same, and Paul also sometimes uses the word *edify* of the church. For example, in his letter to the Ephesians, Paul writes:

> Consequently, you are no longer foreigners and aliens, but fellow citizens with God's people and members of God's household, built on the foundation of the apostles and prophets, with Christ Jesus himself as the chief cornerstone. In him the whole building is joined together and rises to become a holy temple in the Lord. And in him you too are being built together to become a dwelling in which God lives by his Spirit.
>
> Ephesians 2:19–22

In these verses Paul likens the church to a kingdom, a family, and a temple. But in thinking of a temple he thinks of a building into which individuals are being "built together." That is, each one is a part of it.

Take Care How You Build

This image is so well developed in the New Testament, particularly in Paul's writings, that it is useful to think about it carefully. If God is in the process of building his church, as Jesus said he is, and if Christians each have a share in doing the work, we ought to ask ourselves how the work should be done and what this should mean for us personally. We need to keep several things in mind.

1. *To build something properly you need to know what you are trying to build.* You need a design or blueprint. We do not have to go very far to find this idea in Romans 14, because immediately after his first use of the word *edification* (in v. 19) Paul speaks of the project as "the work of God," saying, "Do not destroy the work of God for the sake of food" (v. 20).

This is not a complete blueprint, but it gets us started by reminding us that the church is God's church, not ours, and that what matters is what God is doing in the lives of individual Christians, not whether those people conform to our ideas of what a pious or useful Christian should be. In Paul's day some people thought that it was important that other Christians observe certain rules of eating and drinking or keep certain holy days. But Paul has been saying forcefully that this is not what the kingdom of God is all about. He has just stated that "the kingdom of God is not a matter of eating and drinking, but of righteousness, peace and joy in the Holy Spirit" (v. 17).

For a fuller blueprint, we go again to Ephesians. In one of its best-known passages Paul refers to God's plan like this: "[God] gave some to be apostles, some to be prophets, some to be evangelists, and some to be pastors and teachers, to prepare God's people for works of service, so that the body of Christ may be built up until we all reach unity in the faith and in the knowledge of the Son of God and become mature, attaining to the whole measure of the fullness of Christ" (Eph. 4:11–13).

"The whole measure of the fullness of Christ" is what we should be trying to see in other Christians. Therefore, to the extent that we are following God's blueprint rather than our dim vision of what we think other people should be, we will be doing everything in our power to help them become like Jesus Christ and be equipped to serve others for his sake.

2. *You need the right foundation.* The second requirement for putting up a good building is a solid foundation. In fact, at the very end of the Sermon on the Mount Jesus used this image to distinguish between those who would build well by hearing his words and putting them into practice and those who would not:

> Therefore everyone who hears these words of mine and puts them into practice is like a wise man who built his house on the rock. The rain came down, the streams rose, and the winds blew and beat against that house; yet it did not fall, because it had its foundation on the rock. But everyone who hears these words of mine and does not put them into practice is like a foolish man who built his house on sand. The rain came down, the streams rose, and the winds blew and beat against that house, and it fell with a great crash.

> Matthew 7:24–27

To the Corinthians Paul writes of the foundation as Jesus Christ himself: "For no one can lay any foundation other than the one already laid, which is Jesus Christ" (1 Cor. 3:11).

Jesus meant precisely the same thing when he told Peter, "You are Peter, and on this rock I will build my church" (Matt. 16:18).

Because of the way he said this some people have supposed that he was saying he was going to build his church on Peter. But Jesus was actually making a play on Peter's name to highlight the contrast between his weak disciple and himself. In Greek Peter's name is *Petros,* the masculine form of the noun meaning stone. (It can also mean pebble.) That is what Peter was, a little stone. But when Jesus spoke of the "rock" on which he would build his church, he used the feminine form of the same word (*petra*), which means living rock or bedrock. Peter was a little pebble that could easily be dislodged, as he was soon to demonstrate by his failure at the time of Christ's trial. But Jesus was the solid and living Rock of Ages.

This was how Peter himself understood Jesus' words, because he wrote of Jesus as "the living Stone" in his first letter, drawing on three Old Testament texts to make his point:[2]

---

2. Isaiah 28:16; Psalm 118:22; Isaiah 8:14.

As you come to him, the living Stone—rejected by men but chosen by God and precious to him—you also, like living stones, are being built into a spiritual house to be a holy priesthood, offering spiritual sacrifices acceptable to God through Jesus Christ. For in Scripture it says:

> "See, I lay a stone in Zion,
>> a chosen and precious cornerstone,
> and the one who trusts in him
>> will never be put to shame."

Now to you who believe, this stone is precious. But to those who do not believe,

> "The stone the builders rejected
>> has become the capstone."

and,

> "A stone that causes men to stumble
> and a rock that makes them fall."

1 Peter 2:4–8

Today many people are trying to build useful, solid lives. But they need to know that the only adequate foundation for any stable life or career is Jesus Christ. Are you building on that foundation, a foundation that will enable you to stand against the many storms of life—or are you building on sand?

3. *You need good supplies.* A third necessity if you are going to construct a worthwhile building is enough raw material—and it has to be of good quality. Jesus said, "Suppose one of you wants to build a tower. Will he not first sit down and estimate the cost to see if he has enough money to complete it? For if he lays the foundation and is not able to finish it, everyone who sees it will ridicule him, saying, 'This fellow began to build and was not able to finish'" (Luke 14:28–30).

How are you going to build up another Christian, or your own life, for that matter? By teaching the truths of God's Word. And the Word of God will never run short or prove to be inadequate.

That is why Paul told Timothy:

But as for you, continue in what you have learned and have become convinced of, because you know those from whom you learned it, and how from infancy you have known the holy Scriptures, which are able to make you wise for salvation through faith in Christ Jesus. All Scripture is God-breathed and is useful for teaching, rebuking, correcting and training in righteousness, so that the man of God may be thoroughly equipped for every good work.

2 Timothy 3:14–17

We can also think of the wonderfully moving scene in Acts 20 where Paul is taking leave of the Ephesian elders. He knows that he is not going to see them again, so he says, "I commit you to God and to the word of his grace, which can build you up and give you an inheritance among all those who are sanctified" (Acts 20:32). Paul would never instruct these dear friends again, but he knew he could trust God to continue the work of sanctification in their lives by the power of his written Word.

4. *You need to construct your building bit by bit.* No worthwhile building is constructed overnight. Plans must be drawn, foundations laid, materials chosen, details lovingly applied. In fact, the more substantial and important the building is, the longer the construction will take. Isaiah recognized this when he compared the work of building character to raising children:

> Who is it he is trying to teach?
>   To whom is he explaining his message?
> To children weaned from their milk,
>   to those just taken from the breast?
> For it is:
>   Do and do, do and do,
>   Rule on rule, rule on rule;
>   A little here, a little there.

Isaiah 28:9–10

No one can raise a child overnight, just as one cannot construct a building overnight. Similarly, we cannot edify other Christians rapidly. It takes hard work over time. It means adding a little teaching here and a little teaching there. In terms of a church's ministry, it requires strong consistent teaching week by week.

The Opposite of Building: Tearing Down

There is a negative side to all of this, too. It is also possible to tear down. In fact, this is often done. It is one of the sad things about some forms of Christianity.

One way we tear others down rather than building them up is by fighting over things that are not important: "Do not destroy the work of God for the sake of food" (Rom. 14:20). Another is by insisting on our own rights and pleasures rather than thinking about others: "Each of us should please his neighbor for his good, to build him up" (Rom. 15:2).

Many years ago a missionary executive visited Donald Grey Barnhouse. They talked about problems on the mission field, particularly things that cause divisions, and Barnhouse asked the man to write down things that harm the work of God in other people. The executive spent several hours producing this carefully documented list:

An unforgiving spirit. Self-seeking. A legalistic spirit. Playing God for others. Hypocrisy. Failing to appreciate others' gifts. Failing to make allowances for one another (Eph. 4:2; James 2:12–13). Lack of patience. Not sympathizing with others' infirmities or, perhaps, their lack of gifts that we possess. Evil speaking (James 4:11; Titus 3:2). Assuming, without grounds, that others are at fault (James 5:9). Pulling one another to pieces (James 4:11–12, Phillips). Suspecting the motives of another. A domineering spirit. A rebellious spirit. Snobbery (James 2:1, Phillips). Hatred. Grumbling, arguing, murmuring. Maliciousness. Being a busybody. Greediness. Bitterness. Resentment. A sense of inferiority (i.e., not resting in the Lord, not satisfied with the gifts he has given). Lack of security. Instability. Timidity. Spite. Laziness. Economic sponging. Lying and slander. Malice. Jealousy. Thinking too highly of oneself. A critical spirit toward others. Carrying on controversy. Being ill-informed about the position of another.[3]

All of those attitudes and actions are destructive. They tear down rather than build up. But the missionary executive also prepared a positive list:

Willingness to be in subjection one to another. Considering others better than oneself. An understanding spirit. A sense of intimate relationship to Christ. Not insisting on our rights. Willingness to confess a wrong spirit. Sincerity. A generous spirit. A sympathetic spirit. Trusting others. Having faith in Christ, not necessarily in others, but expressed as trust to others, knowing that we belong to him. Joyfulness. Prayer. Discretion. A critical spirit toward oneself. A gentle and quiet spirit (2 Tim. 2:25). Humility (1 Peter 5:5). Using our gifts for one another. Remembering our own mistakes (James 3:2). Christ-centeredness. Love in word and deed. Fair dealing. Integrity. Recognizing one's place. A forgiving spirit. Doing things decently and in order. Conscientiousness. Faithfulness. Being responsible to perform the tasks assigned to us. Not misusing our authority over others. Being willing to follow those in authority over us.[4]

A Temple Rising to God

Is all this worth it? Is it worthwhile sharpening our skills and developing our Christian character so that others might grow to be like Jesus Christ? Of course, it is. The problem is not that we doubt the ultimate value of the work we are given to do but that we get bogged down in the hard, daily task of fashioning the stones of this building and fitting them to the overall structure. We get our eyes off the blueprint and get bogged down in the rubble.

It helps to remember that what God is building is a temple. Here is an illustration. We are told in 1 Kings 6:7 that when the great temple of Solomon was constructed "only blocks dressed at the quarry were used, and no ham-

3. Donald Grey Barnhouse, *God's Glory: Exposition of Bible Doctrines, Taking the Epistle to the Romans as a Point of Departure*, vol. 10, *Romans 14:13–16:27* (Grand Rapids: Wm. B. Eerdmans Publishing Company, 1964), pp. 21–22.
4. Ibid.

mer, chisel or any other iron tool was heard at the temple site while it was being built." To my knowledge, no other building in history was ever built in this way. Its construction was so well done it was almost silent. Silently, silently the stones were added, and the building rose.

So it is with the church. We do not hear what is going on inside human hearts as the Holy Spirit creates new life and adds individuals to the temple he is building. We do not even fully realize the part we are playing as we seek to build these other people up by focusing on the important matters, laying aside petty differences, and teaching the Word of God to each of them faithfully. But God is working, and the temple is rising. In the days of the apostles God was adding Gentiles to his church. Paul was his chief instrument in carrying the gospel to them. God added the high and low, slaves and freemen, Greeks, Romans, and barbarians. He added many at the time of the Reformation and in the days of the Great Awakenings and revivals.

He is still building his church today, and we are his workmen, laborers together with Jesus Christ. We have a responsibility to do the work well.

218

The Example of Our Lord: Part 1

Romans 15:3–4

For even Christ did not please himself but, as it is written, "The insults of those who insult you have fallen on me." For everything that was written in the past was written to teach us, so that through endurance and the encouragement of the Scriptures we might have hope.

For many years it has been common in the evangelical church to play down the importance of Jesus Christ as an example. This is primarily a reaction to the liberal church's focus on Jesus as an example to the neglect of his deity and atoning work on the cross. Evangelicals have responded by saying, "It is not an example we need; it is a Savior." That is correct, but it is also true that the Bible presents Jesus as an example for those who have been saved by him, telling us that we must be increasingly like Jesus, whom we profess to love and serve. Our text in Romans is one instance of the way the Bible frequently refers to Jesus Christ as our example.

In fact, the chapter we are studying points to his example more than once. In Romans 15:3–4, Paul refers to Jesus as one who did not please himself but rather sought to please the Father and others. In verses 7–9 he denotes him as one who accepted others.

Selfish or Selfless

In this study I intend to follow a line of thought developed by one of my predecessors at Tenth Presbyterian Church in Philadelphia, Donald Grey Barnhouse. His study appeared as part of his extensive radio broadcasts on Romans and was later published in booklet form. Today it can be found in *God's Glory*, volume 10 of the first edition of the Romans series.[1]

Barnhouse began by contrasting the selfishness of human nature with the selflessness of Jesus Christ, noting that the Greek word for the first person is *ego*, translated as *self*. Therefore, to be selfish is to be egotistical. By contrast, our text says that the Lord Jesus Christ did not please himself. In this he is marked with a true, perfect humanity very different from the fallen humanity of the sons of Adam:

> We live in a selfish world, and selfishness is the principle mark of the human race. Stand beside the highway and watch the death toll of automobile accidents rise. What is the cause of most accidents? The attitude of "Get-out-of-my-way!" How many times we see the baleful glare of a driver who comes up beside us in traffic, his whole expression showing his compulsion to be first.
>
> Even when a person becomes a believer in Christ the old Adamic nature remains, and there is warfare between the spirit and the flesh. In the church at Philippi, two people were at odds and Paul thought it necessary to send one of the apostolic company to settle the matter. He explained that he was sending Timothy, perhaps the youngest of the group, because Timothy would put the interests of the Philippians ahead of his own; and Paul added, "For all look after their own interests, and not those of Jesus Christ" (Phil. 2:21, KJV). The purpose of our text in Romans is to teach us to be like . . . Christ, who gave us the example for our daily living.
>
> One need not be a close observer to see that the thoughts of the world are centered in self. We switch on the radio, and the song comes lilting forth:
>
> > Oh! what a beautiful morning!
> > Oh! what a beautiful day!
> > I've got a beautiful feeling,
> > Everything's going *my way*.
>
> We turn the dial and hear a sermon on unselfishness and the glory of becoming like Christ and serving others; but the next program tells you how to get out of helping others.[2]

Here Barnhouse quoted one of the songs from the well-known Broadway musical *My Fair Lady*, based on the play *Pygmalion* by George Bernard Shaw:

---

1. Donald Grey Barnhouse, *God's Glory: Exposition of Bible Doctrines, Taking the Epistle to the Romans as a Point of Departure*, vol. 10, *Romans 14:13–16:27* (Grand Rapids: Wm. B. Eerdmans Publishing Company, 1964), pp. 32–44.

2. Ibid., pp. 32–33.

> The Lord above made man to help his neighbor,
> No matter where, on land or sea of foam.
> The Lord above made man to help his neighbor, but
>> With a little bit of luck,
>> With a little bit of luck,
> When he comes around *you won't be home.*

Barnhouse remarks that when we turn back to the Word of God and consider the example of Jesus Christ, we learn that for Christians, when your neighbor comes around for help, with a little bit of grace you *will* be home.

He Did Not Please Himself

The chief thing our text tells us is that Jesus did not please himself but rather set out to please God for the benefit of others, and it concludes from that truth that we should follow Christ's example. Indeed, the verses teach what Paul repeated in Philippians 2:5–8:

Your attitude should be the same as that of Christ Jesus:

> Who, being in very nature God,
>> did not consider equality with God something to be grasped,
> but made himself nothing,
>> taking the very nature of a servant,
>> being made in human likeness.
> And being found in appearance as a man,
>> he humbled himself
>> and became obedient to death—
>>> even death on a cross!

What would happen to us if Jesus had pleased himself instead of coming to earth as a man and dying for our sins? Where would we be today if Christ had put his own interests first? Once Jesus asked this question of his disciples. As recounted in John 6, the Lord had explained the doctrine of election, pointing out that he alone is the true bread from heaven to whom all must come for life and that no man can come to him unless the Father draws him (John 6:44). Later in the chapter we are told that many of his disciples objected, saying, "This is a hard teaching; who can accept it?" (v. 60). Jesus, knowing that his disciples were confused, said to them, "Does this offend you? What if you see the Son of Man ascend to where he was before!" (vv. 61–62). In other words, "What would happen if I pleased myself and went back to heaven now, instead of dying for your sins?" They would have perished and gone to hell, of course. But he did not do that. Earlier he had told them, "I have come down from heaven, not to do my own will, but to do the will of him who sent me" (v. 38), and he was doing it.

Psalm 69

It is characteristic of Paul to nail down an argument with a passage from the Old Testament after he has made his points well. He does that extensively as he comes to the end of the section of chapter 15 we are studying, quoting Psalm 18:49 in verse 9, Deuteronomy 32:43 in verse 10, Psalm 117:1 in verse 11, and Isaiah 11:10 in verse 12. But he begins this even earlier, in the verses we are studying now, citing Psalm 69:9 to prove that Jesus did not please himself but rather sought to please God his Father for the benefit of others. Romans 15:3 says, "The insults of those who insult you have fallen on me."

Psalm 69 is one of the great messianic psalms of the Old Testament. Seven of its thirty-six verses are directly quoted in the New Testament, and others furnish themes relating to Christ's work that are expanded in the gospels. In the work I referred to earlier Barnhouse noted that if we read this Psalm with Jesus in mind, we will see that he was denied and slandered by his enemies (v. 4), estranged from his own brothers (v. 8), made a proverb by the people (v. 11), criticized by the rulers (v. 12), and was the theme of obscene songs by the drunkards (v. 12).[3] Each of these points lends force to the verse from the psalm Paul quotes and provides examples of the kinds of abuse we should be willing to endure for God and others.

1. *His enemies.* "Those who hate me without reason outnumber the hairs of my head; many are my enemies without cause, those who seek to destroy me" (v. 4). Since Jesus quoted this verse of himself there can be no doubt how we are to apply it. Among the scribes, Pharisees, priests, and Levites, there were men who simply hated him. It is not hard to know why. Barnhouse explained that they looked like good men only until he came and stood beside them. Then they were exposed in their true colors: "Linen bleaching on the grass seems white until the snow falls; it then appears gray. Thus it was for the so-called 'spiritual' leaders of the people. They hated him freely; they hated him without a cause in himself."[4]

2. *His brothers.* Psalm 69 also indicates that opposition to Jesus surfaced in his own home. After Jesus was born, Mary bore Joseph at least six children, as at least two daughters and four sons are mentioned in Mark 6:3. Psalm 69:8 says, "I am a stranger to my brothers, an alien to my own mother's sons." Apparently the presence of Jesus in that household caused problems. And no wonder! It is hard to live with a highly talented person. How much more difficult must it have been to live with absolute perfection, which is what Jesus was. His brothers knew that Jesus was exceptional. They knew he had turned water into wine and that he had healed the sick and fed the multitudes, but they saw this only as a potential source of profit for themselves. John tells us, "When the Jewish Feast of Tabernacles was near, Jesus' brothers said to him, 'You ought to leave here and go to Judea, so that your disciples may see the

---

3. Barnhouse, *God's Glory*, p. 39.
4. Ibid.

miracles you do. No one who wants to become a public figure acts in secret. Since you are doing these things, show yourself to the world.' For even his own brothers did not believe in him" (John 7:2–5). Clearly Jesus had become "a stranger" to his brothers and "an alien" to his own mother's sons.

3. *A proverb.* Still further in Psalm 69 we see that Jesus became a cause for "sport" among the people (v. 11). We know that Christian students can be sneered at on college campuses, called religious nuts, the radical right, or the God squad. We do not know what specific words the unbelieving masses used to make fun of Christ, but the psalm leaves no doubt that he became a joke to the people.

4. *The rulers.* In the next verse we read, "Those who sit at the gate mock me" (v. 12). To sit at the gate was to be an elder and a ruler of the people. Of the model woman described in the last chapter of Proverbs it is said, "Her husband is respected at the city gate, where he takes his seat among the elders of the land" (Prov. 31:23). Thus, those who are referred to in Psalm 69:12 were the rulers of the people, and they were against Jesus.

5. *The drunkards.* Finally, we read that Jesus was "the song of the drunkards" (v. 12). Solomon wrote that "fools mock at . . . sin" (Prov. 14:9), but here we find men who are mocking at the Savior. The Lord Jesus Christ was abused in all these ways, yet he pursued his course because he did not seek to please himself, but the Father.[5]

A Lifetime of Insults

When Jesus began to expose the leaders' sin, they retaliated with hostility. He told them that they were children of their fathers, who had stoned prophets and killed those who were sent to them. "You are doing the things your own father does," he said (John 8:41). They turned on him with anger blazing in their eyes and taunted him with the worst reproach that could be offered. They must have known that Jesus had been born shortly after the marriage of Joseph and Mary. They flung in his teeth that he was known to be an illegitimate child. "*We* are not illegitimate children," they boasted. Jesus knew that he had been conceived by the Holy Spirit and took this reproach in stride, but he let them know their background: "You belong to your father, the devil" (v. 44). "It should be realized that any one who joins the Pharisees in denying the Virgin Birth of our Lord Jesus takes company with the children of the devil, to be judged to the utmost by the Father when he ultimately deals with all the insults that were given to him through his Son," wrote Barnhouse.[6]

When Philip first told Nathanael about the Lord Jesus, he said, "We have found the one Moses wrote about in the Law, and about whom the prophets

5. In these paragraphs I have followed loosely material from Donald Grey Barnhouse, *God's Glory*, pp. 39–40.

6. Barnhouse, *God's Glory*, p. 41.

also wrote—Jesus of Nazareth, the son of Joseph" (John 1:45). Nathanael's answer was a reproach: "Nazareth! Can anything good come from there?" (v. 46). The same reproach was brought against Jesus by the rulers. "How can the Christ come from Galilee?" they asked (John 7:41). When Nicodemus interrupted their tirades with the suggestion that ordinary civil rights demanded that Jesus get a proper hearing, they turned on him, saying, "Are you from Galilee, too? Look into it, and you will find that a prophet does not come out of Galilee" (v. 52).

Barnhouse offers this explanation:

> The first time that Jesus ever spoke in public, even before the Sermon on the Mount, his message on salvation by the simple grace of God aroused in the Pharisees the utmost of fury. He had not spoken twenty lines before they were filled with wrath, and rose up and led him to the brow of the hill on which the city was built, intending to push him over the precipice (Luke 4:28–29). His reminder that God saved the Gentile widow and her son and healed Naaman the Syrian, both examples of his sovereign grace toward undeserving sinners, drew the greatest wrath from the people. Men do not want grace from God, they want him to acknowledge that what they find in themselves he also counts as good. This he can never do, and they hate him for it, and they hated his Son when he came with the same message.[7]

Jesus had not been very long in his ministry before men said that he had gone crazy. When he called the twelve and the crowds began to follow him, his friends, perhaps with good intentions, tried to lay hold of him because, they said, "He is out of his mind" (Mark 3:21). They reproached him with this. When later he showed just a touch of the blazing wrath that God will one day exercise through him, telling them how wicked they were, they again thought he was crazy and sent for Mary and his brothers to lead him away quietly (Matt. 12:47).

When he drove out evil spirits, restoring those who had been demon-possessed, the leaders accused him of working by the power of the devil. "It is only by Beelzebub, the prince of demons, that this fellow drives out demons," they said (Matt. 12:24). "One hesitates to contemplate the depths of iniquity in hearts that can look upon the Lord Jesus Christ and attribute his work to Satan," wrote Barnhouse.[8]

When Jesus was on the cross, the people mocked him with his claims:

> You who are going to destroy the temple and build it in three days, save yourself! Come down from the cross, if you are the Son of God!
>
> In the same way the chief priests, the teachers of the law and the elders mocked him. "He saved others," they said, "but he can't save himself! He's the

---

7. Barnhouse, *God's Glory*, p. 42.
8. Ibid.

king of Israel! Let him come down now from the cross, and we will believe in him. He trusts in God. Let God rescue him now, if he wants him, for he said, 'I am the Son of God.'" In the same way the robbers who were crucified with him also heaped insults on him.

Matthew 27:40–44

It was the height of cruelty to mock a man dying in such agony.

The Bible reveals how the Lord Jesus Christ took these reproaches, which he knew were directed at the Father through him. Matthew paraphrases a passage from Isaiah:

> Here is my servant whom I have chosen,
>   the one I love, in whom I delight;
> I will put my Spirit on him,
>   and he will proclaim justice to the nations.
> He will not quarrel or cry out;
>   no one will hear his voice in the streets.
> A bruised reed he will not break,
>   and a smoldering wick he will not snuff out,
> till he leads justice to victory.
>   In his name the nations will put their hope.

Matthew 12:18–21 (cf. Isaiah 42:1–4)

If there was ever an example of one who was willing to bear even the worst of abuses in order to please God the Father, it was Jesus Christ.

Christ's Life through Christ's Power

The point of this is that Jesus is to be an example for us, that we might behave as he did. We have been told by Jesus that if we seek to please God, we will be hated by the world, because we are not of the world: "If you belonged to the world, it would love you as its own. As it is, you do not belong to the world, but I have chosen you out of the world. That is why the world hates you. . . . If they persecuted me, they will persecute you also" (John 15:19–20). Nevertheless, although we may bear abuse for his sake—and we certainly will if we are living close to him and are bearing a genuine witness for him and for righteousness—we are to bear persecutions patiently without trying to retaliate, that we might please God.

This is an enormous privilege and a daunting challenge. If it were not for the power of Jesus Christ within, we would not respond to either, because we would put ourselves first, as the world does, and avoid the insults. To live as Christ, we must be close to Christ. We must grow in his power by a study of his Word and by close fellowship with him.

F. Godet, the Swiss commentator, wrote, "Divine succor is needed to enable us to follow this line of conduct unflinchingly; and this succor the believer finds only in the constant use of the Scriptures, and in the help of God which accompanies it."[9]

But it's important to remember that in these verses Paul is not talking about Christians standing against the insults and abuses of the world, drawing on the character and power of Jesus to do so, though that is something that is also necessary. Nor is he writing about spiritual warfare. He is talking about a far lesser matter, Christians merely getting along with other Christians, the strong bearing with the limited understandings of the weak and the weak bearing with the beliefs of the strong, whom they believe to be in error. He is simply talking about getting along with one another.

To come back to this point must seem almost a waste of Christ's example, or at least an understatement of the case. But that is exactly the point. Our calling is to be like Jesus Christ, who endured the worst men could do to him in order to please his Father and win our salvation. Since that is our high calling, we should be able to overlook the many ways in which other Christians differ from us and get on with the task of building them up and then striving to grow together with them in the Christian life.

9. F. Godet, *Commentary on St. Paul's Epistle to the Romans*, trans. A. Cusin (Edinburgh: T. & T. Clark, 1892), vol. 2, p. 354.

219

The Encouragement of the Scriptures

Romans 15:4

For everything that was written in the past was written to teach us, so that through endurance and the encouragement of the Scriptures we might have hope.

A number of years ago a German theologian named Juergen Moltmann wrote a book entitled *The Theology of Hope*. His point, which meant a great deal to Bible scholars at the time, was that eschatology (the doctrine of the last things) should not be an appendix to Christian theology—something tacked on at the end and perhaps even dispensable to Christian thought—but should be the starting point of everything. He said that it is confidence in what God is going to do in the future that must determine how we think and act now.

I am not sure that is entirely right. I would call the cross of Christ, not eschatology, the center, arguing that we must take our ideas even of the future from the cross. But Moltmann was correct in stressing that hope is important for living well now. To have hope is to look at the future optimistically. So to some extent a person must have hope to live. The Latin word for hope is *spes*, from which the French derived the noun *espoir* and the Spanish, *esperanza*. But put the particle *de* in front of those words, and the resulting word is *despair*, literally "without hope." People who despair do not go on. When John Milton wanted to depict the maximum depth to which Satan fell when he was cast out of heaven, he has him say to the other fallen spirits in hell, "Our final hope is flat despair."[1]

How can any sane person have hope in the midst of the desperate world in which we live? The frivolous can, because they do not think about the future at all. Thinking people find the future grim. Winston Churchill, one of the most brilliant and influential people of his age, died despairing. His last words were, "There is no hope."

Our text says that a Christian can have hope and that the way to that sound and steadfast hope is through the Bible.

In *The Wizard of Oz*, Dorothy and her friends—the scarecrow, the tin man, and the cowardly lion—make their way down a yellow brick road to find their future. Our text likewise gives us a road to hope. That road leads first through teaching, second through patient endurance, and third through encouragement. The text says, "For everything that was written in the past was written to teach us, so that through endurance and the encouragement of the Scriptures we might have hope" (Rom. 15:4).

The Teaching of the Scriptures

The first and most important stop along this important road leading to hope is teaching, because it is through the teaching of the Scriptures that the other elements, endurance and encouragement, come. Christianity is a teaching religion, and our text is the Bible. It is true that those whose minds have been enlightened by the Bible often go on to learn in other areas too. Some of the greatest scholars in the world have been Christians, and many have traced their love of learning to their Christian roots. Moreover, wherever the gospel has gone throughout the world, schools and colleges and other institutions of higher learning have gone with it. Still, Christians maintain that however much a person may come to know in other areas, if he or she does not know what God has revealed about himself and the way of salvation in the Bible, that person is ignorant and remains a great fool.

Paul said of the Gentile Christians at Ephesus, among whom there must have been many learned persons, that before they had been taught about Jesus and had received him as their Savior, they were "excluded from citizenship in Israel and foreigners to the covenants of the promise, *without hope and without God in the world*" (Eph. 2:12). They may have been educated, but they were ignorant of the things that matter most. After they had been taught and came to faith in Christ, however, they had hope of "the riches of [God's] glorious inheritance in the saints," which was future, and "his incomparably great power for us who believe," which was present (Eph. 1:18–19).

---

1. *Paradise Lost*, Book 2, line 139.

Our text in Romans is about the teaching of the Scriptures and tells us at least three important things about the Bible:

1. *The Bible is from God.* When Paul says that everything written in the past "was written to teach us," he is not saying that when Moses wrote the Pentateuch, the first five books of the Bible, he did so intending that the church in future ages might be blessed by his writings, or that David wrote the psalms so that we might profit by them. His point is that God caused the human writers of the Bible to write as they did, because what he had in mind was the edification and encouragement of his people through the ages, whether or not the human writers understood this.

This also flows from the context. We remember that Paul has just quoted Psalm 69:9, applying it to Jesus Christ, whom he brought forward as an example for our right conduct. Some may object, "How can you imagine that David was writing about Jesus Christ, who was born so many hundred of years after his own age, or that this has anything to do with us?" Paul is answering, in effect, as F. Godet suggests, "If I thus apply this saying of the psalmist to Christ and ourselves, it is because, in general, all Scripture was written to instruct and strengthen us."[2]

Of course, many other verses say the same thing. Peter wrote, "Above all, you must understand that no prophecy of Scripture came about by the prophet's own interpretation. For prophecy never had its origin in the will of man, but men spoke from God as they were carried along by the Holy Spirit" (2 Peter 1:20–21).

Similarly, Paul told Timothy, "All Scripture is God-breathed and is useful for teaching, rebuking, correcting and training in righteousness, so that the man of God may be thoroughly equipped for every good work" (2 Tim. 3:16–17). The reason the Scriptures are so valuable is that they are unlike other books written by mere human beings. They are from God; therefore they have the authority and power of God within them. Besides, God has promised to bless them to the ends for which they have been given (Isa. 55:10–11).

2. *Everything in the Bible is for our good and is profitable.* The second important teaching about the Scriptures in Romans 15:4 is that all Scripture is for our good and is profitable. In 2 Timothy 3:16, Paul wrote, "All Scripture is God-breathed and is useful. . . ." In our text he uses the words "everything that was written," but he means the same thing in both passages.

This is not an endorsement of every piece of ancient literature, as if the words "everything that was written in the past" refer to the writings of the ancient Babylonians, Egyptians, Greeks, or Romans. Paul is not writing about secular literature, but about the writings that are "God-breathed." Other books may instruct and even charm us wonderfully, but only the Bible gives us a sure ground for hope, since only it speaks with full authority and trustworthiness about what God did to save us from sin and give us eternal life.

2. F. Godet, *St. Paul's Epistle to the Romans* (Edinburgh: T. & T. Clark, 1892), vol. 2, p. 355.

Paul's statement is, however, an endorsement of all of the Bible. That is, he is informing us that "*all* Scripture . . . is profitable" and "*everything* that was written in the past was written to teach us."

Some critics of the Bible have found things in it that they do not like and have therefore argued either that the Bible is from men only, not from God, or that it is a mixture of the two—some parts being from God and some from man. The parts that are from God are then regarded as authoritative, but the parts said to be from human beings only are discarded as error-prone and nonauthoritative. This is a convenient way of pretending to submit to the Bible's authority while at the same time avoiding anything in the Bible that is convicting or contrary to the critic's thought. This is not the Bible's teaching. It is not historic Christianity. The Bible teaches that everything in it is the true Word of God and that it is binding upon the minds and consciences of all persons. Therefore, if we are being led by God's Holy Spirit, we will conform our thoughts and actions to whatever we find in his Word.

3. *Nothing in the Bible is without value.* Paul's third point is that not only is everything in the Bible for our good and profitable, but nothing that is in the Bible is without value.

John Calvin was strong in this conviction: "This notable passage shows us that the oracles of God contain nothing vain or unprofitable. . . . It would be an insult to the Holy Spirit to imagine that he had taught us anything which it is of no advantage to know. Let us also know that all that we learn from Scripture is conducive to the advancement of godliness. Although Paul is speaking of the Old Testament, we are to hold the same view of the writings of the apostles. If the Spirit of Christ is everywhere the same, it is quite certain that he has accommodated his teaching to the edification of his people at the present time by the apostles, as he formerly did by the prophets."[3]

Patient Endurance

The second checkpoint we must pass along the road to hope is endurance, which some versions of the Scriptures translate *patience* (King James Version), *perseverance* (New American Standard Bible) or even *patient endurance,* since the word involves both passively accepting what we cannot change and actively pressing on in faithful obedience and discipleship. This word (*hypomonē*) occurs thirty-two times in the New Testament, sixteen times in Paul's writings, six of which are in Romans.

Is Paul saying that endurance comes from the Bible—that is, from knowing the Bible? I raise that question because a detail of the Greek text provokes it. Paul uses the word for through (*dia*) twice, once before the word *endurance* and once before the word *encouragement* (the New International Version omits it the second time). According to the strictest rules of Greek grammar, that

---

3. John Calvin, *The Epistles of Paul the Apostle to the Romans and to the Thessalonians,* trans. Ross MacKenzie (Grand Rapids: Wm. B. Eerdmans Publishing Company, 1973), pp. 304–5.

should mean that endurance is separated from encouragement with the result that the words "of the Scriptures" should be attached to encouragement only. In other words, Paul would be saying that it is through our own personal enduring as well as through the encouragement that we have in studying the Bible that we find hope.

Leon Morris is a fine Greek scholar, and he is led to this position by his grammatical sensitivity. "[Paul's] construction seems to show that only *encouragement* is here said to derive from the Bible," he says.[4]

In my judgment this is a place where it may be wrong to read too much into a fine point of grammar. Grammatically Morris is right. But in terms of the flow of thought it is hard to suppose that Paul is not thinking of the role the Scriptures have in producing endurance too. For one thing, he links the two ideas together in verse 5, saying, "May the God who gives endurance and encouragement. . . . " Again, in verse 4 both terms follow Paul's opening words about the use of the Scriptures for teaching: "For everything that was written in the past was written to teach us, so that . . ." Or again, even apart from what Paul is saying, elsewhere we are taught that endurance comes from reading how God has kept and preserved other believers even in terrible circumstances.

James wrote, "Brothers, as an example of patience in the face of suffering, take the prophets who spoke in the name of the Lord. As you know, we consider blessed those who have persevered. You have heard of Job's perseverance and have seen what the Lord finally brought about. The Lord is full of compassion and mercy" (James 5:10–11). He is saying that we learn to endure by reading about the way God helped others before us.

Although they recognize the grammatical issue, a large number of other writers nevertheless see the matter as I have outlined it here. Among these are John Murray, Charles Hodge and F. Godet.[5]

Encouragement

The third checkpoint along the road to hope is encouragement, which also comes to us through Scripture. *Encouragement* (*paraklēsis*) is found twenty times in Paul's writings out of twenty-nine occurrences in the whole New Testament. It occurs three times in Romans.

The interesting thing about this word is that it is virtually the same one Jesus used to describe the work of the Holy Spirit among believers, saying, "It is for your good that I am going away. Unless I go away, the *Counselor* will not come to you; but if I go, I will send him to you" (John 16:7; see 14:26;

4. Leon Morris, *The Epistle to the Romans* (Grand Rapids: Wm. B. Eerdmans Publishing Company; and Leicester, England: Inter-Varsity Press, 1988), p. 500. Also footnote 25.

5. John Murray, *The Epistle to the Romans* (Grand Rapids: Wm. B. Eerdmans Publishing Company, 1968), vol. 2, p. 200; Charles Hodge, *A Commentary on Romans* (Edinburgh and Carlisle, Pa.: Banner of Truth Trust, 1972), p. 433, original edition 1835; and F. Godet, *St. Paul's Epistle to the Romans*, p. 355.

15:26), and that the apostle John used to describe the work of Jesus himself: "My dear children, I write this to you so that you will not sin. But if anybody does sin, we have *one who speaks to the Father in our defense*—Jesus Christ, the Righteous One" (1 John 2:1). The word *Counselor* and the phrase "one who speaks . . . in our defense" translate the same Greek word *paraklētos*, which is also sometimes translated *advocate*. The literal meaning is "one who comes alongside of another person to help him or her," to back the person up or defend him. So together the passages teach that Jesus himself does this for us, the Holy Spirit does it, and the Scriptures do it too. Indeed, it is through the Scriptures that the Holy Spirit chiefly does his work.

The end result of this is hope. In our text the article is present before the word *hope* ("the hope"), meaning the Christian hope. This is not just optimism that Paul is writing about, not a hope founded on something the world thinks possible. Also, the verb *have* is in the present tense, meaning that hope is a present possession. As Calvin says, "The particular service of the Scriptures is to raise those who are prepared by patience and strengthened by consolation to the hope of eternal life, and to keep their thoughts fixed upon it."[6]

An Example from History

But enough analysis! If we are to travel the road of endurance and encouragement to hope by learning from the Scriptures, we should study how it actually works.

There are hundreds of examples of this in the Bible, of course, but let's examine the familiar story of Joseph. Joseph was the next-to-youngest son of Jacob, and he was favored by his father because he was born of his much-beloved wife Rachel and also perhaps because he was an extraordinary young man. His brothers hated him for his virtue so they threw him into a cistern and then sold him to Midianite traders who were on their way to Egypt. Joseph was just seventeen years old. In Egypt he became a slave of a rich man named Potiphar. Joseph served the man well, and he was placed in charge of his entire household. Then Potiphar's wife was attracted to Joseph and tried to seduce him. When Joseph refused to sleep with her, the proud, angry woman denounced him falsely to her husband, and Joseph was thrown into prison.

Joseph languished in prison for two years. Once when he had correctly and favorably interpreted the dream of Pharaoh's cupbearer, predicting that he would be taken from the prison where he too had been confined and restored to his previous position, Joseph asked the man to remember him when he was released and speak a good word to Pharaoh to get him out of prison. But the cupbearer forgot.

The years dragged on. One day God gave a dream to Pharaoh. No one in the palace could interpret it, but the cupbearer remembered Joseph and his ability to interpret dreams and told the king about him. Pharaoh sent for

6. Calvin, *The Epistles of Paul the Apostle to the Romans and to the Thessalonians*, p. 305.

the young man, and Joseph interpreted the dream, predicting seven years of prosperity to be followed by seven years of severe famine. He recommended that the king appoint a wise man to save grain during the good years so that the people would not starve when the years of scarceness came.

You know the story. Pharaoh appointed Joseph to the task. Joseph served well. The land was saved, and in time, when the famine drove Joseph's wicked brothers to Egypt to buy grain, God used Joseph to bring the brothers to repentance. The family was reconciled, and Jacob moved all of them to Egypt, where the people stayed and prospered for many years.

The climax of this great story comes in the final chapter of Genesis, when Jacob dies and the brothers come to plead with Joseph not to take revenge on them. They had completely misunderstood him. He had no intention of doing any of them any harm. "Don't be afraid," he exclaimed. "Am I in the place of God? You intended to harm me, but God intended it for good to accomplish what is now being done, the saving of many lives" (Gen. 50:19–20). The story teaches that God is sovereign even in such terrible circumstances as those that overtook Joseph. And from it we learn to trust God's sovereignty, endure in hardship, be encouraged, and so grow strong in hope.

I have picked this particular story because of Psalm 105, which refers to it. It may have been written by King David, but whoever the writer was, he was a man who needed encouragement. He found it in Joseph's story:

> Give thanks to the Lord, call on his name;
>   make known among the nations what he has done. . . .
> He [God] called down famine on the land
>   and destroyed all their supplies of food;
> and he sent a man before them—
>   Joseph, sold as a slave.
> They bruised his feet with shackles,
>   his neck was put in irons,
> till what he foretold came to pass,
>   till the word of the Lord proved him true.
> The king sent and released him,
>   the ruler of peoples set him free.
> He made him master of his household,
>   ruler over all he possessed,
> to instruct his princes as he pleased
>   and teach his elders wisdom.
>
> Psalm 105:1, 16–22

This writer clearly knew that "everything that was written in the past was written to teach us, so that through endurance and the encouragement of the Scriptures we might have hope." Do you know that? If you do, you will study what God has spoken and move ahead boldly for him and with hope.

220

A Prayer for Unity

Romans 15:5–6

May the God who gives endurance and encouragement give you a spirit of unity among yourselves as you follow Christ Jesus, so that with one heart and mouth you may glorify the God and Father of our Lord Jesus Christ.

In the great high priestly prayer of the Lord Jesus Christ, recorded in John 17, Jesus prayed for the church he was about to leave behind, and his prayer was that it might be marked by six important characteristics: joy (v. 13), holiness (v. 17), truth (v. 17), mission (v. 18), unity (vv. 20–23), and love (v. 26). Each of these is prayed for distinctly. But it is significant that of the six, the one Jesus prayed for at greatest length was unity:

> My prayer is not for them alone [the disciples]. I pray also for those who will believe in me through their message, that all of them may be one, Father, just as you are in me and I am in you. May they also be in us so that the world may believe that you have sent me. I have given them the glory that you gave me, that they may be one as we are one: I in them and you in me. May they be brought to complete unity to let the world know that you have sent me and have loved them even as you have loved me.

John 17:20–23

1811

Clearly this was an area of church life in which Jesus anticipated problems and for which he therefore prayed at length and in strong terms.

In the letter to the Romans Paul is also concerned about the unity of the church, although he has not been talking about it specifically up to this point, probably because he did not know the Roman congregation personally. He knew the churches of Ephesus, Philippi, and Corinth well, and he had much to say about unity when he was writing to them. He had not yet been to Rome. Nevertheless, he was aware of the potential for divisions within the church at Rome, especially because of the differences between the so-called weak and strong believers.

As I pointed out in chapter 209, Paul's instruction about developing a Christian mind was completed in two verses. To discuss a right estimate of oneself and the need to encourage others took six verses more. A call to love one another filled thirteen verses; material on the relationship of the church to the state took seven verses; right conduct in light of the imminent return of Jesus Christ took seven verses more. But his discussion of how Christians are to accept other Christians when they do not think or behave as we think they should fills all of chapter 14 and the first half of chapter 15, a total of thirty-five verses. Now, as he comes to the end of this section, he prays for unity among these Roman Christians.

This is a typical Pauline touch. He argues passionately, then suddenly interrupts his argument for prayer. Here he says, "May the God who gives endurance and encouragement give you a spirit of unity among yourselves as you follow Christ Jesus, so that with one heart and mouth you may glorify the God and Father of our Lord Jesus Christ" (Rom. 15:5–6). The verses suggest the nature of this unity and give us its source and goal.

What Kind of Unity?

The word *unity* does not occur very often in Paul's writings. In fact, in the New International Version it is found only four times.[1] One place is in Ephesians 4, where it is used in two significant ways. Verse 3 says, "Make every effort to keep *the unity of the Spirit* through the bond of peace." Verse 13 reads, ". . . until we all reach *unity in the faith* and in the knowledge of the Son of God and become mature, attaining to the whole measure of the fullness of Christ."

There are two kinds of unity in these verses. The second type mentioned, in verse 13, is a unity of understanding or of doctrine, and it is referred to as something yet to be attained, since Christians do not have perfect understanding of the teachings of the Bible and therefore differ on some matters. The differences are not desirable—we would like to be of one mind on all doctrinal matters—but they are inevitable given our present, finite understanding of

---

1. Romans 15:5; Ephesians 4:3, 13; Colossians 3:14.

God's truth. These are matters to be worked on together, and they are in areas in which we should see improvement as we mature in Jesus Christ.

The first unity, in verse 3, is different. It is a family unity "of the Spirit," and it is spoken of as something that has already been given to believers and is now their duty to maintain. It is not based on our limited and even mistaken understandings of God's truth, but on the fact that "there is one body and one Spirit—just as you were called to one hope when you were called—one Lord, one faith, one baptism; one God and Father of all, who is over all and through all and in all" (Eph. 3:4–5). It is this unity for which Jesus prayed in John 17 and for which Paul is also praying in Romans.

In the Greek text of Romans 15:5, Paul's prayer is literally "that they might mind the same thing" or, as the King James Version has it, that they might "be likeminded one toward another." The emphasis is not on identity of doctrine but on mutuality, appreciation of one another, and thankfulness to be with one another in the body of Christ.

The one other text from Paul's writings in which the word *unity* occurs makes Paul's meaning clear: "Therefore, as God's chosen people, holy and dearly loved, clothe yourselves with compassion, kindness, humility, gentleness and patience. Bear with each other and forgive whatever grievances you may have against one another. Forgive as the Lord forgave you. And over all these virtues put on love, which binds them all together in perfect unity" (Col. 3:12–14). Obviously, what Paul is concerned with here is a set of accepting and forgiving attitudes that recognize other Christians as being part of that one indivisible body of Jesus Christ to which all true Christians belong.

What Christian Unity Is Not

The kind of unity that Paul is praying for is so important that it will be helpful to look at what it is not before we examine what it is. There are two approaches to unity that are particularly wrong.

1. *Organizational unity.* What most people think of first when they think of church unity is some kind of organizational unity, probably because today we tend to think organizationally but also perhaps because this was emphasized for so long by leaders of the ecumenical movement. The ecumenical movement was an attempt, still somewhat alive but much more lively twenty or thirty years ago, to get all the various denominations of the church to merge. It had several Protestant forms, the best known of which was COCU, the Consultation on Church Union (which became the Church of Christ Uniting), but it also existed in some places as a movement to bring the Protestant churches into the Church of Rome.

There are some advantages to a certain amount of organizational unity, of course. Otherwise there would be no organizations at all—just Christians living in the world. If there are to be places to meet, paid teachers, schools, missionary endeavors, and so on, there have to be structures to support them.

That is why churches that believe alike and have common goals ought to be formally united.

But that is only part of the story. The other part is that in itself organizational unity does not accomplish its goals and, in fact, has actually proved harmful. Church history is the proof. In the early days of the church there was much vitality and rapid growth, but there was very little organization. Later, under the emperor Constantine and his successors, there was a great deal of organization as the church tried to mirror the organizational structure and assume powers parallel to those of the Roman Empire. During the Middle Ages the church was indeed one church. Wherever one went there was one large, interlacing structure with the pope at its head. But this was the period of the church's greatest decadence, to the extent that the world actually cried out against that crushing, tyrannous, superstitious, ignorant thing that called itself Christianity.

2. *Conformity.* Another mistaken notion of the form unity is to take is conformity. This is the chief error of the evangelical church, which, for the most part, is not much concerned with organizational unity. Evangelicals want to maintain their own individual kingdoms and compete with one another for fame and finances. The error of the evangelical church is to strive for an identical pattern of looks and behavior among its members. Some groups train their members in such a way that they end up looking and even speaking alike. Others establish codes of behavior to determine what may and may not be done. Anyone who deviates from these patterns is immediately suspect and may even be judged to be "backsliding" or apostate.

This is not what either Jesus or Paul intended. Paul links his prayer for unity to an acknowledgement that God has made it possible by giving "endurance" and "encouragement." This has to do with our attitudes rather than with organizational structure or conformity. Similarly, Jesus prayed for a unity that was a reflection of the oneness within the Godhead: "that all of them may be one, Father, just as you are in me and I am in you" (John 17:21). A unity like that involves the values, aspirations, goals, and wills of the participating parties.

New Testament Images for the Church

Let's take this a step farther by looking at three images in the New Testament that express the church's unity: the church as a family, the church as a fellowship, and the church as a body.

1. *A family.* Christians belong to the family of God, and therefore they are rightly thought of as brothers and sisters, the most common terms used of Christians for one another in the New Testament and early church. God is called Father, and Christians are called brothers again and again in the Epistles.

What is characteristic of this image is that it speaks of relationships resulting from what God has done for us in salvation. One of the ways salvation is spoken of is God begetting spiritual children. John 1:12–13 speaks of this when it says, "Yet to all who received him [Jesus], to those who believed in his name, he gave the right to become children of God—children born not of natural descent, nor of human decision or a husband's will, but born of God." Jesus spoke of the same reality when he told Nicodemus, "You must be born again" (John 3:7). Those who are born again have become members of God's family and brothers and sisters to each other.

This has two important consequences. First, since the members of this spiritual family are chosen and brought into it by God, we have no say in this matter and must instead welcome whomever God chooses. It is not for us to say whether we will associate with someone or not. Second, we must be committed to each other in tangible ways. We must be willing and available to help each other, and we must defend each other against a hostile world.

But, as one writer notes, "Although God wants us to be brethren, he does not mean that we are to be identical twins."[2] Siblings are usually quite different. One will be artistic and excel in dancing, drawing, and singing. Another may be quite bookish. Still another may have strong organizational skills. One may be a morning person, another an evening person. One may want to be with people all the time. Another may prefer to be alone. It is exactly that way in the church, and we should be happy that it is rather than trying to make everyone alike. Paul told the Ephesians this:

> But to each one of us grace has been given as Christ appointed it. This is why it says:
>
> > "When he ascended on high,
> > he led captives in his train
> > and gave gifts to men." . . .
>
> It was he who gave some to be apostles, some to be prophets, some to be evangelists, and some to be pastors and teachers, to prepare God's people for works of service, so that the body of Christ may be built up until we all reach unity in the faith and in the knowledge of the Son of God and become mature, attaining to the whole measure of the fullness of Christ.
>
> Ephesians 4:7–8, 11–13

2. *A fellowship.* The second term that is used to stress the unity of the church is a fellowship. Fellowship isn't an exact word for what the New Testament has in mind, but it is the best word we have in English. In Greek the word is *koinonia*, which has at its root the idea of sharing something or having something in common. For example, partners who held property in common or had shares in a common business were called *koinonoi*. Likewise, the Greek

---

2. Donald Grey Barnhouse, *The God of Redemption*, booklet 87 in the series of published radio sermons on Romans (Philadelphia: The Bible Study Hour, 1960), p. 7.

of the New Testament period was called Koine Greek, since it was the language most people shared.

As far as Christians being a fellowship is concerned, the idea is that we hold many things in common and that we try to express this in mutually beneficial ways. That which we most hold in common is the gospel, which is why the New Testament can speak of "fellowship [NIV has 'partnership'] in the gospel" (Phil. 1:5). The New Testament also speaks of "fellowship . . . with the Father and with his Son, Jesus Christ" (1 John 1:3), "fellowship with the Spirit" (Phil. 2:1) and "fellowship with one another" (1 John 1:7).

How do we express this interlocking, common fellowship? The gospel is something we share *in*. But there are also things we must share *out*—things we should express to and with one another. We need channels to do this, of course, and that is why Christians regularly meet together not just for the worship of God, which we can also do alone, but for fellowship. Sometimes fellowship takes place in large meetings, but it is generally hard to express it in large gatherings. The best place to express this kind of fellowship is in small groups.

We have tried to encourage small groups at Tenth Presbyterian Church. Tenth Church is not huge, but it is large enough to make fellowship in the larger services difficult. Therefore we have divided ourselves up in several ways. We have age-level divisions, with a graded Bible School and college and young adult groups. We have also divided ourselves geographically, with six regional parishes committed to looking out for those within those six regions. To some extent we also divide by interests: Some adult classes meet around a common theme, groups pray for specific aspects of the church's work, and other groups meet to carry out specific ministries. The most important way we divide ourselves for mutual sharing and fellowship is the seventy to one hundred small-group Bible studies, for it is in these more than in any other church meeting that Christians seem to grow and those who are not yet Christians find Christ.

My own personal experience in this area conforms to what John R. W. Stott found in his greater London parish. He wrote, "The value of the small group is that it can become a community of related persons; and in it the benefit of personal relatedness cannot be missed, nor its challenge evaded. . . . I do not think it is an exaggeration to say, therefore, that small groups, Christian family or fellowship groups, are indispensable for our growth into spiritual maturity."[3]

3. *A body.* The third great New Testament image for the church is a body, more particularly the body of Christ. This image is so prominent that Charles Colson has made it the title of a recent study of the church.[4]

3. John R. W. Stott, *One People* (London: Falcon Books, 1969), pp. 70–71. Stott discusses Christian fellowship at length on pages 69–91.

4. Charles Colson, with Ellen Santilli Vaughn, *The Body: Being Light in the Darkness* (Dallas, London, Vancouver, and Melbourne: Word Publishing, 1992).

A number of New Testament books develop this idea, and with differing emphases. Best known perhaps is the section of 1 Corinthians in which Paul writes of the different ways the parts of the body function and how each is needed: "The eye cannot say to the hand, 'I don't need you!' And the head cannot say to the feet, 'I don't need you!' On the contrary, those parts of the body that seem to be weaker are indispensable, and the parts that we think are less honorable we treat with special honor. . . . If one part suffers, every part suffers with it; if one part is honored, every part rejoices with it" (1 Cor. 12:21–23, 26). In terms of Paul's argument in Romans, this means that the weak need the strong and that the strong also need the weak. There are no dispensable members of Christ's body.

Another important passage is Ephesians 4:16, which emphasizes the work to be done: "From him [Christ] the whole body, joined and held together by every supporting ligament, grows and builds itself up in love, as each part does its work." This stresses the outward witness and service to others of Christ's church.

We might summarize these three images for the church by saying: (1) "family" stresses our relationship to God (since he is the Father who brings his children into being); (2) "fellowship" stresses our relationship to one another (since we share many things together); and (3) "body" stresses our relationship to those who are without (since we exist to witness to and serve those who do not yet know Christ).

To God Be the Glory

Before I end this study, I want to return to the important purpose clause in our text: "*so that* with one heart and mouth you may glorify the God and Father of our Lord Jesus Christ."

According to this verse, the purpose of our unity is not so much that the church might be a pleasant place to be or that weak Christians might be encouraged and strong Christians be channeled into useful work. Rather, it is that God might be glorified. God must be made known as the great and wonderful God he is. Moreover, that is to take place as Christians with *one heart* (that is, in unity) praise him before others *with their mouths*.

From time to time I get letters from or speak to people who say they have trouble with the multiplicity of Christian denominations. In fact, I have a letter on my desk that says this even as I write this paragraph. Their argument is that denominations reflect negatively on the church and weaken its witness.

I am not sure that is the case or even that this is what really concerns these people. No one criticizes capitalism because there are many competing corporations, or the automobile industry because there is fierce rivalry between the Big Three auto makers or between American companies and their Japanese or European counterparts. As I said at the beginning, a certain amount of organization is inevitable and some centralization is desirable. For the most part the world understands organizational multiplicity.

I don't think that the world is even particularly troubled by the fact that Christians disagree on some doctrinal matters. After all, they disagree with other people too.

The real problem is that Christians often do not appreciate and support one another, recognizing that whatever differences may exist, all who are Christ's followers nevertheless belong to the same family, fellowship, and body and therefore belong to one another. That is how, above all other ways, the God and Father of our Lord Jesus Christ must be glorified by us before the watching world.

221

The Example of Our Lord: Part 2

Romans 15:7–9

Accept one another, then, just as Christ accepted you, in order to bring praise to God. For I tell you that Christ has become a servant of the Jews on behalf of God's truth, to confirm the promises made to the patriarchs so that the Gentiles may glorify God for his mercy, as it is written:

> *"Therefore I will praise you among the Gentiles;*
> *I will sing hymns to your name."*

In chapter 218 we studied the way Jesus did not seek to please himself but rather sought first to please the Father and then those whom he had come to serve. Paul taught that we are to be like him in this, as well as in other things. "Each of us should please his neighbor for his good, to build him up" (Rom. 15:2). In the verses to which we come now Jesus is declared an example in the way he accepted others, regardless of who they were or what they had done: "Accept one another, then, just as Christ accepted you, in order to bring praise to God. For I tell you that Christ has become a servant of the Jews on behalf of God's truth, to confirm the promises made to the patriarchs so that the Gentiles may glorify God for his mercy" (Rom. 15:7–9).

This command follows clearly and obviously from the call to unity in the preceding verses, for the way to maintain Christian unity is to accept those other women and men for whom Jesus died.

A Multifractured World

When Christianity burst upon the world after the death and resurrection of Jesus Christ, it found it an extremely divided place. Some of the divisions were nationalistic—Greeks hating the Romans who had overpowered them and dominated the Mediterranean, and Romans looking down on nearly all the conquered and therefore "inferior" peoples of the then-known world. Some divisions were racial, as between Romans and Greeks and Jews and Arabs. Many of those divisions reached back over centuries of hatred and some persist today, fueling tensions that continue to disturb the Near East. There were rivalries between cities, resolved only when one city destroyed the other, as Rome did Carthage and Sparta, Athens. Some of the divisions were religious.

The sharpest and most intractable of all these divisions was between the religion of the Jews, with its strict Old Testament monotheism, and the religions of the Gentiles, with their many pagan gods. The Jews looked down on Gentiles as heathens, just as the Greeks counted as barbarians all who did not know their language.

It is hard for us to imagine how deep these divisions were at the time of Christ's coming, though we can get an idea of it from an honest look at hatreds in our own day. But as real as these divisions were, the remarkable thing is that *they did not divide the Christians.* Christians simply transcended them, so that the church from the very beginning was composed of Jews and Gentiles, slaves and freemen, Greeks and Romans, blacks and whites, rich and poor, and so forth. The church at Antioch, which backed Paul on his missionary journeys, is a superb example. It had as its leaders Barnabas, who was a Jew from Cyprus; Simeon, a black man; Lucius, who was probably a Roman, from Cyrene; Manaen, an aristocrat who had been raised with Herod the tetrarch; and Saul, the Jewish teacher from Tarsus (cf. Acts 13:1). What a collection—and what an effective church!

How could people this diverse come together and function so fruitfully? They knew Jesus, the very Son of God; they knew that he had accepted them without condition, sinners that they were, and therefore they had to accept all others for whom he had also died.

The word *accept* (which also means welcome or receive) is the key, and it goes back to Romans 14:1, where this section of the letter started. Paul did not know the Christians at Rome personally, but he knew human nature, even in Christians, and he wanted to be sure that those who considered themselves to be strong in faith would not look down on those they considered weak, and that the weak would not shun the strong. So he wrote, "*Accept* him whose faith is weak, without passing judgment on disputable matters." In fact, he also made the point he is making again in chapter 15, when he added as an explanation and a motivation for us, ". . . for God has *accepted* him" (v. 3).

In Romans 14:3 he points out that the Father has accepted the other Christian. In Romans 15:7 he reminds us that Jesus has accepted him too. So we ask: With that kind of welcome, who are we to hold to our petty prejudices or keep up our damaging rejection of other Christians?

Jews and Gentiles in Christ's Fold

From Paul's perspective the greatest of all possible divisions was the one between Jews, who were God's specifically chosen people, and Gentiles, who apart from Christ were "foreigners to the covenants of the promise, without hope and without God in the world" (Eph. 2:12). Therefore, that is what he deals with specifically in Romans 15:8, saying, "Christ has become a servant of the Jews on behalf of God's truth, to confirm the promises made to the patriarchs so that the Gentiles may glorify God for his mercy." What he means is that Jesus served the Jews to fulfill the promises made to them regarding his coming to die for sin and be their Savior, in order that he might be not only their Savior but the Savior of the Gentiles too.

1. *Christ became a servant to the Jews.* If Paul said only that "Jesus" became a servant to the Jews, that would not have been a particularly remarkable statement, since anyone could reasonably choose to be a servant to his or her people. But Paul writes "Christ" rather than "Jesus," and *Christ* means Messiah. The Jews expected the Messiah to be a king who would rule on the throne of David to drive the Romans out of Palestine. A king is served by others. They live to meet his needs; he is not their servant. But Jesus was not that kind of Messiah. He told his disciples, "The Son of Man did not come to be served, but to serve, and to give his life as a ransom for many" (Matt. 20:28). He said of his kingdom, "If anyone wants to be first, he must be the very last, and the servant of all" (Mark 9:35).

2. *To confirm the promises made to the patriarchs.* Jesus served the Jews, but he did it in God's way rather than theirs. The people wanted a hero. In fact, they were ready to make him king on several occasions, and when he did not meet their materialistic expectations—giving them free meals, for instance—they quickly turned against him. What God wanted was for him to be their Savior, and that is what the promises to the patriarchs meant. These men were told of a Redeemer who would come, and they were saved by looking to him and trusting him for what he would one day do. Paul explained this to the Galatians, saying, "He [Christ] redeemed us in order that the blessing given to Abraham might come to the Gentiles through Christ Jesus, so that by faith we might receive the promise of the Spirit" (Gal. 3:14).

3. *So that the Gentiles might glorify God for his mercy.* The fulfillment of the promises to the Jewish patriarchs was not intended for the blessing of Jews alone but for the salvation of Gentiles too so that they along with Jews might glorify God for his mercy. This is the argument of Romans 9–11 telescoped

into just one verse. As Paul said to Gentiles toward the close of that argument, "Just as you who were at one time disobedient to God have now received mercy as a result of their disobedience, so they too have now become disobedient in order that they too may now receive mercy as a result of God's mercy to you. For God has bound all men over to disobedience so that he may have mercy on them all" (Rom. 11:30–32).

This, then, is the first important example of Jesus' acceptance of other people: He died for Gentiles as well as Jews. Paul is telling the Jews, who would have tended to look down on Gentile members of the Roman church, that since God has accepted the Gentiles they should not refuse them.

A Friend of Sinners

Jesus' acceptance of others is not limited to Jews and Gentiles, however; it is astonishing and all-embracing. Here are some other types of people he accepted:

1. *Sinners.* "Jesus, what a friend of sinners!" we sing in one of our most popular hymns. It is right that we sing it, for that is exactly what he is. One of his disciples was Levi (Matthew), who had been a tax collector, and when he became a follower of Christ, Levi invited his friends to meet Jesus. His friends were not well thought of by the Jewish leaders—they called them "sinners"—so they demanded of Jesus, "Why do you eat and drink with tax collectors and 'sinners'?" (Luke 5:30).

Jesus replied, "It is not the healthy who need a doctor, but the sick. I have not come to call the righteous, but sinners to repentance" (v. 31).

One of my favorite stories in the Gospels is the account of Jesus' dealing with the woman who had been caught in adultery, recorded in John 8. The leaders of the people were using her to try to trap Jesus and discredit him, because when they brought her to Jesus, frightened and humiliated, they demanded, "Teacher, this woman was caught in the act of adultery. In the Law Moses commanded us to stone such women. Now what do you say?" (vv. 4–5). It must have been a set-up, of course. In order to have witnesses who would satisfy the rigorous demands of Jewish jurisprudence they would have had to have placed spies in the room or at the keyhole. It was a hateful, devilish thing to have done. But it was clever. Because if Jesus had replied, "Forgive her!" they would have denounced him for having rejected God's law. No authentic messenger of God would do that. On the other hand, if he had said, "Stone her!" they would have condemned him for harsh insensitivity, and perhaps hypocrisy too. For he had also said, "Come unto me, all you who are weary and burdened, and I will give you rest" (Matt. 11:28).

"Ah, but what does he do when you do come?" they would have asked. "He tells people to stone you. What kind of a Savior is that?"

We know what Jesus did. First, he caused each of the woman's accusers to be convicted by his own sins, which must have been many. One by one they slunk away. Then, when the people who could have condemned her were gone he said, "Neither do I condemn you. . . . Go now and leave your life of sin" (John 8:11). He did not excuse her behavior. In fact, he told her to change her way of life. But rather than rejecting her, he accepted her as one of those many sinners for whom he was very soon to die.

2. *Outcasts.* Tax collectors were social outcasts. Jesus showed his acceptance of them by having one tax collector, Matthew (or Levi), within the select company of his disciples. Even greater outcasts than the hated tax collectors were lepers. They were banned from all normal human contact and were required to remain outside the city gates, lest they contaminate others with their disease. Jesus accepted even these, and he gave tangible evidence of his acceptance by touching and speaking to them when he healed them. One healing is reported in Luke 5. A poor leper came to him begging, "Lord, if you are willing, you can make me clean" (Luke 5:12).

The text says, "Jesus reached out his hand and touched the man. 'I am willing,' he said. 'Be clean!' And immediately the leprosy left him" (vv. 12–13). It was a remarkable display of grace for him to touch such disease-stricken people. Yet he did it, and when he did the lepers as well as other outcast people were made whole.

3. *The unclean.* In Mark 5 is recorded the story of an "unclean" woman who touched Jesus. She had been suffering from bleeding for twelve years. Any kind of bodily discharge, including bleeding, made people ceremonially unclean so that others could not come in contact with them, even touching their clothing or sitting where they had been sitting, without becoming unclean too. If a person was unclean, he could not go to the temple or share in other normal human activities. The state of the woman must have been one of painful isolation and loneliness. When she learned that Jesus was coming, however, she followed after him and dared to reach out and touch his cloak, thinking, "If I just touch his clothes, I will be healed" (v. 28).

The woman was healed. Her bleeding ceased immediately. Yet she must have been terrified when Jesus suddenly stopped, turned around in the crowd, and asked, "Who touched my clothes?" (v. 30). The frightened woman came forward, no doubt expecting a rebuke for having touched and thus "contaminated" the great teacher. But Jesus did not treat her as one who had done wrong; rather, he commended her for her faith. "Daughter," he said to her, "your faith has healed you. Go in peace and be freed from your suffering" (v. 34).

A few verses later it is told that Jesus went to the home of a synagogue ruler and touched his dead daughter, bringing her back to life. The dead were regarded as unclean too, and coming in contact with a dead body defiled a "clean" person for about a week. Yet Jesus did not hesitate to touch the dead any more than he failed to touch the lepers. He accepted even the most unclean and healed them by doing it.

That would be remarkable if Jesus were only a man. We admire that kind of acceptance when we see it in other people. For the very Son of God to accept sinners, the outcast, and the unclean is utterly wonderful.

Christ's Acceptance of Us

Yet I will tell you something that is even more wonderful than Jesus' acceptance of the sinful, outcast, and unclean people of his day, and that is his acceptance of you and me. True, we may not be "sinners" in the way the righteous persons of Jesus' day meant it when they used that word—that is, those who were in open defiance of the Pharisees' prevailing moral code. We may not be outcasts, pariahs to our neighbors, as the lepers were, or unclean in the Jewish ceremonial sense. But we are sinners in thought, word, and deed. We are outcasts by our own deliberate actions, having turned our backs on God, trampling his mercy underfoot. In the true sense of the word *unclean*, we have by our many moral transgressions become filthy from head to toe. We are unclean even in our supposed righteousness, for in the sight of God "all our righteous acts are like filthy rags" (Isa. 64:6).

Can you imagine how you in your sin, apart from Christ, must appear to the holy God? You cannot. None of us can see ourselves as God sees us. On the contrary, we think highly of ourselves, dismiss our sins as mere mistakes or shortcomings, and compliment ourselves on how well we are doing. But God tells us how he sees us. Remember Romans 3:10–18:

> "There is no one righteous, not even one;
>> there is no one who understands,
>> no one who seeks God.
> All have turned away,
>> they have together become worthless;
> there is no one who does good,
>> not even one."
> "Their throats are open graves;
>> their tongues practice deceit."
> "The poison of vipers is on their lips."
>> "Their mouths are full of cursings and bitterness."
> "Their feet are swift to shed blood;
>> ruin and misery mark their ways,
> and the way of peace they do not know."
> "There is no fear of God before their eyes."[1]

That is how God sees you apart from Christ, as a creature utterly abhorrent to him and as a menace to others. But in spite of that fact, the Lord Jesus Christ, the very Son of God, accepted you and died for you in order to bring you into his righteous kingdom. And God the Father has accepted you too.

---

1. These lines are quotations from the Old Testament: Psalms 14:1–3, 53:1–3, and Ecclesiastes 7:20; Psalm 5:9; Psalm 140:3; Psalm 10:7; Isaiah 59:7–8; and Psalm 36:1.

How, then, can you possibly exclude anyone else? You must accept them, as you have been accepted. And, for that matter, you must not only love Christians; you must also love and seek to bring to Christ all who are not yet Christians—for his sake and for his glory.

To God Be the Glory

As we close, let's reconsider Romans 15:9: ". . . so that the Gentiles may glorify God for his mercy." It is parallel to the phrase that ends the previous two verses, drawing these two sections together: ". . . so that with one heart and mouth you may glorify the God and Father of our Lord Jesus Christ" (v. 6). We are to be united in spirit as God's people, so that God may be glorified; and we are to accept others, as Jesus has accepted us, so that God may be glorified. It is by accepting others that our unity is to be expressed and carried forward.

How God is glorified by that is seen in what I call a biblical understanding of history. Long ago, before God's creation of the heavens and earth and of the people who live on it, God dwelt in glory with his holy angels and everything was harmonious. There was one will in the universe; that will was God's, and it was accepted as good everywhere and unquestionably. But one day Lucifer got it into his head that he could do better than God—that his way was better—and when that happened the original harmony of the universe was broken and division came in. Lucifer became the devil; for devil comes from the Greek word *diabolos*, and *diabolos* means disrupter—one who always stirs things up, bringing frustration, anger, sin, and disharmony.

God could have annihilated Satan at once, blotting out the evil. But if he had done that, he would only have shown that he was more powerful than Satan, not that his way was best or that he could restore harmony even out of chaos. So instead of destroying Satan, God let evil run its course. The devil was allowed to work havoc, doing his best to ruin God's creation. He was even allowed to enter the brave new world that God created, drawing Adam and Eve, our first parents, after him in his rebellion against God. But all the devil was able to show was that he could increase the world's disharmony, not make the universe run smoothly or make people better able to accept and love one another. He could turn paradise, the Garden of Eden, into hell (by God's permission), but he could not turn that hell back into paradise.

But God was not finished. Unknown to Satan, God had planned to redeem a select number of people out of the great mass of fallen humanity that the devil was corrupting. So he did it, sending Jesus Christ to die for them to be their Savior from sin and sending the Holy Spirit to give them a new nature. And thus, these weak, fallen human beings became the arena where God demonstrated his ability to bring his people together again, as they were moved to accept each other in Christ because they had been accepted. Thus they glorified God, and God confounded Satan.

John Calvin said it like this: "As Christ has made known the glory of the Father in receiving us all into his grace when we stood in need of mercy, so we ought to establish and confirm this union which we have in Christ, in order to make known also the glory of God."[2]

---

2. John Calvin, *The Epistles of Paul the Apostle to the Romans and to the Thessalonians*, trans. Ross MacKenzie (Grand Rapids: Wm. B. Eerdmans Publishing Company, 1973), p. 306.

222

Hope of the Gentiles

Romans 15:9–12

As it is written,
 "Therefore I will praise you among the Gentiles;
  I will sing hymns to your name."

Again, it says,
 "Rejoice, O Gentiles, with his people."

And again,
 "Praise the Lord, all you Gentiles,
  and sing praises to him, all you peoples."

And again, Isaiah says,
 "The root of Jesse will spring up,
  one who will arise to rule over the nations;
  the Gentiles will hope in him."

W e have already seen several instances of a striking feature of Paul's writing—developing an argument first, then supporting it with quotations from the Old Testament. Paul did that in Romans 3:10–18, supporting his doctrine of human depravity with at least six Old Testament quotations, and then repeatedly in chapters 9–11 and again in chapters 12 and 14. We also see this here, in chapter 15, at the close of his lengthy explanation of why Christians must accept all other Christians. He quotes four Old Testament texts: Psalm 18:49, Deuteronomy 32:43, Psalm 117:1, and Isaiah 11:10.

Much to our surprise, however, the point the citations make is not the major point of this section, which deals with our accepting other Christians. Rather, they support the point made in a minor way in Romans 15:8–9 only—namely, that Jesus became a servant of the Jews by fulfilling the promises made to the Jewish patriarchs "so that the Gentiles may glorify God for his mercy." This point is not made anywhere else in chapters 12–16 but rather in Romans 9–11.

This tells us that "hope for the Gentiles" was a major component of Paul's thinking. We know this was important to Paul personally, because he often reminded people that he was chosen by God to be the apostle to the Gentiles. In fact, he does so just three and four verses further on, in Romans 15:15–16: "I have written to you quite boldly on some points, as if to remind you of them again, because of the grace God gave me to be a minister of Christ Jesus to the Gentiles with the priestly duty of proclaiming the gospel of God, so that the Gentiles might become an offering acceptable to God, sanctified by the Holy Spirit."

This was also important to Paul as an expression of the fullness of the biblical revelation, which taught that salvation would eventually come to the Gentiles as well as to the Jews. This was a major part of his argument in chapters 9–11. We sense something of the importance Paul attached to this truth from the fact that here, in chapter 15, his citations are drawn from every part of the Old Testament: from the law (Deut. 32:43), the prophets (Isa. 11:10), and the writings (Ps. 18:49; 117:1).

If we are Gentiles, as most in the church today are, this truth should be important to us too.

Without Hope and without God

The first point we need to consider is that there was no hope for the Gentiles apart from Jesus Christ. Earlier in Romans Paul asked whether there was any advantage in being a Jew, and he answered, "Much in every way! First of all, they have been entrusted with the very words of God" (Rom. 3:2). He meant that the Jews had the Bible, while the Gentiles did not. Paul interrupted his listing of the Jewish advantages there, but he picked it up again in chapter 9, adding, "Theirs is the adoption as sons; theirs the divine glory, the covenants, the receiving of the law, the temple worship and the promises. Theirs are the patriarchs, and from them is traced the human ancestry of Christ" (vv. 4–5). The Gentiles had none of these advantages. Therefore, Paul was able to tell the Ephesians, who were Gentiles, that before they had heard about Christ and had believed on him, they were "excluded from citizenship in Israel and foreigners to the covenants of the promise, without hope and without God in the world" (Eph. 2:12).

That is a very grim assessment. But if "salvation is from the Jews," as Jesus told the woman of Samaria (John 4:22), meaning that God had been working with Jews almost exclusively from the time of Abraham to the time of Jesus Christ, then it is accurate. It means that for those many centuries in which God was working exclusively with Israel, there was literally no hope of salvation for the masses of the world who were not Jewish.

The Voice of Prophecy

Fortunately, this former absence of hope is not the final word for Gentiles since Gentile salvation was nevertheless also promised in the Old Testament. Paul has already taught this in Romans 9, supporting it, as he does in Romans 15, by citations from the Old Testament (Hosea 2:23, 1:10; Isaiah 10:22–23 and 1:9); in Romans 10:20, and again in Romans 11, where he spoke of Jewish branches being broken off the Jews' own olive tree so that Gentile branches might be grafted in, concluding, "Israel has experienced a hardening in part until the full number of the Gentiles has come in" (v. 25). When we begin to notice the many verses Paul cites, we get a glimpse of how carefully and persistently he must have had to argue this truth when teaching it to the Jewish and Gentile churches.

There is a progression to the four texts he cites in Romans 15. In the first (Ps. 18:49), the psalmist, a Jew, is praising God *among the Gentiles.* In the second (Deut. 32:43), the Gentiles are called upon to rejoice *along with Israel.* In the third (Ps. 117:1), the Gentiles are invited to praise God *on their own.* Finally, in the fourth (Isa. 11:10), it is shown that this was made possible by him who is *both the Jewish and the Gentile king.*

It is valuable to look at each of these texts individually.

1. *Psalm 18:49.* The first quotation is from Psalm 18, a thanksgiving song in which David looks back over a lifetime of saving interventions and praises God for them.[1] It was apparently written after David's deliverance from Saul, the kings of the many hostile states that surrounded Israel, and the armies commanded by David's rebellious son, Absalom.

At first glance there does not seem to be anything unusual about the psalm, a song by a Jewish king thanking God for, among other things, his victories over the surrounding Gentile nations. But suddenly toward the end of the psalm David declares that he is going to praise God not merely "to" but also "among the [Gentile] nations." This implies that the Gentiles are going to have a part in this praise, listening to it certainly but perhaps also praising God along with David. This is what Paul picks up on when he quotes verse 49

---

1. John Murray sees Paul's quotation as a combination of 2 Samuel 22:50 and Psalm 18:49, but this is without importance since 2 Samuel 22 is almost a word for word repetition of Psalm 18.

in Romans. He is saying that David looked forward to a day when the Gentiles would know the true God and praise him along with Jews, such as himself.

2. *Deuteronomy 32:43*. The second quotation comes from Deuteronomy 32, which contains the Song of Moses composed for the people of Israel shortly before his death.[2] Songs or hymns are a means of praising God, but they also often have a teaching function, and that is the case here. A major portion of the hymn reminds the people of the ways God has been good to them (vv. 7–14), while other portions warn them not to depart from the worship of God lest terrible things happen.

Again, like Psalm 18, one would expect this song to be limited in its outlook, thinking of Israel only. But again, like Psalm 18, it also has the other nations in view. Verse 8 is the first verse to strike this more universal note, for it pictures God as "the Most High" who gives each of the nations its portion of the earth's land as an inheritance. The same thing happens again in verse 21, which Paul has already quoted in Romans 10:19: "I will make them envious by those who are not a people; I will make them angry by a nation that has no understanding." The final place this occurs is in verse 43, quoted in Romans 15, which calls on the Gentiles to rejoice together with the Jewish people when God takes vengeance on his enemies and makes atonement for his land and people.

Paul surely would have taken this as a reference to the death of Christ, after which the gospel was preached to Gentiles specifically. It was at this point that Paul's own ministry came into this prophetic forecast of history.

3. *Psalm 117:1*. The third quotation carries the progression Paul has been developing a bit further. In the first (Ps. 18:49), David was praising God among the Gentiles. In the second (Deut. 32:43), Gentiles are praising God along with the Jews. In this verse, from Psalm 117, the Gentiles are praising God on their own.

Psalm 117 is remarkable for being the shortest psalm in the psalter. But even though it is only two verses long, it has one of the broadest outlooks of any psalm. It is directed to the nations of the world and its peoples, all of whom are called upon to praise Jehovah God for the greatness of "his love toward us" and his "faithfulness," which endures forever. The phrase "his love toward us" might be thought of as meaning his love to Israel only, but that would be contrary to the spirit of the psalm. Therefore, most commentators take it either as God's love "toward the whole family of man," as Charles Spurgeon thought,[3] or of his love for everyone shown by his love for Israel

---

2. Calvin thought that Paul was quoting from Psalm 67:5, but most commentators believe he is quoting from Deuteronomy. See John Calvin, *The Epistles of Paul the Apostle to the Romans and to the Thessalonians*, trans. Ross MacKenzie (Grand Rapids: Wm. B. Eerdmans Publishing Company, 1973), pp. 307–8. There is an excellent evaluation of Calvin's rather unusual views in Robert Haldane, *An Exposition of the Epistle to the Romans* (MacDill AFB: MacDonald Publishing Company, 1958), p. 615.

3. Spurgeon wrote, "The Lord is kind to us as his creatures, and merciful to us as sinners, hence his merciful kindness to us as sinful creatures." C. H. Spurgeon, *The Treasury of David*, vol. 3a, *Psalms 111–119* (Grand Rapids: Zondervan Publishing House, 1968), p. 97.

in fulfilling the promises of blessing made to Abraham by sending Jesus Christ
to be the world's Savior.[4] Because of the way Paul handled this subject in
Romans 9, we are probably right to suppose that he is thinking of God's love
in this way in citing Psalm 117:1.

4. *Isaiah 11:10.* The final quotation comes from Isaiah 11, a chapter that
speaks of a future descendant of David who will rule as a great king and bring
in a day of universal blessing. The opening part of the chapter is often read
at Christmas as a prophecy of Christ's advent:

> A shoot will come up from the stump of Jesse;
>> from his roots a Branch will bear fruit.
> The Spirit of the LORD will rest on him—
>> the Spirit of wisdom and understanding,
>> the Spirit of counsel and power,
>> the Spirit of knowledge and of the fear of the LORD—
> and he will delight in the fear of the LORD.
>
> He will not judge by what he sees with eyes,
>> or decide by what he hears with his ears;
> but with righteousness he will judge the needy,
>> with justice he will give decisions for the poor of the earth.
>
> Isaiah 11:1–4

The chapter goes on to envision a day of glorious messianic blessing in
which "the wolf will live with the lamb, the leopard will lie down with the goat,
the calf and the lion and the yearling together; and a little child will lead
them" (v. 6). It speaks of a time in which "they will neither harm nor destroy
on all my holy mountain, for the earth will be full of the knowledge of the
LORD as the waters cover the sea" (v. 9). Then comes the text Paul quotes in
Romans: "In that day the Root of Jesse will stand as a banner for the peoples;
the nations will rally to him" (v. 10).

Jesse was the father of David. So the text is looking forward to that
promised descendant of David who will bring in the messianic age. Paul is
saying that the age of blessing has begun by Christ's coming, and that the
hope of the Gentiles is in him. This is the main point of Romans 15:9–12, of
course. For Paul is not just saying that the Gentiles should be hopeful in the
sense that people should never give up hope, or that even the Gentile religions have something going for them. He is saying rather that they have hope
because of Jesus Christ. There is hope for Gentiles because Jesus is the Savior
of the world and not just the Savior of the Jews.

---

4. This is Derek Kidner's view. He says, "It may also be that the 'us' of verse 2 has already
found room for the 'you' implied in verse 1, by seeing Israelites and Gentiles as one people
under God." See Derek Kidner, *Psalms 73–150: A Commentary on Books III–V of the Psalms* (Downers
Grove, Ill.: InterVarsity Press, 1975), p. 412.

America's Spiritual Decline

When Paul quotes Isaiah as saying that "the Gentiles will hope in him [that is, in Christ]," he is thinking of personal salvation, of course. Yet I cannot look at this text without thinking that it also applies to cultures, particularly American culture, and of the only hope we or any other people have to avoid utter spiritual bankruptcy and chaos. Romans 15:12 (quoting Isaiah 11:10) does speak of "the nations," after all, and we are one of them.

Not long ago someone gave me a copy of a speech William J. Bennett gave to a special twentieth-anniversary gathering of the Heritage Foundation, a conservative think tank based in Washington, D.C. Bennett served as secretary of education under President Ronald Reagan and later as drug czar under President George Bush. His address, called "Getting Used to Decadence," spoke to America's decline.[5]

Bennett told of a conversation he had with a friend who lives in Asia about how America is perceived today by foreigners. According to Bennett's friend, the world continues to look on America as the leading economic and military power on earth. But, he said, "this same world no longer beholds us with the moral respect it once did. When the rest of the world looks at America . . . they no longer see a 'shining city on a hill.' Instead they see a society in decline, with exploding rates of crime and social pathologies." Foreigners who come to the United States these days no longer come hopefully but in fear. And they have cause to be fearful—a record number of them get killed here.[6]

Early in 1993, through the Heritage Foundation, Bennett released a book titled *The Index of Leading Cultural Indicators*, tracing changes in American behavior over the past thirty years (1960–90). There are a few relatively good signs: Since 1960, the population has increased 41 percent; the gross domestic product has nearly tripled; and total social spending by all levels of government (measured in constant 1990 dollars) has risen from $142.73 billion to $787.00 billion—more than a fivefold increase.

But during the same thirty-year period there has been a 560 percent increase in violent crime; more than a 400 percent increase in illegitimate births; a quadrupling in divorces; a tripling of the percentage of children living in single-parent homes; more than a 200 percent increase in the teenage suicide rate; and a drop of 75 points in the average S.A.T. scores of high school students. Today 30 percent of all births are illegitimate, and, according to Bennett, "By the end of the decade, according to the most reliable projections, 40 percent of all births and 80 percent of minority births will occur out of wedlock."

In 1940 teachers were asked to identify the top problems in America's schools. They answered: talking out of turn, chewing gum, making noise, running in the hall, cutting in line, dress code infractions, and littering. When

5. William J. Bennett, "Getting Used to Decadence: The Spirit of Democracy in Modern America," *The Heritage Lectures*, number 477 (Washington, D.C.: The Heritage Foundation, 1993).
    6. Ibid., p. 1.

they were asked the same question in 1990, they identified drug use, alcohol abuse, pregnancy, suicide, rape, robbery, and assault.

Within my lifetime, says Bennett, the United States was looked upon as the bright moral conscience of the world. Today we have topped the industrialized world in murders, rapes, and violent crime. We are near the top in rates of abortions, divorces, and unwed births. In elementary and secondary education we are near the bottom in students' achievement scores.[7]

And this is not the greatest problem. The greatest problem, according to Bennett, is that we have gotten used to this condition. We have accepted it. There is no shame, no protest, no outrage, no anger.

Not long ago a person who mugged and almost killed a seventy-two-year-old man was shot by a police officer while fleeing the scene of the crime. A jury awarded him $4.3 million in damages, and no one protested. In California the trial of the two Menendez brothers, charged for killing their elderly parents with a shotgun, resulted in a hung jury. The jurors believed the psychiatrists' defense that they must have been somehow psychologically abused.

Bennett traces our problem to what the ancients called *acedia,* borrowing a term meaning "an aversion to and a negation of spiritual things." Aleksandr Solzhenitsyn, the great Russian author and expatriate, called it "spiritual exhaustion." The late American novelist Walker Percy described it as America's "weariness, boredom, cynicism, greed and in the end helplessness before its great problems."[8]

Bennett himself called it "a corruption of the heart." Contrasting America's material prosperity with its spiritual impoverishment, he observed, "If we have full employment and greater economic growth—if we have cities of gold and alabaster—but our children have not learned how to walk in goodness, justice, and mercy, then the American experiment, no matter how gilded, will have failed."[9]

Savior of the Nations

As Christians, we did not need William Bennett to tell us that apart from Jesus Christ all people have "corruption of the heart." But we are indebted to him for tracing so graphically what happens when a culture turns its back on God, as ours has done.

Paul's phrase describing the Ephesians before they came to Christ was "without hope and without God in the world" (Eph. 2:12). Our culture wants to be "without God," but it is discovering that to be without God also means to be without hope. We must remind everyone that where there is God, there is hope, and that Jesus Christ is still what Martin Luther called *der Heiden Heiland,* "the Savior [and, therefore, the hope] of the Gentiles."

7. Bennett, "Getting Used to Decadence," p. 3.
8. Ibid., p. 5.
9. Ibid., p. 6.

223

The First Benediction

Romans 15:13

May the God of hope fill you with all joy and peace as you trust in him, so that you may overflow with hope by the power of the Holy Spirit.

T here is a sense in which the Book of Romans ends with the thirteenth verse of chapter fifteen, because what follows is essentially personal in nature. Paul did not always end his letters with such remarks, and this one would have been complete without them. Besides, Romans 15:13 would have been a great ending.

I have called this study "The *First* Benediction" because there will be two more benedictions before we end—Romans 15:33 and Romans 16:20—followed by a doxology in Romans 16:25–27. Each benediction is important, but this is a particularly important and comprehensive one.

Donald Grey Barnhouse devoted six studies to this verse in his radio series on Romans. (They were reduced to one in book form.) He says, "This verse is a great summary of the blessed life in the brotherhood formed by our oneness in Jesus Christ. The *source* of that life is the God of hope. The *measure* of that life is that we shall be filled 'with all joy and peace.' The *quality* of that life is joy and peace which he desires for us. The *condition* of that life is

1835

faith—we enter it by believing. The *purpose* of that life is that we might abound. The *enabling* of that life is divine power. And the *director* of that life is the Holy Spirit."[1] So clearly, this is a very practical verse.

Romans 15:13 is a prayer, which leads Leon Morris to say, "We should not think of Paul primarily as a controversialist; he was a deeply pious man and it is characteristic that he finishes not with some equivalent of Q.E.D. [*quod erat demonstrandum,* meaning 'which was to be demonstrated'] nor a shout of triumph over the antagonists he has confronted but with a prayer."[2]

The God of Hope

The obvious place to begin this study is with the word *hope,* because it is the first key word and occurs twice, once at the beginning and once at the end.

What is striking here is that Paul links hope to God, speaking of "the God of hope." This can point to God as the source of hope (a subjective genitive), or it can point to God as the object of hope (an objective genitive). Both are true. God is the source of hope because he is the source of every good thing. But he is also the object of hope, since we have hope in him and not in the weak things advanced as objects of hope by our secular sinful world.

Paul is not saying to "keep a stiff upper lip" or "look for the silver lining" or "never, never, never give up" when he speaks of the Christian's hope. To be hopeful is a human characteristic possessed in large measure by great men and women, and we admire it. But if that is all we are talking about in terms of our spiritual state, it would be utter deception and delusion. This is because without God our condition is literally, thoroughly, unmistakably, and unalterably hope*less.* We are indeed "without hope and without God in the world" (Eph. 2:12).

As soon as we bring God into the picture the situation is reversed. Now we have hope through the work of Jesus Christ, because God himself is our hope and has given hope to us.

Nothing else can be that or do that. If you put your hope in other people, they will let you down. If you trust your stocks or bonds or bank accounts, you will find that they can disappear overnight. In any case, they are not ultimately satisfying. Health will fail. Houses can burn. Jobs can be lost. Even great nations enter periods of economic and moral decline. But the one who has his or her hope from God and trusts God as he has revealed himself in Jesus Christ can stand firm in anything. Edward Mots expressed it in one of our best-known hymns:

1. Donald Grey Barnhouse, *God's Glory: Exposition of Bible Doctrines, Taking the Epistle to the Romans as a Point of Departure,* vol. 10, *Romans 14:13–16:27* (Grand Rapids: Wm. B. Eerdmans Publishing Company, 1964), pp. 72–73.

2. Leon Morris, *The Epistle to the Romans* (Grand Rapids: Wm. B. Eerdmans Publishing Company, and Leicester, England: Inter-Varsity Press, 1988), p. 506.

> My hope is built on nothing less
> Than Jesus' blood and righteousness;
> I dare not trust the sweetest frame,
> But wholly lean on Jesus' name.
> On Christ, the solid Rock, I stand;
> All other ground is sinking sand.
>
> His oath, his covenant, his blood
> Support me in the whelming flood;
> When all around my soul gives away,
> He then is all my Hope and Stay.
> On Christ, the solid Rock, I stand;
> All other ground is sinking sand.

Paul spoke of this hope when he wrote to the Christians at Corinth, describing himself as "sorrowful, yet always rejoicing; poor, yet making many rich; having nothing, and yet possessing everything" (2 Cor. 6:10).

Abounding in Joy

Joy is one of Paul's great concepts since, as Leon Morris points out, "the term occurs in his writings twenty-one times and no other New Testament writing has it more than John's nine times."[3] He links it to faith in Philippians 1:25 ("I know that I will remain, and I will continue with all of you for your progress and joy in the faith") and with the other fruits of the Holy Spirit in Galatians 5:22–23 ("But the fruit of the Spirit is love, joy, peace, patience, kindness, goodness, faithfulness, gentleness and self-control").

Yet Paul didn't invent the idea. He received it from Jesus, who spoke of it, along with peace, as his gift to his disciples before his departure. Jesus said, "I have told you this so that my joy may be in you and that your joy may be complete" (John 15:11). Speaking of his death he added, "Now is your time for grief, but I will see you again and you will rejoice, and no one will take away your joy" (John 16:22). Later in his high priestly prayer, recorded in John 17, Jesus said to his Father, "I am coming to you now, but I say these things while I am still in the world, so that they may have the full measure of my joy within them" (v. 13).

This joy has its source in God, since "every good and perfect gift is from above, coming down from the Father of the heavenly lights, who does not change like shifting shadows" (James 1:17).

This means that the Christian's joy is not a matter of natural human endowments or nice circumstances. It is supernatural in origin and in the way it expresses itself in spite of circumstances. Donald Grey Barnhouse wrote, "It is not a question of being an extrovert or an introvert. Some people are by nature gloomy and morose. In the days of superstition it was thought that

---

3. Morris, *The Epistle to the Romans*, p. 507.

such had been born under the influence of Saturn, and so they were called saturnine. Other people are buoyant and outgoing, and this was attributed to their being born under the influence of the planet Jupiter, so they were called jovial. But jovial people are sometimes plunged into the deepest despair and gloom when something goes contrary to their selfish desires. And contrariwise, some who are naturally despondent learn to settle upon the eternal Rock, and are filled with a deep and steadfast joy, which does not have its spring in this natural life."[4]

In the prayer recorded in John 17, Jesus indicated that we should have "the full measure" of this divine joy within. But we don't always; that is why he prayed for it on our behalf.

We find much the same thing in our text in Romans, for Paul is praying that God might fill the Roman believers with "all joy and peace as you trust in him." This teaches that there are degrees of these blessings for Christians; and this must mean that although many have them, not all are filled with them. Instead of being mostly empty of blessings, you should be filled to the brim.

Two Kinds of Peace

Two kinds of peace are spoken of in the Bible: peace *with* God and the peace *of* God. Thus far in Romans the first meaning has dominated, because Paul has been trying to show how sinners, who are naturally at war with God, might find peace with God through the cross of Christ. Here, however, he is talking about personal peace, the peace of heart and mind that God gives.

William Barclay in his commentary on Romans writes about how people naturally want peace but lose it due to inner tensions or disturbing circumstances:

> The ancient philosophers sought for what they called *ataraxia*, the untroubled life. They wanted above all serenity, that serenity which is proof alike against the shattering blows and the petty pinpricks of human existence. One would almost say that today serenity is a lost possession.
>
> There are two things which make serenity impossible. (a) There is the *inner tension*. Men live a distracted life, for the word *distract* literally means *to pull apart*. So long as a man is a walking civil war, so long as he himself is a battleground, so long as he is a split personality, there can obviously be no such thing as serenity. There is only one way out of this, and that is for self to abdicate to Christ. When Christ controls the tension is gone. (b) There is *worry about external things*. There are many who are haunted by the chances and the changes of life. H. G. Wells tells how in New York harbor he was once on a liner. It was foggy, and suddenly out of the fog there loomed another liner, and the two ships slid past each other with only yards to spare. He was suddenly face to face with what he called the general large dangerousness of life. It is hard not to worry, for man is characteristically a creature who looks forward to guess and

4. Donald Grey Barnhouse, *Faith That Lives*, booklet 88 in the series of radio messages on Romans (Philadelphia: The Bible Study Hour, 1960), p. 13.

fear. The only end to that worry is the utter conviction that, whatever happens, God's hand will never cause his child a needless tear. Things will happen that we cannot understand, but if we are sure enough of love, we can accept with serenity even those things which wound the heart and baffle the mind.[5]

What that is all about, if we speak in theological terms, is faith in the sovereignty of God—that God is in control and that he never lets anything come into the lives of one of his children that he has not ordained for that person for his or her ultimate good. A person who really trusts in God's sovereignty will have a peace that others cannot even comprehend.

Trust in Him

The fourth of the key terms Paul puts together in this verse is *faith*, or *trust* as the New International Version has it. Faith is the indispensable channel for blessings, as they come from God but become ours only as we trust in him.

This is not so mysterious. It is simply a matter of believing God when he tells us who he is and what he has done and will continue to do for his people. I am convinced that the most important of all differences between people is precisely at this point, not whether they are intelligent or unintelligent, kind or unkind, joyful or taciturn, people-oriented or loners, but whether or not they will trust God. Christians by very definition are believers; non-Christians are unbelievers. But I mean more than this. I mean that even professing Christians differ fundamentally in regard either to trusting or not trusting God, either believing him or questioning what he says.

In his study of this verse Donald Grey Barnhouse illustrates this by citing the way some Bible critics reacted when so-called errors they believed they had found in the Bible were explained. They began by creating a series of arguments for why intelligent people could no longer trust the Bible—call them arguments A, B, C, and D. These stood for a while because biblical scholarship is slow. Yet as the years went by arguments A and B were refuted by a better knowledge of the Bible and of the times of the writing of the biblical documents. By this time these same unbelieving critics had developed arguments E, F, G, and H. Scholarship crawled on and eventually explained these problems. But now the critics had arguments I, J, K, L, and M. And so it has gone. Eventually they ran out of letters and had to start again!

We might expect that such people would learn from what has happened, but they do not. In the meantime, however, as Barnhouse writes, "While this parade of doubt passes by, there is the quiet march of men of faith who are filled with all joy and peace in believing, because they have been filled by the God of hope who establishes, strengthens and settles them."[6]

---

5. Barclay, *The Letter to the Romans*, pp. 218–19.
6. Barnhouse, *Faith That Lives*, p. 6.

I have often called attention to Charles Haddon Spurgeon's remark that he was willing to be thought a fool today, knowing that in twenty or thirty years his faith in the Word of God would be vindicated, and chiding those who aspired to seem wise now by attacking the Scriptures but who would look foolish in a decade or so's time.

Learn to trust God. You will find that as you trust him you will grow stronger in your faith and that you will become ever more firmly settled in the wonderful doctrines taught us in the Bible. Moreover, you will discover something of the perfect joy and peace of believing God. Hymn writer Thomas Kelly (1769–1855) wrote this:

> Trust in him, ye saints, forever;
> He is faithful, changing never;
> Neither force nor guile can sever
> Those he loves from him.

Powered by the Holy Spirit

The fifth and last of the great biblical words found in Romans 15:13 is *power,* in the phrase "by the power of the Holy Spirit." In the Greek it is the word *dynamis,* not *exousia* (which is sometimes also translated as power but actually means authority). It is a power that gets things done.

This phrase reminds us that nothing of any spiritual value is possible in and of ourselves since, as Jesus said, "Apart from me you can do nothing" (John 15:5). We cannot believe unless we are enabled to believe by God (Eph. 2:8). We cannot find peace unless we submit our requests to God by prayer and earnest petition (Phil. 4:6–7). Joy comes only from God and is a fruit of the Holy Spirit's work within (Gal. 5:22). Hope is impossible (Eph. 2:12). But while these blessings are impossible for any of us to achieve by ourselves, everything is possible for God who makes them possible for us and in us by his Spirit's power. In fact, God promises to bless us in all these ways if we will trust him, and it is for this that Paul is praying in Romans 15.

By ending with a reference to "the power of the Holy Spirit," the prayer that is our text both begins and ends with God. This is an important point, and it is one that should be familiar to us by now since it is exactly what we found in Romans 11:36, which closed the long doctrinal section of the epistle. It ended with a doxology, the final words of which were:

> For from him and through him and to him are all things.
> To him be the glory forever! Amen.

Everything in this whole universe begins with God, is accomplished by God's agency, and exists for God's glory. But if that is true of the inanimate universe—the world of plants and trees, of suns and planets, of quasars, quarks, and black holes—it is certainly true of salvation. It is true of you, if you are a Christian. You exist because God created you. You believe because he worked faith in you and sustains it in you by the power of his Holy Spirit. He does this that you might live to his glory now and indeed forever.

Left to ourselves we can do nothing. Even as saved people we would fall at the first wisp of temptation or the first blast of Satan's death-dealing blows. But because God is for us we can stand firm and triumph. That is why Thomas Kelly continues, in the hymn from which I quoted earlier:

> Keep us Lord, O keep us cleaving
> To thyself and still believing,
> Till the hour of our receiving
> Promised joys from thee.

Finally, we note that according to our text, all this is so Christians "might overflow with hope." That is Paul's emphasis, his conclusion. To put it in temporal sequence: God, who is the source of hope, is asked to fill believers with joy and peace through their learning to trust in him, so that by the power of the Holy Spirit's working they might overflow with the hope of which God the Father is the source.

This is the fourth mention of hope in this chapter (vv. 4, 12, 13 twice) and the third since verse 12. So obviously it is Paul's main concern and should be ours also, especially since we live in an age that is so lacking in hope. As I look around me today I sense that people have lost hope in nearly everything. They have no faith in politicians or the economy or justice from the courts or even safety from those authorized to provide it. They do not even have faith in themselves. And they are without God, and therefore there is no hope for them in this world.

What an opportunity for God's people! Robert Haldane says, "The people of God have high hopes."[7] Indeed we do. We have divine, uplifting, great, overwhelming, and overpowering hopes. So let's *be* hopeful. Abound in hope—and let the world know why.

---

7. Robert Haldane, *An Exposition of the Epistle to the Romans* (MacDill AFB: MacDonald Publishing Company, 1958), p. 617.

PART TWENTY-ONE

Paul's Personal Ministry and Plans

224

Check-off Points for a Good Church

Romans 15:14

I myself am convinced, my brothers, that you yourselves are full of goodness, complete in knowledge and competent to instruct one another.

Have you ever come to the end of something that has been exceptionally nice and found yourself feeling a bit sad about it? Maybe a vacation? Or a night at the opera? Children feel sad when Christmas is over, though their parents are usually rejoicing.

We have something like that now. We are coming to the end of our study of Paul's great letter to the Romans. In it Paul has unfolded the Christian doctrine of justification by faith in all its many ramifications. He has demonstrated its necessity, described what God did to bring it about through the atoning death of Jesus Christ, explained how it works itself out by the power of the Holy Spirit in individual lives to give a permanent and sure salvation, and answered objections rising from the failure of the majority of Jews to believe the gospel. He has unfolded practical applications of this theology in such areas as yielding our minds to Jesus Christ, a proper evaluation of ourselves and others, matters of church and state, how believers are to live in light of the imminent return of Christ, and the need for Christians to accept and value one another.

With Romans 15:14, Paul begins to wrap this up, turning in his final paragraphs to his reasons for writing the letter, suggesting what his future travel plans might be, and sending greetings to people he knew in Rome. But even though he is ending, he still has quite a bit to say.

How does this last section fit in? We can understand the outline of Romans best if we think of it as a doctrinal treatise wrapped up in a letter. The letter began with the first seventeen verses of chapter 1. Everything since has been Paul's treatise. But here, in verse 14 of chapter 15, Paul resumes the letter format and actually harks back to some of the things he wrote about in chapter 1. The words "my brothers" (Rom. 15:14) show that he is speaking personally now and from a concerned Christian heart.

Those Roman Christians

Paul tells the Roman Christians in the opening sentence of his personal remarks that they are doing all right and that he is convinced this is so. The full text says, "I myself am convinced, my brothers, that you yourselves are full of goodness, complete in knowledge and competent to instruct one another." Paul said something along these lines in the first chapter when he took note of their strong faith and of the fact that it was being talked about all over the world (v. 8).

He is renewing his comments along these lines because he had been developing his doctrinal arguments fully and forcefully—the next verse acknowledges that he had written "quite boldly on some points, as if to remind you of them again"—and he knew that they might think that he somehow considers them to be deficient.

Of course, the fact that he has written as he has, far from being a thoughtless slight or criticism, is actually a compliment. Nothing is clearer than that the letter is for people who take their faith seriously. Yet it is not the mere fact of the letter that is a compliment. Paul is aware that his confidence in these believers, whom he had never seen, might nevertheless be misunderstood. So he compliments them directly, using the terms appearing in this verse: (1) "full of goodness," (2) "complete in knowledge," and (3) "competent to instruct one another." John Murray says of this verse, "He could scarcely have devised a combination of words that would more effectively convey to them his own personal conviction of the fruit of the gospel in their midst."[1]

If this really is Paul's way of complimenting the Roman church on being what a church should be, then he is also giving us three criteria by which we can evaluate ourselves—or any local gathering of believers.

1. John Murray, *The Epistle to the Romans*, 2 vols. in 1 (Grand Rapids: Wm. B. Eerdmans Publishing Company, 1968), vol. 2, p. 209.

Full of Goodness

Paul begins with *goodness,* and he says that this is something of which the Roman church was full. This is a rather rare word, not found in classical Greek but used in the Septuagint, elsewhere in Paul's writings, and by some later church writers, no doubt because of its use by Paul. The word is *agathôsunê,* and it is significant because it refers to moral or ethical goodness as well as to what we would most naturally think of—namely, kindness, thoughtfulness, charity toward the poor, and such.

This is important, of course, especially when we remember what Paul had to say about goodness in the earlier chapters. In his study of the nature of fallen man developed in chapter 3 he quoted Psalm 14:1–3 and 53:1–3 as teaching that "there is no one who does good, not even one" (v. 12). Even worse, not only do we fail to do or practice good; we also actively do evil, and that continuously.

> "Their throats are open graves;
>   their tongues practice deceit."
> "The poison of vipers is on their lips."
>   "Their mouths are full of cursing and bitterness."
> "Their feet are swift to shed blood;
>   ruin and misery mark their ways,
> and the way of peace they do not know."
>   "There is no fear of God before their eyes."
>
> Romans 3:13–18[2]

How, then, can Paul speak in chapter 15 of the Roman believers being filled with goodness? The answer, obviously, is that they had become Christians, having been turned from their sin to faith and righteousness by the power of the Holy Spirit. It is true, as Robert Haldane writes, that "in our flesh there is nothing good." But it is equally true that "from the work of the Spirit on our hearts we may be full of goodness."[3] This is to be a normal condition. It is not a matter for some superclass of Christians, what some branches of the church call saints.

We need to remember that Galatians 5:22–23 lists goodness as one part of the Holy Spirit's fruit: "But the fruit of the Spirit is love, joy, peace, patience, kindness, goodness, faithfulness, gentleness and self-control," and that, according to Ephesians 2:10, doing good works is the necessary outcome of our having become Christians: "For we are God's workmanship, created in Christ Jesus to do good works, which God prepared in advance for us to do." If we do not show any evidence of God's goodness in our lives or if we do

2. These verses are quotations from Psalm 5:9, 140:3, 10:7; Isaiah 59:7–8; and Psalm 36:1.
3. Robert Haldane, *An Exposition of the Epistle to the Romans* (MacDill AFB: MacDonald Publishing Company, 1958), p. 618.

not do any good works, it is evidence that we are not Christians. So goodness is a check-off point not only for a good church, but for whether we are genuine followers of Jesus Christ.

Let me illustrate what we should be with this example. Less than two hours before I wrote this paragraph I received word that one of the leading members of our church had died. His name was Cornelius Phillips, and he had blessed many people because of his faith, strong testimony, and good works. When I heard of his death I immediately pulled out a letter that a man I did not even know had written about him a year and a half earlier. It read:

> I'm writing regarding one of your church members at Tenth Presbyterian Church. He's in the hospital now, and I'm sure the folks at church are praying for him. What I wanted to say was that he is a fine Christian. He cares about the Lord; he cares about his family, and also about his church.
>
> I met Cornelius Phillips last August when my father was ill and passed away. He lent a great deal of peace and caring to our family at that time and still does today. . . . Your church has a good reputation, and I would have to say that people like Cornelius and his wife and others like them are part of the reason for that reputation. Cornelius in his humility would be the first to say, "Praise the Lord." I would echo that statement and say, "Praise the Lord" for people like him.

That is genuine Christianity. Wouldn't it be wonderful to be part of a church filled with such people? I dare to say I am part of such a church and that there are many like them. I would say of them, as Paul said of the Roman congregation, "I myself am convinced, my brothers, that you yourselves are full of goodness."

Yet we must not presume along these lines. We must constantly be asking, Am I such a person as Paul describes here? Am I filled with God's goodness? Would anybody ever use Paul's words to describe me? If we cannot answer yes to those questions, it is time for self-examination and for doing what Peter had in mind when he wrote, almost immediately after having spoken of the need for goodness, knowledge, self-control, perseverance, godliness, brotherly kindness, and love among Christians, "Therefore, my brothers, be all the more eager to make your calling and election sure. For if you do these things, you will never fall, and you will receive a rich welcome into the eternal kingdom of our Lord and Savior Jesus Christ" (2 Peter 1:10–11).

Complete in Knowledge

The second check-off point for a good church is the phrase "complete in knowledge." This does not mean learned in an academic sense but rather a sound, practical understanding of the Christian faith that will issue in wholesome, helpful conduct.

At this my mind goes back to our studies of Romans 12:1–2, especially the part where Paul urges us to be transformed by the renewing of our minds.

I made the link between thinking like a Christian and acting like a Christian. I said that you will never act like a Christian unless you begin to think properly.

That is what is wrong with American religion, of course. Pollster George Gallup has described America as richly religious but ethically impoverished. In an interview with *Reformed Theological Seminary Journal* he said:

> Religious belief is remarkably high—certainly, the highest of any developed nation in the world. At the same time, American religious life is characterized by a series of gaps. First, an "ethics gap" exists between Americans' expressed beliefs and the state of the society they shape. While religion is highly popular in America, it is to a large extent superficial; it does not change peoples' lives to the degree one would expect from their level of professed faith. In ethical behavior, there is very little difference between the churched and the unchurched.[4]

The problem is found in the second gap Gallup mentions, a gap between faith and knowledge. "Related to this is a 'knowledge gap' between Americans' stated faith and the lack of the most basic knowledge about that faith. Half of those who say they are Christians do not know who delivered the Sermon on the Mount," Gallup says.[5]

We would like to think this is a problem only for nominal Christians or perhaps, speaking as evangelicals, for liberals. After all, liberals do not even believe the Bible, we think. But it is a problem for us too.

Some time ago I read a book by David Wells, Gordon-Conwell Theological Seminary professor of historical and systematic theology, called *No Place for Truth: Or Whatever Happened to Evangelical Theology.*[6] Wells has a simple but very disturbing thesis: Evangelicalism as a religious force in American life is dead or is in the process of dying because it has abandoned any serious commitment to truth. He is not saying that evangelicalism is dead as a sociological force or presence, for evangelicals have large churches, many members, and a great deal of money. But since they no longer really care about the truthfulness of the gospel and the Christian faith as a whole, they are ceasing to make any significant difference.

I can hear many questioning that. It is the evangelicals, rather than liberals, who believe the gospel, they say.

Well, there is a great deal of difference between what we say we believe or even think we believe and what we believe practically. To judge by what evangelicals do rather than by what they say, which is what Professor Wells is attempting, evangelicals actually believe in Madison Avenue techniques or miracles for evangelism, psychology for Christian growth and sanctification,

---

4. "George Gallup Looks at Religion in America," an interview in *Ministry*, Reformed Theological Seminary Journal, Summer 1992, p. 10.

5. Ibid.

6. David F. Wells, *No Place for Truth: Or Whatever Happened to Evangelical Theology* (Grand Rapids: Wm. B. Eerdmans Publishing Company, 1993).

spiritual voodoo for discerning the will or God, and the power of politics, wealth, or numbers for making an impact on society. This is not what the followers of Christ did in an earlier age, when they proclaimed and trusted in the truth of the gospel.

What is happening to evangelicals is what happened to the liberal church earlier in this century, though most evangelicals are unaware of it. They are losing faith in the power of the truth of God, blessed by the Spirit of God, to make a difference. They are in fact becoming quite worldly. It can hardly be said of most of today's evangelical churches that they are "complete in knowledge," meaning a sound and significant knowledge of the truth of God's revelation, even though they may be proficient in launching and developing churches.

Sadly, if this comparison holds, the prognosis for the future of the evangelical church is prefigured by the history of the liberal denominations that once had plenty of members and money but have been losing both quite rapidly.

Churches will lose their significance, too. In order to influence society, a person or a movement must be different. But Christians will never be different unless they understand, believe, and act upon the revelation of the character and ways of God that we have in the Bible. A while ago I asked the faculty at Gordon-Conwell Seminary what changes they had noticed in seminary students in recent years.

David Wells was present at this gathering, and he replied that he had noticed four things. First, each entering class was more biblically illiterate than the last. Second, each class seemed to be filled with more individuals who were swamped with their own personal problems and thus were thinking mostly about themselves rather than about their studies or how they might help others. Third, they had a greater sense of their own personal rights or entitlements; they expected everything to be done for them. And fourth, they were sold out to and mostly uncritical of the surrounding secular culture.

I find that frightening, now and with a glance to the future. Can it be said of us that we are "complete in knowledge"? We should be. The church in Rome was. What is going to happen to us if we are not?

Competent to Instruct One Another

Finally, Paul says in praise of the Roman church that the believers in Rome were "competent to instruct one another." The Greek word translated *competent* is based on the word *dynamis* (actually *dynamenoi*), which has the idea of being powerful or effective. *Dynamis* was the word used in the phrase "by the *power* of the Holy Spirit" in verse 13. *Instruct* is *nouthetein*, which carries the idea of admonishing another person in order to correct something that may be wrong. In the New Testament the word occurs only in Paul's writings plus once in a speech of his recorded in Acts 20:31.

In Acts 20 Paul has arrived at Miletus on the coast of Asia Minor near Ephesus and has sent for the elders of the Ephesian church in order to say good-bye to them and give them his final admonitions and encouragements.

As part of this helpful instruction he brings forward his own example when he was with them earlier, saying, "Remember that for three years I never stopped *warning* each of you night and day with tears" (Acts 20:31).

He constantly had the health and well-being of the Ephesian church in view and always did everything possible to build it up. Thus, he was always speaking to them about God and the gospel and encouraging them to go forward steadily and boldly in the Christian life.

Do we love the Lord enough to talk about him naturally and often? Do we love others enough to bring spiritual truths into daily conversation? Do we care for Christians enough to point them in the right direction when we see that they are deviating from or falling short of it?

And do we sometimes talk about difficult things, though kindly? Once Donald Grey Barnhouse was sent an appraisal of a man who was under care of the church's session as a candidate for the ministry. It had been prepared by a mature Christian under whom the candidate had worked and was, as Barnhouse said, "a dissection of his spiritual anatomy." Barnhouse met with the candidate and started to review the appraisal with him. He had hardly gotten beyond the first paragraph of the four-page document before the young man reacted strongly. Barnhouse told him to jot down his disagreements while the letter was being read and they would discuss them, which they did. It was easy to see that he was deeply agitated and wounded.

When Barnhouse finished, the man demanded, "Do you agree with this?"

Barnhouse did not reply to that question, but he said, "I do not know when I have ever read a paper that more clearly reveals a heart of love in the man who prepared it. If I were to write a title, I would call it, 'How to Salvage John Jones for the Lord Jesus Christ.'"

That is what the apostle Paul was doing in Ephesus and what he was complimenting the Roman believers as being able to do with one another, not to tear them down or expose each other's faults, but with the goal of training them and encouraging them for the work of Jesus Christ.

If these things can be said of us, thank God. We are not capable of developing these things in ourselves. They are his work. If they cannot be said of us, then they are goals that we can work for: (1) that we might be full of goodness, (2) that we might be complete in knowledge, and (3) that we might be competent to instruct one another. At that point we will have begun to be a mature church, having attained "to the whole measure of the fullness of Christ" (Eph. 4:13).

225

Paul's Priestly Ministry

Romans 15:15–16

I have written you quite boldly on some points, as if to remind you of them again, because of the grace God gave me to be a minister of Christ Jesus to the Gentiles with the priestly duty of proclaiming the gospel of God, so that the Gentiles might become an offering acceptable to God, sanctified by the Holy Spirit.

Christianity has only one priest, Jesus Christ. He alone has made atonement for our sins by his death on the cross, and he alone makes intercession for us before the Father. That is why the church's preachers, pastors, or ministers are never called priests in the New Testament.

In light of this we find something very striking in our text. Here Paul is writing of his ministry to the Gentiles, a ministry given to him by Jesus Christ, and he speaks of his "*priestly* duty." This is striking because the words are not used in that way elsewhere and also because in other places Paul explicitly disclaims interest in what are usually thought of as normal ministerial functions. An example is baptism. He told the Corinthians he did not baptize often and that he was glad he had only baptized a few persons in their city (1 Cor. 1:14–17).

He is making a contrast between what priests are normally thought of as doing and what he was actually called to do as minister to the Gentiles. Priests stand between men and God and offer sacrifices. The priestly duty to which Paul refers is to proclaim the gospel.

The Curse of Priestcraft

It has been a misfortune for the church that its ministers ever got the idea that they were anything else but preachers.

What happened in church history is something like what occurred in Israel in regard to the people's wanting a king. In the early days of Israel's history, after the conquest of Canaan, the land was ruled by judges whom God raised up when leadership was required. But the people began to look around at the other nations who had kings, and they decided they wanted one too. They approached Samuel, who was a judge at that time, and said to him, "Appoint a king to lead us, such as all the other nations have" (1 Sam. 8:5). This idea displeased Samuel, but the Lord agreed to their request, and headstrong Saul became the first of many wayward and even oppressive kings of Israel.

Not content with the role God had given them to teach and so guide the church and its ministry, ministers in the early church looked around at the nearby pagan religions, which had priests, and decided that they wanted to be priests too. So they began to wear special clerical clothes and lord it over the laity. What is worse, they began to think of the communion table as an altar and the observance of the Lord's Supper as a sacrifice in which the body and blood of Jesus were to be repeatedly offered up for sins. From this terrible error came the mass.

Moreover, the clergy taught that they were necessary for the offering to be rightly made and thus that salvation was impossible for anyone without their priestly mediation. The heresy of sacramental salvation was the sad result.

Robert Haldane wrote, "The bread of the Lord's table at length became the body of Christ in a literal sense; the table on which it lay became the altar; the teachers became the priests who offered the sacrifice of the mass; and the contributions of Christians became offerings. In all these things, and innumerable others, the figurative sense has been, by a gross imagination and the artifice of Satan, turned into a literal sense, to the utter subversion of truth."[1]

What a difference between this and what Paul says of his priestly ministry in our passage. Charles Hodge described the contrast this way: "In this beautiful passage we see the nature of the only priesthood which belongs to the Christian ministry. It is not their office to make atonement for sin, or to offer a propitiatory sacrifice to God, but by the preaching of the gospel to bring

1. Robert Haldane, *An Exposition of the Epistle to the Romans* (MacDill AFB: MacDonald Publishing Company, 1958), p. 620.

men, by the influence of the Holy Spirit, to offer themselves as a living sacrifice, holy and acceptable to God."[2]

The Nature of the Ministry

These verses teach that the nature of the Christian ministry is to proclaim the gospel.

The purpose of a court trial is to learn the truth and deal with its consequences. Therefore, witnesses are required to promise to tell "the truth, the whole truth, and nothing but the truth." But since it is often difficult to get at the truth, there are such things as physical evidence, depositions, testimony by experts, and cross examinations. The task of the minister is likewise to proclaim "the gospel, the whole gospel, and nothing but the gospel." But so many other things get in the way and obscure the gospel or its proclamation that in many cases this essential task of teaching is just not done.

Let's follow the outline suggested by the swearing in of trial witnesses and talk about "the gospel, the whole gospel, and nothing but the gospel."

1. *The gospel.* The gospel is good news, which is what the Greek word *euangelion* means. Nothing should be easier to proclaim than that, we think. But let's ask a few questions. First, what is the nature of this good news? Answer: that God has provided a way for us to be saved from sin through the work of Jesus Christ. Now let's explore that: What is sin? The Westminster Shorter Catechism answers this way: "Sin is any want of conformity unto, or transgression of, the law of God." What, then, is the law of God? To answer that question we have to explore the meaning of the Ten Commandments, which is what Jesus seems to have done with the rich young man who came to him, asking, "Good teacher, what must I do to inherit eternal life?" (Mark 10:17), and who later went away sorrowful.

This is also what Paul has done in Romans. He has explored the nature and extent of sin in great detail so we might be able to understand the nature of God's saving grace toward us in Jesus Christ.

The point is that although the gospel is a simple thing, explaining it takes time. But this is what many of today's churches, even evangelical churches, fail to do. It is why David Wells talks about the death of evangelicalism in America in *No Place for Truth: Or Whatever Happened to Evangelical Theology.*"[3] Our churches may appear prosperous on the surface, but thousands of them are dead or dying because in a practical sense they have abandoned truth.

2. *The whole gospel.* Paul also made it his aim to preach the whole gospel. This is very important. I have pointed out that the nature of the gospel is often missed because we do not deal with such underlying matters as sin as

2. Charles Hodge, *A Commentary on Romans* (Edinburgh and Carlisle, Pa.: The Banner of Truth Trust, 1972), p. 439. Original edition 1835.

3. David F. Wells, *No Place for Truth: Or Whatever Happened to Evangelical Theology* (Grand Rapids: Wm. B. Eerdmans Publishing Company, 1993).

defined by God's law. But even when we have done that and have gone on to speak of the work of Christ in saving us from God's just punishment for our sin, we still have not explained the whole gospel. For the good news is not just that God has made a way for us to be saved from sin's penalty but that God is also saving us from practicing sin.

In other words, sanctification is part of what is going on in salvation. Sanctification is not justification. Justification is an act; sanctification is a process. They must be distinguished, but they cannot be separated—you cannot have one without the other. Therefore, if a person claims to be saved but is not going on in the Christian life, that claim, however sincerely stated, is presumption. Jesus said that we must take up our cross daily and follow him (Luke 9:23). He said, "He who stands firm to the end will be saved" (Matt. 10:22). According to the Bible, Jesus died to save us *from* our sin, not *in* it.

This too is what Paul has been teaching in Romans. And not just that. He has taught a Christian view of history and the need to apply the whole of the gospel to the whole of life, which is what chapters 12–16 are about. When we begin to think along these lines, we soon discover that "the priestly duty of proclaiming the gospel of God" is not easy.

3. *Nothing but the gospel.* There is more than one way to tell a lie, and one way is to tell the truth but add to it falsely. The same thing is true of the gospel. The great Christian apologist C. S. Lewis remarked that the greatest heresies in the church have not been the denials of Christian truth so much as they have been additions to it, what Lewis called "Christ and . . .": Christ *and* Buddha, faith *and* works, grace *and* merit, Christianity *and* secularism, and so forth.[4]

In the letter to the Galatians Paul was dealing with people who wanted to add the keeping of the law to faith as a way of justification. He said that if they did that, Christ would be of "no value" to them at all (Gal. 5:2). He said that if anyone preached a gospel of "Jesus and . . . ," this would be another gospel—a false gospel—and that he should be condemned.

The positive expression of what Paul was doing appears in his words to the believers at Corinth: "When I came to you, brothers, I did not come with eloquence or superior wisdom as I proclaimed to you the testimony about God. For I resolved to know nothing while I was with you except Jesus Christ and him crucified" (1 Cor. 2:1). This does not mean that Paul only preached so-called salvation messages or that he failed to relate his teaching to what the Corinthians were dealing with as part of their culture. But he did not attempt to add to Christ's work. He preached Christ and Christ only.

Tact and Boldness

There is an amazing balance in what Paul is doing here between what we would call tact and what he calls boldness. Having stated the gospel fully and

---

4. C. S. Lewis, *The Screwtape Letters* (New York: Macmillan, 1961), p. 126.

applied it forcefully, especially in urging the so-called strong Christians to bear with those they considered to be weaker and urging the weaker Christians not to condemn the strong, Paul apparently sensed that the Roman believers might be offended by his frankness. So he acknowledges that he has written "quite boldly on some points," possibly in an offensive manner, yet tactfully, too. For he not only admits his boldness but explains it in the context of merely reminding the Roman Christians of what they probably already knew.

We learn from this that although it is important to preach "the gospel, the whole gospel, and nothing but the gospel," it is not necessary to do it offensively. We should always be respectful of the people to whom we speak or write.

We also learn from this passage that we need to be reminded of these core doctrines. If Paul is serious about reminding these believers at Rome, then they were already well instructed. Nevertheless, they still needed reminding, as we all do because we tend to forget God's truth or at least neglect it and let it slide away from our active minds. We always need to stir one another up to remembrance (2 Peter 1:12–15).

The Goal of the Ministry

It's important to note in this text how Paul writes about the goal of his ministry. We hear a great deal about goal-setting these days: Companies set goals, individuals set goals, and even churches spend time analyzing the precise nature of their work and state objectives and goals. Paul's goal is this: "so that the Gentiles might become an offering acceptable to God, sanctified by the Holy Spirit."

Paul is not making a formal argument at this point. He does not give us an Old Testament quotation to nail his point down, as he has done many times before. But I suspect, because of his use of the language of sacrifice, that he has Isaiah 66:20 in mind. Isaiah was writing about those who "will proclaim [God's] glory among the nations" (*proclaim* is the very word Paul uses), and he concludes, "They will bring all your brothers, from all the nations, to my holy mountain in Jerusalem as an offering to the Lord."

That is what Paul says God has called him to do: to proclaim the gospel "so that the Gentiles might become an offering acceptable to God, sanctified by the Holy Spirit."

Gentiles were considered to be unclean by Jews, but, according to Paul, they are to become an offering sanctified to God by the Holy Spirit. The word *sanctified* means to be set apart to God and dedicated or consecrated to him. Paul said this of them at the very beginning of the letter: "To all in Rome who are loved by God and called to be saints" (Rom. 1:7). How are people sanctified? The first way is simply by their becoming Christians, for all who become Christians also become saints, since Christians are by definition people set apart for God. It is because of this that Paul can write inclusively of the saints at Corinth (1 Cor. 1:2), the saints throughout Achaia (2 Cor. 1:1), the saints in Ephesus (Eph. 1:1), and so on.

The second way is by their offering their bodies to God "as living sacrifices," which is what Paul urged at the start of this final section of the letter (see Rom. 12:1). Either meaning would fit the context here. But we sense, just because this is the practical portion of the book, that what he has in mind is a dedicated, effective, hardworking, God-glorifying Gentile Christian church.

The Sufficiency of the Word of God

How is all of this to happen? How are the Gentiles (or Jews, or anyone else for that matter) going to become an offering that is acceptable to God, sanctified by the Holy Spirit? By proclaiming the gospel.

Do we really believe that God has given us what we need in the Bible, or do we think we have to supplement it with other man-made things? Do we need sociological techniques to do evangelism; psychology, psychiatry, and counseling for Christian growth; extrabiblical signs or miracles for guidance; and political tools for achieving social progress and reform? To judge from their programs, this is exactly what many evangelicals and evangelical churches believe and are practicing. But it is precisely why they are so weak and why "evangelical" religion is failing.

The Word of God is sufficient in all areas; it is able to do all we need it to do and are commissioned to do as Christians.

1. *Evangelism.* The Word of God is sufficient for evangelism. Indeed, it is the only thing that works in evangelism. Everything else—captivating music, personal testimonies, emotional appeals, even coming forward to make a commitment to Jesus Christ—all that is at best supplementary. And if it is used or depended upon apart from the faithful preaching and teaching of the Word of God, the "conversions" that result are spurious conversions, which is to say that those who respond do not actually become Christians. Worldly methods work, but the results will be worldly as well. The only way the Holy Spirit regenerates lost men and women is through the Bible. Peter said, "You have been born again, not of perishable seed, but of imperishable, through the living and enduring word of God" (1 Peter 1:23).

2. *Sanctification.* When evangelicals think of sanctification today, most of them think of either of two things: a method ("Here are four steps to sanctification; do this and you will be holy"), or an experience ("You need a second work of grace, a baptism of the Holy Spirit"). Paul's approach was to teach Christians what has been done for them by God in their salvation, because if they know that and understand it, then they will know that they cannot go back to being what they were before and they will get on with being Christians. The only rational thing for them to do will be to go forward in the Christian life.

3. *Guidance.* All the guidance we need in the Christian life has been provided in the Bible. It tells us how we are to live and what we are to do to please God. If there is something we want to know or think we need to know that is not in the Bible—what job we should take, whom we should marry, where we should live—there is a sense in which it doesn't matter as long as we are obeying what God teaches about living a godly life. This does not mean that God does not have a detailed plan for our lives. He does. But it does mean that we do not have to know this plan in advance. Indeed, we cannot know it. What we need to know is what God has told us in the Bible.

4. *Social reform.* We are concerned about social renewal and reform today and rightly so, because we live in a declining culture and want to see the lordship of Jesus acknowledged and justice and righteousness prevail. We want to see the poor relieved of suffering. We want to see broken relationships healed. What is needed is not more government programs or increased emphasis on social work, but first and above all the teaching and practice of the Word of God.

This is proved by what happened in Geneva, Switzerland, in the sixteenth century through the ministry of John Calvin. The city was a moral disgrace. It was notorious for its riots, gambling, indecent dancing, drunkenness, adultery, and other vices. People would run around the streets naked, singing bawdy songs and blaspheming God. The governing council of the city was distressed and passed laws designed to restrain vice and remedy the situation, but nothing worked. Public morals continued to decline.

Calvin came to Geneva in August 1536, was dismissed two and a half years later, and was recalled in 1541. He had no money, no influence, and no weapon but the Word of God. But he preached from the Bible every day, and as he did, under the power of his preaching, the city began to change. As the Genevan people acquired knowledge of God's Word and allowed it to influence their behavior, their city became a model city from which the gospel spread to the rest of Europe, Great Britain, and the New World. Geneva was cleaned up physically. Beggars were removed from the streets, but a hospital and poorhouse were provided for them, and they were well run. Education was offered for all classes of people, poor as well as rich, and new industries flourished. There has probably never been a better example of extensive moral and social reform than the transformation of Geneva under John Calvin, and it was accomplished almost entirely by the preaching of God's Word.

The reason, of course, is that the Bible truly is the Word of God and thus carries with it the power and compelling authority of God himself. And that is why Paul made it his business to proclaim the gospel, and why we should too. What God does today he does by his Word. Therefore, it is our priestly duty to proclaim it to a needy world.

226

Paul's Glory

Romans 15:17–22

Therefore I glory in Christ Jesus in my service to God. I will not venture to speak of anything except what Christ has accomplished through me in leading the Gentiles to obey God by what I have said and done—by the power of signs and miracles, through the power of the Spirit. So from Jerusalem all the way around to Illyricum, I have fully proclaimed the gospel of Christ. It has always been my ambition to preach the gospel where Christ was not known, so that I would not be building on someone else's foundation. Rather, as it is written:

> *"Those who were not told about him will see*
> *and those who have not heard will understand."*

That is why I have often been hindered from coming to you.

I do not know how old Paul was when he wrote his letter to the Romans, but to judge from what we are told about him in Acts he must have been coming to the end of both his life and his ministry. Shortly after writing Romans he took his final journey to Jerusalem, was arrested, and was sent as a prisoner to Rome, where eventually he died.

Paul may have had an extensive ministry in Spain after he first came to Rome, after a release from an initial imprisonment.[1] But whether that was the case or not, in this passage of Romans Paul seems to be looking back over the greater part of his lifetime career as a missionary and evaluating it from a spiritual perspective. We know from his letters to the Corinthians that his career had been difficult. He had experienced hardships, threats, beatings, dangers, and rejections (see 1 Cor. 4:9–13; 2 Cor. 4:8–12, 6:3–10, 11:23–29). But he did not judge what he had done to be a failure. On the contrary, in these verses he actually boasts about what God had accomplished through him "in leading the Gentiles to obey God" (v. 18). He uses the words *glory* in verse 17 ("I glory in Christ Jesus") and *ambition* in verse 20 ("It has always been my ambition to preach the gospel where Christ was not known").

Glorying in Jesus Only

At first glance this seems prideful, and we have been taught that pride in any form is wrong. Yet it is not as simple as that. There is sinful pride, but there is also a proper kind of pride, not in what we are or have done by ourselves naturally, but as Christian people who are pleased with what God does through us. This can get distorted and destructive because of sin, but a right kind of pride is helpful—and even necessary—if it is focused properly. Paul had the right kind of pride because he was boasting in Christ and not in his own personal accomplishments or talents.

There was a time in his life when Paul had gloried in his accomplishments, but that was before he met Christ. He wrote about it in Philippians: "If anyone else thinks he has reasons to put confidence in the flesh, I have more: circumcised on the eighth day, of the people of Israel, of the tribe of Benjamin, a Hebrew of Hebrews; in regard to the law, a Pharisee; as for zeal, persecuting the church; as for legalistic righteousness, faultless" (Phil. 3:4–6). That was an impressive list of assets from a human point of view. But when Paul met Jesus on the road to Damascus he learned that these worldly accomplishments did not add up to righteousness before God. They could not earn God's approval. Moreover, his pride in them had been keeping him from faith in Jesus Christ as his Savior.

When Paul saw what he had been doing he wrote those things off as mere garbage, choosing to trust Jesus Christ alone. He told the Philippians, "But whatever was to my profit I now consider loss for the sake of Christ. What is more, I consider everything a loss compared to the surpassing greatness of knowing Christ Jesus my Lord" (Phil. 3:7–8).

Paul did not glory in his natural abilities, either. We know that he had a powerful intellect. The Book of Romans and his other writings are ample proof of that. We know that he could speak persuasively. His speeches pre-

---

1. I will discuss this probability in the next study.

served in Acts give an idea of how tactful, wise, informed, adaptive, and persuasive his speech was. He was the equal of any Greek orator. In fact, he was superior to them, because he believed what he was saying.

Donald Grey Barnhouse wrote, "Paul's greatest talent was his ability to enter a completely pagan city which practiced devil worship and gather a group of transformed believers in the name of Christ. He then hovered over them in prayer and, by constant admonition, lifted them from the most corrupt stratum of heathenism to the highest level of Christian godliness and morality."[2] That was a tremendous achievement based on great talent. It could be said that in time the gospel seeds Paul sowed overthrew the Roman Empire and transformed the European continent. But Paul did not glory in his talents any more than in his amazing accomplishments.

Instead, he gloried in Jesus Christ. He told the Corinthians, "When I came to you, brothers, I did not come with eloquence or superior wisdom as I proclaimed to you the testimony about God. For I resolved to know nothing while I was with you except Jesus Christ and him crucified. I came to you in weakness and fear, and with much trembling. My message and my preaching were not with wise and persuasive words, but with a demonstration of the Spirit's power, so that your faith might not rest on men's wisdom, but on God's power" (1 Cor. 2:1–5). Paul would have loved to sing this hymn by John Bowring:

> In the cross of Christ I glory,
> Towering ov'r the wrecks of time;
> All the light of sacred story
> Gathers round its head sublime.

Yet Paul also gloried in what Christ had done through him. The most glorious thing of all is that Jesus was able to accomplish these things through such a person as Paul. The wonder is that he could take this proud, stubborn, self-righteous murderer of God's people and turn him into the greatest pioneer missionary the world has ever seen. Paul could never take that glory to himself. Yet the more he was able to accomplish, the greater was the glory that went to Christ.

God's Use of Little Things

That should be true of you and me too, which is where this study becomes practical. Earlier I mentioned Paul's claim that he had not depended on wisdom or eloquence when he preached the gospel to the Corinthians, though he had plenty of both, because he did not want the Corinthians' faith to rest on human abilities but on the power of God. He said nearly the same thing in regard to their own mostly undistinguished backgrounds and abilities, as

2. Donald Grey Barnhouse, *The Apostle of the Gospel*, booklet 90 in the series of radio messages on the book of Romans (Philadelphia: The Bible Study Hour, 1960), p. 7.

if to point out that it was precisely through their limitations that God was to be most glorified:

> Brothers, think of what you were when you were called. Not many of you were wise by human standards; not many were influential; not many were of noble birth. But God chose the foolish things of the world to shame the wise; God chose the weak things of the world to shame the strong. He chose the lowly things of this world and the despised things—and the things that are not—to nullify the things that are, so that no one may boast before him. It is because of him that you are in Christ Jesus, who has become for us wisdom from God—that is, our righteousness, holiness and redemption. Therefore, as it is written: "Let him who boasts boast in the Lord."
>
> 1 Corinthians 1:26–31

God is glorified in using us. We are the most unprofitable of servants, even if we have great natural talents. But if we will offer ourselves to God as his slaves, he will use us and will bring glory to himself even through our natural human foolishness, our weaknesses, or our lack of worldly status. And that will be our glory too!

Think of the Reformers, and what God did through them. Luther was a portly little monk. Calvin was what we would call an ivory tower bookworm and theologian. God changed the world through those men. He used another little monk, known as "Little Bilney," to win Hugh Latimer to Christ, and Latimer had a tremendous Reformation influence. William Wilberforce was a cripple, but God used him to free the slaves throughout the British empire. D. L. Moody was only an uneducated shoe salesmen, but one day Moody heard a preacher say, "The world has yet to see what God can do through one man who is entirely surrendered to him." In his heart Moody said, "By God's grace I will be that man."

That is what is required, and it is what Paul did. It is what made him such a powerful ambassador for Christ in the ancient Greek and Roman world.

What Paul Accomplished

In verses 18–20 Paul tells what he accomplished at Christ's direction, by his power, and for his glory. It is not what Jesus is doing with you necessarily. It is personal to Paul. But it is impressive and is a suggestion of what God might be able to do through you, if you truly give your life to him. There are a number of specific points to notice.

1. *The scope of Paul's evangelistic work.* In verse 19 Paul describes the scope of his work, writing, "So from Jerusalem all the way around to Illyricum, I have fully proclaimed the gospel of Christ." Students of Paul's letter have pointed to a problem at this point, but looking into it only gives us greater insight into Paul's accomplishment. The problem is that, so far as we know, Paul did not do evangelistic work in Jerusalem, though he visited it on several

occasions, and he did not evangelize Illyricum. Illyricum refers to the region we know as the former Yugoslavia (Bosnia, Herzegovina, Montenegro, Serbia, Dalmatia) and Albania.

The solution seems to be that Paul is saying not that he evangelized these areas, but that he evangelized from one to the other. It would be as if someone said that he had traveled all over the United States from Canada to Mexico. He would not be saying that he had traveled in either Canada or Mexico but throughout the land in between.

In other words, Paul had evangelized Turkey, Macedonia, and Greece, as described in Acts. He started out in the Near East and pushed on north and west as quickly as he could to establish sound churches in each region. He was obeying the Great Commission as he had received it from Jesus Christ. It was in the furtherance of this goal that he was planning to visit Rome and, if possible, the regions beyond.

The Great Commission was not given only to Paul, of course, but to us. What are you doing to further it, personally or by helping others to go where you cannot?

2. *The nature of Paul's evangelistic work.* In verse 20 Paul gives a glimpse into the unique nature of his work, which was "to preach the gospel where Christ was not known, so that I should not be building on someone else's foundation." He supports this in verse 21 by quoting from Isaiah:

Rather, as it is written:

> "Those who were not told about him will see
> and those who have not heard will understand."[3]

This is not every Christian's calling, nor every minister's. Some are called to build on foundations already laid. Paul pointed that out in 1 Corinthians, where he compared the differing ministries of himself and Apollos, saying, "I planted the seed, Apollos watered it, but God made it grow" (1 Cor. 3:6). My own ministry has had some pioneering elements, but it has consisted largely in watering what others have planted or building on foundations that have been previously laid. My challenge is to build well on what has preceded me.

---

3. Leon Morris points out that this is the last of sixty-four quotations from the Old Testament in Romans, according to the list given in the United Bible Society's Greek New Testament. It is hard to number Paul's quotations accurately, because he sometimes quotes exactly, at other times freely, and at other times only by a passing allusion to a text. The boundary line between a free quotation and the expression of one's thoughts in scriptural language is not easy to pin down. Still, as Morris states, "No one will question the fact that Romans is exceedingly rich in quotations from Scripture." Going by the UBS list, Romans has more quotations than any other New Testament book. The next is Matthew, which is much longer and has only 61. (Leon Morris, *The Epistle to the Romans* [Grand Rapids: Wm. B. Eerdmans Publishing Company, and Leicester, England: Inter-Varsity Press, 1988], p. 515, footnote 108).

At the same time, we need to remember that Paul's ambition has been an important stimulus and challenge to many missionaries who have made it their ambition to take the gospel to new areas. I have friends who want to get into remote areas of the former Soviet Union so that Christ may be preached there to those who do not know him. Others want to reach far into China, and some are doing so. Still others are learning the language of remote jungle tribes so that they can translate the Bible into those languages. That is the ambition Paul had. So even though we may not all be called to do it—real pioneers are usually few in number—we should nevertheless support their efforts whenever possible.

I am reminded of David Livingstone's reply when he was presenting himself to the London Missionary Society and they asked him where he wanted to go. He answered, "Anywhere, as long as it is forward." After he reached Africa he recorded his impressions, saying that he was haunted by the smoke of a thousand villages stretching off into the distance. How can any true Christian be at ease in Zion when there are billions of people who have yet to hear of Jesus Christ?

3. *The power of Paul's evangelistic work.* In verse 19 Paul stated that his missionary work was carried out "by the power of signs and miracles, through the power of the Spirit." According to nearly all commentators, "signs and miracles" is not the best translation of Paul's words. Signs *are* miracles. So the contrast is not between signs and miracles but between two different ways of looking at what is miraculous. The right idea is conveyed by "signs and wonders." In biblical language a sign is a miracle that has significance through pointing beyond itself to truth about God or the gospel. All Jesus' miracles recorded in John are signs in this sense. A wonder is the same event regarded from the point of view of the awe it evokes in a human observer.

There is a fairly popular movement today that claims that doing miracles is the proper and perhaps only truly effective way to do evangelism. It is called the signs and wonders movement, and it is associated with the name of John Wimber, a former professor at Fuller Theological Seminary, and the Vineyard churches that he founded.[4]

Paul only used these words in two other places: 2 Corinthians 12:12, where he used them of himself, calling miracles "the things that mark an apostle"; and 2 Thessalonians 2:9, where they have to do with the work of "the lawless one" who is the Antichrist. These passages teach two important things. First, in themselves signs and wonders prove nothing, for they can be done by demonic powers as well as by God. Second, in the New Testament miracles are associated with apostles ("things that mark an apostle") and were therefore meant to authenticate the apostolic message in days before there was a New Testament. Today the New Testament is our apostolic authority.

---

4. See "The False Religion of Signs and Wonders" (Romans 10:6–7) in James Montgomery Boice, *Romans*, vol. 3, *God and History: Romans 9–11* (Grand Rapids: Baker Book House, 1993), pp. 1181–88.

That doesn't mean that God never does miracles today but that we are not to seek miracles as a way of doing evangelism. All this does is get us away from doing what is really important and effective—teaching the Bible as the Word of God.

Moreover, it is the teaching of the Bible that alone accomplishes the true miracles God and we desire. The miracles that need to be done today are not healing the sick or raising the dead, but bringing dead souls to life to believe on Jesus Christ as Lord and Savior and then to be changed by him. Someone once asked a preacher whether he could turn water into wine as Jesus did. He answered that he could do something better than that. He told about an alcoholic who had neglected his family but who had been brought to Christ by hearing the gospel. The preacher said, "We didn't turn water into wine, but we turned whisky into milk for his babies."

So it has always been. As Christ's people have taken the gospel to the farthest reaches of the world, pagans living in darkest spiritual night have been brought to gospel day, the despairing have been given a sure and lasting hope, liars have been turned into men and women of truth, people of loose morals have become righteous and upright, and those who have been lazy with no real goals in life have been captured for Jesus and have lived industrious lives for his glory. This has fulfilled Jesus' words when he said, "Anyone who has faith in me will do what I have been doing. He will do even greater things than these, because I am going to the Father" (John 14:12).

If even the angels in heaven rejoice whenever a sinner comes to Christ (Luke 15:10), should it not be our goal and glory to work faithfully and industriously to see it happen too?

To God Alone Be Glory

I close by reminding you that although the conversion of the lost is our glory to the extent that we participate by carrying the gospel to them, it is ours only because it is Jesus Christ's first of all, because he is at work within us. Paul said, "I glory *in Christ Jesus*" (Rom. 15:17).

Remember that great scene in Revelation 4:10–11 where the saints lay their crowns before the throne and say:

> "You are worthy, our Lord and God,
>   to receive glory and honor and power,
> for you created all things,
>   and by your will they were created
>   and have their being."

The saints have crowns because of what they have achieved. They have been faithful to Christ, they have fought the good fight, they have triumphed by the blood of the Lamb and by their testimony. That is their glory. But they do not take that glory to themselves. Rather, like Paul, they give it back to God by laying their crowns at his feet.

One day you and I will have a chance to do it too. God grant that what we give him in that day might be bright and glorious, to the praise of his amazing grace.

227

Onward to Spain!

Romans 15:23–24

But now that there is no more place for me to work in these regions, and since I have been longing for many years to see you, I plan to do so when I go to Spain. I hope to visit you while passing through and to have you assist me on my journey there, after I have enjoyed your company for a while.

If a person works for the city or federal government, she might retire after twenty years of service. A man serving in the armed forces might also retire after twenty years. In other work retirement is generally fixed by age. But what about retirement from Christian service or from merely being a Christian? I want to suggest that for a Christian retirement never comes, since we are to live as Christians and serve others until Jesus returns or we die.

David Brainard, the friend of Jonathan Edwards, died of tuberculosis at a young age. But even on his deathbed he rejoiced that he was still able to teach a young Indian boy how to read the Bible. Donald Grey Barnhouse, one of my mentors, said that it was his intention to keep on working until God retired him permanently. And so he did. God took him to heaven shortly after he had completed his studies of the Book of Romans.

Paul had an impressive list of missionary accomplishments, sufficient for many lifetimes, but he had no intention of settling down into a comfortable retirement. Our text tells us that instead of stopping with what was past, Paul wanted to press on west from the site of his present endeavors in Greece to bring the gospel to far-distant Spain.

His attitude reminds us of David Livingstone's response to the London Missionary Society when they asked him where he wanted to go as a missionary: "Anywhere, as long as it is forward."

Forgetting What Is Behind

The passage in which Paul spells out his missionary plans and desires for the future begins at verse 23, but this is one of those places where Paul seems to break off what he is saying without finishing his sentence. The New International Version tries to smooth out the difficulty by adding "I plan to do so" to verse 24, but those words are not in the original Greek text.[1]

The striking thing about verse 23 is that it is a virtual repetition of what Paul said in Romans 1:13, which may be why he breaks off as he does: "I do not want you to be unaware, brothers, that I planned many times to come to you (but have been prevented from doing so until now) in order that I might have a harvest among you, just as I have had among the other Gentiles." In chapter 15 he seems to be saying, "Since I have completed my work in these regions and since I have always wanted to visit you who are in Rome. . . . But you know that, because I have told you that already." What he says then is that although he had often wanted to spend some profitable time with them, he did not want to settle down in Rome permanently but wanted to make it only a stopping-off place on an anticipated fourth missionary journey to Spain.

1. F. Godet provides the most helpful summary of the variations, pointing out that there are three main versions of verse 23: (1) The Textus Receptus and the Byzantine manuscripts add the words "I will come to you" and "for" to the middle of verse 24 so that the passage as a whole reads: "But now that there is no more place for me to work in these regions, and since I have been longing for many years to come to see you, when I go to Spain I will come to you, for I hope to visit you . . ." The major problem is that the words "I will come to you" are absent from the other major texts. (2) The Alexandrine manuscript uses participles ("having no more place" and "having the desire") to subordinate everything before verse 25, so that the main clause becomes "I am on my way to Jerusalem." Verse 24 is treated as a parenthesis. This is a bit awkward, but it would be a possibility except for the word *now (de)* at the start of verse 25, which marks a new beginning. Unfortunately for the Alexandrine solution, the *now* is in all the other manuscripts. (3) The Latin version (supported by the Syriac), which Godet prefers, reads, "Having no more place in these parts . . . but having the desire to see you . . . , when I go into Spain, I hope to see you in passing." But again, this is not the reading of the more ancient and thus presumably more authoritative Greek texts. It is probably best to admit that the sentence just breaks off at the end of verse 23.

Pressing On to What Is Before

Scholars do not agree on whether Paul ever got to Spain. Some read into the pastoral letters that Paul was imprisoned twice in Rome ("The Lord will rescue me from every evil attack," 2 Tim. 4:18). Then Paul could have gone to Spain after his first imprisonment, returned to Rome to report on his activities, and then been arrested again and martyred. Since we know that he was martyred in Rome, if he was imprisoned there only once, he obviously couldn't have gone to Spain.

The only evidence that shows that Paul might have been in Spain are two small non-Spanish records. Clement of Rome, one of the apostolic fathers, writes in *Epistle to the Corinthians* that Paul reached "the limits of the west." He does not use the word *Spain,* but "the limits of the west" would have meant Spain to a Roman, which Clement was. The other record is the Muratorian Canon, which mentions "the departure of Paul from the city on his journey to Spain." These are interesting references, but they fall short of proof.

Regardless of whether Paul actually made it to Spain, we can learn from his plans to go there. Ray Stedman makes several valuable points about these verses:[2]

1. *A place for planning.* Some Christians act as if believers should sail through life on automatic pilot, expecting God to direct their lives in a supernatural way apart from any direct involvement from them. They think planning is wrong. But, of course, Paul did not think like that. He was open to God's special guidance, as we learn from the accounts of his missionary journeys in Acts. He obeyed God's leading. But he also made plans, and one of those plans, which was quite important in his thinking, was to carry the gospel to the far corners of the known Roman world—to Spain. Paul had planned to go to Spain for some time, and he was still pursuing this goal at the time of his writing to the Romans.

2. *The need for flexibility in planning.* Although Paul made plans he was also flexible in the sense that he did not have a timetable. Stedman says that "he went according to the way God opened the doors." He planned to go in a certain direction. He kept that clearly in his mind, but "he did not tell God how or when it had to be."[3] Paul subordinated his plans to God's overall direction, and he did not chafe when the specifics of God's plan or God's timing varied from his own.

3. *The importance of persistence.* Paul did not abandon his plans when they were delayed by God but instead persisted in them. Stedman writes, "He had set his heart on Rome and Spain, and he was going there. No matter how long it took, he kept plodding steadily toward the goal."[4] We do not know if he ever got there, but the evangelization of Spain remained his heart's desire.

2. See Ray C. Stedman, *From Guilt to Glory,* vol. 2, *Reveling in God's Salvation* (Portland, Oreg.: Multnomah Press, 1978), pp. 204–5.

3. Ibid.

4. Ibid., p. 205.

Someone will ask if, in that case, it might not have been wrong for Paul to have made plans to reach that country since, if he did not get there, God obviously did not intend for him to do so. It would mean that Paul's plans were not God's plans, that Paul was in error. Well, if Paul did not get to Spain, it obviously was not God's plan for him to reach Spain. But I do not think it follows that he was wrong to have made this an important missionary goal. If that were the case, it would be wrong for us to plan anything since, as Robert Burns once wrote, "The best laid plans of mice and men gang aft aglee."[5] Our plans frequently fail. I know people who have planned to go to the far reaches of the former Soviet Union but have not been able to get there, at least not yet. I do not believe it is wrong for them to have made those plans. It is better to dream great dreams for God, even if they are not fully realized, than to dream no dreams at all. One thing is certain, unless we see visions, dream dreams, and make plans, there will be no great steps forward in the work of the gospel.

Help on the Outward Journey

Ray Stedman adds another point to what he said about Paul's planning: In his missionary work Paul always tried to work with a team, never alone. We know from the pastoral letters that by the time he reached Rome most of his pioneer team had been left behind—Timothy in Ephesus (1 Tim. 1:3) and Titus in Crete (Titus 1:5). At one point of his imprisonment only Luke was with Paul (2 Tim. 4:11), but even then he wrote to Timothy to urge him to come to Rome and to bring Mark with him. Here in his letter to the Romans he seems to be recruiting the members of this important church to be what we would call a home support team.

How tactfully he does it. First he tells them that he is only going to be passing through. He wants to be able to enjoy their company for a while, but he is not going to stay with them at their expense or take charge of the Roman church. His sights were focused elsewhere.

Second, he wants them to assist him on his journey. The Greek lexicographers tell us that *assist* (literally, "*being brought forward* on my journey by you") is a verb that can be used of a variety of helps, such as food, money, companions, arranging for means of travel, and other matters.[6] The verb could be restricted to items of common courtesy, like prayers and best wishes, but it also allows for more substantial help, which Paul would need and for which he is very gently hinting. Up to this point he had been supported by his home church at Antioch in Syria, but Spain would be too far away for him to receive any tangible help from Syria. Therefore, he is suggesting that

5. Robert Burns, "To a Louse," *The Poetical Works of Robert Burns,* ed. J. Logie Robertson (London: Oxford University Press, 1958), p. 139.

6. See Leon Morris, *The Epistle to the Romans* (Grand Rapids: Wm. B. Eerdmans Publishing Company, and Leicester, England: Inter-Varsity Press, 1988), p. 515, text and footnote 122.

it would be a great help to him and an encouragement if the Roman church could become his new home base and back him as he presses on westward to the Iberian peninsula.

Some Applications for Us

This passage is bursting with valuable applications.

1. *Our missionary task is not ended until every person in the world has heard of Jesus Christ.* It is easy to get tired in Christian work not only as individuals, but as churches. When we are tired it is easy to think of retirement, dropping out of Christian work. That is not right. If God has left us in this life, it is for us to do something good for him. Otherwise he would simply take us home to glory. And if Jesus has not yet returned, it is because there are people who need to be reached with the gospel of God's grace in Jesus Christ. As long as the church is in the world, we have people to reach and neither your task nor mine is completed.

We sometimes sing, "Arise, O God, and shine in all thy saving might, and prosper each design to spread thy glorious light." But we would be more on target today if we cried, "Arise, O church of God, fulfill God's design." Christians are asleep in the world's soft, embracing arms. They need a trumpet call to missions. They need to be told that the gospel task is not ended until every person in the world has heard of Jesus Christ.

2. *"When an opportunity of serving Christ in one direction is shut up, we ought to turn to another."*[7] I can't think of any better way to state this application than the way the Scottish commentator Robert Haldane stated it in his commentary. We do not know why Paul thought that there was no more place for him to work in Asia, Macedonia, or Greece, perhaps only that he felt he had established churches in the key cities and that this was his particular calling from God. But whatever the reason, the closing of his work in one place merely freed him to begin to think of serving in another.

If you are serving God and your work is not done, keep at it where you are. Don't get restless. But if one opportunity has closed—perhaps the people in your Bible study have moved away or you are no longer serving in the Sunday school or on a church board—look around for something else. The needs are great and the opportunities are endless.

3. *A desire to serve God in some place is not unworthy, for God often works his will in us in such ways.* Some people have the idea that the only way we can be sure of doing God's will is if we are doing something we hate or at least would rather not be doing. What an absurdity that is! Look for what you can do and desire to do it. Paul told Timothy, "If anyone sets his heart on being an overseer, he desires a noble task" (1 Tim. 3:1), thereby endorsing a desire to serve God as an elder in a local church. This does not mean that your desire

---

7. Robert Haldane, *An Exposition of the Epistle to the Romans* (MacDill AFB: MacDonald Publishing Company, 1958), p. 623.

will necessarily prove to have been God's will for you. We do not know whether Paul ever got to Spain. But it does mean that the desire itself is not a bad thing. It is certainly unlikely that you will achieve anything for God if you do not aspire to it.

4. *Although the task remains unchanged, God often accomplishes its fulfillment in ways we do not anticipate or desire.* We have to be flexible, for God's ways are not our ways, and he frequently accomplishes what we rightly desire for him in ways we could not have imagined. Who would have thought that God's way of making the Jewish people into a great nation would have been bringing them to Egypt in the days of Joseph and later allowing them to become slaves? Or who would have supposed that God's way of bringing Paul to Rome would have been through arrest in Jerusalem, followed by a two-year imprisonment at Caesarea, culminating in his appeal to be tried in Rome by Caesar?

God's ways are not our ways. Therefore, be prepared for new things and for unexpected circumstances. Although the task of taking the gospel to the lost remains unchanged, God will probably accomplish your part of it in ways you do not anticipate.

5. *Although God could supply his missionaries' needs miraculously, he usually does so through the gifts of his people.* God is a God of miracles. Paul had not lagged behind the other apostles in being a channel through which God performed miracles (2 Cor. 12:12). God could have provided miraculously for Paul. But he did not. Instead, when Paul started out bringing the gospel to Asia Minor he was supported by the church at Antioch. Later when he went from Macedonia into Greece he was supported by the church at Philippi (Phil. 4:10–19). Here he tactfully looks for support from the church at Rome.

It is no different today. God calls his servants to the missionary task, but he also places a duty to support them on those who remain at home. That is your duty if you have a regular income and are not yourself serving on a foreign or other missionary field. Has God blessed you with material things? Are you provided for financially? Then remember your missionaries. Remember that although God could supply their needs miraculously, he has chosen to do so through you.

6. *The fellowship of the people of God is more to be desired than the friendship of emperors or kings.* Paul was going to Rome, the seat of the great Roman Empire, the home of the Caesars. But Paul was not looking to the great of the world to help him out, nor did he covet their friendship. His friends were the Christians, and he wanted to be with them and be helped on his missionary way by them. Learn from his example. The world will not help you do God's work. It will entice you, use you, betray you, let you down. Only God's people will share your godly desires and vision.

Informal Missionaries

When we study an extraordinary person like Paul it is very easy for us to dissociate his achievements from our own plans or expectations, just because we think of him as being so extraordinary. But although he was certainly that, the vision Paul had and the things he accomplished were not really that extraordinary in these early formative years of Christianity. Paul's dreams were the same as those of the great majority of God's people.

In Edward Gibbon's *Decline and Fall of the Roman Empire* we are told about the rapid expansion of Christianity in the first century of the Christian era.[8] Tertullian, writing around the year A.D. 200, said, "We are but of yesterday, and we have filled every place among you—cities, islands, fortresses, towns, market-places, the very camp, tribes, companies, palace, senate, forum—we have left nothing to you but the temples of your gods."[9] How did that occur? Gibbon suggests that it was because in the early church "it became the most sacred duty of a new convert to diffuse among his friends and relations the inestimable blessing which he had received."[10] In other words, each believer considered himself or herself to be a missionary. Adolf Harnack, the great German church historian, declared, "The most numerous and successful missionaries of the Christian religion were not the regular teachers but Christians themselves, in virtue of their loyalty and courage. . . . It was characteristic of this religion that everyone who seriously confessed the faith proved of service to its propaganda. . . . We cannot hesitate to believe that the great mission of Christianity was in reality accomplished by means of *informal missionaries.*"[11]

That is exactly what we need today. If you see this need, you will press on with the missionary task, because you will know that God has given you important things to do for him today.

---

8. Edward Gibbon, *The Decline and Fall of the Roman Empire* (New York: Harcourt, Brace and Company, 1960), pp. 143–91.

9. Tertullian, *Apology*, chapter 37.

10. Gibbon, *The Decline and Fall of the Roman Empire*, p. 147.

11. Adolf Harnack, *The Mission and Expansion of Christianity in the First Three Centuries* (New York: Harper & Brothers, 1961), p. 368.

228

Christian Giving

Romans 15:25–28

Now, however, I am on my way to Jerusalem in the service of the saints there. For Macedonia and Achaia were pleased to make a contribution for the poor among the saints in Jerusalem. They were pleased to do it, and indeed they owe it to them. For if the Gentiles have shared in the Jews' spiritual blessings, they owe it to the Jews to share with them their material blessings. So after I have completed this task and have made sure that they have received this fruit, I will go to Spain and visit you on the way.

When the subject of charitable giving comes up, most people assume they are generous. They are not naturally that way, of course, since people are selfish by nature. It is part of what it means to be sinners. We need to be taught to be generous, which is why instruction about giving is a necessary part of all well-rounded Christian preaching.

The apostle Paul taught those who were converted to Jesus Christ through his ministry to be generous. Here in Romans 15, as he writes to the believers in Rome to explain why he is being delayed in his plans to come to them on his way to Spain, he refers to what he had done to teach the Christians in the eastern half of the empire about giving. In doing so, he gives us important insights into this vital part of what it means to be a Christian. Paul writes,

"Now, however, I am on my way to Jerusalem in the service of the saints there. For Macedonia and Achaia were pleased to make a contribution for the poor among the saints in Jerusalem. They were pleased to do it, and indeed they owe it to them. For if the Gentiles have shared in the Jews' spiritual blessings, they owe it to the Jews to share with them their material blessings. So after I have completed this task and have made sure that they have received this fruit, I will go to Spain and visit you on the way" (Rom. 15:25–28).

The Gentile Offering

When we study what is said about this offering from the Gentile churches for the saints in Jerusalem, in Acts and in Paul's writings, we learn quickly that it was a very important matter for Paul.

The idea of a special offering seems to have entered his mind when he was in Jerusalem to argue the case for Gentile liberty against attempts by Jewish legalizers to force Gentiles to obey the requirements of the Old Testament ceremonial law. We have two accounts of the council at which this took place, in Acts 15 and Galatians 2. In Galatians Paul reports that his view of the gospel, including the rights of Gentile liberty, was upheld by the other apostles and that they endorsed his Gentile ministry. He says that James, Peter, and John "gave me and Barnabas the right hand of fellowship when they recognized the grace given to me. They agreed that we should go to the Gentiles, and they to the Jews." But he adds, "All they asked was that we should continue to remember the poor, the very thing I was eager to do" (Gal. 2:9–10). In other words, the Jerusalem leaders asked aid for the poor in Jerusalem, and Paul agreed to help.

This was a legitimate request. Jerusalem was a poor area of the world, and the Christians there were very poor. Rome was rich, since the wealth of the world poured into Rome. But in order for wealth to flow to Rome it had to flow from other places, and it most often flowed from the outlying provinces, such as Judea. The provinces were impoverished to enrich the capital.

Then, too, the Christians in Jerusalem may have exacerbated their own problems, though with good will. C. H. Dodd, in his commentary on Romans, suggests that the system of Christian communism that the early church established in Jerusalem had contributed significantly to its poverty: "The Jerusalem church contained from the beginning many poor and few rich. Filled with a sense of their unity as 'brethren,' they instituted a system of partial and voluntary communism. But they carried it out in the economically disastrous way of realizing capital and distributing it as income (Acts 2:44, 45; 4:34–5:5). So far as we can gather, no practical steps were taken to replace the capital thus dissipated; and when hard times came, the community had no reserves of any kind."[1] If this is a right assessment, then the Christians in

1. C. H. Dodd, *The Epistle of Paul to the Romans* (London: Hodder and Stoughton, 1960), p. 220.

Jerusalem were not only poor, they were poorer than most of the other poor people around them. It would be a right response for the richer Gentile congregations elsewhere to help out.

Yet even this does not fully explain Paul's preoccupation with this offering, and Leon Morris is right when he observes that Paul must have seen it as an important symbol of the unity of believers: "Some early Christians held that all converts ought to be circumcised and to live according to the Jewish law; Paul had a continuing controversy with people who held such views. His collection would show that those who rejected this hard-line conservatism were nevertheless bound to Jewish believers in ties of genuine Christian love."[2]

Perhaps they would also show the Jerusalem leaders that Paul had been successful in his missionary work. This would not be the noblest of motives, but Paul may have had a bit of pride in wanting to collect this offering and accompany it to Jerusalem himself to show Peter, James, and John and the others how he had honored his agreement to help out and even demonstrate how bountifully he had been able to do it.[3]

How Paul Viewed This Offering

Whatever Paul's motivation for asking might have been, it was right that Christians of means should have assisted those who were in want, and Paul was right to teach the Gentile Christians that they should be generous in responding to the need of their Jewish brethren. How he looked at the collection at this stage is seen in our text. He says three things about it:

1. *It was "in the service of the saints" in Jerusalem (v. 25).* The word that is translated *service* is the one from which we get the word *deacon*. It occurs just a few verses further on in chapter 16, where Phoebe is commended as a "servant" or "deaconess" of the church in Cenchrea. We recognize that caring for the poor is a legitimate function of the diaconate. But since Paul was not a deacon but rather an apostle and yet is saying here that his role in collecting and delivering this offering for the saints at Jerusalem was a diaconal service, we learn that we are all to be engaged in this kind of service. In other words, the role of the deacons is not to minister in our place, so we do not have to care for the needs of others, but rather to show us how to minister—just as

2. Leon Morris, *The Epistle to the Romans* (Grand Rapids: Wm. B. Eerdmans Publishing Company, and Leicester, England: Inter-Varsity Press, 1988), p. 519.

3. Donald Grey Barnhouse argued forcefully that Paul was out of the will of God in how he went about raising this special offering and even more so in persisting in his plans to accompany it to Jerusalem when God told him clearly not to go there but to continue his missionary work among the Gentile nations (Acts 21:4, 10–14; 22:17–18). See Donald Grey Barnhouse, *God's Glory: Exposition of Bible Doctrines, Taking the Epistle to the Romans as a Point of Departure*, vol. 10, *Romans 14:13—16:27* (Grand Rapids: Wm. B. Eerdmans Publishing Company, 1964), pp. 101–4. See also Donald Grey Barnhouse, "The Stupidity of Stubbornness" in *Your Will—Or God's?*, booklet 91 in the series of broadcast notes for the Bible Study Hour (Philadelphia: The Bible Study Hour, 1960), pp. 18–26.

ruling elders show us how to exercise spiritual oversight of one another, and teaching elders lead us in how to study and understand the Bible. Caring for other people is every Christian's job.

Moreover, it is a necessary spiritual fruit, which is exactly what Paul calls it in verse 28. This means that if the life of Christ is really found in us, then we will care for others as a natural and necessary expression of our transformed lives. The apostle James wrote, "Suppose a brother or sister is without clothes and daily food. If one of you says to him, 'Go, I wish you well; keep warm and well fed,' but does nothing about his physical needs, what good is it? In the same way, faith by itself, if it is not accompanied by action, is dead" (James 2:15–17).

One reason we must be generous is because generosity is evidence that we are Christians. If we do not care for other people or the work of God, why should we suppose we are Christians?

2. *The Gentiles "were pleased" to help out (v. 26).* The second thing Paul says about this offering in writing about it to the Romans is that the Christians of Macedonia and Achaia were pleased to share in it. He stresses this point by repeating it twice, once in verse 26 and a second time in verse 27.

Were the Christians of Macedonia and Achaia *really* pleased to do it? I ask this question, because the answer is not a clear-cut yes. It is actually yes and no. The Christians of Macedonia had been willing. Indeed, they had been supporting Paul even before he began to take up this particular collection, and Paul commends them for their generosity on more than one occasion. This was not quite the case with the Christians in Achaia. On the contrary Paul seems to have had difficulty collecting the offering there. We know this because of his two letters to the Corinthians, particularly 2 Corinthians, where he urges the church there to get on with the offering that they had promised but had been slow in taking up.

The problem was that the Corinthians had not followed through on their original early commitment. They seemed to have been willing at first. But like many of us, they had let the matter of their giving to God's work slide. Paul was sending Titus, one of his faithful fellow workers and companions, along with two other unnamed brothers to receive this offering, and he was writing to ensure that the Corinthians would actually take the offering and have it waiting when they arrived (2 Cor. 8:16–18).

Generosity is a natural part of being Christians, but we must be taught to give. That is what Paul was doing in his extensive teaching about giving in 2 Corinthians and in writing to the Romans. We need the same kind of teaching today, even though people dislike being instructed about giving.

3. *The Gentiles who had "shared in the Jews' spiritual blessings owe[d] it to the Jews to share with them their material blessings" (v. 27).* The third thing Paul says about giving in writing to the Christians at Rome is that the Gentiles of Greece owed support to the Christians of Judea because they had received their spiritual blessings through them. It is a simple principle: A Bible teacher ought

to be supported. He should not have to do secular work to support himself, though good ministers are usually happy to do it if that should prove necessary. Paul himself worked as a tentmaker at Corinth, when his support funds were low or slow in coming.

God's Formula for Great Giving

Anyone who has ever tried to get someone else to give to religious or charitable causes knows how difficult motivating another person can be. So it may be useful to ask: How did Paul motivate the Corinthians, who seem to have been reluctant, to be faithful in this area? It is noteworthy that he did not nag, scold, beg, or plead. But neither was he against using some very direct motivation. If we read 1 Corinthians 8 and 9 carefully, we will find him appealing to the need for personal consecration on the Corinthians' part, the example of Christ, the love and grace of God for us, and even to a proper kind of pride and self-interest.

The chief element in Paul's attempt to motivate the Corinthians to great giving was the example of the poorer churches of Macedonia. Like Judea, Macedonia was a poor area. Corinth was a prosperous place by comparison. How is it that the poorer Macedonian churches had been able to set such a good example for Corinth? The answer to this question is in 2 Corinthians 8:2, which I call "God's Formula for Great Giving": "Out of the most severe trial, their overflowing joy and their extreme poverty welled up in rich generosity." Here are three elements: (1) a severe trial, (2) overflowing joy, and (3) extreme poverty. Combined, says Paul, they produced exemplary generosity.

1. *A severe trial.* We do not know what this severe trial was. It may have been persecution. It may have been the poverty. Whatever it was, it represented circumstances that we would probably call unendurable or at least severely trying.

This is not the way we would expect things to be. We think that if a person is going through some trial, his or her attention should rightly be directed to that problem and not to the needs of other people. That is how we would expect to react ourselves. But here, as in so many areas of life, Christian experience is entirely different from what we would expect. When Christians go through trials, they think about others who are also suffering and they reach out to them.

The best example is Jesus, who, when he was hanging on the cross, thought of the soldiers ("Father, forgive them, for they do not know what they are doing," Luke 23:34), his mother ("Dear woman, here is your son," John 19:26) and the dying thief ("I tell you the truth, today you will be with me in paradise," Luke 23:43).

2. *Overflowing joy.* Paul does not say what the Macedonian Christians were joyful about, but we may suppose their joy came from several things. They would have had joy in salvation, for Paul writes in 1 Thessalonians that the believers in that city welcomed the message with "the *joy* given by the Holy Spirit" (1 Thess. 1:6). Before the coming of the gospel they were lost in hea-

then darkness and were, like Paul's description of the Ephesians, "without hope and without God in the world" (Eph. 2:12). After they had believed, they were conscious of having found God and of having passed out of darkness into light, and they were joyful.

Similarly, in Philippians Paul speaks explicitly of the believers' "*joy* in Christ Jesus" (Phil. 1:26), urging them to "rejoice in the Lord always" (Phil. 4:4), that is, to continue as they were doing.

Every Christian should be joyful, of course. But we are concerned with the link between joy and giving, and one thing joy must indicate in this context is that the giving of the Macedonians was unconstrained—it was of their own free will, which is why it was joyful. As long as our giving is constrained, as it is when we give our taxes to the government, it is a burden and is frequently coupled with resentment. But when we give freely, as we ought to do for Christian causes, we give joyfully and our joy is enhanced by giving.

I think here of Frances Ridley Havergal, who wrote lines we often sing with little understanding or commitment:

> Take my silver and my gold,
> Not a mite would I withhold.

Those lines were autobiographical. That is, Frances Havergal did what she described. We know from her writings left behind at her death that at the time she wrote those words she sent to the Church Missionary Society all her gold and silver jewelry, including a jewel chest she described as being fit for a countess. She wrote to a close friend, "I don't need to tell you that I never packed a box with such pleasure." That is a joy generous Christians recognize. They know that joy leads to generous giving, as 2 Corinthians teaches. It is enhanced by it.

3. *Extreme poverty.* The third element in this formula for generous giving is poverty—indeed, extreme poverty. What an utterly contrary principle from what the world teaches! If you hire a fund-raising organization to help raise large sums of money for a secular charity, you will be told that the first third of the goal must be raised by advance gifts from large donors, the second third by nearly as large gifts from very wealthy people, and only the last third from your organization's regular constituency. Or, depending on the cause, the expectations may be even more disproportionate. Sometimes the gifts from large donors are supposed to be at least 80 percent of the whole.

That is not how it is in Christian circles. Large gifts have their place, perhaps to launch a new project or pay for a special need. But by and large, the work of the church is sustained by the regular small gifts of people who are not wealthy. In fact, in many places the spreading of the gospel is underwritten almost entirely by the very, very poor.

Some time ago I came across statistics that showed that giving among the very poor is remarkable. In the United States those below the poverty line give about 5 percent of their income to charitable causes. Those who are in the middle income brackets give slightly more, about 7 percent, because they have more from which to give. But when people move into the highest brackets, that is, above $100,000 per year, the rate falls back to only 2 percent. So, statistically, it is usually not the rich who give generously but those who are not nearly so well off.

The Macedonians were poor and had undergone severe trials. But the result of this unusual combination of circumstances was great giving. It was according to the formula "Severe trials + overflowing joy + extreme poverty = rich generosity." This is something like saying, "Minus one, minus fifteen, minus three equals a million," but that is God's arithmetic, strange as it may seem to us. And it works wonderfully.

The Secret of Great Giving

Verse 5 adds a further explanation of the remarkable giving of the Macedonian Christians: "And they did not do as we expected, but they gave themselves first to the Lord and then to us in keeping with God's will." As we well know, trials and poverty do not in themselves produce great giving, not even among Christians. In fact, they sometimes do the opposite. They produce bitterness in people who thereby become self-centered, mean, tight-fisted, and greedy.

What makes the difference, as Paul explains in this verse, is whether the Christians involved have: (1) first given themselves to the Lord and (2) then given themselves to others as a consequence.

It is hard to emphasize giving ourselves to God too much, because in the fullest sense everything in the Christian life begins, continues, and ends with this necessity. It begins here, because this is what it means to be a Christian in the first place. To be a Christian is to surrender oneself to Jesus Christ, repenting of sin, believing on him, and beginning to follow him as one's Master. It continues here, because Jesus calls us to a life of discipleship, which means serving him as Lord of our entire lives. It ends here, because Christians must persevere in this calling to the very end.

Some years ago I heard a prominent member of a board of directors of an organization say, "To be a good board member you should be able to give one of three things: time, talent, or treasure." That is good worldly wisdom, but a Christian will do better. A Christian will give everything he or she is or has to Jesus Christ because Jesus has first given himself for us. If you have trusted Christ as your Savior, you will want to give yourself and your treasure to others, as he gave himself for you. Or else, you need to be taught to do it!

229

The Full Measure of God's Blessing

Romans 15:29

I know that when I come to you, I will come in the full measure of the blessing of Christ.

We are at the end of a long paragraph in which Paul has been telling the Christians at Rome of his plans to visit them after first going to Jerusalem to present the offering for the poor that he had raised among the Gentile churches. He told them that he had wanted to come to Rome earlier; he had been delayed by his earlier missionary work and by the need to accompany the offering, but he is certain that his proposed visit will at last come to pass. He says, "I know that when I come to you, I will come in the full measure of the blessing of Christ."

Leon Morris points out, as others also have, that these words are a mark of the letter's authenticity and early date, since no one who knew how Paul actually came to Rome (as a prisoner in chains) would have put it this way.[1]

That is an interesting observation, but it is not what ought to occupy our thoughts here. What is important is that Paul anticipated coming to Rome

---

1. Leon Morris, *The Epistle to the Romans* (Grand Rapids: Wm. B. Eerdmans Publishing Company, and Leicester, England: Inter-Varsity Press, 1988), p. 522.

in the "full measure" of Christ's blessing. What is the nature of this "full" blessing? Is it something in which we can share? If it is, how can we be certain of sharing in it? These are questions no true Christian should ignore.

Let's begin with the meaning of the word *blessing*. *Blessing* is not easy to define and has various meanings. Next, we will look at the types of blessing we encounter in the Old and New Testaments. Third, we will study what Jesus had to say about blessing, based on his illustration of the vine and the branches in John 15. Finally, though briefly, we will ask what the requirements are if we ourselves are to be channels of such blessing.

What Does *Blessing* Mean?

What does *blessing* mean, and what does Paul mean when he says, "I know that when I come to you, I will come in the full measure of the blessing of Christ"?

1. *Set apart to God.* *Blessing* has an interesting history. In the early days of the development of the English language, before the Norman conquest, there were more than thirty Anglo-Saxon forms of the words *bless, blessed,* and *blessing,* words like *bloedsian, bledsian,* and *bletsian.* What is common to these words is that they were all based on the Germanic word *blod,* meaning blood, and therefore referred to something that had been set apart to God by a blood ritual.

In today's speech the words that come closest to this are *sanctified* and *consecrated,* though we preserve this earliest meaning of *blessed* and actually use the word itself in two common expressions. First, we speak of "the blessed sacrament," meaning that the communion elements have been set apart for a spiritual purpose. Second, we "bless" people, which is what pastors do at the end of a worship service and what we also do when someone we know sneezes and we respond, "God bless you." We may not know what we intend by that expression, but what it means is that we want the person to be set apart to God and his service.

2. *To speak well of some person.* A second meaning of the word *blessed* comes to us through the French and Latin languages. The Normans, who invaded England in 1066, brought French with them, including the word *benir,* meaning bless, which was based on the common ecclesiastical Latin term *benedicere,* which meant to speak well of somebody. It was used in the Latin Bible for blessing or praising God. This sense of the word occurs in Luke's gospel in reference to human beings when Jesus tells his disciples, "Bless them that curse you." He means that although our enemies speak badly of us, we are to speak good about them. In time this meaning of blessing attached itself to the older Anglo-Saxon expressions so that blessing began to mean not only to be set apart to God but to be well spoken of or well regarded.

3. *An exceptional state of happiness.* A third meaning of *blessing* and *blessed* comes from their being close in sound to another old English word, *bliss,* meaning an exceptional state of happiness or well-being. Because the words were alike, *blessed* soon took on this meaning too, which is the sense it has in the Beatitudes, where Jesus said, "Blessed are the poor in spirit. . . . Blessed

are those who mourn. . . . Blessed are the meek. . . ." and so on. He meant that people who are like this will be deeply and profoundly happy.

In Romans 15:29, the term probably includes all three meanings: to be set apart to God, to be spoken well of, and to be happy. The meanings belong together like this: First, Paul is confident that when he comes to Rome he will do so as an appointed and consecrated messenger of God, who is therefore blessed by God in the sense that God's good words will accompany him and prosper what he does for God. Therefore, because he is God's servant and will be blessed by God in his service, he is profoundly happy and will continue to be so.

Isn't that a wonderful way to face the future? Don't you wish you could face tomorrow like that? The point of this study is that you can, if you will look upon your life and order it as Paul did.

Two Kinds of Blessing

There are at least two types of blessing found in the Bible.

1. *Every spiritual blessing in Christ.* First, there are the blessings that are ours right now because of our being united to Jesus Christ by the Holy Spirit. Many verses speak of this: Romans 8:17, which calls us God's heirs ("heirs of God and co-heirs with Christ"); 1 Corinthians 3:21–23, which tells us that everything is ours ("All things are yours, whether Paul or Apollos or Cephas or the world or life or death or the present or the future—all are yours, and you are of Christ, and Christ is of God"); and 1 Timothy 6:17, which says that God has given us all things richly to enjoy ("Hope in God, who richly provides us with everything for our enjoyment").

The most important of these verses is Ephesians 1:3, which says, "Praise be to the God and Father of our Lord Jesus Christ, who has blessed us in the heavenly realms with every spiritual blessing in Christ." This is important because it teaches that every possible spiritual blessing we could ever have is already ours by virtue of our being united to our Savior.

Not long ago a speaker at one of our 1994 Philadelphia Conferences on Reformed Theology called attention to a fine expression of this truth by John Calvin:

> If we seek *salvation*, we are taught by the very name of Jesus that it is "of him" (1 Cor. 1:30). If we seek any other *gifts of the Spirit*, they will be found in his anointing. If we seek *strength*, it lies in his dominion; if *purity*, in his conception; if *gentleness*, it appears in his birth. For by his birth he was made like us in all respects (Heb. 2:17) that he might learn to feel our pain (cf. Heb. 5:2). If we seek *redemption*, it lies in his passion; if *acquittal*, in his condemnation; if *remission of the curse*, in his cross (Gal. 3:13); if *satisfaction*, in his sacrifice; if *purification*, in his blood; if *reconciliation*, in his descent into hell; if *mortification of the flesh*, in his tomb; if *newness of life*, in his resurrection; if *immortality*, in the same; if *inheritance of the Heavenly Kingdom*, in his entrance into heaven; if *protection*, if

security, if *abundant supply of all blessings,* in his Kingdom; if *untroubled expectation of judgment,* in the power given to him to judge. In short, since rich store of every kind of good abounds in him, let us drink our fill from this fountain, and from no other.[2]

2. *Blessing on our work for God.* The second type of blessing mentioned in the Bible is blessing on our work for God—that is, on our ministry. This kind of blessing is not complete or automatic, as the first is, since it relates at least in part to how closely we are following after Christ and also to whether we seek this blessing and ask God for it. Moses was one who knew this, which is why his hymn on the shortness and frailty of human life ends with this prayer:

> May the favor of the Lord our God rest upon us;
>   establish the work of our hands for us—
>   yes, establish the work of our hands.
>
> Psalm 90:17

Of course, this is what Paul also has in mind as he writes to the Roman Christians. He is not writing about the blessings that are already ours in Christ. He has them, and so do the Roman Christians. Rather, Paul is writing that his future visit to Rome might be spiritually profitable. We remember that he also spoke of this at the very beginning of the letter when he wrote, "I long to see you so that I may impart to you some spiritual gift to make you strong" (Rom. 1:11). Paul wanted his life to count for God wherever he was or would be. Since he was coming to Rome, he wanted his days in Rome to be blessed by God in the lives of the Christians who lived there.

Moreover, he wanted his coming to Rome to count to the greatest degree imaginable. He wanted to experience the full measure of the blessings of Christ in the lives of the Christians.

Have you ever thought of your life in these terms? Most Christians want God to bless them, meaning that they want God to preserve them from physical harm, give them a long life, help them to make a lot of money, and keep their children out of trouble. Those are blessings, of course. But they are self-centered, and they certainly do not represent the fullness of what God is capable of doing or is willing to do in and through us for the spiritual well-being of other people. I encourage you to think of your life as a means by which God might be able to impart spiritual blessings to other people.

The Vine and the Branches

I have mentioned Moses' prayer that the work of his hands might be established and blessed by God and Paul's desire that he might come to Rome in

2. John Calvin, *Institutes of the Christian Religion,* ed. John T. McNeill, trans. Ford Lewis Battles (Philadelphia: The Westminster Press, 1960), vol. 1, pp. 527–28.

the full measure of the blessing of Jesus Christ. This was also the desire of
the Lord Jesus Christ for us, as expressed in his teaching about the vine and
the branches in John 15:1–17:

> I am the true vine, and my Father is the gardener. He cuts off every branch in
> me that bears no fruit, while every branch that does bear fruit he prunes so
> that it will be even more fruitful. You are already clean because of the word I
> have spoken to you. Remain in me, and I will remain in you. No branch can
> bear fruit by itself; it must remain in the vine. Neither can you bear fruit unless
> you remain in me.
>
> I am the vine; you are the branches. If a man remains in me and I in him,
> he will bear much fruit; apart from me you can do nothing. If anyone does
> not remain in me, he is like a branch that is thrown away and withers; such
> branches are picked up, thrown into the fire and burned. If you remain in me
> and my words remain in you, ask whatever you wish, and it will be given you.
> This is to my Father's glory, that you bear much fruit, showing yourselves to
> be my disciples.
>
> As the Father has loved me, so have I loved you. Now remain in my love. If
> you obey my commands, you will remain in my love, just as I have obeyed my
> Father's commands and remain in his love. I have told you this so that my joy
> may be in you and that your joy may be complete. My command is this: Love
> each other as I have loved you. Greater love has no one than this, that one lay
> down his life for his friends. You are my friends if you do what I command. I
> no longer call you servants, because a servant does not know his master's busi-
> ness. Instead, I have called you friends, for everything that I learned from my
> Father I have made known to you. You did not choose me, but I chose you and
> appointed you to go and bear fruit—fruit that will last. Then the Father will
> give you whatever you ask in my name. This is my command: Love each other.

My chief reason for citing this passage in full is the progression Jesus develops using the word *fruit,* which is the equivalent in this illustration of the blessing Paul was seeking on his ministry in Rome. It is fourfold, and it requires
the entire passage to see it.

1. *Fruit (vv. 1–4).* In the first paragraph of this address Jesus stresses that
the purpose of the disciples' union with him, as branches with a vine, is that
they might bear fruit. There are no qualifying adjectives attached to fruit at
this point. Christ's concern is simply that there *be* fruit. Indeed, this is the concern of the Father too, according to Jesus, for the Father is pictured as the
gardener who both trims the vine and prunes the branches to make them
fruitful. The importance of bearing fruit appears clearly in the next paragraph,
for what Jesus seems to be teaching there is that if we do not bear fruit, we
do not belong to Christ; that is, we are not in the vine, we are not his.

The idea of the Father cutting off every branch that does not bear fruit
(v. 2) and the later reference to such unproductive branches being "thrown
away" and even cast "into the fire and burned" (v. 6) has sounded to many
people as if those who have once belonged to Jesus Christ can perish. They

are troubled by what seems to be the teaching that we can lose our salvation. That is not right, of course. Other passages clearly refute it (see John 10:27–30; Rom. 8:31–39; Phil. 1:6). But if these verses from John 15 do not teach that our salvation can be lost due to our being unfruitful, what do they mean?

Various answers have been given. One is that it is the worldly works of unprofitable Christians that are spoken of as being burned up, not the believers themselves, much as Paul speaks of "the quality of each man's work" being revealed by fire in 1 Corinthians 3:10–15. But in John 15 Jesus is clearly speaking of the branches. A second explanation is that it is as "a branch" that the believer is cast out, not as "a son." The problem with this interpretation is that it introduces a distinction into the allegory that is not present and is foreign to Jesus' teaching.

Years ago I tended to either of those two explanations, but today I think that the Puritans (and others) were right when they said that casting out applies to those who are Christians in name only, the bottom line being that Christians must bear fruit if they are truly Christians. I think this fits Jesus' teaching, because Jesus frequently taught that the Jews of his day, who considered themselves to be fruit-bearing children of God, would be rejected at the last judgment. It also fits what Paul developed in Romans 11 by a similar image, when he taught that Jewish branches had been broken off the olive tree of salvation in order that Gentiles might be grafted in.

2. *Even more fruitful (v. 2).* The second step in Jesus' fourfold development of the fruit idea is that the Father's chief object in trimming the vine's branches is that they might be "even more fruitful." "More" is the first qualifying adjective. It is a searching word, as Andrew Murray pointed out in his valuable devotional study *The True Vine*, because "as churches and individuals we are in danger of nothing so much as self-contentment. The secret spirit of Laodicea—we are rich and increased in goods, and have need of nothing—may prevail where it is not suspected. The divine warning—poor and wretched and miserable—finds little response just where it is most needed."[3]

So I ask: Has a torpid spirit of self-satisfaction and vain contentment settled upon you? Do you feel that you have done enough? That your church has achieved all it needs to achieve? That you know all you need to know of Christian doctrine or have witnessed for Christ sufficiently? If so, you should remember how Jesus said that when we have done everything we have been told to do we must still say, "We are unworthy servants" (Luke 17:10).

3. *Much fruit (vv. 5–8).* In the next paragraph of Jesus' teaching a second modifier occurs with the word fruit, *much.* It occurs twice, in verses 5 and 8: "If a man remains in me and I in him, he will bear much fruit" (v. 5), and "This is to my Father's glory, that you bear much fruit, showing yourselves to be my disciples" (v. 8).

3. Andrew Murray, *The True Vine* (Chicago: Moody Press, n.d.), pp. 23–24.

It is sad that so many Christians expect so little of Jesus. It may be because they consider *much* of anything to be worldly—too much money, too much fun. But I suspect the real reason is because they are self-satisfied and lazy. If this is true of you, Jesus' words should be a strong rebuke, for they say that what he desires of you is not fruit only or even more fruit this year than last, but much fruit. If you take that seriously, you will attempt great things for God, knowing that little fruit brings little glory either to the Father or the Son but that much fruit brings much glory to them.

4. *Fruit that will last (v. 16)*. Toward the end of this passage Jesus adds one more step in his fourfold development of the spiritual fruit illustration. He speaks of "fruit that will last" (v. 16). Not all fruit does last. In fact, in purely agricultural terms no fruit actually lasts at all. All fruit decays, rots, and eventually becomes unsuitable to eat. The same is true of much of what we do. Many of our most extensive efforts come to nothing. In time we ourselves die and pass away. The one thing that does remain is the spiritual fruit produced in and through the lives of those who are united to Jesus Christ. God is eternal. Consequently, what he does through us is eternal too. We echo this truth in a bit of Christian doggerel that goes:

> Only one life! 'Twill soon be past.
> Only what's done for Christ will last.

In truth, much of what is done even in the name of Christ will not last because it is not done in the spirit of Christ and by his power. But if Jesus is working in us, we can know that what *he* is doing will be wonderfully fruitful and never pass away.

Are you doing what Christ would have you do? And are you doing it in his name and by his power? Remember that it is possible to build a great monument to self out of wood, hay, and stubble. A haystack can be a very large thing. But it will not last the winter, and all that is done in the power of the flesh and for the flesh will be destroyed too. Make sure that what you do is in "the full measure of the blessing of Christ."[4]

If You Would Be Fruitful

I do not know if Paul had heard of Jesus' teaching about the vine and the branches, but he knew the truths that are in it, and he also knew and practiced the requirements Jesus gave for being fruitful.

First, we must remain in close fellowship with Christ ("No branch can bear fruit by itself; it must remain in the vine. Neither can you bear fruit unless you remain in me," John 15:4). Second, we must know that we are nothing

4. Some of this material on the vine and the branches has been adapted from James Montgomery Boice, *The Gospel of John*, 5 vols. in 1 (Grand Rapids: Zondervan Publishing House, 1985), pp. 1046–47.

in ourselves ("Apart from me you can do nothing," v. 5). Third, we must be filled with Christ's word ("If you remain in me and my words remain in you, ask whatever you wish, and it will be given to you," v. 7). Fourth, we must love each other (vv. 12, 17). That is exactly what we will do if we want to come to others in the fullness of Christ's blessing.

230

Pray for Me!

Romans 15:30–32

I urge you, brothers, by our Lord Jesus Christ and by the love of the Spirit, to join me in my struggle by praying to God for me. Pray that I may be rescued from the unbelievers in Judea and that my service in Jerusalem may be acceptable to the saints there, so that by God's will I may come to you with joy and together with you be refreshed.

I n the last study we looked at how confident Paul was that when he came to Rome it would be "in the full measure of the blessing of Christ." I ended by listing the requirements for such blessing, the basis for Paul's confidence, based on Jesus' teaching about the vine and the branches in John 15. Yet Paul undoubtedly also prayed for God's blessing on his pending visit to Rome and asked other believers to pray too. Paul was confident of God's richest blessing on his ministry because he had asked God for it.

In the final paragraph of Romans 15 Paul passes to the subject of prayer, urging the Christians at Rome to pray for him. This is not unusual. It was Paul's regular practice to request prayers for himself and his ministry. We can think of many passages where he does it: 2 Corinthians 1:10–11; Ephesians 6:19–20; Philippians 1:19; Colossians 4:3–4; 1 Thessalonians 5:25; 2 Thessalonians 3:1–2.

But this is a strong and very impassioned plea, undoubtedly because of the difficulties Paul foresaw in going to Jerusalem. In these verses Paul describes prayer as a struggle and brings in each member of the Trinity: "I urge you, brothers, by our *Lord Jesus Christ* and by the love of *the Spirit*, to join me in my struggle by praying to *God* for me" (v. 30).

John Murray says of this verse, "God answered the prayers but not in the ways that Paul had hoped for or anticipated. The lessons to be derived from verses 30–33 are numberless."[1] I agree with John Murray, for none of us prays as well, fervently, or with as much understanding as we should.

Prayer Is Not Useless

One of the reasons why we do not pray as we should is that we do not realize the seriousness of what is going on or our part in it. According to Ephesians 6, we are embroiled in fierce spiritual warfare, and prayer is our weapon. Paul realized that intensely, which is why he engages the believers at Rome to join his struggles by praying to God on his behalf.

A great Bible teacher of the early part of this century, Reuben A. Torrey, was at a Bible conference in St. Louis. Another minister was speaking on "The Rest of Faith," saying that Jesus has won all spiritual victories for us and that all we need to do is rest on Christ's work. There is a sense in which that is true, of course. But the preacher overextended himself when he exclaimed, "I challenge anybody to show me a single passage in the Bible where we are told to wrestle in prayer." Torrey was on the platform, and he says that although one speaker does not like to contradict another, this was a challenge he had to take up. So he said softly, "Romans 15:30, brother." Fortunately the other speaker was honest enough to admit that Torrey was right. For what Romans 15:30 says is that we are to struggle together in prayer and that much depends on it.[2]

It is helpful to know that the Greek word here is *synagonizomai*, which is a compound made up of the preposition meaning *with (syn)* plus the word from which we get our words *agony, agonize,* and *antagonist (agonizomai)*. An *agon* was an athletic contest. Thus, *agonizomai* described the struggle that took place in an athletic contest and by extension in any other conflict as well. Jesus used the word when he said, "My kingdom is not of this world. If it were, my servants would *fight . . .*" (John 18:36). His word for fight is *agonize.* In Luke 22:44, this is the word that is used to describe our Lord's fervent prayer in the Garden of Gethsemane. Luke says, "And being in *anguish,* he prayed more earnestly, and his sweat was like drops of blood falling to the ground."

1. John Murray, *The Epistle to the Romans*, 2 vols. in 1 (Grand Rapids: Wm. B. Eerdmans Publishing Company, 1968), vol. 2, pp. 223–24.
2. R. A. Torrey, *The Power of Prayer and the Prayer of Power* (Grand Rapids: Zondervan Publishing House, 1955), pp. 88–89.

To return to Paul, both the noun and verb occur in Paul's summation of his ministry, where he says: "I have *fought* the good *fight*" (2 Tim. 4:7).

This, then, is why prayer is not a useless exercise. We are engaged in a great spiritual struggle against the devil and his schemes, and prayer is the only way we can participate in it.

Prayer Is Effective

The second lesson of Paul's important paragraph about prayer is that prayer is useful. As James says, "The prayer of a righteous man is powerful and effective" (James 5:16).

It had to be if it was going to help Paul. In verse 31 of this section Paul asks the Roman Christians to pray for two things: first, that he would be delivered from the unbelievers in Judea, and second, that his service in Jerusalem might be accepted by the saints there. There was ample cause for his anxiety on both counts. Paul was aware of how intensely he was hated by the Jews. They saw him as a Jewish renegade and heretic who was teaching a disastrous theology and undermining Judaism. The proof of their hatred (and of the danger to which Paul was exposed) was seen in their reception of Paul when he arrived in the city and was making his way to the temple. His enemies saw him and stirred up the masses of the people, shouting, "Men of Israel, help us! This is the man who teaches all men everywhere against our people and our law and this place. And besides, he has brought Greeks into the temple area and defiled this holy place" (Acts 21:28). This last charge was untrue, but it was effective in causing the people to seize Paul and try to kill him. He was saved from the mob only because the commander of the Roman garrison sent soldiers into the crowd to take him into custody. Yet even as they did, the people kept crying out for his death (v. 36).

What about Paul's second area of concern, that his service (he means the offering that he had received from the Gentiles) might be acceptable to the Jerusalem saints? We might wonder how any offer of financial assistance could be unacceptable, but we need to remember how fiercely many Jewish Christians felt about the Mosaic law and how fanatically they opposed Paul's insistence that Gentiles should not be subjected to its strictures. Paul wanted the Gentile offering to heal this division, but it was possible that it could have had a directly opposite effect. It could have been seen as a bribe and only have intensified the hostility.

So what was the outcome? Well, in the first instance Paul was indeed delivered from the unbelievers in Judea, though not in the way he would have wanted or expected. When the riot occurred, he was rescued by the soldiers. And though he spent the next two years in custody in Caesarea and at least two years as a prisoner in Rome, he did at last get to Rome and possibly to Spain as well.

There is also reason to believe that the Gentile offering partially healed the breach between Jewish and Gentile Christianity, for the leaders thanked

Paul for his concern and praised God for his ministry, while reminding him that God was also working among them to save many Jews and bless Jewish Christianity (see Acts 21:17–20).

Does prayer work? Yes, in the sense that it changes us. But it also works in the sense that it is God's appointed means to spiritual victory and right ends. Charles Hodge wrote in connection with these verses, "Prayer (and even intercessory prayer) has a real and important efficacy; not merely in its influence on the mind of him who offers it, but also in securing the blessings for which we pray. Paul directed the Roman Christians to pray for the exercise of the divine providence in protecting him from danger, and for the Holy Spirit to influence the minds of the brethren in Jerusalem. This he would not have done, were such petitions of no avail."[3]

Earlier I cited James 5:16 to show that "the prayer of a righteous man is powerful and effective." Another verse from that letter, James 4:2, shows that the reason we do not experience the full measure of the blessing of Christ is that we do not ask for it: "You do not have, because you do not ask God." Unfortunately, we are often woefully deficient in this area.

Let me tell you how Dwight L. Moody became an evangelist. Moody was a shoe salesman who was also the teacher of a boy's Bible class in Chicago. He was there at the time of the Great Chicago Fire, and after he had done his part in getting together some money to help the poor and buy a building for his own work, he went to England for a rest. He did not intend to preach. He only wanted to hear Charles Spurgeon, George Mueller, and some others. But one Sunday he was invited to preach in a Congregational church in north London, and he accepted.

Sunday morning did not go well. Moody said that he had "no power, no liberty; it seemed like pulling a heavy train up a steep grade." It was so bad that he tried to get out of preaching the evening service, for which he had also been invited, but the minister would not let him off.

That evening it was quite different. Moody felt unusual power, and when he got to the end he decided to give an invitation. He asked all who wanted to accept Christ to get to their feet, and about five hundred people did. Moody thought there must be some mistake, perhaps they just didn't understand him. So he asked them to sit down. Then he said, "After this meeting there will be an after-service in the vestry, and I invite all who are serious about receiving Christ to come to that meeting." There was a door to the vestry on each side of the pulpit, and when the service was over the people began to stream through.

"Who are all these people?" Moody asked the pastor. "Are they yours?"

"Some of them are."

"Are they Christians?"

3. Charles Hodge, *A Commentary on Romans* (Edinburgh and Carlisle, Pa.: Banner of Truth Trust, 1972), p. 445. Original edition 1835.

"Not as far as I know," was the reply.

Moody went into the vestry and repeated the invitation in even stronger terms, and the people all once again expressed their willingness to become Christians. Moody still thought there must be some mistake. He said, "I have to go to Ireland tomorrow, but your pastor will still be here and if you really mean what you have just said, come tomorrow night and meet with him again." A few days later, when he was in Ireland, Moody received a telegram from the minister saying, "There were more people here on Monday night than on Sunday. A revival has broken out in our church, and you must return from Ireland and help me." Moody did return, and what happened in those days was the basis for the invitations that later took him back to England and then over the whole world as an evangelist.

That alone is a remarkable story, but here is the rest of it. There were two sisters in that north London church, one of whom was a bed-ridden invalid. After the morning service at which Moody had first preached the healthy sister came home and reported that a Mr. Moody had been there that morning.

"Mr. Moody of Chicago?" asked the sister. When told that he was the one who had preached, the sick sister said, "I have read about him in the newspapers and have been praying that he would come to London and that God would send him to our church. If I had known that it was he who would be preaching this morning, I would have eaten no breakfast and have spent the time praying instead. Now leave me alone. Don't let anyone in to see me. I am going to spend the rest of the day and evening fasting and in prayer." That is what she did, and the revival in north London resulted.[4]

Is prayer effective? Indeed it is! What is more, it is the only thing that is effective in this great spiritual struggle for the minds and souls of men and women. It is God's appointed means to revival.

Prayer Is Necessary

The third point this passage teaches is that prayer is necessary. It is not only effective, it is the only thing that *is* effective. Therefore it is absolutely necessary that we pray to see individuals saved and experience other spiritual blessings and results. Abraham Lincoln once said, "I have been driven many times to my knees by the overwhelming conviction that I had nowhere else to go. My own wisdom, and that of all about me, seemed insufficient for the day."[5]

I include this point on the basis of Paul's reference to the will of God in verse 32: "so that *by God's will* I may come to you with joy and together with you be refreshed." Does that mean that prayer gets God to change his will

---

4. The story is told by R. A. Torrey, who was a personal friend of Moody and his successor as pastor of the Moody Church in Chicago (*The Power of Prayer*, pp. 44–47).

5. Quoted by William Evans, *Why Pray?* (East Stroudsburg, Pa.: Pinebrook Book Club, 1937), p. 15.

so that he conforms to our wishes, or does it mean only that we are changed to accept what he is going to do anyway?

There are two common errors at this point. The first is the error of a superficial Calvinism, which understands that God is sovereign and that his will is always done. It errs in deducing that because this is true, prayer is virtually unimportant except in regard to how it changes us. The second is the Arminian error, which makes God somehow weakly dependent on us. William Evans, in *Why Pray*, writes, "Prayer does not change God's purposes and plans; but it releases them and permits God to do in, for and through us all that which his infinite love and wisdom want to do, but which because of lack of prayer he has not been able to do. . . . Prayer gives God the opportunity to do for us what he wants to do. . . . [We should not] think that God can do whatever he wants to do without our aid. He cannot."[6]

Cannot? Unable? Give God the opportunity? Anyone who knows anything about the majestic sovereign God of the Bible knows that there is something terribly wrong with this approach.

The answer is a better understanding of true Calvinism, which realizes that God does not only appoint the end to be obtained, but he also designates the means to attain that end. Therefore, if God has appointed a widespread revival or the salvation of an individual or any other blessing and if he has determined that the means by which that blessing shall be received is prayer, then it is as necessary that we pray as it is that this predetermined blessing come about. Prayer is inseparably linked to election, just as witnessing and the preaching of the Word are linked to it. If God has determined to do something in response to the prayers of his people, then his people must pray. Indeed, he will lead them to do so.

John Calvin said, "The phrase *through the will of God* reminds us of the necessity of devoting ourselves to prayer, since God alone directs all our paths by his providence."[7] Torrey declared, "Prayer is God's appointed way for obtaining things." He concluded that the major reason for all lack in our experience, life, and work is prayer's neglect.[8]

Prayer Is Difficult

So why do we neglect prayer? Maybe because we do not believe that what I have just said is true or important, but perhaps also because prayer is so difficult. It must be difficult, because Paul calls it a struggle. People who pray well know what that means.

The next question is why prayer is difficult. One reason is that prayer is a spiritual battleground. Our enemy is the devil, and we cannot expect things

6. Evans, *Why Pray?* pp. 66–67.

7. John Calvin, *The Epistles of Paul the Apostle to the Romans and to the Thessalonians*, trans. Ross MacKenzie (Grand Rapids: Wm. B. Eerdmans Publishing Company, 1973), p. 318.

8. R. A. Torrey, *How to Pray* (Westwood, N.J.: Fleming H. Revell, 1900), p. 9.

to be easy when we are struggling with Satan for the souls of men and women. Again, prayer is difficult because we do not know God or God's ways as we ought to know them. Therefore we often do not really know what to pray for. Paul understood this problem well, for he wrote earlier in Romans, "We do not know what we ought to pray for, but the Spirit himself intercedes for us with groans that words cannot express" (Rom. 8:26). In other words, one of the works of the Holy Spirit is to pray for us and with us and so make up for our great spiritual ignorance and deficiencies.

But let me suggest one other reason why prayer is so difficult for us based on what we find in Romans: We are too self-centered in our prayers. Have you noticed how unselfish Paul's prayer requests were? They were for his safety and success in Jerusalem, but not simply that he might have an easy time. He wanted his service to be so well received that it would help heal the breach between Gentile and Jewish Christianity. He wanted to be delivered from the unbelievers in Jerusalem so that his ministry among the Gentiles might be continued with God's blessing. Indeed, the last verse of our passage says, ". . . so that by God's will I may come to you with joy and together with you be refreshed" (v. 32).

I am reminded of the story of a little girl who had been to a Sunday school lesson on prayer and had been taught that Jesus said, "If anyone says to this mountain, 'Go, throw yourself into the sea,' and does not doubt in his heart but believes that what he says will happen, it will be done for him" (Mark 11:23). The child could see a large mountain from her bedroom window, and the next day her mother came by her room and heard her praying that God would cast the mountain into the sea. "Why do you want to pray a prayer like that?" her mother asked. "Why would you ever want that mountain thrown into the sea?"

"Oh," said the little girl, "I'd love to see the big splash it would make when it came down."[9]

Unfortunately, many of our prayers are only a little less selfish than that. And since selfishness is sin and sin is a barrier to prayer (see Isa. 59:1–3), it is not surprising that we find prayer difficult and that our specific prayers often go unanswered.

Prayer Is Commanded

Paul's words are a command: "Join me in my struggle by praying to God for me. Pray that I may be rescued."

Jesus also taught us to pray. Remember his story about the unjust judge and persistent widow who kept coming to him until he finally gave her what she wanted (Luke 18:1–8). Jesus did not teach that God is an unjust judge; but he wanted us to know that we "should always pray and not give up" (v. 1).

---

9. The story is from Evans, *Why Pray?* p. 148.

Jesus prayed! So did the apostles. So have all the saints through all the ages. Can we neglect it? Reuben Torrey was right when he said that whatever else we may learn on this subject, what we must certainly learn is this: "I must pray, pray, pray. I must put all my energy and all my heart into prayer. Whatever else I do, I must pray."[10]

---

10. Torrey, *How to Pray*, p. 7.

231

The Second Benediction

Romans 15:33

The God of peace be with you all. Amen.

Have you ever had the experience of trying to say good-bye to someone or trying to end a conversation, but because new topics kept coming up you found yourself saying good-bye again and again? That happens between lovers all the time. It happened between Romeo and Juliet. In the hands of William Shakespeare it has given us one of the sweetest and most memorable partings in all literature. You might remember these words from Act 2:

> Good night, good night! Parting is such sweet sorrow
> That I should say good night till it be morrow.

We see something like this as we come to the end of Romans. In every one of his letters Paul ends with a benediction, but in Romans he does this more than once. He ends the eleventh chapter with a doxology that could have been a benediction. But even after he gets into the application part of the letter (chaps. 12–16) he seems to be trying to end: first, in the middle of chapter 15; next at the end of the same chapter; then, twice more toward the end of the letter.

Halfway through chapter 15 he wrote, "May the God of hope fill you with all joy and peace as you trust in him, so that you may overflow with hope by the power of the Holy Spirit" (v. 13). Romans 16:20 says, "The grace of our Lord Jesus be with you." The chapter ends, "Now to him who is able to establish you by my gospel and the proclamation of Jesus Christ, according to the revelation of the mystery hidden for long ages past, but now revealed and made known through the prophetic writings by the command of the eternal God, so that all nations might believe and obey him—to the only wise God be glory forever through Jesus Christ! Amen" (vv. 25–27).

Our text is the second of three concluding benedictions: "The God of peace be with you all. Amen" (Rom. 15:33). This is the shortest of the benedictions, but in the judgment of at least one commentator it is the greatest.[1]

A World Turned Upside Down

This verse can be thought of as "the greatest" in the sense that it speaks of peace, the greatest need of sinful men and women.

1. *A world at war.* The earliest of all historical records, a Sumerian bas-relief from Babylon (about 3000 B.C.), shows soldiers fighting in close battle order, wearing helmets and carrying shields. Wars are the chief legacy of every ancient culture. The Peloponnesian War that destroyed Greece at the height of her great civilization lasted twenty-seven years. Rome made war a way of life. In the Middle Ages war ravaged Europe, culminating in the Thirty Years' War, which ended in 1648. The *Encyclopedia Britannica* calls the Thirty Years' War "the most horrible military episode in western history prior to the twentieth century."[2] In it one third of the German-speaking people—seven million—lost their lives. Yet for sheer volume of destruction both of lives and property, the wars of our time have greatly exceeded it. Twenty million people died in World War I. Sixty million died in World War II, while the cost increased from an estimated $340 billion to $1.5 trillion.

In the December 25, 1967, issue of *U.S. News and World Report* an article appeared tabulating that since World War II there have been "at least 12 limited wars in the world, 39 political assassinations, 48 personal revolts, 74 rebellions for independence and 162 social revolutions, either political, economical, racial or religious." A recent book reports that "in 1992 alone, human beings were engaged in ninety-three wars around the world and spent $600 billion dollars preparing for war."[3] There is no end of peace initiatives and

---

1. See Donald Grey Barnhouse, *God's Glory: Exposition of Bible Doctrines, Taking the Epistle to the Romans as a Point of Departure*, vol. 10, *Romans 14:13–16:27* (Grand Rapids: Wm. B. Eerdmans Publishing Company, 1964), pp. 114–21.

2. "War," *Encyclopedia Britannica*, vol. 23, p. 198.

3. David F. Wells, *God in the Wasteland: The Reality of Truth in a World of Fading Dreams* (Grand Rapids: Wm. B. Eerdmans Publishing Company, 1994), p. 158.

treaties, but the ink is scarcely dry on these treaties when guns begin to sound for the next fierce encounter.

2. *No peace for the wicked.* The immediate cause of this persistent lack of peace among nations is that people are not at peace themselves. They are not content. They are not happy to be what they are but are always looking for ways to increase their power, wealth, or reputation at other people's expense. This is what Isaiah was thinking about when he wrote, "The wicked are like the tossing sea, which cannot rest, whose waves cast up mire and mud. 'There is no peace,' says my God, 'for the wicked'" (Isa. 57:20–21). James, the Lord's brother, touched on the same theme when he queried, "What causes fights and quarrels among you? Don't they come from your desires that battle within you? You want something but don't get it. You kill and covet, but cannot have what you want. You quarrel and fight. You do not have, because you do not ask God" (James 4:1–2).

My favorite quotation from the brilliant French apologist Blaise Pascal goes, "I have often felt that the sole cause of man's unhappiness is that he does not know how to stay quietly in his own room."[4] He might have said that this is the chief problem with the world as well.

3. *At war with God.* Yet there is a cause for the turbulence and evil of the world that goes beyond even personal restlessness, and it is that people are also at war with God. What is even more serious, God is at war with them. This takes us back to the very first chapter of Romans, where Paul said that human beings in their fallen state do everything in their power to repress the knowledge of God made known to them in nature, because they are hostile to God and do not want to recognize his demands upon their lives. The key paragraph says, "The wrath of God is being revealed from heaven against all the godlessness and wickedness of men who suppress the truth by their wickedness, since what may be known about God is plain to them, because God has made it plain to them. For since the creation of the world God's invisible qualities—his eternal power and divine nature—have been clearly seen, being understood from what has been made, so that men are without excuse" (Rom. 1:18–20).

Simply put, people are at war with God, so God is at war with them. Their rage against God spills over into their personal lives, so that they are never content, and into their relationships with other people, so that they are a source of turmoil rather than being peacemakers.

But God is also "the God of peace," as Paul says, because he is the author of peace. This means that he has worked to bring peace to sinful human beings and their world. Our experience of this peace is threefold: (1) peace with God, which is all-important; (2) peace with other human beings; and (3) personal peace in all circumstances.

---

4. Blaise Pascal, *The Mind on Fire: An Anthology of the Writings of Blaise Pascal,* ed. James M. Houston (Portland, Oreg.: Multnomah Press, 1989), p. 96.

Peace with God

In his commentary on Romans John Murray remarks on how often Paul in his benedictions "calls God the God of peace or invokes upon his readers the peace that is from God."[5] The reason for this is that a lack of peace is our chief problem. The chief message of the gospel is that God has made peace with us by the blood of Christ's cross.

That is exactly how Paul states it in Colossians 1:19–20: "For God was pleased to have all his fullness dwell in him [that is, in Christ], and through him to reconcile to himself all things, whether things on earth or things in heaven, by making peace through his blood, shed on the cross." Our sin is what causes the state of war that exists between ourselves and God, but God has dealt with sin by having his Son, the Lord Jesus Christ, die for it. The Bible tells us that "the wages of sin is death" (Rom. 6:23), but it also says that Jesus died in our place to take the penalty for that sin upon himself. The result of this, as Paul says in Romans 8:1, is that "there is now no condemnation for those who are in Christ Jesus."

Moreover, as Paul also shows, not only has God brought to an end the cause of hostility between ourselves and himself by the work of Christ, he has also transferred us from the status of rebels against his sovereignty to that of beloved sons and daughters. Paul also writes, "For you did not receive a spirit that makes you a slave again to fear, but you received the Spirit of sonship. And by him we cry, 'Abba, Father.' The Spirit himself testifies with our spirit that we are God's children. Now if we are children, then we are heirs—heirs of God and co-heirs with Christ, if indeed we share in his sufferings in order that we may also share in his glory" (Rom. 8:15–17).[6]

What we are talking about here is "peace with God" (Rom. 5:1), and it has been achieved for us by God himself through the death of Jesus Christ. This is an objective work, and we enter into it simply by receiving or believing what God has done.

Peace with One Another

The second area in which we experience the peace of which God is the author is peace with one another. This is true for Christians in a general sense because Christians no longer need to contend for their own interests at the expense of other people. Instead of continuing as fierce, selfish belligerents on the world scene, they become true peacemakers.

5. Romans 1:7, 15:13; 1 Corinthians 1:3, 16:11; 2 Corinthians 1:2; Galatians 1:3; Ephesians 1:2; Philippians 1:2, 4:9; Colossians 1:2; 1 Thessalonians 1:1; 2 Thessalonians 1:2, 3:16; 1 Timothy 1:2; 2 Timothy 1:2; Titus 1:4; and Philemon 3. See John Murray, *The Epistle to the Romans*, 2 vols. in 1 (Grand Rapids: Wm. B. Eerdmans Publishing Company, 1968), vol. 2, p. 224.

6. For a fuller treatment of this important text see James Montgomery Boice, *Romans*, vol. 2, *The Reign of Grace: Romans 5:1–8:39* (Grand Rapids: Baker Books, 1992), pp. 837–60.

There is also a specific way in which Christians experience peace with one another, however, and this is within the fellowship of the church in which the walls that formerly divided Christians are broken down—walls of race, economic status, nationality, and educational level.

This is an important theme in Paul's letter to the Ephesians, notably in the second chapter, where he writes of the new community that God has created in Jesus Christ:

> For he himself is our peace, who has made the two one and has destroyed the barrier, the dividing wall of hostility, by abolishing in his flesh the law with its commandments and regulations. His purpose was to create in himself one new man out of the two, thus making peace, and in this one body to reconcile both of them to God through the cross, by which he put to death their hostility. He came and preached peace to you who were far away and peace to those who were near. For through him we both have access to the Father by one Spirit.

> Ephesians 2:14–18

In Paul's mind there was a great visible symbol of the hostility that existed between people and races in the wall that surrounded the Jewish temple in Jerusalem. The temple of Paul's day had been built by Herod the Great to replace the inadequate temple that dated from the days of Nehemiah. Much of it was overlaid with gold, and it sat on a raised earth platform known even today as the temple mount. It was surrounded by courts. The innermost court was called the Court of the Priests because only members of the priestly tribe of Levi were permitted to enter. The next court was the Court of Israel; it could be entered by any Jewish male. After this there was the Court of the Women, which could be entered by Jewish women as well as any other Jew.

These courtyards were all on one level. So although there were great differences between them, the differences were not as great as the radical division that came next. From the Court of the Women five steps descended to a level area in which there was a five-foot stone barricade that went completely around the temple enclosure; then, after another level space, fourteen more steps descended to the Court of the Gentiles. The Jewish historian Josephus wrote that the wall dividing Jews from Gentiles was marked at intervals by stone inscriptions warning that no foreigner was to enter the Jewish enclosures upon penalty of death.[7]

These inscriptions were like our signs that say "Trespassers will be prosecuted," except that these read, "Trespassers will be killed." We know how seriously this was taken because of the attempt of the Jewish mob to kill Paul when he returned to Jerusalem on the false charge that he had brought a

---

7. Several of these inscriptions have been found, one as recently as 1935. An inscription unearthed in 1871 read, "No foreigner is to enter within the balustrade and embankment around the sanctuary. Whoever is caught will have himself to blame for his death which follows."

Gentile named Trophimus past these barriers into the inner enclosures of the temple (Acts 21:27–29).

This was the great visible symbol of Jewish-Gentile hostility that Paul had in mind as he wrote of the work of Christ in removing this alienation. In all the ancient world, no wall was as impassable as that between Jews and Gentiles. But Paul says that God has destroyed the barrier in Jesus Christ and has made one new people by him.

He has done this by opening the door to himself to people of all races by faith in Jesus. The temple had another even more significant barrier than those I have mentioned as existing between persons, and that was the great veil that separated the Holy Place, which the appointed priests could enter, and the Most Holy Place, which only the high priest could enter, and only once a year on the Day of Atonement. It symbolized the inaccessibility of God, for God was understood to dwell symbolically within the Most Holy Place between the wings of the cherubim who were perched on the golden covering of the Ark of the Covenant. This was the greatest barrier of all. The entire system of walls and veils was meant to show not only the barriers between various kinds of people, but to highlight the greatest of all barriers, which is the barrier between man and God due to man's sin. The cause of all alienation is sin, and the greatest alienation of all is that between ourselves and the holy God.

But see what God has done! When the Lord Jesus Christ died upon the cross to make atonement for sin, Matthew tells us that "the curtain of the temple was torn in two from top to bottom" (Matt. 27:51). It was a way of showing that because of his death the way to the Father was now open for all who would come to God by faith in him. Because he was the one, perfect, and all-sufficient sacrifice for sin, there is now no longer any need for a line of priests to offer sacrifices. We no longer need an annual Day of Atonement. We no longer even need a temple, because we have been given access to the true heavenly temple by Christ's death on our behalf (cf. Heb. 9:24–28; 10:19–25).

All who believe on Jesus Christ come to God together. There is no reason for any grounds of separation between us. If we have been reconciled to God, which is the greatest chasm to be covered, then it is certain that the chasms between us and other women and men have been obliterated too.

If you are in Christ, you are one body with every other believer—whether Jew or Gentile, male or female, rich or poor. So you must act like it. You may not see eye to eye with every other believer in Christ on every possible point of doctrine or practice, but you must know that you belong to other Christians and they to you, and you must work to make that fundamental unity apparent to the world.

If you are not yet a Christian, you should learn that in the final analysis the solution to all your many problems is to be found in your relationship or lack of a relationship to God. The reason the world is not at peace is that it has rejected God. And that is precisely the reason why you are not at peace, too.

You need to repent of your sin, including your suspicion of, alienation from, and hostility to other persons, and come to God through faith in Jesus Christ.

Peace Passing Human Understanding

Our final experience of the peace of which God is the author is what Paul in Philippians 4:6–7 calls the peace of God: "Do not be anxious about anything, but in everything, by prayer and petition, with thanksgiving, present your requests to God. And the peace of God, which transcends all understanding, will guard your hearts and your minds in Christ Jesus."

The peace *of* God is different from peace *with* God, which is what Romans is mostly about. Peace with God is something that is achieved for us by God himself through the work of Jesus Christ. It is the result of his making atonement for our sins. The peace of God is something beyond this for those who have given themselves to Christ. In this verse, when Paul writes about anxiety he is thinking of the upsetting situations that come into our lives. Perhaps we have lost a job and are worried about earning enough money to provide for our families. Maybe we are sick, or a friend is sick. We are worried about the outcome. Perhaps someone very close to us has died. Elisabeth Elliot, who had one husband murdered by Auca Indians in Ecuador and another slowly consumed by cancer, said that the death of a husband was like having an eggbeater suddenly thrust into the mixing bowl of her emotional life. She called it a time when the earth seemed to be giving way, the waters were roaring, and the mountains were being cast into the sea (cf. Ps. 46:2–3).[8] In such times of personal distress we need peace in our lives, and it is this about which Philippians 4:6–7 is speaking.

But we must ask for it! This is because Philippians 4:6–7 is about prayer—"prayer and petition, with thanksgiving" by which we "present [our] requests to God." The promise is that if we will do that, laying all our troubles, worries, and anxieties before God, then a peace which is manifestly beyond all human understanding will possess us. The hymn writer said,

> What a friend we have in Jesus,
> All our sins and griefs to bear!
> What a privilege to carry
> Everything to God in prayer!
> O what peace we often forfeit,
> O what needless pain we bear,
> All because we do not carry
> Everything to God in prayer.

8. Elisabeth Elliot, *Facing the Death of Someone You Love* (Westchester, Ill.: Good News Publishers, 1980), p. 8.

I find it significant that Paul's second benediction, which is a prayer that the God of all peace might be with the Christians at Rome, follows immediately upon his request for prayer from them. They are to pray, but he is praying too. So should we! We should pray for peace ourselves *and* for one another.

PART TWENTY-TWO

Final Greetings

232

Phoebe, a Deaconess

Romans 16:1–2

I commend to you our sister Phoebe, a servant of the church in Cenchrea. I ask you to receive her in the Lord in a way worthy of the saints and to give her any help she may need from you, for she has been a great help to many people, including me.

The last chapter of Romans contains the names of many people in Rome, to whom Paul was writing, as well as those who were in Corinth with Paul and who joined him in sending greetings—thirty-three names in all. Twenty-four of these people were in Rome. Nine were in Corinth. But there are also two unnamed women and an unspecified number of unnamed men. Far from being an uninteresting listing, this chapter is actually one of the most fascinating of the New Testament.

One fascinating thing about Romans 16 is what it reveals about Paul. Some have the idea that people who are interested in ideas—in this case those who study Christian theology—are not interested in people. They are supposed to immerse themselves in books. They are not "relational," as we say. There are people like this, of course. But Paul is a refutation of the idea that those who are interested in doctrine cannot be interested in those for whom the doctrine has been given. No one could be more interested in the great truths

1911

of God than Paul. The entire Epistle to the Romans has been an unfolding of them. But here we see that Paul was also intensely interested in people. In fact, to judge by this chapter, Paul can be said to show more interest in people than anyone else in the Bible except Jesus.

Another lesson from this chapter is brought out by Leon Morris in his commentary:

> [Romans] was not written to professional theologians (though through the centuries scholars have found the epistle a happy hunting ground). As we consider the weighty matters Paul deals with, we are apt to overlook the fact that it was addressed to people like Ampliatus and Tryphena and Rufus. Clearly Paul expected this kind of person to be helped by what he wrote, a fact which modern experts sometimes overlook. And it is fitting that this letter, which has given us so much solid doctrinal teaching, should end with this emphasis on persons, on love, and on a reminder that humble servants of God perform all sorts of active ministry.[1]

The Bearer of the Letter

The first of these many persons whom Paul mentions is Phoebe. We do not know anything more about her than what we are told here, but we are told several important facts, and there is also solid ground for some additional helpful speculation.[2]

What seems most likely, because of the way she is commended to the church, is that Phoebe was the bearer of the letter to the church at Rome. If we analyze the chapter, we will see that verses 3–16 refer to people at Rome to whom the apostle sends greetings, and that verses 21–24 refer to people who were at Corinth who sent their greetings with Paul. Phoebe stands apart, at the head of this chapter, as one who was obviously traveling to Rome and is therefore commended to the good graces of the Roman Christians. Since she is the only one so commended, it is reasonable to think that she was the one who carried the letter. In the ancient world letters were always sent by individual persons, for there was no postal service outside of the military.

What Paul asks the Christians at Rome to do is "to receive her in the Lord in a way worthy of the saints and to give her any help she may need from you, for she has been a great help to many people, including me." In other words, they were being asked to receive and help Phoebe in exactly the same manner Paul had indicated that he would like to be helped when he would get to Rome himself (see Rom. 15:24).

This woman bore a pagan name. Phoebe is the feminine form of Phoibos, a name given to the god Apollo. But Phoebe had become a Christian, was a

---

1. Leon Morris, *The Epistle to the Romans* (Grand Rapids: Wm. B. Eerdmans Publishing Company, and Leicester, England: Inter-Varsity Press, 1988), p. 527.

2. We can learn things about some of the other persons mentioned in this chapter from other New Testament references, people like Priscilla and Aquila and Timothy.

true "servant" of the church at Cenchrea, and had helped many people, including Paul.

Here is a point at which we may speculate a bit. It was not very safe for a woman to travel alone in the ancient world, so Phoebe probably had people with her. But it is Phoebe who is mentioned and not these other persons—not even a husband—so we are probably right to suppose that she was single and a prominent woman. She must have been wealthy too, because it took money to travel. She was probably like Lydia of Philippi, a dealer in purple cloth who was converted through Paul's preaching and then opened her house to Paul and the other new Christians (Acts 16:13–15).

What a wonderful treasure Phoebe carried in her hands. She had been a servant to the church in Cenchrea, the eastern port of the city of Corinth. In this service she became an even greater servant to the church at all times and in all places. Donald Grey Barnhouse wrote, "Never was there a greater burden carried by such tender hands. The theological history of the church through the centuries was in the manuscript which she brought with her. The Reformation was in that baggage. The blessing of multitudes in our day was carried in those parchments."[3]

Was Phoebe a Deaconess?

Was Phoebe a deaconess—that is, an elected or appointed officer of the church at Cenchrea? This question arises because the word for deacon is the same Greek word as *servant,* and this is the word used of Phoebe in verse 1: "Phoebe, a servant of the church in Cenchrea." The King James Version of the Bible translates the word as *servant.* The Revised Standard Version renders it *deaconess.* The New International Version reads *servant* but adds *or deaconess* as a text note. Without any real justification, the New English Bible has the words "who holds office in the congregation at Cenchrea."

The reason for these various translations is that the word itself is ambiguous. It means servant generally and broadly, but it can also mean deacon or deaconess in a narrower or restricted sense. Only the context can determine how it should be taken, and there is not enough said in Romans 16:1 to be decisive.

As I have looked over what has been written on this question in various commentaries, I have received the impression that judgments, where they occur, come more from the age or ecclesiastical tradition of the writers than from the word *diakonos* itself. For example, John Murray writes, "If Phoebe ministered to the saints, as is evident from verse 2, then she would be a servant of the church and there is neither need nor warrant to suppose that she occupied or exercised what amounted to an ecclesiastical office comparable to

3. Donald Grey Barnhouse, *God's Glory: Exposition of Bible Doctrines, Taking the Epistle to the Romans as a Point of Departure,* vol. 10, *Romans 14:13–16:27* (Grand Rapids: Wm. B. Eerdmans Publishing Company, 1964), p. 124.

that of the diaconate."[4] Murray was from a church tradition that did not ordain women. On the other hand, Leon Morris says, "The social conditions of the time were such that there must have been the need for feminine church workers to assist in such matters as the baptism of women or anything that meant contact with women's quarters in homes. The form of expression here makes it more likely that an official is meant than the more general term 'servant,' . . ."[5]

The bottom line is that the text itself is not decisive, and a judgment on this question must be made on other grounds. In my judgment, based on 1 Timothy 2:12, there are two limitations placed on the function of women in the church: (1) an authoritative teaching position and (2) an authoritative disciplining position. Those seem to me to be restricted to male leaders, functioning together in what the Presbyterian tradition calls a session. But aside from that restriction there is no office or service in the church in which women may not perform.

Again I quote Barnhouse:

> What we owe to [women] in the Sunday school and in the work among women, is shown by the devotion to the Lord of those whom he has called to direct his work. We remember that a group of women followed the Lord Jesus Christ when he was here on earth, for we read that, in addition to the twelve, there were "certain women which had been healed of evil spirits and infirmities, Mary called Magdalene, out of whom went seven demons, and Joanna the wife of Chuza, Herod's steward, and Susanna, and many others, which ministered unto him of their substance" (Luke 8:2–3). And to this day, the faithful ministration of such women makes possible a vast amount of the missionary activity of the church throughout the world.[6]

At Tenth Presbyterian Church we have women serve as deaconesses, in the Sunday school, and on all our committees, with the sole exception of the session, and we encourage them to do so.

But let's step back from the concern for the place of women in society that has been raised for those in our day and notice that our questions were not even being raised in the New Testament era. They are not in Paul's mind as he wraps up Romans, for example, or he would have made his position on church offices clear. Why wasn't this an issue? The answer is not that the apostles were not concerned with women or the exercise of their gifts. Obviously they were. That is why they are mentioned so often, as here. The answer is that the New Testament leaders were just not as deeply concerned with office, as we are. Instead they were concerned with normal Christian

---

4. John Murray, *The Epistle to the Romans*, 2 vols. in 1 (Grand Rapids: Wm. B. Eerdmans Publishing Company, 1968), vol. 2, p. 226.

5. Morris, *The Epistle to the Romans*, p. 526.

6. Barnhouse, *God's Glory*, pp. 123–24.

behavior or functions. What they cared about was that Christian people should actually be the servants of others, as Jesus was, not whether they had a badge saying, "I am a *servant* [deacon or deaconess] of the church."

A Ministry of Service

Service is a necessary function of those who call themselves Christians, and every Christian should be a deaconess or deacon in this sense.

I have been helped in this area by some studies on the role of the diaconate done by George C. Fuller, a minister in the Presbyterian Church of America and a former president of Westminster Theological Seminary in Philadelphia. Although he was concerned with the forms of service peculiar to deacons, Fuller began with an emphasis on the service ministry of each believer in Christ. He pointed out that the world measures greatness by the service a person receives. In business the "important" people are those at the top of the organizational pyramid. The bigger the organization, the more important the top person is. In personal affairs the "great" are those who have servants, and the greater the number of servants, the greater the great one is perceived to be. Jesus reversed all that. He turned the whole thing upside down, making, as it were, "the first last and the last first." In God's eyes, greatness consists not in the number of people who serve us but in the number of people we serve. The greater the number, the better the Christian.

Fuller wrote, "If Jesus had not taken upon himself the 'form of a servant,' if the Lord of glory had not 'humbled himself and become obedient unto death, even death on a cross,' the world's standard would have remained unchallenged." But Jesus challenged it. Now "he is *the* 'deacon,' our ultimate example, and in fulfilling that charge from God he assured power for his people, his body on earth, to do his ministry."[7]

So why do we have official deacons and deaconesses? The reason is that we need people to lead the way in several ministries in which every believer in Jesus Christ should be engaged.

1. *A ministry of mercy.* The first is "the ministry of mercy," the chief service for which the office of deacon was established. You will recall that deacons came into being as a result of the situation described in Acts 6:1–7. There were many poor Christians in Jerusalem. Some Christians had a surplus of goods and gave to assist these poor people. A dispute arose between the Greek-speaking and Aramaic-speaking Jews about a perceived unequal distribution of these resources. The Greek-speaking Jews, the Hellenists, complained that their widows were being neglected in the daily distribution of food. This threatened to divide the church. So after they had prayed about the problem and sought God's direction, the apostles counseled the church

7. George C. Fuller, "Deacons, the Neglected Ministry," *The Presbyterian Journal,* November 8, 1978, p. 9.

to select seven men "known to be full of the Spirit and wisdom" and place this important service in their hands.

The church did this, choosing Stephen, Philip, Procorus, Nicanor, Timon, Parmenas, and Nicolas (v. 5). Judging from their names, these men were all from the Greek-speaking community. So the congregation chose wisely, the food was properly distributed, and the office of deacon was born.

2. *Evangelism.* Another ministry of deacons is evangelism, which arises naturally out of their other work. The first two of the deacons mentioned in Acts 6 are examples. Philip is called "the evangelist" in Acts 21:8. God used him to take the gospel to the Samaritans (Acts 8:5) and later to an Ethiopian nobleman (Acts 8:26–40). He had a gift for what we would call cross-cultural evangelism. Stephen preached with great power before the Jewish Sanhedrin, the same body that had condemned Jesus. In fact, his preaching brought such conviction to these corrupt religious leaders that they killed him too. So he became the first martyr of the church.

3. *Training others.* A third work of the deacons and deaconess is to train others. Some will do this by direct and explicit teaching; all must do it by example.

It is good to remember that in our Lord's parable of the sheep and the goats, told just before his arrest and crucifixion, it was the presence or absence of genuine service to others that marked the corresponding presence or absence of a saving relationship to him. What was done to and for others was regarded as a service to himself:[8]

> Then the King will say to those on his right, "Come, you who are blessed by my Father; take your inheritance, the kingdom prepared for you since the creation of the world. For I was hungry and you gave me something to eat, I was thirsty and you gave me something to drink, I was a stranger and you invited me in, I needed clothes and you clothed me, I was sick and you looked after me, I was in prison and you came to visit me."
>
> Then the righteous will answer him, "Lord, when did we see you hungry and feed you, or thirsty and give you something to drink? When did we see you a stranger and invite you in, or needing clothes and clothe you? When did we see you sick or in prison and go to visit you?"
>
> The King will reply, "I tell you the truth, whatever you did for one of the least of these brothers of mine, you did for me."
>
> Matthew 25:34–40

8. Some of this material on the role of deacons is borrowed with alterations from James Montgomery Boice, *Foundations of the Christian Faith* (Downers Grove, Ill., and Leicester, England: Inter-Varsity Press, 1986), pp. 630–35.

The Church, God's Family

The church of Jesus Christ is meant to be one large and very caring family. The word *church* appears here, in verse 1, for the first time in Romans. It occurs five times in this chapter (vv. 1, 4, 5, 16, 23), where Paul is beginning to write about individual members of the Roman and Corinthian congregations.

It is not the only word for the body of believers, either. Paul calls these Christians *brothers* and *sisters* (Phoebe is "our sister"), *saints, fellow workers, friends, a mother* in one case, and those who are *in the Lord*. What ties these references together is that they regard those who are in Christ as members of a spiritual family. Therefore, the matter is important to Paul, and he emphasizes that these believers belong to each other and serve each other selflessly, without any regard to titles, just as members of a happy and well-functioning family might do.

These people have titles, but not the kind the world would care very much to possess. Barnhouse calls these titles epitaphs, because these people are gone now and are remembered only because of the words Paul spoke over them as he sent this letter to Rome:

> Let us look through this chapter to see the designations of these shadowy figures who walk against the gray stones of ancient Rome. Phoebe is called a servant of the church, a helper of many. What an epitaph! How much can be said in a single sentence. I begin to think of single sentences that described a complete life of a person. For many weeks I glanced at the obituary columns of the *New York Times* and the *Times* of London. It was not long before I had quite a list. "A writer on food and wines" is the sentence left behind by one man. "Developer of trotting races" summed up the life of another. Still another "introduced modern conditions for bottling beer." . . .
>
> In contrast to this, glance through the closing chapter of Romans and read these lines of description. Servant (v. 1), helper (v. 2), fellow workers (vv. 3, 9), four people who are called beloved (vv. 5, 8, 9, 12), two called hard workers (vv. 6, 12), fellow prisoners, men of note among the apostles (v. 7), approved in Christ (v. 10), workers in the Lord (v. 12), eminent (v. 13), a mother to me (v. 13), saints (v. 15). What epitaphs are these! How much greater than the piles of stone that emperors heaped together to preserve their memory. The Colosseum and the Pantheon are great buildings built by two of the emperors, but who knows their names? And if I tell you that one of them was built by Hadrian and the other by Vespasian, who but a few history teachers knows which was which?
>
> But when all the stones have turned to sand, and when the elements melt in fervent heat, and Rome, supposedly eternal, is seen to be the quintessence of that which is temporal, these humble people, beloved, hard workers, and saints, will burst forth in the brilliance of the truly eternal city "which has foundations, whose builder and maker is God" (Heb. 11:10).
>
> We do not pray to these saints; they cannot hear us. But, feeling our oneness with them, we know the true communion of saints and wait for that day when

we, with them, shall be caught up together to meet our Lord when he comes
(1 Thess.4:13–18).[9]

As Barnhouse did at the close of that chapter of his studies, so I also look
back over the years of my life and think of the Christian people who have
helped me along the way. Most of them would be unknown to you, and I do
not know any who have been much honored by the world. But I think of them
and give them these titles: Encourager, Teacher, Counselor, Fellow Worker,
Friend, Companion. I know I am not remembering them all. But they are
known to their Master in heaven, and they will not fail of their reward. Thank
God for these great servants of his. May we be like them.

---

9. Barnhouse, *God's Glory*, pp. 128–29.

233

The Apostle Who Did Not Forget

Romans 16:3–16

Greet Priscilla and Aquila, my fellow workers in Christ Jesus. They risked their lives for me. Not only I but all the churches of the Gentiles are grateful to them.

Greet also the church that meets at their house.

Greet my dear friend Epenetus, who was the first convert to Christ in the province of Asia.

Greet Mary, who worked very hard for you.

Greet Andronicus and Junias, my relatives who have been in prison with me. They are outstanding among the apostles, and they were in Christ before I was.

Greet Ampliatus, whom I love in the Lord.

Greet Urbanus, our fellow worker in Christ, and my dear friend Stachys.

Greet Apelles, tested and approved in Christ.

Greet those who belong to the household of Aristobulus.

Greet Herodion, my relative.

Greet those in the household of Narcissus who are in the Lord.

Greet Tryphena and Tryphosa, those women who work hard in the Lord.

Greet my dear friend Persis, another woman who has worked very hard in the Lord.

Greet Rufus, chosen in the Lord, and his mother, who has been a mother to me, too.

Greet Asyncritus, Phlegon, Hermes, Patrobas, Hermas and the brothers with them.

Greet Philologus, Julia, Nereus and his sister, and Olympas and all the saints with them.

Greet one another with a holy kiss.

All the churches of Christ send their greetings.

I n the last chapter of Romans Paul is thinking about other people, not about himself. But we can hardly read the chapter without thinking seriously about him.

What a remarkable person Paul was! He possessed one of the greatest intellects of all time, right up there with Plato and Aristotle. But unlike those two outstanding Greeks, Paul was not merely a thinker and teacher. He was also the first great propagandist for Christianity, a pioneer missionary with a truly global vision. And he persevered in this vision even though it meant great personal discomfort and hardships. He tells us in one place that he endured "troubles, hardships and distresses . . . beatings, imprisonments and riots . . . hard work, sleepless nights and hunger" (2 Cor. 6:4–5). Yet in spite of such troubles he persevered in the task he believed God had given him to do and by God's grace made a more lasting and beneficial impact upon this world than any mere human being who has ever lived. Only the Lord Jesus Christ was more influential.

Sometimes people with this kind of intellectual ability and drive are hard to get close to, but it is to Paul's credit that he was not at all like that. One commentator rightly says of him, "He was never, for a moment, a professional Christian."[1] He cared for people. What drove him was his love for his Savior and his consuming passion that others might come to know and love the Lord Jesus Christ too.

Friends and Fellow Workers

We have a remarkable picture of this great apostle in Romans 16. It emerges in the way he sends his greetings to more than twenty-four people in Rome. When we remember that Paul had never been in Rome, that there was no postal service for civilians, no telephones or faxes that could have given him quick information about what was going on or who was doing what, it is remarkable that he knew so many people who were there and such a lot about them.

How did he get to know them? And how did he know so many details about their lives? There were two ways. Either these were people he had gotten to know in the long course of his missionary work and then had kept track of,

1. Donald Grey Barnhouse, *God's Glory: Exposition of Bible Doctrines, Taking the Epistle to the Romans as a Point of Departure,* vol. 10, *Romans 14:13–16:27* (Grand Rapids: Wm. B. Eerdmans Publishing Company, 1964), p. 130.

following them in his mind as they left Ephesus, Corinth, or wherever and relocated to Rome, or they were people in Rome whom he had learned about from those who had come to him from that city, like Priscilla and Aquila. As we read over this list of names, we find that Paul knew most of these people personally, which means that most were people he had met in his missionary travels. Either he had led these people to Christ or they had worked with him or he had been imprisoned with them for Christ's sake. Paul loved them all. So he kept track of them and followed what happened to them in their work and travels.

We have telephones and good mail service and other modern means of quick communication. But I doubt that there are many of us who could name twenty-four people in another city, not to mention one we have never visited—people who are believers and whom we remember and support regularly in our prayers.

The Christians at Rome

When we begin to look into these names and what Paul says about them, we find a remarkable picture of life in the early church. In fact, it is one of the best early pictures of the church we have, with the possible exception of the church in Jerusalem described in Acts.

1. *Priscilla and Aquila.* Not many of the people in these lists are known to us in any way apart from what Paul says of them here. Priscilla and Aquila are an exception, because they are mentioned six different places in the New Testament.[2] We learn from these scattered references that Aquila was a Jew from Pontus who had settled in Rome but had been forced to leave Rome, together with his wife, Priscilla, when the Emperor Claudius had expelled the Jews from the capital (Acts 18:2). Aquila was a tentmaker, which was Paul's occupation too. This is what brought them together when Paul had to work in Corinth to support himself during this period of his missionary outreach. When Paul left Corinth for Ephesus, this couple went with him but then stayed on in Ephesus, where they were used "more adequately" to explain the gospel to an influential orator and (later) effective Christian worker named Apollos (Acts 18:24–26). By the time Paul wrote this letter they had returned to Rome.

Aquila and Priscilla had a sound knowledge of the gospel, great ability, and outstanding courage, and they were well known to the churches at Rome and elsewhere, judging by what Paul writes. He calls them his fellow workers, adding that they risked their lives for him and that "all the churches of the Gentiles are grateful to them." We do not know how they risked their lives for Paul, but it may have been at Ephesus when the mob led by the makers of idols of the goddess Diana were rioting.

2. Acts 18:2, 18, 26; Romans 16:2; 1 Corinthians 16:19; and 2 Timothy 4:19. In the Pauline letters Priscilla's name is always Prisca. Priscilla, which is used by Luke, is an affectionate diminutive form.

Priscilla and Aquila had a group of believers meeting in their house. They had opened their home to similar congregations earlier, at Corinth (see 1 Cor. 16:19) and probably in Ephesus. In these days Christians mostly met in private homes, and there were probably many house churches in Rome.

2. *Epenetus*. Epenetus, whom Paul mentions next, was Paul's friend. He calls him "my dear friend," adding that he was "the first convert to Christ in the province of Asia." Since Paul was the first to evangelize Asia, this can only mean that Paul had led Epenetus to Christ. No wonder Paul did not forget him! You always remember those you lead to Christ, especially the first man or woman.

3. *Mary*. There are many Marys in the New Testament, especially the Gospels, but there is no reason to associate this Mary with any of them. Paul says that Mary "worked very hard for you," which means that she was from Rome. Paul had probably been told about her by Aquila and Priscilla, who had come to Corinth about the time Paul had first arrived there. Literally Paul's words mean "Mary the toiler." She may have been one of the earliest members of the Roman church, and her toil may have been largely responsible for its spiritual and organizational well-being. Mary bore no title, but she had the gift of helps (see 1 Cor. 12:28), and Paul is careful to remember those who exercise such service.

4. *Andronicus and Junias*. Paul says four things about these two people: (1) they were his relatives, (2) they had been in prison with him, (3) they were outstanding among the apostles, and (4) they were in Christ before he was.

This is quite remarkable. Calling them his relatives could mean that they were members of his own extended family, but it probably does not. Like other similar references (see v. 11), it probably means only that they were Jews. They had become Christians before he did, however, and this means that they must have gone back to the very earliest days of the infant church in Jerusalem. Interestingly, here are Jews from the very early days of the church who were now in Rome and were part of the congregation there.

The phrase "outstanding among the apostles" is ambiguous. It could mean that they were apostles who were outstanding, or that the apostles considered them to be outstanding. In the first case, Paul would be using the word *apostles* in a less than strict sense to indicate those who are messengers of or for Jesus Christ.

It is possible that the name Junias (NIV) is actually Junia, which being a feminine form of the same name might mean that these two people were husband and wife and that Junia is therefore being commended along with her husband as an outstanding "apostle," in the broad sense, of course. John Chrysostom believed Junia was indeed a woman and was impressed enough to say, "Oh! how great is the devotion of this woman, that she should be even counted worthy of the appellation of apostle."[3] As we saw in the last study, Paul did not belittle women but praised them highly.

3. John Chrysostom, *The Homilies of St. John Chrysostom: Romans* in *A Select Library of the Nicene and Post-Nicene Fathers of the Christian Church*, ed. Philip Schaff (Grand Rapids: Wm. B. Eerdmans Publishing Company, 1975), vol. 11, p. 555.

5. *Ampliatus.* Ampliatus was a common slave name, but it may be significant that in the cemetery of Domatilla, which is the earliest of the Christian catacombs, there is an elaborate tomb with the single word *Ampliatus* on it. Since it bears only the one name, it seems to mark the tomb of a slave—free men had more than one name—but since it is elaborate it seems to be the tomb of an important person in the church. In other words, in the Roman church there were no distinctions based upon whether one was a slave or free. It may also be possible, since Ampliatus is associated with Domatilla, who was a woman of high status in Rome, that this is an example of how Christianity penetrated by degrees into even the highest levels of Roman rank and society.

6. *Urbanus, Stachys, Apelles, and Herodion.* Verses 9–11 mention four men of whom we know nothing other than what Paul tells us here. Urbanus is called a "fellow worker." Stachys is "my dear friend," like Epenetus. Apelles is "tested and approved in Christ." Herodion, like Andronicus and Junias, is called Paul's "relative." It is worth noting that Apelles means called. So putting everything we know about him together, we have one who is "called, tested, and approved in Christ." What a testimony! What a fine thing to be said about any one of us!

7. *The households of Aristobulus and Narcissus.* Neither Aristobulus nor Narcissus is greeted personally by Paul, which is why we count twenty-four names of those Paul knew, rather than twenty-six. Paul speaks only of their households, yet even these households are interesting.

In Rome the word *household* did not only describe a man's family and close relations; it included his household domestics or slaves as well. Now in Rome there had lived a grandson of the Jewish king Herod the Great whose name was Aristobulus. When he died his slaves would have passed to the ownership of the emperor and would have been known as those of "the household of Aristobulus." Thus, Paul's greeting may well be to those Jewish slaves who belonged to this household but who had become Christians and were members of the Roman church. This is made more likely because of the name Herodion, which follows Aristobulus. Herodion is clearly derived from Herod, so he may have been one of the leading slaves in this household.[4]

Narcissus is the name of a wealthy freedman who had been prominent under Claudius but had been put to death by Nero when he took the throne. Again, there seem to have been a significant number of believers in this household.

8. *Tryphena and Tryphosa.* These two female names come from a root that means "to live delicately or daintily," so Paul may be using positive irony when he commends "Delicate" and "Dainty" for actually working hard. None of us should be dainty in practice as long as God has rigorous work for us to do.

9. *Persis.* When Paul wrote about Tryphena and Tryphosa working hard in the Lord he used the present tense, which meant that they were still work-

---

4. This is developed by William Barclay, who is a source of much useful information on the personalities of early Rome. See William Barclay, *The Letter to the Romans* (Edinburgh: The Saint Andrew Press, 1969), p. 233.

ing. Here he uses the past tense, translated "who has worked very hard" in the New International Version. This probably means that Persis was old; her hardworking days were over. Yet although she could no longer work as she once had, what she did was remembered and she was highly regarded. Paul calls her "my dear friend," actually "the beloved."

10. *Rufus and his mother.* William Barclay says that one of the great "hidden romances" of the New Testament lies behind the name of Rufus and his mother. Who was this Rufus? If you look up his name in a concordance, you will find that a Rufus is mentioned in Mark 15:21. That chapter tells the story of Christ's crucifixion, and it mentions that a Cyrenian man named Simon was forced to carry Christ's cross when Jesus was too weak to do it. Mark says that Simon of Cyrene was the father of Alexander and Rufus. Why would he mention that? He would if Alexander and Rufus were well known. Add to this the fact that Mark's Gospel was written for the church at Rome especially, and we have not only the reason why Mark would mention these men but also a probable identification of Paul's Rufus. Quite possibly he was the son of the man who carried Christ's cross.

What a story lies hidden here! Simon was a Jew who, like all Jews, would have hated the Romans. To be pressed into service by a Roman soldier and be forced to carry the cross of a condemned man must have been a hateful, bitter experience for him. But something important may have happened to Simon that day. Instead of merely flinging down the cross at Golgotha, Simon must have been struck by the person of Jesus, stayed to watch the crucifixion, and eventually been converted, perhaps by the same elements that God used to reach the heart of the believing thief. After the Passover he would have returned home to Cyrene and would have told his family about Jesus. They may have become Christians through his testimony.

William Barclay goes even farther, remembering that "it was men from Cyprus and Cyrene" who came to Antioch and first preached the gospel to the Gentile world (Acts 11:20). Was Simon one of the men from Cyrene? Was Rufus with him? Turn to Ephesus. A riot is instigated by people who served Diana of the Ephesians, and the crowd would have killed Paul if they could have gotten to him. Barclay writes, "Who stands out to look that mob in the face? A man called Alexander (Acts 19:33). Is this the other brother facing things out with Paul? And as for their mother—surely she in some hour of need must have brought to Paul the help and the comfort and the love which his own family refused him when he became a Christian."[5]

Much of this is only speculation, of course, but stranger histories have unfolded. It may be that this happened as a result of an apparently chance encounter between Simon and Jesus on the road to Calvary.

11. *Asyncritus, Phlegon, Hermes, Patrobas, Hermas, and the brothers with them.* We know nothing about this group of people except for what Paul tells us

5. Barclay, *The Letter to the Romans,* pp. 236–37.

here, and that is not much. Apparently these were men who in some way lived or worked together. Ray Stedman calls them "a businessmen's group."[6] They may have been slaves of one man or have become freedmen together. Since there are brothers mentioned with them, this may be another reference to a house church.

12. *Philologus, Julia, Nereus, and his sister, and Olympas and all the saints with them.* The most interesting name in this final collection is Nereus. Here again William Barclay provides intriguing information. In A.D. 95 two of the most distinguished people in Rome were condemned for being Christians. They were husband and wife, and their names were Flavius Clemens and Domatilla, the woman who gave her name to the earliest Christian graveyard in Rome. Flavius was executed. Domatilla was banished to the island of Pontia, probably because she was of royal blood. She was the granddaughter of Vespasian, a former emperor, and the niece of Domitian, who was the reigning emperor. The name of this couple's chamberlain, a personal steward who in some cases handled his master's finances, was Nereus.

We do not know, of course, if this is the same Nereus, but it may be that this was the very person through whom the gospel of God's grace entered this prominent Roman household and eventually led to the martyrdoms that doubtless shocked and troubled Rome.[7]

Not to Be Forgotten

When we look back over this chapter we begin to get a sense of how close these people were to Paul, though they were hundreds of miles away, and how much he loved them. For he calls them beloved and praises them for their faithful service to him and one another and for their labor in the Lord.

Do you love other Christians like that, especially people who are not quite like you? Some believers are bookish, working away in libraries in order to understand the Bible better and be more able to explain it to others. Other Christians are visible, popular figures. Some are quiet and self-effacing. Some are loud, enthusiastic, or even awkward in the way they express their Christianity. Some love somber liturgy. Others speak in tongues. No matter! They are all members of the one body of Jesus Christ and should be loved and appreciated by all others who are true Christians. They should be loved by you, if you are following in the footsteps of the apostle Paul in this area.

How did Paul come to know and actually love so many Christians? How did he remember them all? Chiefly because he was thinking about them rather than about himself. I think of the way he handled the delicate situation in Corinth when conflicting loyalties to himself, Peter, and Apollos threatened to divide that church. Paul told the Corinthians, "What, after all, is Apollos?

---

6. Ray C. Stedman, *From Guilt to Glory*, vol. 2, *Reveling in God's Salvation* (Portland, Oreg.: Multnomah Press, 1978), p. 220.

7. Barclay, *The Letter to the Romans*, p. 237.

And what is Paul? Only servants, through whom you came to believe—as the Lord has assigned to each his task. I planted the seed, Apollos watered it, but God made it grow" (1 Cor. 3:5–6). It is this spirit, a spirit that appreciates and values the work of the other Christian, even more than one's own, that flows through Paul's writings.

We need to be like him in this. We need to think about other people much more than we do, instead of always thinking of ourselves. Try making a list of people who have done something for you to bring you closer to Christ or whom God has used you to bless. Write down what they did and begin to thank God for them. If you can't think of anybody, at least start serving others so they will add you to *their* list of people not to be forgotten.

234

A Sudden Warning

Romans 16:17–19

I urge you, brothers, to watch out for those who cause divisions and put obstacles in your way that are contrary to the teaching you have learned. Keep away from them. For such people are not serving our Lord Christ, but their own appetites. By smooth talk and flattery they deceive the minds of naive people. Everyone has heard about your obedience, so I am full of joy over you; but I want you to be wise about what is good, and innocent about what is evil.

Romans is not the longest book in the Bible, or even the New Testament, but it is long for a letter, and Paul has taken a long time ending it. After all, of sixteen chapters fully one and a half contain Paul's final greetings.[1] He seemed to be ending when he commended Phoebe to the Roman church and sent greetings to these he knew who were in Rome, but then suddenly, in the middle of what appears to be his final comments, he breaks in with a completely unexpected warning about people who might "cause divisions and put obstacles in your way that are contrary to the teaching you have learned" (Rom. 16:17).

---

1. From Romans 15:14 to the end.

This warning is so sudden, unexpected, and sharp that some commentators consider it to be an interpolation—something added to the letter later by someone other than Paul. But to approach the paragraph this way is to miss how much Paul loved the Roman church, even though he had not yet been able to visit it, and how concerned he was that something harmful might enter into it to spoil the church and its witness.

Besides, his warning is not really unrelated to what he has just said. Leon Morris suggests that these verses may have been added as a thoughtful response to mentioning the kiss of peace in the previous verse. Paul might have thought how easy it would be for that existing harmony to be disrupted. Or they might have come into his mind as a result of his mentioning the churches he knew and from which he sends greetings in the same verse. Paul knew the problems that had developed in other churches. His letters are full of material dealing with such problems. Recalling them would suggest the troubles that might disrupt the Roman congregation in the future. Or perhaps Paul had received some disturbing reports from Rome just as he was bringing the letter to the Romans to a close.[2]

What we do know is that his fears were not groundless. When he finally did get to Rome he found precisely what he had warned them against. Paul wrote to the Philippians, saying, "Some [here] preach Christ out of envy and rivalry, but others out of good will. The latter do so in love, knowing that I am put here for the defense of the gospel. The former preach Christ out of selfish ambition, not sincerely, supposing that they can stir up trouble for me while I am in chains" (Phil. 1:15–17).

Boars in God's Vineyard

At the height of the Reformation, when Martin Luther was challenging the corruptions of the medieval church by a rediscovery of sound biblical exegesis and preaching, Pope Leo X issued a papal bull against Luther that complained that "a wild boar is ravishing God's vineyard."[3] Luther was not doing that, of course. He was more like an Old Testament prophet, recalling a wayward church to its apostolic roots. But wild boars really have ravished the church from time to time, and that is what Paul is warning about here. He warns against two specific things.

1. *Those who cause divisions.* What Paul has in mind when he speaks of "those who cause divisions" is not so much people who introduce heresies into the

2. Leon Morris, *The Epistle to the Romans* (Grand Rapids: Wm. B. Eerdmans Publishing Company, and Leicester, England: Inter-Varsity Press, 1988), pp. 538–39.

3. The bull was probably drafted by John Eck, Luther's first serious opponent, and the full opening sentences read: "Arise, O Lord, plead thine own cause; remember how the foolish man reproacheth thee daily; the foxes are wasting thy vineyard, which thou hast given to thy vicar Peter; the boar out of the woods doth waste it, and the wild beast of the field devoureth it" (see Thomas M. Lindsay, *A History of the Reformation*, vol. 1, *The Reformation in Germany* [Edinburgh: T. & T. Clark, 1963], p. 247).

church, though this also sometimes happens, but those who divide churches into factions that will be loyal to themselves.

Often these are people who show up in a congregation suddenly, usually from another church where they have also caused trouble, though they give no indication of that when they come. They are knowledgeable. They usually have considerable abilities. They are leaders in the sense that they have enthusiasm and get people to follow them easily. Generally they are used to teaching, and they want to fill this role in their new church. Unfortunately, although the Bible warns us to make full proof of those who want to be teachers, people like this are usually warmly welcomed and quickly put to work, because most churches need able people who actually want to serve.

But problems develop quickly. These new teachers begin to push a particular point of doctrine to the exclusion of other equally important truths. And they are critical of people who do not see things as they do or join them in pushing their personal concerns. When everyone does not go their way—and not all people do, because God always has some in any church who are not so easily taken in, who care for other believers and who are not serving themselves—these unbalanced and divisive teachers pull most of their followers away and start another fellowship. That fellowship is always presented as a more biblical, more faithful, or truer church.

The names of some churches point back to such an origin. They are "*The* Christian Church" or the only "*Full* Gospel Church" or "The *True* Light Gospel Church." I have even seen such names as "The Original Glorious Church" and "Holy Ghost Headquarters." Fortunately, some of these churches mature into less factional and stronger congregations when the founder moves on.

2. *Those who put obstacles in other persons' ways.* The other danger Paul warns the Roman church against is those who "put obstacles in your way that are contrary to the teaching you have learned." The word Paul uses here is *skandalon*, from which we get our word "scandal." He is not thinking of scandalous behavior, though that is also often a problem, but rather of adding things to the gospel that get in the way of those who are merely trying to obey the Bible and follow Jesus Christ.

This is what the Pharisees of Jesus' day were doing and why he spoke so harshly against them. The Pharisees imposed all kinds of extreme, extrabiblical requirements on their disciples. They required hundreds of detailed points of Sabbath observance, strict controls on diet, and the observance of many holy or otherwise special days. Jesus said of them, "They tie up heavy loads and put them on men's shoulders, but they themselves are not willing to lift a finger to move them. Everything they do is done for men to see" (Matt. 23:4–5). He also admonished them directly, "Woe to you, teachers of the law and Pharisees, you hypocrites! You shut the kingdom in men's faces. You yourselves do not enter, nor will you let those enter who are trying to" (Matt. 23:13).

People like this do not deny the essentials of the Christian faith, but they bring in other things that are not in the Bible and insist on conformity in these areas. In the Greek text of this verse Paul uses the words *para*, which means along side of, and *didachē*, which means teaching. So what he is thinking of is those who put some other teaching alongside of what is taught in Scripture.

Because these matters are not specified in Scripture, it is not necessarily wrong for a Christian to practice them. For example, it is acceptable for a Christian to adopt particular ways of observing the Lord's Day or certain standards of dress that he believes point to Jesus Christ or glorify Christ. What is wrong is attempting to impose these standards on other believers and then dividing the church because some Christians will not conform to them.

It is important to remember Galatians 5:1: "It is for freedom that Christ has set us free. Stand firm, then, and do not let yourselves be burdened again by a yoke of slavery." This is the climactic verse of Paul's great treatise on Christian liberty, and it teaches that we must not allow ourselves to be taken into bondage by anyone.

Wolves in Sheep's Clothing

Paul has some rather harsh things to say about people who divide the church over minor matters or insist that other Christians conform to their personal standards of behavior, thus adding to the teaching of Christ. His harsh judgments concern both the motivation behind their actions and their basic methodology.

1. *Their motivation.* When people such as the ones Paul is describing first enter into a Christian congregation, they come as angels of light. That is, they present themselves as teachers who want to instruct and help other believers and move the church forward. They care for them. They want them to experience the fullness of God's blessing.

But this is not what they achieve, nor is it what they are really after. Paul says they really want to serve "their own appetites," not Jesus Christ. What are these appetites? John MacArthur answers, "No matter how seemingly sincere and caring false teachers or preachers may appear to be, they are never genuinely concerned for the cause of Christ or for his church. They are often driven by self-interest and self-gratification—sometimes for fame, sometimes for power over their followers, always for financial gain, and frequently for all of those reasons. Many of them enjoy pretentious and luxurious life-styles, and sexual immorality is the rule more than the exception."[4]

These are sometimes pastors who dominate their congregations, or evangelists who make a great deal of money and live lavishly on the many sacrificial gifts of their followers.

These teachers are described in Philippians and Jude: "Many live as enemies of the cross of Christ. Their destiny is destruction, their god is their stom-

4. John MacArthur, Jr., *The MacArthur New Testament Commentary: Romans 9–16* (Chicago: Moody Press, 1994), p. 374.

ach, and their glory is in their shame. Their mind is on earthly things" (Phil. 3:18–19). "These men are blemishes at your love feasts, eating with you without the slightest qualm—shepherds who feed only themselves. They are clouds without rain, blown along by the wind; autumn trees, without fruit and uprooted—twice dead. They are wild waves of the sea, foaming up their shame; wandering stars, for whom blackest darkness has been reserved forever" (Jude 12–13). No wonder Paul warned the Romans against such false teachers in strong terms.

2. *Their methodology.* The second thing Paul says about teachers like this concerns their methodology. They operate by deception, deliberately setting out to deceive the unwary: "By smooth talk and flattery they deceive the minds of naive people" (v. 18). The New International Version's "smooth talk" captures the idea behind the Greek word *chrêstologia*, but it is useful to note that this compound Greek word is based on the noun *logos*, meaning word or talk, preceded by the adjective *chrêstos*, meaning kind, loving, merciful, or easy to bear. In other words, the term refers to moral talk that appears to be kind and loving. Therefore, it requires a wise person to discern what is going on. We must discern that these people are not what they appear to be.

Apostles of Deceit

It is hard to read what Paul is writing about here without thinking of two recent books: *The Agony of Deceit,* edited by Michael Scott Horton, and *Christianity in Crisis,* by radio host Hank Hanegraaff. Both examine the false teaching of the best-known television evangelists, faith healers, and "health, wealth, and happiness" preachers.[5] These men have been wildly successful in many cases, raking in millions of dollars from their followers. But they have been guilty of precisely the kind of deception Paul was warning the Romans against—smooth talk and flattery.

1. *Special revelations.* Virtually all these teachers pretend to have received special new revelations from God. Robert Tilton built a television empire that at its peak brought in over sixty-five million dollars a year, promising healing to people who would covenant with him by sending in a large financial gift. He claimed, "God showed me a vision that almost took my breath away. I was sucked into the Spirit . . . and I found myself standing in the very presence of Almighty God. . . . He said these words to me, exactly these words."[6] At that point he introduced the plan by which he would raise money. Fortunately, Tilton's empire has fallen on financial hard times since ABC's *Prime Time Live* showed how his listeners' prayer requests were first stripped of money, then quickly disposed of in huge dumpsters.

5. Michael Horton, editor, *The Agony of Deceit* (Chicago: Moody Press, 1990); Hank Hanegraaff, *Christianity in Crisis* (Eugene, Oreg.: Harvest House Publishers, 1993).

6. Horton, *The Agony of Deceit,* p. 39.

2. *Little gods.* These preachers tell their followers that they are "little gods." Paul Crouch said on a Trinity Broadcasting Network program, "We are gods. I am a little god. I have his name. I am one with him."[7] Casey Treat, the pastor of Seattle's Christian Faith Center, said, "When God looks in the mirror, he sees me! When I look in the mirror, I see God!"[8] Kenneth Hagin, another faith healer, said, "You are as much the incarnation of God as Jesus Christ was."[9] Morris Cerullo said, "You're not looking at Morris Cerullo—you're looking at God. You're looking at Jesus."[10]

3. *A merely human Christ.* Surprisingly, because it is utterly contradictory, some of these false teachers deny that Jesus Christ is fully God. Kenneth Copeland claims to have heard Jesus say, "I didn't claim I was God; I just claimed I walked with him and that he was in me. . . . That's what you're doing."[11]

4. *Demoting God.* These teachers also limit God. Kenneth Copeland said, "God cannot do anything for you apart or separate from faith" because "faith is God's source of power."[12] Frederick Price declared, "God has to be given permission to work in this earth realm on behalf of man. . . . Yes! You are in control! . . . When God gave Adam dominion, that meant God no longer had dominion. So, God cannot do anything in this earth unless we let him. And the way we let him or give him permission is through prayer."[13]

5. *Gospel of greed.* This false teaching tells people how God wants them to get rich and how being poor is sinful. Frederick Price says, "If the Mafia can ride around in Lincoln Continental town cars, why can't the King's Kids?"[14] Robert Tilton said, "Not only is worrying a sin, being poor is a sin when God promises prosperity."[15] How different from the Son of Man, who did not even have "a place to lay his head" (Matt. 8:20).

These quotations are enough to show how heretical the evangelists I have just named are. Christians should be appalled at such teaching. Yet thousands of people who consider themselves to be sincere spiritual Christians apparently do not know that this is false, or choose to ignore it. Otherwise they would not give these men millions of dollars or recommend that others watch their programs.

What are we to call this teaching? Heresy, yes. But also deliberate deception. In some cases, as in that of some faith healers, their deception has been documented. Peter Popoff is a southern California-based evangelist. During a large crusade in which he claimed to have supernatural knowledge of the

7. Horton, *The Agony of Deceit,* p. 45.
8. Ibid., p. 91.
9. Ibid., p. 112.
10. Hanegraaff, *Christianity in Crisis,* p. 11.
11. Horton, *The Agony of Deceit,* p. 114.
12. Hanegraaff, *Christianity in Crisis,* p. 65.
13. Ibid., p. 85.
14. Ibid., p. 191.
15. Ibid., p. 186.

names and ailments of several people in the audience a shrewd member of the Committee for the Scientific Examination of Religion named James Randi used a radio scanner to pick up the frequency on which Popoff's wife was broadcasting information to him. She fed him names, illnesses, and addresses of people in the audience to whom she had previously spoken. In the spring of 1986 Randi made his findings public on NBC's *The Tonight Show*.[16]

This is a modern-day parallel to what took place in the Garden of Eden when Satan deceived Eve by promising that if she and her husband disobeyed God and followed Satan they would be "like God, knowing good and evil" (Gen. 3:5). Of course, they already were like God, because they had been made in God's image (see Gen. 1:26–27). After they sinned, Adam and Eve actually became like Satan, who knew evil because he practiced it.

Have Nothing to Do with Them

Not all deceivers and flatterers in the church are this obvious, but they still pose a terrible threat to true Christian people and congregations. Paul gives an answer to what should be done about them in this important paragraph in Romans. It is a simple bit of advice. Yet before we notice what it is, we need to see what it is not. Notice that the Roman Christians were not told to harm the heretics physically, as many church leaders did in the Middle Ages. They were not to have witch trials or burn heretics at the stake. More surprisingly, they were not told to debate the false teachers, to try to prove them wrong.

Quite simply, they were "to watch out for" them and "keep away from them" (v. 17). Then, as if to explain what he is talking about, Paul says, "I want you to be wise about what is good, and innocent about what is evil" (v. 19). Put in today's terms, this means that Christians should not watch false teachers on television. We should not buy their books or attend their meetings. We should ignore them as figures standing entirely outside the fold of genuine Christianity.

In other words, we are to know that they are there but keep away from them. The verb translated "watch out for" in verse 17 is *skopeo*, from which we get our word *scope*, as in telescope and microscope. It has given us our word *bishop*, which means an overseer.

Paul is only telling the Romans in his own words what Jesus said on the issue. Jesus told his disciples, "Watch out for false prophets. They come to you in sheep's clothing, but inwardly they are ferocious wolves. By their fruit you will recognize them" (Matt. 7:15–16). He warned, "False Christs and false prophets will appear and perform great signs and miracles to deceive even the elect—if that were possible" (Matt. 24:24). He also said, "I am sending

16. Horton, *The Agony of Deceit*, pp. 205–6. *The Tonight Show* program was aired April 22, 1986.

you out like sheep among wolves. Therefore be as shrewd as snakes and as innocent as doves. Be on your guard against [them]" (Matt. 10:16–17).

That is exactly what Paul is saying in the last verse of this section when he tells the Roman congregation, "I want you to be wise about what is good, and innocent about what is evil" (v. 19). We are to know about evil, but we are not to know everything about it. We must not want to. Instead, we must fill our minds and hearts with what is good—with the doctrines of this letter, for example—and be on our guard against those who would lead us from the simplicity of what we have been taught to the deception of special revelations, new insights, novel doctrines, or movements that bow before a human teacher rather than glorify God.

235

The Head of Satan Crushed

Romans 16:20

The God of peace will soon crush Satan under your feet.

One of the remarkable things about Christians is that we are able to pass rapidly and naturally from what most people regard as a merely human activity to what is spiritual. For example, we are in a gathering of friends. Everyone is talking and having a good time. We are about to sit down and eat dinner. Then suddenly we stop and pray, thanking God for the food and the opportunity to be together and asking him to bless the evening and guide our conversations in a way that will bring honor to him.

One moment we are walking down the street, enjoying the fresh balmy air of early summer. The next we are praising God as the source of life and the giver of all good things.

One moment we see some great wrong or error. The next moment we are asking God to overthrow the error. The reason we can do this is that for a Christian nothing is ever completely secular.

There is a situation like this as we come to verse 20 of Paul's closing chapter of Romans. Paul has been sending greetings to his friends in Rome and will soon join the greetings of those who were in Corinth to his own. Nothing is more natural than this. He warns about divisions that might harm the church's close fellowship. This, too, is natural. But suddenly Paul moves out of the natural realm into the realm of spiritual realities, predicting for these Roman Christians (and for us, too) that "the God of peace will soon crush Satan under your feet." This short and unexpected sentence immediately lifts what he has been saying from a merely human to a supernatural level.

Spiritual Warfare

Our world is secular and materialistic—it considers as real only what it can see or touch or measure. For our contemporaries the world is a closed system. God is eliminated. True, many people still say that they believe in God; some even believe in Satan. But spiritual beings do not matter; there is no spiritual warfare. Therefore, we are accused by our worldly contemporaries of slighting the battles that in their opinion need to be waged urgently against such visible foes as poverty, oppression, hunger, and injustice.

We do not deny for a moment that poverty, oppression, hunger, and injustice are real problems or that we should not do everything in our power to alleviate or abolish them. But we ask this: If the real problems of this world are merely material and visible, how is it that they have not been solved or eliminated long ago?

Algernon Charles Swinburne called man "the master of things." All right, then, let man master them! If he cannot—and it is perfectly evident that he cannot—let him acknowledge that it is because forces stronger than himself stand behind what is visible. Let him acknowledge that our struggle is not merely against flesh and blood, which we see, but "against the rulers, against the authorities, against the powers of this dark world and against the spiritual forces of evil in the heavenly realms" (Eph. 6:12).[1]

Paul was acutely aware of the cosmic nature of our struggle, so it is as natural as breathing for him to mention it in closing his letter to the Romans.

Three Surprises in One Statement

Leon Morris in his commentary calls Romans 16:20 "a little devotional section with a prophecy and a prayer for grace."[2] It is that. But it is a remarkable statement too, and one thing that makes it remarkable—in addition to the cosmic dimensions that I have been writing about—is that it contains three surprising statements, all in one sentence.

---

1. I have dealt with spiritual warfare and the world's blindness to it at greater length in James Montgomery Boice, *Ephesians: An Expositional Commentary* (Grand Rapids: Zondervan Publishing House, 1988), pp. 195–99.

2. Leon Morris, *The Epistle to the Romans* (Grand Rapids: Wm. B. Eerdmans Publishing Company, and Leicester, England: Inter-Varsity Press, 1988), p. 541.

1. *That the God of peace should crush anyone.* This is surprising because crushing seems ruthless to us, and we do not easily reconcile crushing with peace or peacemaking. It does not seem to be what God or any good personality should do. How can a God of peace be belligerent?

2. *That the crushing of Satan should be under our feet.* This is surprising because Genesis 3:15, which Paul's statement obviously refers to, says that it is *Jesus* who will crush Satan: "He [that is, Jesus] will crush your head, and you will strike his heel." How then are *we* to do it?

3. *That this crushing is going to happen soon.* This is surprising because Paul's words were written to Christians in Rome nearly two thousand years ago, and Satan does not seem to be defeated yet. In fact, the world is precisely what Paul described it as being then (see Rom. 1:28–32).

In the Beginning

Since Romans 16:20 is an obvious reference to the verse in Genesis 3 that prophesies Satan's defeat by Jesus Christ, we should begin with the story of the fall into sin by our first parents.

Adam and Eve had been placed in the Garden of Eden by God and had been given rule over the lower forms of the created order. They were to manage the earth for God, and they were free to do as they saw fit, with but one exception. They could eat fruit from any of the trees of the garden—except the tree of the knowledge of good and evil. God told them that if they ate from it, they would die.

This was what Satan picked up on. When Satan entered the garden he approached the woman with the suggestion that if God prohibited them from eating from the tree of the knowledge of good and evil—that is, if he placed even this one, single restriction upon them—he might as well have forbidden them from eating from any of the trees. His argument was that God cannot be good, nor can he have our best interests at heart, if he makes prohibitions. We should be allowed to do anything. This, the first of Satan's temptations, was a temptation to doubt God's benevolence, and it is exactly what we have today when someone suggests that having to obey the laws of God is burdensome. We ask, If God really loves us, why doesn't he permit us to do anything we want to do?

The second temptation was to question God's truthfulness. For when the woman replied, "We may eat fruit from the trees in the garden, but God did say, 'You must not eat fruit from the tree that is in the middle of the garden, and you must not touch it, or you will die,'" Satan replied with a flat contradiction. He told the woman, "You will not surely die." Whom was the woman to believe? As we know, she decided to trust her own observations and judgment rather than the Word of God, with the result that she ate from the tree and gave some to her husband so that he ate also. This is also a temptation that comes to us today, for we are always tempted to trust our own opinions, however sin-affected and unjustified they may be, rather than the Word of him who is the very embodiment of truth.

The third temptation is what actually turned Eve to disobedience. For Satan told her that God had placed the restriction on her because he did not want her and her husband to reach their full potential: "God knows that when you eat of it your eyes will be opened, and you will be like God, knowing good and evil" (Gen. 3:5; see vv. 1–5).

Eve apparently desired to be like God, which is what Satan had himself tried to do earlier with disastrous consequences. Now, as happened to Satan and the angels that followed him in his rebellion, disaster came upon our first parents too. Their spirits, that part of their beings that had communion with God, died. So they hid from God when he came to them in the garden later. Their bodies began to die, and eventually they did die. For as God said in his words of punishment spoken to the man, "Dust you are and to dust you will return" (v. 19). In addition, God punished the woman by subjecting her to pain in childbirth and the man by subjecting him to hard labor in order to earn a living.

But God made a promise too, and it came in the midst of his judgment upon the serpent Satan had used for his temptations. God cursed the serpent, causing him to crawl on his belly and eat dust all the days of his life. But then he said this:

> "I will put enmity
> between you and the woman,
> and between your offspring and hers;
> he will crush your head,
> and you will strike his heel."

Genesis 3:15

This promise is known to scholars as the protoevangelium, meaning the first announcement of the gospel. It is a promise of peace with God to be achieved by Christ's work. But strikingly, like Romans 16:20, it speaks of conflict, too. There are three levels of conflict: (1) between Satan and the woman; (2) between Satan's offspring—that is, those who follow him—and the woman's offspring—that is, those who would follow in her faith; and (3) finally and most importantly, between Satan and Christ.

We know what Satan did when he was able to strike Christ's heel. He did it at the cross. It included hatred from the religious leaders, mocking by the crowds, severe beatings, and eventually the terrible agony of the crucifixion. Satan must have been delighted by every detail of his apparent triumph. Yet although Satan might have thought he had won, it was a bruising only and not a defeat for Christ, because on the third day after the crucifixion Jesus rose from the grave triumphantly.

Moreover, on the other side, Satan's triumph turned out to be a Pyrrhic victory, for by it his power over us was broken. I do not know what Satan was thinking when he finally saw his great enemy on the cross, but I am sure he must have forgotten this prophecy with its prediction of his eventual and sure defeat. John H. Gerstner wrote of this moment:

> Satan was majestically triumphant in this . . . battle. He had nailed Jesus to the cross. The prime object of all his striving through all the ages was achieved. But he failed. For the prophecy which had said that he would indeed bruise the seed of the woman had also said that his head would be crushed by Christ's heel. Thus, while Satan was celebrating his triumph in battle over the Son of God, the full weight of the atonement accomplished by the crucifixion (which the devil had effected) came down on him, and he realized that all this time, so far from successfully battling against the Almighty, he had actually been carrying out the purposes of the all-wise God.[3]

Satan's only power—unlike his pretensions to power—comes from the character of God that declares that sin must be punished. His strength comes from working within the laws of that character. Satan reasoned that if he could get the man and woman to sin, which he did, the wrath of God against sin must inevitably come down on them. God's good designs would be thwarted. Satan failed to see that Jesus would take the place of sinners, bearing their punishment, and that he, Satan, would have his power broken in the process.

Paul wrote of this triumph more completely in his letter to the Colossians: "[God] forgave us all our sins, having canceled the written code, with its regulations, that was against us and that stood opposed to us; he took it away, nailing it to the cross. And having disarmed the powers and authorities, he made a public spectacle of them, triumphing over them by the cross" (Col. 2:13–15). In view of this triumph, America's great theologian Jonathan Edwards was right to call Satan the greatest blockhead the world has ever known. For although Satan is exceedingly knowledgeable and cunning, he was also supremely stupid to suppose that he could out-think the all-wise God or overpower the Almighty.

Paul's Prophecy in Romans

Having reviewed the Old Testament story to which Paul is referring in Romans 16:20, we now need to go back to Paul to deal with the puzzling features of his statement and learn what he is teaching. Genesis 3:15 is a prophecy. So is Romans 16:20. So let's compare these two prophecies, looking at these three puzzling features.

1. *That the God of peace should crush anyone.* Our problem with this statement, as with many other statements that involve the character of God, is that we do

3. John H. Gerstner, "The Language of the Battlefield," in James M. Boice, ed., *Our Savior God: Man, Christ and the Atonement* (Grand Rapids: Baker Book House, 1980), pp. 159–60.

not understand God very well. When Satan told the woman that God could not be good if he placed even a single restriction upon her and Adam, his temptation was based on our failure to understand what is good. God's goodness is not a quality that allows us to do anything at all, even if it hurts us. It is a characteristic that lays down beneficial rules according to God's moral nature.

In the same way, the peacefulness of God is not a quality that causes God to avoid all conflict or hide from hostility. It is an active attribute that makes peace where hostility existed beforehand. In Romans 16:20 God is called the "God of peace" because he makes peace by destroying the enmity between him and us in our sin, and by defeating Satan.

God makes peace in other areas also. Robert Haldane writes:

> God is the God of peace, because he . . . is the author of all the peace that his people enjoy. Were it not for the overruling power of the Lord, his people would have no rest at any time in this world. But the Lord Jesus rules in the midst of his enemies, and he gives his people peace in the midst of their enemies. This shows us that we ought constantly to look to God for this peace. If we seek it not, but grow self-confident and secure, dangers and troubles may arise from every quarter. Our only security is God, and our duty is constantly to ask peace of him in the midst of a world of trouble. . . . We ought, therefore, constantly to pray for peace to God's people all over the world. We ought to pray for the peace of Jerusalem as our chief joy. . . .
>
> Even in the churches there would be no peace, were it not for God's presence. Such is the cunning of Satan, and the remaining ignorance and corruption of the Lord's people, that Satan would keep them in continual broils, if God did not powerfully counteract him. God is here called the God of peace, with a peculiar reference to the factious persons against whom the believers were warned in the preceding connection.[4]

2. That the crushing of Satan should be under our feet. When we speak of salvation we sometimes say that we have been saved, are being saved, and one day will be saved—three tenses. In a similar way, when we speak of Jesus' victory over Satan, it is possible to say that Satan has been defeated, that he is being defeated, and that he will be defeated. The first and third of these victories has been or will be by the Lord Jesus Christ alone. We have no part in it. But we do have a part in the second of these battles, Satan's being defeated, which is why Paul can say, "The God of peace will soon crush Satan under your feet."

How is Satan crushed under our feet? Here is a point where the link between this text and Genesis 3:15 is very helpful. We must remember that in the Garden of Eden Satan had come to Eve offering her and her husband the knowledge of good and evil: "You will be like God, knowing good and

---

4. Robert Haldane, *An Exposition of the Epistle to the Romans* (MacDill AFB: MacDonald Publishing Company, 1958), p. 644.

evil" (Gen. 3:5). In Romans 16, in the verse immediately before our text, Paul has just told the Roman Christians, "I want you to be wise about what is good, and innocent about what is evil" (v. 19). That sentence is what must have suggested the Genesis story to him and led him to write what he did in verse 20. He must have been thinking that Satan offered the knowledge of good and evil by getting Adam and Eve to do evil. Of course, they did not become like God, knowing good and evil; they became like Satan. What Paul desires of the Christians, by contrast, is that they become like God in this area, knowing and embracing the good but shunning evil, even though they will be aware of its nature and know that it is there. It is when we live like this that God will use us to crush Satan.

In other words, this crushing of Satan has to do with our victory in the sphere of the knowledge of good and evil, the same sphere in which sin first came to Eve and Adam. And it has to do with our knowing and pursuing the good, regardless of the pain Satan or his followers may cause us because of it.

In Revelation 12:11 the apostle John writes of the victory of the saints over Satan, saying, "They overcame him by the blood of the Lamb and by the word of their testimony." There are two parts to this victory: first, the victory achieved by Jesus through his death on the cross, and second, the victory won by our testimony to the truth of God. As for the latter, it is God's victory—God working in us—but it is our victory too, since it is achieved by our testimony. This is what Paul is saying in Romans, for he says that it is God who will crush Satan but that he will do it under our feet—that is, through us.

But let us not forget that we are to use God's weapons in this battle. The world has its weapons, but they are not ours. The weapons of the world are money, numbers, power, and politics. Our weapons are the Word of God and prayer: the Word of God, because it carries within it the power of God to demolish arguments and bring down strongholds; prayer, because even with the Word of God it requires the regenerating power of God to open blind minds to receive it and be persuaded of its truth.

3. *That this crushing is going to happen soon.* The word translated *soon* in Romans 16:20 has two meanings: quickly or without taking much time, and near at hand. So the prophecy that God will crush Satan soon could mean either: (1) that when he does it, it will happen quickly or (2) the victory is just around the corner. Those who choose the second meaning sometimes suggest that Paul was mistaken, since this was written almost two thousand years ago and Satan is not defeated yet.

But what is the victory about which Paul is writing? If it is what I have been suggesting—that is, the victory of believers who live by the truth of God's Word and do the right and good thing, regardless of whatever harsh consequences may come from it—then the victory is immediate, constant, widespread and absolute. For when you do the right thing, God is glorified and Satan is shown to be a failure. This victory is complete in itself. It does not need to be added to. Nothing can diminish it or take it away.

Moreover, every victory for us like this is a promise of victories yet to come. Every act of good in this life is a victory and points to Christ's final victory. Every quiet triumph of faith over fear and pain in the hour of death is a victory, a defeat of Satan, whose ultimate but ultimately ineffective weapon is death. He has been "a murderer from the beginning" (John 8:44). It points to the final victory of the resurrection. All trust in Christ points to faith in his return, when Satan and his angels will be totally destroyed. This is the great and final victory. It is for this that we both long and wait.

Leon Morris says that "the promise of this victorious issue [the defeat of Satan by Christ] undergirds the fight of faith."[5] This is something we must grasp. Satan is our enemy as well as God's, and he is very fierce. But God is our champion and the ultimate victor. Martin Luther wrote wisely in that great Reformation hymn "A Mighty Fortess Is Our God":

> Did we in our own strength confide,
> Our striving would be losing;
> Were not the right man on our side,
> The man of God's own choosing.
> Dost ask who that may be? Christ Jesus, it is he.
> Lord Sabaoth his name, from age to age the same
> And he must win the battle.

---

5. Morris, *The Epistle to the Romans*, p. 273.

236

The Third Benediction

Romans 16:20

The grace of our Lord Jesus be with you.

Christians love benedictions. They love them because they know that they are not meaningless but are based on the character of God, who is gracious, and they are honored by God because they are prayers for the spiritual well-being of other people, which is God's desire and delight.

Paul normally ends his letters with a benediction, usually praying that those to whom he is writing might know and continue to be blessed by God's grace, as here in Romans 16:20. It is a perfect way to end these letters.[1] For when all is said and done, what is most wonderful about God is that he is truly gracious. He has been and will continue to be. Paul has already written two earlier benedictions in this letter. In Romans 15:13 he wrote, "May the God of hope fill you with all joy and peace as you trust in him." In Romans 15:33 he continued, "The God of peace be with you all. Amen." Here he says simply, "The grace of our Lord Jesus be with you."

1. Sometimes this is expanded (as in 2 Corinthians 13:14), sometimes shortened (as in Colossians 4:18). See 1 Corinthians 16:23; Galatians 6:18; Ephesians 6:24; Philippians 4:23; 1 Thessalonians 5:28; 2 Thessalonians 3:18; 1 Timothy 6:21; 2 Timothy 4:22; Titus 3:15; Philemon 25. Benedictions also occur in the introduction to letters, as in Romans 1:7; 1 Corinthians 1:3; 2 Corinthians 1:2; Ephesians 1:2; Philippians 1:2; Colossians 1:2; 1 Thessalonians 1:1; 2 Thessalonians 1:2; 1 Timothy 1:2; and Titus 1:4.

Amazing Grace

A number of years ago I wrote a book in which I studied all the verses in the Bible that have to do with grace.[2] By the time I had finished, I was convinced anew that the most wonderful theme in all the Word of God is God's grace.

Apparently other people have thought so too. Of all the songs that have ever been written, the one that has been recorded most by the largest number of different vocal artists is "Amazing Grace," the classic Christian hymn written in 1779 by John Newton, the former slave trader turned preacher.

> Amazing grace—how sweet the sound—
> That saved a wretch like me!
> I once was lost but now am found—
> Was blind, but now I see.

Grace really is amazing. It is the most amazing thing in this vast universe, more amazing even than neutrons and neutrinos, quarks and quasars, and black holes. Whenever I come to a tremendous word in the Bible, one of the things I do is look in hymnbooks to see what has been written about it by Christians who have gone before me. When I did that for grace, I was surprised by the many words for grace and the many varieties of grace that were listed.

Our church uses the *Trinity Hymnal,* which lists hymns dealing with grace under the following headings: converting grace, the covenant of grace, efficacious grace, the fullness of grace, magnified grace, refreshing grace, regenerating grace, sanctifying grace, saving grace, and sovereign grace. It also has combined listings, such as the love and grace of God, the love and grace of Christ, the love and grace of the Holy Spirit, and salvation by grace.

Moreover, descriptive phrases are used in the hymns themselves: abounding grace, abundant grace, amazing grace, boundless grace, fountain of grace, God of grace, indelible grace, marvelous grace, matchless grace, overflowing grace, pardoning grace, plenteous grace, unfailing grace, unmeasurable grace, wonderful grace, wondrous grace, the word of grace, grace all sufficient, and grace alone.

One of my favorite hymns was written by Samuel Davies, a former president of Princeton University.

> Great God of wonders! All thy ways
> Are worthy of thyself—divine:
> And the bright glories of thy grace
> Among thine other wonders shine;
> Who is a pardoning God like thee?
> Or who has grace so rich and free?

---

2. The material in this chapter is borrowed with changes from James Montgomery Boice, *Amazing Grace* (Wheaton: Tyndale House Publishers, 1993), pp. 3–5, 17–18, 28, 48–60, 121–22, 232–33, 255–57.

Theologians speak of common grace, electing grace, irresistible grace, persevering grace, prevenient grace, pursuing grace, and saving grace. Yet even with these terms, I have not exhausted the Christian terminology. Grace is truly the greatest theme in Scripture.

Common Grace

Let's look at some of the aspects of grace, starting with common grace, grace made available to all persons regardless of their relationship to Jesus Christ.

A number of years ago a New York rabbi named Harold S. Kushner wrote a book called *When Bad Things Happen to Good People*. It was on the *New York Times* best-seller list for months, and its thesis was that bad things happen to good people because God is not omnipotent and things simply get away from him. At the end of the book Kushner advised us to forgive God and, like him, just try to get on with life and do the best we can.

How different from what the Bible teaches!

In Luke 13 there is an incident from the life of Jesus that has no exact parallel anywhere in the New Testament. People had come to Jesus to ask Harold Kushner's question, citing two contemporary examples. In the one example, the soldiers of King Herod had attacked some pilgrims who had come to Jerusalem from Galilee and had killed them while they were offering their sacrifices at the temple. In the other example, a tower in the district of Siloam collapsed and killed eighteen apparently innocent passersby.

The fact that the victims seem to have been innocent in both cases was an important part of the question, because the questioners wanted to know why tragedies like this can happen if God is good and if he is in control of things, as we want to believe. Perhaps he is not a good God. Or is it the case that these apparently good people were actually secret sinners and that this was God's way of striking them down for their transgressions?

For people accustomed to thinking as most of us do, Jesus' answer was startling. He replied, "Do you think that these Galileans were worse sinners than all the other Galileans because they suffered this way? . . . Or those eighteen who died when the tower in Siloam fell on them—do you think they were more guilty than all the others living in Jerusalem? I tell you, no! But unless you repent, you too will all perish" (Luke 13:2, 3–5).

Jesus was saying that when we ask why bad things happen to good people we are actually asking the wrong question. The right question is why good things happen to bad people. For we are all bad people, and good things happen to us every day of our lives. We have food to eat, clothes to wear, houses in which to live, families and friends, and meaningful work to do. The question is Why haven't the *worst* things happened? Why didn't the tower fall on us? Why weren't we struck down by Herod's soldiers? Why did God allow such wicked persons as ourselves to awake this morning, get out of bed, and go to work?

The answer is grace. God is a gracious God. He is gracious even to sinners.

Saving Grace

Common grace saves no one, of course. But although common grace does not save, the special grace of God operating by the preaching and teaching of the Word of God does. When we move into this area of biblical truth we need to speak about (1) sovereign grace, since God displays his saving grace where and upon whom he will; (2) redeeming grace, for we are saved by the death of Jesus Christ on our behalf; and (3) efficacious grace, for it is God's Holy Spirit who both accomplishes our regeneration and works faith.

Sovereign grace is emphasized in Paul's letter to the Ephesians. Like Romans, Ephesians deals with the most basic Christian doctrines. But even more than Romans, Ephesians stresses the sovereignty of God in salvation and the eternal sweep of God's plan, by which believers are lifted from the depth of sin's depravity and curse to the heights of eternal joy and communion with God—by God's grace. This is particularly evident in Ephesians 1:3–14. One commentator calls these verses "a magnificent gateway" to the Epistle, another "a golden chain of many links," still another "an operatic overture and the flight of an eagle."

This long list of interconnected doctrines is arranged in a trinitarian pattern. For Paul says that the blessings listed come from *God the Father* as a result of his electing choice, have been won for us by *Jesus Christ* by his atoning work of redemption, and are applied to us by the *Holy Spirit* through what theologians term effectual or efficacious calling.

1. *Electing grace.* Paul begins with the electing or predestinating choice of God the Father: "He chose us in him before the creation of the world to be holy and blameless in his sight. In love he predestinated us to be adopted as his sons through Jesus Christ, in accordance with his pleasure and will—to the praise of his glorious grace, which he has freely given us in the One he loves" (vv. 4–6). There are a lot of ideas in these verses, including such important ones as holiness, adoption, and the love of the Father for the Son. But the chief thought is of election.

God's electing grace is explained in several ways: as "predestination," another word for election; as being "in accordance with his pleasure and will," which explains election as being by God's will only; by "grace," which is explicitly mentioned; and finally, by the words "which he has freely given." These verses are one of the strongest expressions of sovereign grace in Scripture, for they teach that the blessings of salvation come to some people because God had determined from before the creation of the world to give them to these people—and for that reason only.

2. *Redeeming grace.* Electing women and men to salvation is not the only thing God has done as an expression of sovereign grace, however. Following the trinitarian pattern of this chapter, we come next to the doctrine of redemption (vv. 7–10). Redemption involves all three persons of the Godhead: (1) God the Father, who planned it; (2) God the Son, who accomplished it; and (3) God the Holy Spirit, who applies it to God's people. Redemption is chiefly

associated with Jesus, however, who is specifically called our Redeemer. This is what verses 7 and 8 tell us: "In him [Jesus] we have redemption through his blood, the forgiveness of sins, in accordance with the riches of God's grace, that he lavished on us with all wisdom and understanding."

Redemption is a commercial term meaning "to buy in the marketplace so that the object or person purchased might be freed from it," which is what Jesus did by dying in our place. In this illustration we are pictured as slaves to sin, unable to free ourselves from sin's bondage. Instead of freeing us, the world merely gambles for our souls. It offers everything that is its currency: fame, sex, pleasure, power, wealth. For these things millions sell their eternal souls and are perishing. But Jesus enters the marketplace as our Redeemer. He bids the price of his blood, and God says, "Sold to Jesus Christ." There is no higher bid than his. So we become his forever. The apostle Peter wrote, "It was not with perishable things such as silver and gold that you were redeemed from the empty way of life handed down to you from your forefathers, but with the precious blood of Christ, a lamb without blemish or defect" (1 Peter 1:18–19).

3. *Efficacious grace.* The final expression of the sovereign grace of God emphasized in this chapter is the work of the Holy Spirit in applying the salvation thus planned by God the Father and achieved by God the Son to the individual (vv. 11–14). At first glance the word *chosen* in verse 11 seems to be saying the same thing as Paul's words about the Father's choice in verse 4. But the idea is actually different. In verse 4 the predestinating choice of the Father stands before everything. Here the choice made by the Holy Spirit follows predestination and means that the Holy Spirit now makes God's choice effective in individual cases by choosing those individuals or leading them to faith.

One of the greatest pictures of the grace of God calling a dead sinner to life is Jesus' raising of Lazarus, recorded in John 11. When Jesus got to Bethany he was told that Lazarus had been dead for four days and that he was already putrefying: "By this time there is a bad odor, for he has been there four days" (John 11:39). What a graphic description of the state of our moral and spiritual decay because of sin! There was no hope that anything could be done for Lazarus in this condition.

But "with God all things are possible" (Matt. 19:26). Therefore, having prayed, Jesus called out, "Lazarus, come out!" (John 11:43), and the call of Jesus brought life to the dead man.

That is what the Holy Spirit does today. He works through the preaching of the Word of God to call to faith those whom God has elected to salvation and for whom Jesus Christ specifically died. Apart from those three actions—the act of God in electing, the work of Christ in dying, and the power of the Holy Spirit in calling—there would be no hope for anyone. No one could be saved. Because of those actions even the most depraved of blaspheming rebels can be turned from his or her folly and find salvation.

Abounding Grace

In Romans 5 Paul wrote of the abounding grace of God for those who have been elected to salvation, redeemed by Jesus Christ, and called to faith by the Holy Spirit: "The law was added so that the trespass might increase. But where sin increased, grace increased all the more, so that, just as sin reigned in death, so also grace might reign through righteousness to bring eternal life through Jesus Christ our Lord" (Rom 5:20–21).

Romans 5:20 was a favorite text of John Bunyan, best known as the author of *Pilgrim's Progress* but whose life story is told in the classic devotional auto-biography, *Grace Abounding to the Chief of Sinners.* The title is taken from Romans 5:20, which says, in the King James Version that Bunyan used, "Where sin abounded, grace abounded all the more," and from 1 Timothy 1:15, where Paul refers to himself as the "chief of sinners" (KJV). The title is thus a testimony to the abundant grace of God in Bunyan's life.

Bunyan was born in 1628 of poor parents. His father was a traveling tinker—a mender of pots and pans—and Bunyan practiced this trade for a time so that he became known as "the tinker of Bedford." He had little education. In his youth he was profligate. In time he became troubled by an acute sense of sin. He wrote of himself that in those days it seemed as if the sun that was shining in the heavens begrudged him its light and as if the very stones in the street and the tiles on the houses had turned against him. He felt that he was abhorred by them and was not fit to live among them or benefit from them, because he had "sinned against the Savior."

God saved Bunyan and gave him great peace, and the title of his book is his testimony to what he discovered. He discovered that, no matter how great his sin was, the grace of God proved greater.

Persevering Grace

Another important feature of grace is that it is persevering. God will persevere with those he has called to faith in Christ so that none will be lost and, because he perseveres with them, they also will persevere, resisting and overcoming the world, and thus be ready for Jesus when he comes for them. In other words, God never begins a work he does not graciously bring to full completion. He is the alpha as well as the omega, the beginning *and* the end of all things.

This makes me think of three passages of Scripture that have to do with perseverance. The first is Philippians 1:6: "being confident of this, that he who began a good work in you will carry it on to completion until the day of Christ Jesus."

The second is John 10:27–30: "My sheep listen to my voice; I know them, and they follow me. I give them eternal life, and they shall never perish; no one can snatch them out of my hand. My Father, who has given them to me, is greater than all; no one can snatch them out of my Father's hand. I and the Father are one."

The third is the best known of all, Romans 8:35–39: "Who shall separate us from the love of Christ? Shall trouble or hardship or persecution or famine or nakedness or danger or sword? As it is written: 'For your sake we face death all day long; we are considered as sheep to be slaughtered.' No, in all these things we are more than conquerors through him who loved us. For I am convinced that neither death nor life, neither angels nor demons, neither the present nor the future, nor any powers, neither height nor depth, nor anything else in all creation, will be able to separate us from the love of God that is in Christ Jesus our Lord."

Growth in Grace

Thus far, nearly everything I have said about grace has been in the past tense, meaning that God has revealed his grace to us or has been gracious to us in Christ Jesus, or it has been a promise that God will continue to be gracious. But Paul's benediction is a prayer. That is, it is a request that the grace of the Lord Jesus Christ would continue to be with his readers and that they might experience even more of it than they had before. What can this mean? If God has been so abundantly gracious to us, how can we continue to grow in grace? There are at least four ways Paul's prayer can and should be taken.

1. *We need to be settled in the great grace doctrines.* There are several ways we can fail to be settled in grace. We can allow something other than Jesus Christ to be at the center of our lives. We can forget how gracious God has been and therefore become harsh or cruel with others. We can substitute the mere form of Christianity for the gospel. The cure for these ills is to be so aware of the nature of the grace of God in saving us that we become enamored of Jesus Christ and never forget that it is by grace alone that we have been brought out of death and darkness into God's marvelous life and light.

2. *We need to grow in the knowledge of God's grace.* Knowledge of the grace of God is not a static thing. Therefore, we need to seek continually to grow in that knowledge. Peter wrote, "Grow in grace and knowledge of our Lord and Savior Jesus Christ" (2 Peter 3:18). For this we must study the Word of God and meditate on its teachings.

3. *We need to exercise the gift for serving others that God has given each of us.* We do not often think of the grace of God and the gifts of God as belonging together, but a number of passages combine the two ideas. Peter wrote that each Christian "should use whatever gift he has received to serve others, faithfully administering God's grace in its various forms" (1 Peter 4:10). Paul wrote to the church at Ephesus, "To each one of us grace has been given as Christ appointed it" (Eph. 4:7). Therefore, when we pray that "the grace of the Lord Jesus Christ be with God's people" one thing we might mean is that each Christian should use the gift he or she has been given by God to help others.

4. *We need a continuing supply of grace in order to complete the work God assigns us.* Paul was conscious of having received grace to carry out his calling as an apostle. But he also knew that he needed it constantly, and he was aware that others needed a continual supply of grace to do the work God had assigned to them. Obviously you and I do also.

237

The Church at Corinth

Romans 16:21-23

Timothy, my fellow worker, sends his greetings to you, as do Lucius, Jason and Sosipater, my relatives.

I, Tertius, who wrote down this letter, greet you in the Lord.

Gaius, whose hospitality I and the whole church here enjoy, sends you his greetings.

Erastus, who is the city's director of public works, and our brother Quartus send you their greetings.

When I began this exposition of Romans 16, I said that the last chapter of Paul's letter contains two long lists of names, thirty-three in all, which make this section fascinating. The first list of names (vv. 3–16) was of Christians in the church of Rome to which Paul was writing, and a study of these names reveals a great deal about the early church and of Paul's relationships to these people. The list we come to now (vv. 21–23) is of people who were with Paul in Corinth, the city from which he was writing, and it is even more interesting than the first list.

Paul had been staying in the house of a Roman nobleman named Gaius, who was also a Christian. This man had furnished him with an amanuensis, or sec-

1951

retary, who had been writing down the words Paul dictated. The letter was coming to an end, and now other Christians who may have followed the dictation over a period of several days or weeks gathered and were included in the greetings Paul sent to their fellow believers in the far off capital of the empire.

What is said, though brief, is one of the most remarkable pictures of Christian life and fellowship from the ancient world or, for that matter, from all history or literature.

Number-Three and Number-Four Boy

To begin our study, we need to understand something of the characters who were involved, and the place to begin is with Tertius and Quartus, who are mentioned in verses 22 and 23. In his commentary on Romans, Donald Grey Barnhouse explains that the first time he was in the Orient he was entertained in a beautiful home that had a large retinue of servants. One of these servants spoke English and had everything under his control. The man who was Barnhouse's host said, "He is the best number-one boy in China."

"Number-one boy?" queried Barnhouse. "What are the qualifications of a number-one boy?"

His host explained. "The number-one boy is a Chinese institution. He runs absolutely everything in connection with the household. He hires the other servants. He supervises the marketing. You would never find him carrying a package; a third boy or a fourth boy would be doing that. The number-one boy is the equivalent of an English gentleman's gentleman, plus a nurse, a housekeeper, and many other things. The ambition of third boy is to become second boy, and the ambition of second boy is to become number-one boy."[1]

The same system prevailed in the Roman Empire, and the names of two of these servants, number-three boy and number-four boy, are recorded here. In a prominent Roman household, as this was, the servants would have the names Primus (one), Secundus (two), Tertius (three), Quartus (four), Quintus (five), and so on. So in Romans 16 we have a case of the number-three slave and the number-four slave adding their names to those of the missionaries, plus prominent Gaius and Erastus, as the letter is sent to their fellow believers in Rome.

A Historical Reconstruction

Let's take this social background, add what we can find out about the other characters, and reconstruct this important historical moment in Corinth. And let's follow the text closely for our guidance.

1. Donald Grey Barnhouse, *God's Glory: Exposition of Bible Doctrines, Taking the Epistle to the Romans as a Point of Departure,* vol. 10, *Romans 14:13–16:27* (Grand Rapids: Wm. B. Eerdmans Publishing Company, 1964), p. 169.

First, Paul sends greetings from Timothy, his fellow worker, and from Lucius, Jason, and Sosipater, whom he calls his relatives. Timothy was Paul's young protégé, whom he had picked up in Lystra on his second missionary journey. He had a Greek father but a Jewish mother, which made him a Jew, and Paul used him to build up the Gentile churches he had himself founded earlier. Paul thought highly of Timothy, writing this of him to the Philippians: "I have no one else like him, who takes a genuine interest in your welfare" (Phil. 2:20), and "Timothy has proved himself, because as a son with his father he has served with me in the work of the gospel" (v. 22).

The only puzzle about Timothy is why Paul mentions him here at the end of his letter, rather than at the beginning, as he usually does (see 2 Corinthians, Philippians, Colossians, 1 and 2 Thessalonians, and Philemon).[2] A possible answer might be that Timothy was not present when the letter was begun and had only come in at the end, which is also quite likely the case with the next names mentioned.

It is impossible to be certain who these next men whom Paul calls his relatives (that is, Jews) are, but we can make some probable identifications. Sosipater is most likely Sopater (a variation of the same name) of Berea, who is said in Acts 20:4 to have been one of those who accompanied Paul through Greece on the way to Jerusalem to present the offering from the Gentile churches. He would have represented Berea. Jason was the name of Paul's host when he was in Thessalonica (Acts 17:1–7). Since this is the same general area of the world as Berea, it is likely that he was also part of the party that was accompanying Paul to Jerusalem. Lucius is not Luke the evangelist, as the early church father Origen thought (the names are distinct), but he may be one of the leaders of the church at Antioch who is mentioned in Acts 13:1, though that is uncertain.

What seems to be the case is that these men were part of the group of specially appointed representatives who were gathering in Corinth for the journey to Jerusalem. Timothy may have just arrived. Lucius, Jason, and Sosipater had come. Others were expected momentarily.[3] It may have been the case that the ship they were taking was already in the harbor, that they were leaving the next morning and that Paul needed to draw the letter to a rapid close. It would have been natural for Paul to have dictated greetings from these important representatives as he ended.

---

2. Timothy is not mentioned in the address of 1 Corinthians because, as the letter itself makes clear, Timothy was not with Paul when it was written (1 Cor. 16:10). He is not mentioned in Galatians either, but neither is anyone else by name. He may be included in the general "all the brothers with me" in verse 2.

3. Others are mentioned in Acts 20:4: Aristarchus and Secundus from Thessalonica, Gaius from Derbe, and Tychicus and Trophimus from Asia. It is possible that they were on the way but had not arrived in Corinth yet, or, which is more likely, they just were not present in Gaius' home as Paul finished the letter.

But notice this. Paul used an amanuensis when he wrote his letters, usually adding his own greeting in his own hand at the end (see Gal. 6:11; 1 Cor. 16:21; 2 Thess. 3:17). His amanuensis on this occasion was Tertius, the one I have identified as the number-three boy in Gaius' household, and at this point this number-three slave added a greeting of his own: "I, Tertius, who wrote down this letter, greet you in the Lord" (v. 22).

It may be that Paul paused for a moment, looking around to see who else was present and should be included, and that Tertius simply went on writing, eager to send his own greeting as a Christian in Corinth to the Christians who were in Rome. Or it may be that Paul looked at him and said something like, "Tertius, you've been working on this letter so faithfully and for so long that you must have writer's cramp. Wouldn't you like to send a greeting of your own?" However it happened, this is an example of a slave sending greetings to people he had never met but to whom he felt attached because of their common identity as believers in Jesus Christ.

And there is something else too. The words "in the Lord," which are part of Tertius' greeting, are usually put after the words "greet you" by translators, so that the text reads, "I . . . greet you in the Lord." But in the Greek text the words actually follow "who wrote this letter," so what this lowly slave is probably saying is that he did his work as an amanuensis "in [or unto] the Lord," that is, as Leon Morris puts it, "not as a mechanical project, but as . . . a piece of service" to Jesus Christ."[4]

Do you do that? The work you have may be menial, and you may not have a very prominent position as the world evaluates such jobs. But you can do your work "unto the Lord." Paul told the slaves in Ephesus, "Serve wholeheartedly, as if you were serving the Lord, not men, because you know that the Lord will reward everyone for whatever good he does, whether he is slave or free" (Eph. 6:7–8). God will reward you too if you do whatever he has given you to do joyfully and well.

Gaius, Erastus, and Number-Four Boy

In verse 23 Paul mentions two other prominent people who were present as he drew this letter to a close, plus Quartus: Gaius, who was Paul's host, and Erastus, an elected official in the city. The verse says, "Gaius, whose hospitality I and the whole church here enjoy, sends you his greetings. Erastus, who is the city's director of public works, and our brother Quartus send you their greetings."

Gaius was a common name, and this Gaius is not the Gaius from Derbe who is mentioned as another of Paul's official traveling companions in Acts 20:4. He must have been a rich man at Corinth, since he was hosting Paul in his home, was a host to "the whole church," and owned at least four slaves. He

---

4. Leon Morris, *The Epistle to the Romans* (Grand Rapids: Wm. B. Eerdmans Publishing Company, and Leicester, England: Inter-Varsity Press, 1988), p. 543.

must have been a Roman. He was almost surely the Gaius Paul admits to having baptized in 1 Corinthians 1:14, though it was generally Paul's practice to leave the baptizing to others. This means that Gaius was probably one of the first of Paul's converts in Corinth. There is also reason for believing that he is the Titius Justus of Acts 18:7, into whose house Paul entered when he was forced to leave the synagogue. His full name would have been Gaius Titius Justus.[5]

Since Gaius is said to be not only Paul's host but also the host of "the whole church," the congregation at Corinth probably met in his large home. Christians always met in homes in those days, as they had no church buildings. Gaius was wealthy, so it was natural that he would have opened his home for the Christians' worship services.

Erastus was a public official, undoubtedly a friend of Gaius. He may have been the man by that name whom Paul mentions in 2 Timothy 4:20 as having "stayed in Corinth," but this is questionable since an official like Erastus would probably not have been free to travel with Paul (see Acts 19:22).

It is interesting in connection with Erastus that archaeologists have uncovered an inscription from Corinth that bears his name. It was next to a first-century public sidewalk, and it read, "Erastus in return for his aedileship laid [this pavement] at his own expense."[6] Officials regularly paid for public works, and this is what Erastus seems to have done. This inscription also suggests that he had held more than one office. Paul calls him "the city's director of public works" (actually, it's *oikonomos*, or treasurer), but the inscription says that he served as *aedile*. An aedile could have been such a director, but he would not have been the treasurer.

Robert Haldane writes that the "office of Erastus, although in itself it may appear trifling, is in reality of great importance. It shows us that Christians may hold offices even under heathen governments, and that to serve Christ we are not to be abstracted from worldly business."[7] The inclusion of Erastus rounds out this picture of the early church by showing us that rich and poor, free men and slaves, full-time church workers and public officials, were all part of its diverse makeup.

Barnhouse wrote, "I cannot pass you by, Erastus, without recording that hundreds of Negro mothers, who gave birth to their little black slave sons in the America of a century ago, pored over the names for boys found here. They did not want their boys to be called Number Three and Number Four, so they did not name them Tertius and Quartus. But they picked your name, and hundreds of black boys in early American life were called 'Rastus' because of you."[8]

5. John Murray points out that Gaius Titius Justus would be respectively "the *praenomen, nomen gentile* and *cognomen* of a Roman citizen" (John Murray, *The Epistle to the Romans*, 2 vols. in 1 [Grand Rapids: Wm. B. Eerdmans Publishing Company, 1968], vol. 2, p. 238, footnote 16).

6. Morris, *The Epistle to the Romans*, p. 544, footnote 70.

7. Robert Haldane, *An Exposition of the Epistle to the Romans* (MacDill AFB: MacDonald Publishing Company, 1958), p. 647.

8. Barnhouse, *God's Glory*, p. 171.

And how about Quartus? Paul mentions him in verse 23. Quartus was the least significant of all the people who seem to have been gathered around Paul that day, but he is not left out. It seems that as Paul glanced around to make sure that he had included greetings from everyone, Quartus, off in a corner, raised his hand as if to say, "Don't forget me!" So Paul didn't. He spoke to Tertius: ". . . and our brother Quartus." Tertius wrote it down.

In the Greek text the verb came before the rest of the sentence. So Paul would have spoken it like this: "Greets you Erastus, the city's director of public works, . . . and Quartus, a brother."

A Snapshot of History

We have seen who these people were and have begun to appreciate the picture of the early church that emerges at the end of this important letter. Now it is worth summing up some of the lessons from our survey.

1. *The reality of genuine Christian fellowship.* There is no better picture in all the Bible, or possibly in all the world's literature, of genuine Christian fellowship than this snapshot of the believers in Corinth. In the first centuries none of the Christians worried about brotherhood. They simply ignored the differences that were dividing the rough Roman world and came together as followers of Jesus Christ—the master and the slave, the Roman and the Greek, the Jew and the Gentile, the rich and the poor. "It was an actual oneness, absolutely above and beyond all human distinctions," wrote Barnhouse. "Nothing short of this could have moved the simple number-four slave, Quartus, to ask Paul to send his love to the unknown brothers across the sea."[9]

2. *Each one's special calling to serve Christ.* It was an impressive gathering of full-time Christian workers who were meeting in the house of Gaius of Corinth prior to leaving for Jerusalem, but nothing in the wording of these greetings (or anything else, for that matter) suggests that the others should have followed them in their calling. Gaius could not be an apostle, but he served Christ by opening up his home for the Christians' meetings and by hosting traveling church workers. Erastus could not travel with Paul, but he served the Lord as a public official in the important metropolitan area of Corinth. Tertius served by writing down Paul's letter, and Quartus undoubtedly had his duties too.

It is the same for us. You have your unique calling, given to you by Jesus Christ, and you are to serve him by doing it well, not by trying to do someone else's job. The body has many parts, but it is "one body" (1 Cor. 12:19). You may not be an apostle or be able to serve God as a missionary. But you can open your house to believers who are in need. And if you do not have a house to open, you can open your heart. There are many closed hearts in this harsh sinful world. What a calling, to have an open heart to others for the sake of Christ! It is important for each to do his or her part "unto the Lord."

9. Barnhouse, *God's Glory*, p. 173.

3. *The importance of people the world thinks insignificant.* If this had been a secular rather than a Christian gathering, Tertius may have done his part and Quartus may have been present to attend to the demands of the master and his guests, but the two slaves would never have been allowed to take part in what was going on by sending greetings, as if they were on the same level as those who were writing or those who were in Rome. Things were entirely different here because this was a Christian community! Here each one was important: each was listened to, noticed, and respected.

4. *The importance of world missions.* There is a lesson too about the importance of world missions. Here are Roman slaves, people utterly without status in the ancient world, who were nevertheless contacted by Paul and the other Christian missionaries, brought to faith in Christ, and became members of the body of Christ. Barnhouse asks, "Are you interested when you hear that there are new believers in an Indian tribe on the upper Amazon? Does your heart go out to those who are worshipping in a church in Africa whose mud pews are baked in the sun before the mud walls are built around them and the palm roof goes over them? Quartus knew nobody in Rome and nobody in Rome had ever heard of Quartus, but he loved them and wanted them to know it."[10] God has his people in all these places, and there are others who have not heard the gospel. Shouldn't you help to take it to them?

A Testimony from Corinth

As we look back across the centuries that have passed between Paul's day and ours, we can almost talk to Gaius' two slaves, number three and number four. Suppose you could speak to them, as they speak to us through this letter. Suppose you could ask them questions. Would you like to know what their lives were like? Would you like to know whether they were cruelly treated as slaves? Beaten perhaps? Were their lives empty, cruel, nasty, brutish, or short?

Let Barnhouse answer for them: "No!" they say. "We were slaves, but one day Paul came into the house of our master, Gaius. We saw a great transformation in him. Gaius was transformed. He began to be kind to us. Soon he had Paul tell us about Christ. For two years Paul lived in Corinth, and he came to our house often. We got the bread and the wine ready when the crowd came on Sunday. It made more work for us, but it was delightful. They broke the bread, and we began to eat from the same loaf as our master. They filled a chalice with wine, and our master sipped it and smiled as he handed it to us. Day after day everything was transformed. He put his hand on us and cried as he spoke of the grace of God that had saved us all. He said that he was our master, but he realized that he had a master, Christ. He wanted to treat us the way Christ treated him. Love transformed our lives."[11]

10. Ibid.
11. Ibid., p. 176.

What an amazing transformation! And there are also transformations yet to come. Tertius and Quartus, number-three boy and number-four boy, do you remember how Jesus said that in heaven the first shall be last and the last first? You did your work well here. Did you know that in heaven you would not be Tertius and Quartus, but Primus and Primus, number one? For that is what you are now. Oh, that we all might strive for that distinction and one day hear our heavenly master say, "Well done, good and faithful servant! . . . Come and share your master's happiness!" (Matt. 25:21, 23).[12]

12. The careful reader will notice that there is no verse 24 in the New International Version text. This is because it is missing in the oldest of the ancient manuscripts and seems to have been added in some only because the closing doxology was relocated elsewhere (see my comments in the next study) and it was felt that a benediction was necessary in order to end the letter. It seems to have been added with slight changes from verse 20.

238

Paul's Gospel

Romans 16:25-26

Now to him who is able to establish you by my gospel and the proclamation of Jesus Christ, according to the revelation of the mystery hidden for long ages past, but now revealed and made known through the prophetic writings by the command of the eternal God, so that all nations might believe and obey him—

There is something a bit upsetting about an individual who constantly uses the first-person possessive pronouns *my* and *mine*. Someone who is always talking about *my* car, *my* house, *my* job, *my* vacation, or *my* friends is usually not very likeable, especially if he is implying that what is his is better than what is ours. I am reminded that comedian Chevy Chase once began a television special with "Hello, I'm Chevy Chase and you're not." We do not like anyone to be that self-absorbed or egotistical.

Is that what Paul is doing as he ends his letter to the Romans, speaking of *"my* gospel"? We sense at once that he is not. When Paul says "my gospel" he does not mean that the gospel is his as opposed to being ours or someone else's. The gospel is for anyone who will have it. What "my gospel" actually means is "the true gospel," as the context makes clear. This true gospel is Paul's only in the sense that he has appropriated it personally by a faith that involved committing his life to Jesus Christ, and in the sense that he was teaching it.

"My gospel!" It would be good if the gospel was possessed by each of us in exactly the same way and as intensely. But in order to possess it we need to understand what it is.

The God Who Is Able

Paul usually ends his letters with a benediction rather than a doxology, but it is a doxology that we have here.[1] These last verses are an ascription of praise "to him [that is, God] who is able to establish you by my gospel and the proclamation of Jesus Christ." This has caused some commentators to suggest that the doxology is misplaced, and some of the early manuscripts actually work it in earlier, at the end of chapter 14, for instance, thus ending the letter with the greetings in 16:21–24. Then they add a benediction. Yet the doxology is not inappropriate here. As Brevard S. Childs said, "The doxology is not a liturgical response of the letter's recipients to Paul's words, but a liturgical response of Paul to the subject of his book."[2]

The subject of the book is the gospel. So this tells us from the very beginning that the gospel has to do with God and what he has accomplished for us through the work of Jesus Christ.

This means that the gospel is not human in its origin. Nor is it human in its power or objective. *Gospel* means "good news." This good news is worth talking about. But when we talk about it we are not talking about it as if it were something some great philosopher had thought up or some scientist has discovered. It is not a new insight into human nature or a new discovery of something that is possible for us if we just learn the methodology involved or simply put our minds to it. It is not a matter of human thought or effort at all. It is something that has its origins in God, is accomplished by God, and has God's own goals as its objective.

The words *who is able* are especially important, for they are a way of talking about God's sovereignty. Some years ago I prepared a special series of Sunday evening messages for Tenth Presbyterian Church titled "The God Who Is Able." They were based on seven Bible verses in which the words *God is able* (or their close equivalents) occurred. The titles were: "Able to Save" (Heb. 7:25), "Able to Keep" (2 Tim. 1:12), "Grace Abounding" (2 Cor. 9:8), "Able to Help in Temptation" (Heb. 2:18), "How to Grow Spiritually" (Eph. 3:20), "God Is No Quitter" (Jude 24), and "Able to Raise Our Bodies" (Phil. 3:21). There were so many relevant verses that I didn't even use this text from Romans. My point was that God "is able to do immeasurably more than all

---

1. See 1 Corinthians 16:23–24; 2 Corinthians 13:14; Galatians 6:18; Ephesians 6:23–24; Philippians 4:23; Colossians 4:18; 1 Thessalonians 5:28; 2 Thessalonians 3:18; 1 Timothy 6:21; 2 Timothy 4:22; Titus 3:15; Philemon 25. Romans is the only exception.
2. See Leon Morris, *The Epistle to the Romans* (Grand Rapids: Wm. B. Eerdmans Publishing Company, and Leicester, England: Inter-Varsity Press, 1988), p. 545.

we ask or imagine, according to his power that is at work within us," as Paul told the Ephesians (Eph. 3:20).

For that is where it all begins and ends. We saw that when we studied the doxology at the end of chapter 11: "For from him and through him and to him are all things. To him be the glory forever! Amen" (Rom. 11:36).

The Heart of the Gospel

When we say that the gospel begins and ends in God we do not mean God the Father only. We also mean that the gospel begins and ends in Jesus Christ, God's Son, for it was of him and was centered in him from before the foundation of the world.

This is strikingly apparent in Romans, for these closing verses are a deliberate echo of the opening paragraph of Paul's letter, where Jesus Christ is likewise prominent:

> Paul, a servant of Christ Jesus, called to be an apostle and set apart for the gospel of God—the gospel he promised beforehand through his prophets in the Holy Scriptures, regarding his Son, who as to his human nature was a descendant of David, and who through the Spirit of holiness was declared with power to be the Son of God by his resurrection from the dead: Jesus Christ our Lord. Through him and for his name's sake, we received grace and apostleship to call people from among all the Gentiles to the obedience that comes from faith.
>
> Romans 1:1–5

Romans 16:25–26 echoes at least four of those themes: (1) the gospel is "of God"; (2) this gospel is about God's "Son," Jesus Christ; (3) the gospel was promised in the "Scriptures" of the Old Testament but has only been made fully known now; and (4) the goal is that the "Gentiles," like the Jews, might arrive at "the obedience that comes from faith." Each of these themes is repeated in the letter's closing doxology, but the center is clearly Jesus Christ.

Jesus is the content of the gospel. He is the one who was promised in the Scriptures from the beginning and who has now come. Moreover, it is to him that we are to summon the obedience of the Gentile nations.

One of the great tragedies of the church down through the ages is that Christians have repeatedly allowed other things to rise to undue prominence and so eclipse the preeminence of Christ. Sometimes this has occurred in regard to minor points of doctrine. In such times an observer of Christian affairs might gain the impression that it is far more important whether one holds a right view of the sacraments, or church government, or abstinence from certain kinds of conduct, or eschatology than whether one understands who Jesus is and what he came to earth to do and is committed to him in true, living, and active discipleship.

At other times, and even more seriously, the church has allowed false teaching to obscure Christ's nature (either denying his full deity or his full humanity) and what he has done for our salvation. Any theology that allows human efforts or good works to intrude on Christ's work as the ground of our salvation destroys the gospel and denies the Lord's preeminence.

Revelation of the Mystery

The third thing these verses tell us about the gospel is that it has been a "mystery hidden for long ages past" but that it is "now revealed and made known through the prophetic writings by the command of the eternal God" (vv. 25–26).

When we use the word *mystery* today we are usually thinking of something incomprehensible, or quite possibly a certain kind of detective story where there is a murder at the beginning, an investigation by a shrewd inspector, and a final revelation of "who done it" in the last chapter. The biblical idea refers to something that has been hidden but has now been made known. There are many mysteries like this in the Bible, and most are in Paul's writings.

When I was looking at this word in our earlier study of Romans 11:25, I listed the following mysteries:

1. "The Mysteries of the Kingdom of Heaven" (Matt. 13:11)
2. "The Mystery of the Olive Tree" (Rom. 11:25)
3. "The Great Mystery of Christ and the Church" (Eph. 5:32)
4. "The Mystery of Piety" (1 Tim. 3:16)
5. "The Mystery of the Rapture of the Saints" (1 Cor. 15:51)
6. "The Mystery of Lawlessness" (2 Thess. 2:7)
7. "The Mystery of God Finished" (Rev. 10:7).[3]

The question here is what specific mystery Paul is referring to. The only time that he has used the word *mystery* in Romans is in chapter 11, where it referred to a temporary hardening of the Jews "until the full number of the Gentiles has come in" (v. 25). That is, the mystery was that God was going to extend salvation to Gentiles as well as Jews. This idea had been mostly unknown or at least not understood until Jesus actually came, opened the door to the Gentiles, and gave the Great Commission to take the gospel to all the peoples of the world (see Matt. 28:19; Acts 1:8).

The argument in favor of this meaning is that Paul has stressed the application of the gospel to the Gentiles throughout the letter and, in fact, even ends on this note, saying that the mystery has been revealed "so that *all nations* [that is, Gentiles] might believe and obey him" (v. 26). The problem is that

3. The titles are from H. A. Ironside, *The Mysteries of God* (New York: Loizeaux Brothers, n.d.). Ironside explores these formerly hidden but now revealed doctrines at some length.

this is only part of the gospel, and if Paul is thinking of the whole gospel, then the mystery he has in mind must be bigger.

Most students of Romans think that Paul is instead talking about the gospel of salvation from sin through the work of Christ, which has been the theme of the letter. I agree. But the problem with this view is in seeing how this "gospel" can be said to have been "hidden for long ages past, but now revealed and made known through the prophetic writings." Here are some questions. If it was hidden for long ages past, how can it be said to have been revealed by the prophets? If it has been, it was not hidden. Or again, how can it even be said to have been hidden before the prophets? Don't we speak of the protoevangelium, or first announcement of the gospel, as early as the third chapter of Genesis (v. 15), not to mention intimations of it elsewhere in the Old Testament? Isn't it the case that all who were saved during the entire Old Testament period were saved by looking forward to the Savior who should come?

Most writers think of the gospel being anticipated in the Old Testament prophets, but F. Godet, the Swiss commentator, thinks that when Paul speaks of the "prophetic writings" in which the gospel has been revealed, he is thinking of the writings of the apostles, the New Testament prophets, and of himself and his own book of Romans particularly.[4]

In my judgment this is pressing Paul's words too far. What he is saying is that the gospel is something no human being could have guessed. In the past it was entirely hidden in the mind of God. In fact, when God began to reveal it during the Old Testament period, the details were puzzling even to the prophets to whom the revelation was given, for they were unable fully to understand what God's Spirit had caused them to write. We understand it only because Jesus has now come.

Peter described the situation, saying, "The prophets, who spoke of the grace that was to come to you, searched intently and with the greatest care, trying to find out the time and circumstances to which the Spirit of Christ in them was pointing when he predicted the sufferings of Christ and the glories that would follow" (1 Peter 1:10–11).

The reason we understand the gospel now is that the Holy Spirit has given the apostles understanding of who he is and what he has accomplished in agreement with the prior revelation. Indeed, this is how Paul handled the Old Testament material in writing Romans. First, he explained the gospel. But then, at each major step in the argument, he supported his explanation with direct citations from the Old Testament. These texts were not necessarily clear earlier. But they are now, since Jesus has fulfilled them and the Holy Spirit has given the apostles understanding of what they mean.

4. F. Godet, *Commentary on St. Paul's Epistle to the Romans,* trans. by A. Cusin (Edinburgh: T. & T. Clark, 1892), vol. 2, p. 417.

The Wisdom of God

I want to stress again that not only is the gospel "mystery" known to us today by revelation, but it is only by revelation that the gospel can be known. There is nothing about it that you or I or any other human being could possibly dream up. I wrote about this at the end of the third volume of these studies when I was looking at the wisdom of God, showing that what draws out Paul's awe at the "riches of [God's] wisdom" is not the wisdom God displayed in the ordering of creation, as wonderful as that may be, but rather his wisdom in saving sinners such as you and me.[5] It is what he was unfolding in the first eleven chapters of the letter.

1. *The wisdom of God in justification (chaps. 1–4).* In the first main section of the letter Paul explains the way of salvation. For centuries God had been saving sinners who deserved his just judgment and condemnation. But the question was this: How could God save sinners and at the same time remain a just and holy God? To use Paul's language, how could he be both "just and the one who justifies" the ungodly (Rom. 3:26)? Since God was justifying the ungodly, it would seem that for centuries there was something like a shadow over the good name of God.

This puzzle is beyond the wisdom of mere men and women. But it was not beyond the wisdom of God. Thus it was that in the fullness of time "God sent his Son, born of a woman, born under the law, to redeem those under the law, that we might receive the full rights of sons" (Gal. 4:4–5). Or, to go back to what Paul says in Romans, "God presented him as a sacrifice of atonement . . . to demonstrate his justice at the present time" (Rom. 3:25–26). This means that God satisfied the claims of his justice by punishing the innocent Jesus for our sins. Jesus bore the wrath of God in our place. Thus, the demands of God's justice were fully met and, justice being satisfied, the love of God was then free to reach out, embrace, and fully save the sinner.

Who but God could think up such a solution to the sin problem? None of us could have done it. But God did, and he has revealed it to us in a gospel that is utterly beyond our powers to imagine.

2. *The wisdom of God in sanctification (chaps. 5–8).* The next section of Romans discusses the sinner's need for sanctification. The justification discussed in chapters 1–4 is by the work of Christ, which means that it is by grace. But if that is so, what is to stop a justified person from indulging in his or her sinful nature, since the person's salvation has already been secured by Christ's work? Why should we not continue to sin? In fact, why should we not "go on sinning so that grace may increase" (Rom. 6:1)?

God solves this problem by showing that we are never justified apart from being regenerated or being made alive in Christ. Christians have been given a new nature, and this new nature, being the very life of Jesus Christ, will

---

5. James Montgomery Boice, *Romans, vol. 3, God and History: Romans 9–11* (Grand Rapids: Baker Books, 1993), pp. 1425–32.

inevitably produce good works corresponding to the character of God. In fact, this is the only sure proof of our having been saved by him.

Who but God could think up a gospel like that? We would never do it, because we do not naturally hold grace and works together. If we emphasize morality, as some do, we begin to think that we can be saved by our good works and so strive to do it. We repudiate grace. But if, on the other hand, we emphasize grace, knowing that we cannot possibly be saved by our inadequate and polluted works, we have a tendency to do away with works entirely and so slide into antinomianism. It is a great dilemma. But God has devised a gospel that is entirely of grace and yet produces exceptional works in those who are being saved.

3. *The wisdom of God displayed in human history (chaps. 9–11).* The third section of Romans is concerned with the acts of God in history. The problem is that God made special salvation promises to the Jewish people, and yet, in spite of these promises, the majority of Jews do not respond to the gospel. Doesn't this indicate that the purposes of God have failed? And what about the Gentiles? There are fewer promises for them. Yet in Paul's day the Gentiles seemed to be responding to the apostles' preaching. Does this mean that God has rejected the Jews in favor of the Gentiles? If he has, isn't that wrong? And doesn't it destroy the doctrine of the believer's eternal security? Doesn't it mean that God fails?

Paul's answer is a magnificent theodicy in which he justifies the ways of God with men, showing that God has rejected Israel for a time in order that his mercy might be extended to the Gentiles, but adding that Gentile salvation will provoke Israel to jealousy and so in time bring the Jewish people to faith in their Messiah.

Who could devise a plan of that scope for world history? We could not do it. We cannot understand it fully even though we have it unfolded for us in the Bible. It is complex, manifold. But it is not difficult for God. It is part of the mystery, previously hidden but now explicitly revealed.

Not Just Saved, Established

I close with two important points, each part of this closing doxology. First, the goal of the gospel is not simply that we should be saved from sin's punishment and go to heaven when we die, but that we might be "established" in God's grace now—that is, that we might be settled, strong, and unshaken (Rom. 16:25).

This is exactly the word Paul used in Romans 1 when he spoke of his desire to visit Rome "so that," he said, "I may impart to you some spiritual gift *to make you strong*" (v. 11). Paul knew that there are many things in life that can unsettle us and that the devil wants to make us vacillating in our faith so that we will be of no use to God or anybody else. Paul wanted his converts to be strong Christians, and he tells us that this is also the goal of God for us.

But notice: It is God "who is able to establish" us and to whom we must look, not some other Christian, not even Paul. Paul was God's vehicle for giving us this great revelation that we know as the letter to the Romans. But Romans is not Paul's book. It is God's book. And the power we need to be established in the gospel it speaks of is the power of God. A Christian who leans upon some other Christian—a pastor, a teacher, or someone else—may have to be shaken loose by God through some crisis in order to learn that God alone is the solid rock and only adequate foundation for his people's faith. We must lean upon God to be established.

My second concluding point comes from Paul's last words, where he speaks of God's purpose in the revelation of the gospel where others are concerned, saying that it is "so that all nations might believe and obey him." He means that the gospel must be proclaimed to everyone.

Moreover, Paul links this objective to "the command of the eternal God" (v. 26). We find this command in the Lord's Great Commission in each of the four gospels and the Book of Acts. God has told us to take this gospel, previously hidden but now revealed, to all the peoples of the world. Paul took that command with utmost seriousness. It is why he became a missionary to the Gentiles. It is why he wrote Romans. You and I must also take it seriously by teaching it to everyone we can.

239

Glory to the Only Wise God

Romans 16:27

—to the only wise God be glory forever through Jesus Christ. Amen.

After eight exciting years of pulpit work and 239 separate sermons, I have come to the end of my expositions of Paul's great letter to the Romans, the most important book in the New Testament, probably in the entire Bible, and certainly the most influential letter in all history or all the world's literature. They have been excellent years for Tenth Presbyterian Church in Philadelphia, where these sermons were preached. The church has grown substantially and visibly stronger, Christians have matured in the Lord, and the evangelistic and service ministries that reach out into Tenth's broad city neighborhood have increased.

How should I end a series of this scope? Some might want a word about the greatness of the letter or even the outstanding intellectual, visionary, and creative qualities of the human being who composed it. But our studies should end as the letter itself does, not with words praising the apostle Paul—still less with stories of what has happened at Tenth Church through this teaching—but rather with words praising the great, sovereign, merciful, and eternal God of whose gospel Paul and we have been made missionaries.

1967

The letter rightly ends: "To the only wise God be glory forever through Jesus Christ. Amen." This is a doxology, and it ascribes glory to God in four respects: (1) to God simply as God; (2) to God as the only God; (3) to God as the only wise God; and finally (4) to God through Jesus Christ.

To God Be the Glory

One of the most important things that can be said about Paul is that he was always thinking about God. He saw himself as a creature made by God. He understood his work as having been given to him by God. He wanted to order his life and all the goals of his life in accordance with the will of God. Moreover, when he came to write about the gospel it had to do with God and his purposes from beginning to end.

Donald Grey Barnhouse summarized the content of Romans this way.

> In the opening chapter we find the gospel of God. This is followed by a discussion of the wrath of God. Then the righteousness of God is set forth. Then we find how the righteousness of God can be communicated to sinful men. From then on we see ourselves as the people of God, at peace with God, blessed by God to such an extent that we can cry, "If God be for us, who can be against us?" (Rom. 8:31). Then after a section on the ancient people of God and the unchangeableness of God, we come to our answering obligations to God, all leading up to our text, "To God be the glory."[1]

This is an example of what in an earlier chapter I called a Christian mind—that is, a way of thinking that revolves around God and the truths that he has made known to us. The opposite of possessing a Christian mind or thinking in a Christian way is secularism.

Secularism is an umbrella term that covers a number of other "isms," such as humanism, relativism, pragmatism, pluralism, hedonism, and materialism. But it, more than any other single word, aptly describes the intellectual frame of reference and value structure of the people of our time. There is a right way to be secular, of course. Christians live in the world and are therefore rightly concerned about the world's affairs. We have legitimate secular concerns. But secularism is more than this. *Secular* is derived from the Latin word *saeculum*, which means age, and secularism is a philosophy that does not look beyond this age or world for the whole of reality but instead operates as if this world is all there is.

In an earlier chapter I illustrated this philosophical secularism by something Carl Sagan said in the television series *Cosmos*. He was seen before a spectacular view of the heavens with its many swirling galaxies, and he said in a hushed, almost reverential tone of voice, "The cosmos is all that is or

---

1. Donald Grey Barnhouse, *God's Glory: Exposition of Bible Doctrines, Taking the Epistle to the Romans as a Point of Departure*, vol. 10, *Romans 14:13–16:27* (Grand Rapids: Wm. B. Eerdmans Publishing Company, 1964), p. 190.

ever was or ever will be." That is secularism as clearly as it can be stated. It is bound up entirely by the limits of the material universe, by what we can see and touch and weigh and measure. If we think in terms of our existence here, it means operating within the limits of life on earth. If we are thinking of time, it means disregarding the eternal and thinking only of the "now."

Each of us should understand that well, because it is the philosophy we are surrounded with every day of our lives and in every conceivable place and circumstance. Yet that is the outlook we must heartily oppose and to which we must refuse to be conformed. Instead of being conformed to this world, as if that is all there is, we are to see all things as relating to God and to eternity, which is the true, Christian way of thinking that Paul models for us in Romans.

Here is the contrast, as expressed by Harry Blamires: "To think secularly is to think within a frame of reference bounded by the limits of our life on earth; it is to keep one's calculations rooted in this-worldly criteria. To think Christianly is to accept all things with the mind as related, directly or indirectly, to man's eternal destiny as the redeemed and chosen child of God."[2] We think Christianly when we begin and end with God, as Paul did, and can say with Paul, "To the only wise God be glory forever through Jesus Christ! Amen."

Glory to the Only God

These closing words of the letter not only give praise to God as the beginning and ending of all things but also praise to God as the *only* God—they give glory to him and to no other. These words are opposed to polytheism and to all forms of idolatry.

This reminds us at once of the first of the Ten Commandments, which says, "You shall have no other gods before me" (Exod. 20:3). It demands our exclusive worship. This is what created a problem for the early Christians, of course. In the Greek and Roman worlds of Paul's day an individual was permitted to worship any variety of gods. So there was nothing wrong with worshiping the God of the Bible. The problem was that the Bible demanded that only the Bible's God and no other god be worshiped, and the teaching of the New Testament was that Jesus, who was the only Son of God, the second person of the Trinity, be offered exclusive worship also. Christians were executed not because they worshiped Jesus, but because they refused to worship Caesar too. They would not say, "Caesar is Lord."

To worship any god but Jehovah is to break this command. But to break it we do not need to worship a pagan God like Zeus or Aphrodite, or even a Roman emperor. We do it whenever we give some person or some thing the first place in our affections, which belongs to God alone. In our day people

2. Harry Blamires, *The Christian Mind: How Should a Christian Think?* (Ann Arbor, Mich.: Servant Books, 1963), p. 44.

do it most often when they substitute themselves for God, which they do whenever they assume the right to determine their own moral standards.

Most of the commandments are in negative form ("you shall not"). Only two are positive. But the negative clearly implies the positive, and the positive the negative. Therefore, the command to have "no other gods before me" also means that we are to worship God with all our heart, soul, and mind, as Jesus said when he was asked to state the first and greatest commandment (Matt. 22:37). In order to do this we would need to see everything in life from God's point of view, as disclosed in the Bible; to make his moral will our guide and his glory our goal; to put him first in our thoughts, first in our relationships, first in our work, first in our leisure time and recreation. It would mean exercising responsible stewardship of all the money, time, and talents he has entrusted to us.

Paul put his whole life at the disposal of this one true God. This is what we are required to do too, if we are truly Christians. If we are serious about our faith, we must say with Paul, "To the *only* wise God be glory forever through Jesus Christ! Amen."

To the Only Wise God Be Glory

The third way in which this doxology ascribes praise or glory to God is as the only *wise* God. This is the point I emphasized in the last study when I was writing about the "mystery" of the gospel and how it is now revealed.

Verses 25 and 26, the earlier part of this doxology, emphasized God's power. It is what was meant by the words "to him who is able." It is a way of speaking about God's omnipotence and sovereignty. Here, however, the stress is upon God's wisdom. Why this change? Obviously because this is a natural and proper response to the mystery that Paul has written about. There is nothing about the gospel that could possibly have occurred to the natural mind. We could not think up the way of salvation. How to preserve the justice of God while at the same time allowing him to save sinful men and women is beyond us. We could not think up a way of sanctification consistent with this gospel. Either we would emphasize good works and so repudiate grace and fall into legalism, or else we would emphasize grace, forget about good works, and fall into antinomianism.

And as for the purposes of God in history, who would ever have guessed that God is using history to demonstrate his many glorious attributes—his grace, mercy, and compassion in saving those who are being saved, and his justice and wrath in passing by those who are being passed by? And who would have viewed history as a stage upon which God has hardened the Jews so that the gospel might be extended to the Gentiles, and that he is provoking the Jews to jealousy by the salvation of Gentiles so that in the end all Israel might be saved (Rom. 11:25)?

None of us would ever be able to think up a gospel like this. This gospel is divine in origin, and it displays the supreme wisdom of God in all its parts and on every page of the written revelation. We are therefore right to say with Paul, "To the only *wise* God be glory forever through Jesus Christ! Amen."

The sad thing is that the world continues to regard this gospel as foolishness even after it has been revealed, a point Paul makes in the first chapter of 1 Corinthians:

> For the message of the cross is foolishness to those who are perishing, but to us who are being saved it is the power of God. For it is written:
>
> > "I will destroy the wisdom of the wise;
> > the intelligence of the intelligent I will frustrate."
>
> Where is the wise man? Where is the scholar? Where is the philosopher of this age? Has not God made foolish the wisdom of the world? For since in the wisdom of God the world through its wisdom did not know him, God was pleased through the foolishness of what was preached to save those who believe. Jews demand miraculous signs and Greeks look for wisdom, but we preach Christ crucified: a stumbling block to Jews and foolishness to Gentiles, but to those whom God has called, both Jews and Greeks, Christ the power of God and the wisdom of God. For the foolishness of God is wiser than man's wisdom, and the weakness of God is stronger than man's strength.
>
> 1 Corinthians 1:18–25

Glory to God through Jesus Christ

The fact that Paul preached Christ leads to the last of the four points of the doxology that closes Romans. In these closing words he also ascribes glory to the only wise God "through Jesus Christ." There are two ways glory is given to God through Jesus:

1. *It is only through Jesus Christ that God can be known by us.* Only through Jesus can we know God's glory in the fullest sense. In the Upper Room shortly before his arrest and crucifixion, Jesus gave his final teaching to his disciples. He spoke about going away from them, trying to prepare them for his death, and Thomas said, "Lord, we don't know where you are going, so how can we know the way?"

Jesus replied, "I am the way and the truth and the life. No one comes to the Father except through me."

This was puzzling to the disciples too. It must have shown on their faces. But eventually Philip voiced a deep desire, which was and has always been the deepest longing of the people of God. It was the desire Moses expressed on Mount Sinai when he asked to see God's face (Exod. 33:18–20). Philip said, "Lord, show us the Father and that will be enough for us."

Jesus answered, "Don't you know me, Philip, even after I have been among you such a long time? Anyone who has seen me has seen the Father. How can you say, 'Show us the Father'? Don't you believe that I am in the Father, and that the Father is in me?" (John 14:1–10). This was a clear and unmistakable statement that if we want to know what God is like, the place where we are to find him is by looking to Jesus Christ.

Later on in John's gospel Jesus said the same thing, only this time using the very word of our text, *glory.* Here he is praying to the Father in what we call his high priestly prayer, and the theme of his prayer is glory. Jesus prayed, "Father, the time has come. Glorify your Son, that your Son may glorify you.... I have brought you glory on earth by completing the work you gave me to do. And now, Father, glorify me in your presence with the glory I had with you before the world began" (John 17:1, 4–5). This has to do with the honor given to the Father by Jesus through his obedience and the glory to be given to the Son by the Father through his resurrection and return to heaven.

Then Jesus prayed for his disciples and eventually for the church that would come into being through their testimony, and his point was that he had made God known to them. Finally, summing it all up, he said, "I have given them the glory that you gave me" (v. 22). In other words, God is glorified through Jesus Christ because the nature of God has been made known to God's people through Jesus' life and testimony.

2. *It is only through Jesus Christ that we can glorify God.* It is only through Jesus that we can come to God in worship, for worship means praising or glorifying God. Jesus also taught this in John 14 when he said, "No one comes to the Father except through me" (v. 6).

There is a wonderful illustration of this truth in the Old Testament. The Shekinah Glory was the visible manifestation of the presence of God among the Jews during the days of their wilderness wandering—the cloud that guided the people in the desert and settled down upon the tabernacle when they camped. By day it was a pillar of cloud. By night it became a pillar of fire. When it came to rest upon the tabernacle and actually entered into the Most Holy Place of the tabernacle to abide between the wings of the cherubim above the mercy seat of the ark of the covenant, it became a bright light. This was a symbol of the intense, holy presence of God that was so pure and so terrible that no one could enter the Most Holy Place and live. In fact, some who attempted to do so were at once struck down.

This is what any Jew would immediately have thought about when a person spoke of God's glory, an unapproachable earthly symbol of the greater and likewise unapproachable heavenly glory, concerning which, when Moses had asked God to see his glory, God replied, "You cannot see my face, for no one may see me and live" (Exod. 33:20).

Matthew in his Gospel tells us that when Jesus died "at that moment the curtain of the temple was torn in two from top to bottom" (Matt. 27:51). The curtain separated the room of the temple known as the Holy Place from the room known as the Most Holy Place, which housed the ark of the covenant. So the tearing of the veil showed that the way into the presence of God, into the very presence of his glory, has now been opened to us by the death of Jesus Christ. Apart from his death for our sin none of us could approach God and live. But now, because of his death and through faith in him, even the poorest and least distinguished of God's people can approach God joyfully and without fear and offer worship that the Father will accept.

All this is possible only through the Lord Jesus Christ. It is through him alone that we can know God, through him alone that we can come to God, and through him alone that we can give God glory. So we say with Paul, "To the only wise God be glory forever through Jesus Christ. Amen."

Amen and Amen

And what about the "amen"? We have been working our way through Romans slowly, verse by verse and at times almost word by word. It is appropriate that we also think carefully about this last word of the letter. What does it mean to say "Amen"?

Amen is a wonderfully rich word. It is found in nearly half the languages of the world, and it refers to what is true, firm, or faithful. In its intransitive form it means to be shored up—to be firm, unshaken. It means to be faithful, trustworthy, sure, something that one can lean on or build upon. In this sense it is used as a name for God in Isaiah 65:16, though the New International Version translates it by the word *truth*. The verse says, "Whoever invokes a blessing in the land will do so by the God of truth." But the Hebrews text actually says "by the God of the Amen." It is a way of saying that God is a sure and solid foundation for those who lean upon him. He is utterly reliable.

One of the most fascinating things about this word is how Jesus used it. He commonly prefaced something he was about to say by a double use of the words, as in John 3:3. The NIV has, "I tell you the truth, no one can see the kingdom of God unless he is born again." But the Greek reads, "Amen, Amen, I say to you . . .," which the King James Version rendered, "Verily, verily . . ." There are probably more than twenty or thirty sayings like this in the gospels.

We use this word at the end of something God says. In other words, when God says something he begins with "Amen, amen": "What I am about to say is true; pay attention." For our part, we hear the words, repeat them, and then say "Amen," meaning that we agree with God's declaration. We set our seal to our belief that the Word of God is true and that he is faithful.

That is what Paul is doing as he comes to the end of Romans and offers these last words of doxology. He is setting his seal to God's truth, saying that he believes God's Word. Can you do that? Can you add your "Amen" to what Paul has written?

For my part that is what I am determined to do. There is much in this world that I do not understand. There is much even about the ways of God that I do not understand. But what I do understand I believe, and to God's declaration of these eternal truths I say a hearty, "Amen." "There is no one righteous, not even one" (Rom. 3:10). Amen! "For all have sinned and fall short of the glory of God" (Rom. 3:23). Amen! "For the wages of sin is death, but the gift of God is eternal life in Christ Jesus our Lord" (Rom. 6:23). Amen! "Neither death nor life, neither angels nor demons, neither the present nor the future, nor any powers, neither height nor depth, nor anything else in all creation, will be able to separate us from the love of God that is in Christ Jesus our Lord" (Rom. 8:38–39). Amen!

"Then all the people said, 'Amen'" (1 Chron. 16:36).

Subject Index

Scripture Index